The Frontiersmen
A NARRATIVE

The Frontiersmen

A NARRATIVE

By
ALLAN W. ECKERT

Jesse Stuart Foundation
Ashland, Kentucky
2001

Library of Congress Cataloging-in-Publication Data

Eckert, Allan W.
    The frontiersmen / by Allan W. Eckert.
        p. cm.
    Includes bibliographical references (p.).
    ISBN 0-945084-90-0 -- ISBN 0-945084-91-9 (pbk.)
        1. Kenton, Simon, 1755-1836. 2. Pioneers--Ohio River Valley--Biography. 3.
Tecumseh, Shawnee Chief, 1768-1813. 4. Shawnee Indians--Kings and rulers--
Biography. 5. Frontier and pioneer life--Ohio River Valley. 6. Indians of North
America--Wars--1750-1815. 7. Ohio River Valley--History--To 1795. 8. Ohio River
Valley--Biography. 9. Northwest, Old--History--To 1775. 10. Northwest, Old--
History--1775-1865. I. Title.

F517.K383 E25 2001
976.8'02'092--dc21
[B]   00-069640

Jacket Design by Brett Nance
Original Art by John Alan Maxwell

Published by:

Jesse Stuart Foundation
1645 Winchester Avenue • P.O. Box 669
Ashland, Kentucky 41105
(606) 326-1667

Dedication

*For a friend in the deepest sense
of the word — one who has roamed
with me through many miles and
many years,*

JOSEPH H. CLICK

L. ST. CLAIR
Detroit
MICH.
thames
ONTARIO
LAKE ERIE
Ft. Malden
Frenchtown
raisin
N.Y.
Ft. Erie
PENN.
Ft. Meigs
maumee
st. joseph
Ft. Defiance
auglaize
Ft. Stephenson
sandusky
Cleveland
cuyahoga
OHIO
st. marys
Girty's Town
Upper Sandusky
scioto
tuscarawas
allegheny
Ft. McIntosh
Ft. Pitt
walhonding
Gnadenhutten
Ft. Recovery
stillwater
indian lake
Blue Jacket's Town
Mackachack
licking
Goschachgunk
Provance
Greenville
mad
Urbana
Zanesville
Wheeling
Ice's Ford
Piqua Town
Springfield
Columbus
whitewater
muskingum
Dayton
lt. miami
Chillicothe (Indian)
Kispoko Town
ohio
cheat
monongahela
Ft. Hamilton
gr. miami
Marietta
Chillicothe (white)
hocking
paint
Cincinnati
lt. kanawha
W.VA.
scioto
Gallipolis
Massie's Station
Point Pleasant
Hanging Rock
licking
elk
ohio
Maysville
kanawha
Kenton's Camp
kentucky
Blue Licks
tygart
guyandotte
greenbrier
McClelland's Station
big sandy
Lexington
tug
VA.
rodsburg
Boonesboro
kentucky
new
Danville
Logan's Fort
KY.
cumberland
scale: 1-inch = 39 miles
TENN.
N.C.

The web-fowl nested in the sloo
Beside the sliding otter;
The red maid in her bark canoe
Just skimmed the slumb'rous water;
The red man took the 'wareless game
With sinew-twanging bow,
Till Kenton's cracking rifle came,
An hundred years ago.

> — MAJOR HENRY T. STANTON
> *May in Mason 1775*
> (written for the Kentucky
> Centennial held at Mays-
> ville in May, 1875.)

Only a few white men were ever as good as the Indians at the Indian game. Boone and Kenton were . . .

> — FREDERICK PALMER
> *Clark of the Ohio* (1929)

AUTHOR'S NOTE

T HIS book is fact, not fiction.
In ferreting out the truth of history, the researcher finds that some
of his most important sources are documents of any nature written during
the historical period of which he intends writing. And when, on rare occasions — more rare the farther back in history he digs — he encounters
material written or dictated by the very people about whom he intends to
write, it is indeed a windfall.

For a great wealth of just such material I am deeply indebted to the late
Dr. Lyman Copeland Draper and his incomparable manuscript collection
now in the archives of the State Historical Society of Wisconsin. A great
deal of the material in this book is the outgrowth of material derived from
that source, though by no means to the exclusion of a great many other
respected and important historical sources.

Seven years of extensive research have gone into the preparation of *The
Frontiersmen*. It is the result of a close study of a multitude of documents
written in the period 1700 to 1900, many by the actual principals of this
narrative. These documents include thousands of personal letters, notes
and memoranda, and hundreds of diaries, journals, depositions, tribal
records, logbooks, military reports, governmental records and legal papers.

Within the text there are occasional references to numbered notes.
These amplify the subject under discussion and will be found at the back
of the book in the notes section. Also in this section, listed by chapter, are
the principal sources for the facts and dialogue contained in the text.

To aid the reader further, a List of Indian Characters and a Glossary
of Shawnee Words and Phrases have been included as appendices to the
text; and the index will hopefully prove useful as well.

In order to help provide continuity and maintain a high degree of reader
interest, certain techniques normally associated with the novel form have
been utilized, but in no case has this been at the expense of historical
accuracy.

AUTHOR'S NOTE

More dialogue will be found in this narrative than is normally found in a book depicting actual history. It is true, of course, that no one can know for certain what any other person was thinking or what he actually said in times past unless that individual himself either wrote or dictated these remarks or thoughts. Yet, all of the dialogue of this narrative is very closely traced and, in large measure, represents what the actual principal, then or later, wrote that he had said or thought at the time. Little license has been taken with the dialogue included here, although there is some conversation which was not initially written as dialogue. (For example, the writer of a diary of the time might have written something to this effect: "Today I met Simon Kenton on the trail and he told me that fourteen days ago his good friend and hunting partner, Jake Drennon, had been shot out of his canoe by the Shawnee Indians." In a case such as this — and there were numerous such cases — I felt fully justified, when depicting the actual meeting of these two men, to write: " 'Jake Drennon's dead,' Simon told him, shaking his head sorrowfully. 'Party of Shawnees shot him out of his canoe a couple of weeks ago.' ")

It should be borne in mind, then, that where dialogue takes place in this book, it is actual quoted conversation from another source, or dialogue constructed in the manner above described, or — in a few scattered instances — historical fact utilized in the form of conversation to maintain the dramatic narrative pace. In no case has there been any "whole-cloth" fabrication or fanciful fictionalization.

Equally, every incident described in this book actually occurred; every date is historically accurate; and every character, regardless of how major or how minor, actually lived the role in which he is portrayed.

ALLAN W. ECKERT

Dayton, Ohio
November, 1966

ILLUSTRATIONS

The
Frontiersmen
A NARRATIVE

PROLOGUE

[*April 3, 1755 — Thursday*]

FOR the first time in many hours, Mary Miller Kenton relaxed wholly, marveling in the pleasantness of Mark's ministrations to her body. Although his scarred hands were coarse-grained leather, horny with the calluses of a lifetime of clearing and tilling and building, now they worked with incredible gentleness as they passed a cool, damp cloth over her thighs and amazingly deflated belly, wiping away the clammy perspiration induced by labor. She closed her eyes and smiled weakly, thankful for the cessation of convulsive pains that had begun just after midnight and terminated only with the placental ejection a short time ago.

The first rays of the sun bored though the single, foot-square window of the cabin, paling the light of four guttering candles on the half-round log bench beside the bed. From close outside came the call of a newly arrived robin sounding territorial rights to this small segment of Prince William County, Virginia.[1] The air was balmy, filled with the sweet scent of rich, moist earth and a promise of vigorous growth.

Mark and Mary Kenton had been married for eighteen years and, despite a gnawing poverty that had dominated their existence, they had been good years. Unusually attractive as a young lady, Mary had received several proposals from interesting young men, but it was Mark who had captivated and won her. Now, at forty-one, she was still an extremely handsome woman, exhibiting the best characteristics of her Scotch and Welsh parentage.

Thirteen years her senior, Mark was born on March 1, 1701, of militant Irish ancestry in County Down, but he possessed little of the famed Irish temper and even less of the driving ambition exhibited by so many of Erin's sons. His sole ambitious accomplishment, in fact, was indenturing himself for five years to a Virginia landowner in exchange for passage to the colony, of which so many fascinating stories were told. He was in his late adolescence then and he reasoned, as did many of his contemporaries, that indenture for five years was better by far than permanent existence in this bitter little "Kingdom of Ireland" which seethed in endless frustration under the heel of a despised England.

But ambition was a short-lived phenomenon in Mark's breast, and when his indenture contract was fulfilled he became nothing more than a tenant farmer on the great Carter Grant, eking out a meager living near the little community of Hopewell. Here he had met and married Mary Miller when she was twenty-three; a tenant farmer still, there was little likelihood that he would ever become rich or even wealthy enough to buy her the fine clothing and other possessions she had, as a girl, always dreamed of someday owning.

In some marriages this might have caused trouble. Ambition was an admirable trait in a man and Mary had seen it raise a number of men to enviable heights of fame and fortune. But she had the wisdom to recognize as well that ambition often creates a poor bedfellow and she was content in the knowledge that Mark was not dedicated to some goal which might take him from her. Further, their lives together were in one respect very rich — in family, rather than in property or money.

Less than ten months after their marriage in January of 1737, a son was born to them and they named him William. He was followed by three daughters: Mary in 1739, Jane in 1742 and Frances in 1744. Each time they had expected another son and the anticipation became disappointment and the disappointment gradually gave way to fear as five years passed after the birth of Frances without more children. Mary prayed fervently that she might bear another son for her husband and, at last, so she did. Mark's pleasure was such that he named the infant boy after himself. Two years later had come a third son and he was named John. And now, on this bright April morning in 1755, another baby was born to them.

A brief, high-pitched squalling erupted from the other side of the room and the woman opened her eyes to watch as sixteen-year-old Mary swaddled the babe in a light coverlet at a rough-hewn table and then brought the bundle over to lay it beside her on the bed. She sought her daughter's eyes with silent query and the girl smiled tiredly. It was, she said, another boy. The mother nodded, pleased, but her voice was barely audible.

"His name," she said, glancing at her husband, "is Benjamin."

Mark Kenton did not look up immediately. He tossed the wadded cloth into a wooden basin and pulled the quilt over her. Only then did he straighten to his full height of six feet, and his firm gaze took in both mother and daughter.

"His name," he said quietly, "is Simon."

Mary's smile wavered momentarily, then returned. "His name," she repeated after him, "is Simon."

[*March 9, 1768 — Wednesday*]

As he had done on occasion ever since childhood, the Shawnee chief Pucksinwah contemplated the multitude of stars sparkling with such life and beauty in the deep cloudless and moonless sky. Now that the fire had died to a dim-orange bed of coals and the women squatted around it had lapsed into uncommon silence, these jewels of the night seemed to draw even closer and become more tangible, as if waiting to be plucked.

Only rarely was the stillness broken by a soft cry from within the hastily erected shelter beyond the fire where Methotasa — A-Turtle-Laying-Her-Eggs-in-the-Sand — awaited the delivery of her child. It would have been better had they been able to continue the journey to Chillicothe.[2] The village was only three arrow flights to the northwest of them, but the time to bear fruit had come and further travel, however short, would have been dangerous to both Methotasa and the infant.

Though extremely anxious to reach this principal town of the Chalahgawtha sept, Pucksinwah nevertheless stayed behind with his twelve-year-old son, Chiksika, and ten-year-old daughter, Tecumapese, along with half a dozen women of his clan who would help in the delivery.[3] The remainder of his Kispokotha sept of the Shawnees he sent on to the village with word of his whereabouts and his promise to appear on the morrow at the large *msi-kah-mi-qui*, or council house.

Nearly six hundred strong, these followers of his represented about two-thirds of the population of Kispoko Town on the west bank of the Scioto River. Similar groups from the other four Shawnee septs were also converging for this highly important council at Chillicothe. For over five years tribal representatives had been meeting here at intervals in an effort to decide what the Shawnees, as a nation, must do about the white man who, despite those treaties forbidding it, was crossing the mountains to the east and spilling into the valleys of the Monongahela and Youghiogheny and Allegheny.

Although the Shawnee septs were individual entities and governed themselves, each was an important branch of the Shawnee tribe as a whole and each had a distinct office or duty to perform for the benefit of the tribe. The Peckuwe sept, for instance, had charge of the maintenance of order or duty and looked after the celebration of matters pertaining to Shawnee religion. It was to this sept that Methotasa had belonged before Pucksinwah had taken her as wife.[4]

The Maykujay clan controlled matters pertaining to health, medicine and food. The Kispokotha sept, on the other hand, was in charge of all circumstances of warfare, including the preparation and training of warriors.

But the two most powerful septs were the Thawegila and Chalahgawtha, which had charge of all things political and all matters affecting the entire tribe. These two septs were equal in power and from one of them the principal chief of the Shawnees had to come. The chiefs of the other septs were subordinate to the principal chief in all matters of importance to the tribe but, in circumstances pertaining to their own jurisdiction, they were independent chiefs. The Thawegila, Kispokotha and Peckuwe septs were closely related morally and politically, while the Maykujay and Chalahgawtha septs always stood together, as they had in times past during occasional instances of tribal dissension.[5]

So it was now in this problem of the encroachment of the whites. It was such a serious problem that strong lines of dissension had formed which threatened to cause a permanent breach in the nation; at least so it was feared by the principal chief, Hokolesqua — Cornstalk — a Chalahgawtha Shawnee. His sept and the Maykujays took the stand that "we had better make peace with the white people, as they are outnumbering us and increasing fast. It seems Moneto — God — is with them. Let us make peace with them and be always in peace with them."

"No!" said the Thawegila, Kispokotha and Peckuwe chiefs. "Let us *not* make peace with the white people. Let us fight them until one or the other of us is destroyed to the last man."

Pucksinwah shook his head sadly. To the very marrow of his bones he knew there could never be a true peace between whites and Indians. As surely as summer follows spring, the whites would not stop at the river valleys of western Pennsylvania. Inevitably they would spread down the Spay-lay-wi-theepi — Ohio River — to settle in the great and sacred hunting grounds of Can-tuc-kee. The Shawnee from the north and Cherokee from the south might share the bounty of that land below the great river, but no tribe — nor white man! — must be permitted to take up permanent residence there.

Had not over a century of friction between Indians and whites proven that nothing could be gained by talk of peace? When treaties had been signed and boundaries established in the past, had not these whites treated the Indians with unfeigned loathing and had they not broken the boundaries almost immediately after they were established?

This was why the current council at the Little Miami River village of Chillicothe was so important to Pucksinwah. Largest of the Shawnee towns, it was centrally located to all the septs and more than five thousand Shawnee men would be on hand. And this time it would be his turn to speak without interruption in the *msi-kah-mi-qui*. He would pray to Moneto to bring powerful words to his lips that he might convince the

Chalahgawtha and Maykujay septs that there could never exist an equitable peace between Indians and whites.

He raised his eyes skyward but the prayer died aborning as a huge meteor suddenly plunged into the atmosphere and burst into brilliant greenish-white flame. It streaked across the heavens from the north in an awe-inspiring spectacle which lasted fully twenty seconds.

Pucksinwah had heard of such occurrences, but not before had he seen anything so breathtaking as this and the tales of the old people came back to him now: this shooting star was The Panther, a great spirit passing over to the south where it seeks a deep hole for sleep. Every night it passes somewhere on the earth to go to that home in the south. It was a good sign indeed and Pucksinwah arose and stepped briskly to the fire where the women were clustered, chattering excitedly, for they too had seen it.

From within the temporary shelter came the sharp wail of a baby. Pucksinwah waited quietly, the murmur of voices from inside almost lost in the gurgle of water from the great bubbling spring beside the shelter.[6] Soon the infant's crying faded away and a quarter hour later one of the women came out, beckoned the chief and happily told him he had a son.

Pucksinwah stooped to enter the shelter and the three women inside, giggling delightedly, left to join the others at the fire. Methotasa lay on a bedding of cedar boughs covered with a huge soft buffalo hide, the even softer hide of a deer covering her to the waist. Her breasts were swelled but not yet heavily engorged with the milk which would come in two or three days. In the crook of her arm slept the newborn child, its skin glistening faintly with a protective coating of bear oil applied by the squaws.

Methotasa smiled up at Pucksinwah as he knelt to look at the baby. She told him that the other women had seen a great star, The Panther, passing across and searching for its home in the south. Pucksinwah nodded gravely and told her it was the boy child's *unsoma*.

Shawnee custom declares that a boy baby is not named for ten days after his birth, nor a girl for twelve, during which time an *unsoma* — notable event — would occur which should indicate what Moneto wished the child to be called. But this time the sign had been given at the very moment of birth and this was of great importance. Both Pucksinwah and Methotasa knew there could be no other name for this boy than The-Panther-Passing-Across.

Thus was born and named the Shawnee Indian known as Tecumseh.[7]

CHAPTER I

[*March 24, 1770 — Saturday*]

LIFE on the Kenton farm was a constant drudgery in which all but two members of the family took part. The principal crop was tobacco and the work in the fields was done with mattock, hoe, a pair of jaded workhorses and a great deal of perspiration. Luxuries were unheard of; with not even enough money for necessities, the horses were harnessed with cornhusks braided into makeshift ropes by the girls and hitched to the crude wooden plow with long strips of hickory bark which snapped annoyingly each time a stone or root was encountered.

Somehow the crop never quite measured up to Mark's anticipations and when, about Christmastime each year, the tobacco was loaded into huge hogsheds, to each of which an axle was attached, and then rolled forty miles to Dumfries, the money it brought was barely enough to buy the minimum of supplies necessary for another year. That, of course, was only after the rent had been paid to Richard Graham, the wealthy Scotch merchant who had bought the land when the Carter Grant was broken up.

William, eldest of the Kenton boys, was one of the two who no longer shared the workload of the farm. Seven years ago he had married a Dumfries girl named Mary, daughter of the Reverend Thomas Cleland, so now he had family responsibilities of his own. Still, he came back to his parents' house occasionally and, when he could afford it, contributed a few shillings to the Kenton budget.

The other who adamantly refused to share in the work to be done was Simon. Nearly fifteen, he had long since been labeled by family and acquaintances alike as wild, unresponsive, incorrigible, unmanageable and unbearably lazy — epithets he fully deserved. Remarkably large for his age, he was already approaching his father's height of six feet and his bone structure indicated considerably more growth yet to come. His eyes were the same penetrating blue as the elder Kenton's and his thatch of thick auburn hair was always in a state of disarray.

His aversion to menial labor of any kind was pronounced. True, he would cheerfully set deadfalls for bear or attack a bee tree with an ax and a startling vigor, but when it came to hoeing the fields or splitting rails or pounding hominy, no amount of hickory-switch whipping could make him bend long to the task. Nor, when all other efforts failed, could he even be shamed into work. He was perfectly content to sit by and watch the whole family — even his younger brother and sister, Benjamin and Nancy — perform their allotted chores without offering to help.

"Me work?" he would say. "No sir, I'd rather die first!"

When the whippings became too severe, Simon would work at the designated task only until unobserved and then light out for the surrounding hills he loved so much, or perhaps go to the houses of distant neighbors. He would stay away for two or three days — even longer on occasion, if not bluntly requested to go home — and return only when driven there by the gnawing of an empty belly.

During one such absence [some months before] he met and fell desperately in love with Ellen Cummins, a gangly, hawk-nosed, red-haired, awkward lass three full years his senior. Rarely is love ever again so all-consuming or so totally blind as that which afflicts a young man for the first time. More sedate and longer-lasting loves may come, but seldom do they achieve the burning intensity evoked by the first.

He reveled in her open admiration of his markedly handsome features, his size and his strength. Not surprisingly, he read far more than was prudent into her occasional veiled hints that she was his alone forever and that at some nebulous future date she would become his wife and bear his children — a thought which caused the youth virtually to tremble in anticipation. Ellen alone, of all his limited circle of acquaintances, did not berate him for his refusal to attend school, nor make sport of him because he could neither read nor write.

Simon's lack of formal education was hardly due to lack of opportunity. Time and again he had been escorted to the nearby Bull Run Mountain school where William, young Mark, John and Benjamin had all learned their letters and how to figure sums. But just as he would flee from work, so too he would dart from the classroom at the first opportunity and take to the fields, woods and streams nearby. He did not for a moment regret what he was doing, especially not when Ellen Cummins batted her eyelashes at him calfishly and let him know she thought his refusal to accept formal education was a sign of true independence and self-confidence; besides, no other boy she knew possessed one tenth of Simon's knowledge about animals and plants and nature and tracking. If she had led him to believe he could fly, surely he would have leaped from the highest point of White Rock Ridge to prove her correct.

It came, therefore, as a totally unexpected and devastating shock to Simon when he learned that his beloved Ellen was to be wed the next Saturday to William Leachman, twenty-year-old son of the Kentons' nearest neighbor, widowed Sam Leachman. Until now the two — Simon and William — had had little to do with one another because of their age difference. They had met now and then when one or the other was sent to the neighboring farm to borrow this tool or that; they had been cordial, if not friendly, despite Simon's suspicion that the chunky young man privately condemned him for his lack of ambition.

But now a scalding rage burst in Simon and he cursed the very thought of Leachman. The anger spread to cover every facet of the older youth's habits and existence — his prissy manner of dress, his sixteen-inch queued hair, his flaunted education, his disdainful attitude toward Simon. All became suddenly unbearable. On the day Simon heard the news he fled to the hills and was not seen again for four days.

For the Bull Run Mountain community the wedding in nearby Hopewell was a momentous occasion, as were all the relatively rare weddings performed there. The benches of the little church were filled to capacity and many had to stand along the walls. Vows were exchanged, a nervous kiss presented and then the newly united William Leachmans turned to walk together out of the church. It was at precisely this moment that Simon appeared in the doorway, clad only in his coarse linsey knee breeches and low buckle shoes. His hair was in wilder disorder than usual and the blue seemed to have run from his eyes, leaving them a smoldering gray. The congregation gasped almost as one and mothers shielded the eyes of their offspring against this bare-chested sacrilege.

His huge fists doubled in front of him, Simon scathingly labeled Leachman a thief and a coward and challenged him to step outside to take the reward he deserved. The bride and groom had stopped short in amazement, but now a cold anger stiffened the young husband's face as he gently handed Ellen into the care of his father and stepped forward to meet his adversary.

In calling William Leachman out, Simon Kenton had made two grievous errors. The first was in taking Ellen Cummins and her comments seriously. The second was in very badly overestimating his own pugilistic abilities. For Leachman was not only older by five years, he was heavier, stronger and considerably more experienced in fighting. And so there, in sight of practically every resident of the surrounding countryside, he thrashed Simon as the youth had never before been thrashed.

[*January 30, 1771 — Wednesday*]

Methotasa, who three years ago had achieved for herself and Chief Pucksinwah a great respect among all Indians for having given birth to

Tecumseh at the very instant that The Panther flashed across the sky, now had at least equaled that feat.

In this village of Kispoko on the west bank of the Scioto River just a mile upstream from where Scippo Creek enters,[1] she had lain in the *wegiwa* of her husband and had borne him three sons at a single birth — an event without precedent among the Shawnees.

From all the septs of the tribe scattered throughout the territory came the shamans to view this wonder. Surely Pucksinwah was a favorite of Moneto to have been the direct cause of two such momentous occurrences.[2]

After the ten-day period had passed, the tiny trio was named. The firstborn was called Kumskaka — A-Cat-That-Flies-in-the-Air. The second became Sauwaseekau — A-Door-Opened. The third, a very dark, very ugly and highly vociferous babe was named Lowawluwaysica — He-Makes-a-Loud-Noise.[3]

[*April 10, 1771 — Wednesday*]

The change in Simon Kenton was pronounced. He had become more docile, more willing to do hard work. His energy in splitting rails and chopping firewood, his performance of other menial tasks which he had always before studiously avoided, all these drew grudging admiration from those around him — first from his family, still smarting from the humiliation he had brought upon them, and later, from neighbors. According to spreading word, he had "had some sense knocked into that thick Irish skull."

Only Simon knew it was a façade, behind which lay an overpowering and ignoble motive: one day, in some way, at a time and place of his own choosing, he would wreak a terrible vengeance upon the person of William Leachman. His heavy labors were nothing more nor less than a self-imposed training program to strengthen his body in anticipation of the next encounter with his mortal enemy.

In the year that had passed since the fight Simon had filled out considerably, though not all of this was due exclusively to working his father's fields. He had spent more time than ever in the hills — lifting rocks, climbing trees, hoisting logs, throwing stones and running — all calculated to increase his strength and coordination.

He had succeeded admirably.

On his sixteenth birthday he towered an inch or more over six feet and the muscles of his legs, arms and chest were large and solid. He was casting aside the mantle of boyhood and gracefully pacing into the realm of young manhood. He felt as ready for the encounter now as he would ever be, and opportunity was not long in coming.

Early one forenoon, Mark Kenton decided to cut some pieces of lumber to use as planting stakes. For this he needed the community saw, one of many tools the farmers of the area shared after pooling their funds. As luck would have it, Sam Leachman had used it last and Simon was sent to fetch it.

Crossing White Rock Ridge to get there, Simon heard the rasping of a saw in the woods. He crept up unseen and his eyes narrowed when he recognized the young man cutting cedar fence posts, his long queue flopping haphazardly at each stroke: William Leachman. Without warning Simon burst from cover and flung himself at the man, his head ramming squarely into Leachman's stomach. The result was disappointing. Too low to knock him windless and too high to be damaging, the heavy blow only caused Leachman to drop the saw and stagger backward momentarily. Simon now grasped him in a great hug intended to squeeze the breath out, but Leachman reacted with disconcerting speed. He gripped the youth in turn and twisted sharply as they fell, so that it was Simon's body which slammed heavily to the ground with Leachman on top. Swiftly astride the boy's struggling form, Leachman delivered a deadly rain of blows which left Simon groggy. Desperate now, Simon threw his arms about Leachman and the pair rolled over and over in the clearing.

Once again Simon found himself on the bottom, but now with his foe's fists cupped tightly in his huge hands. Suddenly, with unexpected savagery, he jerked Leachman's hands downward and at the same time snapped his own head forward so that the top of his skull slammed full into the man's face. The impact stung Simon but did considerably more damage to Leachman, mashing his nose and stunning him. As the man fell to one side, Simon slid free, and before Leachman could recover he dragged him a few feet and swiftly tied the long queue of hair to a sapling. Then, holding Leachman's arms down with his knees, Simon permitted his terrible temper to sweep away all reason. He beat the young man unmercifully, stopping only when the raging fury and pent-up anger of more than a year was dissipated.

With the waning of his temper came a sick feeling of revulsion for what he had done, accompanied by a growing fear. Leachman was motionless and scarcely recognizable, his face terribly battered and bloody. Simon untied the queue and tried to prop him up against the sapling, but the flaccid form slid back to the ground. He gripped the man's shoulders and shook him, calling his name, but there was no response. A sudden chilling thought swept through Simon and he pressed his ear to Leachman's chest.

He heard nothing.

Terrified now, he backed off and stared unbelievingly at the body before him, then turned and ran south along the ridge until he could run no more. Gasping, he crept into a crevice in the rocks and huddled there trembling, vaguely noting that he had lost his buckle shoes.

Going home now was out of the question. Shamed once before when their son became a church brawler, what would his parents think of having a murderer as a son? Had he not often been told that the moles on his neck signified he would be hanged? And if the authorities did not arrest and hang him, surely Leachman's kin would eventually catch and kill him. There was but one thing to do. He must flee beyond the reach of any law or sword of retribution.

He remained in the crevice until dusk and, upon emerging, continued to move south along the ridge, following the direction he had taken instinctively upon leaving Leachman. Hatless, shoeless, without gun or knife, provisions or money, clad only in worn linsey-woolsey shirt and trousers stained with blood which he smudged away with dirt and damp leaves, Simon Kenton — aged sixteen years and seven days — headed into the unknown.

[*April 17, 1771 — Wednesday*]

For two days the search parties of men had crawled into every known cave and cranny looking for Simon and they had not found him, even though they had located his shoes. But when they stopped searching, Mary Kenton did not, even though her vision was fogged with uncontrollable tears. Somewhere up there on White Rock Ridge, she knew, was her son and she would seek until she found him.

Her husband, himself haggard, met her at the door of the cabin. She shook her head in answer to his questioning glance and slumped to a bench at the table, laid her head on her arms and raised it only once to shake it in patient negation when he gently suggested that she, too, end her fruitless search.

Mark Kenton paused and fidgeted uncomfortably before telling her the results of the trial. The jury had that afternoon reached a verdict of not guilty by reason of insufficient evidence. Due to his own testimony of what had taken place on the Ridge and the fact that the searchers had been unable to find the body of Simon Kenton, which he was accused of having hidden after their fight, the recuperating William Leachman was acquitted of the charge of murder.

[*April 26, 1771 — Friday*]

From the moment he had left his shelter on White Rock Ridge that first evening, Simon had had no doubt about where he was heading — to the Middle Ground; that mysterious land west of the mountains where civilization ended at a place called Fort Pitt and beyond which lay a fabled land filled with riches and peril beyond imagining. Not that Simon knew very much about it, but the memory of the picture Uncle Tom had unwittingly painted in his mind of that country had never left him.

Thomas Kenton, twelve years older than Simon's father, had come to the Colonies in 1718 with his brother, but they had quickly parted. Soon after, Tom had married Rebecca Stoves of Boston, and a year later a son was born and named after his father. Unlike Mark, however, Tom was not content to settle down in one spot and he frequently left home for long periods of travel. Now and then during Tom's travels he would stop by the Bull Run Mountain farm of his brother to stay a day or so before moving on.

The last visit had been five years ago and Simon vividly remembered the pleasure this had brought his father, who had always idolized Tom. Simon was then eleven and he only vaguely remembered Uncle Tom's last visit before that, when he was seven. During the interval between visits, Mark Kenton often expressed the fear that Tom had been killed, which was not an unlikely possibility. Uncle Tom never bade his younger brother farewell without adding the solemn announcement that it would likely be the last time they would ever see him.

As an Indian trader in the occasional company of John Finley and David Duncan, Thomas Kenton regularly traversed the dangerous route between Philadelphia and the wild Ohio River and he was well suited for the occupation. Although his trading ability would never make him rich, he had a most remarkable memory for detail and had become, in effect, a living newspaper carrying news and messages from village to village, individual to individual, with incredible accuracy. He was a favorite among the settlers because, unlike many, he never fabricated or exaggerated and was normally unbiased in his reporting. And though he received little pay for such service, it brought him meals on a relatively regular basis and a wide range of friends across the country. Few things in life were more dear to him than those.

Thus Simon stood in awe of this man who had seen so much of the frontier and he had listened intently on that muggy July day five years ago as the trader told the family incidents of his travels during his absence. Shortly after darkness fell, Mark had ordered the children to bed; but Simon couldn't sleep, and an hour later he crept from the darkened cabin and lay quietly on the cool grass a dozen feet from where his father and uncle sat on a bench talking, hidden from them by the projecting end of the cabin.

"Yep," his uncle was saying, sucking on a long pipestem, "I've crossed the Ohio River twice since I was here last. It's a great river and an even greater country beyond; the Middle Ground. It's a country where only the brave or foolish enter. The foolish don't come back and pretty regular the brave don't, either. Few of us that've ever been there and back ever go across again.

"Mark, my boy," Tom's voice was growing more animated now, "you couldn't believe what these old eyes have seen. Land so fertile a bean grows like a tree and the grass tickles your belly when you walk. And game! Buffalo so many they shake the ground enough to jar your teeth. Deer, too, by the thousands, and elk. You ever seen an elk? Big deer, they are, big enough that one of them would feed your house for a month or more.

"Mark, they's birds so plentiful they make night out of day when they pass over. Takes hours, sometimes days, for them to fly by and so thick a single ball brings down two, three, maybe five birds. And that's not all. They's wolves and 'coons, beavers, mink, otters, you name it. They's bears by the thousands and panthers ahind every rock. They's wildcats big as hounds, squirrels thick as lice on a hen, turkeys all over. And fish? I never seen such waters for fish; nose to tail in every crik.

"But it's a red land, boy, a bad land. It's a land to die in afore it's time to die. Belongs to them what claims it, and that means the Indians. They's all kinds there and you just get to where you think you understand one when suddenlike he's gone and another takes his place that's all different. They's Iroquois, Mohawks, Senecas, Shawnees, Miamis, Delawares, Wyandots, Potawatomies and a dozen or more others I'd rather forget. That's why they call it Middle Ground. It's smack in the middle where they all come together and no one owns but everyone claims, so streams is oftener than not red with blood from them what lost their claim sudden. Them Indians'll kill other Indians just as quick as they'll kill whites, and they don't do it pretty.

"The whites want that Middle Ground, Mark. Want it bad. But I don't reckon they'll ever get it. The red men'll trade furs and suchlike; but excepting for that, whites that are smart keep out."

Simon had to bite his tongue to keep from asking his uncle if he'd ever killed an Indian. He flicked a bug from his cheek and listened again.

". . . a big land beyond the Ohio," Uncle Tom was saying. "Hundreds, maybe thousands of miles it goes on. Ever hear of the Messipi?"

"Don't think so, Tom, what is it?"

"A river, that's what, but what a river! So big you can hardly see across it. Makes the Ohio a little stream and the Indians call it the grandmammy of all rivers. The stories they tell! Beyond it, they say, there's more land, richer than even the Middle Ground . . . and it's all red buck land!"

The conversation had continued, drifting lazily through topics of the frontier, the villages between here and there, Colonial politics and other subjects, until Simon jerked with a frightened spasm and realized he'd fallen asleep and had better get back to bed before he was caught.

So now, as a fugitive, it was not surprising that Simon should make the Middle Ground his destination. The most direct route from White Rock Ridge would have been directly west to Redstone Old Fort along the Nemacolin Trail and from there straight to Fort Pitt, where the Monongahela and Allegheny joined to form the Ohio River. But evasive tactics were necessary first, and so he had set out to the southwest instead, traveling the mountain slopes to avoid people, particularly traders and wanderers like Uncle Tom who would consider a shoeless boy by himself in the wilderness a newsworthy item to pass on.

The first night of his flight he had moved swiftly, covering eighteen miles and arriving by dawn at Ashby's Gap of the Blue Ridge, where he took "a long, lingering look behind and thought he could still recognize his father's house in the distance, which looked not larger than a thimble."

Simon hid himself in the woods that day and remained there without food, beginning his footsore trek again at nightfall. His first point of aim was to reach Warm Springs, which he'd heard of but never seen. It was ideal because it was on no direct route with his own home area, thus lessening the likelihood of his being recognized by anyone. Further, it was the jumping-off place to the west, for beyond it lay the true frontier.

Hunger forced him into the open on the second day, but he was still reluctant to ask for food for fear they would suspect his hunger was a symptom of illegal flight. The following day he came to a cabin in a clearing where a woman alone with two children barred the door at his approach. She had been baking hoecake on an iron bake-oven lid and out of fear she bade him take some and go, which he did eagerly.

At another place he hired himself out to work in a cornfield for some food, but he was still so much on edge that when he saw a stranger approaching from the path, he dropped the hoe and raced off into the woods, remaining there until hunger once more drove him out. He lived chiefly on roots and young greens, drank from springs and slept in hideaways with dry leaves covering him. Had he remained in one spot any length of time he would have had little difficulty setting snares and deadfalls for squirrels, rabbits, partridge and other game, for he was already well skilled at such activity; but the fear of pursuit drove him ever on.

On the sixth day out he dared to stop at a cabin and ask for something to eat, which was given him. In the course of the conversation he learned the name of a settler a day's journey away, as well as something about the settler's background. The next day he presented himself there under the settler's own last name, and so much interest was shown in a possible relationship between them that he was fed heartily, provided with a pair of used shoes and given a much better shirt than that which he wore. Again he gathered particulars about another family a day's journey on and subsequently presented himself there under that settler's name. The trick worked wonderfully everywhere he went along the way, changing his name each day to coincide with that of the next family ahead.

Finally, on this cloudy Friday evening sixteen days after his fight with Leachman, he arrived at Warm Springs, more than a hundred and forty miles from home. By no means a large town, Warm Springs was still the biggest metropolis Simon Kenton had ever seen. A half dozen or more dusty streets bisected one another and at least two bridges crossed the little stream which rushed past — a sure sign of the permanence of the residents. Several of the buildings were two stories tall and quite well constructed, almost ostentatious amid the extensive cluster of cabins built of rough logs. A welcome smell of wood smoke and food cooking hung in the still evening air and the gnawing hunger that had been his constant companion the past fortnight caused the boy's stomach to growl angrily.

He had no difficulty locating Jacob Butler's mill on the edge of town along the creek, but for some time he stood with his back against a large oak and rehearsed what he would say. The other encounters had been important only for the sake of filling his stomach and resting but this one could well be crucial to the plan he had formulated.

He noted with a start that darkness had fallen and that the glow of a lamp shone through one of the windows of Jacob Butler's fine two-story home. Butler, he had learned at his last stop, was a shrewd businessman and his mill had prospered where several before it had failed. He was a widower who, until now, had done most of the milling himself, but there was a good chance he would welcome a young man willing to work hard.

This fitted Simon Kenton's plans perfectly. He was well aware that if he was to make his way from Warm Springs to Fort Pitt through the essentially wild country in between, he would need proper supplies: gun, ax, knife, powder, lead, bullet mold, clothing and staples.

A short, solid, sandy-haired individual of about fifty with ice-blue eyes answered Simon's knock and looked inquiringly at the youth in the yellow light cast from the lamp on the nearby desk. Simon smiled and removed his hat.

"Good evening, sir," he said. "I've just reached Warm Springs from the east and I wonder if you might be able to tell me where to look for work and lodging? My name is Simon Butler."

Intrigued with the possibility of a relationship between them, the miller invited him in and immediately fired a volley of questions about his origin. He became quite excited when Simon, after fabricating a story about setting out to build his own life, truthfully related that his family had come to the Colonies from Ireland.

Irish himself, Butler considered few things in life more important than family relationships and he lamented the fact that life caused old ties to be broken. In particular he spoke with pride of his illustrious uncle in Ireland, Sir Toby Butler, Duke of Ormond. When Simon casually remarked that he had, as a child, often heard that name spoken at home, Jacob Butler became certain that in some distant fashion he and Simon were related.

Impressed, too, at Simon's size, Butler hired him on the spot. To

Simon's credit, he worked diligently, not only in the grinding and sacking of flour and loading of wagons, but in making long-needed repairs to the milldam and waterwheel. Butler became increasingly proud of Simon and their initial cordiality blossomed into a warm friendship. Yet, Simon still feared discovery and it came as a great disappointment to the miller when Simon announced after two or three weeks that he was thinking of heading for Fort Pitt to see if he could locate his long-missing Uncle Tom. Butler urged him to stay on and Simon wavered. To his amazement, he was enjoying the work and had even managed to save a little bit of his money received as wages. He genuinely liked and admired the miller and so, weighing the fact that he'd been here this long without being recognized, he agreed to stay a while longer.

[*June 5, 1771 — Wednesday*]

Marmaduke Van Swearingen, better known to friends and family as Duke, pulled off an excellent shot at the rabbit he and Charley had jumped beside the creek. It had sprung up from alongside a log and raced in a zigzag along the bank for twenty yards before taking a sharp turn into the woods. Duke's arrow had plunged through its hindquarters only an instant before it would have vanished, impaling on to an emergent root.

Twelve-year-old Charley shouted excitedly at his brother's shot and raced up to dispatch the animal by lopping off its head with his hunting knife.

"You're better with a bow and arrow than most people with a gun, Duke," he said, beginning to skin the rodent.

Duke grinned, pleased. He had been given a serviceable musket for his seventeenth birthday last March and suspected it was just one more effort by his parents to rid him of this strong admiration he felt for the red man and his ways. Ever since he was twelve he had wanted to be like them, and when he heard of encounters between white man and Indian he always, with a perverse loyalty, felt a lift of his spirits when he learned it was the white man who had been bested. He vowed that when he became a man he would take up the free savage life exemplified in the habits and customs of the Indians and live out his days happily with some Indian tribe.

One of the happiest days in the life of Marmaduke Van Swearingen had been when an old crippled trader settled down in a cabin near that of his parents in western Virginia.[4] He spent much of his time after that at the old man's cabin, listening to his tales of dealing with the Indians and learning all he could about them. He even picked up a sizable vocabulary of Indian words which he practiced until he had become relatively fluent. This very bow he had used in bringing down the rabbit had been built of Osage wood by Duke under the old man's tutelage.

Except for Charley, Duke's brothers — John, Vance, Tom, Steel and Joe — had ridiculed him for his preoccupation with and sympathy for the

Indians. But in the past few years, happily, they had not mauled him physically about it as they had frequently when he was younger. In his fourteenth year he had begun to develop rapidly and now, at seventeen, he was unusually muscular, just under six feet tall and more active athletically than any of his brothers.

Now, striding along the creek toward Charley, Marmaduke Van Swearingen even *looked* surprisingly like an Indian. His hair was long and dark and his features angular. He had torn sleeves and collar from the blue linsey hunting shirt his mother had made him and only one low button remained to hold it together, exposing a sizable amount of muscular, well-tanned chest. On his feet he wore buffalo-hide moccasins given to him by the trader for his birthday — along with the fine bone-handled knife now in his belt — and his trousers were tied snugly to his calves. With bow in hand in this manner, he could very easily have been mistaken for an Indian.

He hunkered on his heels to watch the younger boy clean the rabbit and it was in this position that, with breathtaking suddenness, they found themselves the center of a ring of eleven Shawnee Indians, tomahawks in hand. Noting they were not painted, which meant they were hunters rather than a war party, Duke whispered to Charley to keep still and himself arose slowly and tossed his bow and spare arrows to the ground.

"*Manese,*" he said, a grave smile on his face, remembering the word the old trader had told him that meant knife. With his left hand and using only thumb and forefinger, he pulled the weapon from his belt and dropped it to the ground beside the bow. Then he put out his hand, palm upward, toward the leader of the party, a squat unsmiling individual wearing only buckskin leggins and ankle-high moccasins.

"*Ne-kah-noh,*" Duke said pleasantly. "*Was-he-sheke.*"

He almost laughed thinking how he would feel had he come across an Indian who threw down his weapons and said in broken English, "Friend. A fine day." Then he pointed to Charley, who sat petrified with fear, and added, "*Ni jai-nai-nah. Mat-tah tsi*" — "My brother. No kill."

The chief of the party nodded once and his face remained expressionless as he spoke. Marmaduke listened carefully and replied, and then for almost an hour they talked. Now and then one of the other Indians joined in, and at length the youth picked up his weapons and handed them to the leader, then turned to Charley and spoke earnestly.

"Charley, listen. I've got them to promise to let you go home unharmed if I go with them. They say they want to adopt me into their tribe. They're Kispokothas — warrior Shawnees." He held up his hand as the boy, his eyes filling with tears, started to protest. "No, listen; I'm going. It's what I've always dreamed of and it's the only way. If I refuse they'll have to kill both of us. You go tell Ma and Pa and the others what happened. Maybe

I'll see all of you again sometime, but I don't think so. I'll be all right, and so will you. Don't be afraid."

He hugged his brother to him tightly and then pulled him to his feet. "Remember," he added, "they aren't going to hurt me. They're pleased that I want to be like them and they just want to adopt me. They've even given me a name already. Now go!" He thrust his brother from him and Charley ran a dozen steps or so before abruptly stopping and looking back.

"What name, Duke?"

"Weh-yah-pih-ehr-sehn-wah."

"What's that mean?"

Marmaduke Van Swearingen laughed and tapped the breast of his shirt. "Blue Jacket."

[*June 8, 1771 — Saturday*]

Simon was always a little nervous when Saturdays came, for then Warm Springs was a bustle of activity with people from a widely surrounding area walking the streets, chatting by store fronts or converging on the town's four pubs. At such times he preferred to busy himself deep inside the mill where people were less apt to see him and possibly recognize him as a Kenton rather than a Butler.

He had never shared a truly close friendship with anyone before and he felt this was no time to begin. Nevertheless, he had found a friend. Hardly more than a week after moving in with Jacob Butler, Simon had been sent by the miller to get some supplies at a small merchandise depot. There he met an affable chap a year or so older than himself who was also getting supplies for his own employer, a smith, and they had hit it off rather well. His name was Dan Johnson, a lanky, cadaverous-looking individual who drank a great deal and talked volubly about things he might better have left unsaid. One night, before he could put a check on his wagging tongue, Daniel Johnson confessed to Simon that his name was not Johnson after all, but Manlay; that he had stolen a horse in his home colony of New Jersey and was forced to flee when the law had gotten on his trail. The confession had something of a sobering effect upon him and he suddenly became afraid and begged Simon never to tell anyone. The Virginian assured him he would not, but Daniel became even more agitated; not until Simon had confessed that he, too, was a fugitive and that his name wasn't Butler did the thin fellow relax. Simon, in turn, swore Daniel to secrecy and did not elaborate on details regarding his true name or crime. He liked Dan even more for not pressing him with questions about it.

The young New Jersey man was scarcely cut out for life on the fringe of civilization. Highly excitable, he admitted to an unsettling nervousness whenever in the woods and although he had never actually seen an Indian in the flesh, he had encountered thousands in his vivid imagination, no less than half of which had been successful in lifting his scalp. It therefore came as quite a surprise to Simon when this day Daniel sought him out in the mill and suggested he accompany him to Fort Pitt along a trail he had heard about. This was no little excursion and, while the likelihood of encountering hostile Indians was small, the hardships of a wild trail were hardly what Daniel Johnson would seem apt to propose. Naturally, he had a good reason. He loved the sea, he confessed, and wanted to get back to it. Perhaps if he could get back to the coast he could ship aboard one of the many merchant craft that were always coming and going.

While he could not quite comprehend how heading for Fort Pitt would aid Daniel in reaching the ocean, Simon was taken by the proposal. Yesterday, perhaps, he might have refused; but just this morning a stranger had entered the mill and talked some time with Jacob Butler and, whether or not he imagined it, Simon felt the man had looked at him with uncommon interest before leaving. The fugitive fear had again sent a shiver down his back, and so now Simon agreed to go along.

[June 15, 1771 — Saturday]

It was a considerably more self-possessed and better equipped Simon Kenton who left Warm Springs in mid-June than the one who had arrived there seven weeks earlier. He no longer shot occasional furtive glances over his shoulder to detect imagined pursuit and the confidence he exuded even had a relaxing effect on Daniel Johnson, who had ceased expecting Indian attack from behind every tree.

The parting with Jacob Butler had been a wrenching affair, affecting Simon far more deeply than he had anticipated. They had talked long into the night the evening prior to his departure and Butler had done his best to convince him to stay, citing the gathering unrest of the Indians against the whites and the resentment of the Colonials for the British as good reasons not to venture out into unknown country. There were, he felt, bad times coming for everyone before long.

But Simon was again enthusiastic about seeing the Middle Ground, and so Butler had led the youth to his quarters where he removed a fine Pennsylvania flintlock rifle from a peg near the door. The forty-inch octagonal barrel nestled in a forepiece of beautifully grained curly maple and the stock, of the same wood, was decorated with an eight-pointed star and crescent moon in brass. The butt plate, trigger guard and patch box were also of brass and the workmanship of the lock assembly was of the finest.

This rifle he presented to Simon as a parting gift. It had, he said, been given to him over a decade ago by one Samuel Tigue of Lancaster, an old friend who died shortly thereafter. Butler himself had never used it because he'd never had need, but he knew it was a piece matched by none other and was better, in fact, than those manufactured in mother England. It was made by Henry Leman of Lancaster specifically for "those who deal with Indians in one way or another." Butler said he trusted it might someday help bring Simon back to Warm Springs.

Deeply moved by such a generous gift, which included a large shot pouch and finely wrought brass powder flask, Simon promptly — and with Butler's approval — named the weapon Jacob, feeling that in times to come it would stand by him and help him as the miller himself had done.

Besides the weapon, Simon had accepted from Butler a small quantity of clothing and hard goods and, with the money he'd saved from his mill work, he purchased a good belt knife, blanket, condiments and other goods, as well as a back pack in which to store most of his supplies. Finally, as proof against the ever-present danger of copperheads and rattlesnakes, he also bought a pair of well-made mid-calf boots of soft thick leather which clung to his feet as an extra coat of skin might have, permitting him to move safely, yet soundlessly.

Having said their farewells the night before, Simon was pleased when the miller did not rouse in the dawn light to see them off. The man's kindness had already severely shaken his determination to be off. He met Daniel in front of the mill, lashed his pack to Dan's stolen horse and they set off.

They headed just a little north of due west and had soon forded both Deer River and Backaway Creek.[5] That night they camped in a pleasant valley and the next morning found the trail turning north. It ran parallel to the east bank of the beautiful Greenbrier River[6] which, by evening, had become a narrow, rapidly moving brook. From one high point they could see an especially prominent hill ahead — Spruce Knob — and here they camped for the night. Daniel Johnson's informant had told him that the headwaters of the Cheat River began on the other side of the knob, that it soon joined with the Monongahela which would lead them to Fort Pitt.

Simon kept them well supplied with game — turkeys, rabbits, grouse and squirrels — and it seemed that he and the rifle, Jacob, had been made for one another. Although he had little experience with guns, his eyesight and steadiness combined with the superb balance and accuracy of the rifle so well that in a short time he was pulling off brilliant shots at difficult targets. He practiced loading and firing until he had developed a swift smoothness that could well have been the envy of far more experienced woodsmen.

The trip up Spruce Knob and north through the Allegheny wilderness along the ever growing Cheat River was uneventful if rough going. It was near noon on the ninth day after leaving Warm Springs, near where the Cheat emptied into the Monongahela, that the pair found themselves approaching a small settlement, Ice's Ford, western termination of the Nemacolin Trail. Here also began a good, hard-packed horse trail which went north to Fort Pitt and another which struck off northeast to join West Trail, the principal road, if such it could be called, through southern Pennsylvania from Philadelphia to Fort Pitt.

Suddenly excited at the sight of numerous parties of trappers and traders, Simon suggested they stay here for a little while. Daniel declined. He intended taking this northeast trail up to West Trail and then east, adding hopefully that Simon was still welcome to come along if he wanted. The burly young Virginian's outstretched hand of farewell was his answer.

Without further discussion they unloaded Simon's gear from the horse, rearranged Daniel's things so he could ride, and tossed a final wave of the hand at one another. As he watched the thin figure perched high astride the steed, Simon shook his head. It was just as well. Daniel wasn't cut out for a frontier life.

He waited until the rider disappeared around a bend in the trail and then picked up his pack and strolled into the settlement.

[*July 1, 1771 — Monday*]

Ice's Ford, which had been founded prior to 1769 by the brothers Andrew and Frederick Ice, was a rude frontier outpost located at the foot of the beautiful hundred-mile-long Cheat River Valley. There were a number of temporary lean-tos and tents but the only structure of any permanence was a log cabin which had been built by the Ice brothers. It served the combined function of a store, meeting house, drinking place and message center. In actuality, it was little more than a brief stopping point for traders, trappers, scouts and adventurers, either preparing for that last big step into the wilderness beyond or making a welcome first contact with white civilization after having spent an interlude in the unknown country.

Rarely did anyone come here, as had Simon, with no specific plans in mind. He found work easily, for help was always needed in felling and hollowing trees for canoes and in cutting logs for raft construction. There were used canoes — some of them forty or fifty feet long — to be reconditioned for reuse and extra hands were always welcome to help in building temporary residence cabins and sheds for the transients.

Within a week Simon had earned enough at hard jobs to replenish his badly dwindled shot and powder supply, after which he concentrated strictly on hunting and then trading the game he downed for staple goods and more ammunition. His skill with Jacob was considerable and in this short time he gained something of a reputation as an outstanding marksman. No longer did he waste hard-earned lead and powder in unnecessary shooting. When Jacob spoke, it was a rare thing indeed if another turkey, deer, grouse, squirrel or wolf did not lie down and die.

The activity in and around Ice's Ford excited Simon from the start, particularly the crudely lettered sign stuck to the wall of the Ices' cabin. It was read to him by a slatternly woman of indeterminate age who came to the door at his approach and eyed him hungrily. It said:

WARNING

THER HAS 20 PERSONS BEN ROBBED BY INJENS

ALSO 19 HORSES STOLE

AT EAST FORK M RIVER AND TYGERTS VALEY

2 INJENS WAS KILED

The sign stirred considerably more excitement in Simon than the woman, but however pleased he was with the activity here, his expectations of finding a spot with some party heading for the Middle Ground were dimming. Each party he encountered already had as many men as were wanted, although his labors at helping them prepare for their expeditions were always welcome and well paid for. He decided that he'd have a better chance to find a party in the more populous area of Fort Pitt, and so he prepared to follow the river trail the remaining fifty miles or more to that British fortress.

He cached his gear and stalked into the woods in search of meat for his own use along the way. This was a day, however, when game seemed unusually scarce and nervous. Despite his stealth, Simon did not spy desirable quarry until early afternoon, and then it was a difficult situation at best. A considerable distance ahead he watched a fine turkey hen sail across a clearing and alight high in a pine tree close to the trunk. So well did it blend with the shadows there that had he not seen the movement he would have missed spotting the bird entirely. The turkey was edgy and ready to fly again quickly and Simon realized there was no hope of moving closer since protective cover between himself and the bird was sparse.

Steadying against a rock outcropping, he took a bead on the bird's breast, moved the barrel up to that pinpoint of shadow which marked the head and then squeezed the trigger. Quickly he jumped through the cloud of white smoke the gunfire had produced and was in time to see the bird jump convulsively and then plummet to earth. He reloaded and then walked on a straight line to his quarry, counting off the paces.

"Three hundred and thirty-two!" He muttered the words aloud, surprised in spite of himself at the distance. He stooped to pick up the bird lying a dozen feet from the base of the tree. Its head had nearly been torn away by the ball.

"Always shoot that good?" a voice asked. Simon spun around, dropping the bird and leveling Jacob at his hip.

"Easy, boy! No Indian here."

A slender man of about forty, dressed in brown linsey shirt, buck trousers and moccasins, stepped from behind the tree, a flintlock cradled in his left arm and a pleasant smile on his face. Walking up to Simon he extended his right hand and introduced himself as Bill Grills.

Simon's wariness evaporated at the man's evident friendliness. He transferred Jacob to his left hand and held out his right. Grills, instead of taking it, snatched the barrel of Simon's gun to one side and in the same instant shoved the barrel of his own rifle into the youth's stomach. Simon was so completely taken off guard he simply stared. A gradual flush crept up his neck.

"Green," said Grills, his smile grown to a wide grin. He lowered his rifle and released his hold on Simon's. "Haven't been in this country very long, have you, lad? Around here you trust no one you don't know." He added, chuckling, "And damned few of those you do. What's your name?"

Without hesitation he answered, "Simon Butler." The name had served him well in Warm Springs. He might as well retain it and keep his true identity hidden.

In rapid succession Grills fired a series of questions at him. Where was he from? What was he doing here? Did he always shoot that well? Who was he with? Where was he heading? Simon answered them all but stopped short when the man abruptly asked him what he was running from. This was too much. Employing the same tactic used on himself, Simon yanked the weapon from Grills's grasp, at the same time bringing Jacob to bear on the center of the man's chest.

"I don't like being questioned, Grills," he said in a cold voice. "Now you can answer some for me. Why did you sneak up on me and why all the interest in me?'

If anything, Simon's move had made the man's grin even broader and he chuckled approvingly. "You learn fast, boy. That's important around here. Even more important over there." He tilted his head to the west. "I just came from there and I'm soon going back."

Simon was impressed, but not enough so that he lowered his gun. He repeated his questions and Grills shrugged and told him that first of all he didn't sneak up on Simon, that he was already here drawing a bead on the bird when the youth shot it. Secondly, the questions he was asking were important. Did Simon know anything about boat building? Tracking? Indian fighting? Trapping?

Finding himself answering again, Simon was momentarily irritated at how neatly Grills had resumed questioning him. Then the humor of the situation struck him and he smiled, lowering Jacob. Grills indicated a fallen log and suggested they sit and talk.

Grills was shorter than Simon by nearly a head, but what he lacked in height he more than made up in self-assurance. His face was deeply lined where not covered by a scraggly brown beard that matched his hair. Having picked up the bird, he set about cleaning it as they talked and Simon did not fail to note how his knife slid through the carcass as if skin and meat were no more than soft cheese. Swiftly, expertly, he plucked the bird, using his narrow-bladed tomahawk hatchet to chop off the remains of the head and wing tips but leaving the feet attached. His hands were rough but relatively small and quite dexterous, and his brown eyes were so dark they seemed almost solid pupil. Although his hands and face were deeply tanned and weathered, Simon noticed when he pulled up his wide, cuffless sleeve before scooping out the bird's entrails that his arms were quite pale.

Grills's very manner of speaking brought a thrill to the youth. It was as he had expected the real frontiersmen to talk; unhurriedly yet to the point. He was, he related, one of a party of four men, the others being Jacob Greathouse and the brothers John and Raphael Mahon. He evinced surprise and disappointment when Simon confessed he had never heard of them but went on to say the party had been formed previously in the village of Provance, a dozen miles downstream from here. Since then they had taken two major trips down the Ohio, during both of which they had difficult though not disastrous encounters with Indians. He explained that while back east the people generally thought of the Middle Ground as the area lying to west and north of the Ohio, it also included much of the unexplored territory to the east and south of the river, particularly far downstream — most of this area part of western Virginia.

"Down that river," he said, "you'll find game and fur critters thicker than you've ever seen them. That's where we're getting ready to go now, and a lot farther downstream than we've ever gone before. May be all the way to what the Shawnees call the Can-tuc-kee land, which is something of a private game reserve they claim."

Simon was dazzled. His nebulous plans had come into sharp focus now and he knew that this was the land he had to see, regardless of hazard. As the older hunter carefully cleaned the blade of his knife and then touched it a time or two with a small whetstone before returning it to his belt sheath, he remarked casually that the only thing they needed with them on this planned expedition was another man — one with a good gun he could shoot well. He glanced significantly at his companion.

"Simon Butler?" The youth was unable to mask his eagerness.

"Exactly who I had in mind ever since I saw him pull off a shot I'd have been proud to make. Which is why I've been asking you all those questions, too. Let's go see the other boys."

[July 5, 1771 — Friday]

Their reception at Kispoko Town was not exactly what Marmaduke Van Swearingen expected it to be, but it had a profound effect upon him. From what the old trader had told him of Shawnee customs, he knew he would have to run a gauntlet when they reached the village. He was not, however, prepared for it to be as severe as it turned out.

The hunting party had taken its time getting to the Ohio River, which they came upon near the mouth of the Kanawha River on the downstream side, having forded the smaller river some miles back.[7] At this point two of the hunters who might well have been brothers swam the Ohio and struck off afoot diagonally northeast on the trail leading to Kispoko Town. The others, including Duke, followed the south shore of the Ohio downstream.

There were two reasons for this: first, so the pair could alert the village that a white youth was being brought in for possible adoption and, second, because the party had originally come down the Scioto River in canoes which they had hidden opposite that river's mouth on the south side of the Ohio as they had struck inland from there in a wide semicircle.

On the fifth day after leaving the Kanawha they had arrived at this spot and found the canoes still safely hidden in a small protected cove. The boats — three of them — had been weighted with rocks and sunk in about five feet of water and it took only a short while to retrieve, empty, and float them in good condition. The journey upriver on the Scioto to Kispoko Town took two days and they stopped a mile short of their destination to let the leader of the hunting party, with three of his warriors and Duke, alight on the shore and await further word to advance. The canoes continued upstream.

Within an hour a troop of more than a dozen nearly naked boys whooped into sight on horses and galloped madly around the quintet before heading back to the village. This was the signal that the gauntlet lines had been formed and they were to come in.

Expecting perhaps twenty or thirty people to be lined up waiting, Duke experienced a sudden fear when he saw the assemblage. A double line of Indians stretched toward him a full quarter-mile from the central council house. There were many hundreds of them — men, women, boys, girls and even toddlers barely able to stand by themselves. All had some type of whipping device in their hands: willow switches, rawhide strips, light pieces of wood, lengths of blackberry bush bristling with thorns. These were not only the Shawnees of Kispoko Town, but also many from the two villages across the river — those of Cornstalk's Town and the town of his huge sister Non-hel-e-ma.

In the few days he had spent with the hunting party, Duke had quickly improved his Shawnee speech, filling in the gaps between the little he had learned from the trader. By now, although he was by no means fluent in their language, he could converse well enough to be understood — and he could understand them even better.

Reaching the mouth of this double line of Indians, the chief of the hunting party ordered Duke to undress entirely, including even his moccasins. Extremely embarrassed, he obeyed and surprised himself by standing erect with his arms at his sides and not attempting to shield his nakedness despite the jeers and taunts and insulting remarks which arose all down the line.

The squat Indian, a trace of a smile curling his lips, kicked the clothing aside and accepted a rather hefty staff handed him by a small boy who immediately joined the line with his own switch. The Shawnee indicated the staff and said, "When I touch you with this, you are to run down the line to the *msi-kah-mi-qui*. You will not be struck at by anyone until you begin to pass them *unless* you stop running or turn around. If you do that, it will be a sign of cowardice and adoption will be denied."

The implication behind his words was clear enough. There was only one alternative to adoption and that was death. Duke had no intention of either stopping or turning. He intended to run as he had never run before and perhaps he could reach the haven of the council house before too many blows struck him. He was to begin running when the squat Indian touched him with his staff after a drum beat had sounded at the council house. On command from this Indian he bent over, facing down the slot between the double line. An excited silence fell over the assemblage as they awaited the signal.

Duke had expected the "touch" of the Indian's staff might be less than gentle, but hardly the tremendous blow across the buttocks which sent a sickening wave of pain through him and caused him to sprawl face down in the dirt. Instantly a rain of switches lashed his backside and legs and he struggled to his feet and began a headlong run.

Blow after blow struck him, stinging, cutting, welting, ripping the skin of his back. Several times he stumbled but caught himself and ran on and while the blows had never been gentle, they became stronger and the weapons larger the closer he came to the *msi-kah-mi-qui*. Through a haze of pain he saw the big council house a dozen yards ahead and thought he would make it; but just then an awful stroke caught him across the back of the neck and he fell, unable to rise. The Indians crowded around, screeching and flailing their weapons and he believed, as unconsciousness closed around him, that he had failed.

It was more than two weeks before Marmaduke Van Swearingen was able to walk again without the healing wounds on his back and buttocks and legs cracking open and leaving him gasping in pain. He had been unconscious for many hours and, because of several areas which became infected, verged on delirium for a day beyond that. But under the care of solicitous squaws who bathed his wounds and rubbed them with a greasy, foul-smelling concoction, the healing progressed well and this was the day, at last, when he was to be officially adopted.

Taken to the river bank, he was ordered to strip himself of the breech-clout that hung from his waist and peculiarly comfortable woven reed slippers covering his feet. When this was done he was painted lavishly with a variety of colors from head to foot by a trio of young squaws who giggled almost uncontrollably as they worked. As soon as they had finished they snatched up their paint pots and disappeared in the crowd that encircled him.

Now Pucksinwah came forward, stood before Duke with raised arms and chanted an ancient liturgy, very little of which the youth understood except for the last phrases: which were "*Newecanetepa, weshemanitoo weshecatweloo, keweshelawaypa*" — ("The Great Spirit is the friend of the Indians, let us always do good").

This completed, Pucksinwah handed Duke into the care of another trio of squaws, these clad only in a type of pantaloon reaching from waist to knee. One was young and quite pretty, another middle-aged and with stern visage. The third was a very old woman, her face deeply wrinkled about the eyes and mouth with the lines of laughter.

The squaws led him into the water to his waist where they jumped upon him, pulling and tugging until he was knocked off balance and went under. The bottom here was more gravelly than muddy and as he rose sputtering they scooped up handfuls of fine pebbles and sand and scrubbed his body with unrestrained vigor. Not until the paint was all gone and his skin was a bright pink from their scouring was he permitted to return to shore.

Most of the Indians had vanished and Duke was led to the *msi-kah-mi-qui* where they dressed him in a beautiful, tasseled buckskin shirt softer than any he had ever felt and a pair of heavier buckskin leggins decorated with ribbons and beads, porcupine quills and hanks of red hair.

Once more his face was painted, but carefully this time, with lines and spots of brilliant red, dull blue, yellow and pasty white. The hair at the back of his head was interwoven through the perforations of a thin metal disk the diameter of a walnut and into a small hole in its center was inserted an eagle feather so that it projected at an angle downward and its tip touched his right shoulder. As this was being done the Indians — nearly six hundred of them — entered the *msi-kah-mi-qui* dressed in their finest and sat crosslegged on the beaten earth floor, whispering and smiling and pointing toward him.

At a wave of Pucksinwah's hand, the three squaws melted into the assemblage and the prevailing murmur of voices stilled. The chief of the Kispokotha Shawnees now took Duke's hand and led him to a bearskin where he motioned him to sit. Then he handed the youth a pipe tomahawk decorated with blue-tinted feathers, a small cloth bag containing punk, flint and steel, and a pouch made of the entire pelt of a skunk which had been skinned pocket fashion. The tail hung down below it and the white stripes on the back rose to the mouth of the pouch. This bag was filled with *kinnikinnick*, the shredded and dried leaves of tobacco, sumac, willow and dogwood combined in an aromatic blend.

Pipes similar to that which had been given him by the chief were now being lighted all over the room. Now, at a nod from Pucksinwah, Duke ignited his punk with the flint and steel, and with this lighted his pipe and puffed shallowly. Until every pipe had been smoked out and placed on the floor beside its owner, not a word further was spoken by anyone.

At last Pucksinwah rose from the sitting position he had taken for the pipe-smoking ritual and spoke in a strong measured tone, clearly audible to all assembled.

"My son, you are now flesh of our flesh and bone of our bone. By the ceremony which was performed this day, every drop of white blood was washed out of your veins; you are taken into the Shawnee nation and initiated into a warrior sept; you are adopted into a great family and now received with great seriousness and solemnity in the room and presence and place of a great man. After what has passed this day, you are now one of us by an old strong law and custom. My son, you have now nothing to fear — we are now under the same obligations to love, support and defend you, that we are to love and defend one another; therefore you are to consider yourself as one of our people and forever more be known and respected as Weh-yah-pih-ehr-sehn-wah."

Blue Jacket!

[*July 29, 1771 — Monday Morning*]

The twenty-eight-foot canoe slid into the main current with an ease and gracefulness which belied its bulkiness and great weight. With six weeks of tedious and difficult work behind them, the five had wasted no time in packing their gear and launching the craft. Simon could not recall ever before being so thankful a job was completed.

Their hands, even those of Greathouse, were gashed and blistered and full of annoying splinters from the work of laboriously chipping out the canoe in a single piece from the carefully selected straight trunk of an old beech tree. Except for the actual felling of the tree and trimming of its branches, which had been done with a double-bit ax, the entire project had been accomplished with no other tools save their tomahawks. And now that they were on their way, Simon Kenton found it difficult to believe he was riding a current into a land that for so many years had been to him more a myth than reality.

Jacob Greathouse had taken the rear position — the command post — and Bill Grills was in the bow. The other three sat at intervals between them, the accumulated gear for the expedition piled deeply around them: shot pouches tightly filled and lashed to chunks of dry wood so they would float if the boat should happen to capsize; extra powder, nearly half a keg, stored in five watertight oiled bags and in five different locations; flour, salt, jerky and other nonperishables securely sealed and positioned; a greased buffalo-hide bag resembling a fat hog without legs and crammed with sixty pounds of parched corn; extra blankets, linsey shirts, spare knives and tomahawks, greatcoats, coarse linsey-woolsey trousers and knee-length stockings; over one hundred tempered-iron traps of assorted sizes with chains; ropes, rawhide tugs, smoked meat and fish, salt pork, assorted pans and three iron kettles, bear oil, extra paddles and poles, lard and a score or more of other items — all packed and stored carefully.

Only one last stop was contemplated: an overnight stay at Provance Settlement a few miles above the mouth of big White Day Creek on the east bank of the Monongahela.[8] There they would barter for, or buy, what few supplies might still be needed for a trip that was apt to keep them in the wilderness for the better part of a year. It was, Greathouse declared, the last chance they would have for a solid roof over their heads — and whiskey. It would also, he added, be their last chance for real beds in which to sleep or, if they chose, in which to romp with one of the buxom sluts available there for a price.

The booming voice and laughter of Jacob Greathouse, as he alternately dipped his paddle to steer them into the best current for drifting and took heavy swallows from a glazed jug, resounded from the shores and Simon again sensed the awful malevolence which lay just beneath the surface of this man. The feeling had grown stronger ever since that first day when he and Grills had set out for the Greathouse camp a mile or so below Ice's Ford. They had stopped first where Simon had hidden his gear and he had secured the tugs and swung the pack to his shoulder. Half an hour later he dropped it to the ground in the camp and the three men there watched him without expression, wordlessly.

Grills dropped the dressed turkey on a crude table and introduced Simon, briefly explaining how they'd met. Greathouse was a massive, sharp-featured individual who never took his eyes from Simon's, not even while filling a cob pipe from a haired coonskin pouch.

If Simon had thought Grills looked like the typical frontiersman, the appearance of Greathouse proved him wrong. The man's hair was short and very dark, contrasting sharply with penetrating gray eyes. He seemed to be in his late forties and was no less than two inches taller than Simon. Wide across the shoulders and flat as a half-log bench through the middle, his arms and legs were seasoned hickory. He wore no cloth over his chest but, instead, a soft doeskin shirt rubbed deeply with ash and charcoal to impart a gray-dun color which would blend more effectively with wild country background.

The tough buckskin leggins he wore were also grayed and tight to calf and ankle, permitting silent running when necessary. The double-soled moccasins were a dirty-yellow buffalo hide and relatively new. All of his other leathers were well worn, dark with accumulated dirt and grease and sweat across the chest, under the arms, down the back and seat, in the crotch and on the upper legfronts. The skinning knife in a tied-down sheath on his right hip was almost identical to Simon's, and an unusually thin-bladed tomahawk hung in a peculiar sheath under his left arm. Tightly held by his belt beside an odd ornate buckle was a long-barreled flintlock horse pistol. Whatever the emergency, it was obvious that Jacob Greathouse would not be a man easily disarmed.

The brothers John and Raphael Mahon had been squatting near the ashes of a dead campfire, one holding a large hairless buffalo hide steady while the other followed a straight charcoal line with his knife. The pair looked much alike, which was basically nondescript — the type to easily become lost in a crowd of three. Their one unique characteristic was a tight humorless grin more disconcerting than a snarl. The expression seldom altered.

Although Greathouse had said no word, it was immediately obvious that he was leader of this party. Grills, in telling of his encounter with Simon, spoke to the big man alone and the Mahons glanced from Simon to Greathouse as Grills spoke.

When Grills finished, Greathouse approached the youth. He moved with a stealthy grace and Simon watched him warily. He had already taken a considerable dislike to this man and was honest enough with himself to concede that it was a dislike bred mostly of fear.

In the woods Simon had noted the aroma emanating from Grills and it was strong but not repugnant to him — a rather heady combination of woodsmoke, sweat and bear grease. The rancid stench from Greathouse, however, became noticeable when he was still a yard or so distant and grew worse as he came closer. The youth wondered how the others could have become accustomed to it.

Greathouse stopped an arm's length away and stared directly into Simon's eyes, his gaze measuring, calculating. And though Simon felt a strong desire to shift his own eyes elsewhere, he did not look away. At length the leader's right mouthcorner twitched in what might have been a smile and he extended his hand.

"The gun. Give it to me."

Simon's fingers tightened instinctively on the breech and he shook his head slightly. "Jacob fits no man's hand but mine."

The man's eyes narrowed at the soft-spoken words and the twitch evolved into a thin, wicked grin. "Jacob, eh? My name, my gun. Give it here."

Again Simon shook his head but this time accompanied it with a deft movement which brought the muzzle to bear unwaveringly on the man's middle. Though he kept his eyes on Greathouse, peripherally he was aware that the Mahons had looked at one another and then back at him. A wolfish grin showed Grills to be enjoying the scene immensely. Even Greathouse was openly smiling now, but Simon noticed it was only the mouth that smiled, not the eyes.

"Oh ho!" the big man said. "Our babe has teeth, eh? Good. The cub without teeth soon bites into meat he finds he can't tear, eh? Now, young man, point your Jacob at the ground or you will be forced to shoot me very soon and that would be unfortunate, eh? It is never pleasant to kill a man. Necessary at times, yes, but never pleasant. You will lower the gun, eh?"

"When you say you won't try to take it," Simon said flatly.

"Look at me, boy. Look at my eyes. I tell you now that I will not take your gun from you, eh?"

Slowly Simon lowered Jacob and Greathouse erupted in a monstrous roaring laughter. "Not teeth in this babe," he shouted, "but fangs!"

He whooped again and slapped himself on the chest with a huge hairy hand. So swiftly he could scarce follow the movement, Simon saw the hand dart to the side and jerk hard. Instantly a paralyzing blow struck his forearm and Jacob fell to the earth from stunned fingers. With almost the same motion, the big man's half-closed hand swept up and collided jarringly with Simon's jaw. The boy's head snapped back and just that quickly he found himself on his back on the ground, his long auburn hair wrapped in Greathouse's fist and the leader's skinning knife poised in front of his eyes.

"Now see what I have!" Greathouse's voice boomed near his ear. "A red scalp. Never before have I lifted a topknot of red. From red men they are all black!"

He laughed uproariously at his joke and touched the blade of the knife to Simon's hairline. At once a warm red line slid down between the youth's brows, along the side of his nose and into his mouthcorner. Involuntarily he licked and tasted his own blood.

Greathouse tossed Simon roughly to one side and stood astride the youth's outstretched legs as he raised himself to an elbow. Very deliberately the man wiped his knife on the soft leather at the inside of his left elbow and returned it to its sheath. Then he stooped to retrieve the tomahawk with which he'd first struck Simon's arm and slid the weapon back into its underarm sheath. He glanced at the fallen rifle and then back at Simon.

"No man has ever pointed a gun at me that way and lived," he declared. "This is the first time. It is also the last time, eh? Twice, little cub, you could have been dead. It could easily have been the blade of the 'hawk to strike as the shaft — in the belly instead of the arm. Instead of here," he touched his forehead, "the knife could have slid here," and he whipped a stiff forefinger across his throat.

Simon touched the shallow cut at his hairline and stared at the blood on his fingertips. When he looked up at the mammoth frontiersman towering over him, his eyes were bleak. "Mr. Greathouse," he said, "the next time I point a gun at you, I'll kill you. And the next time you touch me, I'll kill you."

Once again Greathouse burst into gales of laughter, but this time it was genuine and the surrounding woods rang with it. When it had slackened enough for him to speak, he rubbed the heel of his hand over the corner of one eye and turned to the Mahons and Grills.

"Eh, what do you think of this cub? Two times he comes very close to my blades and then he lays on the ground in his own blood and tells me he will kill me. I think I like this cub, eh?"

He reached out to Simon who, after an instant's hesitation, accepted his hand and was pulled to his feet with no more effort than if he were made of straw. A heavy arm encircled his shoulders and Greathouse continued, "This one is like me thirty years ago. Strong, big, brave. Soon I think the name Simon Butler will be known on the frontier like Jacob Greathouse is known, eh?"

"Maybe even better, Jake," said Grills softly.

The leader shot him a cold stare lasting a full minute until Grills could no longer hold those fierce eyes and looked away, flushing. Greathouse smiled and again the smile was only on his lips. "Sometimes, Billy," he said, "sometimes I think you are very brave, too. And sometimes I think you are very foolish, eh?"

He turned back to Simon, bent over and picked up Jacob. He looked the weapon over carefully, flicked a pine needle from the lock, nodded approvingly and handed it to Simon.

"I told you I would not take your Jacob from you. Instead, I give it to you, eh?"

That eased the tension and Simon was accepted as one of them. Grills set about cooking the bird and by the time the meal was over the atmosphere was actually congenial, interrupted frequently by their leader's great booming laughter.

Greathouse then told Simon about the canoe they would build together, big enough for five men and equipment enough to last until late spring. Then downriver they'd go to the Shawnees' Can-tuc-kee land where a man's fortune might be made in a winter — if he was lucky.

And now that journey had begun and by this time tomorrow, after their overnight stop at Provance's, they would be approaching Fort Pitt and, more important, the head of the Ohio River.

[*July 29, 1771 — Monday Evening*]

The gait of the man approaching the cabin at Ice's Ford was so smooth he seemed rather to flow than walk and Andrew Ice's eyes lighted in pleased recognition. He stepped from the open doorway where he'd been lazily smoking and watching the sky fill up with night and strode briskly to meet the visitor.

He greeted him as Davey and clapped him on the shoulder, telling him he'd been a long time gone and some of the border men had begun to wonder if maybe he hadn't gotten his powder wet once too often. The newcomer flashed even, white teeth and shook Ice's hand, but he wasted no time in coming to the point of his visit. Had Andy seen or heard anything of the Mahon boys?

He listened carefully as Ice told him that the brothers had been here for weeks but had just left this morning, going downriver with enough supplies for the whole garrison at Fort Pitt. Greathouse was with them; Grills, too, and a feisty youngster new to these parts called Butler. No, he doubted they'd stop at Provance's. Like he said, they were outfitted with damned near his whole stock when they left here.

Davey grunted, squeezed Ice's shoulder and set off down the narrow river trail. Knowing Greathouse, they'd stopped at Provance's for one of two things. Probably both.

[*July 29, 1771 — Monday Evening Late*]

The Greathouse party had put ashore at Provance Settlement several hours before and Simon, as newest and youngest member, was unanimously elected to stay with the canoe to guard the supplies; not so much against theft by other border men, but because it wasn't unheard of for a band of roving Senecas or Delawares to come swooping through and be gone with everything before anyone knew it. As soon as their business, as Greathouse put it, was finished over at the Inn, why, they'd send someone to spell him and they could all get together for a drink at The Cabin.

Simon Kenton had shrugged. His mind was filled with the morrow and he had little interest in the "business" alluded to by Greathouse. Had it been up to him, they would not have stopped here at all. As it was . . . he shrugged again and accepted the delay as philosophically as possible.

Of the four other men in the party, only toward Grills did he feel any real affinity. Bill Grills was an interesting and intelligent man with a vast storehouse of tales, all of which carried the aura of truth, and a woodland ability little short of the miraculous. He boasted he could trail an unshod pony through a thunderstorm over a solid granite outcrop and no one laughed but Simon, and he only once. In the six weeks they were together building the large canoe, Grills taught him a great deal of this woods lore and Simon drew his unqualified praise by proving an eager and amazingly retentive student.

Grills had been born in Baltimore, he said, and attended school there until he was fourteen. At that time his parents set out to claim some of the fertile lands to the west which, as word had it, were there for the taking. Unfamiliar with Indian ways and wiles and even scornful of the "ignorant savages," they left themselves wide open for attack. As if foreordained, the attack came, and the boy's parents were slain and scalped in front of his horrified eyes. For six years Grills lived with the Ottawas, learning their ways and their language. But one day, while on a hunting trip with them, he had simply turned left when the party turned right. He returned to Baltimore and took in a few more years of schooling, but the call of this exciting land was too much for him and soon he drifted back.

"I discovered, lad," he told Simon, "that there were many traits of the Indian that are considerably more admirable than those of the white man. I couldn't go back to the Ottawas, of course, but since I could talk their language I took up trading and did pretty well until — "

"Until?"

"Ah, lad, there was a young squaw name of Match-squa-thi Te-beth-to-kish-thoe — Little Moon is about as close as it comes in English. She was a Thawegila Shawnee. Bit on the chubby side, maybe, but quite a woman. There are times, as you'll find out soon if you haven't already, when something takes over a man and he's just got to have a woman, no matter who she is. So I took her. It wasn't a very smart thing to do because she was already taken. A drunk brave comes in — drunk on my whiskey, mind you! — and lets out a whoop and starts clawing for his 'hawk. So I had to stick him and run off with that squaw screeching loud enough to hear her in Baltimore."

"You killed him? Who was he?"

"Don't recollect his name but I guess he was Little Moon's husband. Hell yes, I killed him. Didn't have any other choice. But that ended any trading I could do with the Indians, so after that I more or less wandered around living off the country, carrying news and making a little money trapping. Had to quit that, though. Got caught in one of my deadfalls one night and got both feet frozen before I could hack my way out. After that I couldn't wade the cold winter creeks anymore. So it wasn't too long after that when I joined up with Greathouse and the Mahons. They needed somebody like me who could read trail well and knew a lot about Indians."

Simon asked about Greathouse, where he came from and how he happened to come here. Grills admitted that while Jake was a man who talked little about his past, he'd been able to put a lot together about him over the years. As he understood it, Greathouse was born on a farm along the Rappahannock in Virginia. He and his younger brother, Daniel, headed west when he was about eighteen and they'd been on one side or the other of the border for over thirty years.

Daniel, Grills said, was milder-mannered than Jake and wanted a little more security than his brother, so he joined the garrison at Fort Pitt and was currently there as a captain. Jake, however, was like a bear — funning and clowning most of the time — but his moods could change in an instant. A dangerous and unpredictable man. A man who would kill without mercy or feeling.

Remembering his own brief and nearly disastrous first meeting with him, Simon realized how fortunate he was. He nodded and asked, "Has he killed many men, Bill?"

"Nine since I've known him, lad, but all but two were Indians. The two white men had a chance, but knowing Greathouse and his ways of fighting, I guess it wasn't much of a chance when you get right down to it. He's a deadly man to have as an enemy and damned nigh as deadly to have as a friend. You've seen him use his tomahawk and knife. There aren't many who have and are alive to tell about it. He can split a pine knot at forty feet with the knife and he's always killing squirrels and rabbits with the 'hawk. He can shoot a rifle about like you but he likes that pistol of his better and you better hope to God he never pulls *that* one on you."

"How did he ever pick up John and Rafe? Looks like they're always with him no matter where he goes."

"Now there are a couple of strange ones," Grills said. "Wouldn't trust either one as far as I could fling a bear. Rafe's oldest by three years but John usually does the talking if there's any to be done. I've never seen either of them laugh.

"Greathouse treats them like dogs and they just lap it up. I've never found out why. They'll do anything he says and the only thing I know they like doing on their own is killing Indians. Any time we cross a trail of a party numbering less than six, those two disappear and before morning comes again they're back in camp saying that those are now "good" Indians. I've heard their house was attacked once, their mother killed and their father taken. Indians probably killed him and threw him in the river before they went a mile. I guess the Mahons don't need any more reason than that for killing them, but you watch out, lad. They're not against killing a white man if they figure he needs it. I've seen them do it a few times. To tell you the truth, I'm scared of those boys. I guess as much as I know about them, they'd do me in in a minute if Jake didn't need me. When he *stops* needing me, that's when I get the hell out of this neck of the country fast as these old frozen feet can carry me!"

"Butler! Eh, Butler!"

Simon jerked erect out of his reverie. Greathouse, pulling a giggling woman behind him, approached the canoe.

"Bess here says she'll watch everything for us, cub," Greathouse said. "Let's you and me go up to The Cabin and join the boys for a drink."

[*July 29, 1771 — Monday Night*]

Sitting around a slivery oak table in The Cabin, the only tavern in Provance Settlement, Greathouse, Grills and the Mahons were immensely enjoying their last hard drinks for some time to come. Surprisingly, Greathouse always refused to carry any whiskey on expeditions, though he did considerable justice to it any other time.

Simon Kenton sat with a mug in front of him, but after the first galling swallow had wanted no more. He was, as a result, considerably more alert than the others and saw the man the instant he entered the door. The stranger cast about with a quick eye that missed nothing, saw the party of five and spoke Jake's name loudly.

"Who calls?" Greathouse muttered, squinting past the sputtering lamp in the center of the table.

"You're still here. I was afraid I'd missed you. Andy Ice said you'd left for Middle Ground this morning."

The stranger strode across the room as he spoke and now stopped where the lamplight struck him fully. He was a striking figure of a man. Of medium height and well proportioned, he carried himself with a boundless assurance. Thick glossy black hair crept from beneath the raccoon skin cap he wore and curled to his shoulders. His buckskins were well worn, yet as clean as any Simon had seen worn on this frontier. His features were not at all rough as Simon had come to expect of border men. If anything, they tended to be close to the line, where they cease being strikingly handsome and become "pretty." The saving grace in this unusual face was a pair of the most intense eyes Simon had ever seen. They moved incessantly, noting every characteristic of their surroundings until, that taken care of, they locked on any object unfamiliar with a scrutiny so penetrating that it seemed no amount of camouflage could hide the truth from his gaze.

In his offhand greeting, which took in the other four members of the party, Simon had watched that gaze settle on him for a quarter-minute; and in that instant he felt that he had been stripped to his basic character and that every secret in his past was clear to the viewer. It was an unnerving experience.

With dawning recognition, Greathouse had risen unsteadily from his chair, knocking it over backward with a clatter which he disregarded. His hawkish features cracked in a great grin of pure pleasure and Simon realized he was witnessing something rare indeed — Jacob Greathouse exhibiting unabashed friendship for a fellow human being.

"Dave!" he roared. "Dave Duncan! By God, where you been for over a year, eh?" He clapped the man a stunning blow on the shoulder which seemed to affect him not at all, then turned to the four at the table.

"You know these boys, Davey," the sweep of his hand took in the Mahon brothers and Bill Grills, then stopped on Simon, "but here's a new one for you, eh? A bear biter if I ever saw one. Tell you a secret, Dave. He stuck a rifle in my gut and after I made him see this wasn't smart and damned near sculped him, the cub looks me in the eye and tells me just as serious as can be that I touch him once more and I'm dead. Now ain't that something? Davey, this here is Simon Butler from down Warm Springs way."

Had Simon been impressed with the newcomer's bearing and appearance, he was infinitely more so at the man's name. David Duncan! It would be a great warrior who could lift this man's raven scalp. In the border lands where many men seemed giants among average people, this man was a giant among giants. Few frontiersmen indeed made names for themselves which were recognizable outside the border areas and those who did could almost be counted on one hand. Simon had heard of only three before leaving Fauquier County. One, of course, was his Uncle Tom, who really didn't count; the other two, however, had a fame which preceded them greatly. One was John Finley, whose activities in southwestern Virginia were already legendary. The other was the famous scout and trader of western Pennsylvania and the Middle Ground who now extended his hand in welcome.

Simon took the firm grip offered and responded in kind, unabashed admiration reflected in his voice. "Mr. Duncan! I've heard an awful lot about you, sir. It's an honor to meet you."

Duncan's smile was a candle in a dark room. "Mr. Butler," he said, "I assure you the pleasure is mine. I've never before had the privilege of meeting a man who pointed a gun at Jacob Greathouse. I rather think I'll be hearing considerably more of you in the future."

"You see, cub, already you are something special, eh?" Greathouse chuckled.

Simon's momentary embarrassment passed while John Provance, owner of The Cabin, deferentially handed the illustrious frontiersman a pint mug half filled with whiskey. Duncan nodded his thanks and Provance withdrew.

"So, Davey," Greathouse continued, "why have you followed us down from the Ford, eh? That's a long way just to say hello. Something big, eh?"

Duncan dropped easily into a spare straightback chair at the table, leaned on an elbow and pointed a finger at the brothers. "John . . . Rafe," he flicked a glance at each in turn, "who do you know who always smiles, has a missing left thumb and a small scar on his forehead?"

For the first and only time, Simon saw real emotion flare in the faces of the brothers. Rafe's jaw dropped. John reached across the table, overturning one almost empty mug without realizing it, and gripped Duncan's wrist tightly. His eyes were burning with a strange fire.

"Duncan, no games. You've seen him?"

Duncan nodded, then stared at Mahon's hand holding his wrist until John abruptly realized what he was doing and jerked it away. Simon was fascinated by the exchange.

"Where?" John Mahon was back on the trail.

"With a hunting party of Delawares camped on Sandy Creek in Middle Ground, two-three days downstream, two-three more by foot."

"How is he?"

"Not good, I think. Thinner than when I saw him last. Looks twenty years older. Good enough to walk, though. Maybe even run a little, if necessary."

"How big a party?"

"Maybe eighteen. Maybe twenty. They'll hunker for a spell, I expect. They made a long-time camp and set up *wegiwas*. Your old friend Running Mink is leading them."

Simon had never seen such naked murder in the eyes of men before. John Mahon's gaze never left Duncan's and his voice when next he spoke was little more than a whisper.

"You know what's next, Duncan."

The scout nodded. "I'll guide you. Reason I came. But one condition: we go out to get him away, not to kill Indians. If we can do it without them knowing it until we're gone, so much the better. I want your promises. John? Rafe?"

Reluctantly the pair agreed and Duncan shot a questioning glance at the others.

"Naturally, Davey," Greathouse said. "Glad to go."

Bill Grills and Simon concurred but Greathouse shook his head. "Not you, cub."

"Why not?" Simon's eyes narrowed.

"Two reasons, both good. First, you've had no experience with Indians and this is no time or place to begin learning. Too much at stake. Second, the boat holds five, that's all. Davey's got to show the way. You couldn't keep those two from going," he indicated the brothers with a big thumb, "since it's their old man who's prisoner. Grills we need for any number of reasons, all obvious, eh? That leaves you and me. I'm going. That leaves you." He turned to the others. "We start in the morning."

Turning back to Simon, whose face reflected stunned disappointment, the big leader said, "You worked hard on the canoe with us, cub. We may be back soon. We may be a long time. Maybe we never get back, eh? So.

We give you your share of supplies and you go your own way, eh? Some powder and lead, some tugs and wearables, some food, some traps. Maybe you soon get some experience trapping, eh?"

Simon was unable to reply.

[*August 20, 1771 — Tuesday*]

Tribal life among the Kispokotha Shawnees was everything Blue Jacket had hoped it would be and more. Not only had his adoption ceremony established him as just as much a Shawnee as any native of the tribe, but it was as if no such thing as his white past had ever existed.

In the months since his capture he had adapted with phenomenal speed to the social, moral, political and religious beliefs and customs and by mid-August he was fluent in the Shawnee tongue. He entered all the sports, habits, games and labors of his fellows with such alacrity and cheerfulness and respect for others that he quickly became very popular.

It was Pucksinwah himself who spent many hours instructing him in the history and culture of the Shawnees and in the religion which played such an important part in their lives. The Supreme Being of all things, the chief told him, is Moneto, who rules the universe — *ya-la-ku-qua-kumi-gigi* — and dispenses His blessings and favors to those who earn His good will, just as He brings unspeakable sorrow to those whose conduct merits His displeasure.

Moneto was not to be mistaken for the Great Spirit, or ruler of destinies, who is subordinate to Him. The Great Spirit — *Inu-msi-ila-fe-wanu* — is a grandmother who is constantly weaving an immense net which is called a *skemotah*. When this net is finished it will be lowered to the earth and all who have proven themselves worthy will be gathered into its folds and taken to a world of great peace and happiness. At the same time, an unspeakably terrible fate will overtake the remainder as the world comes to an end. Good conduct always brought reward, just as evil conduct must bring sorrow.

"No one," Pucksinwah said, "is forced to believe in these matters. Force is not necessary. We know them to be truth. Morality is a fixed law, but each of us is his own judge. From earliest childhood this is instilled in our minds, just as we are taught that deceitfulness is a crime of itself. We live according to our standards and principles, not for what others might think of us. Absolute honesty toward others of our tribe is the basis of character and the standards and rules of conduct are followed scrupulously.

"The foundation of all our intercourse is this: *Do not kill or injure your neighbor, for it is not him that you injure, you injure yourself. But do good to him, therefore add to his days of happiness as you add to your own. Do not wrong or hate your neighbor, for it is not him that you wrong, you wrong yourself. But love him, for Moneto loves him also as He loves you.*"⁹

There was no such thing as a jail among the Shawnees, Blue Jacket learned, but misdeeds did not go unpunished. Punishments were of many kinds and were determined by the gravity of the offense. The chief's word was law and any persistent refusal to obey the unwritten code of honorable conduct was punishable by severe flogging or even death. Anyone refusing voluntarily to take his punishment like a man was ostracized from the tribe as a whole, to which death was infinitely preferable. Nor were the women of the tribe free from the law. The most heinous crime of which a woman could be convicted was *pockvano-madee-way* — gossip about people.

Blue Jacket was impressed at the relatively parallel natures of the Shawnee religion and Christianity. The greatest single fundamental difference was that his people — and he now firmly considered the Shawnees as his people — believed they were only responsible for their conduct toward their own race. To others they owed nothing, except to return in kind the treatment they received.

The closest companion of the newly adopted Shawnee was a strong, vigorous and intelligent young man two years younger than Blue Jacket, named Chiksika. He was son of Chief Pucksinwah and brother to a three-year-old boy who toddled after him adoringly wherever possible; a boy named Tecumseh.

[*August 26, 1771 — Monday*]

It was when he was still a full thirty yards from his secluded campsite that Simon Kenton simultaneously heard the muted laughter and caught a whiff of burning tobacco. With two quick steps he melted into the underbrush and froze with Jacob leveled at waist height for instant use. He berated himself soundly for whatever carelessness he had committed that had left the camp open to discovery, but stood silently for five minutes before ascertaining to his satisfaction that the intruders were stationary. Soundlessly then he crept toward the spot, calmly prepared to kill, if necessary, to protect his property.

During his relatively short tenure in western Pennsylvania, Simon had undergone a remarkable metamorphosis. He looked considerably older than his years and his actions would have done credit to the long-experienced frontiersman; eyes constantly watching the ground as he walked and lifting only occasionally to scan the surrounding area sharply, ears attuned to every sound, nose continually testing the air, all his senses ever on the alert to detect the suspicious.

Since the Greathouse party had left him behind, he had become something of an enigma on the frontier fringe, for no one knew where he lived or saw him except during his regular visits to Provance Settlement or Fort

Pitt to inquire if news had come of the expedition.[10] Simon had had his doubts about what kind of division would be made of the supplies, but his share had turned out to be surprisingly generous, particularly where the traps were concerned. While there were only twelve dozen traps among the five, Greathouse had given him thirty, including the lone bear trap with its huge blunt-toothed jaws and two screw clamps to set it with. A sack each of gunpowder and lead was his, as well as various articles of clothing, staples and food. In a frontier area, this was substantial wealth.

All this material he had hidden carefully in the woods a few miles from Provance and then he had begun to explore. Less than a half mile from his camp he found where someone had felled a beech and begun construction of a twenty-foot canoe and then for some unknown reason deserted it. Simon had since spent much of his time chipping away at it, determined that he would see the Middle Ground if it meant going by himself.

Fort Pitt, smaller than he had anticipated, but nonetheless impressive on that solitary spit of land jutting into the confluence of the great Monongahela and Allegheny Rivers, at once interested and repulsed him. These were the first regular troops he had seen and their rigid discipline and regimentation bothered him. He found it hard to understand how grown men could bow to the many humiliations and ridiculous impositions heaped upon them by their superiors in rank. Even more difficult to understand was that, except for a general complaining which appeared to be the inherent trademark of a soldier, the men seemed satisfied with their lot.

Although he remained in the Provance area, Simon had gone to the fort frequently, where, due to his large size, affability and skill with Jacob, he achieved a pronounced degree of popularity among the men garrisoned there. His natural marksmanship became widely known and there was not a soldier at the fort who had not tried, and failed, to best him in shooting matches.

Newer than most of the British weapons, Simon's flintlock was also lighter, faster loading and easier to sight. His continuous practice in reloading had made him unbeatable in this respect as well; he had even become adept in a feat few men could learn well — that of firing accurately while running, then reloading and firing again without slackening his pace, which meant pouring into the barrel a measure of powder from flask or horn, stuffing in some wadding, putting in a ball and seating each step with the ramrod, all while running.

His early imagined pictures of what border people were like quickly faded. Instead of dauntless, adventuresome woodsmen of high moral character, they were mainly ordinary people drawn to the frontier solely for the possible gain it might net them. Many, in fact, were outright scoundrels for whom the hazards of border life were preferable to the rope or cell awaiting them back east. The knowledge that he had come here because of the same reason was disturbing to Simon. These men were basically an uncouth, obscene and filthy lot given to excesses in drinking, gambling and bedding down with the few available harlots. Except for David Duncan, Bill Grills and Jacob Greathouse, he had met no one who measured up to his preconceived expectations of what a frontiersman should be.

He could have remained in Provance Settlement, but he had neither the money nor inclination to take advantage of the dubious comforts there. Not only did he fear the theft of his store of provisions and personal gear, but he viewed with keen distaste the idea of sleeping in a crowded, vermin-infested barracks of a room with pallets side by side for total strangers.

To some extent, Simon Kenton was lost. His desire to visit the Middle Ground was intense, as manifested by the labor he exerted on the canoe he was making. Yet, fully aware of his own lack of experience and knowledge of where to go and what to do, he hesitated at the thought of setting off downstream by himself. As a result, he spent a great deal of time roaming about the countryside and tracking various animals, particularly deer, wolves, bobcats and raccoons.

He had put to the test and not found lacking the secrets of effective tracking taught to him by Grills during their six weeks together. "Always remember, lad," Grills had told him, "the ground is an open book to those who can read the writing and understand it."

It was true. The bent blade of grass, imprint of toenail or hoof, deserted bedding place or fecal deposits spoke volumes to Simon. From animal droppings, for example, he could determine not only how long ago the creature had passed that point and what kind of an animal it was, but an amazing number of facts which even experienced trackers often overlooked. A day-old deposit of raccoon droppings, for instance, told Simon that the animal was hungry and had passed this way the evening before, shortly after having slept all day. Bits of crayfish shell and frog bones indicated it had spent some time the night before in a small, slow stream — probably Crow Creek, which emptied into the river a mile or so away. With this and other information Simon was able to deduce the exact path the animal had taken with incredible accuracy.

Closely allied to following trail went the ability to conceal his own tracks. With all his goods frequently left in an unguarded camp less than two hundred yards off the trail leading from Provance to Fort Pitt, Simon took great pains to keep the area free of detection from passersby. He seldom entered or left along the same route he had used before and where there was a rock he made certain to step upon it, studiously avoiding soft ground. Fallen tree trunks were used as walkways upon which his soft footwear left no mark and he was well pleased with his cunning.

Thus, it was a severe jolt to him now to know that at least two people had invaded his sanctuary; two, rather than one, because there had been laughter and a lone man rarely laughs aloud.

The pair were sitting propped with their backs against a large boulder, the young one talking steadily and the older one smoking a pipe, his eyes closed. Although Simon could have sworn he made no sound, the older man — without opening his eyes — silenced his garrulous companion with a touch and said, "He's back."

Surprised, the young man turned and his jaw dropped at the sight of Simon fifteen feet away, his eyes as cold and unwavering as the barrel of Jacob as he inspected them.

The older man, who now opened his eyes lazily, had a thick mat of grizzled beard and brows to match. A large ugly mass of scar tissue began high on his brow and formed an island the size of Simon's hand, surrounded by a fringe of the same wiry, grizzled hair. He looked frail in body and his large mournful eyes had deep lines at the outer corners, some of which extended nearly to his ears. What little of his cheeks could be seen above the beard was purplish, due to a pronounced crisscrossing of veins and arteries close to the skin surface.

The youth, on the other hand, was no more than a year or so older than Simon and, in some vague way, reminded Simon of himself when he first reached Warm Springs. Though three or four inches shorter than Simon, he was well built, and his teeth, very even and white, flashed starkly in a wide but nervous grin. His blond hair overlapped his ears, imparting a loutish look, but his eyes were intelligent. His shirt and trousers were of coarse gray linsey, the latter anchored to the waist by a knotted strand of rawhide. His big feet were imprisoned in an ungainly pair of ankle-high, rudely-made brogans. When he spoke, the words had difficulty hurdling the large teeth blocking their passage.

"Say, we sure did have a time finding you, didn't we John?" He glanced at his companion for corroboration.

The old man nodded and smiled toothlessly at Simon. "Hunker down, boy," he said. "We got talk that'll innerest you."

Simon appeared not to have heard and demanded to know who they were, what they wanted and what they were doing in his camp.

"You sure were right, John. You sure were." He explained to Simon, "John said you'd be suspicious as all get out. Said we'd probably be lucky if you didn't shoot before talking. I'm George Strader and him," he dipped his head at the old man, "he's John Yeager. We been hearing a lot about you, Mr. Butler, all about your shooting and tracking and how you got left behind when the Greathouse party —"

"Shesh, boy," Yeager cut in, "you get too excited." He shook his head and indicated Simon's gun still pointed at them. "Put it up son, an' relax. Strader there, he ain't got knife nor gun nor nothin' else 'cept a mouth what kin make five hunnerd words a minute without sayin' a damn thing worth hearin'. Me, I ain't got but this here skinnin' knife . . ." he lifted it out slowly and flipped it aside ". . . an' I reckon a lad your size kin handle an old man an' a green young'un."

Slowly Simon lowered Jacob, propped the gun against a tree beside him and squatted. His mind was racing. Strader acted toward him like he'd felt about Duncan. He was amazed that stories about him were circulating along the frontier and breathed a small prayer of thanks that he'd been prudent enough to retain the Butler identity and hadn't asked Duncan about Thomas Kenton as he'd been tempted.

"I'm gonna tell you a little story," Yeager continued, "but I don't want no inneruptions, so jest hold off any questions you got till I finish. Then you kin ast away all night iffen you've a mind."

Simon nodded and Yeager hacked deeply, spat to one side and began. "Well sir, I'm 'bout sixty, sixty-five year old an' don't know where at I come from, so don't ast. Reckon I was 'bout four when Injens took me. Mingoes, they was. You prob'ly heard 'em called Senecas, which is 'bout the same but not quite. They raised me, them Mingoes, an' raised me good. Taught me 'bout the earth an' sky, birds an' critters an' all. Learned to talk their talk which is called Eery-quoi, plus a couple other kinds, too. Picked up 'nuff Al-gon-qwee-en to figure out what any Injen I meet is sayin'."

He broke off into a rapid barrage of curious grunts and tongue-twisting syllables which surprised Kenton. This was the first true Indian talk he'd encountered.

"Them's samples," said Yeager. "Mingo, Erie, Wyandotee, Tuskeeroras, Kai-yuga, Huron an' lots others, them's all Eery-quoi talk. Ojibway, Micmac, Potty-wotty-me, Chippewah, Deleware, Miami, Ottoway, Shawnee, them's all Al-gon-qwee-en talk. Yessir, boy, them Mingoes taught me.

"I learned huntin' an' warrin' an' trackin' — ain't no better trackers, which is how come we was able to find you — an' ever'thin' else they know, an' I learned it good. Not only that, I learned it in the best Injen huntin' ground they is — the Can-tuc-kee land!"

Suddenly excited, Simon leaned forward to speak but the old man stopped him with upraised hand. "Wait'll I finish, boy. Lived with 'em sixteen winters an' would be livin' with 'em now, but I wanted to move. Wanted to see what kind of people these whites was that was causin' sech a ruckus. So they left me go, figgerin' when I come up on the white man's ways I'd come back glad to stay. Prob'ly would've, too, 'ceptin' I met a pair of Shawnee braves. Them days Mingo an' Shawnee didn't mix much, boy. They caught me an' pulled a few of their games on me, like pullin' out all my teeth an' shovin' their knives under my thumbnails. Then, when I still wouldn't scream or beg, they sculped me. Ever seen a sculpin', boy?"

Simon shook his head, fascinated.

"Ain't fun," Yeager said shortly. "Leastways when you ain't the one doin' the sculpin'. Stuck a knife to the bone here," he pointed to where the scar tissue began above his forehead, then ran his finger in a circle along the fringe of hair, "an' run it around so. Then one buck I ain't never gonna fergit grabs the hair in the middle an' gives a big pull. Well sir, she popped right off. Dunno how it sounded fer them, but fer me 'twas like a powder keg ablowin'. Reckon I did scream then, an' them Shawnees jest laughed fit to bust. They takes my knife an' all my clothes an' turns me loose to wander in the woods, figgerin' I'll die. Well sir, I didn't. Don't 'member a whole lot after that but later on they tol' me at the fort that they run onto me staggerin' 'bout in the woods an' ravin' like a spirit's got holt a' me.

"Should'a died, I reckon, but they was a man there knowed jest what to do. My skull was almost black but that feller, he jest has a couple men tie me down an' puts the tip of a leather awl right on my bare skull an' starts twirlin' it 'twixt his hands. Now, boy, you ever figger on hearin' a real noise, that's the one. Sounded like I was settin' under a waterfall an' right then I figger that iffen this here is the torture the white man's figgered out to work on the Injens, he's got 'em beat sure.

"But that weren't no torture, boy. Leastways it weren't meant to be. They was helpin' me an' but fer them I reckon I wouldn't be here now nohow. Well sir, that feller drills down with that awl, goin' slower an' slower as it goes in 'til a kind of pink juice starts showin' up. Then he quits drillin' there an' starts another hole 'bout a squaw tooth from the first. He does this all over my skull an' by the time he's done I figger I'm either dead or crazy, but let me tell you somethin', boy. That there pink stuff gets all over the top of my skull an' then starts makin' new skin right under the black scabby stuff. I wouldn't of believed it, no sir! 'Fore long the black starts peelin' away an' there's the new skin. Course, it didn't happen overnight. Took nearly two years fer it to heal up like 'tis now. Don't reckon it's much fer pretty, but I don't figger on courtin' no squaw directly, either."

The old man stopped and scratched the bare spot vigorously, as if all the talk about it had brought back the terrible pain and itching that must have accompanied his convalescence.

"I ain't done yet!" Yeager snapped, as Strader began to say something. "Well sir, I been roamin' this here country ever since, keepin' alive somehow an' all the time lookin' fer a couple strong young fellers to go with me back to them Can-tuc-kee huntin' grounds. They's a fortune alayin' there fer them what knows where an' got the iron to go get it. Strader here, I found him a few weeks ago comin' west from over Johnstown way. He's willin' to come along. How 'bout you, boy?"

Simon masked his excitement and paused before answering. There were certain things to be cleared up before he could decide. For example, why had they come looking for him in particular? He put the question to Yeager but it was the younger man who answered first.

"First of all we heard about your shooting and tracking. We need someone who can do it good. John's eyes aren't as good as they once were, he says. I'm pretty good at tracking but not as good as people say you are.

"Secondly," he continued, "we heard about you being all set to go along with the Greathouse party and then being left behind when they took out with David Duncan. That means you're all by yourself now without anything planned, I guess, so you might as well go with us."

Simon considered carefully, weighing the liabilities of such a partnership against the opportunity to see the Can-tuc-kee land. Yeager was a weak old man and apt to become a problem. Strader was very green, seemingly without much promise of learning quickly, and in the country they were headed for, those who didn't learn quickly were dead. He asked Yeager for more details about the fabled hunting grounds and for nearly an hour more Yeager rambled on.

The soil was so rich, he claimed, that parched corn would grow. Bushes, trees, grasses, all the vegetation was thick and luxurious and the game that inhabited the area was so plentiful as to be unbelievable until actually witnessed. There were beautiful flowering hills and cool valleys, and springs which bubbled rivers of the purest cold water, winter and summer.

From his own admittance, it had been nearly fifty years since Yeager had been to the Can-tuc-kee lands with the Mingoes and Simon asked him whether he could find it again. Yeager grew indignant. Of course he could find it! All they had to do was get a boat and float down the Ohio a few days and they'd be there. They would recognize it easily because it was the old Indian crossing and the most beautiful canelands in the world came right down to the south shore of the river. They just couldn't miss.

There was a long silence as each lived momentarily in the glory of the picture Yeager had created of the Can-tuc-kee lands. Then Simon made his decision.

"I'll go," he said.

[November 2, 1771 — Saturday]

The trip down the Ohio was many things for Simon Kenton. It was a thrilling look at a world where few white men had ever ventured before and none stayed. It was a constant awareness of the passing shoreline with the thought never far from mind that they might, at any given moment, come under observation of hostile Indians. It was an exhilarating encounter with a wild, unruly river which might on one day be deep and calm and smoothly rolling and on the next be a windlashed, choppy, rock-filled rapids threatening to smash the canoe and drown its occupants. But of all the things the trip was to Simon, it was mostly a great disappointment, for not only were they unable to find the canelands so praised by Yeager, but there seemed little likelihood that they would in the future.

It had taken them some little time after the decision was made to join forces for the venture downriver to get the canoe completed, to reprovision insofar as they could with their meager funds, and set off on September 12. Simon had left word with John Provance to tell the Greathouse party of his departure if they returned soon.

Yeager's casual reference to the canelands being "jest a few days downstream" was a considerable miscalculation. The few days became a week, a fortnight, a month with no indication of them. Yet, each morning's light found the trio hopeful that this was the day they would reach their goal.

The float down this mighty river was one of unsurpassed beauty. Deep green hills plunged steeply to the water's edge, holding the river into a relatively narrow and swift channel. Their first stop, eighteen miles below Fort Pitt, had been Logstown, once populated by Shawnees before continuous harassment had driven them farther downriver and into the Ohio interior. Here they spent two days with John Gibson, owner of a small trading post, who told them stories of the river traffic over the years.

Past this very spot twenty-two years ago, he said, had gone Pierre Joseph Celeron with his pompous little army of two hundred thirty-five French soldiers, planting engraved leaden plates at the mouths of every major stream he passed, claiming all the land to west and north for France. And it was here also, just eighteen years ago, that a pair of young surveyors named Christopher Gist and George Washington had spent a five-day layover en route to give a "hands-off" order to the French at Fort Le Bouef in regard to the Northwestern Territory, which was the Middle Ground.

Leaving Gibson's, the trio passed Beaver Creek, where the Ohio turns from the northwestward course it has held ever since Fort Pitt and heads south. But ten days and sixty-two river miles after leaving Fort Pitt there had been no sign of the canelands, and so they put ashore at Yeager's suggestion a few miles below Yellow Creek, hid their canoe and took a trail inland to a Mingo village to ask directions.[11] Here they were welcomed and, "as it was a time of peace, they frolicked and danced with the young Indians." But when they asked how to find the Can-tuc-kee canelands, the Mingoes became cool and the lightness of the visit ended.

Afloat again, they saw the little stockade just erected by Ebenezer Zane, but found it empty and continued their journey.[12] Soon behind them were Big Grave, Captina and Big Fish Creeks and the large muddy Muskingum River, entering from the bowels of Ohio.

Now they stopped for more hunting, fishing and dancing; this time at a small Delaware village near the mouth of the Little Kanawha River, one hundred eighty-six river miles from Fort Pitt. Simon was by now beginning to pick up a workable Indian vocabulary and, with a little effort, could make himself understood, although he could still not follow their conversation. Once again they met cool rebuff and their visit was cut short when they inquired about the canelands.

They started downstream again and passed the big mouth of the Hockhocking River.[13] Almost at once they entered the boulder-strewn beach area of the Ohio palisades country, where the shadows of the towering hills shaded the river; then came a forty-mile stretch of sharp bends and rapids climaxed by a treacherous falls which they navigated safely.[14]

Just before reaching the Guyandotte River, the Ohio changed from a southerly direction to a westerly one and, at the Big Sandy River, three hundred nine miles below Fort Pitt, the river angled northwestward again. At length, with October nearly half over — having passed dozens of large unnamed rivers and creeks entering this stream — they reached the mouth of the Kentucky River, well over five hundred miles from the river's beginning.

Arguments, some bitter, had sprung up between them. Where were the canelands that Yeager claimed were a few days down the Ohio? Rattled and confused, Yeager could only insist that they really did exist, that he hadn't been making it up and that they must have drifted past them sometime during one of their many nights afloat.

It was no time to debate. The woods had changed from deep green to scarlet and yellow and rust and winter was rapidly coming on. They must establish themselves before then. The three agreed that the thing to do was to start back upstream to see if they could spot the elusive canelands and, if they could not in a reasonable time, to set up winter camp at the best possible location.

Now the passage became a nightmare of hard work. Hands became blistered and backs ached from the work of paddling against the strong current. As much as possible they stayed close to the south shore, where the current was weaker and attack from Indians less likely.

Time and again they put in to shore and Simon made brief explorations, but still there was nothing that even vaguely resembled their goal. Thus it was that on the first day of November they headed the canoe up the Great Kanawha River, following it to the mouth of the Elk River, where Simon discovered a deeply worn buffalo trail.[15] He followed the trail upstream along the Kanawha to a salt spring which showed much evidence of use by a variety of animals. This looked as good as any place he had seen on the whole journey and so he went back for the others.

The three returned to the site and erected a primitive but highly satis-

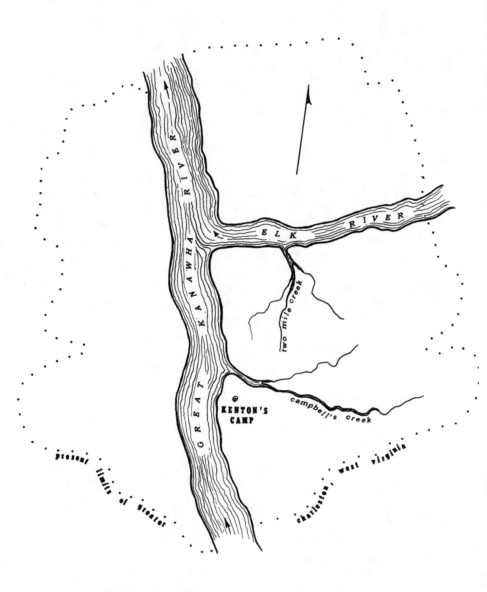

factory half-faced camp. Having located a huge fallen tree, they cleared a space twelve feet square in front of it for the floor area and at the outer corners sunk two large forked poles. Across the forks they placed a heavy pole and from this to the fallen tree they laid a series of smaller poles, finally covering this entire roof with a half-foot of dry grasses and leaves, upon which a layer of dirt and sod was packed. The two open sides were closed with a gradual buildup of heaped logs and more poles and branches, which were in turn covered with leaves, moss and dirt until they were effectively sealed.

Soft mosses and dry leaves were spread on the floor for bedding and a large fire area prepared in front of the open face of the shelter. Here they would cook their meals and, at night, wrap themselves in their blankets and sleep in remarkable comfort with their feet toward the warm coals.

The next day they scouted and found the area alive with game and fur animals. That evening, their stomachs pleasantly filled with fresh turkey and venison and their trapping campaign for the winter laid out, they all felt better and more enthusiastic than they had for many a day.

CHAPTER II

[*April 6, 1772 — Wednesday*]

ALL three of them had been dreading the long upcurrent paddle to Provance Settlement with their furs, but there was no other choice. They needed more lead and powder, more basic provisions and clothing, more tools and more traps.

The winter sojourn on the Great Kanawha just above the Elk had been profitable beyond any expectations and they were greatly pleased with the fruits of their labors. They had seven large bales of fur pelts — muskrat, mink, beaver, otter, raccoon, skunk, weasel, deer, elk, buffalo and black bear — and it seemed they had hardly nicked the surface of the animal population in the area.

Disappointment at not having found the Can-tuc-kee canelands was always with them, but matters had worked out surprisingly well in spite of it and they had gotten along well together. Each had his job and did it well, so there were few disputes.

Simon Kenton covered the country up the Kanawha from the mouth of the Elk, on both sides — hunting and regularly running his trapline. George Strader, a better woodsman now but still unable to learn as he should have from observing the animals and country around him, had as his territory the countryside on both sides of the Kanawha below the mouth of the Elk River. John Yeager, unable to cope with the rigors of running traps and hunting over hills and valleys, remained mostly in camp. It was he who did all the cooking and taking care of camp as well as the skinning, fleshing and stretching of the hides brought in. The arrangement was good and they were satisfied. They were, in fact, loath to leave on the arduous trip upriver.

They had made two smaller canoes shortly after their arrival, one for Simon's use in crossing the Kanawha upstream and the other for Strader as he worked downstream. Now one of these canoes had been carefully hidden in the woods and the other filled with pelts securely tied down, and the smaller craft attached with a piece of braided rawhide to the big canoe in which the three would ride with their immediate supplies.

Even with the Kanawha's spring-freshened current behind them, it took two full days to reach the Ohio and they camped for the night on the triangular point of land where the rivers met, planning to rest well overnight before beginning the hard trip ahead.

In the morning a voice, startling in its unexpectedness, hailed them as they were breaking camp and all three spun about, Simon and Strader with their rifles poised. A huge canoe, fully forty feet long, was putting in to shore from the main current of the larger river where it had been floating downstream. Inside the craft were dozens of bundles of goods — foodstuffs, clothing, powder, lead and a wide variety of tools, cooking utensils and other provisions. Also in the boat were ten husky Thawegila Shawnees and a tall, darkly bearded white man who was now standing with both hands raised as if in benediction. It was he who had hailed them and now he told them they had nothing to fear, that he was a trader on his way back to his trading post near the large village of these Shawnees far up the Omee River or, as they had probably heard it referred to, the Great Miami River.

They hadn't heard of it but they didn't tell him so and he went on. His name, he said, was Peter Loramie and he was an independent Frenchman who three years ago had established his flourishing store on a large creek fifteen miles above the point where it emptied into the Great Miami; a creek, he added proudly, which now bore his own name. He stepped lightly to shore as the craft grounded.

John Yeager had blanched at sight of the Shawnees but his voice was firm and unafraid when he rattled off a comment to the Indian in front and was answered in a curious admixture of grunts and guttural words. He nodded and told Simon and Strader in a whisper that it was all right, that they didn't know him, adding in a louder voice that they had seen the bales of fur and the trader was interested in doing business.

This was indeed a stroke of luck. Simon invited them all ashore and showed the pelts, then inspected the stores in the big canoe. Several hours were spent in the transaction and when the big canoe once again slid into the main current, the three men were provisioned with all the ammunition, clothes, tools and staple foodstuffs they would need to carry them through another year. As a token of friendship, Loramie had added a huge iron kettle to seal the bargain, laughingly suggesting that they could boil in it any Cherokee they might catch. Despite the peace treaty the Shawnees and Delawares had concluded with the Cherokees in 1768, they lost no love on one another.

Before the trading party was very far downstream, Simon directed his companions to get into their own canoe and they too pushed off into the Ohio and began paddling upstream. Simon explained that he hadn't liked the looks of several of the bucks who seemed angry to see white men here. It would, in any event, be foolish for them to announce the fact that they were camped up the Great Kanawha.

As soon as the big boat had passed out of sight downstream, they put to shore and carefully stowed the goods they had quickly tossed into the bottom of the canoe. Then they shoved off once again, returned to the smaller river and headed up toward their hunting grounds, well pleased with themselves and their good fortune.

[July 18, 1772 — Saturday]

John Murray Dunmore, in less than one year as governor of the Colony of Virginia, had succeeded in making himself extremely unpopular among the Colonists.

A rather heavy, pompous individual of forty, he had become an earl at the age of twenty-four and had taken his seat in the House of Lords in 1761. Two years ago he had become governor of New York Colony and then, last year, his Lordship had taken on the additional responsibilities of governing Virginia as well.

Lord Dunmore of late had become quite perturbed at the growing antagonism of the Colonists and their overt dissatisfaction with English rule. It was time to put a decisive end to that. Accordingly, he sent forth an order to be posted in all public places which dissolved the right of assembly because of its expression of revolutionary sentiment.

It was a highly combustible stick with which to poke the fire of resentment already burning so brightly.

[September 30, 1772 — Wednesday]

Throughout the summer Simon Kenton, George Strader and John Yeager had explored, ostensibly seeking the elusive canelands which, by now, none of them really believed they'd find in this area. Mostly they covered the ground on the south side of the Ohio River between the Great Kanawha and the Big Sandy, roaming the hills as much as twenty miles inland but mostly staying within an hour or so of the Ohio. Here and there they discovered sign of Indian encampment, but it was always many days or even weeks old and they saw no one. There were numerous elk and some buffalo in this area, along with a wide variety of small game, and Simon came to the conclusion that it wasn't only their own camp area near the mouth of Elk River where they could make profit with their trapping.

In early October they once more paddled up the Kanawha to their half-face camp and settled down for another winter, which they anticipated would be at least as profitable as the last.

[March 2, 1773 — Tuesday]

With five large canoes and fifteen men under his command, Dr. John Briscoe put ashore at a fine bottomland opposite a nearly mile-long island close to the Ohio shore, just six miles above the mouth of the Little Kanawha River.[1] A quick inspection showed the ground to be rich indeed, level and well drained by two small creeks. He announced that this was where he would start his settlement and immediately the unloading of the canoes commenced.

It was a good selection; high enough above the river level to be safe from spring and fall flooding, forested just enough to provide logs for the proposed cabins, with little more left to clear to commence planting in a month or so. They would make a fine settlement which he would name Briscoe. As a start, he named the little creek at the base of the hills to the north, Briscoe Run, and glowed with the thought that perhaps this day he had founded a great river port.

[March 9, 1773 — Tuesday]

Simon Kenton did not at all mind the sometimes heavy snow which blanketed the hills and valleys throughout the winter. It drove the fur animals to follow the creek beds more closely and this was where the majority of their traps had been set. But rain was another matter. With it the creeks rose high, covering their traps and making the ground everywhere a slick mire where mud clung to the feet in great lumps and a mile's walk was more tiring than ten on dry land.

This was one of those hateful days, raw and blustery, with the light a dismal gray at best and the rain a constant depressing drizzle. It was cold and the wind bored through wet clothing, chilling them thoroughly. And now, even though an awful weariness enveloped the pair, the glow of the fire twinkling ahead of them through the naked trees caused them to quicken their steps.

With the passing of the snows and the coming of the rains, the take in their traps had dwindled sharply and so Simon Kenton and George Strader had taken to running their traplines jointly, each starting at a different end of the line and eventually meeting somewhere in the middle, then returning to camp together, the work of it always easier when it ended in company. There had been no possibility of staying dry this morning and so they had delayed leaving the camp until late in the forenoon, hoping the rain would stop, then setting out resolutely anyway to cover the ground they must cover in the shortest possible time.

The trapline lay in a wide semicircle around the camp, covering a total distance of something more than fourteen miles, and they slogged their uncomfortable rounds until meeting about four miles due east of their base. It had hardly been worth the effort. Strader had three raccoons and two opossums, Simon just one small mink not yet fully grown. The only bright spot of the day occurred as they trudged a straight line back to the camp just as the gray and gloomy light deepened even further with dusk. They jumped a large turkey gobbler with plumage so wet it elected to run rather than fly. Simon swiftly jerked away the oil-heavy opossum hide wrapped around the lock of Jacob to keep the powder dry and threw the weapon to his shoulder, firing instantly. The ball ripped a tuft of feathers from the bird's back and then passed through the neck, severing the spine. At least they would eat well tonight.

The fire was crackling cheerily as they reached the camp and old Yeager grunted appreciatively at sight of the bird. It had been nearly a month since one of them had brought in a turkey. He began plucking it while his two companions dried and oiled their weapons and leaned them against the bales of furs beside the back treetrunk wall, then removed all their clothing and hung it to dry from sticks stuck into the ground around the fire. Their teeth chattering with the cold, Simon and Strader wrapped themselves in their blankets and crouched on the ground at opposite sides of the fire.

With the coming of nightfall the rain had finally ceased, only now it grew colder. Yeager had sectioned the bird so it would cook faster and was spitting it on the ramrod of his rifle when Simon suddenly stared out into the darkness at a slight noise and saw, ten yards away, half a dozen Indians in a semicircle, two with guns already raising to fire.

Simon blurted a sharp warning but it was lost in the crash of one of the guns and Yeager, his back to the intruders, stiffened unnaturally, dropped the spitted bird and clawed for his back.

"Meet at the bear trap!" Simon shouted, at the same time diving toward the darkness on his side of the fire, stumbling for a moment as he lost his blanket and then dashing on into the woods. Strader leaped away in the opposite direction just as rapidly, losing his own blanket to a low broken tree branch as he reached the woods.

Yeager had no chance. He turned with one hand raised and the other covering the hole in his lower back where the ball had entered. He looked puzzled and took one faltering step toward the Indians, his mouth working to say something, then crumpled to the ground as one of the Indians raced up shrieking triumphantly and buried his tomahawk to the haft in the old man's head.

This much Simon saw in a swift glance over his shoulder and then he was out of sight, running as hard as he had ever run before, stumbling as branches lashed his naked body and sharp rocks and sticks gouged his bare feet. Not until he had run for more than a mile did he stop and try to halt his ragged gasping to listen for pursuit. For five minutes he stood motionless against a tree trunk and then, satisfied that they were not immediately following, slipped away in the direction of the lone bear trap in a ravine many miles away.

Now the rain began again and, though he was thankful that it helped obliterate his trail, its touch was a horribly icy film upon his bare skin. He wondered if Strader had made it safely away and his mind filled briefly with the grisly picture of Yeager being tomahawked. It was then, for the first time, that the full enormity of his predicament crashed down upon him and he trembled with a fear never before experienced.

[*March 15, 1773 — Monday*]

It was clearly obvious that the two young men could not much longer continue in their progressively worsening condition. This was their sixth morning of travel and they could do little more than stumble along, their feet severely lacerated and swollen to nearly twice normal size, their bodies deeply gouged by encounters with blackberry briers and bruised everywhere from frequent falls. They had slept little, unable to remain motionless very long without clothing.

On that awful night of the attack, soaked and exhausted, Simon Kenton had pressed on steadily, but it was still close to dawn before he reached the ravine where the bear trap was set. He was fearful that Strader had not made it, but the youth was there waiting for him, cowering in a fetal huddle in a small dry spot beneath a rocky ledge, dangerously near abject panic.

So relieved were they at finding one another safe that both of them wept as they hugged each other in greeting. Simon joined him under the ledge, though there was scarcely room for two, and they crouched there shivering, discussing what had happened at the camp and since they parted. Strader had not seen what happened to the old man and when Simon told him the blond youth broke into a spasm of uncontrollable trembling. He was all for fleeing immediately, but a measure of confidence returned to Simon and he reassured his companion that they were reasonably safe from pursuit, that there was enough plunder at the camp to keep the Indians there for some time. Besides which, the all-night rain would have made trailing virtually impossible.

The problem was not so much in what lay behind them as what now lay in front. They were both ravenously hungry, having been out many hours the day before without food and then forced to flee the camp before eating anything. They had no clothes and there was nothing available at this time of year in which to clothe themselves—unless in some way they were fortunate enough to kill a deer or elk, which was unlikely since they were also weaponless. All three of their flintlocks, including Jacob, were back at the camp. There had not been time even to snatch up knife or tomahawk.

Their only hope, Kenton said, lay in reaching the Ohio and walking up the shoreline until they found help, which might not be until Zane's Station or beyond, or perhaps until someone came by in a boat, as had the Frenchman a year ago.

They rested for a few hours and then set off, angling northwestward until they hit the Elk, which they swam across at a narrow point, then continued half-frozen in the same direction until they struck the Great Kanawha and followed it down.

This was the worst possible time of the year for them to find food. Here and there they discovered black walnuts or hickory nuts not eaten by the squirrels and cracked them open for the morsel of meat each contained, but there was little else available. If they found a dry cleft or small cave, they would scoop up leaves and cover themselves, lying close together for warmth, and try to sleep, but the cold quickly penetrated and before long they stumbled off again.

Now, on the morning of the sixth day, they glimpsed through the trees the bright welcome expanse of the Ohio and staggered toward it. They broke away from the woods onto the same gravelly beach where they had traded their furs for provisions a year ago . . . and were stunned to see three canoes pulled high up on shore and a group of men, white men, casually sprawled about a small fire.

The men saw them at the same time and leaped to their feet. It was too much for Strader, who fell unconscious where they stood, but Simon surged forward. The world was tilting crazily for him when a great bear of a man ran up and caught him just as he was falling. He scooped the large youth up into his arms as if he were a baby and carried him back toward the fire as two others ran toward Strader.

Joel Reese and Bill Grills spread out a blanket for the big man to lay Simon down upon and then Reese said, "They're more dead than alive. You fellows know 'em?"

Jacob Greathouse grunted as he deposited Simon on the blanket and covered him with another. "Eh, Bill, do we know this cub?" He answered his own question. "We know Simon Butler very good. I think pretty soon everybody knows him, eh?"

[*March 25, 1773 — Thursday*]

It took a full day for the Reese and Greathouse party to reach the Briscoe Settlement above the Little Kanawha River and nine days after that for Simon and George Strader to fully recuperate from their six-day ordeal in the woods.

Jacob Greathouse and Joel Reese had been on their way downriver with a party of seven other men, including the Mahons and Grills, for the purpose of locating game lands for possible settlement, winter hunting and trapping. Reese was particularly interested in locating lands suitable for future settlements to be founded by a land company whose name he would not divulge but which he said he represented. The party had planned going downstream at least as far as the mouth of the Scioto.

Shortly after Greathouse carried Simon Kenton to the fire, however, the young frontiersman roused only long enough to eat some food and disjointedly tell of the attack, the death of Yeager and their flight from the Indians, immediately following which he passed out again. Worried lest this attack should mark a general uprising, the party turned back upriver to return to the newly established Briscoe Settlement they had visited only the day before.

It was to Simon's and Strader's benefit that John Briscoe was not only an adventurer and land speculator; he was a tolerably good doctor as well. The two young men were bedded down comfortably in the only cabin so far completed and carefully nursed back to health.

During this interval the Greathouse party was undecided what to do. Five of the nine men had abruptly lost their taste for acquiring new lands and wanted to return to the east. Strader, too, had had enough and would return with them. The other four — Greathouse, Grills and the Mahon brothers, John and Rafe — were not particularly worried by the attack after Simon had explained it more fully, considering it an isolated affair, but decided to escort the others to Fort Pitt, pick up more supplies and men and return late in the summer to stay all winter. Simon, however, elected to stay at Briscoe's for a while.

Bill Grills told Simon the results of the expedition after John and Rafe's father: they had floated down the Ohio for forty miles or more and then turned up Little Beaver Creek, took the first fork to the left and followed it as far as they could. Caching the canoe, they had traveled overland almost due southwest until they hit the waters of Sandy Creek, then followed this watercourse downstream another twenty miles to where David Duncan had spotted the camp of the Delawares led by Running Mink. But despite the frontiersman's belief that it was a long-time camp, the site was deserted when they got there. For three days they followed the trail farther into the interior of Ohio, but then a severe storm had wiped out the trail and they were forced to return.

They got back to Provance Settlement less than a week after Simon's departure and were disappointed to find him gone. Only a few nights after that, Duncan set off again on his own and since that time the four had been up and down the Ohio River several times. But the mouth of the Kanawha, where they had found Simon and Strader, was thus far their deepest penetration into the unknown country.

So it was, with promises to return in a few months, the ten men set off up the Ohio this morning. Simon was sorry to see Strader go. Even though the big youth was something of a misfit in the wilderness, he had learned to like him well.

Enough extra clothing had been available among the Greathouse party to outfit Simon and Strader again and Grills gave his young friend a good knife, which was matched by a gift tomahawk from Greathouse, but they had no gun available. Dr. Briscoe, however, had an extra flintlock which he offered and Simon accepted it gratefully, though not without the promise to work at any task the doctor indicated until his debt of medical care and arming was repaid. Glad for the help, Briscoe agreed.

[May 2, 1773 — Sunday]

Sitting guard by the campfire not more than a quarter mile from the mouth of the Big Sandy, Simon Kenton reflected upon the incidents since the Greathouse party left Briscoe's.

Late in April, a month after their departure, a party of fourteen men under the joint command of Dr. John Wood and Hancock Lee, arrived at the settlement. A rugged-looking pair of men in their mid-thirties, Wood and Lee had been commissioned by the Virginia governor, Lord Dunmore, in the name of George III, to survey lands for future development. The Colony of Virginia stretched all the way from the Atlantic Coast to the Mississippi River, but precious little was known about sprawling Fincastle County — that whole territory to the west of the mountains and south of the Ohio River. The Wood-Lee party was one of several coming down the river which had been commissioned for the same purpose.

Another such party, eighteen men under the command of stocky little Captain Thomas Bullitt, arrived two days later. They stayed only overnight and then shoved off in the morning after cementing plans to meet the Wood-Lee party at the mouth of the Scioto River on June 1. Bullitt's party would survey much farther downriver.

The Wood-Lee party remained at Briscoe's for five days, making a few preliminary surveys of the area and questioning Simon carefully about what lay ahead, what he had seen, the lay of the land, the proximity to Indian villages and the best locations for settlements. Having hunted most of the southern side of the river as far down as the Big Sandy and having a phenomenal memory for landmarks, Simon described this segment carefully and had suggested this wide flat bottomland just above the mouth of the Big Sandy for their base.

He had readily agreed to guide them and today, a week after their departure, the party of fifteen men put ashore here in the forenoon to establish a settlement. The idea was to use this place as a base of operations for further explorations downriver. It was a good site, and the respect of the surveyors increased for their huge guide whose bearing and ability belied the fact that only a month ago he had turned eighteen.

The day was spent investigating the location and selecting a site upon which to build. Simon had struck off into the woods at once and returned a little more than an hour later with a fine fat doe draped over his shoulders. At nightfall, on Simon's suggestion, camp was made several hundred yards from the water's edge so that the light of their fire could not be seen from the river in case Indians should pass. It was decided, too, that a guard should be posted.

Simon volunteered for first watch, and now, when it came time for him to be relieved, he lay down fully clothed with his rifle in the crook of his arm. He would not again be caught unprepared at a campsite.

[May 18, 1773 — Tuesday]

Nothing had ever shocked the Chalahgawtha sept of the Shawnee nation so much as when, on this bright warm spring day, the lone white man appeared. Never before had a white man been within twenty miles or more of the Chillicothe town on the Little Miami River and never had anyone, white or Indian, ever approached the center of the Shawnee tribe without his approach being known long before his arrival.

Yet here, stepping along briskly with his rifle upside down over his shoulder, his hand clenching the muzzle and the stock angled upward above and behind his head with a white cloth dangling from it, was a man — a white man — already entering the edge of the sprawling village. The boldness, the inconceivable audacity of it, stunned them; but not for long.

They flocked about him in a milling mass until he was walking forward in a circle twenty feet in diameter. He smiled pleasantly and nodded but did not stop until he was fifty feet in front of the *msi-kah-mi-qui*. He regarded the large structure — one hundred twenty feet long by forty wide — with interest, as if his whole purpose in coming here had been to study the construction of a council house.

While he stood thus, Chief Black Fish stepped out of his nearby *wegiwa*, largest in the town, and came toward him, frowning slightly. He was not an especially large Indian, not more than a couple of inches taller than the white man's own height of five and a half feet. But he carried himself with a grace and authority that made him seem larger. Black Fish was not only chief of this Chalahgawtha village, but second to the principal chief of the entire Shawnee nation; an outstanding warrior whose bravery and intelligence were widely known in the Middle Ground.

His only garb was a pair of loose leggins of suedelike doehide and bead-adorned moccasins of the same material. About his neck he wore a necklace made of upward-curved bear claws separated from one another by inch-wide pieces of beaten silver. His straight black hair hung loosely to his shoulders and his eyes were extremely dark. A rosette of smooth scar tissue, almost like a medal, stood out clearly on his right breast between nipple and collarbone.

The crowd, easily two thousand strong, parted magically to let him through and he came to a stop between the white man and the *msi-kah-mi-qui*. The murmur of surrounding voices stilled at a scowl from the chief and then he looked at the white man and spoke.

"What news do you bring? Are you from the *Shemanese?*[2] If you are an ambassador, why did you not send a runner?"

The man showed even white teeth in a smile and he answered in the Shawnee tongue, slowly but fluently. "I have no bad news. The Long Knife and the Shawnee are at peace, and I have come among my brothers to have a talk with them about settling on the other side of what we white men call the Ohio River or, as it is known among the Shawnees, the Spay-lay-wi-theepi."

"Why," asked Black Fish, "did you not send a runner?"

The white man chuckled. "My name is Thomas Bullitt. I had no runner swifter than myself and, as I was in haste, I could not wait the return of a runner. If you were hungry and had killed a deer, would you send your squaw to town to tell the news and wait for her return before you would eat?"

A genuine smile tugged at the lips of Black Fish and a whoop of laughter erupted from the crowd. There was a relaxing of the strained atmosphere that had surrounded them and Black Fish now stepped forward and led Bullitt into the council house.

They settled themselves in the middle of the building and quietly smoked together a fragrant *kinnikinnick* mixture which Black Fish lighted in a long ceremonial pipe tomahawk. When the other Indians had all filed into the building and seated themselves, a company of squaws entered at intervals, each carrying a large bowl, each bowl containing a mixture of raw vegetables and chunks of venison which were cooked, but cold. Bullitt and Black Fish shared one of these and there arose a considerable din as the assemblage ate, chewing the meat and vegetables with much lip-smacking and finger-licking. The squaws returned to take away the empty bowls and once again pipes were lighted. Not until all of them had been smoked out and were put aside did Black Fish nod at Bullitt to speak.

Bullitt stood and first opened his pack, from which he brought forth a variety of gifts for the chief: many yards of bright calico, a large container holding an assortment of beads, and little statuettes. There were also a half dozen fine new tomahawks and two dozen equally good skinning knives. All of these items he placed on the ground before Black Fish, stating that it was little to give, but nonetheless a token of friendship from the whites to the Shawnees. He then raised his voice slightly so that all assembled could hear, though he still addressed himself to the chief.

"I am sent with my people, whom I left on the Ohio, by the white father of Virginia, Lord Dunmore, who was in turn directed by his great white father across the eastern sea, King George, to send me. The treaty made five summers ago between your people and mine — known to us as the Fort Stanwix Treaty — fully acknowledges your claim to all lands to the north and west of the Ohio River, as well as your right to hunt and trap as you always have in the land to the south of the river.

"Now we come from Virginia to settle that country on the other side of the river, as low down as the falls.[3] We only want this country to settle and to cultivate the soil. There will be no objection to your hunting and trapping in it, as heretofore. I hope you will live with us in friendship."

Black Fish was not pleased. His face had hardened at Bullitt's speech and when Bullitt resumed sitting, he arose and stood silently for many minutes. There was an intensity about all the men gathered here as they waited for their chief to speak. They had signed the Fort Stanwix Treaty, yes, soon after the meeting of all the septs of the Shawnee nation here, but the white man had broken the agreement. He had come time and again without permission into this land west and north of the Spay-lay-wi-theepi and he had killed Shawnees without provocation.

Black Fish spoke at length, discussing the Treaty and subsequent events. He warned that the Shawnee would no longer allow the *Shemanese* to step one foot from the river onto their land and that those who did would die. The time was ended when the white man could kill the Shawnee with impunity and then feel safe from retaliation simply because he recrossed the river to his own country. He spoke in detail of the Shawnee history in this land and of how he had been forced back from the land of his ancestors farther and farther until now there would be no more backing away and the line of the Fort Stanwix Treaty must be an inviolate line for the whites.

"The Shawnees," Black Fish said, "cannot tell you that you are allowed to settle in the Can-tuc-kee lands. We have never owned that land. It belongs to the ghosts of murdered Azgens — a white people from an eastern sea.[4] Their bones and ghosts own and occupy every hill and valley of the country. They protect the game there and have more and better right there than any of the Indian tribes, including our own Shawnee nation, because they do not need or use material food themselves and do not like it. Long ago our fathers and our grandfathers killed off the Azgens, but we now fear more the spirits of these people than our fathers and grandfathers feared them when they were flesh."

Black Fish paused and there was a murmured assent and nodding of heads among the assemblage. "When our food is all gone," he continued, "and our squaws and children starving, we appeal to the ghosts of the white mothers who were killed there and, by saying the right words, we are allowed to kill an elk or deer or bear or buffalo. But," and now his voice lost its almost chanting quality and he fastened an unfriendly gaze on Bullitt, "we are never allowed to kill the game wantonly and we are forbidden to settle in the country of Can-tuc-kee. If we did, these ghosts would not rise from their caves and mounds and slay us, but they would set father against son and son against father and neighbor against neighbor and make them kill one another."

Finally, homing in on the subject at hand, Black Fish concluded, "You have come a hard journey through the woods and the grass. We are not pleased to know you plan to settle in the Can-tuc-kee land and we cannot stop you, but since the *Shemanese* are determined to settle south of the Spay-lay-wi-theepi, they must be aware that they are not to disturb us in our hunting; for we must hunt to kill meat for our women and children, and to have something to buy powder and lead, and procure blankets and other necessaries. We desire you will be strong in discharging your promises towards us, as we are determined to be strong in advising our young men to be kind, friendly and peaceable towards you.

[*May 22, 1773 — Saturday*]

Thomas Bullitt was no little bothered by the misfortune that had over-taken them. It would have been bad enough had one of the canoes been damaged, but for both of them to have been so badly smashed was wholly exasperating. It would take many days to repair them — *if* they were reparable — and by the time the survey was finished and the work could be done on the boats, the time for the meeting at the Scioto would have come and gone.

It was just tough luck, of course, that they had not reached the Falls of Ohio until after dark. Even then he should have had enough sense to order the boats ashore until daylight rather than to try to navigate the fierce rapids in the darkness. He cursed his own stupidity at the memory of the two boats hitting the rocks and breaking like kindling within seconds of each other.

It could have been worse, much worse. Though the bows of both boats were smashed, neither had capsized and no supplies or, worse yet, men had been lost. Half drowned, they had managed to pull the damaged boats ashore and make camp.

Angrily, Bullitt kicked a rock into the water and hoped McLygger would have the sense to realize something like this had happened and send someone to inform Lee's party.

[*May 28, 1773 — Friday*]

The eight men Captain Thomas Bullitt had left on the south shore of the Ohio River opposite the mouth of the Great Miami River had now completed their surveys and wondered why they had heard nothing further from their leader.

Bullitt, with the rest of the party, had continued down to the Falls of Ohio to survey there, but had said he would return to this spot no later than May 27 and then the whole party could move upstream to meet the Wood-Lee party at the mouth of the Scioto. He was already a day late and the eight were worried.

A nearly bald, though relatively young surveyor named Jeff McLygger had been left in charge of this detail and he now suggested they get into their canoes and move out into midstream to get a better look downstream and perhaps spot Bullitt's boats. Not until they were within ten yards of the north shore, however, were they able to get an unobstructed view several miles downstream. There was nothing in sight.

Close as they were to the alien shore, they put in to the wide beach there and discussed the matter. The consensus was that Bullitt was in trouble, that they by themselves were not enough of a force to come to the rescue and that a detachment of them should return upstream to the Scioto to enlist the aid of the others in the Wood-Lee surveying team.

This decided upon, McLygger and two others set off upstream in one of the canoes with orders to the others to return across the Ohio after they'd rested a bit and wait there. They were, McLygger instructed, to keep a sharp lookout for Captain Bullitt.

[May 29, 1773 — Saturday]

Peshewa — Wild Cat — patted his horse's neck to quiet it and looked down the slope at the five men camped on the rocky shore several hundred yards above the mouth of the Great Miami River.

"They still have not gone," he told his four companions. "Now we must tell them to go to the other side as Black Fish said. I will ride in alone, but if something happens come quickly."

He kicked his heels to the horse's sides and started down toward the group of surveyors. Under orders from their chief they had followed Bullitt until he reached his men and then trailed them until the party split at the Great Miami. They were satisfied to see that, as the little white man had promised, the party stayed to the south shore of the river.

But yesterday they had come across the river unexpectedly and the party had split again, with these five remaining here. Peshewa thought soon they would return to the south shore but at nightfall they were still here, as they were when dawn came.

Now, going to them alone so they would know he had come in peace, he would tell them they must return to the other side. He was glad that he had left his rifle with Wepe-nipe — Cold Water — lest these men mistake his intentions. One could never guess accurately how a white man would think.

The surveyors did not hear Peshewa's approach until the unshod hooves of the pony, muffled on the earth, clattered noisily onto the loose rocks behind them. Four of them leaped to their feet in surprise, but the fifth reacted differently. Scooping up his flintlock he leveled it and snapped off a shot that caught Peshewa over the left eyebrow.

The Shawnee's body made an ugly thump as it struck the ground.

[*June 4, 1773 — Friday*]

Simon Kenton was last to give in to the majority opinion and then only because he had no other choice. Captain Bullitt had told Dr. Wood and Hancock Lee to meet him here at the Scioto on the first of June. The fact that he had not arrived spelled trouble to the young frontiersman and, having himself only recently escaped serious trouble, he was loath to abandon one who might be needing help.

For three days he had been fighting a losing argument with the members of the Wood-Lee party, some of whom were ready to leave when Bullitt had not shown up by daybreak on the first. Little by little the others had convinced themselves that Bullitt had either forgotten about their planned meeting or else had become so enrapt in his surveying that he had decided against returning. John Wood, Hancock Lee and a rough-and-tumble Irishman named Michael Tygart had held out until this morning, but now even the two leaders of the group had capitulated and there was nothing to do but leave. For Simon there was little comfort in the fact that Tygart still sided with him and he could not help but feel they were making a very bad mistake.

The group's work at the mouth of the Big Sandy had been completed three days before the end of May. Not only had they built fifteen fairly good cabins, each ten feet square, one for each of them, but a great portion of this previously unmapped section of Virginia's Fincastle County had now been surveyed.

Simon had alternated at helping with the cabins and accompanying the surveying teams and it was from these men that he learned of tomahawk improvements — the means by which an energetic young frontiersman might well become fabulously wealthy at some later year. The term was a general one but what it meant, as Simon understood it, was that any white male citizen of Virginia could claim land in the western portion of Fincastle County through the simple expedient of using the tomahawk to blaze trees and drive stakes to mark one-thousand-acre plots of land. Having thus "claimed" the land, it belonged to the tomahawk wielder. As soon as this became widely known, Hancock Lee gravely predicted, there would be an influx of emigrants to this wilderness such as people had never seen before. What better way to quickly populate an area? It would be the wise individual who spent time making his tomahawk improvements before the great land rush began. Simon was extremely interested in this and, as might have been expected, quickly decided to count himself among the "wise individuals." In an unusually short time, under the tutelage of Hancock Lee, he had become a rather good surveyor.

Shortly after completion of the surveys and cabin building, the party set off for the Scioto River, arriving there just at dusk on May 30. The hope that Bullitt would already be there died quickly, as did the hope that he would soon arrive. No doubt the fact that Simon would not permit fires to be built, that he had ordered the canoes hidden away from the water and the men themselves to stay in general concealment, added to the strong desire of the members of the party to be off and away quickly. The whisper that only a day or two up this very Scioto River were several huge Shawnee villages made them extremely edgy.

Looking back now at the mouth of the Scioto receding behind them and the wide empty expanse of the Ohio below, Simon shook his head. God forbid the day might ever come when he would have to depend upon such a party in an emergency!

[*June 7, 1773 — Monday*]

At Simon Kenton's insistence, as well as his assurance that they were now reasonably well out of the danger area, the Wood-Lee party camped for two days at the mouth of the Great Kanawha, a spot Simon cheerfully dubbed Point Pleasant, since it was here that a most pleasant coincidence had occurred for him — his being saved by the Greathouse-Reese party.[5]

He still had hope that they would soon see the Bullitt party coming and this time it paid off. Toward evening of this day he spotted a tiny speck far down the river which resolved itself into a canoe carrying three people. The entire party waited anxiously for it to arrive and were already shouting questions at Jeff McLygger when his craft was still fifty yards away. McLygger and his companions remained silent until their boat was beached.

Swiftly then, McLygger filled them in on all he knew about Bullitt's failure to return, adding that he thought it would be a good idea if they all returned to the Great Miami together, by which time Bullitt might have rejoined the men there or, for that matter, might even meet them on their way upstream.

Simon, Hancock Lee, John Wood and Michael Tygart agreed instantly, but the remainder were considerably less than enthusiastic. After some spirited wrangling, it was decided that just one canoe, their largest, would go downstream with six men: Wood, Lee, Tygart, McLygger, Simon and a brawny surveyor in Lee's group, Daniel McAfee. The rest would return immediately with all the surveying equipment and report to Briscoe's Settlement. If nothing further was heard at the end of ten days, this party was to set out for Fort Pitt with an alarm.

With no further ado, they parted.

[*June 11, 1773 — Friday*]

Except for Hancock Lee's "Oh my God!" there was a stunned silence among the six. They stared in revulsion at the bloated bodies of the five surveyors sprawled on the north shore. McLygger abruptly turned away and vomited.

Simon was first to act. Swiftly he inspected each of the remains and then walked back and forth in an ever-widening semicircle until he reached the point where the rocky shore gave way to earth vegetation. Then he returned to the others who had watched him uncomprehendingly.

"We better move and move fast," he said. "There'll be the devil to pay in a right smart time."

"You mean they'll be back?" John Wood looked horrified.

"We're gonna have the whole Shawnee nation down on us 'fore we know it," Simon said.

"How do you know, Butler?" Lee demanded. "Maybe it was just a small raiding party long gone now."

Simon shook his head. "Two good reasons why not: first of all, the scalps have been taken but that's all. They didn't mutilate the bodies, which means they were in a hurry. Next, one of the Injens was killed. Big pool of blood over there. The others tossed some gravel over it and took the body so's we wouldn't know, but there was one killed all right. What it means is they're heading back home in a hurry with the news that one of their braves was killed just about at his own back door. The chief won't like that. And don't think for a minute they don't know we're on this river. They know and they'll be coming for us. All's we can hope for is to make it back up 'fore they can set up an ambush."

There was a hurried consultation over what to do with the bodies and Dr. John Wood quickly put in that there was no time to be worrying about the dead when their own fat was in the fire. He suggested that the bodies be consigned to the Ohio River immediately and the party leave this place with all haste.

They were on their way within five minutes.

[*June 14, 1773 — Monday*]

The closer their canoe came to the Three Islands, the more convinced Simon became that if they were to be attacked it would be there.[6] Already they had passed the mouth of Limestone Creek — so named by one of the surveyors on the way downriver because of the bluffs flanking this stream entering from the south shore — and it was not far now to where these islands split the Ohio River into relatively narrow channels, where anyone on shore could fire with certainty of a hit and a crossfire would be disastrous.[7] Thus, when the river ahead of them angled north in a huge,

S-curve, with the Three Islands out of sight five miles ahead around the bend at the top of the S, Simon steered the boat ashore at a little creek at the foot of the double-curve of the river.[8]

The other five stepped ashore at his bidding, not understanding his action. He explained their position and the possibility of ambush ahead, telling them that from this point on they traveled by land. There was considerable objection and Simon's judgment was seriously doubted. To all but Mike Tygart, it appeared that travel on land was far more dangerous than in the canoe. Wood, Lee and McLygger were all for getting back into the boat and continuing their upstream progress. McAfee vacillated.

Knowing they had little time to stand in the open and discuss the matter, Simon nodded to Tygart and the pair unloaded their gear from the canoe. Before anyone realized his intention, Simon gave the boat a mighty shove, sending it skimming far out into the swift current.

This very nearly resulted in an open battle between them. The choice taken from them, however, they grudgingly shouldered their gear and followed Simon into the woods.

Ninety minutes later they clustered in a silent, white-faced group behind Simon, two hundred feet above the river atop a steep ridge. Below them the long narrow islands looked like huge dark boats in the setting sun and with the wide ribbon of river sliding past the whole scene had a peaceful quality to it . . . except for the Indians.

All three of the islands, as well as the shorelines on both sides of the river, were alive with Shawnees. Some were hauling canoes far up onshore to hide them in weeds and driftwood. Others were selecting strategic vantage points so that all avenues of river passage would be covered without the Indians themselves being seen by their quarry until it was too late.

Within ten minutes the majority of them were hidden except for the lookouts at the lower end of each island watching the north shore downstream where another lookout would signal them as soon as he caught sight of the expected whites.

His finger to his lips to demand silence, Simon Kenton beckoned the five to follow him in single file. There was now no reluctance on anyone's part to follow this shrewd young frontiersman. The sight of the Three Islands had unconditionally wiped away any doubt they may have harbored concerning his ability.

[*June 30, 1773 — Wednesday*]

The enforced stop for two weeks to treat Dr. John Wood's wound was a blessing in disguise — at least for Simon and for Michael Tygart.

After leaving the Three Islands area, Simon had led them inland about four miles and then struck out to the east, gradually angling back toward the river. When once again they reached it, he kept the party distant enough from the shore so they would occasionally see the water from atop steep ridges; but mostly it was out of sight.

When they reached a bend in the river where the stream was suddenly coming toward them from the north, Simon recognized it as the approach to the mouth of the Scioto, perhaps ten miles ahead. Here he again led them directly east through the hills until the crooked course of a large creek was reached — a creek which flowed north and emptied into the Ohio not far above the Scioto.[9]

Almost exactly a year earlier, Simon had explored up this very creek with Strader and Yeager, and he was familiar with the lay of the ground. By following this creek upstream some ten miles from its mouth to a point where he knew the hills closed in on either side, they could then strike due east up a small feeder creek valley, over a small hill and almost instantly hit a fine spring branch flowing east.[10] In a few miles this branch met the Ohio, again coming south, only a mile below where the Little Sandy River emptied.[11]

However, coming down into the large creek valley, John Wood stepped on a big copperhead and was struck deeply in the calf. A halt was called and Wood, who had occasionally treated his own patients for snakebite, now directed Simon in cutting the wound open in a deep X incision, and Simon unhesitatingly sucked and spat out the poisoned blood.

Within two hours the doctor's leg was swollen to nearly twice normal size and further travel was out of the question, so they established a camp. John Wood was delirious all that night and the next day, but on the second night he slept peacefully. After that it was simply a matter of giving the wound time to heal before pushing on.

Their diet during this period consisted of blackberries, soup made from a variety of roots Simon dug, wild onions and the eggs of a wild turkey, which were on the verge of hatching yet which all of them ate with gusto. Simon cautioned them all against using their guns and what fires they built were small, used briefly for cooking and then extinguished. It was something of a paradox that while Simon Kenton was by far the youngest man here, he had undoubtedly become the leader and his every suggestion was obeyed promptly.

It was while Dr. Wood was recuperating that Simon and Tygart set about making tomahawk improvements. Tygart in particular was taken with the beauty of this creek valley and he promptly named both creek and valley after himself. By the time Wood was ready to travel again, both men had claimed many thousands of acres. But the party that found the spring branch and followed it back to the Ohio the next day was made up of five men, not six.

Michael Tygart had found himself a little empire.

[*August 15, 1773 — Friday*]

Simon Kenton was distinctly bothered upon reaching Provance Settlement to learn that the exploits of one Simon Butler were the talk of the frontier. Stories were told about him that were pure imagination and others were amazingly expanded versions of relatively minor things that had occurred. For example:

Simon Butler had rescued thirty government surveyors from sure death; Simon Butler had single-handedly, with only a tomahawk, fought and killed four Shawnee Indians simultaneously at Three Islands; Simon Butler had carried a snake-bitten doctor a hundred forty miles on his back; Simon Butler could shoot a turkey on the wing in deep woods at one hundred yards with his rifle; Simon Butler was the greatest thing to hit the frontier since David Duncan and John Finley.

The journey back to Provance Settlement had been little more than an enjoyable frontier hike once they crossed the Big Sandy. Shortly after that Simon had deposited his four charges at Briscoe's Settlement where they immediately made plans to canoe back to the Fort Pitt area the next day, so as to get the surveys and word of Indian attacks back to the government immediately.

Kenton declined going with them. He had had as much of these surveyors as he could take. Instead he elected to trek cross-country until he hit the upper Monongahela and follow it down to Provance. This was a disappointment to Dr. John Wood, Hancock Lee and the other surveyors. They had come to respect him highly and to depend a great deal on his judgment. However, if that was his desire, they would go ahead and look forward eagerly to meeting him again, perhaps at Provance Settlement where they would stop for a few days' rest before pushing on to Williamsburg.

Simon took his time getting there, often interrupting his march to follow an interesting trail or to study out-of-his-way places which looked interesting. The surveyors had reached Fort Pitt without difficulty, spent several days in the little adjoining village of Pittsburgh, and then went on to Provance where they stayed two days more. Nevertheless, they had come and gone long before Simon arrived and everywhere they stopped they were more than lavish in their praise of the young frontiersman. Hancock Lee had made it plain that he was going to make a special point of telling Lord Dunmore about him. The story the surveyors told of their weeks with Simon Butler may have been exaggerated a little, but not much. Yet, as stories of this nature often are, they were immediately blown all out of proportion and long after the surveyors were gone the name of Butler was on every tongue and each story told was told a little better than the last time.

Thus, when Simon entered The Cabin pub, John Provance recognized him immediately and made quite a fuss about his return, treating him with the same deference he had shown to David Duncan. Men he didn't know came up to shake Simon's hand, to ask him what his plans were and to beg for stories of his exploits. This had no more effect than to make Simon rather taciturn and he left soon to find the Greathouse party which, Provance had told him, was encamped a half dozen miles or so upstream.

He found them without difficulty and the reception he got was a jubilant one. Even the perpetual smiles of the Mahon brothers seemed less formidable and more sincere. Grills thumped him on the back delightedly and remarked with a chuckle that maybe sometime Simon would show him how he whipped four — or was it six? — Shawnees using nothing but a penknife.

Greathouse shook his hand vigorously and his smile was broad, if not quite as genuine as it might have been. "Eh, cub," he said, "just like I predicted. Now everybody talks about Simon Butler, eh? Even more than they talk about Jacob Greathouse." He laughed loudly but his eyes did not join in the laughter.

At length they got around to talking about where they might go for a good winter of hunting and trapping. Simon suggested using the cabins he had helped the surveyors build at the mouth of Big Sandy. There was plenty of game and fur animals and as long as they cleared out when the thaws came, they shouldn't have any Indian trouble.

Just that quickly the plan was adopted.

[*March 5, 1774 — Saturday*]

Five canoes, each carrying six surveyors, put in to shore without delay upon seeing the string of tiny cabins at the mouth of the Big Sandy. These were the first sign of white habitation since leaving Briscoe's Settlement and, from what they had learned there, the last.

The leader of the surveyors, James Harrod, talked for many hours with the members of the Greathouse party, who were eager for news. Only rarely had boats come this far down and none had gone farther. The reports of Indian attacks, thefts of gear and horses and occasional murders of isolated travelers had spread frighteningly up and down the entire frontier bordered by this river.

Harrod, dispatched to lead another of Lord Dunmore's surveying parties, was en route to the Falls of Ohio to finish the surveying begun there by Captain Bullitt. Bullitt, he said, had gotten back to Virginia's capital safely by traveling overland after the bodies of two of his men, scalped and long dead, had floated past the Falls where he had been repairing damaged boats. Now Harrod was to finish Bullitt's survey, after which he planned to head upstream on the Kentucky River into the heartland of Fincastle

County's unexplored interior, there to establish a station and survey at length.

The news he brought was not encouraging. Although the hunting and trapping done by the Greathouse party here all winter had been excellent and their bales of fur were rich and thick, all their activities had been overshadowed with the knowledge that hostilities between whites and Indians were worsening and their little station here might be attacked at any time, as had a number of other isolated posts between here and Fort Pitt.

Equally sobering, however, was the news that relationships between the English and the Colonists had degenerated to a crucial point now. All of the Greathouse party, including the two new members — Samuel Cartwright and James Lock — who had joined them before they left Pittsburgh late last September, had heard the explosive news about the massacre of citizens in Boston by the British troops. But for the first time they learned of last December's so-called Tea Party in Boston which had not only resulted in the closing of that city's port, but in the installment of four regiments of redcoats to take control of the Massachusetts government from Colonial hands. Rabble-rousing Sam Adams was being sought by the authorities in an effort to end his incitement of the leading Colonists all the way down to North Carolina through a Committee of Correspondence; the word was that Adams was calling for a Continental Congress, which could be interpreted in no other sense than as an act of outright rebellion.

Despite the ramifications of the news, it remained the Indian problem which most concerned the party at this isolated post and they plied James Harrod with questions about it until the fire had died to embers. Harrod knew little more about it than they themselves had already heard — principally that there was talk of an Indian War coming. At this, Greathouse and the Mahons showed animated interest and even after Harrod and his men had rolled into their blankets for the night, the Greathouse party sat up, talking about what they should do. They had been fortunate in that no incidents with marauding bands of Cherokees or Shawnees had marred their stay here; but now, with the winter's hunting and trapping almost over, it would be foolish to take a chance.

Shortly after Harrod's party shoved off downstream in the morning, Greathouse, Grills and the Mahon brothers set off upstream in the large canoe with all their furs, leaving Simon, Cartwright and Lock behind to make some more tomahawk improvements in the area. The plan was for the Greathouse party to trade the goods for money and provisions, while Simon's party would claim more land; when they met again in a few weeks or so, they would split equally all around.

[*March 16, 1774 — Wednesday*]

Blue Jacket was deeply impressed by Tal-ga-yee-ta, the tall angular Mingo chief of the Cayugas — better known to both Indians and whites as Logan — not only because he had heard so much about this highly revered man, but because he was the first Cayuga the youth had ever seen. It seemed incredible that Logan's influence could be so great that with his encouragement alone the unaligned tribes might side with the Shawnees to repay the whites in kind for the harassment to Blue Jacket's adopted tribe.

In his three years with the Kispokothas, Blue Jacket had entered into their work, games, hunting, politics and religion with such fervor and sincerity that already he had become a leader among those of his own age and was looked upon with high favor by the older members of the sept. This was why he had been permitted to accompany Pucksinwah and his party in their important journey to visit Logan at his little village on Yellow Creek on the Ohio side of the big river.

No other Indian on the frontier was as widely respected by both whites and Indians as this Mingo. Time and again his wisdom and persuasiveness had prevailed to smooth strained relationships between the two races and his word carried great weight, not only among the Cayugas and Senecas, but among the Delawares, Shawnees, Miamis and Wyandots as well. But it was not for this reason alone that before him now sat the stern-faced delegation from the Shawnee tribe, come to ask him to raise both voice and hand against the whites. There was a more personal reason involved: Logan was especially sympathetic to Shawnee problems because many years before he had married a Shawnee maiden.

That Tal-ga-yee-ta should be known by the English name of Logan was not surprising. His father, Shikellimus, had many years ago formed a close personal friendship with James Logan, intimate of William Penn and founder of the Loganian Library at Philadelphia. So firm was this friendship that Shikellimus had named his second son after him. And now, just as Shikellimus had been a good provider and friend of the whites on the shores of Cayuga Lake in New York, so his son Logan's *wegiwa* was framed as an abode of warm hospitality, friendship and kindness to all, without distinction, along the shores of the Ohio River.

From Cayuga Lake, Logan had moved as a youth to the banks of the Juniata — a lovely, rambling river in central Pennsylvania which empties into the great Susquehanna. Here he built a cabin and later met and married the beautiful Shawnee girl. In spite of the many outrages committed upon the Indians by white men, Logan continued to remain a friend to all and not only refused to take part in the French and Indian War of nineteen years ago and that of Chief Pontiac which followed, but became a notable peacemaker during both. He was welcomed equally in the councils of various tribes and in the homes of white settlers; all of them knew they could trust him completely. He was a highly skilled marksman and brilliant hunter with either bow or gun and he had a certain aura about him that commanded unblemished respect. As one crusty old white trader put it: "Logan is the best specimen of humanity I ever met with, either white or red."

But now the visage of the chief was troubled as he listened carefully to Pucksinwah's plea: the whites were not only increasing their harassment of the Shawnees, but were spreading into the Can-tuc-kee hunting lands and must soon cross the Ohio to drive them away from their villages. Some whites in the border areas were masquerading as Indians in order to steal horses or other possessions of their fellow men, were even murdering and scalping them so the blame would be placed upon the Shawnees or other Indians. The Shawnees could fight their own battles with the whites, but the word of Logan was needed to encourage the other tribes to stand fast and to stop, by battle if necessary, any whites crossing into the Ohio country; the Shawnees alone could not and should not be expected to guard the entire frontier against encroachment for the benefit of all the tribes; there was word that the white fathers in the east were massing armies to come against the Shawnees and all tribes must do their part to stem this flood.

Blue Jacket was moved by the impassioned plea of his chief, but the reply of Logan, no less moving, was a deep disappointment. Never had Logan raised his hand against the whites, even when some members of his own family had been slain in battles with them, for there was no future in warring with a nation having unlimited resources and more men by far than all the tribes together. Were not the Shawnees themselves guilty of stealing horses and equipment from the border whites? Had they not, when occasion prompted it, slain whites? Would defiance of the armies make the war wither and die or would it, instead, cause violent and immediate retribution against which there could be no standing? The Shawnees were brave and their complaints to some degree justified, but how much better to attempt to reach an understanding, how much better to be guided by clear thought than blind emotion? There must be a way in which whites and the red men could live in harmony and peace, but this could not be consummated without restraint on both sides. Logan would not raise either his hand or voice against the whites, but he would send emissaries to them to ask of them the same restraint that he was asking of the Indians.

Pucksinwah argued no further. The meeting adjourned, and as the small party of Kispokothas mounted their horses for the ride back to their village on the Scioto, the Shawnee chief addressed the Mingo one final time: Logan was a wise man but he must beware lest Matchemenetoo, the Bad

Spirit, blind him to the inevitable and he one day find himself in grave peril from the white man. There was not now, nor could there ever be, a true and equitable peace between Indian and white.

[*April 26, 1774 — Tuesday*]

John Murray Dunmore had just completed one of the most eventful weeks he had experienced since becoming governor of the New York and Virginia Colonies. A few days earlier, Sir William Johnson had made his blunt statement that the western boundary rivalries between Pennsylvania and Virginia frontiersmen had now degenerated to a virtual state of war between Indians and whites, and there had been an immediate clamor for action. Johnson, a powerful voice in Colonial and Indian affairs, condemned the Earl of Dunmore for sending out surveying teams with the view of getting more land, not for Virginia or Pennsylvania or New York, but for the Earl of Dunmore; and this in defiance of the Fort Stanwix Treaty, and with the certain knowledge of stirring up further animosity between red men and white. He had even hinted that perhaps Lord Dunmore fancied himself an empire builder and warned that any man this ambitious bore close watching, lest his allegiance to King George be undermined by a greater allegiance to self.

Dunmore had strongly denied the insinuations and stated that it was necessary to have the surveyors he had sent out establish the boundaries of the Colonies with accuracy so there could be no grounds for further disputes. The very fact that the Virginians and Pennsylvanians were at this moment embroiled in a heated argument over their westernmost boundaries, he asserted, proved this. Further, the difficulties with the Shawnees were being instigated solely by the Indians themselves who continued to prey upon settlers up and down the Ohio; this was a situation he must see to at once.

To his local militia commandant, Captain John Connelly, a doctor by profession, he issued an order immediately to raise an army of three thousand men to go against the Scioto River Indians. Half of these men were to be inducted at Fort Pitt under Connelly's direction and the other half would assemble at Fort Union, under Colonel Andrew Lewis, on the western frontier near the Greenbrier River.[12]

Dunmore was pleased to note that this decision met with instant approval from the Colonists. As the letters and bulletins issued by Connelly and Lewis were displayed at various border posts, men began flocking in to volunteer for service; in Richmond and Williamsburg, as well as Forts Pitt and Union. To substantiate the claim that he was motivated not by desire for self-gain but only to aid the Colonies, Lord Dunmore announced that he, himself, would lead the Fort Pitt wing of the army against the Indians when the raising of the force had been completed. This was an effective move in winning some of the Colonists back to his side.

One final matter had been settled today. He had asked for two good men to volunteer for a mission that might be hazardous: the various surveying teams now out would have to be warned of the forthcoming hostilities and be withdrawn before they began. The first volunteer was a huge German immigrant who spoke English brokenly but had a reputation as a solid man who would complete to full satisfaction any mission assigned him. His name was Michael Stoner and he was directed to go down the Ohio to the Falls, then inland, following the string of surveyors and ordering them in Dunmore's name to return.

The second man was to go to the same country, but from another direction. He would go southwest through North Carolina and the wilderness beyond and then head into Fincastle County from the south, following the Clinch River until he reached the headwaters of the Cumberland. He would find James Harrod's party somewhere on the upper reaches of the Kentucky River and warn him, then follow the string of surveyors north until he should meet Stoner or reach the Ohio River.

The man who volunteered for this staggering job was a lean, black-haired man of thirty-eight from Reading, Pennsylvania. Along with Stoner, he had been a wagoner and blacksmith at Braddock's defeat nineteen years before. Since then he had spent a good deal of time in the North Carolina and Tennessee wilderness with John Finley, who had also been at Braddock's defeat. In fact, after telling him about the fabled Can-tuc-kee land for years, it was Finley himself only five years ago who had led this man for the first time through the Cumberland Gap. By now he had come to know this country as few white men did and he was a good selection for the job. His name — Daniel Boone.

[*April 30, 1774 — Saturday*]

It was customary, when canoes bearing whites met on the Ohio, to put ashore and pass along whatever news each might have about the direction from which they had come. Rarely, however, did both parties have news as momentous as when the single large canoe bearing Jacob Greathouse, Bill Grills and John and Rafe Mahon encountered the six canoes of the Michael Cresap party near the mouth of Little Beaver Creek.

The news from Cresap, who was coming upstream, was the killing two days before of a pair of Shawnee warriors at their Pipe Creek camp.[18] Except for Cresap himself and his husky young companion, the party of twenty-four men was jubilant about it. Their only regret seemed to be that one of the trio of Shawnees had escaped and that Cresap, as leader of their surveying party, had sternly forbidden them to carry out their half-formulated plan of completing the job by wiping out the Yellow Creek village of Chief Logan.

Cresap's companion was a strikingly handsome individual of twenty-one. He was from Albemarle County, Virginia, and his name was George

Rogers Clark. At this moment he was still almost beside himself with rage at what he termed "the brutal, savage, senseless killings."

Roaring with bullish laughter, Greathouse slapped him on the back and told him not to worry about it, that the men were justified in the deed. At Pittsburgh, he explained, they had learned that Lord Dunmore was gathering an army with the intent of striking the Shawnees on the Scioto River. "So, just as well those two are killed now as later, eh?"

After some more discussion, and in a rather casual way, Greathouse asked where Chief Logan's village was located and learned that it was some miles up Yellow Creek from its mouth, but that there was a contingent of about twenty Mingoes from Logan's village camped right at this moment along the Ohio River shore quite close to the mouth of that creek, directly across the river from Baker's Bottom.[14]

At this news Greathouse shook his head and remarked that he hoped they could pass them by unseen at night so as to avoid possible trouble, but he winked at the Mahon brothers and Bill Grills. A wicked fire sprang to life in the eyes of John and Rafe.

The two parties camped together that night and parted in the morning's early light; Cresap and his men continued their paddling toward Fort Pitt and the large Greathouse canoe drifted downstream. By late afternoon the four men had reached Baker's Bottom and put ashore, there to be met by a scraggly-bearded individual with rotted teeth and evasive eyes whom Grills recognized as a rather disreputable character named Tomlinson. With him were twenty-seven men and they made up a motley group — loud, mostly drunken and filthy. They shouted familiar greetings and jovial obscenities at Greathouse and the Mahon brothers.

Within minutes of the landing, Tomlinson and Greathouse had their heads together discussing something in undertones. Once they sauntered to the river's edge where, by looking diagonally downstream, they could just make out the Mingo camp on the Ohio shore. Greathouse grinned and nodded and thumped Tomlinson on the back.

After dinner the two leaders discussed a plan with the rest of the men. Of them all, only one objected — Bill Grills — and he was quickly sneered down. Less than an hour later, shortly after full darkness had come upon them, Greathouse and Tomlinson crossed the river to the Mingo camp where they were greeted in a friendly manner by Shikellimus, father of Chief Logan. Old and wrinkled and mostly toothless, he was pleased to be honored by a visit from the whites. Greathouse, reasonably fluent in the Iroquois tongue, smiled pleasantly and wished him peace, happiness and a full belly. His party of six men were camped just across the river, he said, and they would be pleased to have the Mingoes join them for some fine rum spirits and perhaps also engage with them in a marksmanship competition.

Shikellimus shook his head regretfully. It was a disappointment, he said, that most of them had work to do, since they were breaking camp in the morning. However, he did not wish to offend these kind white men and so he would send five good marksmen to represent him and his party. They shook hands again and the two white men paddled back to their camp.

Ten minutes after their return, a light canoe scraped ashore and from it stepped five Mingo braves and a decidedly pregnant squaw. She was sister of Logan and daughter of Shikellimus and she declined to drink any rum, as did her brother, Tay-la-nee, and her husband. The other three men, however, tilted the jug frequently, not noting that the six white men took only tiny sips when they drank. There was laughter and some small talk between Greathouse and Logan's brother and before long the three drinking Mingoes had become very unsteady.

Greathouse cut four sharp little pegs from a twig and tacked his handkerchief to the trunk of a tree within the light of the fire. With a piece of charcoal he made a small circle in the center, marked off thirty paces and invited the braves to show their skill. In succession the three tipsy Indians fired, two missing the handkerchief entirely and the third hitting just the edge of it. Logan's brother, however, sent a shot into the exact center of the little circle and his sister's husband cut the charcoal line with his ball.

Engrossed and laughing with their own fumbling efforts to reload, the Indians did not realize anything was amiss until Logan's sister suddenly ran toward the river, screaming an alarm in the still night air. The Mingoes looked up in surprise to find themselves quite alone in the center of an arc of men who had leaped from hiding, their rifles at ready. Rafe snapped off a quick shot at the squaw and her screaming was cut short as she flopped disjointedly to the ground. The Mingoes dropped their useless guns and clawed for knives and tomahawks, but a volley of shots rang out and all five fell, dead or dying.

A barely audible shout came from across the river and within a half a minute a lookout from Tomlinson's group warned that the remaining Mingoes were on their way over to investigate. Those who had fired reloaded swiftly and the entire party of whites crouched in the darkness along the shore until the boats came within range. At a shout from Tomlinson, thirty-one rifles roared — all except Grills's — and most of the occupants of the boats were killed instantly. Those few who were not dove into the water and struck out for the Ohio shore, but only three made it. Shikellimus was not among them.

Now the whites returned to the camp and methodically scalped the five dead men lying there. Logan's sister, they found, was still alive. The rifle ball had entered her back and lodged in her right lung and she was only semiconscious. Under orders from Greathouse she was lashed by her wrists to a pole which was then raised and angled into the fork of a tree so that her feet hung a foot or two off the ground. The frontiersman cut away her garb and tossed it aside; then he jerked the tomahawk from his underarm sheath and with one vicious swipe, laid open her belly, spilling its pitiful contents in an obscene hanging mass.

No one had even noted that Bill Grills was no longer with them. From fifty yards away in the heavy darkness of the woods he had been watching, but now he turned and slipped silently away. His association with both Jacob Greathouse and the frontier had just ended permanently.

[May 1, 1774 — Sunday]

With a gentleness belying the great anger that raged in him, Chief Logan cut loose the body of his sister and laid her on the ground between the bodies of her husband and brother. Wordlessly he touched her lips with his fingertips and then did the same with his brother and his sister's husband.

He recalled now the warning given him six weeks ago by the Kispokotha chief, Pucksinwah, that he should beware lest Matchemenetoo blind him to the inevitable. He had been blinded then; just as he had been blinded several nights ago when the young Shawnee, Blue Jacket, had come with an account of the death of two companions by Michael Cresap's party and his warning that he had overheard the men planning to destroy Logan's own Yellow Creek village.

And now, because of that blindness, his family was dead, viciously murdered without cause. A cold, frightening fire burned in his eyes as he raised his tomahawk high and told the Mingoes with him that peace had ended, that they would not return to the Yellow Creek camp but to Kispoko Town on the Scioto River and that his tomahawk would not again be grounded until he had taken ten lives for every one that was slain here last night.

[May 15, 1774 — Sunday]

Hokolesqua — Cornstalk — was afraid; not for himself nor even for his own village on the Pickaway Plains, since the Chalahgawthas were a great warrior sept and welcomed any battle. His fear was for the Shawnee nation as a whole, at least half of which was strongly against engaging in a devastating war with the whites.

Since early spring this year there had been scattered murders of both Indians and whites along the border, but after Logan's family had been butchered and the Mingo chief had moved his little band to nearby Kispoko Town and taken up the tomahawk against the whites for the first time in his life, there had been a sharp increase in killings.

Now it was known that the white father from the east, Dunmore, was raising an army to come against the Shawnees. Such a war could not help but be damaging to the whites, but it would be even more so to the Shawnees. And so, though personally he would rather fight, Cornstalk stayed his belligerence. As principal chief of all the Shawnees, he was responsible for putting personal desire aside and considering nation rather than self, and so he had sent runners to the chiefs of the other four septs and to all the individual village chiefs, entreating them to maintain the peace, to urge the young men eager to fight to ground their tomahawks and avoid encounters with whites wherever possible.

It was in this frame of mind that he was found by one William Wood, messenger from Colonel George Croghan who was the Indian agent at Fort Pitt. Wood approached Cornstalk's village under a flag of truce and invited the chief to come to the fort to talk of peace with the commandant and the Colonists' delegates.

It was customary for a chief to bring along a very sizable retinue of his warriors for such meetings but, because feelings were running so high among the whites, it was feared that the men at Fort Pitt might mistake this as an attack; therefore Wood asked that Cornstalk come with just a very small party.

Cornstalk considered this. To attend a peace negotiation without a sizable retinue would cause him to lose face among all the Indians. Yet it would also set a good example of the very things he had been preaching to his own tribe, and so he agreed. When they set off for Fort Pitt, he took along only his brother, Silverheels, and his sister, Non-hel-e-ma. Because of her bearing and her great size and strength — she was six and a half feet tall and remarkably well proportioned — Non-hel-e-ma was known to the whites as the Grenadier Squaw. When necessary, she could fight with the ferocity of any warrior. Fighting, however, was not the object of this mission. Cornstalk welcomed this one last chance to reinstate the peace.

Already many of the newly established white posts along the southeast bank of the Ohio had been abandoned by whites as a result of the increased killing along the border and in fear of the coming conflict. While they were en route to the fort, the three Shawnees and Wood met just such a party breaking up their station to return to the safety of the garrison. They offered to escort them there so that no unfortunate incidents might occur along the way. With William Wood there to assure them of their safety and the wisdom of such a merger, the Indians agreed to it.

Pittsburgh was a great bustle of activity when they arrived. No longer the tiny outpost of two or three years ago, it had become a substantial city of hundreds of relatively well-made cabins surrounding the fort. There were trading posts and taverns and merchandise stores, several large stables and blacksmith shops, even a boat-building establishment. Pittsburgh was becoming a sizable town, but whether it was to be Pittsburgh, Pennsylvania or Pittsburgh, Virginia, yet remained to be seen. Dispute as to boundary lines was a hot issue here, as well as in Philadelphia and Williamsburg.

Right now its population was swelled to several thousands, exclusive of the garrison, by the incoming traders and trappers deserting their lonely frontier stations and camps. Added to this was the influx of men from the east come to volunteer in the militia Lord Dunmore had ordered be raised.

As Wood led the three Shawnees toward the in-fort quarters of Colonel Croghan, a huge knot of angry frontiersmen gathered, as if drawn together by magnetism, and rushed upon them without warning. A wild melee ensued, lasting for several minutes, until Croghan rushed to the scene and fired his pistol into the air, demanding that the mob fall back.

Fall back they did, in a wide silent circle around the Indians. Silverheels lay on his back gasping, a deep knife wound in his right chest and frothy red bubbles at his lips. Cornstalk and Non-hel-e-ma crouched back to back, each with knife in one hand and tomahawk in the other.

The profuse apologies were not enough. That the principal chief of the Shawnees should be invited to come here to talk peace and be thus treated was unforgivable. Refusing offers of assistance, Cornstalk and Non-hel-e-ma packed Silverheels's wound with a plugging of soft downy breast feathers of buzzards, always carried for just this purpose, made a chair of their arms and carried their brother away with no further talk.

All hope of peace was thereby shattered.

[May 18, 1774 — Wednesday]

Three days later, Simon Kenton reached Pittsburgh. Reports of killings along the border had come to him and his two companions, Lock and Cartwright, within two weeks of the departure of Greathouse and from that time on the rare boat that came that far downstream had told of additional killings.

With their strength slight and their position vulnerable at the mouth of the Big Sandy, Simon proposed near the end of April that they start upstream to Briscoe's Settlement where they could wait in greater safety for the return of their companions. Briscoe's, however, was deserted when they reached it, as were five other small new stations they encountered during the next two weeks of following the shoreline. Not until they reached Zane's Fort did they learn from Ebenezer Zane himself that Lord Dunmore had declared war on the Shawnees and that volunteers for the militia were assembling at Fort Pitt and Fort Union.

For the first time, too, they heard of the massacre of Logan's family and the very fact that Logan, so long a friend to the whites, had taken up the tomahawk was more cause for consternation than anything else. At least twenty whites, Zane declared, had been killed along the river since then and he urged the trio to strike out to the east and hit the Monongahela and follow it downstream rather than to continue to follow the Ohio. It was sound advice and they followed it.

And now, having left Cartwright and Lock at Provance Settlement, Simon had arrived at Pittsburgh to find the atmosphere charged with excitement and the whole area swollen with new arrivals, most of whom were immediately being sworn in as militia. At this moment his curiosity was piqued by a large group of men gathered along one of the walls and he headed toward them. He was surprised to see a short, thickset man with black hair come stumbling violently backward through the edge of the crowd and fall when one of the onlookers inadvertently tripped him. His face was bloody and one eye was partially closed, but he struggled to his feet as three men in uniform closed in on him. One grasped him by the hair and hauled him to his feet, thrusting him at the other two who struck him heavily at the same time, one in the face and the other in the stomach. He tumbled to the ground again but this time had more difficulty in attempting to rise.

The officer who had hauled him to his feet by the hair stepped up again and drew back his booted foot to kick him, but it never landed. Instead, he was spun around by a huge young man who gripped him by the throat in one hand and shoved him against the other two with such force that two of them fell to the ground and the third staggered.

Simon leveled his rifle at the three, who remained frozen where they stopped and calmly announced he would kill the next man who laid a hand on the smaller fellow. Not a person there doubted his word. Slowly and cautiously the two fallen officers stood up. One of them, a man of about thirty and nearly Simon's size, glared at the young frontiersman and absently brushed the dust from the white bands that formed a large X on his chest. His voice was tight and his lips barely moved as he asked his assailant who he was.

"Simon Butler."

There was an excited murmur from the crowd. Simon knew none of them but apparently there were few here who had not heard of him. The officer's eyes widened for a moment and then narrowed again. "If you were in the Army," he said, "I'd have you hung for that." He appeared on the verge of saying more but abruptly pivoted and shouldered his way through the crowd, followed by his two companions.

Simon paid little attention to the muffled cheers and the calls of his name that came from the crowd. He lowered his rifle and gave the smaller man a hand to his feet. The man's good eye was a piercing black but now the corners crinkled with the effort to produce a lopsided grin. He motioned Simon to follow him and they walked several blocks toward the east end of the fort area where there stood a cluster of cabins. Into one of these the man walked and, after a moment's hesitation, Simon joined him.

The man was pouring water from a pewter pitcher into a basin. He began mopping the blood from his cracked lips with a cloth and spoke without turning around. "So you're Simon Butler. I remember now seeing you here about three years ago. You've changed a lot since then."

Simon was embarrassed. This man remembered him but he had no recollection of ever seeing him before. The dark-haired man glanced at the youth and grinned, then winced as the cracked lip split again. He indicated a chair between the two beds with a dip of his head and Simon sat.

"Those boys were a little rough," the man said, resuming his cleanup. "Good thing you came along. I was about ready to kill one of them." He lifted his buckskin blouse and pulled out a fine knife which he flicked away with hardly a glance. The knife arrowed across the cabin and thunked heavily into the handle of a makeshift broom leaning against the wall. Broom and knife fell with a clatter. "They don't like me much," he added. "Call me an Indian lover. Say I'm spying for them on the side. I'm not, but I don't hate 'em. Hell, lived with 'em for years. That was Dave Williamson you shoved. He's a captain, believe it or not. The other two don't matter. I'm translator here. Scout, too, among other things. Deal with the different tribes a lot. Sort of a go-between when Croghan wants to talk to the chiefs. Oh," he turned around and held his hand out to the youth, "my name's Simon, too. Simon Girty."

[May 25, 1774 — Wednesday]

It took a week for Simon Kenton to make up his mind to join the militia for the proposed move against the Indians. It was an unusually eventful week climaxed with an announcement that Colonel Angus McDonald would lead the first punitive force against the half-dozen Indian towns called Wapatomica above the forks of the Muskingum River within two weeks.[15] It would be the young frontiersman's first opportunity to see what some of the Middle Ground looked like and he had no intention of being left behind. Every day new faces were appearing in Pittsburgh and it had become a city of tents as well as cabins. The air was alive with sound; axes biting into trees, saws constantly rasping, horses neighing and snorting, shouts of men overriding all.

In this short time he had met many men, most of whom impressed him not at all; but several of them he immediately admired and respected. One of these was Jacob Drennon, a frontiersman Simon had heard much about; a tall, friendly man of serious nature, with the ingrained stealth and watchfulness of the experienced border man. Simon helped him finish a small cabin he was building and accepted gratefully when Jake insisted he share it with him. Drennon, too, planned to enlist in the militia, but as scout and spy rather than rank and file. He encouraged Simon to do the same, not unaware of the big young man's ability and past exploits.

Through Drennon he also met Michael Cresap and George Rogers Clark, both of whom had already taken the oath of allegiance and were raising companies. They were quiet, assured men who seemed to know what they were about. In some intangible way, Clark reminded Simon of David Duncan. There was about him the same aura of leadership which generated in those about him the feeling that here was a man to follow and rely upon.

They also met Colonel McDonald, an old regular army officer, who sized them up, approved of what he saw and urged them to enlist and raise a company of men, over which he would make them officers. Simon and Jake agreed to do so. At once McDonald called for two witnessing officers and the two frontiersmen raised their right hands and repeated the oath of allegiance after the senior officer.

No little confused by what he had just sworn to, Simon accepted the limp handshake of the colonel and he and Jake left with orders to see about gathering a company of men.

[June 2, 1774 — Thursday]

With the influx of men into the Pittsburgh area, Jake Drennon and Simon Kenton had little difficulty in raising the company requested by McDonald, but by now both of them were having second thoughts. McDonald was reputed to be a good fighter when fighting others who fought by the same rules he observed — which meant conventional, straight-line ranks. His ability to fight Indians, however, was suspect and there were even rumors that he was apt to keep himself carefully safe from danger while his men met the enemy in those suicidal lines.

Drennon decided, and Simon agreed with him, that somehow he just couldn't see himself leading a bunch of soldiers in such fighting. They were loners, he and Simon, men used to acting on their own initiative. Any one of hundreds of the men here could act as officers and command a company, but few could properly scout the way or spy out the movements of the enemy as could they. Jake suggested they explain this to McDonald.

The colonel listened to them carefully, occasionally nodding. Aware of the reputation of these two, he agreed that their value to the army would be far greater in the position of scouts and spies. Without further discussion he assigned them both to Clark's company.

At this point there was a question about just who the militia wanted to fight most — the Indians or themselves. The companies quickly aligned themselves on one side or other of the argument which was so disrupting affairs on this frontier; whether Fort Pitt — or Fort Dunmore, as the post had recently been renamed, even though practically everyone still called it by the former name — and the surrounding area was a part of Pennsylvania or Virginia territory.[16]

The Pennsylvanians were disturbed that Virginia was laying claim to too much of what the colony considered her own territory along the eastern bank of the Ohio River. The fault, however, apparently lay in Pennsylvania not having established sharply delineated boundaries.

Just the year before, Westmoreland County was formed by Pennsylvania out of the western portion of Bedford County and even the new county name was cause for rancor among the Virginians, signifying, as it allegedly did, the desire of the Pennsylvanians. Hannastown, about thirty miles east of Fort Pitt, had been selected as the county seat.

The matter came to a head when Lord Dunmore, a few weeks later, visited Fort Pitt and the western country and immediately adopted measures looking to a contest with Pennsylvania for jurisdiction over it. Not until six months ago, however, did the frontiersmen become heated over the issue. Lord Dunmore had chosen Dr. John Connelly as his agent in the disputed territory and Connelly let no grass grow under his feet. On January 25 he had posted his proclamation:

His Excellency, John, Earl of Dunmore, Governor-in-Chief and Captain-General of the Colony and Dominion of Virginia, and Vice-Admiral of the same, has been pleased to nominate me captain commandant of the militia of Pittsburgh and its dependencies, with instructions to assure his Majesty's subjects, settled on the western waters, that, having the greatest regard for their prosperity and interest, and convinced from their repeated memorials, of the grievances of which they complain, that he proposes moving to the House of Burgesses the necessity of erecting a new county, to include Pittsburgh, for the redress of your complaint, and to take every other step that may tend to afford you that justice which you solicit.

Pennsylvania did not take this lying down. Her champion in the dispute was a portly gentleman of vigorous nature and short temper named Arthur St. Clair. A justice of the peace in Westmoreland County, St. Clair soon had Connelly behind bars in Hannastown. His big mistake, however, was in releasing Connelly on parole. The doctor, leading a battery of militiamen, stormed the Pennsylvania Court at Hannastown and sent three of its justices — though not St. Clair — to jail in Staunton, Virginia. This coup effected, Connelly took possession of Fort Pitt and changed its name to Fort Dunmore.

Had it not been for the burgeoning Indian trouble from the mongrel bands of Mingoes and Delawares and stronger Shawnees, open warfare between Pennsylvania and Virginia factions might have resulted. But now, with a common enemy to fight, an uneasy peace prevailed.

Dunmore, still marshaling a large body of militia under regulars back in "civilized" Virginia, did not expect to reach Pittsburgh himself until late summer and so it was no surprise when the express had arrived authorizing Connelly to send McDonald's army alone against the Wapatomica Towns.

[June 16, 1774 — Thursday]

Nearly one hundred miles south of the Ohio River in the vast unexplored interior of Virginia's Fincastle County, a small group of permanent buildings was being raised not far from the Kentucky River, close to the east bank of Salt River. It was the first settlement of whites ever to be established in the Can-tuc-kee lands and the leader of the party, toward the close of this day, eyed his men's handiwork and nodded approvingly.

"I've always dreamed of establishing a town and naming it after myself," he said. "I therefore name this settlement Harrodsburg."

At practically the same moment on the west fork of the Monongahela River half a thousand miles away, the Mingo chief Logan expertly removed the glossy raven-black scalp from the buckskin-clad white man lying dead at his feet. It was the thirtieth scalp he had personally taken since the murder of his family, but his vengeance was yet far from sated.

The white man had never even heard the shot that sent a lead ball crashing through his spine at the base of his neck. And because of his solitary habits, he was not apt to be missed for a long time.

His name was David Duncan.

[October 5, 1774 — Wednesday]

Summer had passed swiftly and by now few people living on the frontier were not familiar with the name, if not the person, of Simon Butler. He had proven himself well in the events leading up to the forthcoming battle. Where messengers had to traverse dangerous, Indian-infested country, Simon was first choice to get through. Usually three couriers were dispatched with the same message and twice only Simon had delivered it, not only himself unscathed, but considerably faster than had been anticipated. Bareback or in saddle, he rode as if he had been bred to it and when it became necessary, as occasionally it did, he could run all day without dropping.

Thus far the war, if such it could be called, was a success. McDonald's campaign in June resulted in practically nothing except the relocation of the Wapatomica towns from the Muskingum River to some unknown place deep in the interior. A minor ambush before the army reached the towns killed a few of the militia and Simon Girty had managed to wound one of the Shawnees with a spectacular long shot. But by the time the army reached the villages they were deserted and what few buildings of a permanent nature were there, such as the council house, Simon Kenton had helped to burn. From the time they left Pittsburgh until their return, the young frontiersman had fired his gun only once; then just to clear the weapon of powder slightly dampened by a storm.

Simon and the other scouts had been sent out on occasional spying missions, but there was little to spy upon in this deserted country and so, by the time they returned, he was heartily disillusioned with army life in general and officers in particular. Colonel Angus McDonald had remained far in the rear throughout their trek; the single time gunfire sounded, he had dived to safety behind a log and huddled there fearfully until the skirmish ended. He had been observed, however, and the story of his cowardice raced through the ranks. Respect for McDonald disintegrated and, with it, discipline. At their camps a man way off on one side would call loudly in the darkness, "Who hid behind the log?" and a hundred voices or more would immediately thunder in chorus, "The Colonel!" Shortly thereafter Captain George Rogers Clark nipped in the bud a minor rebellion of the troops by soundly whipping Private Strother Crawford, a hulking, harelipped malcontent who, with some justification, decided McDonald was not the man to lead him into combat.

For Simon, the only truly bright spot of the campaign was his growing friendship with Girty. Increasingly during their spying expeditions together, the little interpreter told the young man of his background. Eighteen years ago, when he was just fifteen, his entire family had been captured by the French-led Indians who seized and burned Fort Granville on the Juniata River of Pennsylvania near its junction with the Susquehanna. His stepfather, John Turner, had been tortured to death in a grisly manner and the boys were taken for adoption — Simon by the Senecas and his brothers, thirteen-year-old James and eleven-year-old George, by the Shawnees and Delawares respectively. When the war ended and peace treaties were signed at Fort Pitt in 1759, all the prisoners had been released and Simon Girty stayed on at the fort to act as interpreter for the Crown under Indian agent Alexander McKee.

One night, as Kenton and Girty were resting in a small cave along the Muskingum, Girty suggested that the two of them bond themselves together in brotherhood in a sacred rite he had learned with the Senecas. What it meant, he explained, was that their blood became one and they were brothers and would vow to forever help and protect one another at all times, regardless of risk. There weren't many people a man could depend on in this country, he added, and it would be good to know there was at least one.

Simon agreed readily and Girty, with shallow flicks of his knife, laid open his own and Simon's right wrists. They then gripped each other's forearm so that the incisions met and pressed tightly together and their blood mingled. The grip was held for several minutes, during which first

Girty and then Kenton swore eternal friendship, brotherhood, devotion and protection, one for the other, as long as they both should live. It was a solemn and impressive ritual and the youth felt a great warmth for his companion. He hoped one day to be able to prove the strength of this bond. Yet, even though he trusted Girty implicitly and felt great friendship for him, he could not bring himself to reveal that his name was Kenton, not Butler. The threat of the noose was still too distinct a reality for carelessness.

In mid-August, James Harrod had passed through Fort Pitt again on his return trip to Williamsburg. Daniel Boone had arrived to warn him of the impending war, but Harrod was already preparing to leave when he got there. Two of his best surveyors — Jared Cowan and Hancock Taylor — had been slain and scalped by Shawnees just a few days before Boone's arrival. Boone had turned down an invitation to join their return party, electing instead to return south to a small settlement in the Powell Valley of Clinch River to warn the residents and help defend them if necessary.

Not until Lord Dunmore's arrival at Fort Pitt the last of August had Simon's true skill as a scout been put to the test. With the troops he had brought with him, the governor's army here had swelled to nineteen hundred men and there were still eleven hundred more under Colonel Andrew Lewis at Fort Union. The plan was for the two armies to meet at the mouth of the Great Kanawha River; Dunmore's by floating down the Ohio in a huge armada of canoes and rafts, Lewis's by marching down the Greenbrier River to where it joined the Bluestone River to form the New River, then down the New to its confluence with the Kanawha, and down the Kanawha to its mouth at Point Pleasant. This would be an extremely rugged march over mostly unmapped territory and there was some indication that Dunmore anticipated with approval that it might lead to dissatisfaction, dissent and desertion of the Colonial militiamen under Lewis. From the mouth of the Great Kanawha, according to Dunmore's initial plan, the converged army of three thousand would cross the Ohio to march against the Shawnee stronghold on the Pickaway Plains along the Scioto River — Kispoko Town, Cornstalk's Town and Non-hel-e-ma's Town.

Annoyingly for Dunmore, the expected dissatisfaction among Colonel Lewis's men did not occur. The unit seemed to grow stronger with the rigors it experienced and marched much faster than anticipated. Dunmore sent Lewis changes of orders not once but several times, each change designed to slow this wing of the army, exhaust its men even more, force it to travel farther over more difficult terrain to reach the same destination.

Simon spent most of September carrying messages back and forth between the two armies and some of the trips were extremely hazardous. The very first express to Lewis was given to Simon, Jake Drennon and another scout named Austin Parchment. The three were surprised and fired upon by Mingoes and separated. Drennon and Parchment, concerned over what lay ahead, returned to Fort Pitt, but Simon spurred on, clinging to the back of his mount with the tenacity of a burr, thrashing through woods and fields, across swamps and streams.

These initial change-of-march orders were, to Lewis's mind, utterly senseless. He could not comprehend why Dunmore would order him to march over the worst possible terrain to reach a point on the Ohio eighty-five miles above the mouth of the Great Kanawha. Nor did he believe Kenton's story of having slipped through the Indians to reach him in such record time, so he continued his march and held Simon prisoner until his own runners could check with Dunmore. When Simon's story was substantiated — with jubilation back in Dunmore's army, since it was thought he had been killed when he did not get back with the other scouts — he was again the object of much admiration, but Lewis ordered him back to Dunmore with word that he was continuing downriver in accordance with the original plan.

Dunmore was furious and the friction between the two commanders deepened. The Virginia governor seemed determined to shame and discredit the Colonial colonel and his backwoods militia in the eyes of the Colonies. Failing to accomplish this by diverting the little army and making it too late to join the forthcoming battle, he now sent Simon to Point Pleasant with word for Lewis to cross the Ohio immediately upon arrival there and engage the enemy by itself, while Dunmore's army would join them by moving up the Hockhocking River. Ostensibly this would catch the Indians in a pincer movement and defeat them. However, it was now obvious to everyone that Lewis's army would reach the Scioto villages many days in advance of Dunmore's if this plan were followed, only to receive the brunt of the Indian forces at a time when they were exhausted after weeks of marching through wilderness. If they were defeated, the arrival of Dunmore to wipe out the battle-weary Indians and save the remainder of Lewis's troops would not only show graphically the superiority of British-led troops over Colonials, but would tend to give the rabble rousers in the east — Sam Adams, for one — pause for thought where revolution was concerned. If an army of militiamen could not vanquish a horde of savages, how could they hope to take on the British Army?

And so, swiftly following the Ohio River downstream, Simon came once again to Point Pleasant, only to find it devoid of Lewis's troops. In accordance with Dunmore's instructions in case he arrived there first, Simon hid the dispatches in a hollow tree and marked the tree so Lewis would know where to find them.

The young frontiersman was well aware that Lewis would be enraged over the orders. It would be worse than folly for that little army to leave this Point Pleasant position before some sort of stockade for the beeves and provisions had been erected and the men given a rest. But if they followed the orders, they would certainly see fierce combat and for a moment Simon considered waiting for the army to appear and joining it. Not only was he more sympathetic toward Lewis, but he had not yet been tested in battle and he was eager to be in the thick of things.

With Dunmore's explicit orders still ringing in his ears that he return immediately, however, he shrugged regretfully and left.

[*October 6, 1774 — Thursday*]

For the first time since he had become principal chief of the Shawnees, Cornstalk's advice and counsel had been overruled. He had not become one of the great war chiefs of Shawnee history by avoiding battle, but this time he urged his tribesmen to consider again what was in store and to make another effort to establish peace with the whites.

"We are eight hundred Shawnee warriors," he said in the final council, "and only one thousand strong with the aid of our brothers, the Mingo and Delaware and Wyandot. The *Shemanese* have three men to our one and their guns are newer and better. I ask you once again, think to the future of our race."

His plea made little impression. They had had enough of peacemaking. Now was a time of war and if Cornstalk would not lead them, then they would be led by Pucksinwah and the Kispokotha chief's second-in-command, She-me-ne-to — Black Snake. There was no other way. Reluctantly, Cornstalk agreed and for some hours they listened to reports of spies who had been watching both wings of the army.

The white father, Dunmore, had the most men, but he was still far up the Ohio River at Wheeling and it would be many days before he could reach the Great Kanawha. On the other hand, the white warrior, Lewis, was almost at that point already and his force was much smaller, not much larger than their own. In addition, a three-hundred-man detachment of Lewis's force was a full day behind the main army, bringing up the beeves and supplies. If they could strike while Lewis had only eight hundred men, they would have a distinct advantage, even though the army was better armed than they.

Cornstalk listened carefully and then arose to speak a final time: "We will attack the *Shemanese* under Lewis at once, but remember this: now there will be no turning back; now the seed of war has been planted and watered and already it sprouts. Whether it thrives and grows or is cut down remains yet to be seen."

Within the hour they were riding southeast through the hill country of Ohio along the trail which would take them directly to the mouth of the Great Kanawha. On horses a short distance behind Cornstalk and his partially recuperated brother, Silverheels, rode Pucksinwah, who had fought many battles in his life. Beside him to his right rode his taciturn but devoted friend, Black Snake. Flanking them were two young men, their eyes alight with excitement and anticipation. It would be their first battle with the *Shemanese* and they were eager to prove themselves. To the left of the chief of the Kispokothas, tall and strong upon the back of a chestnut mare, rode his eighteen-year-old son, Chiksika. To the right of Black Snake, on a dappled gray, rode a remarkably muscular young man called Blue Jacket.

[*October 9, 1774 — Sunday*]

At the mouth of the Hockhocking, Lord Dunmore directed his company commanders in the erection of a fortification which he named Fort Gower before construction was even begun. It was really not a fort at all, but merely a cattle stockade and a place to store their extra provisions in preparation for the march into Indian territory. The men fell to the work, but grudgingly. Their thoughts lay with Lewis and his force downstream and the feeling was general that Dunmore should continue down until the two wings of the army were joined. Rumors were widespread that the Indians might number five thousand and they were worried.

That evening, some seventy miles away on the same shore of the Ohio, nearly a thousand warriors lay hidden and surveyed the frenetic activity on the opposite shore. The white commander, Lewis, had established camp on a piece of ground presenting problems where attack was concerned. The triangular point was bordered by the Great Kanawha on one side and by the Ohio on the other. The only way to attack was from the rear.

Cornstalk, his son Elinipsico, Red Eagle, Silverheels, Black Snake and Pucksinwah held council and the plan was drawn. After dark they would move upstream, cross the river silently and align their forces to form the third side of the triangle. If they could succeed in doing so undetected, they would have the army neatly trapped with nowhere to retreat. With Moneto at their sides to protect them, to guide and lead them, they would wipe out the entire opposing force.

On the other side of the Ohio, with dusk closing in, Colonel Andrew Lewis strolled once more around the camp before turning in. He was deliberately disobeying Dunmore's orders which had been found secreted in the hollow tree. They were suicidal. So today had been declared a day of rest and the men appreciated it. They greeted him and smiled as he passed and he felt a warmth for them that he had rarely felt for troops beneath him. Their trust in him and willingness to obey orders without question had been proven over and over again during the rugged weeks of marching. He had every confidence in their sustained fidelity, even should they come under fire. The final contingent of three hundred men behind them would arrive sometime tomorrow and then only would they obey the orders to cross the Ohio.

At noon today they had held Sunday services with himself officiating, though he was unaccustomed to acting the part of minister. He had read to them from the Twenty-fourth Psalm and really felt that the Lord, mighty in battle, was with them. As he closed with a prayer asking the Lord to lend them strength in the days ahead, the militiamen clutched their cloth or fur caps in their hands and bowed their heads and a silence settled over them so that every word of the commander's was audible. Even as he finished the stillness held on for some time and there was the feeling that the Presence was here among them and it was a good feeling.

As he moved about the camp now, Colonel Lewis spoke briefly with each of his company commanders. Then he returned to his own tent, rolled himself in his blanket and was almost instantly asleep.

At this moment, just one mile upstream, light bark canoes that had been carried along strapped between horses, each craft capable of ferrying ten warriors at a time, were being launched. A thousand painted warriors under Cornstalk had begun a silent crossing of the Ohio.

[October 10, 1774 — Monday]

The first chill gray light of dawn was outlining the hills to south and east when the scout raced into the encampment and virtually threw himself into the tent of the commander.

"Indians, sir!" he gasped. "Hundreds. Maybe thousands. Creeping through the woods towards us." He pointed.

Colonel Andrew Lewis frowned and sent the man to get his two company commanders, James Fleming and Charles Lewis — the latter his own brother. As the pair of colonels came running up to him from different directions, the commander was calmly lighting his pipe.

"Charlie," he directed, "take your men and spread out to cover a third of the distance across the point here, starting from the Kanawha shore. Fleming, you do the same from the Ohio shore. I'll cover the middle. Advance as soon as the line is formed."

There was a flurry of activity as the word passed. The men sprang to their feet and saw to their guns and powder, their knives and tomahawks. In fifteen minutes the line had formed, making the third side of a triangle whose other sides were the rivers. At a wave of the colonel's arm, they moved into the woods.

They were nearly a half mile from the point and the sun was just bathing the tree-covered hilltops when gunfire broke out sporadically on the Ohio side of the line and then spread to a general barrage on the entire front. Gunsmoke filled the woods and lay close to the ground, obscuring both friends and enemies with a pungent screen. The noise was incredible

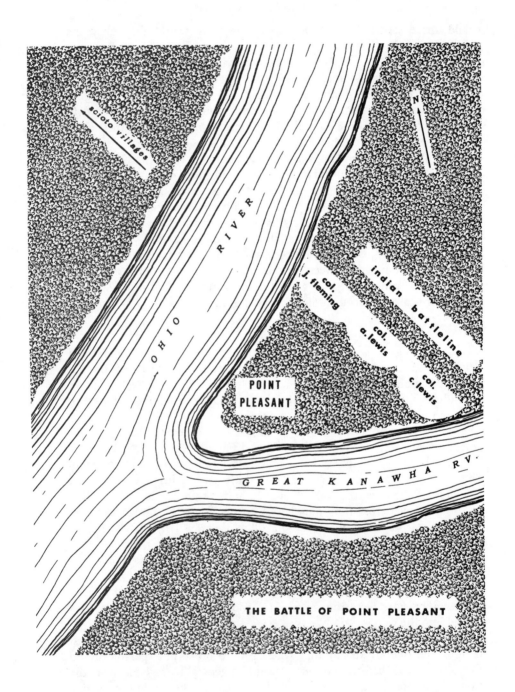

THE BATTLE OF POINT PLEASANT

— a constantly fluctuating chorus of screams and harsh cries, gunfire and grunts and curses. And moans.

At the first firing, a ball tore through the skull of Colonel Charles Lewis and, at almost the same moment on the other end of the line, Colonel James Fleming was put out of action when a shot passed through his body just beneath the ribs.

The first onslaught was strong and broke the line of defenders, forcing them to give ground for some minutes until they took cover behind trees, logs, rocks, anything that might provide protection from the withering fire. The acrid smoke was now so heavy that eyes were blinded and tears streaked the cheeks of Indians and whites alike.

Andrew Lewis and Cornstalk were both well aware of the same important factor in this battle. If the whites could force the Indians back, the foot of the triangle would grow longer and the line of warriors thinner and weaker. If the Indians could thrust the whites back toward the point, the enemy would become more hampered by its own movements, more apt to have greater casualties even with unaimed shots sent toward their lines. Each force was determined to gain the advantage by forcing the other back and the result was a particularly savage battle in a small area.

Back and forth through the forenoon the fight raged, first the whites giving ground, then the Indians. After firing only twice, Blue Jacket had discarded the clumsy flintlock and relied on his bow until his quiver was emptied. Then, tomahawk in one hand and knife in the other, he darted about engaging each white he encountered in hand-to-hand combat. Five, six, seven times he left behind him the bodies of militiamen, pausing only an instant after each had fallen to cut off his scalp and scream triumphantly. A bullet had grazed his neck and the blood running down his broad chest and back gave him the look of some apparition from Hell. More than one white turned and gave ground when he appeared.

A quarter-mile away fought White Wolf, a warrior of thirty-three. Like Blue Jacket, he was white, but he remembered only a very little of his heritage. His name had been John Ward and he had been captured and adopted by the Shawnees when still a relatively young boy. He was not an aggressive fighter, but he was deadly nonetheless. He relied mainly on his flintlock, took his time and fired at incautious white heads poked from behind trees and logs. His aim was excellent and those he hit moved no more.

Among the whites, fifty-four-year-old Captain James Ward exulted in the battle. For twenty-two years there had burned in his breast a great yearning for vengeance against the Shawnees who had killed his wife and stolen his son, John. Cautiously he peered over the log behind which he lay and in that moment his vengeance was forever unfulfilled as a well-aimed rifle ball caught him in the center of the forehead.

Pucksinwah and Chiksika fought side by side until just before noon when a bullet smashed into the chief's breast and he fell. Stunned, Chiksika cradled his father's head and wept. With his dying breaths the chief directed his eldest son to take his place as the head of the family and to preserve the dignity and honor of that family. He must instruct his six-year-old brother, Tecumseh, along with the triplets, in the ways of war and teach them courage and stamina and ability in battle.

All morning long up and down the line could be heard the deep powerful voice of Cornstalk urging his warriors on, praising them where they were fighting well and, where they were weakening, rallying them with stentorian cries of *"Oui-shi-cat to-oui! Oui-shi-cat-to-oui!"* — Be strong! Be strong![17]

Still weak from the chest wound sustained at Fort Pitt, Silverheels fought near his brother until he collapsed with exhaustion and was carried out of range by the only woman in the battle, his giant sister Non-hel-e-ma.

For five hours the battle was fought at fever pitch within an area less than two hundred yards deep. It was a remarkable thing, for this was not usual Indian strategy. It was customary procedure for them to outnumber the enemy, preserve their own flanks and overreach those of the enemy, but there was no chance to do that here. The very nature of the ground upon which they fought was against them, so they clung tenaciously to every inch of woodland they had gained.

At noon the firing began to taper off and both sides rested along a front of a mile and a quarter. There was desultory gunfire during the remainder of the afternoon but no more hand-to-hand fighting. At five in the evening a spy brought word to Cornstalk that the final detachment of Lewis's army was approaching from the rear and would arrive in three hours. With evening closing in, the Indian force melted into the woods behind them, taking along their wounded and all the dead they could reach.

Lewis did not pursue, afraid this would be playing into their hands. He maintained the same quiet line until just after eight in the evening, when his trailing company arrived, then withdrew to the point. About the same time his scouts reported observing what was apparently the last of the Indians returning across the Ohio.

The men rejoiced in their "victory," as they termed it. The term was debatable. Certainly there had been no routing of the enemy, nor had he cried quarter And though the militia was jubilant over the retreat of the Indians, Colonel Andrew Lewis was by no means confident that it was a retreat.

The whites had lost half their commissioned officers and fifty-two militiamen, for a total of seventy-five killed. There were also one hundred forty injured, eighty-eight of whom were beyond further fighting on this campaign.

The Indians, on the other hand, had twenty-two killed and eighteen wounded.

If it was a victory at all for the whites, it was indeed a hollow one.

[October 11, 1774 — Tuesday]

Cornstalk permitted no stopping until the Scioto villages were reached. Anger rode in him as he overheard the warriors behind him speaking not of further battle but of suing for peace before the arm of the *Shemanese* retaliation should sweep down upon them.

Stronger even than his anger was his contempt for his allies—the Mingo, Delaware and Wyandot factions. Shortly after recrossing the Ohio and mounting their horses, these parties had turned away to return to their own more distant villages by divergent routes. He did not bid them stay nor did he accuse them of cowardice and desertion, though they were guilty of both, but their eyes dropped before his and they rode off with the mantle of shame over their shoulders.

The principal chief of the Shawnees called for a council immediately upon their return to the villages and the assemblage was strangely subdued as compared to the battle-eager crowd of less than a week ago.

"You have fought well, my children," Cornstalk said, "and my heart sings the song of praise for your strength in battle, just as it sings the song of mourning for our brave warriors and chiefs who fell. Now I must ask of you, was this all in vain? Many among you have already said to me, 'Let us now seek peace with the *Shemanese*, lest they come against us even more strongly.' My heart is filled with shame that my ears have heard these words. If it was peace you wanted, why did you not say so when I begged you to do so five days ago?

"What do we do now?" he asked loudly, angrily. "The *Shemanese* are coming upon us by two routes, far stronger than those we met alone, while we are weaker in the return of our brothers to their homes where they will be safe." He paused and the contempt in his voice was a palpable thing. Then he repeated, "What do we do now? Shall we turn out and fight them?"

Again he paused and, when no one replied, he continued: "Shall we now kill all our women and children and then fight them until we ourselves are all dead?"

Still there was no reply and some vital spark seemed to go out of the chief. He drew out his bloodstained tomahawk and held it high for all to see, then hurled it savagely at the ground so that nearly the entire head was buried when it struck. With great vehemence he shouted, "Since you are not inclined to fight, we will go and make peace!"

There was a roar of approval and runners were dispatched immediately to Dunmore with treaty proposals. Five days ago he would have welcomed this but now, for Cornstalk, it was the saddest day of his life.

[*October 24, 1774 — Monday*]

Lord Dunmore's army was very close to open rebellion and he knew it. For ten days, ever since runners had arrived with offers of peace from the Shawnees, an ugly undercurrent of disgust, distrust and anger had seethed in the men. The whisper among the militia was strong that Dunmore, jealous of Lewis's success, was now determined that no further glory should come to the militia through the destruction of the Indians — an accomplishment practically within their grasp. The belief was just as strong that the commander's every move was geared to the widening gap between England and her Colonies. What Dunmore was doing now was almost certain to firm this belief, but there was no help for it. Even at personal risk, he had to stop Lewis.

Much as he was averse to fighting and much as he wanted to believe the offers of peace from the Indians, Dunmore was not fool enough to take the word of the runners alone. Immediately after their arrival he had sent Kenton and Girty to see the chiefs. If these two scouts did not return in a proper time, the army would listen to no further word of peace. At the same time, in case the offering was legitimate, he sent Drennon and an older scout named John Gibson to Lewis with orders to make camp and desist in further advance on the enemy until ordered to proceed.

Results had been gratifying on the one side but disturbing on the other. Kenton and Girty had returned considerably before the deadline with confirmation from Cornstalk himself that the Shawnees wished no more warfare. But Colonel Lewis had ignored the dispatches from Dunmore and kept his army on the move with the intent to fight at first contact. The river crossing had slowed him down, but now he was moving at full speed in the Ohio hill country toward the Scioto Towns. Another order was sent for him to stop and this, too, was ignored.

The Pickaway Plains were an oval grassland of unusually rich soil about a hundred fifty feet above the bed of the Scioto River. The greatest diameter of the oval was seven miles and its width four. In anticipation of talking peace, Dunmore had established an unprotected camp at the eastern edge of the plain along Scippo Creek, which bisected it. He named it Camp Charlotte and it was in view of the villages of both Cornstalk and Non-hel-e-ma, separated from one another by this same Scippo Creek.

A quarter mile below these two villages, Congo Creek joins Scippo Creek and it was a mile up the former where Colonel Lewis, late the day before, had made an overnight camp preparatory to assaulting the enemy. Now Dunmore was on his way to stop the attack which could only be disastrous to everyone concerned.

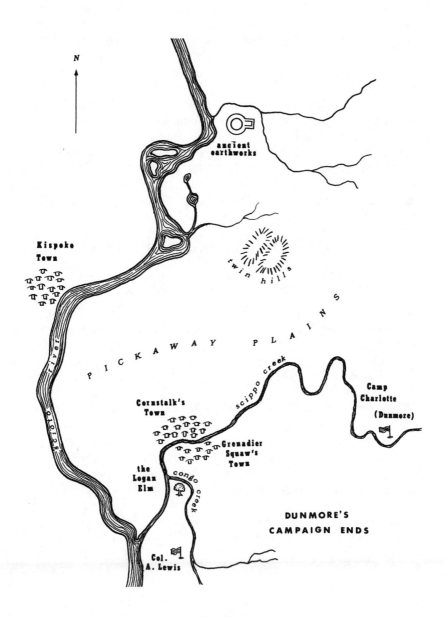

N

ancient
earthworks

Kispoko
Town

twin hills

P I C K A W A Y   P L A I N S

scippo creek

Cornstalk's
Town

Camp
Charlotte
(Dunmore)

Grenadier
Squaw's
Town

the
Logan
Elm

congo creek

DUNMORE'S
CAMPAIGN ENDS

Col.
A. Lewis

river

scioto

The governor was almost too late. Lewis had his troops on the move and was hardly a half mile from the villages when Dunmore intercepted him. After a heated argument between the two officers, Lewis agreed to obey the order only when Dunmore drew his own sword and threatened his second in command with instant death if he persisted in further disobedience.

Lewis's capitulation was not, however, through fear of Dunmore's swordsmanship; rather, knowing the Colonies would be proud of his moves up until now, he feared the reaction would change swiftly and detrimentally were he to engage in mortal combat with his commander.

With the enemy in their grasp, the men were furious at being cheated out of their revenge; but they remained loyal to Lewis and they turned at his bidding and headed back for the Congo Creek camp. From there they would return to Point Pleasant and erect a permanent fort.

Still seething and trembling, but satisfied at the outcome, Dunmore sheathed his sword and returned to Camp Charlotte to commence negotiations.

[*October 26, 1774 — Wednesday*]

Girty, Kenton and John Gibson found Chief Logan where they had been told his little camp was located: beneath the branches of a great spreading elm along the south bank of Congo Creek. They had come when it was learned that Logan had refused to attend the peace conference but would dictate a message to be read there. Girty would translate and Gibson would take it down on paper.

Logan stood before them silently, a figure commanding the respect of any who might look upon him. He was clad only in fresh doeskin leggins and high moccasins laced to mid-calf. At the back of his head he wore four white-tipped brown eagle feathers and on each wrist and his left upper arm were wide bands of beaten silver. Around his neck was an intricately fashioned necklace of colorful beads and silver and down his well-muscled bare chest hung two queues of straight black hair held near their ends by smaller circlets of silver. He wore no weapon of any kind. Despite the primitive costume, his bearing was as regal as any king in royal garb.

Most striking, however, was his strong face, etched by sadness, his deep dark eyes reflecting an inner pain beyond description. The expression did not change as he shook hands briefly with the three white men, nor did it alter to any appreciable degree as he began to dictate in a soft voice:

"I appeal to any white man to say if ever he entered Logan's cabin hungry and I gave him not meat; if ever he came cold or naked and I gave him not clothing.

"During the course of the last long and bloody war, Logan remained idle in his tent, an advocate for peace. Nay, such was my love for the whites that those of my own country pointed at me as I passed and said, 'Logan is the friend of the white man.' I had even thought to have lived with you, but for the injuries of one man. Colonel Cresap, the last spring, in cold blood and unprovoked, murdered all the relatives of Logan, not sparing even my women and children. There runs not a drop of my blood in the veins of any living creature. This called on me for revenge. I have sought it. I have killed many. I have fully glutted my vengeance.

"For my country, I rejoice at the beams of peace; but do not harbor the thought that mine is the joy of fear. Logan never felt fear. He will not turn on his heel to save his life.

"Who is there to mourn for Logan? Not one."

[*November 10, 1774 — Thursday*]

There was a great sadness in the family of Pucksinwah. Methotasa had mourned him deeply, with tearful lamentations at first but, later, during the journey to Chillicothe on the banks of the Little Miami River, with painful and silent grief. They were leaving Pucksinwah's town forever, taking with them even the name of the Kispoko Town, for hereafter it would be known by the name of the new chief of the Kispokotha sept, She-me-ne-to. Hereafter it would be called Black Snake's Town.

The husband of Methotasa was gone and now she and her eldest son, Chiksika, had brought the rest of the family — her daughter, Tecumapese, the second son, Tecumseh, and the triplets, Lowawluwaysica, Sauwaseekau and Kumskaka — to the Chalahgawtha town where, in accordance with Shawnee law, they would all become charges of Chief Black Fish.

The oversight and care of a fallen battle chief's family, because of his rank and service, always became the peace chief's duty until time and circumstance eased their necessities. Even then this relationship would remain unbroken. In effect, even though Methotasa would still have no husband, her sons and daughter would have, in Black Fish, a pseudo-father.

It was a sensible arrangement, but Methotasa withdrew in her shroud of grief. Her life had been so much a part of Pucksinwah's that when he died, something in her died, too. She never had loved another man and she never would. The flame that had lighted her soul was forever extinguished.

[*November 28, 1774 — Monday*]

It was with mixed emotions of pleasure and disappointment that Simon Kenton beached his canoe at the mouth of the Big Sandy and contemplated the charred remains of the cabins he had helped build there. Once again the elusive canelands had remained hidden from him and now he and his new companion would make winter camp here. This time, however, due to the treaty made with the Shawnees at Camp Charlotte, they would be able to hunt and trap in relative safety.

More than anything else, the huge young frontiersman was happy to be free of the army and once again be his own agent. The months with Dunmore's army had instilled in him a strong distaste for military life in any form. It had been a bright day indeed when the force was disbanded upon return to Fort Pitt.

The treaty had been swiftly concluded after the reading of Chief Logan's speech — a speech that had moved the whites as much as the Indians. Many of the soldiers had committed it to memory and it was the subject of much conversation around the campfires; especially the last lines. One militiaman would ask the question aloud, "Who is there to mourn for Logan?" and another would reply with great feeling, "Not one."

At the first public reading of it, George Rogers Clark had turned to Michael Cresap who stood beside him and muttered, "You must be a very great man that the Indians shoulder you with every mean thing that ever happened."

Cresap scowled. "If I ever encounter Greathouse again, I swear I'll tomahawk him."

The treaty was a temporary one which reestablished a peace between the whites and Shawnees as well as once again confining the Indians to the Ohio side of the river, except for hunting, and the whites to the Virginia side. The chiefs agreed to meet with the whites again at Fort Pitt the following spring to make a fuller treaty, and with that the war ended.

Following the disbandment at Fort Pitt, Simon sought out Girty and asked him if he would like to seek the canelands with him, that he had had enough of large parties of men and wanted only one companion with him. Girty declined, preferring the life around rapidly growing Pittsburgh. It was then that Simon turned to Thomas Williams who, nineteen years old like himself, had more or less attached himself to Simon during the weeks of the campaign and frequently expressed the desire to accompany the noted frontiersman on his next trip "down the river."

Although Kenton would have preferred Girty as a companion, he was pleased with Williams's request. Throughout the campaign the youth had proved himself a steady individual with a desire to see the new country that was almost as strong as Simon's. And so they had pooled their resources, gathered their supplies and set off in early November in quest of the elusive canelands.

At Letart's Falls, some thirty miles above the mouth of the Great Kanawha, they met the French trader, Peter Loramie, heading for Pittsburgh. They put ashore and for several hours discussed news of the frontier. Loramie was particularly anxious for news of the war and the two young men filled him in on what had transpired.

"And what of the strain between the English and the Colonists?" Loramie asked. "Will there be the war everyone expects?"

"Wouldn't be surprised," Williams answered. "The boys made a resolution when they got back to Fort Gower that even though they respected Dunmore and all, they aimed to protect American liberty at all costs. Ol' Dunmore didn't like it much."

Williams, who had an excellent memory, provided the Frenchman with a detailed account of how, at Fort Gower, the troops had held a meeting to consider the grievances of British America and there was little he left out.[18]

Loramie seemed pleased with what he heard, but mostly by the fact that the war had ended. They chatted amiably for a while longer and then the trader asked them where they were headed.

"Maybe chasing wild tales," Simon said. "We've heard of a place downriver called the canelands where there's game like no one's ever seen before. Looked for it twice but never yet found any place where the cane comes down to the river."

"Son, that's because it doesn't grow in the area where you've been looking," Loramie said. "I know them canelands you're talking about. They run in the same direction as the river and don't come down to it until way below the Falls. But you don't need to go down that far. You go down maybe a day below Three Islands and watch for a creek emptying into this river from between big limestone bluffs. You put ashore there and go straight south overland for two, three miles and you'll find 'em."

Simon was jubilant. He had almost come to the conclusion that Yeager's story was the fantasy of an old man, but now it was strongly confirmed. He thought he remembered the creek Loramie mentioned and was sure he could find it easily now from this description. With an exchange of good wishes, the boats set off in opposite directions and Kenton and Williams paddled along with their hopes high.

They soon found the creek mouth a few hours below Three Islands which roughly matched the description given them by Loramie. Enthusiastically they struck off into the hills, but though they wandered through heavily wooded slopes for two days, the canelands continued to elude them and they returned to their canoe disheartened. Winter was close at hand now and they must establish camp very quickly or be in serious trouble.

And so they returned once again to the mouth of Big Sandy to stay the winter in one of the burned surveyors' cabins, which they rebuilt, convinced that the canelands were a myth and that they could probably spend their lives looking and never find them.

About this same time, thousands of miles away in London, an Act of Parliament annexed the whole of the Northwestern Territory as part of the Province of Quebec, as created and established by the Royal Proclamation of October 7, 1763.[20]

CHAPTER III

[*March 12, 1775 — Sunday*]

PETER LORAMIE put in to shore at the Mouth of the Big Sandy and greeted the two young frontiersmen heartily.

"I did not," he said, eyeing the bales of furs inside the little cabin, "expect to see you here. I thought you were going to the canelands."

Simon Kenton stifled an angry retort but Tom Williams told him they had looked where directed and found nothing but hills and woods. Loramie was puzzled and asked them to describe the creek mouth where they went inland. As Williams did so he broke into a smile.

"It is simple," he said. "You stopped at the wrong creek. The one you wanted is more than an hour below that one. It is what we call Cabin Creek where you stopped. The next creek, that is the one where you find your canelands and I tell you again, they are there! You go look. You will find them."

Once again he described the mouth of the creek he meant and now the description triggered a memory in Simon's mind and he remembered that this was the stream that one of Bullitt's men had called Limestone Creek. Suddenly excited again, he described it to Loramie and the Frenchman nodded. "Now you have it!"

They finished their trading with considerable haste and took, in addition to powder and lead, blankets and staples, an extra large supply of corn for both parching and planting. Less than an hour after the trader left, they themselves had broken camp and pushed off into the muddy river.

It was as Loramie had said. Every detail of his description tallied and they paddled up the creek for a mile before stopping. A camp was hastily made and Williams suggested they get some meat, cook a meal and do some exploring first thing in the morning. Simon agreed and said he'd shoot something, but his eagerness to see the country he'd sought for so long carried him far from the camp. He set off up the creek for a mile or two but then, as it angled to the southeast, he struck away from it toward the southwest.

The canelands!

He was there at last. Great fields of dry cane, some rising twice his own height, swayed in the gentle afternoon breeze and, as if to reward him for his discovery, a fine fat doe stepped gracefully out of the cover and he downed her with a single quick shot.

That night at camp they celebrated the end of their search with Simon's favorite food: "the hams of a young deer." They slept well and the next morning, and during many of the days which followed, they explored their new domain.

On a sixty-foot elevation just above the two righthand forks of a little creek they established a permanent camp. Here, about four miles from the mouth of Limestone Creek and near a fine gushing spring in a hillside, they erected a half-face lean-to. From this site they could see the spot near the edge of the canebrake where Simon had shot the doe.

A buffalo trail so well trodden that it was a better road than many Simon had seen in the east passed near their camp and they followed it into the interior. It led directly to a tremendous bubbling spring of the clearest blue water imaginable. Its shoreline was heavily trampled and, tasting the water, the young frontiersman found it to be heavy with salt. In the pockmarks caused by the hooves of the buffalo, deer and elk which came here, evaporation had caused pure salt to encrust and rim the edges like frost on the ground. Nowhere before had the pair seen such a profusion of game. Buffalo by the many thousands roamed the land, their great herds following the "roads" which, at some points, were as much as fifty yards wide. Twenty or thirty abreast, these bison herds often took two or three days to pass. The elk were more solitary, but even they would congregate in dozens by the great blue springs which fed a fine river. Hundreds of whitetail deer, dainty and relatively unafraid, also came here and stared curiously at the two hunters.

The streams—rills, creeks and rivers—were alive with fish; great yellow catfish weighing a hundred pounds or more and with a white flaky flesh better than any eaten before, huge spotted garfish with alligator-like jaws, fine large bass, silver catfish and blue catfish and huge humpbacked white perch, mammoth turtles, some with ridged mossy backs and tails, and others with greenish shells as soft and smooth to the touch as good leather.

There were otters there and beaver, mink and raccoon, weasels and skunks and opossums. Great lumbering black bears were so common as to be frightening and now and then when they shot one of these, the pair would roast the feet all night in hot coals and have, for breakfast, "the richest conceivable delicacy."

The trees and fields were full of turkeys and squirrels, pigeons and quail and grouse. It was a land of dreams, a land that far surpassed even the extravagant tales Simon had heard about it. And because the game from miles around came here to lick salt at the springs which fed the large river, they named it the Licking River and the bubbling springs themselves were called the Blue Licks.

Even when they widened their explorations they found nothing to disappoint them and they marveled that a land so rich as this had so long remained uninhabited. On the other side of the river they found another trail leading to a similar salt spring which was named the Upper Blue Licks. Here again the profusion of game was staggering.

There was no sign whatever that anyone, Indian or white, had ever lived here. But there was much sign that the Indians came frequently to hunt, as evidenced by the trails obviously made by the moccasined feet of men. These trails were quickly distinguished by marks and blazes on trees, and frequently on the flat outcroppings of rocks were scratched rude sketches of the moon and sun, men and animals. These roads, except where they followed streams, were invariably forest trails and moved with straight-line directness from point to point.

The difference between the two twenty-year-old frontiersmen now became apparent. Thomas Williams looked at the country and appreciated it, but Simon Kenton *saw* it in detail and committed every detail to memory. Every point, every unusual tree or rock, every game trail or Indian road, every spring or creek, every stretch of skyline — all were so indelibly impressed in his mind that once having covered a piece of ground, he never forgot it, nor the avenues of escape it offered should the need arise.

For Simon, this was indeed a promised land if there ever had been one; for the first time since leaving his father's house on that fateful day four years ago, Simon Kenton felt that he had come home.

[*March 17, 1775 — Friday*]

It was an unseasonably warm and delightful day. It was a good day for trading and hundreds of miles to the south of the Ohio River a significant trade was being consummated. On the banks of the Watauga River the company of men under Judge Richard Henderson carefully established an ironclad treaty with the Cherokee Indians at a place known as Sycamore Shoals.

Henderson was many things; farmer, adventurer, hunter, explorer, member of the North Carolina judiciary. But more than anything else, he was a man obsessed with the knowledge that land was wealth and wealth was power and he craved power the way some men did alcohol or women.

He organized his own land company and called it the Henderson

Company until he expanded and brought in associates with more money or especial skills and then renamed it the Transylvania Land Company.

Richard Henderson had a dream and this dream was of an empire of his own, a country separate from other countries, over which he would be supreme ruler. Now was the time to secure the land and this was the purpose of the meeting with twelve hundred Cherokees here on the Watauga. For several days they had dickered and discussed boundaries and now the lines were firmly established, the transaction completed.

With $10,000 in guns and provisions of all kinds he bought an enormous expanse of territory — all the land enclosed in the area bordered by the Appalachians to the east, the Ohio River to the north, the great Mississippi to the west and the Cumberland River to the south.

For the Cherokees, it was an excellent transaction. Their neglect in mentioning that they did not own this land but only used it in treaty with the Shawnees was perhaps understandable under the circumstances. There was no love among them for their northern brethren and if difficulties ensued for them or the whites over the occupancy of the land, it would be their problem.

Henderson was jubilant. The first great step in the establishment of the country of Transylvania had been taken. At once he directed his most experienced scout to blaze a wilderness trail over the mountains and lay out a town which would become the capital of his country.

With thirty men, Daniel Boone prepared to set off at once. Just before he left, however, the Cherokee chief, Dragging Canoe, took his hand and wrung it firmly. He seemed to want to say a great deal, but finally he muttered a single sentence veiled in warning:

"We have given you a fine land, Brother, but you will find it under a cloud and a dark and bloody ground."

[*May 15, 1775 — Monday*]

Simon Kenton and Thomas Williams extended their exploration of the country around them before and after clearing an acre of ground in the midst of the canebrake and planting in the rich soil the first corn ever planted by white men in the Can-tuc-kee country. It was as beautiful a rolling countryside as either of the young men had ever seen and they quickly made tomahawk improvements at the corners of the sections they most admired, claiming them for themselves.

They were none too soon in doing it. The end of Dunmore's War and the treaty of peace with the Shawnees had opened the Ohio River as a highway for emigrants into the wilderness. They came down the river in great numbers and in anything that would float — small canoes, rafts, flatboats, huge oversized canoes, whatever would carry them and their families, horses, cattle and belongings. Almost overnight towns sprang into

being along the upper Ohio below Pittsburgh and above the Great
Kanawha and those already established before Dunmore's War, such as
Ebenezer Zane's Wheeling, grew with remarkable speed.

Fewer of the emigrants were daring enough to descend the Ohio as far
as the uncharted Can-tuc-kee lands, but there were still many; usually large
parties of men in flotillas of canoes who planned to follow to their
headwaters the larger streams entering the Ohio from the south, there to
establish their stations.

Among the first to return was James Harrod with his party to reestablish
the Harrodsburg settlement begun and abandoned last summer. Twenty
miles or so to the southeast of him, Benjamin Logan's party had followed
the Kentucky River to a good site and set about building a station which
he named St. Asaph but which his own men more commonly referred to as
Logan's Fort.[1]

Coming up from the south, Daniel Boone's party had stopped to
establish the capital of their Transylvania empire on a plain south of the
Kentucky River near a salt lick frequented by great herds of buffalo and elk
and the fort they erected, by popular acclaim of the party, was named
Boonesboro.

In April, John McClelland and his family, along with several other
settlers, put their flatboats into Salt Lick Creek not far from Limestone
Creek and were amazed to be met by a young giant named Simon Butler
who appeared to possess an incredible knowledge of the land about them.
He guided them to a beautiful prairie land bordering South Elkhorn Creek
where a magnificent spring of cold crystal water bubbled forth in such
volume and so beautifully that it was named Royal Spring. McClelland
and his party were greatly taken by the site and immediately set about
putting up a station named after the leader.[2]

On his return, Simon was near the South Fork of the Licking River
when a stampeding herd of buffalo made him take to a tree and while they
were passing he saw another man in a tree some distance away. An hour
later, when the herd had passed, he held his rifle ready and called, "Come
out — show yourself!" In a voice filled with relief, the man replied, "By
golly, you come out yourself!"

It was introduction enough for each to know the other spoke the
common language and both descended. The stranger was John Hinkson
who had, a month ago, come up the Licking with fifteen other men, some
with families, and built fifteen good cabins at a lovely place he called The
Cedars, about forty miles from Kenton's place.

Simon went with him to the new settlement, stayed a day and then
returned to his own camp to help Williams with further planting, cultivating and clearing. But Simon was learning, as long ago he had learned at
home, that he simply wasn't cut out to be a farmer. Williams enjoyed

tending the corn and clearing more land, but Simon was only content when prowling through the woods or fields with his flintlock gripped in one hand. The fact that the treaty with the Shawnees seemed to be holding up rather well did not cause him to become any less alert. Treaties had been broken before and they would be broken again.

At the end of the first week in May, he was hunting at Blue Licks when he spied four men walking purposefully along a buffalo road. Unseen, he slipped through the cover and was waiting for them when they came by. All four were greatly startled to see this young giant nonchalantly leaning against a tree. They exchanged greetings and introductions and Simon learned that this was the surveying party of Captain Robert Patterson on its way to build a station on the Kentucky River. Simon offered to lead them there over the best route and, when they accepted with appreciation, he led them directly southwest along a hard-packed buffalo trail.[3] At a beautiful site in rolling bluegrass country, they paused to camp and it was while they were there that Thomas Williams intercepted them.

"Simon," he said as he came up, not waiting for introductions, "I just got word. We're at war with England. They attacked us at Lexington, Massachusetts, on April nineteenth and we whipped 'em good. Killed near three hundred of 'em and they only got eight minutemen. It's a fact now, we're really having a revolution. Whole East's in an uproar."

The party was very interested and questioned Williams for all the details he knew, which had been given to him by a party heading downriver. The hopes of them all were for the success of the minutemen, but none of them considered at the moment heading east themselves to join in the affray.

"This spot," Patterson said as they sat around the fire that night, "is one of the most beautiful places I've ever seen. One of these days I'm going to come back here and lay out a town and do you know what I'm going to call it? In honor of the victory we just heard about, I'm going to name it Lexington."[4]

Meanwhile, near the mouth of the Kentucky River, another surveyor was busy at his own work and very excited with the new land that was opening for settlement. His name was George Rogers Clark and in a letter to his brother he wrote:

I have engaged as deputy surveyor under Cap'n Hancock Lee for to lay out lands on ye Kentuck, for ye Ohio Company, at ye rate of 8o£ year and ye privilege of taking what land I want . . . Colonel Henderson is [here] and claims all ye country below Kentucke. If his claim should be good, land may be got reasonable enough, and as good as any in ye world . . . We have laid out a town seventy miles up ye Kentuck, where I intend to live, and I don't doubt but there will be fifty families living in it by Christmas.

Again on his way back to their own camp with Williams, the young frontiersman encountered a man at Blue Licks. He was a great beefy individual with hands like small hams and a German accent so thick they could scarcely understand him. His name was Michael Stoner and he described himself as chief hunter for Henderson's capital which he called "Daniel Schpoon's fort." He told them that on May 23 — just eight days from now — Judge Henderson would convene a meeting of delegates from all the forts between the Ohio and the Cumberland. It would be held at Boonesboro and be called The House of Delegates or The Representatives of the Colony of Transylvania. It would be the first legislative assembly ever held west of the Alleghenies and its purpose would be to establish laws to govern the settlement. He invited them to attend but both Kenton and Williams declined. Theirs was neither fort nor station and they had no desire to establish or be bound by a set of rules proposed by a man neither even knew.

But George Rogers Clark attended and it was a blessing for all the frontiersmen that he did.

[*July 2, 1775 — Saturday*]

An aura of strong resentment and anger filled the gloomy silence of the large *msi-kah-mi-qui* at the Little Miami River Chillicothe Town. The three hundred fifty chiefs and subchiefs and delegates of the five Shawnee septs waited quietly for Cornstalk to speak. As principal chief of the nation, he would be next-to-last speaker, but the honor of speaking last would go to Black Fish of the Chalahgawthas, in whose council house the meeting was being held.

For many hours the chiefs had risen one by one to air their grievances and demand freer rein to repay like with like. The great trouble had begun with the peace treaty at Camp Charlotte. Like the crumbling of a great dam, it had permitted a frightening flood of whites to swarm down the Spay-lay-wi-theepi in every manner of floatable craft. They came like the locusts and where they stopped they cut down the trees and burned the prairies. Worse yet, in their sacred hunting grounds of the Can-tuc-kee the whites had not only wantonly slaughtered the buffalo and elk by the hundreds, often for only the tongue or liver or hide, but they had brought with them hundreds of cows and horses which competed with the game for the food that grew there.

The angry words filled the *msi-kah-mi-qui* with a great bitterness: only half a year had passed since the *Shemanese* came but already the buffalo seemed fewer and the elk had become solitary, always on the alert and difficult to down.

"But that is not the worst. The worst is the men themselves who float down the Spay-lay-wi-theepi and shoot to kill whenever one of us shows himself on our own shore. Nine of our warriors have been found dead on our shores since the Hunger Moon.[5] Four of our men have crossed to the Can-tuc-kee hunting ground for meat and have never returned. Whites have landed on our shores and have tried to build their cabins and have been angry with us when we tell them that they may not. They insult us and our wives and our children and our way of life. We are losing our dignity, our self-respect. Why must it be we who turn our backs and walk away when it is we who are the injured? Why may we not, as we always have, repay in kind for what we receive at the hands of our enemies?"

For long minutes Cornstalk stood before them without speaking and his voice, when it flowed past strong white teeth, was sad and soft and yet distinct to all who sat here.

"It is a bad time for us, yes, and as your war chief the fire in my breast wishes to burst forth in vengeance for those crimes that have been committed against us. I hold back in this desire for I have given my word, as have many of you here, that we will remain at peace. Do not think now or ever that Cornstalk so advises through fear, except that it is fear our nation will perish. If once again we war with the *Shemanese*, it will be the beginning of our end. The white man is like the worm who, when cut in half, does not die but merely becomes two. For each one that is killed, two or three or even four rise to take his place. As the treaty last autumn opened the dam to let the whites down the river in a flood, so warfare against them will be opening the dam to permit them to flood into our country here and take it from us. It is no easy matter to say that we must not fight, just as it is no easy matter to bear the injuries being turned upon us. Yet it may be that if these injuries can be borne for a while, better relationship will come and we will be able to live with the whites as neighbors."

Many of the older members of the Maykujay and Peckuwe and Thawegila septs nodded and murmured in approval, but the undertone of exasperation and disgust and anger became even greater from the younger men, especially those of the Chalahgawtha and Kispokotha septs. Cornstalk waited until the council room quieted again and went on:

"My young men are hard to hold and want to strike back when struck and it is not in my heart to tell them they are wrong. They are not wrong! But look deep into your hearts, each of you, and ask if any personal insult or injury is worth the destruction to our nation which retaliation must surely bring."

He returned to his place beside Black Fish and as he sat down, the little chief arose. He was a peace chief and it was expected that he would concur with the words of Cornstalk, but he surprised them. Tossing behind him the queue of hair that hung over his right chest, he tapped the roseate scar there.

"This is my memory," he said slowly. "It tells me that no white man can be trusted at any time, any place. It tells me that when I accepted injury and insult from the white man, believing it would not happen again, it became worse than before. The Shawnee must live in dignity. He must not only demand respect of others, white or Indian, but, even more important, he must retain his self-respect and he can never do this by turning his back on injury and insult. My memory," he tapped the scar again, "tells me this."

He shook his head. "I do not say we should make war unless war is visited upon us, but I say we must protect ourselves. If our men are killed, we must kill. If our buffalo and elk are destroyed, then so must the cattle of the whites be destroyed and their horses taken away. If our woods are cut and our fields burned, then so must the cabins of the whites be burned. Only in this way will the *Shemanese* know that we will not allow our country to be ravished and they will think well on it before giving us further injury."

The trend, clearly, was toward instant retaliation, but the chiefs were sobered by the memory of what had been said earlier in the council by the oldest leader, Chief Ki-kusgow-lowa of the Thawegila Shawnees:

"The septs have always been joined together closely in all important phases of Shawnee life, yet I tell you now that the Thawegilas have seen their last war with the *Shemanese*. If once more the tomahawk is struck into the war post, the Thawegilas will leave the Shawnee nation and cross the great grandmother of rivers to the west, never to return."

[October 26, 1775 — Thursday]

The Indian trouble had come, as it always seemed to, swiftly and unexpectedly. On the first of September Simon and Williams had met a pair of would-be settlers — named Hendricks and Fitzpatrick — stumbling about after having lost their canoe and gear in a storm. Fitzpatrick had wanted nothing more than to get back to Pennsylvania, and so the two young frontiersmen had left Hendricks in a temporary camp at Blue Licks while they took Fitzpatrick to the mouth of Limestone Creek, outfitted him with food and a small canoe and sent him on his way. They were gone five days and when they returned to where they had left Hendricks, they found his mutilated and charred body atop a huge bed of coals. They didn't need to discuss what they must do next.

It took a couple of days for the two young frontiersmen to break up their permanent camp at the edge of the canelands. Most of one day was spent bringing in the corn, stuffing the dry ears into greased skin bags and burying them in the constantly dry ground beneath an overhanging ledge of the nearby creek. What gear they would not be carrying with them — extra tomahawks, knives, clothing and the like — they tied into bundles and hid in the widely separated hollow trees so that if something happened, they would not be left naked and defenseless as had once happened to Simon.

On the morning of the third day they had started on their round of the forts to warn them of Indian attack. They went first to Hinkson's on the South Fork of the Licking and then to McClelland's Station on South Elkhorn Creek. From here they continued southeast along the buffalo road to Harrodsburg and from there upstream and eastward again along the Kentucky River to Boonesboro where for the first time they met the pioneer leader Michael Stoner had told them about and for whom the fort was named.

They finally settled at Hinkson's again, having gone full circle and somewhat disappointed that the news they carried was not as momentous for the settlers as they had imagined it would be. Nearly all the forts and stations, including those they hadn't visited, had been having Indian troubles for some months now. Horses were being stolen, cattle shot and left lying, outlying cabins burned, several settlers and their families killed and at least half a dozen men were missing. All the forts were throwing up stronger defenses against possible attack and though the warning from the two young men was appreciated, it came as no surprise.

The great hope was that with the influx of emigrants from the east next spring — expected to be larger by far than this year's had been — the whites would be so numerous as to discourage further raids by the Shawnees.

Simon had decided to stay at Hinkson's for the winter because of two things; it was the closest station to his own camp, to which he fully intended returning in the spring, and it was the one least well defended and most in need of more men and arms to stand off any attack that might come.

Just a week after his arrival there, while out hunting near the Ohio for the settlement, he heard a faint cracking sound and spun about to see an Indian thirty yards away aiming his rifle at him. Simon dived to the side, rolled over, came up on one knee and snapped off a shot. The bullet caught the Shawnee in the center of the throat and killed him.

A few hundred yards beyond the downed Shawnee, two more Indians raced into view from the woods. Simon turned and ran, reloading all the while, but when he stopped and looked back from cover, he saw the pair had only run up to their fallen companion and one of them now shook a fist in the direction in which Simon had disappeared from their sight. The pair picked up the body and moved off in the direction of the river. Simon trotted off toward Hinkson's, suddenly acutely aware that he had just slain his first Indian.

He was quite certain it would not be the last.

[*December 28, 1775 — Thursday*]

George Rogers Clark was now more glad than ever that he had taken it upon himself to report the status of affairs in Fincastle County to the Continental Congress. Little by little he had watched Richard Henderson developing his purchase of the Transylvania empire during the summer, with all its feudalistic implications, and it bothered him. It was then that he wrote: *I am now thinking about concerning myself with the future of this country.*

The journey back to Williamsburg last fall had been an arduous one, but well worth the effort. Henderson's agents were already there, asking the Congress to validate his treaty with the Indians. With Shawnee troubles once more coming down on them, Clark was well aware that if Henderson's request was approved it would make this frontier area, at best, a separate colony and unentitled to any military protection from Virginia.

With matters of the swelling Revolution of utmost importance, Virginia was ill prepared to consider saddling itself with the possibility of having to send away troops for the defense of the settlers when these very troops and arms were needed closer to home. Yet there was an awareness that these Fincastle lands could be extremely valuable and this — along with some degree of irritation at Henderson for his unauthorized and illegal treaty with the Cherokees and his purchase of land whose ownership was not fully established — swung the scale in Clark's favor.

His petition that Virginia create a new county out of the most westwardly portion of the Fincastle lands and call it Kentucky County appealed to them. He was directed to provide authorization for himself and another man — or two other men elected by the settlers — to represent this frontier country and to this he readily agreed.

At once an express was sent to each of the various forts and stations, in which he explained what had transpired and the need for these men to help dissolve the anomalous political situation in which they now existed. The men in the Kentucky area, he stressed, would eventually be in grave need of military assistance from Virginia and this was the best and most feasible way to get it. He had written: . . . *I therefore request that all persons in the Kentucky country who are interested in resolving ye situation assemble at Harrodsburg on June 6 next, at which meeting I will be present to explain everything.*

[*January 26, 1776 — Friday*]

The final thin thread which still bound the Colonists to England snapped irrevocably.

Since the outbreak of actual armed conflict at Lexington last April, the fighting had not been to establish a new country but simply for rights as

British subjects. George Washington himself, as he took command of the Continental Army in June, did so with the belief that it was for such rights they were fighting.

"I abhor," he declared, "the idea of American independence."

In October, 1774, exactly fifteen months ago, the first Continental Congress had sent a petition to King George imploring him "as the loving Father of your whole People" to redress their wrongs.

But now the King's proclamation reached John Hancock, president of the Continental Congress, and its only reply to the plea for justice was for his troops to put down the rebellion in America. As if anticipating this precisely, tens of thousands of pamphlets entitled *Common Sense* were distributed by their author, Thomas Paine. He had written: *The time has come ·for the final separation from England and arms must decide the contest.*

And then came word that since the English people would not volunteer to fight their friends and relatives in America, the King had hired thirty thousand Hessians to do the job. That was the final crushing indignity. The Americans had sought justice, not separation. But now King George — not the English people — had forced it upon them.

There was no longer any choice.

[*April 30, 1776 — Tuesday*]

If last spring's influx of emigrants down the Ohio and into the Kentucky country seemed extensive, it was dwarfed by the swarms of boats descending now. They came in every conceivable craft: rich men and poor, men with great amounts of property — tools and supplies, horses and wagons, Negro slaves and herds of cattle — and men with nothing but an ax and a knife, a wife and children and a dream of a new land away from the Revolution that was threatening to engulf the entire East. New settlements were springing up everywhere, usually named after the man who founded them: Henry Lee came out and settled Leestown to the west of McClelland's Station; "Big" Daniels and Roscoe Crow started the little settlements of Danville and Crow's Station just south of Harrodsburg. And there were others more distant.

Meanwhile, Simon Kenton and Thomas Williams had returned to their camp along the little creek at the edge of the canebrake and, in a burst of hard work, cleared another acre of ground for planting. But Simon's inclination to farm became less and less as the work progressed. He was infinitely more interested in the settlers coming in, and before long he was spending much more time encamped at the mouth of Limestone Creek to greet the new arrivals and help them find land to settle upon than he was at helping Williams with the farm chores.

First among the settlers to arrive had been the Samuel Arrowsmith family. With Kenton's encouragement and help, he cleared an acre of ground close to Simon's. Others came and settled nearby, too: Major George Stockton's party of five; the John McCauseland, George Deakins and William Graden families, which totaled thirteen people; the John Virgin party of three, and then a familiar and very welcome face — that of Simon's fellow scout in the Dunmore campaign, Jake Drennon, with his party of five.

Few were the spring emigrants who landed at the mouth of Limestone Creek without being met by the self-appointed welcomer, counselor and guide known as Simon Butler, whose love for this land flowed over into the new arrivals, filling them with a zeal to make this their permanent home. As far away as Pittsburgh, "Limestone" was being recognized as the landing port for the interior settlements of wild Fincastle County.

With his twenty-first birthday less than a month behind him, Simon Kenton now looked, walked and reacted like an Indian. It amused him to see new settlers gape when they first met him upon arriving. Only the bright blue eyes and the long auburn hair as he swept off his fur cap in greeting, the soft and musical tone of his voice welcoming the strangers, let them sigh in relief at his appearance. As it had in the upper Ohio River frontier, so now Simon's fame as pilot and scout and trailsman grew here. He seemed to have an incredible knack for being at the right place to help someone just when he was most needed. Other men who came to this country remained reasonably close to their own camps or to their stations or forts or settlements, but not Simon. From the Big Sandy to the Kentucky River and beyond, and into the mountains rising to the south where the Cumberland River thundered over a magnificent falls, he came to know this Kentucky country as well as any man had ever known it, Indian or white.

But with this influx of new settlers came chilling news. There was much talk — and fairly well substantiated it was — that the British were nurturing their alliance with the Ohio Indians and that they were deliberately encouraging them to harass or even kill the white settlers in the Kentucky country.

No one could tell where or when the Indians would strike, but it was a foregone conclusion that strike they would and no man but a fool would walk about in the frontier country without a rifle in his hand and both tomahawk and knife in his belt.

[May 15, 1776 — Wednesday]

For an eight-year-old, Tecumseh was unusually tall. He stood very erect and was a remarkably intelligent and good-looking youngster. His abilities were apparent in whatever he found it important to excel. He reveled in the games and sports engaged in with his many companions at Chillicothe and listened carefully to the lessons received from his brother Chiksika and others who taught him. More than a few times Chief Black Fish had eyed him approvingly and had thought how proud of this son Pucksinwah would have been.

None of the youngsters his own age were a match for him and even those in their early adolescence were hard put to keep up. His body was slim and solid; impressive young muscles rippled beneath his skin as he ran or swam, jumped or wrestled with the others. Chiksika had been teaching him well, as their dying father had bade him do. The boy could ride a horse expertly and could shoot his little bow with the greatest of accuracy, even from astride his galloping mount.

Chiksika felt a deep love for Tecumseh — more so than for the younger triplets — and dedicated himself to training his brother in all phases of Shawnee life. He taught him the history, traditions and codes of the tribe by word of mouth, since nothing was written. It was not enough that he merely be told of them; he must, as was custom, commit these matters so perfectly to memory that he could repeat them verbatim with nothing added, altered or omitted.

In his eighteen years with their father, Chiksika had been taught a great deal and, in the year and a half since Pucksinwah had been killed, the young warrior passed on much of what he had learned to Tecumseh. He taught him keenness of observation and how to bear pain without grimace, loss without depression, danger without fear and triumph without pride. He taught him mastery of self, the need to control and direct his passions and not let them rule him.

They fished together in the streams and together roamed fields and woods. Chiksika taught him the art of tracking and stalking, the best way to hunt for various types of game, how to build deadfalls and snares for fur animals and traps for birds and rabbits. He also showed him how to foretell the weather.

"When dew is on the grass in the morning," Chiksika told him, "it will not rain during the day and when it is not there just after darkness has fallen, it will rain before morning. When birds fly low and silently, a bad storm is coming, and when the dove sits close to the trunk of the sapling during the daytime, a great wind will soon blow. When the leaves of the maples turn over to show their underside, thunder and lightning will come soon. When the blackbirds flock together and start south when late summer is still with us, there will be much snow during the winter. When the swamp muskrat builds a low house of reeds and mud, the winter will be mild, but the larger and higher the house he builds, the worse the winter will be. And when he builds no house at all, but instead burrows beneath the ground, prepare for severe cold, for the waters of swamps and ponds and smaller streams will freeze to the bottom and even the great Spay-lay-wi-theepi will freeze so that a horse may walk upon it."

From Chiksika, Tecumseh learned the names of plants and trees, birds and four-legged animals. He learned to find roots that were edible and was taught what plants could cure illnesses or blunt the knife of pain. He learned the names and meaning of the thirteen Moons of the Shawnee year and that each year began in spring with the Green Moon.[6]

He even learned how to build the *wegiwa* — not the movable, conical tepee of some of the tribes here and most of those west of the great river, but a fixed square or rectangular structure of poles and treated bark which was cool in summer and warm in winter, easily erected in a short time and therefore easily abandoned if the need arose, yet stronger and roomier than the tepee.[7]

But it was not from Chiksika alone that the boy learned. His graceful, fine-featured sister Tecumapese, now eighteen, taught him important things as well, such as the value of patience and the need for pity for those unfortunate or powerless. She taught him the essentials of honesty — especially to self — in all matters and the value of speaking truth at all times. Cruelty for the sake of cruelty, whether to animals or man, degraded a person, and the man who stole or cheated or lied could never secure the most priceless possession of a Shawnee: honor among his fellows or in his own soul.

The most important lesson of all, taught him by everyone, was that of respect for his elders, a trait which went hand-in-hand with respect for authority. Not only the individual's parents and chiefs, but any person of the tribe who began to show advanced years assumed some degree of importance and authority. And when talking was done, whether in councils or just about the campfires, it was always the older people who spoke first and they were listened to closely and their wisdom and advice deeply respected. Revering the aged became an ingrained characteristic.

Even at his tender age, Tecumseh was exhibiting important signs of leadership. Where sides were chosen in the games played among the youngsters, he was the one selected to do the choosing for his side and always he had a company of companions about him, eager to follow his lead in doing anything he suggested.

It was a clear, crisp morning last October when his foster-father, Chief Black Fish, had summoned him and with solemn admonitions and instructions, informed him that it was now time for him to prepare for his *Pa-waw-ka* — that is, to become possessed of some material object through which he could approach and receive power from Moneto and the Great Spirit in times of need. He was sent to Chiksika's *wegiwa* to strip himself, run naked from there to a deep hole in the nearby Little Miami River and plunge into it, then return and dress. Each morning thereafter he was

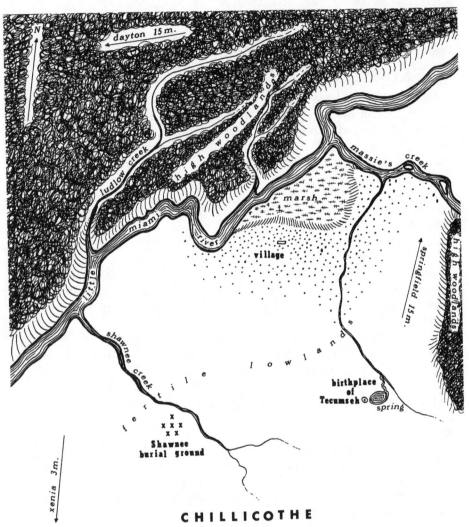

CHILLICOTHE

SEAT OF THE CHALAHGAWTHA SHAWNEE SEPT

(On the site of present Oldtown, Ohio.   The distances indicated
are to modern cities.)

required to do this, right into the bitterest depth of winter. As the weather grew colder, the task became harder to bear and frequently he was forced to break the ice before he could take the plunge. The icy water and frigid air were a severe test of courage and endurance, but his mentor's directions remained unchanged and his own obedience unswerving. He was being disciplined in obedience and in reverence for the command of his earthly father to make him worthy of receiving the protection and loving care of both Moneto and the Great Spirit.

In mid-January, on the morning of his final plunge, Black Fish informed him that the time of preparation was at an end. He must now seek his *Pa-waw-ka* symbol. He instructed the boy this time to dive deeply, to the very bed of the river, there to close both hands over whatever they touched. Without looking at what was grasped in his hands, he was to return to Black Fish.

This he did and, as he stood shivering with cold and anticipation, the chief pried open one hand and found some gravel and a piece of water-logged twig and, in the other, a soggy leaf and some sand and a piece of white quartzite rock.

Black Fish took the rock between his fingers and held it up. It was about the size of a pigeon's egg. He inspected it closely, turning it over several times, and then he grunted approvingly.

"This," he said, "is forever your *Pa-waw-ka*, to be carried by you and used as an intermediary between yourself and the Great Spirit when you are in need of help and direction."

It had taken weeks for the boy to chip a groove all the way around the stone so that he might securely tie it and wear it around his neck and he was sure that wherever it touched his skin it imparted an inner warmth.

And now, with the fundamentals of childhood training already deeply ingrained in his little brother, Chiksika began the long and important business of training Tecumseh in the matters of warfare.

[*May 12, 1776 — Sunday*]

Despite the warnings they had been given against attempting anything so foolhardy, this day the party of Moravian missionaries reached the Muskingum River just over two miles below the forks. They were led by the Reverends David Zeisberger and John Hickswelder and had with them eight families numbering thirty-five persons.

"This is the place where we will build our mission village," Zeisberger announced, "and we will call it Lichtenau — that is, Pasture of Light; a green pasture to be illuminated by the Gospel."

The site was a pleasant one and had been selected in deference to the wishes of Netawatwees, a friendly Delaware chief who, with his family, had previously become converted to Christianity and now lived at the

Forks in his village of Goschachgunk.[8] The chief and his villagers were there in full force to meet the missionaries and they assembled on the riverbank beneath trees heavy with great green buds; here Zeisberger preached the first Christian sermon ever given in the Ohio country.

"Thus it is written," he intoned, "and thus it behooved Christ to suffer, and to rise from the dead on the third day; and that repentance and remission of sins should be preached in His name among all nations, beginning at Jerusalem."

[June 6, 1776 — Thursday]

Simon Kenton had just finished guiding a party of newcomers to Leestown on the first of the month, when John Todd, who had come out with Henry Lee, told him a meeting would be held at Harrodsburg to select somebody to go to Williamsburg to get aid for the settlements.[9] The young frontiersman was impressed with the number of people who showed up at Jim Harrod's settlement and was especially delighted to see many familiar faces, some of whom he had not seen since the Dunmore campaign or before.

George Rogers Clark called the meeting to order and explained the perplexing situation facing them. Richard Henderson had, he said, consummated a purchase of this whole territory from the Cherokees, but he deeply doubted its legality. It was, he admitted, an intriguing idea to think of establishing an entire new country named Transylvania, but it wasn't too practical. Even if legal, how would they defend themselves? Right now they needed an armed force to stand off the Indians' repeated and growing attacks, and they had neither the men nor arms to do this themselves. Nor did they even have enough powder and lead for the guns at hand. They must have help and this help must come from Virginia. It was extremely important, therefore, that instead of trying to follow Henderson's grandiose plan, they urge Virginia to divide the Fincastle County lands and make of this section the County of Kentucky, with its own delegates to the Virginia General Assembly and its own right to demand, and get, military aid from the colony.

There was little opposition to the plan. Even those of Henderson's capital city of Boonesboro had to concede that there was little likelihood they could defend themselves against any invaders. It was proposed, therefore, that two men be elected as delegates to represent the frontiersmen in all matters politic before the Virginia Assembly.

George Rogers Clark was almost a foreordained nominee as one of the two and the other was a very well-liked lawyer from Boston, John Gabriel Jones, one of McClelland's settlers. A vote was called and the pair won by acclamation. A petition was immediately drawn up asking that the Virginia government recognize these two as authorized delegates of the frontier settlements. This petition was signed by the leading representatives of the various settlements and the few free agents such as Kenton and Williams who owed their allegiance to no specific fort. Those who could not write but were in accordance with the petition had others sign their names for them. Among those whose names appeared were Robert Patterson, James Wilkinson, Joshua House, John McClelland, Daniel Boone and his brother, Squire Boone, Isaac Shelby, Joseph Crockett, Samuel McDowell, John Hinkson, Benjamin Logan, Levi Todd, Jacob Drennon and, of course, Simon Butler.

[July 4, 1776 — Thursday]

During the June session of the Continental Congress, Richard Henry Lee had risen to present a momentous resolution, which was : "Resolved: that these United Colonies are, and of right ought to be, free and independent states." Instantly John Adams seconded it and a committee of five — Thomas Jefferson of Virginia, John Adams of Massachusetts and Benjamin Franklin of Pennsylvania, Roger Sherman of Connecticut and Robert R. Livingston of New York — was chosen to draw up a declaration embodying that resolution. It was Tom Jefferson who did the lion's share of the work.

On this date, as president of Congress and in a bold hand which "the king of England could read without spectacles," John Hancock was first to sign the Declaration of Independence. It was a great day for America and the patriots in Philadelphia rang the great bell in the State House joyously, while in New York City others pulled down the huge gilded lead statue of the king and melted it into bullets.

The Colonies were no longer colonies, but states — provided they could make this Declaration stick. It would not be easy.

There came an immediate call to enlarge the Continental Army and various state militias. As an inducement to enlistment, Virginia, Massachusetts and Connecticut promised bounties of land to all in those sections of the Northwest Territory which their charters included. It was a powerful inducement. These were lands many men had dreamed of owning but had been kept out of by treaties with various Indian tribes.

But the offer caused an uproar among those states whose charters did not embrace large portions of western unappropriated lands. They insisted that these lands be appropriated for the benefit of all the states, according to the population, as the title to them, if secured at all, would be by the blood and treasure of all the states. Congress thereupon urged the states owning western unappropriated lands to make liberal concessions of them for the common benefit of all; at once Virginia set the pattern by ceding her lands north of the Ohio River on condition that if her lands south of the Ohio should prove insufficient for her legal bounties to her own troops, the deficiency should be made up from her lands north of the river and between the Little Miami and Scioto Rivers.

And so, before the Revolution had hardly begun, America was haggling over the division of the spoils — land now occupied by Delawares and Shawnees, Wyandots and Potawatomies, Mingoes, Miamis and Ottawas, none of whom could be expected to give up willingly any of this land to which they were entitled.

[*July 30, 1776 — Tuesday*]

For a long time Simon Kenton had foreseen the breakup of his partnership with Tom Williams and he shouldered full responsibility for it. He liked Tom well enough and trusted him as a steady, dependable partner, but their very natures were too dissimilar for them to remain together any longer. The wonder of it all was that they had stuck together this long.

In recent months Williams had taken to mooning about the camp, unwilling to go very far away, uncommonly eager for news about eastern Pennsylvania from any emigrant who came through, and suddenly possessed with a powerful yearning to return to the East, even if it meant fighting the British.

Their two acres of corn this year had been a dismal failure. There had not been enough rain and what the buffalo had not trodden beneath their hooves, the deer ate up. It was obvious they would realize far less corn, despite doubling their acreage, than they had last year; as a result both of them took to neglecting the hoeing and cultivating which should have been done.

And so they had parted, sorrowfully to some extent, because they had shared much together, but with relief as well. With Williams went also Sam Arrowsmith, who first carefully greased his plow and other tools with bear oil and then buried them in anticipation of returning "in a year or so."

Now Simon was free once more to roam the Kentucky country unencumbered, secure in the knowledge that his "tomahawk claim" was still waiting for him back there along the stream known now as Lawrence Creek. Soon after Williams and Arrowsmith had left, Simon spent a few days at Hinkson's Station where he helped to erect a blockhouse. While he was there, a hit-and-run attack of about thirty Shawnees occurred and, while no one was hurt on either side, many cows were killed and some horses stolen; moreover, the realization was implanted in John Hinkson's mind that the little settlement was still not strong enough to stand by itself. With Simon guiding them, they went to McClelland's Station and found that the settlers from Leestown, similarly attacked and having reached the same conclusion, had arrived there only a day before.

Simon moved on and everywhere he went the story was the same:

Indian attacks were growing ever stronger and more vicious; the only hope of succor was from George Rogers Clark and John Gabriel Jones, who had returned to Williamsburg for recognition and military aid. Jones, a personal friend of Virginia's new governor, Patrick Henry, was certain they would be successful and return with men and arms by autumn.

Not until he reached Boonesboro did Simon discover that only a couple of weeks ago Daniel Boone's daughter, Jemima, and her two companions, the sisters Betsy and Frances Callaway, had been captured by five Shawnees while canoeing in the Kentucky River within sight of the fort. Boone, John Floyd and several other men had set out in pursuit, tracking the party for nearly fifty miles before catching up to it. They took the Indians by surprise. Boone killed one and Floyd another and the remainder fled, leaving the captives behind.

Although Daniel Boone was twice his own age, Simon got along with him very well. They were, in many ways, cut from the same pattern — happiest when away from civilized life, even that of these rude settlements, and sharing the same near-reverence for the beauties of nature abounding all about them. In their first week of hunting together they found themselves even more compatible than either had first realized. It was a rare pleasure for them both to share the wilderness with someone who could fully take care of himself — who did not have to be told to avoid unnecessary noises, who knew how to read and interpret sign, whether natural, Indian or white, and who could be depended upon fully in event of an emergency. Such companionship is a rare commodity indeed, even in the world of frontiersmen.

For most of this summer the pair rambled the Kentucky country together, ranging from as far east as Tygart Valley, where they stayed with Michael Tygart for two days, to as far west as the Falls of Ohio, but mostly in the area of Lawrence and Bracken Creeks near Limestone. It was, for Simon, the beginning of as close a friendship as he had ever had with any other man, with the possible exception of Simon Girty.

[*December 27, 1776 — Friday*]

Tracking was ridiculously easy for Simon Kenton in the two-inch snow that had fallen during the night. This was only the third snowfall of the season and, as with the previous two, it showed every sign of melting quickly. Day was only a few hours old and already the temperature was well above freezing. Thus far December had been very mild.

Over four hundred yards ahead of him, a heavy-antlered buck stepped along purposefully on a treeless hillside. Simon placed the long barrel of his rifle in the crotch of a sapling, took careful aim and fired. The buck leaped high into the air and fell in a thrashing tangle, regained its feet and ran thirty yards or so before falling again. This time it lay still and Simon grinned.

He waited motionlessly for several minutes after reloading to see if his shot had attracted the attention of any marauding Shawnees. A little movement near a grove of trees a half-mile east attracted his attention and he watched carefully as three men moved into sight. They were too distant to identify their features, but the distinctive bobbing pace of the leader was familiar to him. The only man he knew who walked like that was George Rogers Clark.

Simon stepped into the open, cupped his mouth and let out a far-carrying halloo. As the party stopped and looked toward him, he swept off his coonskin cap and waved it high. At once Clark waved in return and the three started toward him. In a few minutes they met and shook hands warmly, Clark admitting that the snow-covered ground was confusing to him and that he was trying to find Harrodsburg. Could Simon lead him there quickly? Simon could.

The buck he had downed was meat for that very settlement. They walked to the deer and Simon removed the viscera, saving liver and heart, scrubbed out the body cavity with handfuls of snow and then replaced the two organs, tying the body incision shut with two strips of rawhide. He hoisted the animal to his shoulders, draped it about his neck and tied its feet together in front of him, and off they went for Harrodsburg. All during this activity, Clark explained what had happened and why there was need of haste in reaching the settlement.

Shortly after last summer's meeting, he and Jones had returned to Virginia — but they had arrived too late. The General Assembly had just adjourned and would not be seated again until fall. They had immediately gone to see the governor to lay the matter before him. Patrick Henry was sympathetic but he could not personally authorize sending arms and men to Fincastle County. With the Revolutionary War in full swing, there were neither men nor weapons to spare, even had he the power to grant the request, which he did not.

Henry had listened carefully as Jones and Clark told what had transpired in the Kentucky country and frowned deeply at the news of increased Indian attacks. He was in full agreement that the settlers and their families needed, and should have, military support from Virginia, but the matter was not that simple. Richard Henderson was still here and gaining ground in his battle to have his purchase of Transylvania legalized. If that occurred, no help of any kind from Virginia could be sent.

They had talked long into the night and made a plan. Patrick Henry would, on the morrow, personally take the pair to the state's executive council and add his own voice to theirs in a plea for help. If approved, Clark and Jones would remain over until the fall session of the General

Assembly and do what they could to quash Henderson's move. The governor felt strongly that retaining the Fincastle lands of the Virginia Charter was imperative and no one could put the point across better than the two men before him.

Unfortunately, the executive council was less than inclined to share the governor's enthusiasm for retaining the western lands. It would be nice, they agreed, but the war took precedence; also, there was no legal way, unless the Kentucky country became a separate county of the state with its own elected representatives, for the state to send aid. Powder and lead were available, the council admitted, but legally it could not be allotted for their purpose.

Now Clark and Jones resorted to a last-ditch try to bring pressure to bear. If the council did not give them at least a good supply of powder and lead, perhaps the Pennsylvania or North Carolina councils would be more inclined to help.

Such a prospect was not at all pleasant for the Virginia council to contemplate and, as their talks continued for three days, there was a perceptible weakening on the part of this body. They were most impressed by the fact that an election had already been held and that Jones and Clark were authorized representatives. On August 23 a decision was reached: Clark and Jones would be given five hundred pounds of gunpowder and plenty of lead. In return, they were to remain in Williamsburg until the General Assembly reconvened. If they could succeed in having Henderson's purchase declared illegal and the new County of Kentucky formed, perhaps actual military aid could be forthcoming.

And so they had stayed on and, when the General Assembly met, made their plea in the strongest possible terms. The matter was taken under consideration and put into committee, with a vote to be made before Christmas. Having done all they could, the two delegates set off for Fort Pitt with a written order from the excutive council that the five hundred-weight of powder and sufficient lead be issued them at that place.

They recruited seven men to help — men anxious to get to the Kentucky country but without means of their own to do so. One of these was the cheerful fifteen-year-old son of Clark's sister. His name was Joseph Rogers and he admired his Uncle George with something approaching reverence. Clark had misgivings about bringing the youth along, but he had finally given in to his pleas and the party had set off downriver in three canoes with the meager supplies.

As they passed the mouth of the Scioto River, five canoes filled with Indians started in pursuit. Clark's party had gained distance on their pursuers gradually, but there was no indication that the Indians would give up the chase. Under cover of darkness they landed at Three Islands and hid the powder and lead in five different locations. Then they continued paddling downriver until Limestone Creek was reached. There they set the boats adrift and struck out overland for Hinkson's Station. It was nearly deserted when they reached it; but when they learned there how much more serious the Indian situation had become during their absence, they left immediately for McClelland's Station where there might be enough men to retrieve the ammunition in safety.

But, Clark told Simon now, most of the men remaining at McClelland's were off on a hunting expedition and so he had left Jones there with five others and struck out for Harrodsburg to get the help needed.

This was a serious situation. The settlers desperately needed these supplies and it could mean the end of everything if the Indians found them first. The four men increased their pace but, even though he was carrying the deer, Simon had to hold down his own speed so the other three could keep up. Left to his own devices, he could easily have run all the way to Harrodsburg with the animal.

A meeting was called the moment they reached the settlement and the situation quickly explained. James Harrod called for volunteers to return to McClelland's, pick up the Jones party and go after the supplies. There was not a man unwilling to go and Harrod selected thirty. Less than an hour later Simon was leading them on horseback by the shortest possible route to John McClelland's little station where just a few months before he and John Todd had helped erect the blockhouse.

McClelland met them with shocking news. John Gabriel Jones and a settler named William Graden had been killed and two of the new men in the Jones party had been captured. McClelland hurriedly gave them the details. On Christmas Eve the hunting party of eight men under John Todd had returned here and Jones had talked them into teaming up with his men to go after the supplies. About noon on Christmas Day, at Johnson's Fork near the Blue Licks, they had been ambushed by a party of forty Indians under a vicious little Shawnee subchief whom the settlers called Pluggy.

At the first volley, Jones and Graden had been killed. Two of the former's party, unused to horseback riding, had fallen off their mounts in the mad scramble that ensued and were captured as the main body retreated at full speed. One of those captured was Clark's young nephew, Joseph Rogers. Now there was strong belief that Pluggy was on his way to attack McClelland's and, after that, Harrodsburg. If Harrodsburg could be taken, the backbone of the settlers' existence here would be broken.

James Harrod became greatly worried. Numerous families had moved into Harrodsburg for protection, including most of the women and children of this whole frontier area. Hardly a handful of men remained there to fight off Indians if they should appear and this could turn into a wholesale massacre. The recovery of powder and lead, if it was still on the islands, would have to wait.

The only women and children at McClelland's were the families of John Todd and McClelland himself. They were swiftly bundled up and sent back to Harrodsburg with Harrod and most of his party of volunteers to prepare the defenses of that station with what little ammunition remained. This left Hinkson, McClelland, Kenton, Todd, a husky young man named Bates Collins, whom Simon had first met at Leestown, and perhaps a dozen others to defend the McClelland blockhouse.

The attack was not long in coming. At dawn Pluggy and his warriors attacked. They rushed the blockhouse firing their rifles as they came and, through a freakish accident, a bullet buzzed through a tiny niche in the logs and struck John McClelland in the head, killing him.

A burst of gunfire flamed from the gunports and several of the advancing Indians fell, among them Chief Pluggy, two bullets having pierced his breast. The Shawnees hesitated at the dropping of their leader, then fell back to cover, carrying their fallen with them. They milled around out of gun range for an hour or so and then, to the amazement of the men in the fort, rode off to the east.

Certain that this direction had been taken to deceive them, Simon and Bates Collins volunteered to follow the Indians to see if they would begin a wide sweep around to the southwest to attack Harrodsburg. But the death of their chief at the very onset of the fighting had been taken by the Shawnees as a bad omen and they were returning home. The two frontiersmen followed them to the mouth of Limestone Creek where they had crossed the Ohio.

Satisfied that they were really gone, Simon and Collins raised the former's own little canoe, which a few months back he had filled with rocks and sunk into hiding in a little cove a short distance above Limestone Creek. Clinging close to the Kentucky shore, they paddled up to Three Islands and were overjoyed to find all five deposits of powder and lead still where they had been hidden by Clark and Jones.

They returned with the good news to McClelland's and then Simon set off alone for Harrodsburg to get together a party of men to bring the heavy supplies to safety. There was sorrow at the news of McClelland's death but considerable relief at word that the supplies were undetected and the Indians had returned to Ohio.

And Simon, in turn, was also given good news. Word had come that the Virginia General Assembly had, on December 6, declared the Transylvania Land Company illegal and officially created Kentucky County out of the Fincastle lands.[10]

[*January 20, 1777 — Monday*]

Though not permitted to attend the council meeting with his brother Chiksika, Tecumseh crouched in the cold near the door and listened in excitement to what was being said inside the *msi-kah-mi-qui*. As the best hunter and shooter among all the boys in Chillicothe, he considered himself something of a warrior already. After all, his ninth summer was looming.

The voice of Black Fish as he addressed his warriors was harsh and it frightened Tecumseh a little. The chief had always been so pleasant and warm outside the council house. Tecumseh shivered and tucked the buffalo robe more firmly around him and strained to hear.

Black Fish was telling them that their great chief, Cornstalk, had said they must honor the treaty made with the *Shemanese* at the Chief Dunmore's camp. But now, with the death of one of Black Fish's own subchiefs, Pluk-kemeh-notee — Pluggy — it had become a personal affront to the Chalahgawtha Shawnees and a matter which must be settled by them without delay. He personally would lead two hundred warriors, only Chalahgawthas from this village, and destroy every settlement in the Can-tuc-kee lands.

There was a murmur of assenting voices and, lest he be seen there, Tecumseh scurried away from the doorway and back to the warmth of Chiksika's *wegiwa*. But later, even after becoming thoroughly warm before the fire, he shivered again as he thought of Black Fish's words and what they might mean to the Shawnees.

[*February 26, 1777 — Wednesday*]

Even though Simon Kenton had led a party of thirty men back to Three Islands and safely retrieved the supplies Clark had hidden there, the frontier settlements were in bad shape. The deaths of the two highly in-fluential and respected frontiersmen — Jones and McClelland — and the attack on the latter's station had depressed everyone. For the past seven weeks there had taken place a veritable exodus of families back to the comparative safety of the east. Already such settlements as McClelland's, Hinkson, Leestown and Danville were abandoned. And now even Benjamin Logan was deserting his own small fort. When he arrived at Harrodsburg with his people, the only two occupied settlements left in the whole of Kentucky were Harrodsburg and Boonesboro, with a total of only one hundred three able-bodied men left to fight.

While James Harrod welcomed Logan and his group and was pleased at the added strength they lent his settlement, there was no doubt but that their very coming was weakening to the fort because of the tax on its resources to house, feed and clothe everyone. It also meant that now Simon Kenton must spend all his time at the most dangerous job there; he became hunter for the fort, going out alone to shoot game and bring it back to feed the hungry within the walls. It was no job for the faint-hearted.

In the depths of night he would slip out of the fort and go to the place where he intended hunting the next day. There he would crouch for hours, waiting for daylight. On some of these nights the temperature was far below zero and, except for an ingenious method shown to him by John Yeager during that first winter they had spent together on the Kanawha, he would surely have frozen.

White oak bark had wonderful qualities; it burned almost without smoke and generated a remarkable amount of heat for a small amount of fuel. Simon would locate a white oak tree and remove strips of bark from it. These he would put into a small pile on the ground. Beside it he would dig a hole the size of his own head and in this he would criss-cross narrow strips of the bark until it was filled. Then, tossing his blanket over his head and shoulders so the sparks would not be seen, he would "make fire" with flint and steel.

As soon as the bark strips were glowing well, he would cover the hole with the earth he had dug out, leaving only two small holes for draught. Then he would sit crosslegged with the hole in the space between his legs and his entire body and the hole covered with the blanket. Inside the blanket it quickly became as pleasant as a warm room and, hunched over in this position with one hand on his rifle, Simon would sleep in reasonable comfort in the bitterest of weather. More than once he had awakened surprised to find that many inches of snow had fallen.

In the morning, often many miles from Harrodsburg, the hunt would begin. Sometimes it meant lying in wait for game, but mostly it was a matter of tracking. Cautious of his movements and keeping to cover at every opportunity, there was little danger he would be seen by roaming Indians. But there was no way to muffle the crashing report of the rifle, and this became the instant of greatest danger.

Once the shot was fired and the game downed, he would remain hidden and motionless for long periods. Only his head would swivel slowly from one side to the other, his sharp eyes taking in every detail, every movement. For an instant he would catch the flick of wings as a chickadee hopped from one branch to another fifty yards away. A fox gliding silently through the edge of a wooded fringe would hold his attention for a moment. A deer standing in deep cover a hundred yards away might twitch its ear and immediately Simon's piercing gaze would home in on it and gradually make out the outline of the entire animal.

Even when certain the shot had not been heard, he took his time reaching the fallen quarry — usually a deer. He would drag the carcass to the nearest large tree and, with his back to the trunk and his gun leaning within quick grasp, he would skin the animal, lay the skin open on the ground and pile on it the quarters of meat as he cut them. Then, when a second kill had been heaped high on the first pile, the two skins were punctured along the edges and tied together with lengths of rawhide into a pack often weighing fully two hundred pounds. With this fastened to his back, he would begin his careful trek back to Harrodsburg. For the past several weeks, wild meat without salt or bread was the only food available at the settlement.

And Simon Kenton was the salvation of Harrodsburg.

[*March 5, 1776 — Wednesday*]

Five days ago the commission from Governor Patrick Henry had arrived at Harrodsburg, appointing George Rogers Clark a major and in command of the entire County of Kentucky and the defense of the western frontier. He was also directed to appoint officers and so he called the meeting of the men before him this day to announce his appointments for the first militia of Kentucky.

"I hereby commission," he said, "Daniel Boone, James Harrod and John Todd as captains. Joe Lindsay will be officer in charge of commissary. For these officers the rate of pay is fixed by the Virginia government. We are, unfortunately, provided with no authority to appoint spies and scouts. Yet, since it is the latter group upon which so much will depend and, because they are so badly needed, I am asking Silas Harlan, Samuel Moore, Benjamin Linn, Thomas Brooks and Simon Butler if they will accept such a post without payment except that I pledge to them the faith of Virginia."

They accepted, of course, for the job was little more than they would have been doing anyway. Each of the men was given a specific round of territory to cover to watch for the approach of Indians; Simon's assignment was the area surrounding Boonesboro, the weaker of the two remaining inhabited settlements.

"We have at present, both here and at Boonesboro," Clark said, "a very serious shortage of clothing and sugar. Later today I will form a party of four men to go up to the large maple grove four miles northeast of here at the place some of you call Shawnee Springs, to set about tapping trees and boiling down the sap.

"Along the same vein, I want John Haggin and three other men to leave in the morning for Hinkson's to get the flax that was left there. And also to harvest some of the hemp nearby.[11] We must have it so our women can make some clothing. I'll ask Simon Butler and Michael Stoner to go along and they can take a portion of it to Boonesboro. At all times keep alert for Indians. The remainder of us — *everyone* — will continue to work at improving the fortifications here."

[*March 6, 1777 — Thursday*]

Simon Kenton had met a number of men in his twenty-two years whom he considered fools, but few were the rival of John Haggin, a diminutive man with a pinched expression and a seemingly endless amount of nervous energy seldom expended in constructive directions. From the moment they left the gates of Harrodsburg he had been aggressive and domineering, particularly where Simon was concerned. It seemed likely he detested the big young man who had brought him meat for weeks simply because of Simon's large size and well-earned reputation on the frontier.

As if he were a banty-hen caring for a brood, Haggin kneed his horse round and about the other five men, exhorting them to stay in line, to speed up or slow down. It amused rather than angered Simon and he winked at Stoner who grinned and winked back. Abruptly putting his horse into a gallop and shouting something over his shoulder about needing a scout up ahead, Haggin swept out of sight along the buffalo road. It was the consensus of the others that John Haggin would not last long in this country. If the Indians didn't kill him, some angry settler was sure to.

A few hours later Haggin showed up again, galloping toward them with all the speed his poor lathered horse could muster. The party pulled up and clods of earth flew in all directions as Haggin jerked his mount to a stop. His eyes were alight with a strange fire and he told them in a jerky, nearly incoherent manner that hundreds of Indians had surrounded Hinkson's and were camped only a short distance away.

"Then its time we get back to Harrodsburg," Simon said.

"Back!" Haggins voice was a shriek. "The big brave scout sticking his tail between his legs and running, eh? Well I say it's our duty to spy on 'em and anybody who's not afraid can come with me. We'll leave our horses here."

He leaped down lightly and, amazingly, all but Simon and Michael Stoner followed. Simon couldn't believe it when the dismounted men tied their horses and started slinking down the road. He held up a hand for Stoner to wait and vaulted off his own horse, tied the reins hurriedly to a bush, then ran to catch the men and, if necessary, knock some sense into their heads. They were just going around a bend in the road when he reached them and spun Haggin around. Haggin flushed and brought his fists into position, his legs braced wide apart.

Before either man could speak there came the thunder of hooves and with a wave of his arm Simon motioned Stoner to go on back. He clapped a huge hand over Haggin's mouth and dragged him into the bushes, whispering to the others to follow. They weren't an instant too soon. Ten mounted Indians led by Chief Black Fish swept past them and broke into shrill cries when they saw the horses ahead. Stoner was already crouched low over his own mount's neck as he raced away.

For a moment, as they thundered past the riderless horses, the Indians seemed bent on chasing Stoner; but after only a hundred yards Black Fish raised a hand and they wheeled about and returned to the animals. Puzzled, they looked around sharply for the riders, glanced back in the direction in which Stoner had disappeared and held a muttered conference. It was apparent they were worried that this might be advance indication of a large army of whites and without delay they loosened the reins and led the horses after them in the direction from whence they had come. Only when they were out of hearing did Kenton release his hand from over Haggin's mouth.

"You want to be a big man," he said icily, "so now's your chance. Those Shawnees'll be back soon. You get back to Harrodsburg fast with word they're coming. Likely the Injens'll try to pick up our trail. Backtrack every now and then to throw them off. Walk in water where possible. Stay off soft ground. Go in twos, stay off the road. Two on one side, two on the other. Don't stop for rest or anything. If Mike doesn't get through, the lives of everyone at Harrodsburg'll depend on you. Get through! Tell Clark I've gone on to Boone to warn him."

With that he took one last look down the road and then loped away in that mile-eating run toward Boonesboro.

[*April 5, 1777 — Saturday*]

Boonesboro considered itself lucky. Until today, Harrodsburg had undergone three severe attacks by the two hundred warriors under Black Fish. Boone's people knew little about these attacks other than that they had occurred, but they were thankful that the force had not been thrown against them at Boonesboro, for here the fortifications were weaker and they had only twenty-one fighting men as compared to about seventy-five at Harrodsburg.

The three separate day-long attacks on Harrodsburg might well have succeeded but for the weather. Michael Stoner had arrived three hours after the surprise on the road to Hinkson's, but this wasn't the first time that the fort had heard of approaching Indians. A half hour before Stoner arrived, a wounded man had staggered into the settlement and collapsed. He was one of the men from the sugar camp. Brought around, he told them his three companions had been killed by "about seventy" Shawnees that swept down on them from nowhere. Wounded, he had eluded them in the brush and returned here. The work of fortification now moved along in frantic haste.

Early in the morning, having walked all night, Haggin and his three companions reached the settlement and told of the "attack" on the road and of Simon Butler having gone to Boonesboro to warn them. Less than an hour after their arrival, one of the lookouts in the blockhouse shouted an alarm and the attack was on. A shouting horde of Shawnees charged the fort, some riding but most afoot. There was a furious exchange of shots but with little effect. A few Indians were hit and one of the whites took a ball in the shoulder.

About noon the skies darkened, a stiff wind came up and it began to snow — tiny sharp crystals which peppered like hail. As the afternoon progressed the weather grew worse and by dusk it was a howling storm. Black Fish withdrew his forces.

For days the storm continued, alternating snow and rain with the temperature hovering near freezing. Slowly and reluctantly it began to clear and the settlers braced themselves for another attack. It came on March 18, but once again the battle was only an hour or so old when the weather closed in and heavy black clouds dumped rain in torrents.

For the next ten days it rained off and on, then began to grow colder. The temperature fell to just below freezing and held there for a day. And just as Black Fish began his final attack here on March 28, the temperature plummeted in a matter of hours to only a few degrees above zero. Disheartened, Black Fish withdrew his men and headed toward the Ohio River to establish a camp, leaving behind only a handful of men to continue harassment of the whites.

Simon Kenton had reached the Boonesboro area in midafternoon of the day they lost their horses, but he didn't go immediately across the clearing to the fort. He had seen a great deal of Indian sign along the way and feared they might be lying hidden in the woodland fringe, waiting to shoot anyone who might leave. He decided to wait until nightfall to approach. Late in the afternoon, however, a small group of whites came out of the gates and began picking up firewood in the area that had been cleared of timber to build the fortifications.

Simon sprang to his feet and ran toward them shouting an alarm. Simultaneously several shots rang out from the woods on the other side and three men in the work party fell. Two regained their feet and hobbled toward the gate while two others took the fallen man's arms and dragged him as they ran clumsily after the others. They reached the gate about the same time Simon did and it was swung closed with a reassuring thud. An instant later the heavy locking timber fell into place.

Daniel Boone ran up to Simon, who explained the situation as he knew it. The man who had been dragged into the fort was dead but the wounds of the others were not too serious. Helplessly the settlers watched from chinks in the logs as, one after another, their cattle were shot to death in the little corral just outside the gates.

Then, today, had come Mike Stoner and two others with a message from Clark to Boone, apprising him of what had happened at Harrodsburg and the fact that the vast majority of Indians had left the area, "although for where and for how long cannot yet be known." Benjamin Logan, Clark wrote, was so confident that Black Fish had given up and returned across the Ohio that he and his fourteen men and their families had returned to his station, St. Asaph. It was, in Clark's opinion, a premature move and he cautioned Boone not to become overconfident, lest this mood precede disaster.

It was advice to heed well.

[*April 24, 1777 — Thursday*]

The attack on Boonesboro after so long a delay since the last attack on Harrodsburg was a great shock. Even though they had observed caution religiously, they were surprised.

Simon Kenton and two other guards had posted themselves with their guns at ready at the open gate when two men went out into the clearing a short distance away just after dawn. The pair had picked up anything that could be used as firewood and, their arms full, were returning to the fort when the shots came. One of the men fell and the other dropped his load and burst into a frantic run to reach the gate sixty yards away. The man on the ground got to his hands and knees and began to crawl toward the fort, but six Indians rushed out of the woods and overtook him.

The lead Indian slammed his tomahawk into the man's spine and then whipped out his knife and began scalping him. Kenton and the two other guards ran out and Simon fired while running, dropping the one Indian just as he freed the scalp; a tremendous shot at fifty yards. The other five turned and ran lengthwise down the clearing instead of back toward the woods, while at the same time Boone charged out of the gate with ten men at his heels. The same thought was in everyone's mind: that this was a small raiding party bent on mischief. It was a tragic miscalculation.

Simon was past the dead man, his gun already reloaded, and Boone's group was fully forty yards from the gate when the deception became clear. A wave of warriors, at least a hundred of them, burst from the edge of the woods and ran to cut them off from retreat into the fort.

"Back!" Boone cried. "Back to the fort!"

It was a desperate race. Except for the women and children, only eight men had remained behind to defend the fort. Spinning around, Simon fired scarcely without aiming as he saw an Indian drop to one knee and aim at Boone. The Shawnee screamed and then lay motionless. Again Simon reloaded as he ran and shot another; he had already reloaded a third time when, at last, supporting fire came from the fort. Many of the Indians dived to take cover behind stumps and one of these, hidden to Boone, raised up as that frontiersman approached and shot. Boone pitched to the ground, his leg broken.

The Shawnee ran to him, his tomahawk upraised to administer the finishing blow, but he crumpled silently as Simon's fourth shot ripped through his chest. Boone raised himself on his hands and swiveled around, shaking his head imperatively as Simon ran toward him.

"Can't get up," he said, gasping. "Go on. Don't stop. Get to the fort!"

Simon didn't answer. Pausing only for an instant he dropped his gun and scooped Boone into his arms as if the man were a baby, then set off running just about as fast as he had been running before. Two Indians rushed side by side to cut him off and instead of veering from them, he continued his course. Both braves had tomahawks in their hands and triumph in their eyes. When only ten feet separated them, Simon dived, thrusting Boone's body away from him as one might shove away a log being carried. Boone sailed through the air and crashed solidly into the pair, stunning one and knocking both to the ground. Before the uninjured one could scramble to his feet, Simon's tomahawk buried itself in his head. The huge frontiersman again picked up Boone, now unconscious, lashed out a foot viciously at the stunned Indian who was dazedly attempting to rise, and felt the rib bones cave in under the impact.

Now the way to the fort was clear and he ran as if all the devils of Hell were at his heels. Under the circumstances, it was no extravagant comparison. Bullets kicked up the ground around them and several thunked solidly into the heavy logs of the gate as they neared it. And then they were through and the gate slammed and latched behind them.

It was no time for rest. Simon lay Boone on the ground gently, dashed into the blockhouse and scaled the ladder to the upper room. For the first time it dawned on him that he had no gun and he called down for another. One of the women pitched a rifle up to him and then climbed up after it with more powder and lead.

Amazingly, except for the dead and scalped settler on the ground outside, none of the whites had been killed. But of the twenty-three men left alive, seven were wounded and three of them very seriously.

Throughout the remainder of the day and all through the next two the siege continued. Finally the major force of Indians disappeared, but it couldn't be known whether they had gone home or not. It was certain not all of them had gone, for cattle continued to be killed here and there, horses stolen and the incautious shot at.

[May 25, 1777 — Sunday]

At best it was a difficult month which followed. It daily became more apparent that Black Fish and his men had not returned over the Ohio after all. There were just too many Indians moving about the countryside and creating havoc.

Simon Kenton and Michael Stoner did all the hunting for Boonesboro and it was even more difficult now than it had been during the winter. Indians were everywhere and the sound of a rifle shot was an invitation to all Indians within hearing to investigate. The men hunted together now and then, but mostly they struck off by themselves, each feeling safer when relying on his own woodland ability. Stoner did not range quite as far afield as did Simon, nor did he have as many encounters with scattered parties of Indians, but whenever either of the men went out, no man in the fort held much hope of ever seeing him again.

It was no longer possible for those at Logan's Fort, Harrodsburg and Boonesboro to stay inside for great lengths of time as they did during the winter. Ground had to be broken, corn and other vegetables planted if there was to be any food next winter. Wood had to be chopped and brought in, salt and sugar boiled at the salt springs and maple groves. New and better cattle stockades and horse corrals had to be built and enclosed so as to be free from depredation. All of this work necessitated people going outside the walls to work and it was a dangerous time for everyone. Each work party had to have guards along with it and this, of itself, weakened each fort.

Over and again, so frequently as to become monotonous, the settlers, both men and women, were writing in their diaries or journals or letters fundamentally the same sentence: *Simon Butler saw an Indian about to fire upon me* [or a friend]: *he fired first and the Indian fell.*

His fantastic ability with the rifle was a phenomenon commented upon by virtually everyone on the frontier. No other person they had ever seen or heard of had such deadly aim nor so frequently pulled off such incredible shots which not only saved the lives of his friends but eliminated the enemies.

Since Daniel Boone was still helpless in his convalescence, it was Simon who took command of the fort. The suspicion that Black Fish had not returned to Ohio was confirmed when, at sunrise May 23, the Chalah-gawtha Shawnee chief led another strong attack on Boonesboro. All day long they traded shots and two men firing from stockade portholes were wounded slightly; one of them a man who had been creased across the shoulder by a bullet on the day of the first siege a month ago. Ironically, the ball narrowly missed Simon and creased the opposite shoulder of this same man in practically the same manner.

The attack ended at dark but began again the following dawn. Twice on this day Indians were seen to fall and were believed wounded or killed, but no one could be sure. One fact was certain — the stockade walls were holding up well under the attack and, unless the Indians came up with some new strategy, the settlers should be able to hold them off.

On the bright morning of May 25, the Indians were gone.

[*June 1, 1777 — Sunday*]

"Something," Benjamin Logan announced, "*has* to be done. First Harrodsburg, then Boonesboro, now us. Who knows how long Black Fish can keep picking at us until we fall apart? There has to be outside help brought in."

St. Asaph — or Standing Fort, as the Indians were calling it now after it had withstood such concerted assault by them for two days — came under attack beginning May 30 at dawn. It was by far the weakest of the three remaining Kentucky County forts, but that weakness was one of manpower, not construction. That eleven men could hold this place against the sizable force he led against it was infuriating to the Shawnee chief.

The attack had begun, as all of them had, with disconcerting surprise despite their caution. Three of the fort's women, under the guard of four men, left the gate to go the few dozen feet to the cattle compound to milk the cows. A barrage of shots came, died away, then came again as a few of the seven tried to crawl away. All were killed and then one at a time, as if taking turns, the Indians shot down the cattle from concealment. The rest of the day a desultory fire continued from both sides.

During the night there was quiet, but when dawn came it brought a shock. Six of the victims had been scalped and the only one who had been saved this debasement was the attractive young wife of one of the men who had been killed. One of the cows that had been shot had fallen upon her, covering her head and upper body.

Ignoring the pleas and warnings that met his announcement, Benjamin Logan went ahead with his plan. Tonight, after dark, he would slip out of the fort with two good horses, both with muffled hooves. With any luck he would get through and, once free of the siege line, strike out overland for Virginia's capital. He was convinced that if they could know what was happening here, aid would be sent.

He would go by the back route, through Cumberland Gap along the trail blazed by Boone and then through Roanoke and Richmond. If luck rode with him, he might be able to get through and back by the twentieth of June.

He was luckier than he knew. An hour and a half before he began his long journey, Black Fish assembled his men — all of them this time — and headed for the Ohio and home. He was not satisfied with the results but not greatly disappointed, either. Chief Pluk-kemeh-notee's death had been avenged many times over and perhaps these three months of continued harassment had shown the settlers that no longer would the Shawnees step back and allow themselves to be injured in any way.

[*June 7, 1777 — Saturday*]

"Gentlemen," George Rogers Clark said, "I have sent for you four because I know of no other men as well versed in spying as you. You've all had a great deal of experience in it and I feel I can rely on you completely."

Simon Kenton, Benjamin Linn, Silas Harlan and Sam Moore looked at one another uncomfortably, as modest men are inclined to do when publicly praised. They waited quietly for the commander of Kentucky's militia to go on.

Clark frowned. "I have an extremely dangerous mission in mind for you. An important one. Two men will suffice for the job but I want all of you to hear me out and consider well before deciding who will undertake it.

"The British have three major outposts west of here," he continued. "I am convinced that much of our Indian trouble is at the instigation of the officers of these forts. If we can eliminate them, we can eliminate a possibly severe hazard at our back door, so to speak. At the same time we would certainly weaken the British hold on the entire Northwestern Territory."

He opened a map on the crude desk and they gathered around as he pointed out the forts. The largest and most important was Kaskaskia, located at the mouth of a river with the same name in the Illinois country. It was on the Mississippi River about a hundred thirty miles above the mouth of the Ohio. The second was Cahokia, some miles farther upriver, a few miles below and across the river from the French port of St. Louis. The third was Vincennes, also called Port St. Vincent, on the Wabash River in the Indian country.

"The first two, especially Kaskaskia, are the immediate concern," Clark said. "I want two men to spy in Kaskaskia thoroughly and bring back details on population, both native and white, armament, horses, food, defenses, weaknesses. I want a fast job and a good one. Now then, bearing in mind that if you're caught you will probably be executed, do I have any volunteers?"

He had four of them. Pleased at the vindication of his judgment, he picked up four straws from his desk. Two were short and two were long. He cupped them in his hand so that four equal lengths projected.

"Pick. The long straws go."

They drew and Simon felt a stab of disappointment when he saw that his was one of the short ones. So was Harlan's. Linn and Moore grinned wolfishly, already anticipating the mission.

"My thanks to all of you," Clark said. He shook hands with Sam and Ben. "God go with you. I'll expect your report no later than the first of September."

[*August 1, 1777 — Friday*]

Of all the men Virginia could have sent to aid Kentucky County, hardly a worse choice could have been made than the officer who rode into Harrodsburg this date at the head of a column of one hundred regular cavalry soldiers.

The appearance of the disheveled and weary Benjamin Logan in Williamsburg and his disquieting news of the frontier attacks had a major effect on Patrick Henry and many members of the General Assembly. They heard his story fully and, obligated to the defense of their western-most county, promised to send help immediately.

Logan had rested but one day in the east and turned right around to return to his settlement. His pace returning was not quite as rapid as going, but it was nonetheless a remarkable record, averaging about sixty miles each day. He was stiff and sore for days after his return and delighted to find the little fort still there and its inhabitants as numerous as when he left them.

Colonel John Bowman did not endear himself to the settlers, however. In fact he alienated many within minutes of his arrival. He was a too-young commander, highly impressed with his own importance and no little disgruntled at having been sent to the west instead of to the British-American battle lines where men such as Anthony Wayne and Arthur St. Clair were gaining much recognition.

He crinkled his nose disdainfully at the rude living conditions and was extremely put out when he discovered there were neither sleeping quarters for his men nor stable facilities for the horses. He was muttering something about "primitives" when Major George Rogers Clark stepped up to greet him with outstretched hand, explaining he was commander here.

Bowman looked over Clark's frontier costume with unfeigned distaste, ignored the extended hand and bluntly told him that he was no longer in command; that Clark fell under his command now, as did his militia.

"Perhaps my militia, sir," Clark replied frostily, withdrawing his hand, "but not I. I'm afraid it has become something of a habit for me to be able to respect the officers under whom I serve."

He turned away and returned to his quarters, followed by the faintly amused gaze of the colonel. Bowman slowly surveyed the crowd clustered around him and his voice was clipped and unfriendly as he said, "Well, let's get this over with. Where are these savages we hear are causing so much trouble?"

There was an embarrassed silence. Hardly an Indian had been seen since the first of June and at that moment none of the settlers had much of an idea at all about where they were.

[*August 29, 1777 — Friday*]

Sam Moore and Benjamin Linn did a superlative job of spying, Clark concluded, but the most fortunate break was the fact that they brought with them on their return "Gentleman" Shadrach Bond. Clark asked Bond to wait until he finished his discussions with the two spies, after which they would dine together and talk. Bond nodded and, at Clark's suggestion, retired to the major's quarters to nap in Clark's bed. For hours then, Clark questioned Moore and Linn, sketched maps and learned every detail he could of their reconnaissance.

The job had been amazingly simple. The pair had casually meandered into Kaskaskia, presented themselves to Governor Rocheblave and asked to be hired as hunters, claiming they were just back from a long trip into the western territory beyond the Mississippi.[12] They feigned surprise at news of the Revolution and evinced disgust at their stupid countrymen for thinking they could stand against England, greatest power in the world. Rocheblave warmed to them immediately and they were hired. They did a little hunting for game and a great deal of hunting for information, which was readily accessible to anyone actively seeking it.

Their only fear of discovery had come when they encountered Bond, who recognized them, but "Gentleman" Bond had quickly sensed their mission here and assured them he was with them all the way and would, in fact, return to Clark with them when they left.

With the information they obtained, Clark was sure he could take the garrison there if the plans could remain a secret. The important thing now was to get these plans down in writing and present them personally to Governor Henry in such a persuasive manner that the military command he would ask for could not be denied him. He was certain that Patrick Henry would, for a change, be pleased with the news from the west.

From Bond, Clark got news of a different sort, but no less valuable. Shadrach Bond was something of a enigma. On a frontier where men were rough and coarse and dirty as well as frequently illiterate, he stood out like a beacon. He was tall and handsome and very blond, almost white-haired, and though Clark didn't know for sure, he suspected Bond's age to be about forty.

Bond was, as his nickname indicated, refined and gentlemanly, the result of a birth in good station in England and an early life of the best in education and worldly needs in Boston. His manners were courtly and even under the worst of circumstances he managed somehow to keep himself clean and well dressed. He would have been an attraction at any fancy ball in the East, but Bond had a flair for adventure and bravado. For a short while he was in the army as a lieutenant but, tiring of military routine, he drifted to Kentucky and visited his old companion in arms, George Rogers Clark, for some weeks before continuing downriver. For all his gentle airs and quiet nature, he was a deadly shot and almost as deadly with the thin-bladed knife concealed under his arm — as several men, both red and white, had already learned.

Now Bond told Clark of his stay at Kaskaskia, of the character of her people and their likely reaction to an attack. He dwelt for some time on the beauty of the only true lady he had ever seen in the west; a fine figure of womanhood named Rachel, wife of the trader John Edgar. Her sympathies lay with the American struggle for independence, possibly because of her close friendship in the past with none other than Martha Washington.

The fort itself at Kaskaskia was not much, he said. As with Cahokia above it, the British garrison was small and the population of the town mostly French and Indian. The French, he was inclined to believe, would as gladly live under Virginian rule as British.

Long into the night they talked and when at last they turned in, Clark was positive that not only Kaskaskia and Cahokia but Vincennes, too, could be taken swiftly and without much bloodshed.

[*October 10, 1777 — Friday*]

The heart of Cornstalk was heavy in his breast. Three years ago to the day, at this very point where the Great Kanawha River emptied into the Ohio, he had led his warriors in the single battle of Lord Dunmore's War. Since that time his world seemed to have gone all wrong.

He and his son Elinipsico, along with the subchief Red Hawk, had come to Fort Randolph today under a flag of truce and were received in Captain Arbuckle's quarters with suspicion and a certain fear.

"I come with grave news," Cornstalk said slowly. "At the Camp of Charlotte three years ago I gave my word as principal chief of the Shawnees that our tribe would keep the peace, would remain on its own side of the river and refrain from retaliation if grievances arose between my people and yours. This was a talk-treaty and papers were to be marked later at the Fort of Pitt where the Spay-lay-wi-theepi begins. But this meeting never came about because of the war between your own peoples.

"Now I say to you that the grievances have become too great to be borne. I can no longer restrain my young men from joining the raiding parties encouraged by our friends, the British. I no longer *wish* to restrain them. We have suffered much at the hands of the *Shemanese* who have repeatedly broken the treaty. Now there is a treaty no longer. It is a matter of honor that we have come here to tell you of this."

Captain Arbuckle arose from behind his desk and, without a word to the chief, motioned to the small squad of soldiers standing along the wall. "Take them," he ordered. "Apparently we're at war with the Shawnees again. We'll hold these three hostage."

Perplexed at the ways of white men, Cornstalk and his two companions allowed themselves to be flanked and led to a small room in which there were only three small slits for a window.

The news of the imprisonment of this great chief spread rapidly through the garrison. In a short time angry voices were calling back and forth and suddenly the Indians heard a door open roughly and numerous heavy footfalls approaching. Cornstalk placed his hand on Elinipsico's shoulder.

"My son," he said gently, "the Great Spirit has seen fit that we should die together and has sent you to that end. It is His will, and let us submit."

The three of them stood erect and calmly faced the door. In a moment it was swung open fiercely and a mixed group of soldiers and frontiersmen armed with rifles crowded to the doorway.

"By God," said Captain John Hall, "it *is* Cornstalk!" He flung his weapon to his shoulder and fired. Instantly the other guns belched flame and smoke and even when the three Indians had crumpled to the floor in death, more shots came as men, eager to do their bit in "fighting the enemy," shot the corpses.

So fell Cornstalk, principal chief of all the Shawnee septs, with no less than nine bullets in his body.

[*December 31, 1777 — Wednesday*]

The year of the "three sevens" wound up with the distinct feeling among the border people that they were precariously balanced on a needle point, with grave peril in every direction. The coming of winter had lessened the scattered Indian attacks, but those which did occur now were much more severe. The entire Shawnee nation was aflame with a great desire to avenge the deaths of Cornstalk, Elinipsico and Red Hawk. There was the certainty that, come spring, the attacks would become even worse.

Simon Kenton spent most of the winter at Logan's settlement, St. Asaph, which remained the weakest of the three Kentucky settlements. Once again he engaged in hunting to keep the residents in meat, enduring long lonely nights crouched over his hidden fire, occasionally encountering small Indian parties and somehow always managing to elude them. The Indians knew him now, by sight as well as by reputation, and they feared him greatly, calling him "the man whose gun is always loaded" and sometimes by his name which they pronounced "Bahd-ler." Great honor would come to the warrior who could take the auburn scalp of this huge frontiersman.

The fears of the remaining settlers were eased a little with the return of Colonel John Bowman and his hundred cavalrymen. Knowing himself to be disliked, Bowman kept pretty much to himself. It was rumored that he had been severely reprimanded for returning to Williamsburg with his men after staying in Kentucky County for only a very short while and the fact that he resented being sent back was evident in his treatment of the settlers at Harrodsburg where his men were quartered.

There was no lifting of the animosity between Clark and Bowman, either, and shortly after the latter's return to Harrodsburg, Clark left to see Patrick Henry with his bold plan to take the British forts on the Mississippi.

Clark had difficulty getting to see the governor but, when he did, Henry was much impressed with the plan. He could give Clark no men, he explained, but he would give him the authority to raise and command what men he needed and proceed on the mission. Clark was enthusiastic. He sent agents to the Watauga settlements in Tennessee to get recruits there and also sent word to the Kentucky settlements that he wanted volunteers for a mission. He would gather what men he could at Fort Pitt, proceed down the Ohio and set up a temporary camp at Corn Island at the Falls of Ohio. The Tennessee and Kentucky men could meet him there. With his plan for taking the British forts, he felt he would have no difficulty, even if the army he gathered amounted to only the little maximum figure of three hundred fifty men predicted by Henry.

He was convinced that 1778 would be a year of great victories for his little army.

CHAPTER IV

[*February 7, 1778 — Saturday*]

WITH game surprisingly scarce in the vicinity of the three Kentucky settlements, it was only logical that Simon Kenton would strike out for the Blue Licks, where there had always been great numbers of buffalo, elk and deer. He was not planning to hunt now, only to scout out the game for future hunting. At the moment he was headed for Redstone, a settlement near Pittsburgh, to join Clark. He could hunt on the way back.

Not having stopped off at Boonesboro, he was unprepared to find Boone already at Blue Licks with a large party of men. The older frontiersman showed no trace now of the injury received at the hands of the Indians last year.

Boone greeted him happily and they talked for some time about frontier news. Boone was here with his men to make salt and he shook his head sadly at Simon's concern over the lack of game around the settlements, telling him that the situation was no different here. Already there was a nostalgia growing for "the old days" when game was so plentiful.

Simon told his friend he was on his way to meet Clark for the "secret" mission that had people so curious, but when he asked Boone if he was going to join up the older man shook his head. With Cornstalk and his son and Red Hawk getting themselves murdered at Fort Randolph, there was going to be hell to pay as soon as the weather warmed.

"Clark better bring plenty of men with him," Boone said soberly, " 'cause he won't get 'em here. Ain't nobody here to spare to go along. 'Cept maybe some like you and Jake Drennon and a few others who don't have forts and families to take care of."

"Not Jake," Simon said, just as soberly. "He's dead. Got shot out of his canoe on the Kentucky. Guess it must've been just after your party here left Boonesboro."

Boone was shocked. He hadn't heard about it. His party of thirty men had left Boonesboro for the Blue Licks on the first of January. Since then they had spent every day here tending the fires over which the huge kettles bubbled and steamed as the water evaporated and left behind the pure white crystals. It was a picturesque thing to see the men tending a dozen or more of these fires and the distinct aroma of the boiling blue water was very much like that which emanates from salt marshes along the seashore, except that this was stronger. The work party was so large because it was a big job just to supply enough wood to keep the fires going and every day the area rang with the clean strokes of axes biting into timber. Each of the big iron kettles held ten gallons of water and it took a dozen kettlefuls boiled down to produce a single gallon of salt, which was then distributed equally to the three settlements. This salt was very white, fine-grained and better than any they could import — if such importation had been feasible — mainly because the quality of the nitre in it was especially effective in the preservation of meat. Already enough salt had been boiled down so that Boone had sent three men off with a quantity, each to a different settlement.

Boone did not take part in the actual salt-making himself, preferring to act as meat hunter for the party. He invited Simon now to go along on a hunt with him, but the young frontiersman declined. There was little enough for the Boone party as it was and besides, he had to move along to the mouth of Limestone where his canoe was hidden and join Clark as soon as possible.

Boone was disappointed. He would have enjoyed Simon's company on a hunt. It seemed a long time since they had roamed the countryside together. He watched Simon leave and then set off by himself downstream along the Licking. Less than thirty minutes later he found himself abruptly surrounded by one hundred and two Indians led by a muscular young Shawnee named Blue Jacket.

[*February 8, 1778 — Sunday*]

Blue Jacket was exultant. What a coup for his party! Not only the capture alive of the twenty-seven saltmakers at the Blue Licks without a life lost, but the capture as well of the able frontiersman who had stood off Black Fish's assaults so well last year — the man called Boone.

He was delighted with Boone's wisdom in capitulating not only for himself but for all of his men. Not that the Shawnee would have been loath to kill the saltmakers, but live captives were worth so much more in Detroit than scalps.

It had seemed strange to him to speak in English again while questioning Boone. He tended to slip into Shawnee idioms and had to catch himself time and again. This fact alone convinced Boone that Blue Jacket was an Indian who had learned English rather than a white man who was rusty in it.

At first Boone had told him he was out hunting alone "for the soldiers garrisoned now at all three forts," but just an hour later a warrior had come in and told about discovering the camp of the saltmakers. Boone was given a choice: either he could go in and convince them to give up and their lives would be spared, or the entire party, Boone included, would be slain. It wasn't much of a choice.

Not until the Indians had silently encircled the salt camp did they permit Boone to return to his companions. True to his word, he explained the situation and stressed the fact that there could be no escape if they fought. Inside an hour they were all captives, their equipment loaded on horses and themselves being marched to Chillicothe prior to being taken to Detroit.

At the head of the party Blue Jacket smiled tightly. Black Fish would be pleased indeed.

[*March 28, 1778 — Saturday*]

There was no need for Simon Kenton and Simon Girty to reaffirm their pledge to one another or to state in so many words that what they said to one another this day would remain in confidence and not be used against each other. They both were well aware of the danger in what they had discussed and yet neither had any fear it would be used against them. They were brothers and had been since the day of their blood-pledge to one another and nothing could change that, not even the knowledge that from this night on they must be, technically, deadly enemies.

It had been a wonderful reunion for them when Simon got to Pittsburgh. They had hugged one another and thumped each other's backs and laughed inanely at anything said and then Girty had proposed they go on a day-long hunt, just the two of them, as they often had in the past.

There was little hunting done. Instead they walked through the woods, stopping now and again and then ambling on, talking all the while. It was a sad time for them because it quickly became clear this must be their last time together.

"Butler," Girty said at one point, in his usual direct way, "tonight I'm joining a party that is going to desert and go to Hamilton in Detroit."

Simon was momentarily speechless. That his beloved friend, a Pennsylvanian by birth, could turn his back on his fellow Americans was unbelievable. Nor could Simon's pleas make him change his mind.

Girty's reason was not so much the pledge of allegiance to King George, which he had taken and never renounced, as it was his disgust at the way Americans were treating the Indians in general and himself in particular. His own life here at Fort Pitt had been made miserable because of his admiration for and dealings with the red men. Because of alleged "intercourse with the Indians" for purposes not in keeping with the American policies, he had been castigated and imprisoned. He broke out of jail, returned the following night and said he had broken out only to show them he could and had returned to show them he was not guilty of the charges against him. Once again he was imprisoned and a court-martial held, at which time he was found innocent and freed again. Since then, however, any kind of promotion or advancement had been denied him.

But, Girty explained, there was more to his reason for leaving than that. There were others here who felt as he did, that the Americans had no right to declare themselves independent when everything they had was a direct result of what they had started with in England. Tonight, along with Fort Pitt's chief Indian agent, Alexander McKee, and five other men, he would leave for Detroit.

"But how can you do this when you're an American?" Simon protested.

"Four years ago," Girty replied, "we were all British subjects. We pledged allegiance to the Crown. Nothing I've seen has made me want to change that and I won't. Just as nothing can change the fact that we are brothers and are pledged to one another."

They dropped the subject then and Kenton told him of Clark's plan to go against the Mississippi River forts and of the instructions he had received from Clark to return to Colonel Bowman at Harrodsburg and inform him of Clark's pending start down the river with a small army. Bowman was to supply Clark with as many men as possible, and they would meet at the Falls of Ohio in May. From there they would go down the Ohio to the mouth of the Tennessee River and cut across the Illinois country to take Kaskaskia by surprise.

Girty laughed derisively. "Where's he going to get men enough when everyone's fighting already? Bowman won't be able to help him out, either. Clark'll be lucky if he can find ten per cent of the men he needs."

They parted soon after that with a lingering handshake and warm wishes of luck, one to the other. As far as either man was concerned, this was very likely the last time they would ever see one another.

[*April 30, 1778 — Thursday*]

Of all the white men he had ever known, Black Fish had never found one he liked and respected as much as Daniel Boone. Here was a man who would have made a wonderful Indian; a man who excelled in whatever he did, and never complained; a man who could be trusted to keep his word and a man who understood the Indian. He was happy that Boone had consented to being adopted by him and become known as Sheltowee — Big Turtle.

It had taken the captives ten days of extremely uncomfortable travel in terrible weather to reach Chillicothe and there they remained for a few weeks until, on March 10, they were taken to Detroit. Black Fish sold Boone's companions to Governor Hamilton but refused to sell the noted frontiersman, even turning down the governor's generous offer of 100£ sterling.

Boone's magnetic personality was as attractive to the Shawnees as to his own countrymen and they admired him greatly. After their return to Chillicothe he put them off guard by becoming as friendly as possible with them, joining in their work and talk with a cheerfulness which bespoke an apparent happiness. He hunted with them frequently and gained added respect for his skill in shooting, both at game and at targets. He could easily outshoot any of them with a rifle, but he was careful to win the matches only once in a while, recognizing that they were extremely envious of his shooting ability and afraid their liking for him would turn into suspicion and distrust if he proved too good. In their stern and steady expressions, he thought he could detect great joy whenever they exceeded him in competition and great envy when the reverse was true.

One thought was dominant in Daniel Boone's mind through all of this. Sooner or later, he knew, he would attempt his escape and he must be successful, for there was no second chance. The penalty for white men recaptured — those who had been adopted before escaping — was a hideous death at the stake.

[May 31, 1778 — Saturday]

"This is all of them?" The handsome features of Major George Rogers Clark were grim as they took in the twenty-five men Simon Kenton had just piloted to Clark's Corn Island camp at the Falls of Ohio.

Simon nodded. "Some of Boone's men had been planning to come, but they were captured. Now it seems like everyone here is thinking that if you attack those forts, both the Indians and British will retaliate on the settlements. Most everyone's decided to stay here to help fight 'em off when they come. Can't blame 'em much." He looked at the young commander speculatively. "Colonel Bowman, he wasn't much help. Said he couldn't be expected to send any of his soldiers and he wasn't about to order the militia to come."

Clark's lips tightened. Instead of the minimum figure of three hundred fifty men he had expected to march against Kaskaskia, this addition of twenty-five men from Kentucky and Tennessee gave him a sad total of a hundred seventy-five. Not much of an army with which to attack

England's holdings in the American west. His spies had reported the population of Kaskaskia alone to be over a thousand.

Disappointed though he was, the lack of manpower didn't deter him. He climbed atop a log and raised his arms for silence. When he had everyone's attention, he spoke:

"I want to thank those who are here for coming. We are not many but it is altogether possible that this may help rather than hinder us. If we reach Kaskaskia by surprise, as anticipated, we can take it simply. We start downstream in the morning."

[*August 15, 1778 — Saturday*]

The new subchief of the Kispokotha Shawnees, Blue Jacket, stood straight and proud in the line of twenty young men facing a similar line of young women standing fifteen feet away. He was excited over what was to come, but his face showed little expression.

Quite the opposite was true on the women's side. Their eyes danced with eagerness and they smiled boldly at the men, occasionally shaking themselves so that their long loose hair flared wildly and the contours of their bodies were outlined momentarily against the simple knee-length garments of soft buckskin. Now and then one or another would stamp her bare feet on the hard-packed earth.

Directly across from Blue Jacket stood the tall and beautiful visitor from the Maykujay Shawnees who, for nearly a moon now, had been visiting her Kispokotha mother's parents. Her eyes were large and dark and bold and her features finely chiseled, the high cheekbones giving way to smooth tan cheeks framing a wide smiling mouth set with beautifully even white teeth. This was Wabethe — the Swan — daughter of Wabete — the Elk — who was the younger brother of Moluntha, chief of the Maykujay Shawnees.

Blue Jacket and Wabethe had been unusually aware of each other's presence ever since she came here and the young man felt himself drawn to her as never before to another. That this feeling was reciprocal became obvious on the night of the frolic dance ten days ago. Then it was that the circle of men and women had formed around the fire, facing the circumference of the circle rather than the fire. Each man put his hands behind him and the woman who took her position behind him took his hands, holding a cloth between them so that their skin did not touch. If the contact of hands was made without benefit of cloth, it was an acknowledgment of the woman's admiration and possible love for the warrior.

Blue Jacket had seen Wabethe run lightly to take a place behind him, and then the chant had begun and the shuffling forward movement had started. He had put his hands behind him, and they were quickly grasped by hers and there was no cloth between them.

Tonight, at the far end of his own line, Blue Jacket heard the oldest man begin a queer compelling chant, fluctuating in tone, monotonous and yet gripping. Over and over he chanted the words — "*Ya ne no hoo wa no . . . ya ne no hoo wa no . . . ya ne no hoo wa no.*" Both lines had begun swaying to the weird tune and now they were inching toward one another. When they were less than a foot apart, the participants themselves took up the chant, alternatingly, each having his turn. Some gave the same meaningless words of the original chant, but others chanted words to the rhythm.

The men and women were separated now by only an inch or so and when it came time, it was Wabethe who was first of the couple to sing. She leaned forward so that her breasts pressed against the broad chest of Blue Jacket and her face was very close to his and in time with the chant she sang softly, "*Psai-wi ne-noth-tu*" — Great warrior.

They leaned the other way and it was Blue Jacket's turn. He pressed himself firmly against her and, feeling the warmth of her full breasts against him, he replied, "*U-le-thi e-qui-wa*" — Beautiful woman.

Back and forth they swayed, each holding his hands clasped behind him, letting words and eyes and the touch of bodies relay subtle meanings.

"*K-tch-o-ke-ma,*" she murmured. Great chief.

"*Ke-sath-wa a lag-wa,*" he replied. You are the sun and the stars.

"*Oui-shi e-shi-que-chi.*" Your face is filled with strength.

"*U-le-thi oui-thai-ah.*" Your hair is lovely.

"*Oui-sha t'kar-chi.*" Muscular legs.

"*U-le-thi ski-she-quih.*" Pretty eyes.

None of the dancers was saying the same thing except for the continued undertone of the initial meaningless chant by the old singer. There was a gripping murmur of sensual whisperings as each of the dancers in turn complimented his own partner in his own way. The couples, lost in themselves, heard nothing of what the others said, not even those beside them in line. Only their own chanting was important to them and now the tempo of the dance picked up and they swayed back and forth faster and with greater dips. Small beads of perspiration on Wabethe's upper lip and Blue Jacket's forehead reflected the firelight in tiny sparkles.

"*U-le-tha beh-quoi-tah,*" she said, pushing her own stomach against his. Your belly is handsome.

They leaned the other way and he pushed back against her. "*Ah-quoi-teti beh-quoi-tah.*" And yours is warm.

"*Cat-tu-oui ni-i-yah.*" Your body is perfect.

"*Psai-wi uske-to-ma-ke.*" Your breasts are ripe melons.

"*Ps' qui ah-quoi te-ti.*" Your blood runs hot.

"*Qui-sah ki-te-hi.*" Your good heart is full of understanding.

Abruptly the tempo slowed and the dips were longer lasting, the contact of bodies stronger and more passionate, the heat of the dance an aura which surrounded them all. Blue Jacket leaned over her and his chant was a hoarse whisper, filled with words of a more personal nature, describing the more intimate portions of her body, and she responded in kind. For the first time their hands came into play, fondling and caressing one another, and their passion grew.

This was the crucial time. If Blue Jacket remained silent now or told her "*Oui-sah meni-e-de-luh*" — good dance — they would part at the end of the chant and go their own ways.

But now he leaned hard against her and his words were urgent. "*Ni haw-ku-nah-qa.*" You are my wife.

Wabethe smiled and placed her cheek against his and murmured in his ear. "*Ni wy-she-an-a.*" And you are my husband.

[*August 22, 1778 — Saturday*]

"He did *what?*" Colonel John Bowman's voice was filled with disbelief.

"He took Kaskaskia and Cahokia without firing a shot," Simon Kenton repeated, "and pretty soon he'll be moving against Vincennes."

He went on briefly to explain how Clark's little army had managed to take the two forts by surprise — largely due to the information supplied by Gentleman Shadrach Bond and, as Bond had later intimated to him, to certain inside assistance from the beautiful Rachel Edgar — and then how Clark had sent Bond, Elisha Batty and himself to spy on Vincennes. Dressed as Indians, the three had entered this Wabash River fortification and, notwithstanding several very close calls, had spied closely on it for three days. Then they had parted, Bond and Batty returning to Clark by different routes and himself, as directed by Clark, returning here to seek aid.

Bowman's eyes narrowed and his mouth compressed into a tight line. For the first time, Simon realized the depth of jealousy the young colonel harbored for Clark. It was a bitter pill for the officer to swallow that a backwoods, untrained, self-proclaimed soldier could have taken the British western forts so handily. It was obvious that he now wished he had taken charge of the expedition and led it to such victory.

Simon went on to explain that Clark now needed every available man to be sent to him for the projected attack on Vincennes, adding that he was to lead them to Clark. Bowman's reply was too quick.

"There are none to send. We have our problems here. When word spreads of what that damned fool has done, the whole Shawnee nation will sweep down here to wipe us out. I can't afford to send anyone — not even an express with these despatches from Clark for Governor Henry. Fortunately, Captain Harrod is planning to leave tomorrow for Williamsburg. I'll entrust the messsages to him to deliver. In the meantime, you can join

Major Boone at Boonesboro. There's word that they expect an attack — a major one — at any time."

"Boone! He got back?"

Colonel Bowman nodded. "Escaped just after you left. He was adopted by the Shawnees and living at their Chillicothe Town. Saw a big war party, about four hundred fifty men under Chief Black Fish, getting ready to come against Boonesboro. He needs all the help he can get. I've sent a detachment there, all I can spare from Harrodsburg and Logan's Fort, but it may not be enough."

Simon left, more than ever disliking Bowman's arrogant and superior nature, but greatly relieved to learn that his companion had escaped the Indians and was now a major. He saw Harrod briefly, reclaimed the horse and saddle he had left with him, and set off immediately for Boonesboro, arriving there late in the evening.

Boone rushed up and embraced him in a hug that threatened to crack the young frontiersman's ribs and Simon grinned with pleasure. His friend looked better now than he had at any time since being wounded. Boone rapidly recounted the details of his capture and Simon listened with interest.

"It's a big village, Simon," Boone continued. "Five, mebbe six thousand Injens. Mebbe more. 'Long about first of June I went with a party to the salt springs on the Scioto and we spent ten days there making salt. I'll tell you something, son. The land above the Ohio is rich. Lots of springs and better ground than we got here.

"Anyway, when we got back to Chillicothe I got a surprise. They was four hunnerd fifty warriors all painted an' ready to march against Boonesboro. I'd been thinking about getting away and knew then I couldn't put it off no longer. Took out early the next morining when they sent me out to gather up some horses. Took a horse and made off. Hunnerd an' sixty miles back to here. Made it in four days, with just one meal along the way when I kilt a 'coon and roasted it.

"Well, when I got back here, things was in bad shape. I got ever'one busy repairing the walls and gates and posterns and then we formed double bastions. This took ten days. Then we waited. Frank Goode come in about then. He was being held in Chillicothe when I left. Escaped a few days later hisself. Said my going got 'em all riled up and made 'em change their plans. They sent out a call for more warriors from the Maykujays and Peckuwes to the north and Thawegilas and Kispokothas to the east. He figgered it'd be about three weeks 'fore they started out from Chillicothe against us. We been waiting ever since and I'm getting tired of it. Think I'm gonna mount a party and scout a bit north of the river toward Paint Crik. They's a little Shawnee town near where it dumps into the Scioto.

Might be we could surprise 'em and get back some of the horses they been stealing. You game to go along?"

Simon Kenton was game and plans were made to move on the expedition with seventeen other men from the fort.

[September 3, 1778 — Thursday]

Simon Kenton very much liked the quiet confidence of Alexander Montgomery. A relatively new arrival who had been living at Boonesboro with his wife and two children, he was a pleasant, capable man who could, when occasion demanded it, be daring without being foolhardy. He was thirty-four years old and a great tangle of unruly sand-colored hair covered his head and crept out from beneath his beaverskin cap. His smiles were frequent and his frowns rare and he didn't often speak unless he had something of importance to say.

It was not unexpected, therefore, when Boone asked Simon to pick another man and scout ahead after they crossed the Ohio River, that he chose Montgomery. It was a good feeling to have a solid dependable man riding beside him.

They were two days into the Ohio country and within four miles of the little Shawnee village near the mouth of Paint Creek when Simon abruptly raised a hand and they stopped. A short distance ahead was the sound of laughter and the frontiersman leaped lightly to the ground.

"Take my horse with you," he said, handing Montgomery the reins, "and go on back. Tell Boone to get up here in a hurry."

With a single bob of his head, Montgomery turned and disappeared into the woods. Simon checked his rifle and crept toward the sound until he came to a narrow path. Here he crouched behind a tree and waited expectantly for half an hour, but, when no one came into sight, finally started forward cautiously. The path took an abrupt turn and with shocking suddenness he found himself staring up at two Shawnees, one quite old and the other a lad of no more than fifteen, both riding the same horse less than fifty feet away.

The old man saw him at the same time and let out a whoop, digging his heels into the horse's side so that it sprang toward Kenton. At the same time he was clawing for the tomahawk at his waist. Simon flung the rifle to his shoulder and fired. The ball struck the old man in the left breast, smashed through his heart and out his back and then plunged high into the chest of the boy behind him, passing through him, too. Both Indians fell.

Simon ran up to take the horse but, frightened, it spun about and thundered back toward the village. He reloaded swiftly and turned back to the young Shawnee who lay on his stomach, trying to get to his feet. He was groaning deeply and when Simon rolled him over onto his back and saw the amount of blood that had already escaped, he knew the wound had to be mortal.

"How many warriors in the village, boy?" he asked, not ungently.

The youth blinked at him and frothy red bubbles came to the corners of his lips. "Old men, young boys here," he gasped. "Enough to kill you. Others join Black Fish to kill all *Shemanese*." Strangely, there was a triumphant ring in his voice, but now he closed his eyes and his breathing grew more labored.

A shriek of rage split the air as a half dozen or more Indians galloped into sight. Simon shot too hurriedly and though one of the Indians, a skinny old man, toppled from his mount, the frontiersman was certain he hadn't killed him. He turned and sprinted away, reloading as he dodged from tree to tree and each time firing behind him as quickly as possible.

Doubtless he would have been caught, but now there came a chorus of cries from the other direction and Boone, with Montgomery beside him and sixteen horsemen behind them, thundered into sight. The air was rent with the crashing of rifles and Simon continued his run until he reached the party, which now stopped and took cover behind trees.

The exchange of shots was greatly one-sided. No more than four or five shots came from the Indians and then there was silence. Simon crept forward and found them gone and waved the others in. The old man he had shot was still there, dead, but the wounded boy and the thin man were missing.

Simon watched with mild distaste as two of Boone's men rushed up to the old man and scalped him. It was not an unusual practice among the frontiersmen, but one in which he had never felt inclined to engage. He was glad the boy had been taken away, knowing he too would have been scalped, alive or not.

Boone hurriedly called a meeting and Simon told him what the boy had said. Obviously worried, the older frontiersman said, "We have to get back to Boonesboro fast. Let's go."

"I'll catch up," Simon said. "We came after horses. I aim to get some. Want to come along, Alex?"

Montgomery looked at Boone and the latter shrugged. "You might as well," he said, "but don't take too long about it. We're going to need every man."

He wheeled his mount around and led the party away. Simon and Montgomery walked their horses down a little spring branch for half a mile and then moved off straight toward the village. It was nearly dark when they reached the edge of a small cornfield adjacent to the little town. They tied the horses in the woods and crept froward for a better look. There was no smoke rising from the *wegiwas*, but here and there could be seen the muzzle of a flintlock projecting from doorway or niche. Between the cornfield and Paint Creek were four horses hobbled with rawhide about their front knees, and on the other side of the village were eight others.

Not until full darkness came did the two frontiersmen inch forward along the rows of corn, pushing the occasional pumpkins out of their way. At the edge of the cornfield they found themselves no more than a dozen feet from the four horses. The animals stood watching them curiously, their ears erect.

Simon crooned gently and gradually the nervousness left them and one even moved toward him. Simon touched Montgomery's arm and slowly they arose and stepped out to the horses. They were surprised when the animals didn't bolt, but then Simon saw why. The horse that had moved toward him was one he knew well — the favorite horse of Benjamin Logan which had, Montgomery whispered, been stolen over a month ago. The other three were also apparently horses from Logan's Fort and obviously far from alarmed at seeing white men.

Muttering softly to them, Simon grasped the rawhide bridles of two and Montgomery took the other pair. Flicks of their knives sliced the hobbles away and then slowly, quietly, they moved parallel to the last row of corn to the woods. Within ten minutes they had rigged lead-lines, remounted their own horses and were easing through the woods toward home.

They were very pleased with themselves.

[September 5, 1778 — Saturday]

It was with reluctance that Black Fish accepted the plea of the two white men to halt his party of four hundred warriors at Blue Licks for a day's rest before beginning the onslaught against Boonesboro.

The arguments of Isadore Chene, the British captain, and Captain DuQuesne, the Frenchman in charge of eleven of his own soldiers, were strong. It had been a long journey and a hard one from Detroit to Chillicothe and another difficult march to the Ohio and across it to reach this spot. The white men were exhausted and could not fight at their best unless rested before the battle. It would not, they added, do any harm either for the Shawnee warriors to rest. There was some feeling among the whites that it was not a good thing to start a battle on the Sabbath and it was this argument which Black Fish could best understand.

"I would not," he said, "have you offend your God and so I will tell my warriors they must rest here until the morrow has passed. On the day after, we will begin our march against the fort of Sheltowee — the man you call Boone."

Shortly after nightfall a party of sixteen men led by Daniel Boone made a wide silent circle around the huge encampment of the Indians and, as soon as they were out of hearing, roused their horses into all speed to reach the fort and prepare for the long-awaited attack.

About six hours later Simon Kenton and Alexander Montgomery, leading the four horses they had taken from the Paint Creek village, passed the encampment about six miles to the east, unaware of its existence. Only the fact that they had crossed the Ohio to the mouth of Cabin Creek rather than to the mouth of Limestone prevented their heading directly to the Blue Licks and head on into the war party.

[*September 6, 1778 — Sunday*]

Colonel John Bowman was highly pleased with himself. If matters went as planned he would make Clark's feat of taking the British forts look like child's play. In years to come it would be known that he, Colonel John Bowman, was the man who had wiped out the Shawnee race and opened the Northwest Territory to settlement.

Ever since that big young frontiersman, Simon Butler, had come with the numbing news of Clark's victories, Bowman had been thinking. He had deluded himself in believing he could make a military name for himself only by joining in the battles with the British to the east. Look at what Clark had done with his ragtag crew of less than two hundred. If Clark could do that, why couldn't he, a far more experienced and able officer, pull off a coup that would greatly outshadow anything Clark had done?

Gradually the plan formed in his mind. Boone's escape from captivity had provided the intelligence of the whereabouts of Chillicothe, the principal Shawnee village; a fact only roughly known until now. If he could get two or three good men to scout out the village and discover its weaknesses, he could march against it and destroy it in one fell swoop.

And then, as luck would have it, he was visiting Benjamin Logan this morning when Simon Butler and his friend Montgomery came in with four recovered horses belonging to Logan's Fort. As soon as they had eaten, Bowman summoned them to report. His face darkened in anger as they described the expedition mounted by Boone and at one point he jumped to his feet and swore he would court-martial Boone for deserting his fort in the face of the enemy.

With a wave of his hand he brushed off the intelligence Simon had gotten from the dying Indian boy about the war party moving against Boonesboro. He no longer believed that any such attack was to take place and that even if they were coming, they would prefer to attack the far richer Harrodsburg.

As for Simon and Alexander Montgomery, he had other plans. He informed them that they were now under his exclusive command and that they were to spy out the center of the Shawnee nation, Chillicothe. They were to leave at once, find out all they could about the village and return as swiftly as possible. The prospect of seeing the fabled Chillicothe stirred their imaginations and they became eager to go. But there was one bothersome hitch: Bowman had another man he wanted to go with them; a young admirer of his who had often expressed a desire to become a scout and spy. He was only twenty and his name, coincidentally, was George Clarke.

It was, Bowman thought, a pleasantly ironical similarity.

[*September 9, 1778 — Wednesday*]

Daniel Boone was worried. Early in the morning yesterday the four hundred forty-four Shawnees, after crossing the Kentucky River at a ford a mile and a half above, had surrounded the fort and Captains DuQuesne and Chene had come here under a flag of truce to order him to surrender it or be wiped out. He had no intention of surrendering, of course, but he let on that he was seriously considering it and wished to discuss the matter with his people. He asked that they be given until this evening to make up their minds and the request was granted.

Throughout the remainder of that day, last night and today, every preparation for the defense of the fort which could be made was done. What cattle or horses could be collected were brought in and all firearms were checked and rechecked, loaded and primed.

Now the two officers were once again striding forward to meet him just outside the gate. They were somewhat disconcerted when he told them bluntly that he considered the idea of surrendering as being ridiculous and that they would defend the fort while a man was living. The officers stepped a little apart and put their heads together for some muffled discussion, then returned to Boone.

"We do not wish you any harm here," Captain Chene said, "and we are agreeable to a treaty of nonaggression between us if you are."

Boone nearly laughed in their faces but managed to keep his expression serious and replied that they would be happy to enter into such an agreement. Captain DuQuesne told Boone to bring out his nine ranking men to sign the treaty papers and they would have the Indian forces withdraw.

Boone brought out his men — the poorest he could find — and warned those left behind to watch for the ambush he felt sure would come. The papers were signed sixty yards from the gate, not far from the place where Boone had had his leg broken in the earlier Shawnee attack. Then the two captains, DuQuesne and Chene, and the Shawnee chiefs, Black Fish, Black Hoof, Moluntha and Black Beard, made their marks. Black Beard then announced that it was custom for two Indians to shake hands with every white man signing the treaty. As Boone expected, there came an immediate grappling as an attempt was made to take prisoner the ten from the fort.

Boone's men were prepared, however, and jerked free to race back toward the fort. A few shots were fired by the Indians but only one man was slightly wounded before the heavy gate swung shut behind them.

And now began the siege of Boonesboro.

[*September 13, 1778 — Sunday*]

For an expedition that had begun so well, this one had taken a severe turn for the worse and Simon Kenton was torn between leaving the horses behind or making further attempt to get away with them.

They had moved swiftly, the three of them, after leaving Logan's Fort. Each carried provisions enough for two weeks, but the weight of the salt and halters they carried for use in capturing horses far outweighed their essentials. It was Simon's plan to replenish the dwindled horse supply at the settlement by capturing and bringing back the entire herd of Shawnee horses.

Montgomery was delighted with the bold plan, for it would hit the Indians where it hurt. But George Clarke was not at all happy. From the very beginning he was something of a thorn in the side of the two frontiersmen. A very short and pudgy man, he complained all the way, frightened at every moment that they would be ambushed, certain that at every river or creek they had to cross his horse would stumble and he would drown because he could not swim.

Simon and Alex did not make it any easier for him. They rode hard and frequently talked with mock gravity of how they would be tortured if taken and how, if they were surprised, Clarke would undoubtedly be the first caught since he was too fat to ride well enough to escape or to stand and make a fight.

They followed the directions Boone had given Simon for reaching Chillicothe, crossing the Ohio below Limestone and striking northeastward through the river hills until they reached the Little Miami River.[1] Then they followed the river upstream. By the time they came within shouting distance of their goal, George Clarke was in a state of perpetual fear one step removed from panic, willing to do whatever he was directed if only it meant getting back safely.

They parked him far out in the woods several miles from Chillicothe to watch their horses and set off alone to spy. The village was huge, covering twenty or thirty acres of ground, but though they saw many women and children and older men, there were relatively few warriors in their prime; probably not more than threescore.

For two days and a night they watched the village carefully. It was during that night, while making a cautious circle around the village, that they discovered something which set their blood atingle. Apart from the village, not more than forty yards from the junction of a substantial tributary meeting the Little Miami, was a fenced compound in which stood half a hundred horses.[2]

They considered briefly trying to herd the horses together and take them all, but the plan seemed too risky. It would be necessary to get away without alarming the Shawnees, and so they decided to take only as many as they could lead easily and still make good time. This meant three apiece for Simon and Alex and one for Clarke, who even then might have difficulty.

The second night they quietly entered the compound and, using their salt liberally, selected seven of the best horses there and bridled them.

They were almost ready to move silently away when one of the horses became frightened. A contagious whinny of fear erupted from the animal and in seconds the entire compound was in an uproar. Dogs began barking furiously at the village and Simon realized at once there was only one thing to do. Working with frenzied haste, the big young frontiersman tore the fence down, raced to the far side of the corral, screeched loudly and fired his gun. Instantly the horses bolted, thrashing through the gap in the fence, some falling and regaining their feet and all of them quickly thundering off into the darkness.

Simon vaulted into his saddle, took his string of horses from Montgomery and they set off at a fast pace, making no attempt now to hide their trail, only putting distance between themselves and the Shawnees. The Indians would not be able to catch the horses until daylight and even then it would be a good while before they could get on the trail. But not one of the three men had any doubt that they'd be followed as soon as possible.

Near the spot where they had first struck the Little Miami, a smaller creek entered from the south.[3] Now, to throw off pursuit, they rode their horses up the stream a quarter mile to where a still smaller stream entered from the south as the larger creek turned eastward. They followed the smaller watercourse for well over a mile before leaving it and then put their heels to the horses and made time. They traveled just a shade east of due south and each time a small stream was passed they rode their horses in the water for hundreds of yards before resuming their heading.

At a branch of the Little Miami they swam the horses downstream a half mile before emerging on the south bank and striking off southeast again.[4] And finally, at dawn on September 12, they reached the Ohio.

The weather was bad with a very high wind and the river was high from storms upstream, full of floating driftwood and speckled with whitecaps. Time and again the trio tried to make the horses swim across, but they would no more than get them into the water when the animals would turn and scramble frantically back for shore, their eyes bulging in panic.

Knowing that the wind often settles at sunset, Simon ordered the horses hobbled and told Clarke to stay with them while he and Montgomery backtracked a way to see if they were being followed and, if so, to ambush any party that came along. But this time the wind did not die and all night they huddled shivering, waiting for the expected attack.

When the Indians had not shown up by morning, they began to have hope that their maneuvers in the creeks had thrown off their pursuers. A stiff breeze still blew but the water was nowhere near as rough as it had been the day before.

Immediately upon returning to the river through the gap in the hills a little below Red Oak Creek and just above the mouth of Eagle Creek, Simon took his string of three horses and attempted to lead them across on his own.[5] But the animals, still frightened by the water of the day before, refused to cooperate. It was a sticky situation and this was the position they found themselves in now: should they abandon the captured horses and get away, or should they continue to try to save them? Clarke was all for leaving them and getting back across the Ohio themselves, but both Simon and Alex, their goal so near, were reluctant to do this. After much discussion they finally agreed to Simon's plan to move downstream along the shore until they reached the Falls of the Ohio. With Corn Island there to break the long swim, perhaps the horses could be persuaded to cross. At once they set out to round up the remaining four horses liberated from the Indians, plus the two saddled mounts belonging to Montgomery and Clarke.

The horses had scattered farther than anticipated and now Simon grew apprehensive. He had the "feel" that the Shawnees were close by and so, while Montgomery and Clarke went off in different directions to continue the roundup, he returned to the first small ridge behind them to look over the backtrail and make certain they were still safe.

They were not.

As he cautiously poked his head up over the ridge he saw five mounted Indians coming up the other side. They had not yet seen him, their eyes directed to the trail they were following, and Simon raised his rifle, took aim on the lead man and squeezed the trigger. With an ugly, sinking feeling he saw the rifle flash in the pan without firing and a great cloud of blue-white smoke drifted above him. The Shawnees saw him then and screamed triumphantly and the lead warrior spurred his horse to the crest after him.

With such pursuit as this there was no time to reload and Simon turned and ran as he had never run before, heading for a huge thicket of fallen timber where a horse could not follow. The Shawnee, an agile warrior named Bo-nah, galloped to the spot where Simon entered and leaped from his horse to follow him as two of his companions circled the thicket on their mounts.

Simon crashed through the awful clutter of branches and logs in a dead run, heading downhill; just as he broke free the two mounted Indians galloped into sight on either side. He stopped and made to turn back into the thicket, hoping to elude pursuit in there, but the delay was too long. As he began to turn, Bo-nah grabbed his shoulders fiercely and kneed him so savagely in the small of the back that he fell to the ground.

Bo-nah stood panting above him, tomahawk in hand and ready to strike should he move. The two horsemen rode up, followed in a few moments by the other two. There was nothing to do now but submit. He allowed himself to be pulled to his feet; then his ankles were tied tightly and his wrists were bound behind him. They lashed him to a tree and, as they were doing so, Simon saw Alexander Montgomery appear on the slope a hundred yards away and raise his gun to shoot.

Simon quickly looked in another direction and then shouted loudly, "For God's sake, Alex, don't shoot! Run! Get away!"

But Montgomery shot and the bullet buried itself in a limb close to Bo-nah's head. The frontiersman turned then and ran and Bo-nah ordered his companions after him. As they dashed away, Bo-nah positioned himself in front of Simon with his gun barrel less than a foot from his breast, cocked and ready to fire at the least sign of further resistance. Even as he watched the panting Shawnee, Simon was sure that the red man's finger was closing on the trigger and every instant would be his last.

He forced himself to relax and stared back at the Shawnee who regarded him with such living hatred. The gun barrel never wavered until at last there came the distant report of a gun. Bo-nah grunted in a satisfied manner, stepped back a little way and lowered his weapon.

Simon prayed that the shot he heard had come from Alex Montgomery's gun. Certainly he had had time to reload. If he had managed to kill one, he might yet be able to get away. His speculations ended a few minutes later, however, with the return of the four Shawnees, one of them carrying the bloody, sandy-haired scalp of Montgomery.

Loosening Simon, they took off his clothing and then retied him in a sitting position against the tree. Then, in turn, they wrapped the long hair of Montgomery's scalp in their fingers and slapped the still-warm, bloody-fleshed portion of it across his face and repeated in English at every slap, "You steal Shawnee horse!"

Then they made a willow hoop and laced the scalp to it to stretch and dry and propped it up before him so that he could see it. Now each of them took turns urinating upon him until he was saturated and threw dirt at his face and body so that it would stick wherever he was wet. One of them took a slender switch and whipped him repeatedly across the face until great welts appeared and broke and his own blood mingled with that from Montgomery's scalp.

A little later another group of five Indians rode up to join them and Simon was relieved to see that they did not have George Clarke's scalp; apparently they had no suspicion of the little fat man's existence. Actually, Clarke was already far down the river and nearing the opposite shore. He had been close to the river's shore and at the first sound of trouble had rushed to the water's edge, tossed in a small log and clung to it. Kicking until he felt his heart would burst, he finally made it to the Kentucky shore — his escape the crowning irony of the day.

Though his original captors had not recognized Kenton, one of the new-comers now did. He stared into Simon's swollen, bloodied face and suddenly stepped back with a start.

"Bahd-ler! Bahd-ler!"

The whole party of them now ringed the captive and inspected him with new respect and a certain fear. This was the man whose rifle was always loaded, the man whose shots never missed, the man a hundred or more Shawnees had sworn to capture or kill, only to be killed or routed themselves. Only the recapture of Boone himself would have been a coup equal to this!

The recognition saved Simon's life; for the time being, at least. A captive of his stature would not just be killed here and his scalp taken. No! This was an enemy to take before the whole Shawnee nation before he was put to death. The glory of capturing him would ride with them all their lives, especially with Bo-nah.

Now that lanky, athletic Indian swelled visibly with pride and basked in the admiration of his companions. For this act alone he would be famous for the rest of his life. He vowed he would stay by the side of this dreaded *Shemanese* until the last tormented breath wheezed from his dead lungs.

The Indians, themselves weary from the long trail, now made camp. Simon was again released from the tree and made to lie spreadeagled on his back. A thong of rawhide attached each wrist and ankle securely to a stake pounded deep into the ground. In addition, a pole was laid across his neck and tied to each wrist. A rawhide halter was slipped around his neck and tied to a tree behind him in such a way that he could not even turn his head. And then, as the flies and ants came, attracted by the smell of blood and the meat cooking over the little fire, he began for the first time to wish that Bo-nah had killed him.

[*September 14, 1778 — Monday*]

It was a night of absolute horror for Simon Kenton and he got neither sleep nor rest. The manner in which he was bound made movement practically impossible and the hours from nightfall until dawn were one torment after another. Every now and again one of the warriors would come to stand over him and look at him, still finding it hard to believe that they had captured alive their dreaded enemy. Rarely did the individual return to his companions without first spitting in Simon's face or kicking him in the ribs or grinding a heel into his unprotected groin.

The insects were maddening. First the flies, which crawled and bit and crawled some more and then the ants, which were nearly as bad. When darkness deepened and they disappeared, mosquitoes took their place and whined continually over him for hours, glutting themselves on his blood before droning sluggishly off, their bodies a deep swollen red. And finally, when it became too cool for them, the cool night air clamped down upon him with a hand of sheer misery and his teeth chattered and his body trembled until he felt he must be shaken apart.

At last blessed dawn came and the fire was rebuilt and more meat cooked. A greasy, almost raw chunk heavy with fat was thrust into his mouth by Bo-nah and he chewed it greedily and swallowed. Then he was untied and ordered to stand up; but his limbs would not cooperate and he rubbed and kneaded the stiffened and cramped muscles under the readied guns of the Shawnees. When at last he was able to stand again, Bo-nah handed him a water-filled gourd which he drained in one great draught.

Immediately his wrists were bound behind him again and he was propped against a tree and tied to it while the Indians prepared to break camp. They gathered up the horses, and among them was a wild, unbroken three-year-old black which had been in the string Simon was leading. Even the Indians had trouble with it, and not until they had tied a blanket around its eyes did it become tractable and allow itself to be led. Now Bo-nah came over to Kenton and asked him if he spoke the Shawnee tongue. When Simon nodded, Bo-nah smacked him smartly across the face and said, "You steal Shawnee horses, yes? Now we let you ride Shawnee horse."

It took the combined effort of six of them — two to hold the wild black horse and four to maneuver the frontiersman — but finally they got him astraddle the horse, facing backwards. They bound his ankles beneath the belly of the black and then placed a loop over Simon's head and drew it snug around his neck. The other end of this line was tied around the horse's neck.

The Shawnees mounted their own horses and led the black into a small clear area and here Bo-nah jerked away the blanket blinding the animal and whipped it smartly on the rump. Instantly the horse screamed in panic and began to buck and spin, doing all it could to dislodge its rider. It smashed against trees, scraping the hide off Simon's legs, and galloped under low branches which slammed into his back or head with numbing blows. It tore through areas thick with brush and thorns and his body was raked and grooved in a hundred places while the Shawnees shouted and laughed.

But somehow the frontiersman stayed on. If he were thrown off he would surely be strangled or his neck broken, and so he locked his legs as tightly as he could around the animal and managed to catch some of the mane hair in his bound hands behind him. He leaned forward and bowed his head as low as the throat halter would allow and closed his eyes tightly so that he would not be blinded. There he clung for what seemed an eternity, while the world turned into a swirling, slashing, pounding hell.

Finally, utterly exhausted, the wild black stood spraddle-legged, its head low and its sides heaving. Even when the Indians rode up to it there was no will left to shy away. Dully, Simon felt his feet released. Arms gripped and lifted him and his leather leggins were put back on, covering the buttocks worn raw. Then he was replaced on the animal's back so he faced forward and his ankles tied again, though loosely this time. Through a fog of hurt he felt them begin to lead his horse, but for a very long time he rode in misery so severe that nothing about him existed except a faintly flickering hope that if he could hold out long enough, somehow, in some way, he would escape.

[*September 17, 1778 — Thursday*]

Bo-nah and his party of nine Shawnees took their time returning to Chillicothe with the prisoner. Their treatment of him improved but little on the journey. Only once in a great while was a morsel of food crammed into his mouth and a drink given him. Each night he was staked out in spreadeagle fashion again as he had been the first night and there were more cuffings and kickings, but not once did he ask quarter from them. Kill him they might, but he would never beg mercy from them.

A few improvements in his lot had been made. On the second night Bo-nah had concocted a pasty mixture of water and mud with mashed herbs and roots and this he spread over the multitude of wounds on Kenton's body after the frontiersman had been permitted to bathe in a meandering little creek. Amazingly, much of the sting and hurt of the slashes and scrapes was immediately relieved.

It took them three days to reach a point about a half mile from Chillicothe and here they had camped last night while several of the warriors had ridden on ahead to alert the village to their successful return. He was staked out again on his back and all through the evening until late at night there came a steady procession of Shawnees to see the famed enemy helpless. Women and little children stared at him from a few feet away and some of them whipped him across face and body with slender stinging switches.

Finally, close to midnight, Simon felt his hair gripped savagely and his head shaken hard. His eyes snapped open and in the light of the fire he saw that a huge Negro dressed in Shawnee garb was standing above him. At the fire several of the guards watched amusedly.

The Negro slapped his face resoundingly and said, "*Shemanese mat-che-le ne tha-tha.*" Long Knife, you are my enemy. But then, in a whisper which barely reached Kenton's ears, he spoke in English. "You're in bad trouble, sir. They're going to burn you."

As Simon regarded the black, wide-nostriled face hovering above him, the Negro yanked his hair again and shook his head, immediately apologizing. "I have to do that so they won't suspect. My name is Caesar. My master was coming down the Ohio a couple years ago when they killed him and the missus and took me prisoner. I been adopted here."

"You certain they're going to kill me?" Kenton's whisper was a hoarse rasp.

Caesar slapped him again, gently this time. "No doubt about it. They all know you'll be condemned soon's Black Fish gets back."

"From where?"

"You don't know? He gone to take Boonesboro. When he come back, they hold trial for you in *msi-kah-mi-qui* — that's the council house. That's when you get condemned. You important man."

"Can you help me get away?"

Caesar jerked back and rolled his eyes, his expression one of fear and dismay. He caught himself and took Simon's hair again and shook his head lightly. "No!" he whispered. "No! They kill me too, for sure. But in the mornin' you got to run gauntlet. You in bad shape for it. If you can get away tonight, go straight south till you hit creek. That's where I hunt most of the time now. Ain't far." He grinned and added proudly, "I calls it Caesar Creek. You follow it downstream till it join Little Miami. Shawnee trail on west bank of river. You stay on east side and it go to Ohio River. Then you safe."

One of the warriors near the fire got to his feet and walked toward them and Caesar slapped Simon's face viciously. "Horse thief!" he said in Shawnee. "We teach you tomorrow to steal Indian horses!"

The Indian touched Caesar's shoulder and shook his head, saying gutturally, "*Mat-tah tschi yah-ma*" — Don't kill him — Caesar nodded and, as the Indian walked back to the fire, he leaned a final time over Simon.

"If you don't get away and got to run the gauntlet, get to *msi-kah-mi-qui* fast. Once you there, Shawnee law say you no more get whipped."

With that he slipped off into the darkness and Simon was alone, knowing with a sinking finality he could not hope to release himself and get away tonight.

In the morning, Simon was fed a bowl of a tasty gruel called *takuwah-nepi* — bread water. It was made of pulverized corn from which the chaff had been removed and then the corn boiled until it became a thick white fluid. Then more water was added and a small quantity of seeping fluid — made by letting water seep through clean wood ashes — was stirred in. To this was added chunks of venison or buffalo meat and the whole concoction was then stewed for some time. Simon couldn't remember having eaten anything that tasted so good.

When he finished they untied his ankles and Bo-nah led him toward the town. At the foot of the hill southeast of the village, a double line of men and women — from ancient ages all the way down to the smallest children who could wield a stick — stretched a full quarter mile to end at the massive council house. There were easily four hundred people in the line, each with stick, switch or club four to six feet in length.

They stripped his clothes from him again and Bo-nah pointed at the council house with his hickory stick. "You run to the *msi-kah-mi-qui*. If you stop or fall, you start over."

He stepped behind the frontiersman and, at the beat of the starting drum from the council house, laid his stick across Simon's back with such force that the frontiersman thought his shoulder blades were broken. Simon ran, ignoring the pain in his body from the previous injuries, taking great bounding strides that often got him past the waiting Indians before they could react enough to land their blows. Even then he was hit often, though seldom with very great force because of his forward speed. Near the end of the line and with safety close, he was suddenly confronted by a warrior who stepped into his path, his club at ready. Simon increased rather than slackened his speed and with his clenched fist punched the man between the eyes such a tremendous blow that he broke his nose and sent him sprawling senseless into his companions in the line.

But the pause this occasioned was disastrous. A heavy stick thudded against his temple and as he grasped his head in pain, more blows rained down upon him until he fell dazed. Dimly he was aware of other blows falling on him but then they stopped and he felt himself lifted and half propelled, half dragged back to the starting point amidst the howls of delight from the Indians in the lines.

They let him rest for perhaps ten minutes when once more they reached the head of the line. When the drum sounded again, Bo-nah struck him with his stick while he still sat on the ground and then struck him again as he scrambled to his feet. Once more he was on his way, but the blows had told on him and his speed had diminished. More and more frequently he was being struck. Abruptly he turned and leaped high, his feet catching a squaw full in the stomach and bowling her over and then, outside the lines, he raced for the council house.

From the line ahead of him a squaw rushed toward him and as she raised a hefty club over her head he knew he should dodge around her, but somehow his body wouldn't answer quickly enough and the club hit his neck and knocked him sprawling. Instantly he became the center of a growing circle of people striking him with clubs and switches, fists and feet.

Even after he was unconscious they beat him for a long time.

[September 24, 1778 — Thursday]

Sutawnee was as beautiful an Indian maiden as Simon Kenton had ever seen. She was tall, inches taller than the average Shawnee woman, and neither slender nor plump but well proportioned in every respect. Her hair was long, falling to her waist and of a rich dark chestnut color rather than black. She smiled frequently and her small even teeth shone with startling whiteness against the deep tan of her face. She appeared to be about eighteen or nineteen years old.

During the first few days of her ministrations to him, Simon was too full of pain to appreciate the incredibly gentle touch of her hands over his body as they washed his wounds and rubbed into them a greasy and remarkably soothing poultice. From his head to his feet she treated each wound individually, no sooner having washed and medicated him all over than she began again at his head, washed the poultice free, kneaded the flesh gently and rubbed in another mass of the curative.

By the fourth day after his double-run of the gauntlet, he was well on the mend and now, though his muscles were still very sore and his wounds pulled with sharp pain when he moved, he was startled at the overpowering desire for this Shawnee woman that swept through him. During those brief intervals when she was gone out of the *wegiwa* on some errand he would feel an awful hopelessness and aloneness but, when she returned, it was as if she brought into the *wegiwa* with her a glow and warmth which made his cares and fears fade.

This afternoon she was gone for more than two hours, her longest absence, and he was afraid she would not return. He considered escape but knew there was no possibility of it. His weapons were gone and, though he was free of bonds, Sutawnee had told him how Bo-nah had taken up vigil outside the door to the *wegiwa* and that they were almost in the center of Chillicothe. The gauntlet beatings had taken much out of him and he could not trust himself to outrun pursuit even if he could get a good headstart. He wished again Sutawnee would return and, as if he had called to her aloud, the heavy buffalo hide at the door was pushed aside and she entered.

She carried two large bowls of the same delicious food she had been bringing him twice daily — a strange mixture of corn, turnips and squash in a kind of paste sprinkled with nuts in one bowl and strips of roasted meat in another; meat which, she told him in an offhand way, was **with-si** — dog meat — but which he chewed and found himself enjoying.

He ate the meal rapidly, picking up the meat strips with his fingers and scooping out the vegetable dish with a short flat stick which served as a spoon. Then he set the bowls aside and, wincing a little, raised himself so that his shoulders rested lightly against the side of the *wegiwa*. Sutawnee took the bowls to the other side of the little room and brought back a larger one filled with the greasy medication. She placed it beside him on the floor and pulled her long doeskin blouse off, but before she could thrust her hands into the poultice, he reached out suddenly and pulled her to him and kissed her fiercely. She pulled away quickly but appeared neither angry nor pleased. She nodded seriously.

"*Ki-luh-weh agh-queloge mat-tah met-chi. Oui-sah.*" You are sick no more. It is good.

He held out his arms and said, "*Pe-e-wah*" — come — but she shook her head.

"I am not your woman and you are not my man. You are strong and handsome and big and my body would like yours, but it must not be."

She shook her head again and her voice was even more serious now. "Tomorrow you will be *cut-ta-ho-tha*, the condemned man."

He started to reach for her, but then paused as what she had said registered. "*Cut-ta-ho-tha?* Why tomorrow?"

"Because Black Fish and our warriors have returned today and tomorrow they will hold council and condemn you. There is no way else."

The heat left him almost as suddenly as it had come and he took her hand and squeezed it urgently. "Did they take Boonesboro, Sutawnee?"

She shook her head. Boonesboro was a strong fort. For thirteen suns they had tried to break in, but they had failed and they were angry. Thirty-seven of their men were killed and many wounded and only one white man was known for certain to have been killed. The news of Kenton's capture had been greeted by them with fierce pleasure and early tomorrow morning they would hold the council that would proclaim the end of the frontiersman.

Was there no hope at all? Might not he be adopted into the tribe? Sutawnee's reply was an unequivocal no; Bahd-ler was too great an enemy, had killed too many Indians and outwitted too many others. They would gain strength and respect and prestige among all the other Shawnee septs to have captured and executed the deadly foe and this act alone would offset much of the disgrace of failing to destroy Boonesboro.

"I will ask my father, White Wolf, to vote to spare you," she said, "but that is all we can do and I know it is not enough."

She bade him lie down again and pulled the blanket over him, dipped a cloth in a water container and wiped from her own arms and breast and stomach the spatterings of grease and put her long blouse back on. Without another glance at him she picked up the emptied food bowls and left.

[*September 25, 1778 — Friday*]

During those early minutes of the assemblage of the Shawnees, Simon Kenton was tied in a sitting position to a stake outside the *msi-kah-mi-qui* while Bo-nah stood guard nearby. A large gathering of children collected about him and snickered and jeered at him. Several of the older boys spat upon him from a distance, which was cause for great laughter among the others, including many of the warriors on their way into the council house.

But one of the boys watching the activity was strangely quiet and took no part in torturing this captive. He was Tecumseh, a strong, serious boy of ten who was rather more disgusted than anything else over the actions of his companions. Chiksika had taught him to be brave and courageous and he could see nothing but fear and cowardice among these boys. His expression changed only once; when a boy called Stand-Under-the-Tree approached close to Simon, dug a foul mucous mass from his own nose and rubbed it in the frontiersman's eyes and mouth. Simon suddenly lashed out with a foot and caught the boy full in the stomach, knocking his wind out and sending him sprawling. Tecumseh laughed along with the others as the boy regained his feet and rushed away. But a few minutes later he returned with his mother, a fat and ugly squaw carrying a thorny branch from a bush. She shook her fist at Simon and cried, "You no kick Shawnee boy!" and with that she lashed him with the branch until his head and shoulders were bloody, stopping only when Bo-nah waved her off and untied Simon to lead him into the council house.

This *msi-kah-mi-qui* was much larger up close than Simon had expected and inside it was amazingly roomy. It was built of logs a foot in diameter and was square, sixty or seventy feet to a side. There were numerous shoulder-high holes, smaller than a man's head, chipped out between the logs and Simon gathered that these would be used as portholes to fire from in event of an attack. The roof was gabled and criss-crossed by an intricate and obviously sturdy system of interlocked poles several inches in diameter.

The floor was hard beaten by the passage of many feet over the years and when Bo-nah led him in with his hands tied behind him and a loop around his neck, it took several minutes for his eyes to become accustomed to the dimness. The warrior led him to a post projecting from the floor just off to one side from the center of the room and made him sit with his back against it and wound the neck cord many times around, then sat down himself a few feet away, his tomahawk loose in his lap. It took the better part of an hour for the building to fill up and Simon had never seen so many Indians so close before. Only the men were here, some appearing incredibly ancient, most of them in young middle age or even younger. Their faces were grimly set and their eyes, meeting his, held hatred.

It soon became obvious that these were more than just the warriors of the Chalahgawtha sept. Kispokothas were here, as were Maykujays, Peckuwes and Thawegilas. No other tribes were represented, however. When about five hundred men had assembled and others were still coming, Black Fish himself entered and there was a sudden hush.

Since the murder of Cornstalk, Black Fish had been principal chief of the Shawnee nation and he was deeply loved and respected by his tribesmen. He carried a staff in one hand and limped a little as he walked. Simon noted an ugly red furrow on the inside of his right calf and guessed this was caused by a bullet. Fleetingly he wished it had struck a couple of feet higher.

Black Fish stepped up to Simon and regarded him with a stern expression. He pointed a finger at the captive and said, "You are the man the *Shemanese* call Bahd-ler, our great enemy. You have been stealing horses?"

"I took seven horses from the Shawnees who have taken many times that many from the whites," Simon answered calmly.

"Did Sheltowee, the man you call Captain Boone, tell you to steal our horses?"

"No, I did it by myself."

"Don't you know it is wrong to steal Indians' horses?"

Simon snorted. "It is no more wrong than for you to come and steal our horses."

Displeased with the way the conversation was going, Black Fish took another tack. "The Shawnees have no cattle about their doors like the *Shemanese*. The buffalo are our cattle, but you come here and kill them. You have no business to kill Indians' cattle. Did you know that?"

"No, I did not. Did you know the Shawnees have no business killing the white man's cattle?"

Black Fish's lips became a tight line and without speaking further to the young frontiersman, he struck him ten or twelve hard strokes with his staff over the shoulders and legs. Then he turned and walked to his place beside his two chief subordinates, Black Hoof and Black Beard. He looked around at the assemblage — now close to six hundred men — and addressed them.

"I say the man Bahd-ler is guilty and vote that he be declared *cut-ta-ho-tha* and burned immediately here. How say the chiefs?"

Then began a series of speeches, mostly short but some lengthy, as the various chiefs and subchiefs spoke their pieces, mainly bringing up complaints in general about the whites and praise for Bo-nah in capturing this great enemy and then winding up with their vote of death or mercy for the frontiersman. Black Fish had resumed his cross-legged sitting position on the floor and before him was a smooth dry branch some five feet long. For each man who voted death he notched one side of the log with his knife and for each who voted mercy he notched the other. The speeches took several hours and when they were finished there were only four or five notches on the left side of the branch and more than two dozen on the right.

Black Fish thereupon declared Simon *cut-ta-ho-tha* and ordered that his body be painted black as was the custom for the condemned. Bo-nah and two other warriors began this task with bowls of inky fluid already on hand and now the discussion moved to when and where the execution should take place. Black Hoof and Black Beard wished it to take place here and now in the main village of the Shawnee nation, but the other chiefs — especially Moluntha, powerful chief of the Maykujays — argued that this was an execution of national importance and, as such, should take place at the town of Wapatomica, geographic center of the Shawnee nation, so that the greatest number possible of their tribe could witness it.

Black Fish agreed that the importance of this execution made it a national affair and that it should take place at Wapatomica. Another vote was taken and the decision of Black Fish so swayed the remainder that the national execution site was agreed upon. Bo-nah, as Simon's original captor, was ordered to select a party of braves and start off first thing in the morning for Wapatomica with their captive, being sure to stop at every village en route in order that the residents there might have the opportunity to participate in a gauntlet.

Despite the predictions of Caesar and Sutawnee that he would be condemned, Simon had hoped that somehow he might have been given mercy, perhaps even been adopted as Boone had been; but now there was no doubt in his mind that he would be executed and he resolved that he would attempt an escape at the first opportunity. Should he fail and be recaptured, his lot would be no worse than it was now.

[*September 28, 1778 — Monday*]

Colonel John Bowman was as furious as he had ever been in his life. He should have known better than to expect these ignorant backwoodsmen to know the meaning of justice. He should, in fact, have had more sense than to agree that the court-martial be presided over by members of the Kentucky militia rather than by his own officers, with himself as president of the court.

Just two days after the Boonesboro siege had been lifted and Black Fish had withdrawn, Bowman sent a detachment to the fort to arrest Daniel Boone and bring him back to Harrodsburg for trial on the three charges Bowman levied. James Harrod acted as president of the court and those officers sitting in judgment included Ben Logan, Mark McGohan, John Todd and the Reverend John Lythe. From such men Colonel John Bowman had expected justice.

It was James Harrod who read the charges brought by the military commander:

"Major Daniel Boone, you are brought to court-martial under the principal charge that you have British inclinations; to wit, that you, one, did voluntarily surrender your party of saltmakers into captivity last January with no attempt at defense; two, that you did undertake an expedition into the Ohio country, absenting yourself from your station at a time when Boonesboro was expecting attack hourly; and, three, that you did assent to the British proposal for a surrender talk which was a ruse to get into Boonesboro. How do you plead?"

There was some snickering among the spectators at the charges and it came as a surprise to no one when Boone pleaded not guilty. The actual trial was very nearly as brief as the deliberation of the court-martial board following it. It was James Harrod again who read the decision of the court:

"Daniel Boone, this board of court-martial finds you innocent of all charges brought against you and believes that not only did you act properly and with wisdom at all times, but that your actions undoubtedly saved Boonesboro and possibly the other settlements from destruction. In view of this, it is the considered view of this board that you be elevated to the rank of colonel of the militia."

There was a roar of approval from the spectators and thus it was that Daniel Boone became, on this date, the first true Kentucky colonel.

No one paid much attention when Colonel John Bowman unobtrusively slipped through the crowd and returned to his own quarters. He was positive now that he would never understand the mind of a frontiersman and hoped that he would never have to depend upon one in an emergency.

[*October 1, 1778 — Thursday*]

A hundred or more escape plans had been formulated and as quickly dismissed by Simon Kenton during these torture-filled days. As he was marched along he would fix his eye upon a bush or tree ahead and say to himself, "I will make my escape attempt when I reach that point," but always before he got there he would recognize the futility of it and look ahead to another point.

In large measure, it was only the constant planning for escape which kept him going. He hadn't known it was possible for the body to be such a shell of pain. The composite agony of a thousand or more bruises and cuts, welts and small burns, bumps and scratches was almost unbearable.

And now, before him, lay another gauntlet to run — his sixth — and he honestly doubted he could make it. The very thought of the clubs and switches, branches and sticks whipping across the multitude of injuries already covering his back and head and shoulders was enough to set the muscles of his calves and thighs atremble. If he was to escape at all, it must be here and now. One more gauntlet and he would be unable to muster the strength for it.

All the way from Chillicothe he had been hounded and teased and tortured by following Indians. Worst of all were the squaws and children who made life a living hell for him; they were the first to meet them as he approached a village and they would whip him with switches and throw mud at him and small rocks. It was they who made up the majority of people in the gauntlet lines and they were the most fierce in their intensity to inflict real injury.

After leaving Chillicothe under guard of Bo-nah and four other warriors, they had reached the village of the Peckuwe sept called Piqua Town on the bank of the Mad River and the quarter-mile gauntlet here had been a severe one, even if it was the first one in which he had successfully reached the *msi-kah-mi-qui*.[6]

From here they had moved north the next day through a countryside of beautiful prairies and islands of woods, where the ground was more fertile than any land Simon Kenton had ever before encountered. One night, as they rested beside a huge bubbling spring of the clearest coldest water imaginable, he vowed that if he could get away, that someday he would return and make his home here when the Indians were no longer a threat.[7]

A dozen miles north of that point he was forced to lie face down to form a human bridge across a little muddy creek, and each of the five warriors and the dozen or so women and children following after them made certain to step on the back of his head and force his face deep into the muck. He was nearly unconscious from suffocation when they dragged him out.[8]

More and more Indians came to meet them the farther north they traveled, as word of the famous captive spread rapidly from village to village. The inhabitants of Wapatomica and Moluntha's Town remained in their villages waiting, knowing Bahd-ler would be brought to them, but those inhabitants of other Shawnee villages, as well as nearby villages of tribes other than Shawnees, came in a hurry to be sure they got in their licks on this dreaded frontiersman. From Mackachack and Buckangehela's Town they came; from the new little Blue Jacket's Town, established a few months ago by the brave young subchief; from McKee's Town, where Alexander McKee, former Indian agent for Fort Pitt, had built a British-supplied trading post; and from Mingo Town and Solomon's Town and Girty's Town they came.[9]

With this influx of Indians, each gauntlet was larger, longer and more painful than the last. Before reaching the Mackachack Towns he was forced to run two more gauntlets and both times he was beaten to the ground before the run was completed. The second time, when it appeared he would make it through, a squaw had heaved a double handful of sand into his eyes and, while he groped about blinded, he was beaten into unconsciousness.

Each time he awakened from these ordeals it was to find that, in a strange paradox, his wounds were being treated with great care — washed and medicated and, where necessary, bound. He was given good food and water to drink to rebuild his strength and he took it willingly, knowing it was just to restore him for another gauntlet run, but knowing as well that he must retain what strength he had for whatever opportunity might present itself for escape.

And now, with the huge double line of this sixth gauntlet stretching before him to the *msi-kah-mi-qui* in Moluntha's Town, he knew he would make his determined bid for freedom — a bid that would have to be made *before* the gauntlet run, else he would not have the strength left to make the escape. Despite the beatings and other mistreatment already received, he still felt strong enough to run; he was sure that if he could once gain a lead on his pursuers, he could outdistance them.

Bo-nah positioned him at the mouth of the terrible twin lines and stood waiting behind Simon with his own staff at ready to strike as soon as the drum at the council house door should sound. But this time Simon didn't wait. With complete unexpectedness he leaped forward and raced down the line and had sped by a full thirty of the club wielders before they realized it. Suddenly he turned and sprang into the air directly at a short squaw who ducked instinctively. He cleared her by a foot and was running at full tilt when he touched ground behind her.

So amazed was the entire gauntlet line that for a long moment the Indians just stared. But Bo-nah's shrill cry of rage galvanized them into action and the entire assemblage thundered out in pursuit. As Simon had anticipated, this worked to his advantage. The women and children got in the way of the more speedy young men and there were several collisions and upsets. By the time the young men had gotten up to full speed behind him, Simon was easily seventy yards in the lead.

Naked and shoeless, the agony of running was severe for him at first and it was all he could do to hold his own. But then his tormented muscles began loosening and he increased his speed, running in great smooth strides that carried him through fields and over fallen logs and little creeks as if they weren't even there. At one point he came to an erosion groove through the prairie. It was five feet deep and twenty feet wide at its narrowest. Without hesitation he catapulted himself across it, landing on the other side with a couple of feet to spare. At least a dozen of the pursuing Indians tried it but only two were successful, and even one of these tumbled over and over when he hit. The others jumped down, ran across and climbed up, but now the distance between them and their prisoner was over a hundred yards and a desperate howl of anger and frustration arose from them.

The single Indian to leap the groove successfully after Kenton was Bo-nah, but though he was a good jumper he was not an endurance runner and by the time Simon had run a mile, Bo-nah was a quarter mile behind him and losing ground.

A great feeling of triumph now filled the frontiersman and he increased rather than slackened his speed. He raced into a woods to the east until out of sight, made a sharp right turn for fifty yards, then a sharp left for a similar distance, then struck off diagonally to the southeast.

There was a half-mile prairie on the other side and he sped through this at full tilt and entered the opposite woods just an instant before Bo-nah emerged from the first, far from where Kenton had come out. He stared around him anxiously as he ran and then paused as if uncertain whether Kenton had continued or was still in the woods behind him. He couldn't believe the frontiersman could have made it across the prairie to the other woods in so short a time, and so now he turned back into the first woods to continue his search.

In the woods ahead, Kenton found a little creek and ran in the water for another quarter mile before running up the slanted trunk of a fallen tree and jumping far off onto rocky gound. It would be a while before they untangled this part of the trail.

Now he found himself entering a wide ravine between large rolling hills and he raced into it, exulting in the escape, knowing he could continue this pace for an hour or more if it became necessary. Ahead of him the ravine made a sharp turn to the right and he raced around the bend without pause, only to slam to a stop so suddenly that he slipped and fell, rolled over, regained his footing and raced back in the direction from which he had come.

En route with six other horsemen from his village to Moluntha's Town to see the famed captive, Blue Jacket was as startled to see Simon charge around the bend as the frontiersman was to see Blue Jacket. The Shawnee assessed the situation instantly and spurred his horse into pursuit, at the same time jerking his tomahawk from his belt and holding it high.

Simon now turned from the easier footing of the ravine bed and raced up the steep brushy hillside, gasping for breath. Behind him he could hear the cries of his pursuers and, even worse, the drumming of hooves as Blue Jacket's horse closed the gap between them.

He gained the top and struck off for a large woods fifty yards distant where he might be able to force his pursuers to dismount. His lungs were afire with the need for oxygen and he felt as if he were in the midst of some awful nightmare from which he would awaken sweating and exhausted. But this was worse than any nightmare.

He was still a hundred feet or more from the edge of the woods when Blue Jacket caught up to him, leaned far forward on the horse's neck and swung his tomahawk fiercely. Fortunately for Simon, it was the pipe end rather than the cutting end of the blade which struck him. The rounded metal end smashed into the very top of Simon's skull, punching a section of bone the size of a shilling into his head, and he fell senseless.

[October 7, 1778 — Wednesday]

General Henry Hamilton, governor of the western lands and commandant of Detroit, the greatest British fortification in the Northwest Territory, returned the salute of Captain Lernoult. He stood high in the stirrups to inspect a final time the regiment of mounted men behind him and then returned his attention to his adjutant.

"Captain Lernoult, in my absence you are to command this fort as I have done. You will see that the annuities are paid on time to the assembled tribes at the principal trading post of Upper Sandusky, and you will make certain that none of your men do anything to offend the chiefs.[10] You will continue to honor our obligations, paying fifty dollars for each white scalp and one hundred dollars for each living prisoner. Wherever it is possible, prisoners are to be bought in preference to scalps."

He raised his right hand and the assembled horsemen behind him steadied their mounts. "We should reach Vincennes by the seventeenth," Hamilton added, his expression sour as he considered anew the effrontery of the Frenchmen there who had ousted the British garrison after learning of Clark's victories at Kaskaskia and Cahokia. Now the general's voice matched the expression he wore as he continued. "We will teach the rebellious Frenchmen there a lesson in fidelity and take command of the garrison again. We will hold the fort throughout the winter and move against Clark at Cahokia immediately when the weather breaks in spring. Until our return, you will keep a tight command here, is that clear?"

"Yes sir," Lernoult said. "I will dispatch Captain Drouilliard with the trade goods to Upper Sandusky within the week." He saluted again. "God speed to you, sir."

Hamilton dropped his arm and the British Western Army set off for Vincennes on the River Wabash.

[September 13, 1778 — Tuesday]

Simon was not dead, though by rights he should have been. As it was, he did not regain consciousness for two days after Blue Jacket brought him back to Moluntha's Town. The mood of the Shawnees there had changed in an instant from one of great gloom to one of deep joy when they saw their captive returned. Some of them ran up, gauntlet weapons still in hand, and began pummeling the frontiersman as he lay unconscious across the horse's back.

Moluntha, most ancient of all the Shawnee chiefs and, for this reason, known as King of the Shawnees, ordered the attackers to desist.

"What kind of courage do my people have," he asked scornfully in his raspy whisper, "that they can beat a great enemy while he lies unconscious and helpless before them? What kind of respect do my people have for a great man who can best them when his body is already weak with injury and pain? Do not make your kind ashamed of you. This prisoner is a man of mighty courage and strength. Since when does the Shawnee show his respect for such attributes in such manner?"

He pointed to his huge cousin, the Grenadier Squaw. Since the death of her brother, Cornstalk, she had resided close to Moluntha and now she stepped forward.

"Non-hel-e-ma," he said, "take this brave white warrior to your *wegiwa*. Nurse him as you would your own son. He may now be dying, but yet nurse him well that he may survive. If he should live, another council of judgment will be held to determine whether or not the punishment he has already received at our hands is not payment enough for the theft of seven horses."

The frontiersman did survive, although for four days after recovering consciousness he was in something of a daze from the pressure of that circle of skull bone resting on his brain. But incredibly, his mind cleared and by the end of the seventh day after being struck he could sit up and even walk about some. His treatment under the hands of Non-hel-e-ma was excellent and the wounds of his body healed as rapidly as that to his head. Moluntha himself came by several times each day to check on his progress and, when Simon was able, to talk with him. Repeatedly he told the young frontiersman that as far as he was concerned, the punishment already sustained was enough.

Simon appreciated the unexpected kindness but had little belief that even the Shawnee King could prevent the execution. The term king was an honorary one only. Black Fish was principal chief and it was Black Fish's ruling that he should die.

And so it was. The council held the next day was small as compared to that held at Chillicothe, but the death sentence was reaffirmed over Moluntha's counsel and the aged chief reluctantly turned the prisoner back over to Bo-nah to be taken on the morrow to Wapatomica where the execution was to take place.

Another gauntlet faced Simon at the end of their eight-mile walk to Wapatomica, northeast of Moluntha's Town. This town was situated on a beautiful plateau on the west side of the upper Mad River, with a fertile bottom intervening. On the west the village was skirted by a high ridge from which issued many springs and rivulets. It was a fine location, but at the moment Simon had no eyes for it. The prospect of another gauntlet caused his stomach to churn.

This time it was not so severe. Most of those in line were armed with switches rather than clubs, stinging when they hit rather than bruising muscle and bone. But toward the end of the line a lone, club-wielding squaw landed a savage blow over the same spot where his skull had been fractured by the tomahawk and, when he regained his senses, he found himself once more at the head of the gauntlet line and forced to run this torturous route for the eighth time.

He could do little more than stagger along now. For the first time since becoming a captive, he lost absolutely all hope of salvation. His feet dragged as he ran and it was in something of a haze that he felt the fire of the switches across his back and buttocks and legs. But this time no one struck his head and, though several times he stumbled, he managed to carry on and reach the open doorway of the grandest *msi-kah-mi-qui* of the Shawnee nation, far larger than that at Chillicothe. He collapsed unconscious across the threshold.

The rest of the day was one of continuous teasing and debasing, which was as hard for him to bear as the whippings. Still nude, he was staked again in spreadeagled fashion on his back. Women and children flitted about him, hurling ugly remarks and dropping handfuls of fiercely biting ants on his chest or groin. The little boys took great delight in standing with a foot on either side of his chest and urinating into his face. The worst of these acts came when a fat squaw attempted to defecate upon him. She stepped astraddle his head, raised her greasy buckskin skirt and squatted over his face. But in a rage, Simon jerked his head upward and buried his strong teeth in the soft flesh of that very tender portion of her anatomy. As she shrieked and screamed and thrashed in an effort to get away, he felt as if his head would be torn off. Only when the blood gushing from her torn body threatened to smother him did he finally release his hold. With that the whimpering squaw scrambled away through the crowd, which was roaring with laughter at how this unbelievable captive had turned the tables on her. There was no sympathy at all for the squaw: she had earned what she got through carelessness and underestimating her enemy.

The Wapatomica Council held the next day differed only in that the question was not whether or not Simon should be put to death, but when. Once again long speeches were made and votes cast, and when it was over he was told that when the sun arose three days from now, the fire would be kindled to consume him.

Still, there was indeed a deep respect in the attitude of the Shawnees toward their prisoner those last two days. He was provided with dirty leggins and moccasins and a ragged linsey shirt of faded gray. The minor pestering by squaws and children had ceased. And this night — the evening before the third sunrise — he was provided a fine meal of roasted venison and strips of dog meat, fresh vegetables and fruit. Understandably, he had little appetite for them. Less than fifty feet from where he sat tied, a sturdy post was erected and around this on the ground, in a circle beginning five feet from the post, a crew of squaws was laying out firewood.

[*October 14, 1778 — Wednesday*]

One hour before dawn Simon Kenton was roused from his fitful sleep and marched into the council house in which five different fires were burning to dispel the chill of the night. Already more than half a thousand warriors had gathered inside and yet, in this giant *msi-kah-mi-qui*, there was room for easily twice that many or more. It was built of split poles standing upright to a height of sixteen feet and was, both outside and inside, covered with fitted pieces of bark to act as insulation. The building was easily seventy-five feet wide and twice that in length, covered with a flat roof.

Simon recognized few of the Shawnees and other Indians assembled. Blue Jacket he saw at once, sitting with his own people near the door. Further inside he recognized Bo-nah and, near him, Black Beard and Black Hoof. A brutish-looking Indian with a hideous scar down his left cheek and the ear on that side of his head missing had to be the well-known Delaware, Chief Buckangehela. Close by him was the chief of the Kispokotha Shawnees, She-me-ne-to — Black Snake. At the center of the room sat Black Fish and Moluntha and, off to one side of them were Moluntha's son, Young King, and the son of Pucksinwah, Chiksika.

Simon's shirt was removed and once again his face, arms and upper body were painted black. Then the talk began. Only a few speeches had been given, proclaiming this a great and memorable day and referring to Simon not only as *cut-ta-ho-tha* but also as *ne-noth-tu ou-ki-mah shemana* — great warrior chief of the whites. Suddenly there was a hubbub from outside; a runner rushed in and whispered something to the principal chief.

Almost immediately Simon was led outside and ordered to sit unbound in the center of a circle of warriors. Beside him sat Bo-nah, who seemed very pleased. Simon asked him what was happening.

"You are very lucky," the Shawnee answered. "Your beginning-to-die has been delayed for a while. A hundred and twenty of our warriors have just returned from near your fort of Wheeling and they have brought with them many fine scalps and eight prisoners.[11] These prisoners must be tried immediately before we begin your execution. You are lucky."

Simon Kenton didn't feel lucky at all. The delay merely prolonged his agony. Nevertheless, in the growing daylight, he watched the large war party come in, saw them file into the council house with their prisoners and then vaguely heard the mumble of speeches from inside. For over an hour the talking continued and then a summons was sent and Bo-nah brought Simon back into the chamber and stood him along the wall apart from the other prisoners who sat exhausted and frightened fifty feet away.

A short man with war paint on his face was finishing off his recounting of the expedition. At least twenty whites had been slain, he said proudly, and perhaps many more. No Indians had even been wounded. There was something strangely familiar about the speaker and Simon studied him carefully across the dimness. Suddenly his eyes widened with the tremendous shock of recognition.

Simon Girty!

When his report was finished, Girty stepped through the crowd to see the "important prisoner" who stood there along the wall all blackened with the mark of the *cut-ta-ho-tha*. With no sign of recognition on his part, Girty threw his blanket to the floor and sat down upon it. To the prisoner he said in English, "Sit down!" When Simon did not immediately obey, Girty jerked his arm and half threw him to the blanket.

"You are from south of the Ohio River?"

Kenton nodded. Girty continued the questioning.

"What is your name?"

Simon smiled tightly. "I never thought to see the day when Simon Girty would fail to recognize his own blood brother."   .

Girty started and gripped the blackened arm and stared into the eyes. "Who is it?"

"The man who spied beside you at Fort Pitt and Point Pleasant and in between. Don't you remember Simon Butler?"

"Butler!" There was an instant of disbelief and then Girty saw that it was indeed his good friend and he hugged him fiercely and tears came to his eyes. He talked to him rapidly and then listened carefully as Simon explained what had happened since his capture. Then he jumped to his feet and pulled Kenton up beside him.

"My brothers!" he called, silencing the scattered mumbling in the room. All eyes turned to him and when he had their attention he placed an arm around Simon and spoke earnestly. "My brothers, this *cut-ta-ho-tha* must not be killed. This is my friend. This is my brother whom I love. Long years ago he and I, lonely men on the banks of the Spay-lay-wi-theepi, we vowed our lives to one another, hand in hand, for life and death, when there was nobody present in the wilderness but the Great Spirit and us. For long now I have ridden with you against the whites. I have been your voice to the white father Hamilton in Detroit, who is the voice to the great white father across the sea, King George. With your other British friend, Alexander McKee, I have devoted myself to your cause, which cause is to drive away the white settlers who threaten this land. Never before have I asked you for any gift but that of your friendship, which has been readily given and returned. I know this man has been condemned for stealing Shawnee horses, but consider: he has eight times since Chillicothe run the gauntlet and each time, to near the point of death, he has proven himself a man. At Moluntha's Town he was nearly killed and his head bone broken and yet still he begged not and had the courage and strength to run the gauntlet here. This is no ordinary man. This is a brave man among brave men! A man whose life should not be burned away needlessly. Long I wandered with him before the war on the Scioto and I know him for a friend like no other. Our attachment has remained unbroken. We have shared each other's secrets and participated in each other's joys and sorrows. He knew it first when I was preparing to leave the Americans to join the British and you, yet he stayed me not but instead wished me well and our friendship grew. We have pledged ourselves one to another and our wrist blood has mingled in the oath of brotherhood. If he is killed, you are also killing a part of me and this you must not do in haste or anger. I have not asked favor of you before but I ask it now. Spare to me the life of my friend and brother. Spare to me Simon Butler!"

There could be no doubt that the Indians were moved by the impassioned plea. Simon Girty was well liked and more than once he had proven his interests lay with the Shawnee. Now Chief Moluntha rose slowly to his feet and reiterated the remarks he had made in this prisoner's behalf at his own town, asking that a new vote be taken on this great young white man's life.

The speeches were brief and the vote unusually swift. It was an extremely close vote this time, but now the margin was in Simon's favor. There were many who were disgruntled at this but none who disputed the validity of the voting. Black Fish now walked over to Girty and Kenton and placed his hands on Kenton's shoulders.

"I hereby declare you *mat-tah cut-ta-ho-tha* — not condemned. On the morrow you will be adopted into the Shawnee nation and forever after be our son and our brother."

Simon Kenton very nearly wept.

[*November 5, 1778 — Thursday*]

For twenty days after his adoption by Melassa Te-qui — Sugar Tree — Simon Kenton roamed the area surrounding Wapatomica with Simon Girty. He still had frequent dizzy spells, and each morning when he awoke there was a period of excruciating pain as stiffened muscles were put back into use. But day by day his strength and health improved.

The adoption ceremony had taken half of one day and he felt quite proud of his introduction into the tribe. Melassa Te-qui had lost her only son in the Green Moon last year when he had gone with Black Fish to attack Boonesboro. Simon, whom she named Psai-wi Wuh-ker-ne-kah Ptwe-o-wa — Great White Wolf — was to take the place of this lost son.

The woman was as good to him as his own mother could have been and all through the adoption ceremony a deep sense of guilt rode him. He was at that fight at Boonesboro and had killed Indians there. It was altogether possible that he was the one who had killed Melassa Te-qui's son. .

The squaw, a rotund and happy individual, smiled constantly as she hung the huge kettle over the fire and hummed a strange tune to herself as the water heated. When a faint whisp of steam began rising from it, she dipped her hands into it and scrubbed them together and then she cupped the water and rubbed it over Simon's arms and chest. She then held her hands up in front of her face with the palms up and fingers pointed toward the sun and blew on them, then made a motion as if thrusting something from her and called out loudly, *"Puck-e-ton!"* — Throw it away! — meaning Simon's white skin. This was repeated with water on his head, after which she repeated the same incantation all over his body. Then she wiped him dry and dressed him in Indian leathers belonging to her son, which were considerably too small for Simon but better by far than the uncomfortable nudity he had been enduring in large measure. When she was finished she hugged him to her massive breasts and said, "Now you are Great White Wolf, beloved son of Sugar Tree. Let Moneto always walk beside you."

After that, Simon had gone with Girty to the latter's own town, a sleepy little village of a dozen hastily-erected *wegiwas* which everyone called Girty's Town, where the renegade had a small trading station. Here he gave Simon clothing that fit him — hat, coat, moccasins, breechclout, leggins and kerchief for his neck — and provided him not only with tomahawk and knife, but with horse and saddle.

Simon still did not feel altogether comfortable in the midst of the Shawnee nation; had it not been that things would have gone poorly for Girty, he would simply have ridden off and returned to Kentucky. He decided to wait about a month and then perhaps he could one day disappear.

From town to town he and Girty traveled. They visited McKee's Town, Solomon's and Buckangehela's Towns, Tarhe's Town, Blue Jacket's Town and, finally, the little winter hunting camp of a great Indian chief Simon had thought must be long dead — Logan.

The Mingo chief's camp was on the headwaters of the Scioto River some twenty-five miles northeast of that swampy body of water known simply as Indian Lake.[12] No mention was made of the Pickaway Plains or Logan's speech there, but the chief shook Simon's hand gravely and said he had heard of his capture. He added that he would have come to Wapatomica for the council but he needed to get the winter quarters built for his small band.

By mutual consent, Simon and Girty gave him their help and showed him how to erect a sturdy pioneer-type log cabin ten feet square which would be warm and cozy all winter long. Logan was very grateful and invited them both to come back anytime. The pair had just reached

Solomon's Town again when they were met by the subchief Red Pole and four other Shawnees. An important council, Red Pole told them, was being convened at Wapatomica and the two white men were to ride back with them immediately.

Several hundred men were already inside the *msi-kah-mi-qui* when they arrived and many of these warriors stood to greet Girty and shake his hand, but none of them offered his hand to the frontiersman and Simon's heart sank at the omen. It did not take long to discover the cause for the snub.

Red Pole, who had been one of those voting for Simon's death at Chillicothe during the first trial, spoke at length. He and a party of sixteen men from Chillicothe had ridden to the Can-tuc-kee land to attack Standing Fort. They had fallen into ambush and seven of the party were killed, three others wounded. Red Pole, hearing upon his return of Bahd-ler's adoption, was furious. The white man had been declared *cut-ta-ho-tha* by the principal chief of the Shawnees and no one — not even Black Fish himself — had the right to reverse this decision once it had been made. The death of Bahd-ler was now more necessary than ever to appease, by the sacrifice of him, the injury dealt to the Shawnees by the deaths of Red Pole's warriors. It was equally necessary if the Shawnees were to be able to hold up their heads among the other Ohio tribes.

Moluntha, one of Simon's strongest protectors, was not here now and, as Girty spoke in rebuttal and other Indians made their comments, it became clear that things were going badly for the young frontiersman. Twice Girty was chided for assuming too much importance for one who had been among them for less than a year.

The need for revenge in the Shawnees was strong. A vote was called for and taken and, by an overwhelming margin, Simon Bahd-ler was once again declared *cut-ta-ho-tha* and nothing Girty could say would change their minds. At last the little renegade stood and spoke softly but fervently:

"My heart lies heavy in my breast. Are the adoption vows of the Shawnees no longer sacred? Many times in the last twenty suns my friend could have gone away, but he did not. It is sad to know that this is how the Shawnee rewards faithfulness. These words I speak as a friend and brother of the Shawnees. Yet, I can understand why the execution is now desirable, so now hear me speak as a British agent anxious to help all of the Ohio Indians, especially my friends the Shawnees.

"At this time," he continued, "delegations of the Shawnees and Wyandots, Cayugas and Ottawas and Tuscarawas, Chippewas, Potawatomies, Mingoes and Delawares are assembling at the British trading post of Upper Sandusky fifty miles to the northeast of here. They will receive their annuities of powder and lead and other supplies to carry them through the winter. Therefore, let not the death of Simon Butler be an act of revenge hidden in a Shawnee village. There is now a growing alliance between the various Indian tribes and the death of so great an enemy as this carries much importance for every Indian. Let his execution become one of symbolic significance for all these tribes as well as vengeance for the Shawnees. Let this execution take place at Upper Sandusky under the eyes of all so that the Shawnee tribe may gain respect and honor in the eyes of the other tribes. Do not lose such an important opportunity as this to increase the stature of the Shawnee in the eyes of all the other tribes. Let the execution of the *cut-ta-ho-tha* take place at Upper Sandusky!"

The assembled Indians had been listening intently and nodding frequently. There was wisdom in the words of this powerful little friend of theirs. It would indeed be better to hold an intertribal execution of this great enemy than to kill him here, for it was not only the Shawnees who had long sought to still the deadly fire of this young frontiersman's rifle. The plan was accepted and once again Simon's original captor, Bo-nah, was placed in charge of four other warriors and directed to march the *cut-ta-ho-tha* to Upper Sandusky immediately.

Within the hour — the five warriors mounted and their prisoner afoot, tethered to Bo-nah's horse by a long rawhide cord attached to his throat — they set off for the town. They were no more than three miles from Wapatomica when Girty came riding up behind them on his horse. He waved to the guards and called out to Simon in English, "They will be stopping for a night at Logan's camp and he is our friend. I'll ride ahead to see if he can help us. Have courage, my friend."

Of courage, Simon had more than his share. Of hope, he had considerably less.

[*November 6, 1778 — Friday*]

Chief Logan listened carefully as Simon Girty explained what had transpired, but he was shaking his head sadly as the little man finished.

"My son," he said, "you credit me with far more influence than I have. This is a Shawnee matter and I am Mingo. I do not approve that young Bahd-ler be executed, especially after having been lawfully adopted, but this has become a matter of Shawnee pride against which my words and beliefs are as nothing."

Girty's expression registered great disappointment and Logan put his hand to the renegade's knee and smiled. "Do not let gloom surround you, my good friend. Return to your own village, leaving this problem with me. You have the word of your friend Logan that whatever can be done for Bahd-ler will be done."

But Simon was already having serious troubles. This morning the little party had stopped to drink at Silver Creek a few miles south of Solomon's Town. Simon was first to rise and he stepped across the little rivulet and sat down on the opposite bank. At this movement of the prisoner without orders, Bo-nah's rage — growing continuously during these weeks of frustration in getting the *cut-ta-ho-tha* executed — reached a peak and he leaped across after him, swinging his heavy stone-headed war club. The blow caught Simon on the left arm several inches beneath the shoulder and snapped the bone. Bo-nah grabbed him by the hair and pulled him to his feet, ordering him to continue marching along the trail. The other guards had their clubs or tomahawks out and stood ready but, even so, Bo-nah stood back several paces from the fierceness of Simon's gaze. Without a word or even a moan of pain, Simon began to walk again, cradling his injured arm in his right hand.

To his immense relief, no gauntlet was run as they entered and passed through Solomon's Town, but a crowd hovered close and hurled insults at him and followed for half a mile before withdrawing. Simon had not even indicated that he was aware they were there and this had the effect of increasing their growing awe of him. But an old Shawnee and his squaw whom they encountered along the trail were not awed. The slaying of their son by whites not long before was still too fresh in their minds. They had been chopping firewood and stopped to watch as the party approached. Suddenly the old man cried, "Bahd-ler!" and snatched up the ax he had been using and swung a blow at Simon's head. Simon ducked away but the weapon struck and broke his right collarbone, at the same time cutting a deep gash. Simon stumbled and fell and it took the combined effort of two of his guards to keep the old man from completing the job.

When assured that Simon was to be executed at Upper Sandusky, the old man grinned toothlessly and muttered, "*Oui-sah, oui-sah!*" — Good, good!

There was little concern for Simon's condition. He was hauled erect and prodded along the trail, enveloped in an aura of extreme pain.

[*November 11, 1778 — Wednesday*]

Simon Kenton had no hope whatsoever. Tomorrow at sunrise he would be tied to the stake already erected here in the center of Upper Sandusky and he knew that now he was a dead man. The additional day given to him by the "Great Spirit" made little difference.

He took scant interest in the many Indians who now came to look at him, even though most of them were in different costume than those he had seen before and of different tribes. For the third time his body was blackened and he sat staring at the ground in front of him, ignoring the jeering cries and occasional blows and pokings he received as if they were not even happening.

Not until they had left Logan's camp did he realize fully just how much hope he had placed in the venerable old chief. For two days they had stayed there and, though Simon's guards were anxious to move on the remaining twenty-three miles to Upper Sandusky, they could not insult the chief by refusing to accept his hospitality.

The miles of walking to Logan's camp had been a living hell for the young frontiersman, whose sole concentration had been devoted to simply placing one foot in front of the other and forcing himself to plod onward step by step.

Logan had greeted both the guards and Simon cordially and told the Shawnees that he had a *wegiwa* for them to use and that since this white man had once been a friend, he would stay in Logan's cabin and Logan would be responsible for his safekeeping while he was here. It was only with the greatest of reluctance that Bo-nah and his companions acceded.

Immediately Logan had summoned a squaw and directed her to treat Simon's injuries. She did so with great care and skill, setting the broken bones, splinting his arm and binding his chest. They ate together, Simon and Logan, and it was dark by the time the meal was finished. The chief directed Simon to remain where he was and went outside. In a few minutes he returned.

"I have sent two runners to a man of great influence at Upper Sandusky," he said. "When they return we will know if you can be saved. These people are very angry with you and talk of burning you there, but I am a great chief and my runners will speak good of you."

The next evening Logan's runners returned and sat with the old chief for some time but, to Simon's growing concern, Logan neither approached nor spoke to him. In fact he seemed deliberately to avoid the young frontiersman. Simon thought perhaps he was waiting for the morning to tell him what had happened, but at daybreak Logan merely gave him some bread and meat and told him he had to go with his guards to Upper Sandusky. That had been the end of Simon's hope.

Ten miles or so from the major trading post on the Upper Sandusky River, a troop of twenty Indian youths on horseback met them and galloped around the captive and his guards with shrill cries and threatening gestures, then disappeared in the direction from whence they had come. In another mile the six came to a clearing where these boys and several dozen others had aligned themselves for Simon's ninth gauntlet. Even the fact that they were armed only with light switches failed to raise Simon's spirits and he walked rather than ran the thirty-yard gauntlet, hardly aware of the stinging blows raining upon his backside.

No white man ever *walked* through a gauntlet! No white man did not feel the burning bite of willowy switches — not unless he was under the special protection of the Great Spirit. As a result, the blows that struck him at the end of the line were hardly more than gentle taps and some of the boys, out of fear, refrained altogether from striking.

Apparently word of this phenomenon had spread to Upper Sandusky and this time there was no gauntlet line awaiting him. Nor did he receive as much of the heckling and minor torturing as before. He was simply tied to the post and told that at sunrise he would be burned. Once again fate intervened. The ring of firewood was laid around the fire post and Kenton was led toward it in the early light. Before he could be tied to it, however, the skies suddenly broke and a heavy pelting rain drummed down on the entire area, soaking the wood and adding fuel only to the belief that the life of this great white man was being protected.

Nevertheless, the ritual burning was merely postponed until tomorrow at the same time and Simon Kenton could conceive of no other possible twist of fate which might again save him. This time tomorrow he would be dead.

[*November 12, 1778 — Thursday*]

Usually when away from Detroit dealing with the Indians, Captain Peter Drouilliard wore the garb of a trader: soft leather moccasins, leggins and loose blouse, all well frilled. But today, following the advice passed on by Chief Logan through his runners, he donned the striking scarlet and gold uniform of his rank. Logan had said it would do much to impress the tribesmen gathered for their annuities at Upper Sandusky.

Logan was right and Drouilliard smiled faintly as he saw the respectful looks sent his way by the Indians as he walked into the center square of the town. Nevertheless, when he observed the fresh dry faggots ringing the fire post and the paint-blackened form of the captive tied to the post alongside the council house, his smile faded. So did his confidence that he would be able to effect a rescue of Chief Logan's friend. The poor wretch looked half dead anyway.

Drouilliard had an enormous amount of prestige among the Indians gathered here. It was he who brought them food supplies and fine cloth, jewelry and beads, tomahawks and knives, gunpowder, lead and rifles. It was he who gave them the best prices for their furs and who never tried to cheat them in any way. His words were always listened to with great respect and his wishes had an undeniable influence upon their actions.

Now he approached the assembled chiefs in the open, shook hands with each, wished them full stomachs and strong wives and long lives. Then he pointed to the prisoner who sat watching him closely.

"Brothers," he said, "it is well known among you to be the wish and interest of the English that no American should be left alive; that the Americans are the cause of the present bloody and distressing war. Neither peace nor safety can be expected while these intruders are permitted to live here. However, it requires cunning as well as bravery for the war to be carried on successfully.

"Brothers, your English father in Detroit wants this man. He has heard grave news that the *Shemanese* chief called McIntosh has moved an army into the eastern quarter of your country and has built a fort there which is called Fort Laurens. It is the desire of the white father in Detroit that all American prisoners be brought to him immediately so that they can be questioned as to the strengths and weaknesses of this army."

The atmosphere was not as friendly now as it had been a short while ago, but Drouilliard continued: "I know this man is a great enemy of yours; that he has stolen your horses and killed your warriors in battle. But he is also a man who must be filled with the plans of the *Shemanese* and this information is worth more to the British interests, which are your interests, than the lives of twenty prisoners.

"This man is condemned to the stake not because he slew your warriors in battle, which is a noble matter, but because he and a companion stole seven Shawnee horses. In my heart he has already suffered enough and the Shawnees have had retribution enough. Was not his companion slain? Has not he himself run nine different gauntlets? Have not his bones been broken? Is this not lesson enough? Or is it that the brave warriors so fear this man that they wish him dead so that they need no longer worry about his skill in battle? No, I cannot believe the brave Shawnees would be guilty of this shame.

"However, it is not for me to question the decisions reached by the Shawnee nation. I ask only that you consider this: what we may be able to learn from this prisoner could well save the lives of many Shawnees, as well as those of the Delawares and Wyandots and other tribes gathered here. If I am allowed to take him to Detroit, when we are finished questioning him, then you may have him back to do with as you will. Surely a short delay can be of no harm and possibly of immeasurable good."

A few of the chiefs were nodding now at this logic and Drouilliard turned to Bo-nah. "This prisoner is in your charge," he said, "and therefore it is expected that you would return with us to Detroit until after the questioning, when you could take him back again for execution. For your fatigue and trouble, however, I will pay you one hundred bucks.[13] And for the others of you here who must be inconvenienced as well, for the privilege of taking this prisoner to Detroit I will pay you one hundred bucks' worth of rum, tobacco, salt, powder or whatever other articles you may choose."

The chiefs and many of their men immediately retired to the council house where an hour-long conference was held. When they emerged a runner was sent to the trading post to tell Drouilliard that his plan was acceptable.

Simon Kenton was now in the hands of the British.

[*December 31, 1778 — Thursday*]

Bo-nah had the attributes of a leech. Every step of the way he clung close to Simon, occasionally reminding him that this trip to Detroit was only a temporary delay and that soon again he would be at the stake.

They went overland along the Sandusky River, following it downstream to Lower Sandusky where a small British detachment was camped and where Drouilliard's canoes were waiting.[14] Not until they started down the last of the river to Lake Erie by canoe was Drouilliard able to be alone with Simon, demanding that Bo-nah follow in the canoe behind them — far enough behind so that Drouilliard could question the captive and his answers would not be influenced by having the threat of death at his side. Reluctantly, Bo-nah agreed.

And then, for the first time, Simon Kenton was told that he no longer needed to fear the death penalty; that although he was a prisoner of the British he would be well treated and that they had no intention of returning him to Bo-nah once they reached Detroit. For this, Drouilliard said, he could thank his friends Girty and Chief Logan, who had arranged it all.

They talked together then of many things and Drouilliard told Simon he had been along on the recent attack on Boonesboro. He shook his head. "They were lucky," he said. "Weather was against us. We started running a tunnel from the river bank to undermine the fort, but it rained so much it kept caving in. Got so dangerous we had to give it up. Better luck next time maybe."

Not much older than Simon, Drouilliard was several inches shorter and lean. His eyes and hair were very dark and he was possessed of a restless energy which gave extra push to his paddle strokes and caused Bo-nah to labor to keep up with them.

Through Sandusky Bay they paddled and then past the islands just off shore. Four different nights they camped along the lakeshore and on the fifth day they reached the British fort. By then they had come to know one another rather well and Simon found that he liked the captain considerably. He told him of his cabin near Limestone Creek and of how, if ever he got the chance, he would return there. It was remarkable how much better he felt now that he could envision a future which didn't end at the stake.

Still in bad shape from his injuries, Simon was taken without delay to the quarters of Captain Donald McGregor, Governor Hamilton's own physician. The doctor ordered that the frontiersman be given a bath and after that he checked him thoroughly. He was disgustingly cheerful and whistled or hummed as he pushed or probed at Simon's wounds. At last he announced quite jauntily that although the collarbone was knitting well, he'd have to break the arm again and reset it. The inflamed tissues were so tender that the pain of the breaking caused Simon to faint. When he regained consciousness he was once again splinted and the pain in his arm had diminished considerably.

"Quite a constitution you have, young man. Can't remember ever seeing anyone with such a variety of injuries. Cuts, scrapes, burns, punctures, scratches, breaks, the whole lot. Looks like somebody tried to grind you up in a gristmill. Fact is, looks like they succeeded. Amazing you're still walking around with what's happened to your body but, even more than that, I don't know how you're living with that hole in your head. That piece of bone on top is depressed a quarter inch or more. Amazing."

For the first night in many weeks, Simon Kenton slept comfortably; in the morning he was given a new set of clothes and Drouilliard took him before Captain Lernoult. Detroit's temporary commander listened carefully to Drouilliard's story and then began asking questions, most of which dealt with General McIntosh's army. Kenton shrugged. He had never served under McIntosh and consequently knew nothing about him or his army. Well then, what about the strength of the Kentucky settlements? Casually, Kenton resorted to the subterfuge of naming every officer he had ever heard of in Kentucky and elevating each in rank so as to give the impression of a larger force there.

Lernoult was not particularly aggressive. He jotted down a few notations and told Simon he was to consider himself a prisoner of war. He would be given the freedom of the city; he would be given quarters and a job to perform; he would report each Sunday to the commandant, either Lernoult himself or, when he should return from Vincennes, Governor-General Hamilton.

"I would strongly discourage any thoughts you may harbor of escaping," he concluded. "Some have tried. None have succeeded. We are deep in Indian territory here, and there is no way to get through to your American settlements. If you should attempt escape and somehow the Indians do not kill you and you are brought back here alive, you will be executed. There is no second chance. Is that clear?"

It was quite clear and, for the time being at least, Simon Kenton had no intention of attempting escape. Here was a perfect opportunity to spy with immunity on the entire Detroit military establishment; besides, winter was upon them. Summer would be soon enough to take his departure.

When the meeting was over, Drouilliard confronted Bo-nah and told him apologetically but firmly that the prisoner was so important he could not be given up. Governor Hamilton would not be back until next year and he would want to question the frontiersman personally, so they would have to hold him. For this additional disappointment, Bo-nah was given more presents, both for himself and his tribesmen, and he left reasonably satisfied that he had done all he could in the matter of getting Bahd-ler executed.

CHAPTER V

[*January 8, 1779 — Friday*]

IN the Moravian mission at Lichtenau two and a half miles below the forks of the Muskingum, the Reverend David Zeisberger raised his hands in benediction over the more than two hundred fifty Indians assembled before him. How proud he was of his congregation and how thankful to God that more than three fourths of them had discarded their heathen beliefs and accepted Jesus Christ as their true and only Savior.

His eyes filled with tears that this was the conclusion of the last service he and his fellow missionaries would hold here in the "Pasture of Light." In May it would be three years since they came here and they had accomplished much. He thought briefly of the changes that had been wrought. Above the Muskingum forks on the river called Tuscarawas, the influence of the missionaries had manifested itself in the construction of three new Christian Indian villages, each with its own mission building. The closest was Salem, eighteen miles upstream;[1] five miles above that was Gnadenhutten and eight miles farther up was Schoenbrun.

"My children," he addressed the congregation, "it is known to us all that we can no longer stay here. The presence of white men at Lichtenau has been an abomination in the eyes of the Mohawk chief whom you know as Thayendanega and we as Chief Joseph Brant. Now he has announced that we must leave and we have agreed to do so, not for our own protection, which is as nothing, but for you assembled here who have accepted the True Belief.

"Chief Brant has said he will burn this House of God and slay all converts if we do not leave and he shows his intention by bringing his warriors to assemble here on our very Pasture of Light and from here to sally forth to kill and plunder in the white settlements to the east. And so we go with heavy hearts, yet with our hearts singing in the knowledge that you here have come to know the true God and the true Son of God and that you will continue to believe in Him and have faith."

He wiped his eyes and smiled beatifically. "Now it is you who must become the missionaries among your own people, teaching them the Word of God as it has been taught to you and converting others in the gospel of Christianity. Perhaps one day we will return, perhaps not. But may God rest His blessings upon you now and forevermore. Amen."

A number of voices in the congregation mumbled "Amen" in response and then the old Delaware chief once known as Netawatwees but now called Abraham stood. He waited until he had the attention of all and then spoke.

"We are grateful to you and the other missionary fathers for directing our paths. You have shown us the True Light and we will carry it in our hearts wherever we go. We will continue here as before, working our fields and bearing no malice toward man and continuing in our worship of our Lord Jesus Christ.

"Thayendanega does not understand Christianity; will not permit himself to understand. He is more content in the field of war than in the field of peace. He is angry that we have not joined his Confederacy of Wyandots and Mingoes and Delawares, but we will not. We will continue here in peace with all men for all time. Our hearts, too, are heavy at your leaving, but you will be in our prayers and, when our time here is finished, we will be reunited in great joy in Heaven."

[*February 25, 1779 — Thursday*]

The fledgling United States of America had few victories with which to compare it, but certainly the taking of Vincennes and the army of General Hamilton by George Rogers Clark was one of the greatest — if not *the* greatest victory — in the nation's history.

Aware that Hamilton had reoccupied Vincennes with his sizable force and would undoubtedly move against his own pitiful army of less than two hundred in spring, Clark had no intention of waiting to be put on the defensive. It was a bitterly cold winter and no time for an army to consider a long march to assault a considerably larger army safely fortified, but Clark martialed his forces and set off cross-country for Vincennes.

For seventy-one brutal days his men waded to their knees, their waists, even their necks across creeks and vast swampy areas and, except for the iron control of the commander, would certainly have rebelled or deserted. He worked harder than any of the others, deprived himself of food, harangued and cajoled, joked and threatened. And finally, haggard and half frozen, he invaded the British stronghold by complete and devastating surprise and demanded the surrender of Hamilton. With no other choice and considerably awed by Clark's feat, Hamilton handed over his sword. Clark accepted it and instantly claimed the entire region between the Ohio River and the Great Lakes in the name of Virginia.

Only eighteen miles away on White River the news of Hamilton's unconditional surrender reached the Delaware village of Running Fox, chief of the Rabbit clan.[2] He called an immediate council of the elders and gravely they discussed the matter. The future was inevitable now. With a toehold north of the Ohio River, the white woodsmen would soon overflow the countryside and the streams would run red with blood and the skulls of brave men would bleach in the sun.

The Rabbit clan of the Delawares was small in number — less than two hundred, counting women and children. Once they had numbered thousands, but that was before the coming of white men. Since then they had fought and died and migrated and then fought and died and migrated again. Time after time they were forced to leave their lands until finally it became clear that fighting gained them nothing but death, for the eviction always came. The course of wisdom lay in migrating before the trouble came to them.

A half dozen times or more since then they had moved, always farther west. The decision of the elders was the same this time. Less than twenty-four hours after learning of Clark's victory, Chief Running Fox led the Rabbit clan to the west, away from the village where they had lived at peace for the last seven winters, ever since leaving their previous village on the Little Kanawha River.

"This has become a bad land," Running Fox told his assembled people just before they started their trek, "and the smell of death is heavy in the air. Our land here will soon be a delight only to the carrion eaters. This time we will not sink our roots until the grandmother of rivers lies a hundred days to the east of us."

[March 10, 1779 — Wednesday]

Over three months of good food, medical care and rest had worked wonders on Simon Kenton. His bones had knit well and the cuts and bruises had healed. For the rest of his life he would bear the scars of his ordeal — the great wide ax scar at his collarbone, the deep indentation in the center of his skull, the criss-crosses over his entire backside — but on the whole he was well again and at the very peak of his physical prowess.

He had developed a distinct fondness for Peter Drouilliard, whom he saw frequently. On his own part, Drouilliard was something of an enigma. Although apparently a loyal Redcoat, he occasionally shocked Simon with his comments, such as when he nonchalantly told the young frontiersman that when he was ready to make his escape to let him know and he'd do all he could to help. It was something to consider, but Simon was still not altogether sure he could trust the captain. Anyway, he wanted to study Detroit a bit more before making his dash for Kentucky.

In less than a month he would be twenty-four years old and he was an extremely handsome young man. His eyes were still that penetrating blue and his thick auburn hair curled to his shoulders, adding to the aura of strength and self-confidence that surrounded his well-proportioned frame. Many of the residents of Detroit now called him "the Giant" and it was an appellation well deserved. He was easily the largest man there, towering some five inches over six feet and weighing fully two hundred fifty pounds, all of it muscle and bone. He had the look of ruggedness and indestructibility about him. His fists were like small hams and no clothing, no matter how loose, could hide the swell of bulging biceps and calves, thighs and chest muscles. He was, in short, a most fascinating creature to the women of the city, including one in particular.

Simon had met Rachel Edgar only briefly at Kaskaskia when that fort was taken by Clark, and even then he had been struck by her beauty and poise. But at that time she had indicated an interest in Shadrach Bond. Now, however, John Edgar had moved his trading post to the more stable atmosphere of the principal British fort and, naturally, his wife had come along. For her own part, Rachel Edgar remembered Simon well and was as delighted as Simon was surprised at their meeting again. During these intervening days and weeks and months, their association had become quite close.

Rachel Edgar was many things. Above all, she was an incredibly beautiful woman. She was a tall, cornsilk blond with eyes a deep marine blue; she moved with an innate gracefulness so pronounced that nearly any man who saw her stopped dead in his tracks just to watch her pass. But it was not surface beauty alone that made her attractive. She was highly intelligent, a gifted conversationalist, capable of expressing herself admirably, though not imperiously, on a wide variety of subjects. It was, in fact, this trait more than any other that had endeared her to George and Martha Washington some years ago. In those happy days she had always been in demand to attend the many balls and other social functions; but in this western country, where the greater majority of the women were illiterate and rough, she stood apart as might a gorgeous white swan in a hog yard.

It was whispered about that her marriage to portly John Edgar had been one of convenience. Edgar was wealthy and Rachel had a weakness for fine laces and furs and jewelry. Certain it was that little evidence of love was exhibited between them, although there seemed to be an understanding of one another, a tacit agreement to share one another's lives to a certain point but, beyond that, to keep apart, aloof.

It was a monument to his colossal naïveté that Simon Kenton believed

Rachel's interest in him was platonic. She was, after all, nineteen years his senior. He was, in the beginning, blind to hunger in her eyes and the depth of feeling which lay behind every word she spoke to him. When he hinted of his plans to escape Detroit, therefore, he was amazed at the fright she registered and the degree to which she attempted to dissuade him. She begged him not to go, to consider the horror he had undergone on the way here and the worse horror that he had so narrowly escaped. Captured again, he would have no hope of getting away.

But at last she gave up, seeming to recognize that a spirit such as Simon's could not remain fettered for long, even with the generous freedom of movement he was permitted here in Detroit. She kissed his cheek gently and smiled through a mist of tears.

"You'll need provisions," she said. "I'll see what I can do. Promise you won't leave until I can help you."

Simon promised. There would be only one chance at escape and he intended to plan it well. Besides, the weather was still too uncertain to leave immediately. He would wait until the spring rains had slackened, perhaps in early June. But there was no doubt whatever in his mind that he would go.

[*March 19, 1779 — Friday*]

Never before had such a sense of grief and loss and despair smitten the Shawnee nation. The hearts of her people were breaking and there was a pain beyond description in the eyes of all of them.

For so many years it was difficult to remember exactly when they had started, the representatives of the five septs of the Shawnee tribe had been solemnly discussing what to do about the problem of the whites. At each such deliberation it had become progressively clear that there would never be full agreement among them. Those who advocated peace and the adoption of the white man's ways were more than ever strongly convinced that this was the only means by which the Shawnee nation could survive. Those who advocated war were equally certain that survival under such circumstances would be a life without honor, dignity or respect, to which death was infinitely preferable. And now, at last, a decision had been reached — beyond any doubt the most important event that had ever occurred in the tribe.

The Shawnee nation split irrevocably.

There were no tears, but there was a grief of unbelievable depth among all. Not an individual among those leaving this land forever was not leaving behind a member of his family or a friend; and not one of those staying was not saying farewell for the last time to parents or children or other kin or to friends.

Moluntha and Black Fish, flanked by Black Hoof and Blue Jacket,

Chiksika and Black Snake, stood silently together by the side of the *msi-kah-mi-qui* and watched the loading of the packhorses. The French trader, Peter Loramie, shook hands with each and wished them well, promising that he would return immediately after he had guided the great exodus to a new home across the Mississippi River and report on the journey.

At the head of the migrating septs were the chiefs Black Stump and Yellow Hawk and Ki-kusgow-lowa and behind them were nearly four thousand Shawnees, of whom twelve hundred were from Chillicothe alone. Only the aged and infirm rode horses, the remainder walking and the horses used to transport their goods. It would take them nearly a month to reach their new land — a grant of twenty-five square miles on Sugar Creek near Cape Girardeau in the Missouri country. Peter Loramie had nego-tiated with Spanish officials on behalf of the Shawnees and had been heard sympathetically by the Baron de Carondelet, who authorized the grant.

And so now the assembled remaining chiefs and the one hundred warriors left at Chillicothe watched in stoic silence as the cleavage of the Shawnee nation took place. Leaving the Ohio country forever to seek peace were the majority of the Kispokothas, the Peckuwes and the Thawegilas. Remaining to fight until the last man of them should die were the broken remnants of the Chalahgawthas and Maykujays. A large number of the latter two septs had joined those who were migrating, just as a few of the former three had remained behind to fight; among them, most notably, was Black Snake, who gave up the leadership of the Kispokothas to Yellow Hawk in favor of remaining behind, declaring he would never make peace with the *Shemanese*.

And now an emptiness filled the breasts of all the Shawnees, the like of which, until now, was unknown in their entire history.

[*June 3, 1779 — Thursday*]

The warm pressure of Rachel Edgar against him very nearly swayed Simon Kenton at the last moment. This was the hour of good-bye and it was more painful than he imagined it would be. They kissed lingeringly and the wetness of her cheeks was a coolness on his own. Gently he disengaged himself from her arms and held her a little away from him. Her eyes were beseeching but there was no need to ask again if he would stay. In his own eyes the answer was clear and the furrows in her brow deepened and she bit her lower lip.

"I will watch the bundles of trophy scalps the Indians bring in," she said, her voice a dull whisper. She touched his thick hair with one hand and added, "I know that one day I will see yours among them."

Simon put his hand under her chin and lifted her face so he could look into her eyes. He shook his head and kissed her softly on the lips. Silent tears welled from her eyes and he wiped them away with his index finger and then kissed each eye in turn. "I'll miss you." It was all he could say.

"Oh Simon, Simon!" Rachel pulled herself away and fled from his room with a strangled sob and Simon found he was trembling. He stood there for a long, quiet time and thought of what it would be like to stay near her, to forget about returning to Kentucky County. But it was no good. The yearning was strong in him to be his own man again and nothing could sway him from it. Nor was he unaware of the importance of his intelligence about the weakness of Detroit. The fort was undermanned and the city frightened by Clark's success at Vincennes. He was certain that a determined force marching against it could take it easily. But it had to be soon, before the British command could send a new force of men and officers to take the place of those captured at Vincennes. There could be no other way. Tonight, with the supplies provided by John Edgar, he would escape.

Simon couldn't quite understand Edgar, but he was grateful to him. Surely by now the man must know of the close relationship between his wife and Simon, yet he continued to treat the young frontiersman with cordiality; moreover, his help was to be the key to Simon's escape.

"A prisoner who wanted to escape from Detroit," Edgar commented idly once, "would be a fool to follow the shoreline of the lake or even go inland a little way and then cut due south. That's what every man who has tried to escape has done. They've all been caught. The Indians know this country better than anyone and as soon as the word goes out that a prisoner has escaped, it doesn't take them long to track him down. Now if I were a prisoner here and planning an escape, I'd go a few miles northwest, then head straight west through the prairies and marshes for three days at least before turning south. This would take me out of heavily Indian-populated country. I'd travel by night, stay off trails and leave no sign behind. That way I'd take longer to get to the Ohio River, but I'd get there safely."

On another occasion, after Simon casually mentioned that two of his fellow prisoners — Jesse Copher and Robert Bullock — might go on a "little walk" with him, Edgar dumped a large boxful of moccasins on the floor and then left the room after commenting that the box was obviously too full and perhaps Simon could level it off a bit for him.

But it was Rachel who passed on the word to him where the most important supplies would be: hidden in an abandoned outhouse at the edge of the city. There he would find guns and ammunition obtained by Peter Drouilliard and extra clothing and food from her own husband's store. And so he did, an hour after dark, when he arrived with Bullock and Copher. With Simon leading, they filed away toward the deep shadows of a thick wood to the northwest.

As John Edgar had said — and Peter Drouilliard had seconded him — it would take longer, but it was safer.

[*July 2, 1779 — Friday*]

Chuckling to himself, Colonel John Bowman read over the report he had written to Governor Henry about the proposed attack against the principal Shawnee stronghold, Chillicothe. They would leave Kentucky over two hundred fifty strong, catch the Shawnees by surprise and utterly destroy them. Then would the officials in the east see what a militarily conducted campaign was like! He had heard so much about George Rogers Clark's exploits this past year that he was sick of the name.

The knock at his door at this time of night startled him and he called for the visitor to enter. For an instant he thought he was looking at a ghost, for the disheveled giant of a man who strode into the room was a man long supposed dead — Simon Butler.

Simon greeted the colonel and told him that he had hoped to find Colonel George Rogers Clark here at Fort Nelson but was directed, instead, to Bowman.[3] It was perhaps characteristic of Bowman that the first words he spoke to this man were in the nature of a reprimand. He seemed to take a queer delight in driving home the point that the two experienced frontiersmen, Butler and Montgomery, had been taken while the novice, fat little George Clarke, had come home with the intelligence he'd been sent after. Simon cared little about what the offensive young colonel thought of him, but when he maligned Montgomery, a dangerous spark came alive in Simon's eye.

"Alex Montgomery was killed trying to save my life," he said. "I'll listen to nothing said against him."

Bowman caught himself abruptly, as if suddenly realizing the peril of pushing this man too far. He became businesslike then and asked Simon to tell him what had happened. Quickly and with much skipping of details of his treatment by the Indians, Simon gave him the essentials, including the arduous thirty-day march through unknown Indian territory — a trip he could have made on his own in two weeks but during which he was hampered by his two fellow escapees who were next to helpless in the woods. He had dropped off the pair here at Fort Nelson and come immediately to report. Toward the end of his narration Simon became more animated.

"Colonel," he said, "Detroit's a ripe plum ready to be picked. They're undermanned, underarmed and scared. Fresh troops and supplies can't get there for a long time yet and the whole city can fall to us easily if we go in now. Can you raise the men to march against it?"

Bowman reflected. If he could take Detroit! Almost instantly he rejected the idea. The march against Chillicothe was all set. Besides, what did this

backwoods lout know about military strength? Suppose they marched all
the way up there and met a force that routed them. Where would his
career be then?

He waved his hand as if brushing off a fly. The answer was no. Frankly,
he didn't feel he could trust Butler. Why didn't he go see his good friend
Colonel Clark at Vincennes? For a man as good at pulling off surprise
attacks as he, this might be just his meat. That was all. Dismissed.

Simon didn't trust himself to speak. He stalked from the room and very
nearly shattered the door when he slammed it behind him. Go to Clark,
eh? By God, that's exactly what he'd do!

[July 5, 1779 — Monday]

"Simon! Simon Butler! My God, man, you're supposed to be dead!"

George Rogers Clark leaped from his chair and embraced the big
frontiersman in a great hug, beside himself with joy. Grinning widely,
Simon allowed himself to be pulled into the room and seated at the table
before a fine roast.

The colonel couldn't get over the fact that his spy was back again and he
fired a whole series of questions at him, scarcely giving the frontiersman an
opportunity to swallow. Catching himself at last, he apologized and let the
man eat. But now it was Kenton who questioned Clark on details of the
Vincennes campaign. Clark smiled with pleasure at his friend's open
admiration of the feat and insisted that it was because of the admirable
scouting done by Simon, Bond and Batty. But there was a note of disappointment in his voice as he told how the reinforcements he had
expected in June had not come; and now he had received word from
Virginia that the government could not spare anyone for a good while.

"I've turned command of the post here over to Colonel Hugh McGary,
Simon. Know him?" Simon shook his head and Clark continued. "Came
out here with Bowman. Cut pretty much from the same cloth. You
probably won't like him, but he does know soldiering and I needed him.
Wanted him to keep control here while I went against Detroit."

"Detroit! George, that's why I came. You could take Detroit with a
handful of men. Less than you had for Kaskaskia. The only really good man
they had there for fighting was Captain Depeyster and he went up to Fort
Mackinac three hundred miles north of Detroit to command the little
garrison there. All that's left at Detroit is Lernoult with a few men and
he's no fighter. We could take it easily!"

Clark momentarily became enthusiastic but at length he shook his head.
"God knows I want to take it, Simon. And, like you say, there's no better
time. But since the campaign I've lost nearly half my men, some in holding
the three forts we took and others who've gone back to work their settlements. Even if I could take Detroit with what I've got, I couldn't hold

it without reinforcements — and Virginia says they're just not available."

Kenton asked about Bowman's company and was stunned when Clark told him of Bowman's planned expedition against Chillicothe. With such a force of men, Clark admitted, he would not hesitate an instant in marching against Detroit. More than ever now, Kenton disliked Bowman; he found it hard to believe that the arrogant little colonel could be so disdainful of Simon's services on the expedition that he hadn't even told him it was planned. And now even the meeting with Clarke, upon which he'd pinned so much hope, had proven a dismal failure.

They continued their talk and Simon told Clark all he knew of Detroit and its men; but gradually the conversation drifted to Kentucky County and Clark filled him in on what had happened there since his capture. The settlements were growing ever larger and stronger and the whole area was filling out with land jobbers and surveyors. More than a thousand new emigrants had come, counting women and children, since he left and new settlements were forming everywhere. An occasional Indian raid took place, but these were mostly horse-stealing forays that didn't amount to much. There was even a possibility — remote, but a possibility nonetheless — that a peace treaty could be reaffirmed and the settlement of the Kentucky lands could go on in comparative safety. But Bowman's invasion of Chillicothe would certainly end that.

And now, suddenly, there was a strong yen in Simon to get back again to his beloved canelands and Blue Licks, to see again the forts and his companions — Boone and Logan and Harrod — all of whom thought him dead.

He spent the night with Clark; but early in the morning he was on his way again to Kentucky.

[July 10, 1779 — Saturday]

It was, for Colonel John Bowman, fortunate beyond words that only a few months previous to his attack the great split in the Shawnee nation had occurred. It was equally fortunate that at the time of his assault on Chillicothe, considerably more than half its remaining warriors were attending a council meeting at Wapatomica. Had the first not been true, his army of two hundred sixty-four men would have been annihilated to the last man. Had the second not been true, he would have been met by a hundred warriors instead of a total fighting force of thirty-five men and boys.

He was fortunate in these matters because even though his army outnumbered the defenders nearly eight to one, he suffered an awful loss, due almost entirely to his inept commanding. Certainly he had everything going for him at the onset.

The army had come within sight of Chillicothe at night, but through poor judgment in allowing a few men to show themselves, it had lost the element of total surprise. Immediately the Indians sounded the alarm and an exchange of shots commenced. Women and children could be seen running from cabin to cabin in great confusion, finally gathering in the most central and strongest places for defense.

Although the return fire indicated a scarcity of the enemy, Bowman was afraid to rush the cabins and overwhelm the foe by force of numbers. Instead, he ordered a sporadic fire be kept up until daylight. By then all the inhabitants had gathered in the council house and several *wegiwas* close to it, as the strongest points of defense.

By daylight it was obvious that, except for these few structures, the sprawling town was empty; and so Bowman ordered his men to move in and fire the buildings. This was done, but the soldiers and militiamen, suddenly more concerned with the loot they might get than with the object of the mission, took their time going through each *wegiwa* before setting it afire. By the time the flimsy structures were burning, a great mass of kettles, blankets, fur robes and silver ornaments had been gathered — and, in the process, the Shawnee defenders had managed to pick off ten of Bowman's men. Not a single Indian had yet been wounded.

With the enemy in the very palm of his hand, Bowman now ordered his troops to withdraw. A militiaman had reported finding a huge drove of horses in the woods and Bowman ordered them rounded up and driven back toward Kentucky. By ten o'clock in the morning, Chillicothe was abandoned and the army, jubilant with the loot it had gotten, was driving over twelve dozen horses toward the Ohio.

The Shawnees, hardly daring to believe the large force had pulled away, quickly took advantage of the situation. Two dozen horses which the whites had been unable to catch were rounded up and mounted and now began a nagging harassment that ate away at the army's rear.

Bowman's army had not marched more than eight or ten miles before the attacks of sniping began. One by one the riders at the rear were cut down, until Bowman was forced to draw his army into a square for defense. With that, the attackers disappeared; but as soon as the army started forward again they returned and more of the rear guard were shot down. Again the army was formed into a square by Bowman's orders and again the attackers disappeared. Three, four, five times the same thing happened and finally, almost beside themselves with rage, Captain James Harrod and two of his lieutenants, acting on their own, ordered a hundred of the army to throw down their loot and attack the small party besieging them.

Rushed upon in this manner, the twenty-four warriors now dispersed and abandoned the harassment. By now more than thirty whites had been killed and double that number wounded — yet Bowman, upon reaching the Kentucky shore with the horses and much of the valuable plunder, had the unmitigated gall to declare the expedition a great victory!

Camp was made for the night and the booty disposed of by auction, following which the army was disbanded on the spot and each man sought his own home in his own way.

Back in Chillicothe, the warriors absent at the Wapatomica council had returned to find their homes burned, their possessions taken and two casualties among the Indians — their subchief Red Pole was dead and the principal chief of the Shawnees, Black Fish, was lying in his *wegiwa* in great pain from a severe bullet wound. The ball had shattered his hip socket, shooting splinters of bone into the surrounding flesh. In his eyes was the knowledge of death but, with it, the belief that it would be a long time in coming.

The torch Bowman had held to the village of Chillicothe was as nothing to the fire this action ignited in the remaining Ohio Shawnees. No longer were the assaults on the Can-tuc-kee lands to be hit-and-run attacks with a few horses taken. The firing of Chillicothe was an outright declaration of war and it had exactly the result George Rogers Clark had feared. It drove the remaining Indians not only to accept the arms and supplies of the British, but to ask for a British army to join them in attacking the *Shemanese* settlements.

Britain was delighted to oblige.

[August 24, 1779 — Tuesday]

The door was shoved open with a crash that rocked the room and John Edgar and his wife both leaped to their feet. Rachel hurriedly pulled her robe less revealingly around her and Edgar moved angrily toward Lernoult, who stood in the doorway flanked by soldiers.

"Captain Lernoult! What is the meaning of this? How dare you enter —"

"*Major* Lernoult, if you please!" the officer snapped. "Mr. Edgar, you and Mrs. Edgar are under arrest."

"On what charge?" Edgar's voice cracked a little and Rachel paled.

"Primarily for helping numerous American prisoners to escape, among them Simon Butler, Jesse Copher and Robert Bullock. Generally, for corresponding with Americans and counseling savages against the British cause." He stepped to one side and motioned to the squad with him. "Put them in irons," he said. "Both of them. They will be transferred aboard ship day after tomorrow and taken to Niagara for permanent imprisonment there."

He spun on his heel, ignoring the words of protest rising behind him; as he strode toward the quarters of Captain Peter Drouilliard, a second squad fell in behind him. Drouilliard's door was opened just as unceremoniously and the officer looked up in surprise from a letter he was writing at a small desk.

"Major?"

"Peter Drouilliard, consider yourself under arrest for suspicion of aiding three American prisoners — Simon Butler, Jesse Copher and Robert Bullock — to escape. Confirmation of the charge is expected soon. Until that time, however, you are to consider yourself stripped of rank and all your goods and monies are to be confiscated. Since you are — were — a member of the military, summary execution will follow upon confirmation of the charges. For the time being you will be confined to a cell but not shackled unless you show it to be necessary for us to do so."

Again he spun about and left the room and this time he walked away alone. He rounded the corner of the nearest building and then leaned against the wall and released a deep breath. He was not used to this role of inquisitor and he found, somewhat to his own amusement, that his face was beaded with perspiration and that he was trembling.

[*October 2, 1779 — Saturday*]

Simon Kenton found a deep peace and contentment in once again roaming the hills and valleys of the land he had sought so long in vain. How many times just a year ago had he been certain he would never again see any of it?

The experience with the Shawnees had marked him. No longer was there any trace of boyishness about him. Even though he smiled frequently, his laughter was a rare thing and his eyes reflected depth and experience. Already there were definite lines forming around his mouth and eyes; lines which could, in an instant, deepen and harden in a frightening scowl.

More and more often now he was coming back to the canebrake cabin he and Tom Williams had lived in together for so long. He planted no corn but it was nice to know he actually had a home of his own where he could stay as long as he wished without feeling beholden for the pleasure.

This night a rapping came on his door — the first time it had ever happened. Instantly he snatched up his rifle and trained it on the entry. Quietly he lifted the latch and then stepped back and called the visitor to enter. A bedraggled, scraggly-bearded man walked in and stopped, his shoulders slumped in weariness. He saw Simon, but when he spoke it was more to himself at first than to the frontiersman.

"It's a long way here from Detroit." He smiled and added faintly, "Greetings, friend of Logan." With that he slumped unconscious to the floor.

Simon did not recognize him until after he had closed and barred the door, picked the man up and carried him to the bed. When the light of the lamp shone on the man's face he caught his breath. It was Peter Drouilliard.

It took some time to bring the man around and then there could be no questions until he had eaten. It had obviously been a long time between meals, for he nearly choked in his haste to wolf down the meat and bread and corn pudding that Simon placed before him.

At last he was able to tell the story: after being arrested he had let on that for some time he had been hiding small amounts of the Crown's money in the woods nearby. As principal contact with the Indians, it would have been an easy thing for him to do. A gullible guard, too greedy for his own good, had been coaxed into letting Drouilliard lead him to the site. Instead of money, he wound up with a huge lump on his head and an escaped prisoner. Since the Indians knew Drouilliard well and knew nothing of his trouble, they welcomed him at each village. It was the last portion of the journey — from Chillicothe to Kenton's cabin — that was the hardest. He was no frontiersman.

The ramifications of what he had done struck him solidly now and he became afraid. Everything he had was gone: money, property, goods, rank, citizenship, friends, even his wife and son. Simon shook his head, reached out and squeezed the small man's shoulders. "Not everything, Peter. You still have my friendship and you always will. And as for land, across the creek are two hundred prime acres I claimed during my first year here. They're yours. This house is yours as long as you want to stay. For the rest of your life, if you like."

[*October 15, 1779 — Friday*]

Black Fish was dead.

Since Bowman's attack on Chillicothe last July he had lived an existence of agony unending. Little by little and day by day he slipped toward the brink and finally, just before the light of dawn three days ago, the final breath of the principal chief of the Shawnees had wheezed out.

The word spread immediately to all the Shawnee villages and from near and far they came to witness the laying away of their great chief. It was, for many who came, the first they had seen Chillicothe since Bowman's attack and, though it had been rebuilt to the needs, it was only a shell of the great Shawnee center it had once been and they were shocked and angry. Instead of a thousand or more *wegiwas*, there were only a few hundred and the ugly mounds of ash of those which had been burned still bore mute testimony to the attack by the *Shemanese*.

Inside the *msi-kah-mi-qui*, Black Fish was stretched out on his back on a sort of low table. He had been washed and shaved and cleansed and now was wrapped only in a fine new blanket. On the edge of the table and on the earth beneath and around it were a great collection of goods brought

by his tribesmen, mostly calicos and belts and ribbons. Beside the body lay
his four most important possessions in life: his rifle, tomahawk, knife and
pipe.

A great number of Indians were present and all of them wore loose
clothing and their hair was unbraided. Many of the braves had painted
their faces in whorls of yellow and blue and vermilion and all of the men
were smoking. As they entered the huge room they looked first upon the
corpse of him who had been their leader, their old and beloved and
courageous chief, their counselor in peace and war. Then they sat in silence
on the floor wherever there was room. No one spoke and for hours they sat
thus. Not an individual present was without tears of mourning in his eyes
over the death of his chief. This was no affectation or showy display for
effect, but a deep and heartfelt grief.

Outside the *msi-kah-mi-qui* was accumulated a large quantity of wild
meat downed by young men of this village who had been sent out expressly
for this purpose. There were twenty deer and forty wild turkeys, three bear,
two elk and a bison, a dozen raccoons, fifty quail and twenty ducks and
twenty geese. And there were more than a hundred flat loaves of hard
bread. Tecumseh was in charge of this horde and he commanded six other
boys, all equally armed with six-foot sticks. They were positioned strategi-
cally around the pile to keep any dog from molesting it.

At last, toward evening, Chiksika and seven other warriors entered the
msi-kah-mi-qui and gently slid four wide rawhide straps under the body.
Each of the men gripped one end of a strap and together they lifted the
body and carried it directly from the room to the burial site in the
Shawnee graveyard two miles southwest along the banks of a small creek.[4]

No child under eight was permitted to accompany the procession lest he
make some noise or cry during the solemn rite. Immediately following the
body walked the three daughters and two sons of Black Fish and the family
of Pucksinwah, his charges. Behind them came Black Hoof, now the new
principal chief of the Shawnees, and behind him came Moluntha and
Black Beard and Black Snake and all the other chiefs and subchiefs
according to rank. In this group was Blue Jacket. Finally, some distance
behind the chiefs, came first the warriors of Chillicothe, then those of
other Shawnee villages, all of them followed by their squaws, behind whom
came the children between ages eight and fifteen.

The grave was already dug — a narrow rectangle scarcely two feet across,
seven feet long and three and a half feet deep. At the bottom a split
puncheon lay and another the same size was placed on edge along each of
the length-walls of the grave. Carefully, Black Fish's body was lowered
until it lay on its back on the bottom puncheon and then the last clothing
he wore in health was placed atop his body. His old moccasins were cut
into strips and pieces and put with the other clothing. No weapon or food

or other memento was put into the grave. A final puncheon was laid over the chief and the effect of these puncheons was now something of a rectangular open-ended box in which lay the chief.

At length Black Hoof stepped to the head of the grave and removed a cloth bundle from his belt. From the throats of the thousand or more mourners there now came the eerie, fluctuating notes of the death chant — a throbbing, melancholy sound that at once embodied tenderness and regret, sorrow and despair and a deep pervading grief. Black Hoof opened the little bag and dipped his fingers into it and sprinkled some coarsely ground material into the grave. This was *nilu-famu* — sacred tobacco — a final sacrament. Slowly around the grave Black Hoof moved as the chant continued, sprinkling more of the grains at each step onto the puncheon below. When the bag was empty and he was back where he had begun, he dropped the empty cloth onto the center of the puncheon and turned and headed directly back to the *msi-kah-mi-qui*. Still chanting, all but three men followed him.

Chiksika was one of the three who remained behind and only when the chant had become a barely audible sound in the distance did they set about scooping up the earth in their cupped hands to fill the hole. It took them half an hour to finish and then a single smooth stone the size of a small pumpkin was placed at the foot of the grave and the trio left and went straight to the Little Miami River.

Here they stripped themselves and threw away their clothing. They entered the river and with handsful of sand they scrubbed their bodies until they were pink and each man thrust his fingers down his throat and forced himself to vomit. They moved upstream a short distance, drank until they could drink no more and once again forced themselves to vomit, thereby cleansing their bodies both inside and out. A short distance upstream they found and donned the fresh loin cloths awaiting them on the bank and jogged back to the village.

When they reentered the crowded *msi-kah-mi-qui*, quiet discussion was being held, each person who cared to contributing some special little memory of his own personal contact with the great chief. Outside the squaws were roasting the game and as it was finished it was brought in and distributed to everyone present. And so the ceremony continued far into the night, concluding only as the first gray shafts of dawn streaked the eastern sky.

Black Fish had been greatly loved by his people.

His death would be avenged.

[October 31, 1779 — Sunday]

Simon Kenton did not dislike the skinny, rawboned young surveyor he met again at Danville as much as he felt sorry for him. Not too many men came to the Kentucky settlements wearing chips on their shoulders; but lately, with constantly more people coming in and the settlements growing into substantial towns, there had been an influx of all kinds. Over the past few months, Danville and Crow's Station had become somewhat notorious as places where the taverns were always crowded and whiskey flowed copiously. Rarely a night went by without fights, some of a serious nature, breaking out among the rowdies and the more established settlers in the area.

Not a drinking man himself, Simon did not normally spend much time at the taverns but occasionally, as now, it became necessary. Henry Lee had left his own settlement of Leestown in the hands of John Todd and was making the rounds of the various settlements in an effort to get some idea of what the current strength of Kentucky County was, and how many men might be available should it become necessary to defend the county in the spring against retaliation by the Shawnees for the destruction of Chillicothe by Bowman. Simon, who happened to be at Leestown at the time, was glad to accompany him.

They traveled on horseback together to Ruddell's Mills and Bryant's Station, McClelland's and Harrodsburg and Boonesboro. It was at this latter place where they first came across the lean surveyor who was a member of a large party of line-cutters led by Dr. Jonas Walker. They had been running the boundary line between North Carolina and Virginia but, with winter coming on, had come in to stay until spring.

From their first encounter there at Boonesboro, the big frontiersman and the rangy surveyor had hit it off badly. The surveyor, whose name was Andrew Jackson, seemed to resent Simon for no better reason than for his size and reputation. They were no more than a year apart in age and Jackson, it seemed, was enormously proud of the fact that he was in command of the packhorse men, a rough-and-tumble crew, every one of whom was older than he and every one of whom he had whipped. Simon appeared to him as something of a challenge and his comments to and around the big frontiersman were such as might have made a less even-tempered man fly into a rage. But Simon refused to rise to the bait.

It was because of Jackson's crew that most of the tavern fights broke out; they seemed to delight in moving from one settlement to another in search of donnybrooks. And because Crow's Station, four miles from Danville, was apparently the most riotous town and within easy riding distance of both Danville and Harrodsburg and even Logan's Fort, here was where they finally settled. There was another reason, as well: Jackson had become rather enamored of Rachel Donelson, the beautiful young daughter of Colonel John Donelson who was temporarily living at Harrodsburg after he had laid out Nashville to the south.

Simon was never quite sure how the fight started there in Gill's Tavern.

He and Henry Lee had ridden into Crow's Station late in the afternoon and stopped to eat dinner. They were on hand when Jackson and his crew stormed in. The men drank heavily and became noisy and rough. Quite unexpectedly Simon was struck a terrific blow and knocked out of his chair. He looked up to find Jackson, wild-haired, his face flushed and eyes bright with the liquor he had drunk, standing over him with his fists clenched.

The fight was brief and conclusive. Within two minutes Jackson realized he had bitten off far more than he could chew. Three minutes later he lay battered and bloody on the tavern floor, looking through dazed eyes at the huge angry man towering above him.

A wild light was beginning to show in Simon's eyes, the same rage kindling in him that had burned during his fight years ago with William Leachman. It would undoubtedly have gone further here, except that Lee stepped in and took Simon's arm and coaxed him away.

Jackson had learned two important things about the frontiersman. The first was during the fight: here was a man he could not whip. The second occurred as he lay on the floor looking up at him: here was a man who did not fight for fun, a man who fought with a deadly seriousness and who would probably have killed him if his friend hadn't stepped in just in time.

Andrew Jackson may have been wild, but he wasn't without common sense. Simon Butler was a man he would hereafter leave strictly alone.[5]

[November 2, 1779 — Tuesday]

At Upper Sandusky the assembled chiefs sat silently on the ground of the *msi-kah-mi-qui* floor, their blankets firmly wrapped about them and the air slightly fogged with the smoke from their pipes and the several small fires. There were Shawnees, Wyandots, Hurons, Ottawas, Tawas, Tuscarawas, Chippewas, Delawares and a few Miamis and Potawatomies. Their attention was directed to the center of the room where, resplendent in his full dress uniform of scarlet and gold, Captain Henry Byrd, flanked by Alexander McKee on one side and the three Girty brothers on the other, now stood and raised his arms for silence.[6]

"Brothers," he said, "I come bearing news of great moment to you. Our father across the eastern sea, King George, has become deeply concerned over how you have been treated by the Americans. He has wept over the burning of Chillicothe this past summer and the death of the great Shawnee chief, Black Fish, and he fears for the sanctity of your lands unless steps are taken to wipe out this threat.

"Brothers, my heart is glad that I am able to tell you that now Lieutenant General Frederick Haldemand, governor of Canada, upon instructions from the King, has authorized an invasion not only to crush the Kentucky forts, but also to force the Virginia frontier back east of the

Allegheny Mountains. Such invasion, brothers, will not only regain for you your traditional hunting grounds south of the river, but it will prevent the western growth of American Colonies now threatening your lands."

There was a deep murmuring as he paused and he smiled faintly at the favorable reaction. He raised a hand again and continued:

"My brothers, listen! My chief has empowered me to lead this invasion of the Kentucky lands and it will be an invasion the like of which this country has not heretofore witnessed. My chief will provide an army made up of British regular soldiers, Tories and officers from Detroit and green-coated rangers from Canada. The Kentucky forts are strong and have withstood attack before, but they will not be able to withstand this attack. We will march against them not only with tomahawk and knife and flintlock, but with cannons as well — the great brass guns which can knock down the wall of a fort with a single shot. For this they have no defense.

"Brothers, the winter season is upon us now and in the spring there is planting you must do so that your grain may grow for next winter's use. Therefore, the invasion will not start until the corn and melons and vegetables have been planted. Until that time, my chief will continue to buy scalps and prisoners from you at Detroit. And when the time comes to go, your friends beside me, Agent McKee and Simon Girty and his brothers, will come to you with the news and we wish for every warrior who can, to come along. The day of reckoning will be at hand for the *Shemanese!*"

For a long time the *msi-kah-mi-qui* rang with the screams and howls of approbation for the plan. There was no doubt that the Indians would join this invasion when the time came.

[*March 30, 1780 — Thursday*]

As usual, Simon Kenton spent most of the early winter — November and December — lending his hand and his gun at one of the newest and weakest of the Kentucky stations. As Robert Patterson so long ago had vowed he would, he had built his settlement of Lexington, but it was a weak station at best, founded after his return from a trip to the east; he had brought back with him a number of families anxious to start life anew in a city they would help to develop.

The work of building continued throughout the fall and winter and it was obvious that Patterson was not going to be content with a second-rate station any longer. The stockade he laid out embraced an acre rectangularly, with substantial blockhouses at each angle. Instead of a high log-paling fence surrounding a series of individual cabins, the homes were built as an integral part of the wall. These cabins adjoined and ran on a line between respective blockhouses; in those areas where the cabins did not yet join, pickets were erected in the intervening space, three or four inches thick. At either end of the stockade was a heavy gate with huge wooden hinges and log bars.

In between stints of working with Patterson and his men on the fortifications and bringing in meat for them, Simon once again began to use his tomahawk to claim various parcels of land he admired. Up until this winter he had made his tomahawk improvements on something like a thousand acres of land at various points in Kentucky, mostly in the area of Limestone and the cabin he had built along Lawrence Creek at the edge of the canelands. Now, however, he expanded his operations. Within a month of his arrival at Lexington he had claimed settlement and preemption rights to fourteen hundred acres on South Elkhorn Creek and from this time forward he planned to increase his efforts considerably at claiming good land wherever he found it.

By early January, with much of the Lexington fortification completed, Simon again started on rounds of visiting the newer stations — Martin's, McAfee's, Bryant's and Ruddell's — the latter a rebuilt version of Hinkson's abandoned station on the South Licking, where Isaac Ruddell had begun construction of a grist mill. In all these areas Simon claimed more land, but once again he was most often to be found in the Limestone Creek area.

It was an especially cold winter this year and the first time since he had come to the Kentucky country that the ground was snow-covered from late November through early March. This made difficulties for the settlers but still they welcomed it. With weather like this there was little likelihood of Shawnee attacks. There was, in fact, a prevailing fear of when the weather should break, for rumor had penetrated every settlement that retaliation for Bowman's attack on Chillicothe would come then.

And so it did.

As if atoning for the severe winter it had delivered up, nature now provided a month of March more like early May. Warm zephyrs filled with the scent of fresh rich earth chased one another in little eddies and only twice during the entire month did the temperature dip below freezing overnight. With the warmth came a sharp increase in depredations by small roving Shawnee bands. Cattle were slaughtered by herds, abandoned cabins and settlements were burned, scores of horses stolen and all too frequently men, women and children were either killed or captured. In Boonesboro, just three days ago, in the very shadow of the fort where they were digging out a poplar log for a canoe, Colonel Richard Calloway, Pemberton Rollins and Ebenezer Eliot had been killed by a party of twenty Indians. But there were many others. Fortunately, no attacks had yet been made this year on the inhabited forts, but individuals were rarely safe.

As had to happen sooner or later, the forts were no longer large enough to house the increase in population and lonely cabins were springing up all over. If these appeared well defended they were left alone, but it was always a moment of extreme danger in the morning to open the door and step outside. More than one settler, his wife or child had been met by arrow or bullet and crumpled dead on the threshold.

And the frightening suspicion remained that all this was but a prelude.

[*May 13, 1780 — Saturday*]

Tecumseh and his younger brother, Lowawluwaysica, were almost exact opposites in virtually every respect. At twelve, Tecumseh was quiet and polite to his companions. At nine, Lowawluwaysica was loud and boisterous and rude to everyone his own age or younger. Tecumseh was modest and when he spoke of his accomplishments, as it was proper to do during the talk-times in the evening, he did so with a great truthfulness, playing down his exploits rather than boasting of them. Lowawluwaysica was a decided braggart and took great pleasure in crowing extravagantly over anything he did.

Even physically the pair differed. Lowawluwaysica was rather short and scrawny, on the very borderline of what might have been termed a true runt. He was the last born of the triplets and the other two were just normal little boys, undistinguished in looks or actions. Not so Lowawluwaysica. He was perceptibly bucktoothed and his features seemed to have been thrown together carelessly. His laughter was a shrill and irritating cackle and he was quick to take offense and fly into blind rages. Tecumseh, on the other hand, was tall for his age, well proportioned, even-tempered and, with his smooth symmetrical features, certainly the most good-looking youth in the whole of Chillicothe.

Tecumseh could, with ease, best anyone his own age or up to three years older in virtually anything; but Lowawluwaysica was hard put to hold his own, even with those one or two years his junior. Perhaps it was for this reason that he followed Tecumseh adoringly wherever his older brother went. As Tecumseh loved and admired his elder brother, Chiksika, so Lowawluwaysica exhibited love and admiration for Tecumseh. And as Tecumseh learned rapidly and well those lessons taught him by Chiksika and emulated his twenty-four-year-old brother's characteristics, so Lowawluwaysica attempted to emulate Tecumseh. But mostly he failed.

Chiksika and Tecumapese took great pains to instill in Tecumseh a deep and abiding love for truth, a wholehearted contempt for meanness and sordidness and a steadfast courage in all circumstances. But Lowawluwaysica always hovered on the fringe of censure from his elders because of his lackadaisical nature in such matters. While he didn't quite dare to be blatantly untruthful with his elders, he more often than not skirted the edge of veracity through embroidery or omission. He could be diabolically clever, and he was skillfully adept at concealing his deceptions and meanness.

This was not to say the love Lowawluwaysica felt for Tecumseh was false. It was honest within the bounds of honesty as he knew it, but it was a love that constantly wrestled with an equally powerful jealousy and envy of his brother's character and popularity. Strong though this feeling was, he somehow managed to keep it as covert as his love for Tecumseh was overt. The only one in the family who suspected this duality of his emotion was their twenty-two-year-old sister.

Lowawluwaysica was happy this day. He realized that Tecumapese had this suspicion, even though she had not yet put it into words. And now chances were that she never would. At last night's dance she had swayed to the chanting rhythm in exact time with Wasegoboah — Stand Firm — a nephew of their late Chief Black Fish. She had whispered to him and he to her. Their bare hands had met and Tecumapese had smiled and recipro- cated when Wasegoboah's hands had searched out her body. She had gone with him then to his *wegiwa* and had thus become his wife and the mother- to-be of his children. And this morning she had returned and taken her few belongings to her new domicile and her brothers were happy for her, for Wasegoboah was a fine man and a brave warrior.

And Lowawluwaysica was happiest of all, for Chiksika was easier for him to fool than Tecumapese and from this time forward the care and educa- tion of Pucksinwah's children would be the sole responsibility of Chiksika.

[*May 30, 1780 — Sunday*]

It was obvious to Simon that the party of eight men camped near their beached canoe on the shore just below Three Islands was new to this country. Their fire was much too large and the wood they were burning too green and smoky. It was this smoke that he had detected over a mile distant and stealthily followed to its source. These had to be newcomers. No Indians or seasoned frontier people would have broadcast their pres- ence in such manner.

Simon was amused and yet disgusted. Little wonder so many of the river travelers were being killed by Indians. These men were prime examples of fatal carelessness. He was able to get within twenty feet of them and still they had neither seen nor heard him. Of the eight, only one had his rifle in his lap; two had theirs leaning against rocks nearby and the rest had apparently left theirs in the well-loaded canoe, its bow pulled a few feet up onto the sand. He marveled that they had made it this far safely and guessed they wouldn't live long if they continued in this manner.

The frontiersman nearly laughed aloud at the awful start he gave them when he called hello. One of them, a friendly, florid-faced man appeared to be spokesman and, after the initial start, welcomed Simon to the camp. He looked over the big man carefully and then nodded.

"Expect," he said, "you're the feller we heard about upstream who helps all the newcomers get to the settlements. Be your name Simon Butler?"

Simon told them it was and then carefully explained the danger they were letting themselves in for with their carelessness or ignorance. He helped them drown the fire until every last puff of smoke was gone and then together they pulled the canoe the rest of the way out of the water and into concealment. Simon then showed then the proper way to build a hot and yet essentially smokeless fire, warning them as well to keep their guns primed at all times and never farther away from themselves than arm's reach.

Sam Childers, the leader who had initially welcomed Simon, was properly chagrined, admitting that they had a lot to learn about this country. They had come from Virginia and were hoping to settle in one of the new towns they had heard about here — Harrodsburg or McClelland's or Danville. Simon agreed to lead them wherever they wanted to go.

One of the men looked vaguely familiar to Simon and as they ate he sat beside him, a little bit apart from the others, and struck up a conversation. The man talked about the east and how the war was going and how, shortly after his younger brother Benjamin had been killed in a battle with the British, he had decided to leave the rest of his family and seek land in the west. He said he hailed from Fauquier County in the Bull Run Mountain area and Simon caught his breath. Very casually the frontiersman mentioned how he had once been through that very area and remembered that at the time the countryside thereabouts was in something of a turmoil about a young man named Kenton who had killed another fellow named Leacher or something like that.

His companion laughed. "You've got it all backwards," he said. "His name was Leachman. Bill Leachman. And it was he who killed Simon Kenton. They tried him for murder and I was in the party that searched for Simon's body up on White Rock Ridge." He shook his head. "We never did find it and so Leachman was acquitted for lack of evidence."

Simon was stunned. It was only with the greatest of self-control that he maintained an outward calm. "You knew this Simon Kenton, then?"

"Knew him! Why, man, he was my younger brother!"

Simon was overwhelmed. His own brother! No wonder he had thought the man looked familiar. Nine years had made a considerable difference in John Kenton but there was no doubt in Simon's mind now who he was. He reached out and grasped the newcomer's arm with unexpected fierceness.

"Then you must be John Kenton!"

John looked startled but nodded and admitted that was his name, but how did Simon know him? They had never met, had they? A rush of hot tears nearly blinded the young frontiersman and he blinked rapidly to hold them back. His voice was hoarse as he spoke now.

"Aye, John, we know one another well. Don't you recognize your own brother?"

John Kenton looked incredulously at the man beside him. When finally he recognized the frontiersman for who he was, he was beyond speech. They embraced and tears streamed down the cheeks of both. The other men gathered around and there was rejoicing and congratulations extended.

The brothers could not seem to hear enough from one another and they talked long into the night. John told him that both their parents were still alive, although their father was now seventy-nine and his health was beginning to fail some. Their mother was very well and, as he had mentioned earlier, Benjamin had been killed early in the Revolution. The rest of their brothers and sisters were married now and had their own families, except for himself.

Simon, still unable to comprehend the fact that Leachman wasn't dead after all, asked about him. John told again of the trial and acquittal and how Leachman had gone back to his father's farm where, less than a year later, he and Ellen had had a son. Ellen, unfortunately, suffered severely in the birth and within a few months had died.

"And so all these years, Simon," John concluded, "you've been running from something that never happened. Lord, but it's good to see you alive and well. I'd never have recognized you, you've changed so much. It's hard to believe that the man the whole frontier knows about and calls Simon Butler is my own brother."

"Simon Butler no longer, John," the frontiersman answered. "From this day on, everyone's going to know me by my right name."

He spoke his own name aloud and smiled at the savor of it on his tongue.

[June 22, 1780 — Thursday]

Captain Henry Byrd was beginning to wonder if perhaps he hadn't let himself in for more than he had anticipated — not where the enemy was concerned, but in connection with his allies, the Indians.

When he had told the council of the various chiefs last fall of the proposed expedition against the Kentucky forts and asked their help, he had expected that at the most only about a hundred warriors would join him. But when he arrived at the mouth of the Auglaize River leading his own hundred uniformed Redcoats and the seventy Canadian green-coated Rangers, he was met by a force of over three hundred war-painted warriors — mostly Delawares, Hurons, Wyandots, Ottawas and Mingoes, but with a scattering of Chippewas, Tawas, Miamis and Potawatomies as well. Nor was this to be all. The Shawnees, he was told, would join them en route.

He had a small stockade built at the point where the Auglaize joined the Maumee River, here to store some emergency provisions.[7] When the work was completed they paddled their canoes up the Auglaize until they reached the portage point called Wapakoneta by the Indians.[8] From this point the canoes were carried fifteen miles due south along the portage trail to the upper Great Miami River where they were once again launched.

Every day as they floated farther down this stream more Indians joined them, now mostly Shawnees. By the time they reached the mouth of the Great Miami at the Ohio River, the Indians numbered eight hundred fifty and the total force was twelve hundred fifty men — plus six cannons, the first pieces of artillery ever seen in this country. Five of them were French swivels mounted on horseback and the last a large brass cannon on wheels.

Along with the Shawnees had come four white men: the Girtys — Simon, James and George — and the Indian agent, Alexander McKee. Captain Byrd was no little disturbed at how these four kept the Indians at a peak of savage anger by recalling to them constantly the deaths of their great chiefs Cornstalk, Pucksinwah and Black Fish, exhorting them to fully avenge these deaths.

At the mouth of the Great Miami River they turned upstream and followed the Ohio to the mouth of Licking River,[9] then on up the Licking until they reached the point where the South Licking joined. Here they erected huts and shelters for most of their stores and baggage, girded themselves for war and started overland.

They followed the South Licking for a distance, went down the dry bed of Snake Lick Creek and then crossed the river at a sweeping curve near the recently abandoned Boyd's Station, felling trees and placing tied logs — first crosswise to the current and then lengthwise atop them — to form a temporary ford over which to haul the wheeled cannon. They then forded Raven Creek, Mill Creek and Gray's Run.[10] Once more they crossed the South Licking at Lair and in the first dim light this morning had crept up the embankment below Ruddell's.

They were seen by the guard and an alarm was called out. Within minutes a hundred men — nearly a quarter of Ruddell's population — were peering fearfully over the stockade walls. Without wasting any time, Byrd ordered the wheeled cannon loaded and aimed. The boom of the gun shook the earth and there was a tremendous crash and splintering of wood as one whole outer section of the north blockhouse was smashed apart. Consternation inside the fort bordered on panic. Against such a weapon as this there was no defense.

John Ruddell raised a white flag and the gate was opened far enough for himself and several other men to emerge. His brother Isaac, who had established the fort, was unable to accompany them as his foot had been injured several days before by a falling rock. Byrd and three of his officers cantered up to meet them. In the name of King George III he demanded unconditional surrender of the fort, upon which Ruddell and his men would be taken prisoner and their women and children permitted to travel on their own to safety at the nearest settlement. There was not much choice and Ruddell accepted.

But the Indians had no intention of being cheated out of their long-promised revenge. The instant the gates were opened, they rushed inside with terrifying shrieks. Their tomahawks fell with unerring accuracy and as the whites dropped they were scalped without regard to sex or age. Mrs. Ruddell's infant son was torn from her arms and thrown into a fire and when she leaped to save him, she was tomahawked and fell into the flames herself. John Ruddell hastened to her aid and he, in turn, fell with his head broken and his scalp lifted.

It had all happened so swiftly that Captain Byrd was stunned. It took him a considerable time to bring order to bear, but by then over twenty of the inhabitants had been murdered. Byrd's face was white and pinched with anger and, though he himself was deeply afraid of the Indians, he did not permit it to show.

With sternness and scorn he berated the chiefs for allowing their men to treat in this manner prisoners who had surrendered — prisoners who had laid down their arms and accepted the terms of surrender in good faith. Was this the great bravery of the Indians about which he had heard so much? How much honor came to a warrior who butchered a baby or tomahawked and scalped a defenseless woman?

They were telling words and at a few commands from Black Hoof and the other tribal chiefs, the Indians stopped their killing and stood back. But the slaughter was not over. If prisoners were to be taken back, the army could not allow itself to be hampered by those who were too sick or too old or too young or too weak to travel. Those who fell into these categories were executed where they stood and their scalps taken. Among them was Isaac Ruddell.

Byrd was powerless to stop this logical, if inhuman, carnage. Finally the remaining white survivors, knotted together in a crying, fearful group, were put under guard by the British regulars and once again the Indians leaped away to ransack the quarters and stack their loot.

Byrd's plan had been to attack Martin's Station next, just five miles away on Stoner Creek.[11] But he was sickened and disgusted with this kind of warfare and, when the looting was finished, called a meeting of the chiefs. If, he told them, he did not get their unbreakable promise that there would be no more massacres such as this he would, as of this moment, call off the expedition and return with his men and cannons to Detroit.

From past experience the Indians knew they could not breach the walls of the Kentucky forts without artillery, and so they listened soberly as Byrd continued. If, he continued, the chiefs would give their word that all prisoners would be turned over to the British for transferal to Detroit, and that at Martin's Station there would be no repetition of the shameful massacre that had taken place here, they would go on to that fort and take it and all the plunder therein would become the property of the Indians. With great reluctance, the chiefs gave their word.

Each of the prisoners was now loaded with all he could carry and the march began for Martin's. Two of Byrd's lieutenants, with a deputation of three of the settlers from Ruddell's, were sent ahead to demand Martin's surrender. They were assured by Byrd personally that there would be no reenactment of the massacre — *unless* Martin's failed to surrender at once.

Again, there was no choice. Martin's Station surrendered and its population of close to a hundred was taken prisoner. Now the Indians wanted to march against the next station, Bryant's, but Byrd was facing something of a dilemma. He could not leave nearly half a thousand prisoners behind to be guarded by the Indians lest there be another massacre, to which he was unalterably opposed, nor could he leave his soldiers behind to guard them and lead the Indians against the remaining forts. He had, in fact, in these few hours, gotten more than a stomachful of this campaign and he therefore decided to end it.

The Indians were furious, but they were forced to accede. Both parties were all too painfully aware that they needed one another. The Indians took everything of value, including the plunder which the captives were forced to carry, mounted the horses belonging to the settlers and herded the laden prisoners before them like cattle, pushing them back toward the forks of the Licking. Those who objected or fell beneath the weight of their load were executed.

The Indians now regarded Byrd with deep contempt. There was no doubt in their minds, nor in anyone else's, that had he continued this campaign he could have wiped out each of the settlements in turn. But Byrd wanted to fight a war without the letting of blood, and they could not take the forts if they had to burden themselves with prisoners at each one. All too late, they realized that Captain Henry Byrd was a squeamish man.

[*June 30, 1780 — Friday*]

A sickening rage burned in Simon Kenton as he and Charles Gatliffe peered through the underbrush and watched the many prisoners being ferried across the Ohio River. It was a rage first ignited at Harrodsburg when word of the slaughter at Ruddell's Station and the capture of Martin's had been reported. A youth of sixteen, taken by the enemy at Ruddell's and then marched to witness the surrender of Martin's, had escaped neatly by wriggling into a hollow sycamore tree and remaining there until the entire procession had passed. He had then fled to Harrodsburg and spread the alarm.

Never had such an anger spread through the Kentuckians; immediately three messengers were dispatched by James Harrod to go to George Rogers Clark by different routes and ask him to lead them against the enemy. It was significant that Bowman, back again at Fort Nelson, was not even considered for this position.

At the same time Simon Kenton and Gatliffe — a lanky, hawkish newcomer — decided they would trail the enemy on horseback and spy on them, with the hope of returning to warn the forts should a change in plans send the British-Indian force back against them. At Ruddell's they walked in a stony silence among the sprawled, scalped bodies and were awed by the damage caused by a single cannonball to the blockhouse. At Martin's they found only the smoldering shell of the fort; and now, several miles upstream from the mouth of the Licking, they had caught up with the enemy and the pitiful procession of prisoners.

It was the frustration at their very inability to do anything to help the prisoners which most affected Simon. To remain hidden here and watch helplessly as hundreds of Kentucky settlers and their families were led into a captivity with which he was only too familiar was unbearable and his eyes glittered icily as he considered what to do. With the coming of cannons, the entire future of Kentucky County was jeopardized.

Carefully Simon scrutinized the operations taking place on the Licking riverbank. There were not enough canoes for everyone, and so boatload by boatload the prisoners were being taken across to the Ohio side where they would resume their land march. More than half of them were across already; by nightfall the crossing would be completed.

Abruptly Simon gripped Gatliffe's arm and pointed. The prisoners and plunder were being loaded aboard the canoes about a quarter mile from the Licking's mouth. Just fifty yards from the mouth a point of land, mostly sandbar but with a dense clump of willows growing on it, jutted into the river and the individual boats came quite close here as they passed around it and disappeared from sight of those behind. Kenton whispered at length to Gatliffe and his companion slowly brightened and nodded.

The pair backtracked to where they had tied their horses and then rode in a wide circle through the woods to come up fairly close to that point. Once again they tied them out of earshot and crept through cover until they reached the point. Here they flattened themselves on the ground and peered unseen from the dense tangle. For two hours they remained motionless. Grasshoppers alighted on their clothing and flies droned lazily over their heads. Once a water snake gliding smoothly through the water came ashore less than three feet away; so still were they that it slithered off into the willows without even suspecting their presence.

In the late dusk the canoes began their last crossings. The horses had already been taken across and the prisoners were all on the other side. Now the remaining soldiers and Indians passed in a fairly compact group of canoes, followed at greater intervals by a dozen craft carrying the remainder of the army's supplies.

The two frontiersmen had figured that somehow they might be able to help some of the prisoners escape, but clearly there was no opportunity for that. The canoes ferrying them across were too close together and each boat too well guarded. In darkness they might have been able to do something, but it had been too light. It was heart-wrenching to lie there and watch friends and neighbors in such dire straits so short a distance away and still be unable to help.

But now, barely visible in the gathering gloom, they watched the final boats push off. Of the five, each with four soldiers in it, four moved along briskly, pulling far ahead of the last. By the time the four leading boats were around the point upon which the two frontiersmen lay, the final craft had two hundred yards yet to come.

Then, as it drew closer, the reason for its sluggishness became clear. Precariously balanced athwart the center of the canoe was Byrd's wheeled cannon. Its weight caused the canoe to sit low in the water, making a considerable drag, and it was obvious that, while they might be able to get across the Ohio well enough, it would take a good bit of hard work to buck that heavy current.

After a few whispered sentences between them, Simon and Gatliffe shed their powder horns and other gear, stripped off moccasins and shirts and slid soundlessly into the water. Walking along the muddy bottom in five feet of water, the frontiersmen hunched down so that except when they raised up slightly to breathe, only the tops of their heads were visible. From a few feet away in that deep twilight, they were well nigh invisible.

The canoe came directly toward them, slicing through the moderate current to cut close to the point of land. When it was still twenty feet away the pair submerged and hugged the bottom. Simon raised his arm and felt back and forth until there was contact. Then instantly he braced his feet on the bottom and shoved hard on the right side of the boat, his head clearing the water as he did so. One of the men gave a brief startled cry as the boat overturned, but the only other sound was that of the small supply of cannonballs smacking against one another, lost in the deep splash of the cannon striking the water.

A soldier's head broke water near him and at once Simon dived, thrust his knife and felt it plunge into the man's body. Even as the man sank, Simon wrenched it free and turned. Of Gatliffe he saw nothing, but two of the remaining three soldiers were struggling to their feet, apparently still not sure that the capsizing was due to anything more than striking a sunken log.

As he surged toward them Simon caught a glimpse of Gatliffe struggling with a man to the right. The struggle ended quickly and with it the soldier's life. Gatliffe swirled about and struck out to join Simon. The remaining pair of Redcoats still appeared confused, apparently thinking the frontiersmen were their companions until they were only an arm's length away. Then it was too late. Simon grappled with one and, in turn, was grabbed around the neck by the other. The water boiled with their exertions, but then Simon's knife slid between the ribs of the man he was holding and, almost at the same time, he felt the grip around his neck relax as Gatliffe's knife found its mark.

By now, the overturned canoe and one of the paddles had drifted into an eddy near the point and the two men moved toward them quickly before they could drift away. As quietly as possible they emptied the canoe and righted it, then got in. Hugging the west shore closely, they glided lightly toward the mouth of the river. En route they bumped into another of the paddles and scooped it up. Within a few minutes they had reached the Ohio and far out on that broad expanse of water they could hear voices from the last canoes, and across the river the faint glows from three different campfires could be seen.

As the Licking gave way to the Ohio they put ashore, overturned the canoe and shoved it far out into the strong current. Back they went then along the Licking shoreline to the original point, recovered their goods and slipped on their shirts and moccasins.

Simon cut a leafy branch, daubed the projecting stub with mud to disguise it and swept away the sandprints of their passage out onto the point. When they reached the grassy slopes he shoved the cut end of the branch into the earth, so it stood erect like a growing sapling, and then they raced back to their horses.

Within fifteen minutes they were riding rapidly back toward Harrodsburg. There was little likelihood that the cannon would be recovered by the enemy. They would probably conclude that the boat had overturned when it struck the faster current of the Ohio. Even if they searched farther up the Licking, the murky waters would hide the cannon and its ammunition until the settlers could retrieve it for themselves.

All in all, the pair had done an extremely good job.

[*July 10, 1780 — Monday*]

Just who does he think he is?" Bowman's voice rose with indignation. "God? He has no authority to issue orders like these." He flung the paper down upon his desk and added, "None at all!"

Colonel John Slaughter put a hand to his mouth and tugged seriously at his moustache in an effort to disguise the smile touching his lips. He and his company of a hundred fifty men had just arrived here at the recently established Fort Jefferson overlooking the Falls of Ohio. They had been sent by newly elected Governor Thomas Jefferson with orders to protect Kentuckians and to establish, in accordance with an act passed by the Virginia Legislature in May, a town at this Falls of Ohio, to be called Louisville.

Slaughter, a mild-mannered man, was definitely amused at Bowman's reaction to Clark's proclamation. He said, "Clark takes a lot upon himself, doesn't he." Then he added softly and carefully, "But he *does* seem to get things done in quite a remarkable fashion."

John Bowman spun about and stared at his fellow officer, as if suspecting him of ridicule, but Slaughter's expression was bland. Bowman made a rude sound. "All I've heard since I came to this damned country is Clark this and Clark that. I'm sick of it. And now this!"

The paper he held minced no words. Hastening to Harrodsburg upon word of the attack on Ruddell's and Martin's, Clark had sent runners to all forts, stations, settlements and scattered individuals throughout Kentucky County to come to Harrodsburg immediately for emergency meeting. Those attending were to include all members of the Kentucky militia, without exception.

Grimly he had listened to the accounts of the massacre at Ruddell's and dispatched a party of thirty men to bury the dead there. As titular commander of the Kentucky militia he had certain limited authority and responsibility, but when he heard Simon Kenton's report and learned of the capture of the British cannon — the only bright news of the entire affair — he did not let lack of authority stand in his way.

At the meeting in Harrodsburg and in his proclamation which followed, Clark made it clear what his plans were. He would, immediately, organize an offensive expedition against the Shawnees and their allies. If he was taking the law into his own hands, then that was just too bad; but he was, as of this moment, ordering that all exits from Harrodsburg be blocked and each and every man be assembled here. Of these, seven hundred were drafted into the army, regardless of whether resident or transient. Until the termination of this campaign, Clark was ordering that all land speculation cease. He commandeered all available resources — guns, powder, lead, food, clothing, horses — "without compunction of conscience." More runners were sent with his proclamation to every fort, including Fort Jefferson, demanding that all Kentucky men, or men then visiting Kentucky, gather their equipment and horses and prepare to assemble to march against Chillicothe. The army, he declared, would rendezvous at the mouth of Licking River on August 1. Any man found deliberately shirking this duty would be dealt with summarily.

It was quite a strong proclamation.

Bowman now paced about his office, glaring at Slaughter who was casually lighting his pipe. The officer sucked on the stem until he had wreathed himself in a cloud of blue-white smoke and then he said, "I suppose you aren't planning to send some of your own men to give aid on this expedition?"

"Aid! Don't be a fool! I'll not only not send aid, I'll forbid any man here to join him under threat of court-martial for desertion and I'll discourage the civilians and militia from joining him. I'm tired of Clark getting whatever he wants whenever he wants it!"

But Bowman's indignation fell mostly on deaf ears. The Kentuckians were fighting mad and they turned as one man from Bowman to Clark. They would probably have retaliated on their own if Clark had not come to lead them, but now, with such a leader, they flocked to join him. Some even left their homes and forts immediately to camp at the mouth of the Licking to be there waiting for the time when Clark would arrive.

But an even worse shock awaited Bowman. Colonel Slaughter now chose to interpret his orders from Virginia to "guard and protect the people of Kentucky County" as justification for offering to Clark the services of his own men and himself.

George Rogers Clark welcomed him.

[*August 2, 1780 — Wednesday*]

There was a forbidding grimness about the thousand mounted men who had met at the mouth of the Licking River yesterday, along with a willingness — even an eagerness — to follow George Rogers Clark's orders to the letter, so long as it meant destruction to their dreaded enemies.

During most of the afternoon and much of this morning the crossing of the Ohio was completed. About half a hundred of the horses had refused to swim the river and rafts made of logs bound with wild grapevines were constructed to ferry them across. Most of the supplies and ammunition for the army were brought across by canoe in a steady procession which had only now ended; and by far the prize possession was the fine six-pounder brass cannon on wheels that had been recovered, along with twenty cannonballs, from the Licking where Simon Kenton and Charles Gatliffe had scuttled them.

A camp was established and the business of naming officers and setting up companies was concluded, having begun yesterday on the south shore. Five companies were formed, each commanded by a colonel: James Harrod, John Floyd, Benjamin Logan, George Slaughter and Benjamin

Linn. Clark personally appointed Simon Kenton to the rank of captain and placed him in charge of all scouts and spies.

While the army was thus shaping itself, a small blockhouse was swiftly put under construction. Here would be stored emergency supplies and a contingent of forty men would be left behind to guard both them and the small flotilla of canoes and rafts until the army's return. It was not much of a building but it was the first real construction on the north side of the Ohio River by the Kentuckians.[12]

Clark now instructed Simon to take a half dozen of his men and scout ahead, marking the trail for them to follow. He was to keep himself about twenty miles in advance of the army and to send back messengers with news of anything important. Simon nodded, selected his men and left.

Since more than half the day was already gone, most of the men who hadn't served before under Clark figured that they would camp here for the night. As usual, Clark surprised them. By 2 P.M. the army was mounted and moving out.

[August 3, 1780 — Thursday]

The first great journey of Tecumseh was coming to a close and he was disappointed it was over. The exhilaration he felt as he rode or walked beside Chiksika over the country was beyond expression. The gentle, musical voice of his older brother as he explained things about the wonders they saw — the streams and springs, the lakes and hills, the trees and wildlife and heavens — carried something of a hypnotic quality. The words lulled him into a kind of daze in which he seemed somehow to leave the shell of his body and become as one with all of which Chiksika spoke. Yet, even though he experienced this detachment, he not only heard but remembered practically verbatim every word Chiksika uttered, and when he asked occasional questions they were neither shallow nor idle. In fact, Chiksika was hard put to answer many of the questions Tecumseh asked. In some cases the penetrating nature of the questions astounded him and he often found himself wondering why he had never thought to ask that. Time and again he berated himself for his inability to answer the boy and it was surprising how often Tecumseh made him feel as if he were the younger instead of the elder.

The long journey they were soon to complete was something both brothers had long looked forward to; Tecumseh because of an insatiable curiosity about everything and a burning desire to know more; Chiksika, because not only did it give him the opportunity to be alone with his beloved little brother to tour the countryside at their leisure, but because his heart had been so heavy with the prevailing worry of his people over the *Shamanese*.

They had ridden far, these two; far to the north into the country of pine trees until they were stopped by the great blue lake many days to the north and west of the western edge of the lake below Detroit which the Wyandots called *Erige* — Lake of the Cat — and which the British called Lake Erie. But this body of water was a much bigger lake; bigger and bluer and deeper and far more beautiful. It was called, Chiksika said, *Mis-e-ken* by their northwestern brothers, the Fox tribe. This name meant, simply, large lake. From this term the English called the land which lay between the two lakes, Michigan.

At this *Mis-e-ken* shoreline they had turned south and followed its great southern arc until soon they were passing through Sac territory and heading north again on the other side of the lake. Here they entered the Fox tribe's land. Before long they had turned to the west and gone through a fresh-scented pine-forested land bejeweled with myriad little lakes of incredible beauty. It was here, at last, that they came to the magnificent grandmother of all rivers where she ran clear and sweet and cold from the north. They followed the stream a long way southward to where, on the opposite side, another great river entered from the land of the Sioux and swelled the grandmother of rivers to nearly twice her size. It was at this point that the brothers turned their mounts and headed straight again for the rising sun.

For more than three moons they had been gone and while in some ways it would be nice to be back again in their own *wegiwa* in Chillicothe, it would be nice, too, if the journey could go on and on. Now, approaching the villages of the Maykujay Shawnees, they would stay a few days to visit and tell of their great journey before the fires at night. Only then would they go on to their home village.

Tecumseh was silent and withdrawn, thinking of what they had seen and the great goodness of Moneto to create a world of such variety and beauty. And why was it that a world of this nature became so complex to the men who lived in it? There were so many questions he had asked of Chiksika for which he had received answers that left him dissatisfied. Why, for example, since Moneto was all-powerful, did He permit the *Shemanese* to take the lands and lives of the Shawnees? Why were not all the Indian tribes one — the Shawnees and Wyandots, the Kickapoos and Sacs and Foxes, and the multitude of other tribes that they had not seen which were in all directions — why were they not one? Why did they fight each other instead of uniting to oppose their common enemy? And, closer to home, why was it that the principal chief of the Shawnee nation could be only a Chalahgawtha or a Thawegila? Why were he and Chiksika, as Kispokotha Shawnees, ineligible to become principal leaders of the tribe? Why was it that their own father, Pucksinwah, had had to prove himself in battle time and again as a superb leader before his talents were at last recognized and he was permitted to become a chief, even then only a secondary chief, a war chief, of the Shawnees? These last few questions he put to Chiksika now.

The older brother sighed. Such questions from one so young. Yet, what better time than as they rode along like this to tell the boy more fully of the tradition which declared that principal Shawnee leaders be only Chalahgawthas or Thawegilas, and of the origin of the Shawnees and the first meeting of the tribe's two most powerful septs?

The Chalahgawtha, unlike the other four Shawnee septs, Chiksika explained, did not originate on this continent. In the beginning it was created and dwelt in a foreign country and the Thawegila alone was the Shawnee sept out of which the chief ruler of the nation was chosen.

The Chalahgawtha sept, migrating eastward toward this continent, came to an end of the land upon which they lived. From this point they continued to the east upon thick, unbroken ice until at length this gave way to a narrow and shallow open sea. The chief thereupon told his people to call upon the *opa-wa-kon-wa*, which is the living creature each individual had merited, through possession of which the individual aid and inspiration of the Great Spirit are obtained. This was done as he requested and out of all those animals which appeared at the summonses he chose the turtle and the grizzly bear, since they were most accustomed to water.

Those Shawnees for whom these two animals were *opa-wa-kon-wa* at once entrusted themselves in this exodus of theirs to the backs of the creatures and were thus carried through the water to dry land across the strait, thereby becoming the leaders of the rest of the people in this part of the exodus. In this way all the Chalahgawtha people were brought across to the shores of this continent and continued their journey eastward.

In the meanwhile, the Thawegila sept had begun a journey westward and camped one night at a small brook. Far into the night these Thawegila people suddenly heard voices approaching on the other side of the brook and, at the warning from their chief, they listened in silence. To their great surprise they found that the language of those approaching was their own Shawnee tongue. Finally the ones approaching stopped for the night in the same manner the Thawegila had done, unaware anyone else was near.

They were amazed, next morning, to find a camp of people so near and at the same time the Thawegila chief demanded to know who they were and how they knew the Shawnee language. The Chalahgawtha chief told him where they had come from and that he and his people were Shawnees whose blood was unadulterated. The Thawegila then inquired if the Chalahgawtha had a *Meesawmi*.

Now the *Meesawmi* is known only to the Shawnee tribe. It is a free gift of the Great Spirit with which he originally endowed each sept composing the Shawnee nation. Its potency or inspiration always remains with the sept as the very symbol of its life. It is represented by some material object, but what this object is no one knows save those who have the right and authority to open the parcel in which it is contained after having undergone the ceremony connected with it; something very seldom done unless absolutely necessary. A strange thing about the *Meesawmi* of the two chief septs is that the parcel in which it is contained is never kept in the *wegiwa* of the chief who has charge of it, but it is always on his premises somewhere — sometimes atop a pole set in the ground. It is wrapped with layers of buckskin and covered over with some common material to protect it from the elements. The ground about the pole is always carefully swept and no weed is allowed to grow there. The *Meesawmi* is held sacred and secret by all and it is considered wrong to speak of it outside or in public. Therefore, no one except the chiefs who have charge of it know its true nature.

When the Chalahgawtha chief replied that he had a *Meesawmi*, he was then questioned as to its powers and, upon learning them, the Thawegila chief said there must be a test to determine which of them had the most powerful *Meesawmi*. This was agreed to.

First to be tested, the Chalahgawtha chief prepared a small bow and an arrow with a sharp point. He said that his test would be to shoot at the sun and if it turned bloody, this would show the power of his *Meesawmi*. At noon, in the presence of the people, he shot this little arrow at the face of the sun, which quickly became blood red and the air became dark for a while. Then it cleared.

Impressed, the Thawegila chief then tested his *Meesawmi*. Preparing a still smaller bow and arrow, he took a wooden basin filled with water and set it in the midst of the two septs. He then shot at the reflection of the sun in the water, whereupon the water became blood red and the air darkened as before.

Upon completion of these two tests, the chiefs and their people declared the power of these two *Meesawmis* as equal and at once the chiefs grasped hands and decreed that henceforth the chiefs of the Shawnee nation must be chosen only from one or the other of these two septs. By tradition, the greatest Shawnee leaders could not come from the Peckuwes or the Maykujays or, Chiksika concluded sadly, the Kispokothas.[13]

While he had been fascinated by the story, Tecumseh was not at all satisfied with it. If his questions were ever to be answered, he realized, he would have to find those answers for himself, for there was none who could tell him. And so he rode in a deep meditation which remained unbroken for many miles until suddenly Chiksika grasped his arm and announced that Moluntha's Town was in sight.

Tecumseh kicked his heels into his horse's sides and galloped away toward the town, his head bent low to the mane so that the following

Chiksika could not see his face. A feeling of deep confusion had abruptly engulfed Tecumseh and he was crying and he didn't have any idea why.

[*August 5, 1780 — Saturday*]

George and Simon Girty, along with the party of four Shawnees, watched with growing consternation the approach of the army of one thousand men. The six had stopped beside a little bubbling spring to refresh themselves while out hunting some twenty miles south of Chillicothe when the army hove into view two or three miles from them, following the course of the Little Miami River. Even as they watched, the army pulled up, apparently to make camp. It was clear what they intended — a rest here until some time in the early morning and then a swift assault upon Chillicothe.

At once the brothers and their companions wheeled about unseen and galloped off toward the town to sound the alarm. They rode silently and steadily until reaching a point not more than six miles from the army when one of their warriors, Red Snake, grunted a warning. Ahead, four riders were coming toward them and the six wheeled and slipped into the brushy screen of a small ravine to let them pass.

While two of the Shawnees stayed with the horses to keep them quiet, the Girtys and Red Snake, along with another warrior, crept forward to watch the smaller group. Suddenly Red Snake made a sound of surprise and whispered urgently, "*Cut-ta-ho-tha* — Bahd-ler!"

Simon Girty looked closely and, though his eyes were not as keen as any of the others, even he could recognize the enormous figure of his young friend leading the little party of horsemen. Undoubtedly they were scouts returning to the army. They watched until the quartet was less than fifty yards away, and then a slight movement to his left caught Girty's attention and he saw that Red Snake had aimed his rifle at the center of Simon's chest and was already squeezing the trigger.

As swiftly as thought, Girty slapped his hand over the pan of the rifle just as Red Snake fired. The flint chip in the hammer mechanism leaped forward and made a soft thump as it struck the back of Girty's hand. Red Snake looked in amazement at the white renegade and Girty now hissed a warning to them all. "Wait! Let them go. Don't shoot unless you have to."

George, himself ready to fire, looked at his brother in surprise, but all of them held off. When the four horsemen had passed by without seeing them and were pulling out of range, Girty nodded to his companions and they crept back to the ravine. By the time they reached the horses he had formed a good logical reason — other than his bond of brotherhood for the young frontiersman — for his action.

"They don't know we saw them," he said. "If we had shot at them and even one of them got away to give the alarm, the army would have moved against Chillicothe immediately. But now we can ride back unknown to them and give the warning and the Chalahgawthas will have the rest of today and most of tonight to prepare."

Red Snake considered the wisdom of this and nodded. "You are right," he said. After a brief pause he added, "The Shawnees made Bahd-ler *cut-ta-ho-tha* several times, but Moneto took him away little by little until he took him away from us entirely. He is under the hand of Moneto, that is clear. It is well we did not shoot. Come. We will go to Black Hoof now."

[*August 6, 1780 — Sunday*]

Chief Catahecassa — Black Hoof — was only five feet eight inches tall but he was nonetheless a distinguished-looking man. For four decades his word had carried great weight among the Shawnees and since he had become their principal chief at the death of Black Fish, their respect amounted almost to reverence.

He was fifty-four years old and had lived a very full life, being one of the few living Shawnees who had been born in Florida and still remembered bathing and fishing in salt water before encroaching whites had forced the nation gradually north and west to seek new land.

Black Hoof was an esteemed warrior who had fought at the defeat of Braddock near Fort Pitt in 1755, and who had taken part in practically every major battle since that time. He was a man of sagacity and experience and imbued with a fierce and desperate bravery and love for his people. With the possible exception of the ancient chief of the Maykujays — Moluntha — no Shawnee knew more of the tribe's history and traditions.

It was he, over the many years since he had first become a subchief at the age of sixteen, who spoke out against the Shawnee customs of polygamy and the burning of prisoners and, as a result, both practices had been sharply curtailed over the intervening years. No Shawnee law had been established making these practices illegal, but because of Black Hoof's influence, Shawnee society had come to frown upon a man taking more than one wife. Old Moluntha, in fact, was the only Shawnee at present who still practiced the old custom and only because he already had three wives before the views of his society altered.

Prisoner burning, on the other hand, was a practice Black Hoof had considerably more difficulty discouraging. There were, to his way of thinking, far too many instances of it today. But he was pleased to see that, as compared to its prevalence in the past, it had become in these days a rather uncommon event.

The chief was eating in his *wegiwa* when Simon Girty and Red Snake asked permission to enter and were welcomed and offered food, which they declined. There was little time for amenities and the two narrated what they had seen. When they finished, Black Hoof sat for several minutes in thought, his fingers toying absently with the bear-claw necklace he wore. At last he spoke and his voice was melancholy.

"At most we have only few more than a hundred warriors here. We could not stand against a thousand horsemen. No. The time has come, for now at least, when we must abandon our town. We must dispose of our belongings and treasures and move to join our bothers at Piqua Town on the Mad River.[14]

It was already late afternoon and Black Hoof called in his subchiefs and told them what must be done. The atmosphere of the village became electric as squaws, children and warriors rushed about, each carrying to the edge of the sharp slope dipping from the village's level a hundred yards behind the *msi-kah-mi-qui* the possessions they could not hope to carry with them. In a very short time there was a huge pile of goods stacked here — kettles, pans, utensils, items wrapped for preservation in greased buckskin, tools for planting, crude shovels, hoes and mattocks, sealed bundles of extra clothing and furs, leathers, balls of rawhide tugs, ceremonial pipes, small carved figures, spare tomahawks and knives and even a few guns that could not fire because of need of minor repairs. But most valuable and heaviest was the silver. Nearly a ton of it was deposited here — rings, necklaces, bracelets, armbands, medallions, plates, long narrow bars and heavy formless wads. This was the silver mined over generations by the Shawnees in the great gorge of the Little Miami River a short distance to the north and east of them and in the steep banks of the little tributaries to north and south.[15] It was a treasure they valued highly. Now the individual pieces were securely tied in buckskin parcels, each about the size of a raccoon, and stacked in a pile until there were about fifty of them.

Through the evening hours and into the night the Chalahgawthas worked, foregoing the light of a fire and working in strict silence. A circle of guards squatted at intervals around the entire village site, keenly alert to give warning of anyone's approach. From the top of this slope behind the council house a line of warriors and squaws formed, stretching nearly a thousand feet, down the incline and out into the large marshy area below, between the village and the river. Only one tree grew in this marsh, a magnificent old oak that had somehow taken root in the only spot of firm ground throughout this area of several hundred acres. To this tree and perhaps a dozen feet beyond it the line stretched and at the very head of the line was Black Hoof himself.

Now began the big job of moving the massive pile of treasure and goods. From hand to hand the items passed along the line and when they reached the chief he thrust them out from him and they fell into a pool of black water perhaps fifteen or twenty feet in depth. Here they would remain hidden until the Shawnees could once again return and gather them up.[16]

Disposal of the goods having thus been accomplished, Black Hoof led his people back to the village and directed that every *wegiwa* and the large *msi-kah-mi-qui* be set afire. Dry grasses, brush and twigs were placed at the base of the walls and ignited. When the fires were going well, the Chalahgawtha Shawnees began their march to the north and west for the village called Piqua Town, thirteen miles distant. Here, perhaps, if there were men enough on hand, they could make their stand against the dreaded *Shemanese*.

A mile or so north of Chillicothe, Black Hoof stopped momentarily and looked back. The fires glowed brightly and yet, hot though they were, they struck in his breast a numbing coldness and he was thankful that the Shawnees who had split away from the tribe and migrated west last year would never see this disgrace. An enveloping weariness and sadness settled over him as he turned and resumed the march while the first gray light of August sixth brightened the eastern sky.

At this moment, five miles below the burning village, the army of General George Rogers Clark was approaching at a smart canter.

[August 8, 1780 — Tuesday]

Joseph Rogers trembled, as much with excitement as with fear. Well over three years he had been captive of the Shawnees and a hundred times or more he had thought of escape, but he lacked the confidence in his own ability to survive in the wilds, even should he manage to get away, which he doubted. But now his reunion with Uncle George and the other Kentucky men appeared not only possible, but quite probable.

The mounted men had attacked Piqua Town in a furious onslaught several hours ago and since then the battle had been a hotly contested one. But young Rogers took no part in it. All he could think of was that if he could hide from his captors for just a little while, he'd be able to reach the whites. Or they would reach him.

Shortly after the initial onslaught he had crawled into a narrow cleft between craggy rocks and pulled some brush over himself. From this hiding place he could not see much, but what he heard thrilled him. The shouts of men speaking English made his arms and legs break out in gooseflesh and occasionally he shivered, though it was a very hot day.

He thought again of the time he had been captured and the many months he had spent among the Shawnees here at Piqua Town. He remembered vividly the details of his last free hours: how after Uncle George had gone for help to get the hidden gunpowder off Three Islands, those other men who had been out hunting had come back to McClelland's Station; and how John Gabriel Jones had convinced them they could retrieve the powder and lead with ease; and how they had subsequently been ambushed. He could still see the look of stunned surprise on Jones's face as he clutched his chest at the first shots and then tumbled dead from the saddle. How many times had he cursed himself for stupidly falling off his own horse and getting himself captured? How quickly then his first thoughts of escape had been erased. Less than an hour after the attack, the man who had been captured with him — he couldn't even recall his name now — had tried to run off. They ran him down and brought him back, tied him to a tree after stripping him and then took turns throwing their knives at him until his belly and loins and legs were bathed in blood and he screamed in agony. And then they had taken off his scalp while he writhed and twisted beneath the knife. Even then he remained alive until one of them sharpened a stick and held it to his eye and then shoved hard and the stick plunged in until it struck the inside rear of his skull. They had thrown his body into the river and with gestures made it clear that this was what would happen to Rogers if he tried to escape. Three long years had passed, during which he had never attempted escape; and yet the awful picture of his tortured comrade was still vivid in his mind. But now, at last, he would be free!

The battle had begun an hour or so after noon and now, in the early evening, the firing was slackening. Cautiously he crept out of his hiding place and nearly cried with joy. Directly below him, at the base of the hill he saw not only a group of white men, but his own uncle!

He burst from cover, waving his arms and shouting incoherently in his relief. But instead of rejoicing, the men looked startled; several of them raised their rifles and young Joseph felt the tremendous blows as the bullets slammed into his chest and he tumbled over several times. He had forgotten something very important — he thought of himself as a white, but in appearance he was as much a Shawnee as his captors.

The group walked toward him carefully and he raised himself on one hand and his voice was a hoarse croak as he said, "Uncle George . . . it's . . . it's Joe . . ."

George Rogers Clark sprinted the remaining distance to the youth and turned him over and cradled his head in his arms. Anguished tears streamed down his cheeks and over and over he said, "We didn't know, boy . . . we didn't know."

But Joseph Rogers did not hear him.

[August 22, 1780 — Tuesday]

Colonel George Rogers Clark sat with his head buried in his hands for a long time at the desk in his temporary quarters at Fort Jefferson. The lantern shed a warm glow in the room. He had bathed and eaten at his leisure and had even taken a little stroll through the newly developing village of Louisville adjacent to the Fort, but the knowledge of what he was putting off was a heavy weight upon him and he returned to his desk. He took an inordinately long time setting up his ink pot and cutting a fine point on his goose quill and getting his paper in position and then, with nothing else to do to put off the task, he simply cupped his face in his hands and sat this way for a long time.

At last he looked up and dipped the quill into the ink and began to write, but this letter was not the letter he had been prolonging. That would come later. He wrote:

> *Fort Jefferson at Louisville*
> *Kentucky County*
> *August 22, 1780*

To His Excellency
Thomas Jefferson
Governor of Virginia

   Sir:

By every possible exertion, and the aid of Colonel Slaughter's corps, we completed the number of 1000, with which we crossed the river at the mouth of the Licking on the first day of August and began our march on the 2nd. Having a road to cut for the artillery to pass, for 70 miles, it was the 6th before we reached the first town, which we found vacated, and the greatest part of their effects carried off. The general conduct of the Indians on our march, and many other corroborating circumstances, proved their design of leading us to their own ground and time of action. After destroying the crops and buildings of Chillecauthy we began our march for the Picaway settlements, on the waters of the Big Miami, the Indians keeping runners constantly before our advanced guards.[17] At half past two in the evening of the 8th, we arrived in sight of the town and forts, a plain of half a mile in width lying between us. I had an opportunity of viewing the situation and motion of the enemy near their works.

I had scarcely time to make those dispositions necessary, before the action commenced on our left wing, and in a few minutes became almost general, with a savage fierceness on both sides. The confidence the enemy had of their own strength and certain victory, or the want of generalship, occasioned several neglects, by which those advantages were taken that proved the ruin of their army, being flanked two or three different times, drove from hill to hill in a circuitous direction, for upwards of a mile and a half; at last took shelter in their strongholds and woods adjacent when the firing ceased for about half an hour, until necessary preparations were made for dislodging them. A heavy firing again commenced, and continued severe until dark, by which time the enemy were totally routed. The cannon playing too briskly on their works they could afford them no shelter. Our loss was about 14 killed and 13 wounded; theirs at least triple that number. They carried off their dead during the night, except 12 or 14 that lay too near our lines for them to venture. This would have been a decisive stroke to the Indians, if unfortunately the right wing of our army had not been rendered useless for some time by an uncommon chain of rocks that they could not pass, by which means part of the enemy escaped through the ground they were ordered to occupy.

By a French prisoner we got the next morning we learn that the Indians had been preparing for our reception, moving their families and effects:[18] that the morning before our arrival, they were 300 warriors, Shawnees, Mingoes, Wyandotts and Delawares. Several reinforcements coming that day, he did not know their numbers; that they were sure of destroying the whole of us; that the greatest part of the prisoners taken by Byrd, were carried to Detroit, where there were only 200 regulars, having no provisions except green corn and vegetables. Our whole store at first setting out being only 300 bushels of corn and 1500 of flour; having done the Shawnees all the mischief in our power, and after destroying the Picaway settlements, I returned to this post, having marched in the whole 480 miles in 31 days. We destroyed upwards of 800 acres of corn, besides great quantities of vegetables, a considerable portion of which appear to have been cultivated by white men, I suppose for the purpose of supporting war parties from Detroit. I could wish to have had a small store of provisions to enable us to lay waste part of the Delaware settlements, and falling in at Pittsburgh, but the excessive heat, and weak diet, shew the impropriety of such a step. Nothing could excel the few regulars and Kentuckyans, that compose this little army, in bravery and implicit obedience to orders; each company vying with the other who should be the most subordinate.

I am, sir, your most humble
and obedient servant,
George Rogers Clark, Colonel

Clark sat back in his seat and rubbed his eyes with one hand. He was tired, very tired, and would like nothing better than to collapse into bed and sleep for a week, but the worst task still lay ahead. Sighing, he set Jefferson's letter aside and began to write on a fresh sheet:

August 22, 1780
Ft. Jefferson, Louisville

My Dear Sister:
I fear I have grievous news about my nephew, your beloved son, Joseph Rogers . . .

[*September 30, 1780 — Saturday*]

Four times since coming to the Ohio country the Chalahgawtha sept of the Shawnees had been forced to move out of the spreading ring of danger caused by white men. From the first Chillicothe on the Scioto River three miles above its junction with Paint Creek they had moved straight upriver to a fine rich ground on the west bank three miles below the junction of Darby Creek. From here they had moved southwest to the North Fork of Paint Creek to establish the third Chillicothe but, as with the other two, they were still too vulnerable to interlopers coming up the Scioto valley. At last they moved to the site of the Little Miami River where already there was a small village called Piqua, after the Peckuwes, their brothers, who established it. When the Chalahgawthas moved in, the Peckuwes moved out, most of them establishing themselves on the Mad River at the site just destroyed by Clark's army, while other factions traveled up the Great Miami River and established two Piqua Towns there, one just below the junction with Loramie Creek and the other three miles above that, also on the Great Miami.[19]

Now, with the Little Miami Chillicothe and the Mad River Piqua Town destroyed, the survivors once again migrated. Since most of the Peckuwes had gone west of the Mississippi when the tribe split, few residents were left at the Upper and Lower Piqua Towns, as those two along the Great Miami were called; it was to these villages that the dislocated Shawnees now moved, to the west and slightly south of the Maykujay and Wapatomica villages on the upper Mad River.

It was a gloomy procession at best and the downhearted septs — the Chalahgawthas settling at Lower Piqua Town and the remaining Peckuwes at Upper Piqua Town — were disappointed in the land. It was flatter and less attractive than that which they had left; the ground seemed not as fertile nor the springs as numerous, nor the game as abundant. It was a new home, to be sure, and far enough away from the *Shemanese* to be relatively safe, but their hearts yearned for the old Chillicothe in the beautiful Little Miami valley and in the night the muffled sound of crying from the squaws was a dagger thrust into the hearts of Black Hoof and his warriors.

Many of the warriors were talking about going back to the two towns and reestablishing them and now plans were already in the making to do just this; if not right away, then next spring when corn and vegetables could again be planted and new *wegiwas* constructed. It was something to look forward to.

Chiksika and Tecumseh and their younger brothers had built a suitable *wegiwa* here at the new location in the north, but the eyes of all of them were hollow with misery in the knowledge of what they had lost on the

Little Miami River. While his brothers slept, Tecumseh lay with his hands behind his head and stared unseeingly into the darkness. He heard a faint stirring and the voice of Chiksika came to him very softly.

"You are troubled, little brother. Tell me what is in your heart."

Tecumseh remained silent for a dozen heartbeats and then he spoke in a voice old for its years. "After we joined with our people on their flight from our village, I heard a little girl ask her mother why, if Moneto loved them, He allowed the *Shemanese* to kill her father and destroy her home and make her flee. Her mother hugged her and told her not to think of such things. But now I think of such things and now I ask you, Chiksika, if Moneto loves us as we love and respect Him, as well as the grain and animals and birds He provides for our use, why then does He permit the white men to hunt us down? Why does He let them kill us? Why does He let them destroy our forests and our crops and our fields? Why does He let them destroy our homes and our families and our friends? Why does He hurt us so? Why, Chiksika?"

And the sorrow of Chiksika became even deeper because he had asked these very questions of himself and he did not know the answers.

CHAPTER VI

[*January 16, 1781 — Tuesday*]

EVEN including the most pessimistic, there remained no doubt in anyone's mind that the settlements in Kentucky County were now permanent and no longer balanced so precariously on the brink of extinction. Emigration had jumped from the scores to the hundreds, and then to the thousands, and the traffic on the Ohio River was a sight to behold. Rare was the day when, from any given point, one could not look in one direction or the other and see at least one boatload of settlers. Usually the number was greater.

But though the permanence of the settlements was now obvious to all, this was not to say all danger was gone. To the contrary, marauding bands of Delawares and Wyandots and Shawnees still terrorized the country, but these were mainly in-and-out attacks, designed to get rifles and ammunition and food, along with new horses.

The settlements themselves were becoming more than that; they were substantial villages and some, such as Harrodsburg and Danville, Stanford and Lexington were becoming small cities. Log cabins were giving way to new and better types of structures. Carpenters and masons were among the emigrants and now frame houses, very large and two stories high, were being built, as were sturdy brick homes.

Regular stores were being erected as well as a variety of shops — livery stables, blacksmith shops, general merchandise establishments, barber shops and many others. Schools were being built and among the emigrants were teachers for them. And in Harrodsburg, whose population had now grown to exceed twenty-five hundred, plans were under way to erect a courthouse.

New laws were being enacted locally and one of these declared gambling illegal. It was ironic that among the first cases to be tried in the first

Kentucky court which convened this date in the Harrodsburg blockhouse was one in which Hugh McGary, late a colonel at Vincennes under Clark and now a settler on his own, was charged with "playing the races" — giving and accepting bets on the popular Sunday horse races.

McGary, not at all chagrined, laughed uproariously when he was found guilty and the court proclaimed him ". . . an infamous gambler . . . not to be eligible to any office of trust or honor within the State of Virginia."

Most of the residents laughed with him, but there were some who labeled McGary a "dangerous man," one who would knowingly and cheerfully bring disaster upon his fellows. Unfortunately, there were few who listened.

[April 13, 1781 — Friday]

The destruction by Clark's army of the grain and vegetable crops of the Shawnees resulted in an extremely difficult winter for the tribe. Without corn to parch or grind and without vegetables, particularly those of the tuber variety, their diets were badly imbalanced and the men had to hunt practically all the time in order to get enough meat to keep their women and children alive. Although Lower Piqua Town was not much more than thirty-five miles northwest of their old village site, the terrain was different. Without the hills and valleys to protect them, the winter seemed colder, the snow deeper, existence tougher.

As their hardships grew, so grew their resentment and hatred of the whites. With bare survival a constant tax on their resources, relatively few forays could be made into the Kentucky country and nearly all those made by the Shawnees were for the prime purpose of obtaining food, especially grains.

But though the attacks on the frontier settlements during the past winter were the lightest the pioneers had yet enjoyed, the picture changed drastically as winter broke and warmer weather came. The Shawnees struck back in a relatively new and terrible way, taking a grim toll of lives and supplies from the new settlers coming down the Ohio River. Temporary camps were established near the mouth of the Scioto River and near Three Islands and from these points they could hurl destruction upon the unsuspecting river travelers with virtual impunity.

The confidence of the Shawnees, which had been dealt such a devastating blow the previous summer, was returning, and with the reconstruction of both Chillicothe on the Little Miami River and Piqua Town on the Mad they felt their fortunes were changing for the better. The easy victories over the river traffic gave them even more confidence. Frequently in the new little settlement at the mouth of Limestone Creek the settlers had seen upset canoes drift by, mute testimony of attacks upriver. And then there were the bodies — dozens of them already this spring — seen floating along in grisly fashion, many of them horribly mutilated and their scalps gone.

Over and over through March and the first part of April panic-stricken survivors of attacks reached the little port settlement called Limestone and told of the horrors they had undergone — of how the peaceful river had suddenly come alive as a dozen or two canoes, each carrying ten or twenty warriors, sped from hiding in little coves or creeks and converged on the boats of the emigrants. More often than not, no one escaped.

It now became wise for river travelers to remain as close as possible to the Kentucky shore. Boats coming down along the Ohio side or even in the swift current of the middle were apt to find themselves targets of snipers who rarely showed themselves and were content with picking off individual parties one by one as they passed. In those rare cases where survivors arrived to tell of their experiences, Simon Kenton somehow always seemed to be on hand to raise a party of men and travel upriver to the spot where the attack had taken place, hoping perhaps to find other survivors who were too weak or too frightened or too injured to travel and would die unless help came.

Such was the mission he was on now with eight men from Limestone and the surrounding area. A man of about thirty — no one knew who he was — was brought ashore after he had been spotted clinging to a log. He had suffered a severe tomahawk blow in the back and one lung was punctured. He was far gone when they brought him in and it was obvious he wouldn't live.

But he hung on for a few hours and regained consciousness long enough to tell of the attack. They were two boats out of Wheeling, he said: sixteen men, twelve women, eight children, three infants. As they passed three large islands upstream a little way, what must have been half a hundred screaming savages put out after them in eight canoes and their only hope was to head for shore. They got there only seconds before the Indians and raced into the underbrush, but the dying man had little hope for the others. He had heard them screaming in agony as they were overtaken and as three of the Indians converged on him he leaped off a high bank into the river. But he hadn't been fast enough; just as his feet left the ground a tomahawk buried itself below his shoulder blade.

There had been no attempt to recover him. He managed to grasp the log which drifted past and somehow, in the hours that elapsed, the tomahawk had worked loose and fallen away.

That was all he could tell them, except that there was a rather wide sandy beach where they had landed, within sight of the lowest of the three islands. Kenton knew the place. He and his men had left at once on horseback, following the Kentucky shoreline upstream a dozen miles or so to the beach the survivor had indicated. They tied their horses a half mile from the spot and advanced cautiously afoot. They heard no sound, but abruptly Simon saw before them in a clearing an awful scattering of bodies guarded by an Indian; he was sitting erect, but his head was bent as if in sleep, his rifle in a ready position over his knees and a blanket draped over the back of his head and shoulders and tucked around his body.

Simon motioned the others to silence and began a careful stalking. The Indian certainly appeared asleep, but it might well be a ruse. Every nerve in the big frontiersman's body was poised for instant flight and he moved to within twenty yards of the clearing with less noise than a sunbeam makes as it slides across the forest floor.

Now he began to suspect something wasn't right. The sitting figure was altogether too erect; he felt sure the man was dead, and yet there appeared to be nothing holding him in this position. For long minutes he studied the figure and the careless scattering of bodies around it, and then abruptly he grunted and strode boldly into the open, calling the others to join him.

The scene in the clearing was terrible. Every last one of them was dead and, in addition to being scalped, most of the bodies had been disemboweled with tomahawk blows. Fingers, hands, arms or feet had been chopped from four of the men and from two of the women and from the amount of blood in evidence it was apparent that these atrocities had been committed before the victims were killed.

Of them all, only the three infants and the blanket-wrapped sitting figure had not been scalped. The latter had been used merely as a tactic to delay pursuit should it come; it had been positioned and draped to look like an Indian, but when Simon touched the shoulder the head lolled and the blanket fell back.

In his years on the frontier Simon had seen death in many forms, but what he saw now almost caused him to retch. An inch-thick stake had been sharpened and the dull end buried firmly so that the tip projected nearly two feet above the ground. The man's clothing had been stripped from him. Though he was unbound now, marks on wrists and ankles indicated that he had been tied and then lifted over the stake and positioned so that when released, the point of the stake entered his rectum and the weight of his body drove it through him until he was sitting on the ground with the entire exposed portion of the stake inside him. From the marks where his heels had dug into the ground in his struggling and the amount of blood beneath his buttocks, it was apparent that he had not been killed instantly by being so impaled, but had gradually bled to death. Then his hands and feet were untied, the blanket draped about him and his knees propped up so that the battered and useless flintlock could be positioned.

They buried them all in a shallow common grave, placing the infants under the arms of the women whose breasts showed them to have been nursing mothers. The lone survivor was dead by the time they returned to Limestone. All the way back they had been silent, each man visualizing the horror they had witnessed and hearing again the single sentence the big frontiersman had spoken as they mounted to return.

"I got a bad feeling," he had said softly, "that this is only the beginning."

[*September 1, 1781 — Saturday*]

Since his companion of old, Daniel Boone, was tied up in domestic, political and military affairs at Boonesboro, Simon Kenton once again became the solitary giant who restlessly roamed the Kentucky landscape.

Even though there had been over three thousand newcomers to Kentucky this past spring, Simon still felt strongly that more major attacks by the Shawnees would strike the Kentucky settlements; and so, rather than take the chance of being away when and if the blows should fall, he put aside his home-going plans and resumed his work of rescuing attacked emigrants on the Ohio and guiding newcomers to wherever they wanted to settle in Kentucky, claiming ever more land and occasionally engaging in combat with lone Indians or small parties of two or three, from which he emerged, thus far at least, the victor. Although he was often seen visiting friends in the various taverns that had sprung up all over, Simon Kenton did not drink, in fact, he was often strong in his remarks against it. His contention was that liquor was a poison which gradually destroyed the consumer. Certainly he had a basis for this belief. Peter Drouilliard, still living at Simon's old cabin on Lawrence Creek, had become a hopeless sot, deeply depressed when drink was unavailable and bleary-eyed, staggering or unconscious when it was handy. He constantly wheedled for whiskey, whining to Simon or anyone who came to the cabin to get him some.

Nor was Drouilliard the only example upon which Simon based his prejudice. He was well aware that the worst of the Indian atrocities were committed after the attacking savages had discovered and consumed stores of whiskey. He could also name off a score or more white men who had been slain because they were too befuddled by drink to protect themselves. If more basis was needed, it had come with a shock this summer when Simon learned from a Detroit escapee that liquor had, indirectly, caused the death of his Mingo friend and benefactor, Chief Logan.

Logan, he was told, had also become addicted to whiskey, and when it was refused him at Detroit one night he had mumbled an angry retort to the effect that if the British wouldn't give it to him, perhaps the Americans would and that he would go to Clark in Kentucky. The fear that he would influence his Mingoes equally in this matter was enough to seal his fate. He had been followed and, while on the path to the very cabin Kenton and Girty had helped him build, was murdered by a tomahawk blow from behind.

While Kenton still considered the old Lawrence Creek cabin his home base, he did some preliminary work in setting up other settlements of his own elsewhere. When sent with a message from Colonel Trigg — Colonel Bowman's replacement — to George Rogers Clark, now a brigadier general due to his highly successful campaigns, Simon marked his K on a double ash sapling and cleared a little ground at the forks of Clear Creek. And a little later, after having guided a newcomer party from Limestone to Danville, he began to erect another cabin on land he had claimed along nearby Quick's Run.

More and more these days he thought about visiting his home and parents in Fauquier County, hoping to persuade the elder Kentons to give up the mean little tobacco farm at Bull Run Mountain and return with him to Kentucky where he would give them ten times as much — and better! — land of their own to settle on. John Kenton, who had built his own cabin a couple miles southeast of Simon's place, thought this an excellent idea and encouraged him to go, but somehow things kept coming up to delay execution of these plans.

[*October 19, 1781 — Friday*]

Abraham, chief of the Moravian Indians, listened in disapproving silence to the words of Chief Thayendanega of the Mohawks and the Delaware chiefs, Pimoacan and Pipe. They had failed to convince him he must unite with his Delaware brothers and join the confederation being led by Thayendanega against the white settlements in western Pennsylvania. Now they urged him, for the safety of himself and his three hundred Christian followers, to leave their towns and move to the region of the Upper Sandusky River.

"You know well," Thayendanega said, "that the white chief Brodhead came here and murdered nearly all the residents of Goschachgunk who remained behind while their neighbors fled. Thus was their trust in the white man rewarded. That is what can happen to you. Even Chief White Eyes was murdered by them while in the very act of talking peace!"

Abraham was not impressed. The white men, he said, knowing the Moravian Indians were no longer Delawares and not their enemies, would leave them alone. No, they would not leave. God would protect them as he already had.

Captain Matthew Elliott from Detroit, representing the British, who were demanding that these Indians be moved away, stepped forward with an angry wave of his hand. He had had quite enough of this coaxing; they were not offering a choice but delivering an order. "What do *you* know of God?" he said condescendingly. "Can you really be so ignorant as to believe that because you have been, as they say, 'converted' and changed your name from Chief Netawatwees to Abraham, that this provides you protection of God? I tell you that God will not help you here once we begin to attack these Pennsylvanians in earnest. The whites will try to retaliate and you will be killed. Can't you understand that it is for your own protection that we have requested you to leave? We hoped you would be wise enough to do so without being forced. Instead, we find you a stupid, stubborn old man." He pointed to Thayendanega. "Chief Brant here has three hundred warriors waiting outside the village. Once again I say you *must* take up new residence on the Sandusky River. You have no choice. Go, or we will destroy your homes and your missions."

"But what of our corn, our other crops?"

Elliott shook his head. They would have to leave them behind. But there was no need to worry. He would see to it personally that the Moravian Indians would be given sufficient food to sustain them throughout the winter.

Abraham sighed. He could not believe his friends, the Americans, would hurt them, but this ultimatum worried him. They had worked long and hard with the missionaries to establish their three towns on the Tuscarawas — Salem, Gnadenhutten and Schoenbrun — and the thought of the homes of his people and their missions being destroyed was distressing to contemplate. There was really no need for him to be unreasonable about it. Perhaps after a winter on the Upper Sandusky River matters would have settled down enough so that they could come back. He nodded resignedly.

"We will go," he said.

[*November 10, 1781 — Saturday*]

The electrifying news had finally reached Kentucky and the populace was nearly delirious with joy. On October 19 Cornwallis had surrendered his entire army to Washington at Yorktown, Virginia. It had to be the beginning of the end, even though no cessation of British-American hostilities had yet been called and no peace conferences held. For all intents and purposes, America had won her independence as a free nation. The fighting was over. At least that was what they were saying in the east.

They were not so sure in the west.

[*February 4, 1782 — Monday*]

General Daniel Brodhead returned the salute of the young colonel who had just entered his quarters. He had heard rumors about this young man — that he was cruel and a hothead — and felt that such a temperament might now prove an asset.

"Colonel Williamson," Brodhead said, "the western Pennsylvania settlements, as you know, have been severely harassed all winter long by Mohawks and Delawares. They have stolen, burned and, on occasion, engaged in killing outlying settlers. They have done so with virtual impunity. I intend to change that."

"Yes sir?" David Williamson's dark eyes glittered.

"I'm tied up with details here and can't go myself, but I'm going to give you command of a hundred men. A week from today I want you to move out on a retaliatory expedition against the Delawares. You may have a free hand in this operation. That's all."

Williamson saluted smartly and turned to leave, but then stopped abruptly and swiveled around as Brodhead said, "Colonel!"

"Sir?"

"Do a thorough job. I want those Delawares taught a lesson they won't forget."

"Yes, sir!" Williamson said confidently. "You have my word, we'll give them something to remember."

[*February 20, 1782 — Thursday*]

Regardless of the British promises to provide food enough to sustain them through the winter, the Moravian Indians suffered severe famine. What supplies did occasionally come out of Detroit were meager in the extreme and nowhere near enough to tide them over, even on far less than adequate rations. The Wyandots and the few Delawares in the vicinity of Upper Sandusky were of little help. Not only had their own crops been skimpy last fall, but they were too engaged in their frequent raids into the Pennsylvania country. Besides, they looked rather scornfully upon any Indian who would willingly renounce his own tribal designation to take up the name Moravian.

Abraham had thrice journeyed to Detroit to plead for food; and now, at last, he returned with good news. No, the British had no food for them, but they had given Abraham permission to lead a hundred and fifty of his followers back to the three Tuscarawas River towns on a temporary visit for the purpose of gathering up what portion of their unharvested corn crop still remained on the stalks.

They would leave at once.

[*March 8, 1782 — Friday*]

Most of his people had fallen asleep now and Abraham stared unseeingly into the darkness of the big room. During the past two days of talk with the white chief Williamson and many of his men, he was able to reconstruct how such an unbelievable thing had happened. Yet, even as he reviewed it there was something of a nightmare quality about it all, a pervading unreality; in one corner of his mind he still felt that with the dawn he would awaken to find that all that had transpired was nothing but a wild dream.

Exactly two weeks ago he had led his hundred and fifty Moravian Indian followers on the overland journey to the forks of the Muskingum, arriving at the southernmost of their three towns, Salem, late in the afternoon. They had been delighted to find more corn had survived the winter than anticipated, and so Abraham had directed the fifty residents of this town to gather up the corn while he and the remainder continued upriver to Gnadenhutten and Schoenbrun, fifty staying at each of those villages also.

The days had gone by swiftly as the three separate parties worked in their fields, gathering and stripping the corn from the husks during the day and then, around the evening fires, shelling it off the cobs into large buckskin bags.

Meanwhile, Colonel David Williamson and his company of one hundred had arrived within a mile of Gnadenhutten and camped there. In the morning, observing Abraham and some of his followers at work in the cornfield on the opposite side of the river, fifteen volunteers had accompanied Williamson to the location. They crossed the river unseen in a large boatlike sugar-sap trough, two at a time; a vine rope was used by those still on shore to pull the empty boat back to them. When all sixteen were safely across, the remainder of the army marched into Gnadenhutten. There they found only two Indians, a man and his wife, both of whom they killed instantly with tomahawks lest they raise an alarm.

Williamson's squad, on approaching the Indians far out in the cornfield, found them much more numerous than expected. There were forty-eight — men, women and boys — nearly all of whom had weapons with them. His men behind him, Williamson approached in a friendly manner, holding up his hand in greeting. The Indians smiled and waved and followed Abraham as he moved to greet them.

"I come with good news," Williamson said blandly. "We have been sent here to take you back with us to the neighborhood of Fort Pitt where in the future you will be protected from all harm. You may quit your work here now, for there is no need. Soon you will be given good food in abundance, warm clothing and sturdy shelter.

Abraham broke into a wide smile and shook Williamson's hand warmly and, for those of his followers who had only partially understood, he translated. There were cries of joy and relief from all.

These Indians remembered how last year some of their people had been taken to Fort Pitt in similar manner and had been well treated by the commander of the fort and finally dismissed with fine gifts and tokens of lasting friendship. Under these circumstances it was not at all surprising that Abraham ordered his people, at Williamson's request, to surrender their arms as a token of good faith.

Abraham placed himself and his people under Colonel Williamson's protection and, again at the officer's request, sent a pair of runners to nearby Salem to tell his people at this village to come at once to Gnadenhutten.

Now the entire party recrossed the Tuscarawas, but as they came into the center of the village they found themselves surrounded by men with weapons aimed at them. Puzzled, Abraham asked what was wrong. Williamson refused to answer, but instead ordered the wrists of each Indian bound behind him. The mission and the largest house in the village were side by side and the prisoners were marched into the two buildings, men and boys into the former and the women into the latter. Once inside they were forced to sit on the floor and their ankles were thereupon bound as well.

After two hours the Salem group showed up, walking along happily, talking and laughing. They were greeted outside the town by Williamson and some of his men who shook their hands and smiled and told them their brothers were waiting for them in the mission and that Abraham had said for them to turn over their arms to him. Without suspicion they did so and then followed him into the village, only to have the same scene that had greeted Abraham reenacted.

The chief shook his head sadly as the new prisoners were brought in. How could this have happened? Did it mean that they were to be taken back and held as hostages at Fort Pitt for some purpose? For only one thing was he grateful — that he had not mentioned the third village of Schoenbrun above them, to whom he had planned sending another messenger after crossing the river.

A total of ninety-eight men, women and boys now sat or lay bound in the two buildings. Outside, a strong ring of guards had been stationed and there was no hope of escape. Thus they remained the rest of the day and through the night, being provided with neither food nor water nor toilet facilities. It was a terrible night and few of the captives slept.

In the morning, Colonel Williamson called a meeting of all his men to determine what should be done with the Indians. He spoke to them in a flat, emotionless voice.

"The question before us now," he said, "is whether these Moravian Indians, who are Delawares, should be taken as prisoners to Fort Pitt or be put to death." Some of the men were startled at this, but Williamson went on: "I might remind you of the damage nearly all of you have suffered at the hands of the Indians. And I might further remind you that General Brodhead's strict orders were that the Delawares should be taught an unforgettable lesson. To my way of thinking, imprisonment is hardly such a lesson."

He shot his cold dark glance over the assembled men and then concluded, "I now ask those of you who are in favor of saving their lives to step out and form a second rank." The manner in which he said it, and the thinly masked violence in his eyes, was clear indication that he expected no one to step forward.

A few braved his wrath, but only a few. One at a time they stepped out, but when the movement had ended only eighteen of the hundred had voted for mercy. The majority had ruled; the ninety-eight captives would be executed. It was Williamson himself who told Abraham of the judgment of his "court" and he seemed to revel in the sound of the phrase — "put to death" — as it rolled off his tongue.

Shocked and unbelieving, Abraham finally recovered enough to speak. "I call upon God as witness that my people are perfectly innocent of any crime against you. We are prepared and willing to suffer this death. Yet this much I ask of you: when we were converted from our heathen ways and baptized, we made a solemn promise to the Lord that we would live unto Him and endeavor to please Him alone in this world. But we know, too, that we have been wayward in many respects, and therefore we wish to have the night granted to us to pour out our hearts before Him in prayer and beg His mercy and pardon."

Williamson considered and then shrugged. It made little difference, actually. God had better have mercy on them, because he certainly wouldn't. The request was granted.

As word of the sentence spread through the captives in the mission and then jumped the gap to the women prisoners next door, a great wailing of terror arose which gradually subsided to weeping among the women and some of the smaller boys. Abraham spoke to them at length, reassuring them that God had not forsaken them and that, if it was His will that they should die thus, they should accept it with calmness and a certain joy in the knowledge that they would soon be in the presence of their Heavenly Father. At one point he put his back against the wall and managed to slide himself up along it until he regained his feet.

"My children, hear me," he said. "Our sentence is fixed and we shall soon all depart unto our Savior. This I must say now: I have sinned in many ways and have grieved the Lord with my disobedience, not walking as I ought to have done. But still I will cleave to my Savior, with my last breath, and hold Him fast, though I am so great a sinner. He will forgive me all my sins and not cast me out."

Together then they prayed long into the night, until at last only Abraham remained awake, staring into the darkness and asking himself again how this incredible thing could have happened. But now, as it became lighter in the big mission room, where so many times over the years he and his people had prayed and held services, he could hear them coming and called aloud to his people to awaken and say their final prayers.

Fully twenty men entered the room, led by Captain Charles Builderback who, by the drawing of lots, had been given the honor of starting off the executions. Builderback ordered that the captives be stood on their feet and faced against the walls, shoulder to shoulder around the room. There was just barely space enough for this.

The day before, as the lots were being drawn, the remark had been made that Abraham's long flowing hair would make a fine scalp and so now Builderback, having been handed a large cooper's mallet by one of his men, stepped up behind Abraham and without a word dealt him a blow which caved in the entire back of his skull. The Indian dropped instantly, and even as the chief's legs and arms jerked spasmodically, Builderback cut away the scalp and held it aloft in triumph while his men cheered lustily.

Moving now in a clockwise fashion from Abraham, Builderback felled thirteen more in succession, each blow making a hideous smacking sound. Following this fourteenth execution, however, Builderback blew out a great gust of air and handed the mallet to Private George Bellar.

"My arm's failing me," he said. "You go on in the same way. I think I've done pretty well."

Bellar grinned wickedly and, as Captain Builderback began scalping his last thirteen victims, the private carried on, using both hands and bringing the mallet down with such force that often bits of skull and bloody gray matter splattered his front. But Bellar played out quickly, too, and only managed to murder eleven before he was forced to hand the mallet to the next man. In the distance, sounds of a similar nature could be heard coming from the house next door. But still there were no cries, no pleas for mercy. It was too much for Private Otho Johnston, who abruptly vomited and then fled out the door with the laughter of his companions following him.

But Johnston had left the door ajar and now two of the victims closest to this portal — both of them boys of about fourteen — glanced at one another and nodded. All through the night they had worked on their bonds until they had finally gotten them off. With great care they had replaced them, but so loosely that a single exertion would cast them off both wrists and ankles.

At the instant the club next thudded into the head of a victim, the two boys threw off their ties and leaped out the door. They darted around the building and were practically into the woods before the cry was raised of their escape, but there was no pursuit. The consensus among the soldiers was that once in the woods no one would be able to find them. Besides, they were only boys. Let them go.

And go they did, running as they had never run, until they felt their hearts must burst, and crying as they ran — crying for their lost chief and their lost parents and brothers and sisters and other relatives, crying for their lost companions and neighbors, crying for their lost world.

They ran the full seven miles to Schoenbrun.

Back in Gnadenhutten the massacre continued until all ninety-six of them — thirty-five men, twenty-seven women and thirty-four boys — had been killed and scalped, not including the pair who had been tomahawked on the army's arrival here. Then, Colonel Williamson ordered both the mission and the house containing the women to be set afire. As the roaring flames made ashes of their crime, they set off to the north. While the executions were in progress, a scout had come in to report that he had found another village like this one just a little way upstream.

But when they got there, they found Schoenbrun abandoned.

[April 25, 1782 — Thursday]

Reaction to the Moravian Massacre, as it quickly came to be known, varied in different areas of the country, but mostly it was disapproving at best. The frontiersmen in Kentucky were shocked and dismayed at the barbarism of the act and a distinct undercurrent of fear ran through them that the retaliation, when it came, might spread to involve them. The frontiersmen in Pennsylvania were somewhat awed that such a thing had happened, but there were remarkably few who spoke out against it and many who asserted that the Indians had "got what they deserved." There was even speculation among them of mounting a second invasion of the same type. Leaders in the east were deeply disturbed by the news, but few, if any, had a true realization of what a cold-blooded, premeditated mass murder it had been. Besides which, they had worries of their own; the peace treaty negotiations with Great Britain in Paris were bogging down; political problems were besieging the new states; and the problem of establishing a federal government was rearing its head.

The Moravian missionaries were utterly devastated by the news, scarcely able to comprehend the enormity of what had happened, realizing with guilt that had they stayed at Lichtenau with their converts the tragedy might have been averted. The British in Detroit were appalled by it and yet were quick to assess its propaganda value, using it to light even brighter fires of unrest among the Indians. They even went so far in trying to prove the benevolence of "the great white father across the sea" that a company of Redcoats was dispatched at once to the Upper Sandusky River region to escort the remaining Moravian Indians to a quiet area to build a new village far from danger, a site along the banks of the Thames River in Ontario.

The Indians — all of them in general, and the Delawares in particular — were infuriated as they had never been before. They considered this massacre a wanton outrage of the blackest nature and a clear depiction of the real character of the *Shemanese*. They lived with one thought paramount in their minds now — total annihilation of these enemies. They had more than enough courage and fighting ability for the task. All they lacked were horses, cannons, gunpowder, firearms, food, supplies and manpower.

[June 12, 1782 — Wednesday]

For perhaps the hundredth time since accepting command of this army, Colonel William Crawford berated himself for ever joining the campaign. All his life, it seemed to him, he had been plagued with a sharply critical hindsight of his own actions, coupled with a distinct inability to heed his premonitions, most of which proved correct in the end. This time was no exception.

Ever since David Williamson's massacre of the Moravian Indians, a sort of blood lust had taken over the Pennsylvanians. Instead of seeing it for what it was, these settlers were calling that campaign a "great victory" and clamoring for another of the same to wipe out that other Moravian village along the Upper Sandusky River.

Their wish was granted.

Almost from the start it was dubbed "the Second Moravian Campaign" and, with the exception of Colonels Crawford and Williamson, who were both "loaned" by Fort Pitt for the expedition, the army of four hundred eighty men was made up entirely of western Pennsylvanian volunteers. The object of the campaign was to finish the work of the first one — marching to and destroying the Moravian town on the Upper Sandusky. After that they would march upstream to the south and wipe out the Delaware and Wyandot towns on the same river, principally the large village of Upper Sandusky.

It was the resolution of all those concerned in the expedition to kill instantly any Indian falling into their hands, Christian or heathen, friend or foe, man, woman or child. No quarter was to be given. Bulletins stressing this were tacked to trees in the campgrounds. The thirst for revenge for the long period of harassment the Indians had given them was all-encompassing.

The rendezvous point for the army was the old Mingo Town on the Ohio.[1] They came mounted on the best horses they could procure, for this was to be a "dash" campaign — in and out before any sizable force could be assembled against them. Each man furnished his own supplies, except for some ammunition provided by the lieutenant colonel of Pennsylvania's Washington County.

Upon assembling on May 25 they held an election for their commander, with Williamson and Crawford the candidates. Crawford won and accepted only with the greatest reluctance. They followed Williamson's

Trail, as the route to the Tuscarawas River villages was now being called, and camped at Schoenbrun, where they found much of the unharvested corn still on the stalks. During the evening a pair of Indians was seen by three of the militiamen; the moment the news of the discovery of Indians reached camp, the men rushed out into the woods in a tumultuous mass without any sign of order. It was at this moment that Crawford experienced a definite premonition of disaster.

The march continued uneventfully to the west until on June 6 they had reached the town of the Moravian Indians on the Sandusky River. Instead of being full of peaceful Christian Indians to murder and plunder to take, however, the village was abandoned. Only the broken remains of a few huts projected from the weeds.

Now they were confused and no little worried about what to do next. Crawford called a meeting of the officers and a decision was reached to march one day longer in the direction of Upper Sandusky; if the village was not reached by then, they would retreat in all haste.

Thus, on the morning of June 7, they rode through the Plains of Sandusky. About 2 P.M. the advance guard was suddenly attacked by Indians hidden in the high grass. The guard galloped back to the main army and a general engagement broke out. Heavy firing continued incessantly until darkness fell, when it ceased. The casualties were the same on both sides: three men killed. Both armies kindled large fires along the line of battle and then retired some distance from them to prevent surprise attack. Not long after the fires were built, a man bearing a white flag showed himself in the glow between the fires. Crawford sent a man to see him and in a few minutes he returned.

"He talks English, sir," the militiaman reported. "Asked for you by name. Says he wants to talk with you right away but that you're not to come nearer to him than twenty steps."

Crawford went at once, alone, stopping at the required distance and trying to make out the features of the short figure in the flickering light.

"Colonel Crawford," the man called, "do you know me?"

Crawford hesitated. "I seem to have some recollection of your voice," he admitted, "but I can't see your face well enough and those Indian clothes you're wearing don't help. Do I know you?"

"We shared lodgings once," came the reply. "My name is Simon Girty."

Girty! The deserter and renegade. How well Crawford knew him. They had once been very closely acquainted in those months before McDonald's campaign eight years ago.

"A surprise to meet you here, Girty. What do you want?"

Girty's voice lowered. "The Indians think I've come out here to tell you you're surrounded and to demand your surrender. I'll tell them you refused. Crawford, if you don't surrender, the Indians plan to take you tomorrow.

They're three times as strong as you are and they'll cut you to pieces. Tonight they really are surrounding you. When the move is completed you'll hear some guns fire all around the ring. But there's a large marshy ground to the east of you. It isn't covered. It'll be hard going, but you have no choice. Listen for the gap in the sound when the firing goes round the ring. Take your men and ride for that gap. It's your only chance."

"Why are you doing this, Girty?" Crawford demanded.

But Girty only threw down the white flag and disappeared back into the darkness. Crawford returned at once to his camp and called a meeting of the officers to discuss this alarming situation.

Williamson and many of the men distrusted Girty and figured the whole business smelled of a trap. They could not believe there were that many Indians about; indeed, Williamson wanted to take a hundred fifty men and move straight into Upper Sandusky, but the commander refused him permission.

"Even if you reached the town, Dave," he said, "all you'd find would be empty dwellings and the army would be weakened by the division. I can't allow it. These Indians don't care anything about saving their town. It's worth nothing. Whatever squaws and children and goods were there have been taken away long ago."

Williamson started to object but Crawford cut him off. "I said no and that's an order, Colonel! These Indians want our lives, our horses and our equipment. If they get us divided they'll soon have them. We've got to stay together and do the best we can."

They continued to talk about the visit from Girty. Crawford and quite a few of the men were inclined to believe the renegade and the scales tilted in their favor when a firing of rifles broke out indicating a circle around them, but with a gap on the east side. A retreat was decided upon along the route suggested by Girty as the only means of saving their army. They would leave as soon as the fires died down. In the meantime, the three dead men were buried and ashes spread over the common grave so the Indians would think it a campfire site and not dig up the bodies for their scalps.

Crawford suddenly gave the order and they moved to the east quickly, expecting ambush at every step. They soon found themselves in the marsh and safely through the Indian lines, whereupon Crawford began swinging the column in a wide circle to the left to get back to their original trail, which they reached in a couple of hours.

During the whole of June 8 the retreat progressed with occasional long-shot harassment of the rear guard. Once again Williamson and Crawford were arguing. About three hundred of the men sided with their commander in his contention that they must stick together, but Williamson succeeded in convincing the remainder that the best escape possibility lay in breaking into small parties, avoiding the trail by which they had come and making their way back by different directions. The argument turned into near open rebellion until finally Crawford allowed them to go.

Williamson's group split into nine parties of twenty men each, one of which he led, and all nine groups set off in different directions, leaving Colonel Crawford and his weary main army. They calculated the Indians would follow the bigger prize and leave them alone.

They were wrong.

Seven of the small parties were followed and wiped out almost immediately. The remaining two, including the detachment led by Williamson, joined forces and, with severe losses, managed to return to the main army. But now this army was a pitiful thing, weak and straggling and spread out all over the countryside. Many of the men simply fled on their own, alone, and were never seen again.

Toward late afternoon, Crawford suddenly discovered that his son, John Crawford, his son-in-law, Major James Harrison, and his two nephews, James Rose and Bill Crawford, were all missing. He had no way of knowing that all four were already dead, so he halted and called for them as the line of militia passed by — but there was no answer. Then, when he attempted to regain the lead, he found his horse was so weak it couldn't even catch up with the rearguard.

A straggler came along and he saw that it was the army surgeon, Dr. Edward Knight. They stayed together and a little later they were joined by Lieutenant Timothy Downing and another man Crawford didn't know. They traveled all night, directing their course by the light of the north star. On the following morning, June 9, they encountered Captain John Biggs and Lieutenant Bruce Ashley, but the six of them made little headway and camped together early in the evening.

At dawn they were discovered by Indians and Crawford and Knight were captured almost at once; Biggs and Ashley were killed and Downing and the other man escaped. The arms of the captives were bound and rawhide halters placed about their necks and they were led to a Delaware and Wyandot camp less than a mile from their own campsite. Here they found nine other prisoners and seventeen Indians, and here they stayed all day.

On June 11, Crawford and the other ten prisoners were marched to the main Delaware village, called Big Spring, on a bottom land on the east bank of Tymochtee Creek, about eight miles above its mouth at the Sandusky River.[2] And this morning two of the major Delaware chiefs, Pipe and Wingenund, had arrived.

Abruptly Crawford's hopes skyrocketed. Wingenund! Years ago at Fort Pitt, Crawford and Wingenund had become good friends when Wingenund had acted as guide and interpreter for the British under Alex

McKee. They had drunk together in Crawford's own quarters and become attached to one another. Now Crawford watched closely and hopefully as the two chiefs talked with the Indians; except for one brief glance in his direction, however, Wingenund paid no attention to him. In a few minutes the chiefs retired to a *wegiwa*.

At once nine of the prisoners — all but Crawford and Dr. Knight — were led to the edge of the village where they were unceremoniously tomahawked and scalped. Knight was left tied where he was but Crawford was now taken by five of the Indians, stripped of all clothing and led to a thick post projecting fifteen feet from the ground. His wrists still tied tightly behind him, a long rawhide cord was run between his arms and then brought around the post and tied firmly in a large loop. In this way he was able to walk around the pole, stand, sit, even lie down, but was unable to move more than four feet in any direction from the pole.

In a little while Pipe came toward him with another man, followed by a large crowd of warriors and squaws. Crawford recognized the other man as Simon Girty and once again his hopes began to rise. But not for long. While the pair stood twenty or thirty feet away, the crowd of Indians rushed up with sticks and switches and beat Crawford unmercifully, withdrawing only when his body was badly welted and bloodstained and he appeared on the verge of unconsciousness.

The group then raced over to where Dr. Knight was tied and subjected him to the same punishment, while Girty and Chief Pipe watched quietly and in apparent approval. At length Crawford came around enough to call to Girty and both the renegade and the chief approached him.

"Girty," Crawford said, his voice hesitant with pain, "are they planning to burn me?"

"Yes they are, Colonel."

"My God, Girty, you're a white man, too. Can't you help me?"

Girty shrugged and grimaced, indicating he doubted it but he would try. He turned to Chief Pipe and spoke rapidly in the Delaware tongue. This prisoner, he said, was a good soldier with whom, many years ago, Girty had shared a cabin at Fort Pitt. It was Colonel Williamson, not Crawford, who had murdered the Moravian Indians. Would Chief Pipe sell him this prisoner for three hundred fifty bucks?

Chief Pipe took a step backward, his expression as shocked as if Girty had slapped him. Then a great rage came over him at the effrontery of this white man, at the great insult of his remarks. When he spoke his words hissed between his teeth and were frightening in the malevolence they carried.

"Do you think I am a *squaw*, white man? How dare you make such a proposition to me? If you speak one more word on the subject I will have a stake erected beside his and burn you along with the white chief!"

He stalked away toward his own *wegiwa* at the other edge of town, nearly three quarters of a mile distant. Girty had paled at the threat in the chief's retort and now he blew out a gust of air and came closer to Crawford. He explained what they had said and then shook his head.

"I would like to save you, Crawford, but I will not give up my own life needlessly nor jeopardize my position among the Indians. But there is one thing I can still do. There are two parties of important British traders not beyond reach — one on the Black Fork of Mohican River, the other on the Sandusky below Upper Sandusky. They both have much more influence than I among the Delawares. I'll send runners for them at once. Perhaps they may be able to buy you, but I cannot hold out much hope on that."

Crawford nodded that he understood and Girty started away, but then turned back. "One thing more," he said. "The death they have in store for you is a very slow and painful one. If all hope becomes lost, I will do what I can to end your suffering more quickly."

Crawford watched him walk away, not cheered by Girty's final remark. He had little hope where the English traders were concerned. There remained, in fact, only one real hope for him.

Wingenund.

[*June 13, 1782 — Thursday*]

Shortly after sunrise, still shivering from his night of nakedness at the stake, Colonel William Crawford saw Girty threading his way through the crowd already assembling and called him to come over. Girty hesitated and almost walked on, then turned and came toward the captive.

A foot-high circle of kindling had been placed all the way about Crawford's stake at a distance of about five yards. About a hundred dry hickory poles, each an inch or so thick and upwards of twenty feet in length, had been placed so that they lay with one end atop the kindling and the other stretching outward, away from the circle. Girty stepped between them until he could come no closer without stepping upon them and he stopped.

"Any word from your friends, Girty?" Crawford's eyes were pleading.

Girty shook his head and turned to leave but Crawford cried, "Wait!" Girty turned back, and Crawford hurried on. "Listen, do you know Chief Wingenund very well?"

"Well enough."

"He and I used to be friends at Fort Pitt. I don't think he knows who I am. Maybe he could get me out of this."

Girty was shaking his head even as Crawford spoke. "He knows you. That's why he hasn't come to see you. He's afraid you'll ask him to help you. He doesn't think you know who he is."

"Do me one last favor, Girty," Crawford begged. "Go to him right away. Tell him I ask to see him in the name of the friendship we once shared. Tell him he can't deny me this."

"I'll give it a try, Crawford. Don't expect much."

A quarter hour passed before Wingenund finally came up, his embarrassment and agitation obvious. He stepped over the ring of hickory poles and stood in front of Crawford and feigned surprise.

"Are you not Colonel Crawford?"

"I am."

"So! Yes! Indeed!"

Crawford held back his irritation at this play-acting. "Wingenund," he said, "don't you remember the friendship that existed between us? I recollect we were always glad to see each other."

Wingenund smiled. "Yes! I remember all this and that we often drank together and that you have been kind to me."

Crawford relaxed a little. "Then I hope the same friendship still continues."

"It would, of course, were you where you ought to be and not here." Wingenund was frowning now.

"And why not here? I hope you would not desert a friend in the time of need. Now is the time for you to exert yourself in my behalf, as I'd do for you if you were in my place."

"Colonel Crawford! You have placed yourself in a situation which puts it out of my power — and that of others of your friends — to do anything for you."

"How so, Wingenund?"

The chief was becoming angry now. "By joining yourself to that devil, Williamson, and his party. Only the other day, this man murdered a great number of Moravian Indians, knowing them to be friends, knowing that he ran no risk in murdering a people who would not fight and whose only business was praying!"

"Listen, Wingenund, believe me! Had I been with Williamson at the time, this would never have happened. Not I alone, but all your friends and all good men, whoever they are, reprobate acts of this kind."

The Indian nodded. "That may be. Yet these friends, these good men did not prevent him from going out again to kill the remainder of these inoffensive, yet foolish, Moravian Indians. I say foolish because they believed the whites in preference to us. We have often told them they would one day be so treated by those people who called themselves their friends! We told them there was no faith to be placed in what the white man said; that their fair promises were only intended to allure us that they might the more easily kill us, as they had done many Indians before these Moravians."

"I am sorry to hear you speak thus, Wingenund," Crawford said sadly. "As to Williamson's going out again, when I found out he was determined to do it, I went out with him to prevent his committing fresh murders."

Wingenund broke into a harsh, scornful laugh. "This story, my friend, the Indians would not believe were even *I* to tell them so."

"Why would they not believe?"

"Because it would have been out of your power to have prevented his doing as he pleased."

"Out of my power!" Crawford's voice rose indignantly. "Have any Moravian Indians been killed or hurt since we came out?"

"None," Wingenund replied, but now his voice became harsh and bitter, "but do not try to deceive me, Colonel! We know well what you have done. You first went to their town and, finding it deserted, you turned on the path toward us. If you had been in search of war- riors only, you would not have gone thither. Our spies watched you closely. They saw you while you were gathering on the other side of the Ohio. They saw you cross the river. They saw where you camped for the night there. They visited every one of your camps the moment you were gone from it and they found bits of paper with writing on them that had been stuck to the trees by your men and which said that no Indian — friend, enemy, heathen, Christian, man, woman, boy, girl or infant — should be spared. How brave an army! Our spies saw you turn off from the path at the deserted Moravian town. We knew you were going out of your way to attack Upper Sandusky. Your steps were constantly watched and you were permitted quietly to proceed until you reached the spot where we wished to attack you."

Crawford's shoulders slumped and he could not deny the truth of anything Wingenund had said. Those words destroyed his last ray of hope and now his voice was filled with emotion as he asked, "What do they intend to do with me?"

The harshness in Chief Wingenund's features softened. He placed his hand on Crawford's shoulder as he replied. "I tell you with grief. As Williamson, with his whole cowardly host, ran off in the night at the whistling of our warriors' balls — being satisfied that now he had no Moravians to deal with, but men who could fight, and with such he did not wish to have anything to do — I say, as he has escaped and they have taken you, they will take revenge on you in his stead."

"And is there no possibility of preventing this?" Crawford was pleading now and did not see the look of disgust which crossed the Indian's face at such unmanliness. "Can you devise no way of getting me off? You shall, my friend, be well rewarded if you are instrumental in saving my life."

Wingenund shook his head. "Had Williamson been taken with you, I and some friends, by making use of what you have told me, might perhaps have succeeded in saving you; but as the matter now stands, no man would dare to interfere in your behalf. The King of England himself, were he to come on this spot with all his wealth and treasure, could not effect this purpose. The blood of the innocent Moravians, more than half of them women and children, cruelly and wantonly murdered, calls loudly for revenge. The nation to which they belonged will have revenge. The Shawnees, our brothers, have asked for your fellow prisoner and on him, *they* will take revenge.[3] All the nations connected with us cry out, Revenge! Revenge! The Moravians whom you went to destroy, having fled instead of avenging their brethren, the offense is become national and the nation itself is bound to take revenge!"

Numbly, Crawford nodded. "My fate is then fixed and I must prepare to meet death in its worst form?"

Wingenund sighed. "I am sorry for it, but I cannot do anything for you. Had you attended to the Indian principle, that as good and evil cannot dwell together in the same heart, so a good man ought not go into evil company, you would not be in this sorrowful position. You see now, when it is too late, after Williamson has deserted you, what a bad man he must be. Nothing now remains for you but to meet your fate like a brave man. Farewell, Colonel Crawford. They are coming. I will retire to a solitary spot."

Chief Pipe had moved into the center of the milling mass of Indians and stepped up on a log so that he was head and shoulders above them. As he raised his arms the laughter and shrieking and murmur of conversation that had been going on died away. There were about forty warriors in this throng and sixty or seventy squaws and children.

For more than half an hour the chief spoke, his voice filled with controlled anger and emotion. Crawford understood nothing of what was being said and he looked around. In only two faces — and even one of those he was not sure of — did he detect any compassion: Dr. Knight and Girty, the latter sitting close to the tied doctor.

There was a hideous triumphant screaming as Chief Pipe completed his speech and immediately all the warriors and at least half the squaws rushed up until the closest were within a few feet of Crawford. All of them carried flintlock rifles. Into the barrels they poured extra-large quantities of gunpowder but no balls, and now they shot at him in turn.

The grains of powder, saltpeter still burning, peppered his skin, some of it puncturing and continuing to burn just beneath the skin. Crawford screamed until he was hoarse and then only a kind of whimpering grunt issued from him. More than seventy powder charges had struck him everywhere from feet to neck, but the greater majority had been aimed at his groin, and when they were finished the end of his penis was black and shredded and still smoking.

The crowd thinned momentarily as the guns were returned to the *wegiwas*, but as soon as all the Indians had reassembled, Chief Pipe stepped up to Crawford and with two swift movements sliced off his ears. From where he sat watching in horror, fifty feet away, Dr. Knight could see blood flowing down both sides of Crawford's head, bathing his shoulders, back and chest.

Now came squaws with flaming brands and they lighted the kindling all the way around the circle, igniting the material every foot or so until the entire circle was ablaze. The poles quickly caught fire on their tips and the heat became intense, causing the closest spectators to fall back. A peculiar, hair-raising animal sound now erupted from Crawford. He ran around the post in a frenzy, finally falling to the ground and wrapping his body around the stake. After the better part of an hour the fire died down, leaving behind a fanned-out ring of long poles, each with one end a glowing spike.

Crawford's back, buttocks and the skin on the back of his thighs had blistered and burst and then curled up into little charred crisps. The animal sounds from him were fainter now. About this time there was something of a disturbance and the British traders Girty had sent for cantered into the village. They greeted both Pipe and Wingenund in friendly fashion, complimented them on Crawford's capture and moved closer to the fire ring to look. Both men paled at the sight, but they turned back to Chief Pipe and announced their pleasure at being able to witness the execution. In a few moments the chief waved for the continuation of the torture and the traders stepped over to join Girty and watch. As they came up, one of them looked directly at Girty and gave a barely perceptible shake of his head before turning around.

In groups of four the Indians now began taking turns at a new torture. Each of the four would select a pole and jab the glowing end onto Crawford's skin where they thought it would give most pain. Dr. Knight thought Crawford near death by now, but was amazed to see the officer scramble to his feet and begin stumbling about the stake, attempting to avoid the glowing ends which hissed and smoked wherever they touched him. One of the glowing points was thrust at his face and as he jerked to avoid it he ran into another which contacted his open eye, and a fearful shriek erupted from him.

When the poles had all been used and tossed on a pile to one side, some of the squaws came up with broad boards and scooped up piles of glowing embers to throw at him until soon he had nothing to walk upon but coals of fire and hot ashes.

"Girty! Girty! Where are you?" These were the first coherent words Crawford had spoken since before the guns were fired. "Girty, in the name of Christ, kill me! Shoot me. Oh my God, Girty, *kill me!*"

Chief Pipe, hearing Girty's name, shot the renegade a stern glare and Girty neither moved nor replied to Crawford's plea, knowing he was closer to the stake now himself than he had ever thought to be. Most of the Indians did not understand what Crawford was saying, but the beseeching tone of voice pleased them and they clapped their hands and shouted aloud in triumph at having forced the white chief into this outburst.

When there was no answer to his cries, Crawford began a shuffling walk round and round the stake as if in a trance, scarcely flinching as he stepped on the hot coals. Finally he stopped and slowly raised his head and his voice came out surprisingly loud and clear.

"Almighty God, be with me now. Have mercy upon me God. I pray you end this suffering so that I might be with you where there is no pain and suffering. Oh God, dear God, help me!"

Once more he began the same shuffling walk until at last, two full hours after having been prodded with the glowing poles, he fell on his stomach and lay silent. At once Chief Pipe stepped over the ring of ashes and cut a deep circle on the top of Crawford's head with his knife, wrapped the long dark hair around his hand and yanked hard. The pop as the scalp pulled off was clearly audible to Girty and Dr. Knight.

Chief Pipe now stepped clear of the circle and advanced on the captive doctor. He held the dripping scalp in front of his eyes and shook it. "This is your great captain!" he said. With rapid strokes he whipped the fleshy portion of the scalp back and forth across Knight's face a dozen times or more, stopping only when there came a deep murmur from the crowd behind him.

A squaw had entered the circle of ashes with a board heaped full of brightly glowing coals, and these she scattered on Crawford's back and held them with the board against the officer's bare skull. The murmur that had arisen was occasioned by what seemed wholly unbelievable: Crawford groaned faintly and rolled over and then slowly, ever so slowly, drew up his knees and raised himself to a kneeling position. For perhaps two minutes he stayed like this and then he placed one foot on the ground and stood erect again, beginning anew that queer shuffling walk. A few squaws touched burning sticks to him but he seemed insensitive to them, no longer even attempting to pull away. It was the most appalling sight Dr. Knight had ever witnessed and, unable to control himself any longer, he suddenly vomited and then screamed at his captors, cursing them and calling them murderers and fiends and devils, blaming Girty more than anyone else.[4]

Chief Pipe made a motion and one of the warriors cut the thong binding Knight to the stake at his back and then propelled him toward the Chief's *wegiwa*. When he was gone from sight, Pipe issued some more commands and a bevy of squaws scurried away and returned with armloads of fresh kindling. This was tossed into a pile a dozen yards from the stake and lighted. The hickory poles were thrown atop the new fire.

When the fire reached its peak, two warriors cut the rawhide cord that bound the still shuffling Crawford and, one on each side, let him shuffle toward the fire. When the heat became too intense for them to advance closer, they thrust him from them and he sprawled onto the blaze. His legs jerked a few times and one arm flailed out but then, as skin and flesh blackened, living motion stopped and all that remained was a gradual drawing of arms and legs close to the body in the pugilistic posture characteristic in persons burned to death.

So ended the life of Colonel William Crawford.

[*August 22, 1782 — Thursday*]

The pleasure General George Rogers Clark felt at seeing the huge frontiersman died aborning at the expression on Simon's face. The usual smile was missing and there was a heaviness, a gravity in his every movement as he approached. The handsome features were frozen into tight, stern lines and he walked with an unnatural stiffness. They shook hands warmly, Clark's hand nearly lost in the big man's grip.

"Trouble, General," Kenton said. "Bad trouble."

Clark listened carefully as the scout reported. What he had to say was based on his own observations, the accounts told him by other frontiersmen and information extracted from several dying prisoners. It was not a pleasant report.

The British Captain, William Caldwell, along with Alexander McKee and Chief Joseph Brant, had been leading an attacking force of a thousand Indians and fifty Redcoats en route to destroy Wheeling when Simon Girty intercepted them with news of Crawford's defeat and subsequent death at the stake. Reasoning that the escaped whites of Crawford's army would by now have made their way back to Pennsylvania and alerted the forts there, Caldwell ordered the invasion to be diverted and to go, instead, against the newest and weakest of the Kentucky settlements: Bryant's Station, six miles north of Lexington.

This change in plans had not met with much enthusiasm from the northeastern Ohio Indians under Chief Brandt, their interest being more in the closer, more dangerous Pennsylvania forts. As the march progressed toward Kentucky, arguments broke out among the various tribes represented — Wyandots, Shawnees, Delawares, Ottawas, Chippewas and Mohawks — with the result that great numbers of the Indians simply broke away to return to their homes. By the time Caldwell's army reached Bryant's Station it numbered only two hundred forty men.

They had come upon the station on August 16 and attacked it by surprise. Nevertheless, two men there managed to escape and go for help.

The little fort suffered badly under the concerted attack but everyone fought doggedly — even the women and children — all of them aware that if they could just hold on, help would come.

Having expected almost instant capitulation, Caldwell was amazed when wave after wave of his forces were held off and driven back. Instead of an easy conquest in a matter of minutes, the siege had continued all day, sporadically through the night and all the next day.

The men who had gotten away fled to Lexington and, as a force was being gathered there under Colonel John Todd, messengers were sent to Harrodsburg, Boonesboro, Danville and Stanford for more help. First to arrive was a small army from nearby Boonesboro, led by Daniel Boone himself. Todd, realizing that Bryant's could not long hold out without help, took command and led the force toward the little station, certain that Harrod's and Logan's men would soon be coming behind them.

But by this time Captain Caldwell realized that he had taken far too long in his effort to crush Bryant's. He knew the area would soon be swarming with retaliating Kentuckians and so he ordered a retreat, swinging eastward toward the Blue Licks.

They were gone a few hours when Todd's army of one hundred seventy-six men arrived and set off immediately on the enemy's trail. Within twenty-four hours they had reached the ford of the Licking River at Blue Licks and saw that the attackers had crossed here so recently that fresh mud still swirled in the eddies along shore.

Boone advised against going across, knowing the terrain beyond was a maze of ravines and ideal for ambush. Todd agreed, as did Lieutenant Colonel Stephen Trigg. It was obvious that they were outnumbered and the results could be devastating to them. But now stepped forward that hotheaded gambler, Hugh McGary, who had been named a major for this enterprise. Irrationally angry about the attack on Bryant's, he demanded revenge at all costs. Many of the men seemed inclined to agree with him and he swayed them all the more by bellowing that they must push on after them lest the enemy escape. It was obvious they had them on the run, so why quit? Were there no men here? He, Hugh McGary, would go after them if it meant going alone! With this he plunged his horse into the water, calling that any who were men and not rabbits could follow him.

Emotion prevailed over reason and the men swarmed after him. There was nothing for the officers to do but accompany them, though with great reluctance and warnings. Within a mile their fears proved true. Indians and Redcoats sprang from behind every tree and rock and in a fierce battle lasting only fifteen minutes, more than a third of the Kentuckians were killed and seven captured. The slaughter was awful and Caldwell could easily have wiped out the remainder but, still fearful of further reinforcements for the Kentuckians, he chose to resume his retreat. This time his soldiers and Indian allies were not followed.

Simon Kenton's voice was nearly breaking as he told Clark the rest of the story. He, himself, had been at Logan's Fort — Stanford — when word of the attack on Bryant's came. Logan gathered four hundred seventy men and, with Kenton as captain of one of the companies, they rode hard. On reaching Bryant's they learned that Todd's party had already been gone a day and without hesitation they followed.

In the early morning light of the day after the battle — August 20 — they crossed the ford and viewed with sick horror the defeated army. The bodies were still being gathered and brought to a central location and an unspeakable rage and sorrow filled Simon as he saw stretched out in death the forms of so many friends and companions: John Todd, one of the first to be killed, lay beside the body of Stephen Trigg. Only Boone, of the three principal officers, had survived, although he was wounded and his own son, Israel, had been killed. And there was Simon's former fellow spy and companion, Silas Harlan, and the Bulger brothers, Major Edward and Captain John. Here, too, were Captains Clough Overton and John Beasley, Joe Kincaid and John Gordon. All five of the lieutenants had been killed — Bill Givins and John Kennedy, James McGuire and Barnett Rogers and pleasant little Thomas Hinkson. And the man who had been to blame for it all, Hugh McGary, had emerged unscathed.

Simon paused, unable for the moment to continue, his head bowed and seeing again in his mind's eye the terrible picture of violent death that had overtaken seventy men — good men, all of them; men who had done much to help carve Kentucky County out of this wilderness.

At length he raised his head and continued. He had stayed to help bury these men, these friends of many years' standing, and then he had ridden here to Louisville to Clark. Would the general mount an expedition to go against the Shawnees in the same villages of Chillicothe and Piqua Town his army destroyed two years ago?

General George Rogers Clark would.

[*September 6, 1782 — Friday*]

Simon Kenton took considerable pleasure in visiting Ruth in the one-room cabin at Quick's Run not far from Harrodsburg. His affair with her had lasted many months but he had never really considered marrying her and so now he was disturbed at her abrupt comment that she would not marry him.

He frowned and raised himself on an elbow, the linsey-covered cornhusk matting of the bed crackling with the movement and the light of the single candle across the room causing strange shadows to flicker across their nude forms. She was looking at him intently but when he opened his mouth to speak she stopped him with light kisses and he lay back and felt her small hand come to rest on his and cup it even more firmly to her ample breast.

"You wonder why I say this," she said slowly, "and I'll tell you. I see you now and then, Simon. One day you are here, the next you're gone. You may come back, but then again you may not; one never knows for sure. Other men put down roots and fight if danger comes to them, but you go to danger and one day you will not come back from it. I will not be the woman at home waiting for her husband, wondering if he will ever return. I couldn't stand that."

Ruth paused and though he sensed she didn't expect him to speak, he felt he had to say something. He shook his head. "I'm not one to put down roots," he admitted. "I could never stay too long in one place. But I would marry you if you like."

Her eyes suddenly glistened and she sat up and kissed him full on the mouth, then let her lips pass lightly over his bare shoulder as she lay back beside him. She shook her head and continued, "What we have had is good. What we can still have will be good, too, perhaps even better. I am your woman, but not your wife. You do not love me and I do not yet love you, as I could if I let myself. I won't do that. I can stop being your woman, but I could not stop being your wife. Will you promise not to force me — or even ask me — to be your wife?" She sat up again and their eyes locked. "Will you promise me that?"

Distinctly puzzled, Simon nodded and now Ruth took the hand that cupped her breast and placed it low on her soft belly and pressed it firmly to the warm flesh there.

"I'm glad, Simon," she said. "Do not forget that promise when I tell you that beneath your hand at this moment is growing your child."

[*November 3, 1782 — Sunday*]

From everywhere in Kentucky County the men came and now, as they assembled here on the Ohio shore opposite the mouth of Licking River, Simon Kenton was amazed at the similarity of this rendezvous with the one that had taken place at this same spot two years ago. Even their destination, in part, was the same; it was as if the pages of the calendar had been turned back and a segment of life was being relived.

A thousand and fifty mounted men were gathered here, armed and fully confident in the ability of General George Rogers Clark to lead them on a successful campaign. Hardly a man there was not known personally to Simon Kenton. These were the men whose lives he had helped to save, whose forts and homes he had helped to build, men whom he had guided across the wilderness to the places where they wanted to settle. Strong men and silent, men driven with a desire for revenge and an equally strong desire to possess the lands and goods and country of the Indians against whom they were preparing to march.

Here was Benjamin Logan, himself a general now, second in command of the army under Clark. And here were the Pattersons and the Todds, the Harrods and Boones and McGarys, the Stewarts and Lees and Cassidys and Galloways. Here were the men Kenton knew and respected, the men he had watched mold their own little kingdoms in trackless woods and prairies and canelands of the Kentucky country. Over a thousand of them had assembled here and it was hard for Simon to believe that only seven years ago there was no white man here at all save for himself and his companion, Williams.

Again in charge of scouts and spies, Kenton would guide the army to a permanent campsite at the point where two creeks came together a half day's ride from old Chillicothe and from where they could launch their attack.[5] At this point the army would divide in two, Clark's half pressing on to destroy Chillicothe and Piqua Town again and Logan's force going against the Shawnee towns on the Great Miami River, Upper and Lower Piqua Towns, as well as against the principal source of their supplies, Peter Loramie's trading post. Clark's larger force would be mostly afoot, while Logan's hundred and fifty men would all be mounted. They would strike hard and fast and perhaps this time the destruction could be made so complete that the Shawnees would not return.

[November 9, 1782 — Saturday]

General George Rogers Clark uncorked the ink bottle and carefully began printing the final order for his men before engaging the enemy. Scouts had reported both Chillicothe and Piqua Town bustling with normal activity, indicating that the army's approach was unknown to them. It looked as if this time, at last, they would catch them by surprise.

Clark wished momentarily that he had kept Ben Logan with him, for this was a man of great ability and excellent judgment — a good right arm in which to have perfect faith. But this, of course, was why he had chosen Logan to lead his horsemen against the upper Great Miami River towns. He would do the job and do it well, Clark knew, and the very assurance of this had been transmitted one to another in their final handshake this afternoon when Logan and his men rode off.

Clark smiled, thinking of the report Simon Kenton had given him a short while ago following a spying mission at Chillicothe. Not only were the inhabitants unsuspicious, but the population of the village was less than during the last expedition and the same was true of Piqua Town. Apparently not all the ousted Shawnees had moved back after all. It was good news.

Clark tapped out his pipe, put it into his pocket and bent to the task of writing out the final general orders. His handwriting was poor and his spelling less than perfect and he grunted with exasperation at the necessity which somehow, even on the eve of battle, always seemed to force him to paperwork, which he detested. He wrote:

November 9, 1782

GEN'L ORDERS

as an action with the Enemy may be hourly Expected the Officers are Requested to pay the Strictest attention To their duty as Suffering no man to Quit his Rank Without leave as Nothing is more dangerous than Disorder. If fortunately any prisoner Should fall in to our hands they are by no means to be put to Death without leave as it will be attended with the Immediate Masseerce of all our Citizens that are in the hands of the Enimy and Also deprive us of the advantage of Exchanging for our own people, no person to attempt to take any Plunder untill Orders Should Issue for that purpose under penalty of Being punished for Disobedience of orders and to have no share of Such plunder himself. The Officers in perticular are requested to Observe that the Strictest Notice be paid to this Order, as much Depends on it all plunder taken to be Delivered to the Quarter Master, to be Devided among the Different Batallions in proportion to their Numbers any person Concealing Plunder of any kind Shall be Considered as Subject to the penalty of the Above Order.

G. R. Clark

Clark blew on the ink, squinted at the paper sideways to make certain it was dry and would not smudge and then called on his orderly to post it in plain sight on the huge oak along the creek bank, with word to pass that all the men were to read it or have it read to them.

At first the crowd around the posted orders was large but, as evening drew on, it diminished as the men returned to their fires to eat and get their gear in readiness for the attack tomorrow. Shortly after dark only three men stood before the order, one on each side of the man in the middle who read it aloud slowly and laboriously in the flickering light of the nearest campfire. All three were dressed similarly — worn leathers and linsey-woolsey and moccasins. Each had a knife at his belt and carried a flintlock and one wore a tomahawk at his waist. All of them wore fur hats made of raccoon skin.

When the man had finished reading he spat a stream of brown juice to the ground and grumbled something about Clark taking all the fun out of things. The man to his left grunted an affirmative but the tall fellow on the right continued to stare silently at the general orders. The reader squinted at him and spoke again.

"Don't recollect I've seed you afore. You new to Kentuck?"

The tall man nodded. "Got here just in time to come along," he said. "Came from my folk's place along Cherry River south and east of Kanawha."

"That right? Me an' Jaybo here, we're from Pittsburgh. Never been down around that way. What's your name?"

The tall man shrugged. "Just call me Duke. Well, I'm going to eat now." He turned away and sauntered off into the darkness.

Jaybo looked at his companion and grinned. "Them Virginny men talk funny, don't they Mike?"

Moments later and fifty yards away the man who had identified himself as Duke slipped through the undergrowth and silently crossed the creek in water just over his knees. On the other side he broke into a quiet run which continued until he reached a little clearing a quarter mile away. There he ripped off the fur cap and shook his long black hair free and literally tore the linsey shirt from his back. He untied the horse awaiting him and threaded his way through the woods for more than a mile before finally breaking into open prairie country.

Blue Jacket curled his lips, the very fact that he had spoken English distasteful in his mouth. He had been surprised at how difficult it had been for him to read Clark's orders. How many years now had it been since he had tried to read English? Not enough, he decided.

In a few hours he reached Chillicothe and spread the news; the *Shemanese* under Clark were coming again. And again there were not enough warriors here to face them. Retreat was the only answer, both from here and from Piqua Town. He would warn the others at Moluntha's Town and Mackachack, in his own town and Girty's Town, in Upper and Lower Piqua Towns and in Solomon's Town. They would all assemble at Wapatomica and there, with proper strength and weapons, meet the enemy.

As Blue Jacket rode off, a fourteen-year-old youth moved into the shadows behind his *wegiwa* and clasped the piece of quartzite tied on a leather thong about his neck. It felt warm in his hand.

"Moneto," he whispered, "I call on you through this *opa-waw-ka* to help us. Let us escape without harm except to our *wegiwas*, which can always be built again. Spare our elders and our women and our children and keep our warriors strong. Let not the *Shemanese* destroy them. And most of all, Moneto, spare my brother, Chiksika, and my sister, Tecumapese, and the members of our family. I, Tecumseh, ask this of you through the *opa-waw-ka* which I earned here."

Then he went where the others were to help with packing their belongings.

[*November 25, 1782 — Monday*]

The expedition was a success on both fronts. For the second time Clark's army destroyed Chillicothe and Piqua Town, burning not only every *wegiwa* but setting fire to prairie grasses which, tinder dry, burned with a fierce whipping flame for miles in all directions, charring trees and bushes and destroying game. What dried corn was found was fed to the horses and what stored vegetables were discovered were tossed into the burning remains of the *wegiwas* to be rendered inedible.

Logan had been just as successful. He burned both Upper and Lower Piqua Towns on the Great Miami and he destroyed Peter Loramie's store after the transportable plunder there had been packed on their own horses.

But the victories, while complete, were hollow. These villages were deserted when they arrived and few things of value remained. Occasional scattered shots had come from cover to harass the troops and twice small parties of Indians attacked openly, but mostly there was little actual fighting. It was a conquest without resistance and the taste of it was bitter in Clark's mouth.

Simon Kenton, too, felt uneasy about the relatively simple destruction of the towns. It was too easy, in fact, and he did not believe the rumor being spread that the towns were abandoned because the Shawnees had given up at last and had gone away to live west of the Mississippi with their brothers who had moved there three years ago.

The only man wounded had been riding beside Simon when he was shot. They had just ridden into the deserted Piqua Town on the Mad River when a rifle sounded from the hillside and Captain Victor McCracken cried out and lurched in his saddle, grasping his upper arm. Kenton and a half dozen others had spurred their horses up the hill and flushed the solitary Indian who stood his ground and watched them come, a devilish smile on his face, tomahawk in one hand, knife in the other. Even when he flopped to the ground, dying from the three different bullets which struck him, still he smiled what seemed to Simon, queerly, a smile of victory.

McCracken's wound was bad. The bone had shattered and by the time they were halfway back to the Ohio the wound had become gangrenous and it was obvious McCracken was dying. He held out until the day they reached the same spot on the Ohio shore where the army first assembled, and there he died as they were descending the final hillside to the riverbank. He was buried on the spot.

Half an hour later, the army of General George Rogers Clark was disbanded and Simon Kenton went immediately to Quick's Run to see Ruth.

[*November 30, 1782 — Saturday*]

Commissioner John Adams, acting on behalf of the United States in the peace negotiations at Paris, allowed a faint smile to appear as he signed with a flourish the preliminary articles of the treaty. This was only a step, but it was a major one and not gained without considerable effort.

These provisional articles to the Treaty of Peace between Great Britain and the United States dealt with boundaries and the consensus had been that the fledgling country would be so pleased at having won her liberty that she would make ample concessions over the treaty table; one of these being that the westernmost boundary of the United States be the Ohio River.

They had reckoned without the influence and stubbornness of John Adams who, though the other commissioners would gladly have conceded this, violently opposed it and demanded that the western boundary be established at the Mississippi River. If it was not, the peace talks could go no further. It was that simple.

They begged him to reconsider, to realize what was at stake here; if the negotiations bogged down or broke off, they might again find themselves in an all-out war. But Adams remained firm and at last the British commissioner, Oswald, acceded to the demand.

The United States was now half a continent wide.

[*February 8, 1783 — Saturday*]

Vincent Calvin glanced nervously at Simon and said for the tenth time: "Probably very soon now. And . . . and you're positive you don't mind, Mr. Kenton? I mean about Ruth and me?"

Simon scratched his head. He'd never encountered such a situation. After Clark's expedition he had returned to the Quick's Run cabin and at once Ruth had told him of meeting young Calvin in Harrodsburg and falling in love with him — *really* in love, she insisted — and he with her. They wanted to get married and she wanted Simon's word he'd hold no grudge against Vincent.

Simon had dipped his head at her distended belly and, though she flushed, her eyes had remained on his. Vincent knew all about it, she'd said, and didn't care. He'd gladly raise the child as his own. Would Simon meet with Vincent and talk with him — the three of them together — about it? Simon agreed.

The frontiersman had been prepared to dislike the thin, nervously smiling man of twenty-two, but it didn't work out that way. Embarrassed though Vincent was, he'd been direct and unassuming. Yes, he was very much in love with Ruth and wanted to marry her. Yes he knew of her affair with Simon and of the unborn child. He was not only agreeable to providing a home for this child and raising it with the love he would have for his own, but he even insisted that it bear the last name of its father, provided Simon didn't object.

Simon didn't and they'd parted friends and now, after remaining at his own cabin or in Harrodsburg most of the winter, he and Vincent Calvin stood together in the little cabin beside the one where Ruth lay in labor. Vincent repeated his question and Simon smiled as he replied:

"No, Vincent, I don't mind at all. I admire you for it. Not many men would do it. You must realize you're apt to get some harsh criticism from the people around here though. We all are."

"Nothing anyone can say makes any difference," Vincent said heatedly. "I love Ruth and as soon as she's able to, we'll get married."

He was interrupted by an older woman who stuck her head in the doorway, nodded first at Simon and then at Vincent.

"Ruth?" Calvin asked quickly.

"Couldn't be better. And you've got a fine healthy son!" Suddenly unsure as to whom she should direct her comments, she bobbed her head again and withdrew. Simon and Vincent, both a little embarrassed now, looked at one another and grinned.

"I'm proud that he's your son, Mr. Kenton," Vincent said. "What are you going to name him?"

Simon hadn't considered this and was taken aback. Then he cleared his throat self-consciously and said, "Simon for me. Ruth for her. His name is Simon Ruth Kenton."

[*April 27, 1783 — Sunday*]

In the Shawnee camp close to the mouth of the Scioto River, Tecumseh stood silently to one side and watched the preparations being made to burn the single white survivor of their attack upon the party that had landed on the Ohio shore. Ever since he could remember Tecumseh had heard tales of the burning of prisoners but until this time he had never witnessed it. And though he remained mute while these preparations were taking place, he strongly wished it was not to happen here.

Had he not been so extremely active and courageous in the taking of this party of whites, his reluctance now might have been considered a sign of weakness, but no man among them could claim this after the fight. In fact the bravery and fierceness he had exhibited during the attack had been startling to behold and was the talk of the entire camp. Not a warrior there had failed to approach him later and compliment him as a "great young warrior." The fact that at the age of fifteen he had outshone even the ablest warriors of the party was not only accepted without jealousy, but with deep and warm approval.

The party of whites had included thirteen men and when the Shawnees swooped down upon them as they cooked their meal on shore, the fighting had been particularly hot. The most that any other warrior had slain was two, but Tecumseh had leaped about with remarkable agility and daring, narrowly missing death a half dozen times or more; when finally the fury of the fighting had died away, the youthful warrior had slain four men by himself and had helped Chiksika in the dispatching of another. He seemed to be everywhere, not only moving with tremendous grace and speed, but endowed with the ability to anticipate his opponent's next move before it was made and thus himself strike more effectively.

Chiksika was highly pleased. Never had he seen or heard of a young warrior who, in his very first battle and at such a tender age, had so excelled. He wished Pucksinwah could have been here to witness this. How proud he would have been.

Without expression Tecumseh watched the single live prisoner being bound naked to the stake, watched the fire being set and heard his screams as the burning wood was pushed closer with long poles until finally his feet and lower legs had become black. He watched as the victim finally fell into the flames and writhed in agony as more fire was pushed toward him and thrown atop him. Even then it had taken him a long time to die and his moaning was a forlorn cry of utter despair, as terrible a sound as the youth had ever heard.

Through it all a deep revulsion arose in Tecumseh's breast for what they had done to this man. And when it was all over and the body charred and lifeless, he could contain himself no longer and he strode forward and raised an arm and spoke with an intensity that shocked his older fellows into respectful silence.

"You will say that I am young and inexperienced in such matters," he said, "and you will be right, but I cannot keep from speaking. What I have seen here has made me sick and ashamed for you and for myself. What bravery, what courage, what strength is there in the torturing of a man unable to defend himself? Are we so unsure of ourselves that in order to prove our superiority, our own excellence, we must resort to something as disgusting and degrading as this? Hear me now, my older brothers, for I speak from my heart and my heart is heavy with shame and revulsion. Our dearly loved chief, Black Fish, was strongly opposed to death at the stake, but until today I never really understood why. Now I do. Now I see that in the very act of committing it we lower ourselves to something beneath animals, to something evil and hideous and revolting. I do not and can not believe Moneto could approve of such cowardice, of such desire to inflict unnecessary pain. An enemy he was, yes! Death he deserved, yes! But the death of a man, not that of a rat cornered and tied and burned alive. How have we the right to call ourselves warriors, or even men, if we act in such manner? My heart is sick and heavy and what I have seen here will never be erased from my mind and I will never stop being ashamed of it. Young I may be. Inexperienced I may be. Yet this I can say with certainty: Never again will I take part in the torture like this of any living creature, man or animal. *Never!* Nor will I consider as friend any man who will allow himself to take part in so degrading a measure."

For a considerable time there was silence and even an increased respect for this stripling warrior. Had anyone ever heard such eloquence or such uncomfortable truth from one so young? When, before, had a fledgling warrior shown his elders not only how to fight in battle but how to behave with humanity? At last Chiksika stepped to his brother's side and spoke softly but loud enough for all to hear.

"What my little brother has said is truth," he began. "Who among us, despite provocation, has not felt himself lowered and shamed to treat a human being — regardless of whether an enemy — like that!" He pointed an accusing finger at the grotesque body. "But who among us has had the courage to speak up and tell us of the cowardice and shame of such an act? No man here today fought with greater skill or courage than Tecumseh and therefore his words must not be taken lightly. This I say to you: though he is yet not far beyond being a boy and I am a man twelve summers his elder, yet I am constantly learning from him and left feeling humble and unworthy in his presence. And this, too, I say to you now: that though he is a Kispokotha, yet will Tecumseh one day become the most powerful chief and greatest warrior the Shawnees have ever known!" He let his flashing gaze swing across the assembled men. "I therefore vow here and now that from this time forward I will never again take part in any such cruelty as this. Are there others here who will so vow?"

"I will," said one of the oldest, a one-eyed warrior called Frog Hunter. "The words of young Tecumseh have stirred me deeply. They are words wise beyond his years or yours or mine. He has won the respect and admiration of us all and Shawnees everywhere will learn of this bravery and wisdom."

One at a time then, each of the Shawnees stepped forward with similar remarks and the heart of Chiksika swelled with pride. He had no doubt whatever in the truth of what he had said of Tecumseh becoming a great leader. Was not Pucksinwah's family blessed with the ability to see — dimly at times, but at other times clearly — events of importance in the future? And was not this young warrior born under the momentous sign of the shooting star? There could be no question of it; Tecumseh was destined to become the greatest leader the Shawnee tribe had ever known.

[*May 13, 1783 — Tuesday*]

The negotiations were concluding and all that remained now was the final signing of the Paris Treaty between the United States and Great Britain.

This was expected by late summer and, with the possibility of continued war with the mother country all but lifted, the States now became extremely aware of the value of their western lands — lands saved for them through the perseverance of John Adams.

It was obvious, particularly in the case of Virginia, that there would not be enough lands south of the Ohio River to fulfill bounty obligations to Continental and State troops. Having already ceded to the Congress her nebulous claim to all lands north and west of the river Ohio, Virginia now claimed — and was granted by Congress — the previously stipulated tract of land in the Ohio country from which to bestow land bounties.

This tract was called The Virginia Military Lands, and it was enormous in area, taking in all the country bordered by the Ohio River to the south, the Scioto River to the east, and where it changed course in central Ohio and headed west, to the north, and the Little Miami River to the west. The only portion not bounded by a stream was that between the headwaters of the Little Miami and the Scioto, and so a diagonal connecting boundary line was drawn, moving northwest from the Little Miami headwaters to those of the Scioto. This tract included a total of some four million two hundred acres of extremely rich land, which Virginia felt was adequate to satisfy the claims of her troops. Without benefit of being surveyed into townships of regular form, the land was declared open for settlement. Any individual holding a Virginia Military Land Warrant could locate wherever he chose within this district and take land in any shape that he desired wherever the land had not been previously located. No one paid any attention in particular to the fact that settling on such land would be in violation of treaties with the Indians.

At the same time, Connecticut reaffirmed her northwestern territory along the south shore of Lake Erie, claiming — and being granted by Congress for bounty purposes — over three and a half million acres. This area was termed Western Reserve Lands.

It was time the settlement of the Ohio country was begun, everyone agreed; everyone, that is, with the exception of some thousands of Shawnees, Delawares, Wyandots, Miamis and other Indian tribes currently living there.

[*June 6, 1783 — Friday*]

To all but one person in Kentucky County, Simon Kenton had disappeared God knew where. No one had seen him for many weeks and rumors were rampant about what had happened to him.

Only George Rogers Clark knew for certain.

The frontiersman had roamed the countryside for some weeks now, concentrating on making tomahawk improvements and claiming ever more land. By the time he reached General Clark's home to spend a few days with him, his land holdings were undoubtedly in excess of one hundred thousand acres.

Simon was amazed at how tired and drawn and how dissipated Clark looked. The pewter mug in his hand was no sooner emptied than he was again filling it and now Simon began to give a little more credence to the stories he had heard of the excessive drinking Clark had been doing. It was something to do with intermilitary rivalry and disputes with the governor but Simon didn't inquire further and Clark did not elaborate. He did think, however, that a trip would do the officer a world of good and it was then that he asked him to go along with him; Simon was at last going back to Virginia to the Bull Run Mountain settlement, not to stay but to bring back with him, if he could convince them to come, his entire family.

Clark was wistful in his refusal. He would very much like to go along with Simon, if for no other reason than to witness the expression on the faces of the Kenton family upon seeing Simon after believing him dead for the last dozen years. But unfortunately he had duties he could not leave and so he wished his friend good luck and Godspeed and Simon set off alone.

The trip up the Ohio and then overland to Fauquier County was essentially uneventful. When at last Simon stood on the final ridge and looked down at the tiny cabin below, an almost overpowering nostalgia gripped him and his eyes filled with mist.

Halfway down the ridge he met a man who seemed vaguely familiar. He was about thirty-three years old but looked much older, his face puffy from too much drink and too little sleep, his hair mostly gone, his eyes rimmed with red and his cheeks interlaced with little broken veins. His shoulders slumped as with the weight of fourscore years and his whole attitude gave the impression of wretchedness.

They greeted one another cordially enough and the older man nodded when Simon asked if the Kenton family still lived in the little cabin below. And then it came to Simon with a jolt that the man to whom he was speaking was none other than William Leachman, his old rival for the hand of Ellen Cummins. Bracing himself, Kenton told Leachman who he was and was surprised at the lack of reaction; a mere lifting of the eyebrow, a little closer appraisal and a muttered comment to the effect that he had told them he hadn't killed anyone. And then he shuffled off.

Simon shrugged and continued down the hill. How much smaller the cabin looked to him now, and how the memories came crowding back upon one another in an engulfing rush: there was the same old bench where his father and Uncle Tom had eons ago discussed the Middle Ground; there was the rock upon which he used to stand and pretend he was king; here and there were the thousand and more little things that brought back clearly those all but forgotten memories of childhood. And as he stepped to the door that had always before seemed so large to him, he smiled faintly as he realized he would have to duck his head to enter.

He recognized his mother instantly when she answered his knock, but she did not know him. She seemed taken aback at the size of this giant of a man at her doorway. Behind her he could see an old man, his father, sitting in a rocker with a quilt covering his legs.

"Yes?" she said.

"You don't recognize me?" His smile was broad.

She frowned and studied him and then shook her gray head. "No," she said slowly, "I'm afraid not, sir. Should I?"

He laughed. "You should, since you gave birth to me!"

Her eyes widened and she pressed the back of her hand to fragile lips and then she whispered, "Oh my God, can it be? Is it . . . Is it . . ."

"It is, mother," he said and wrapped his arms around her and lifted her clear off the ground. "It's your son, Simon, come home at last."

Blinded by tears, she kissed him fiercely on the mouth and then on both cheeks and then the mouth again, finally burying her face in his shoulder and crying over and over, "Oh Simon, my boy . . . Simon . . ."

[*September 3, 1783 — Wednesday*]

The Treaty of Paris was signed!

The months of negotiations had finally concluded and at last the formal documents had been signed and given their official seals. The joy among the erstwhile Colonists was unprecedented, but there was considerable gloom on the North American continent as well.

The Loyalists were now ruined. During the progress of the Revolution great numbers of them had fled to the eastern and western ends of Lake Erie. Niagara was their stronghold and Detroit their might and both places had remained unmolested in Loyalist hands throughout the war, mainly because the Colonists could not get at them. Actually it was just as well. As Detroit had fallen to the British without battle when Montreal was surrendered by the French, so now both Niagara and Detroit were expected to fall to the Americans in the same manner. Such expectations were a bit premature. While theoretically both strongholds became American territory, they were still populated by British subjects; military, civilian, Loyalist. When Lake Erie was split in accordance with the terms of the Paris Treaty to make the boundary between the two countries, Britain agreed to abandon these places "in due time and with all convenient speed."

It was a dangerously nebulous clause to have in any treaty.

[*December 1, 1783 — Monday*]

Mary Kenton had been almost sick with the joy of her son's return and there was, for a short while, serious concern that the shock of seeing Simon again after all these years would kill old Mark Kenton, now eighty-two. He was only a pitiful and feeble shell of the man Simon had remembered as his father but his eyes had come alive again at the sight of his son and for days there was little done but talk. Neighbors arrived in droves and the room was constantly filled with people as he told them of the Kentucky and Ohio frontiers, his captivity and escape and the various military campaigns in which he had participated.

And they had much to tell, too. Not as momentous or as exciting news, perhaps, but of abiding interest to Simon. His sister Frances had died and, as John had told him, his younger brother Benjamin had been killed at the outset of the Revolution. His brother William was the father of six children now and his brother Mark had also served in the Revolution and had been on hand to watch the hanging of Major André, Benedict Arnold's contact in the matter of treason, at Yorktown Heights. His sisters Mary and Jane were both married and had children of their own. And the last time Simon had seen Uncle Tom Kenton was the last any of them had seen or ever heard of him. Ellen Cummins, his old sweetheart, had died very young and now William Leachman lived alone, still on the same farm, with his eleven-year-old son.

But it was Simon who had fired the imagination with his tales of the Kentucky country and he had urged them to abandon this mean little farm and return with him to that land where he would give each one of them no less than two hundred fifty acres of prime land all his own. It was a land to build in, he had told them, a growing land and a land of opportunity. It was a land where a man could be his own master, beholden to no one.

Old Mark Kenton's eyes had glittered at the words and not even Simon's mother could remember when he had become so enthusiastic about anything. Nor was he the only one. Quite a few of the neighbors were interested in going along and to each of these Simon had offered at least a hundred acres of good land free. He even went out of his way to extend a special offer of similar magnitude to William Leachman.

Such offers made the tiny farms here on the Virginia mountains dwindle to mere lots and at length quite a few of the neighbors and all of the Kenton family except Mark and sister Mary's family had agreed to migrate with him on the great adventure.

It had taken some weeks to prepare, for there were teams and wagons to be bought or hired to carry them and their goods over the mountains to the Monongahela; but at last, on September 16, they had started. There were forty of them in the party, including Simon, and the journey was not an easy one by any means.[6] It was, in fact, much too hard on the elder Kenton. After some days of riding in the pitching wagons his health began to fail and so a litter was fashioned for his comfort — a bed attached to two long poles and these poles fastened to the collars of two horses, one ahead and one behind. This made for much slower traveling and so Simon had spurred on ahead to the Boat Yard on the Monongahela near New Store to order their boat made.[7]

It was to be a tremendous boat. A hundred and twenty feet long, it would provide quarters for all, room for all their gear, enclosures for horses and cattle, food stores and other equipment. The largest boats going down the river at present were those being built at the Boat Yard and these were normally not larger than sixty feet long and cost thirty-five dollars. Eyebrows were raised at the size of the boat Simon ordered but, when Simon paid them the demanded sixty dollars in advance, they set to work with special work crews at once.

On returning to the wagon train, the frontiersman had found his father failing rapidly and though they did all they could to restore his health, the old man's time was clearly running out. At the mouth of Peter's Creek, about thirty river miles above Pittsburgh and just three miles below New Store, Mark Kenton finally died on October 16. He was quietly buried at the mouth of the creek. Sadly, the party had continued their journey to the Boat Yard to await completion of their huge keelboat and to send back the hired teams and sell whatever wagons and gear they would have no further need for.

Although the size and bulk of the boat was great, it could be easily navigated by four pole-wielding men. It was rectangular and flat-bottomed and drew a minimum of water. At one end were the stock pens, protected from Indian rifle fire by sides as high as a horse. In these pens were herded the cattle and the nineteen horses being taken along. At the other end of the boat was the multi-roomed cabin, well sided with planks and roofed so as to give the appearance of a large frame house, inside of which was a fine fireplace for cooking.

The voyage had been crowded and long, but pleasant for all. Simon had quite naturally taken over as leader of the party and his decisions were final. The trees along the river were ablaze with fall color and every now and then they had stopped for a short span to take on firewood and to hunt game. When they left Fauquier County they had taken a large number of cattle with them, some being slaughtered along the way to supply them meat. But when they reached the Boat Yard, all save a handful had been butchered, dressed, quartered and salted down in huge barrels for use through the winter in Kentucky. They were well stocked with corn, salt and flour but whenever they stopped for wood Simon left the woodcutters to their chores and went off to hunt, usually returning with turkeys and deer and, one time, a fine young bear.

As they had passed the Scioto River mouth and Three Islands, Simon noted but did not mention a considerable amount of Indian sign on the Ohio shore, but none on the Kentucky side. None, that is, until at length they had reached Limestone and there they found it in abundance.

And so, instead of settling here as Simon had originally planned, they had continued to the Kentucky River and up this meandering waterway walled in by great cliffs until they reached the Danville area. Here, at last, they disembarked for the final time. It had taken many days to dismantle the boat to build cabins with the lumber and still more time to transport all their supplies to the Salt River land Simon had selected to give them.

But now, with December beginning, once again Simon was on his own. He decided he would stay occasionally during this winter with Clark, but mostly he would keep on the move, marking more trees with his K and claiming more land and moving always toward the site he liked best in Kentucky — his first little station on the banks of Lawrence Creek a few miles from the mouth of the Limestone.

[December 31, 1784 — Friday]

The year 1784 produced significant, if not momentous, changes in Kentucky County. Despite continued attacks by the Shawnees on river travelers and occasional forays south of the river to burn isolated cabins and capture horses, the settlers continued to come here in an ever-increasing flow and the interior of Kentucky gradually began losing its frontier aspect.

Lexington, Harrodsburg, Danville, Stanford, Frankfort and Georgetown could no longer be considered small towns. They were cities with populations running into the thousands, each with streets and churches, shops and stables and schools. The initial log cabins were being rapidly outnumbered and overshadowed by fine frame and brick buildings, some of these as much as three stories in height.

Dozens, even scores, of new settlements were springing up all over the countryside, most of them far in the interior but a few in areas still dangerous — along the south shore of the Ohio River. One of these was Simon Kenton's Station on Lawrence Creek, rebuilt into a sturdy two-story brick house high on the hill overlooking the two springs. A cluster of a dozen or more smaller cabins surrounded it, though the closest was over three hundred yards away; as soon as they had finished, Simon recruited a group of sixty men from the Salt River area to help build a good blockhouse at the mouth of Limestone Creek and then settle there on land he would sell them. Within months Limestone had become a respectable community of half a hundred or more structures.

The frontiersman continued to survey land for himself and others, ranging far to east and west and into the heavily wooded hill country to the south. Off and on he stayed for short periods with Daniel Boone or George Rogers Clark, but soon the old urge to move would be upon him again and he would drift away. Often during these rovings he saw small parties of Indians and they him, but rarely did they approach one another closely

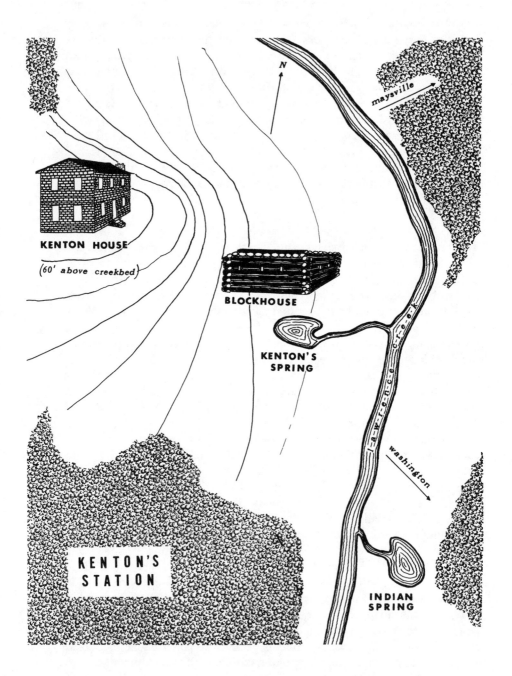

KENTON HOUSE

(60' above creekbed)

N

maysville

BLOCKHOUSE

KENTON'S
SPRING

l-a-w-r-e-n-c-e c-r-e-e-k

washington

KENTON'S
STATION

INDIAN
SPRING

enough to engage in combat. Most of the Shawnees recognized the huge *cut-ta-ho-tha* from a distance and deliberately avoided him, convinced that having survived all their tortures and having eventually escaped, he must be under the protection of Moneto; they would bring disaster upon themselves if they attempted to harm him further.

The settlers had named the blockhouse at Limestone, Hinkson's Fort, and it was a welcome sight to water-weary travelers who had made the long journey from Pittsburgh. But it didn't last long. On June 22, a large party of warriors led by a daring brave stormed it and forced the whites to flee and then burned it to the ground. None of the whites was injured but a single Maykujay Shawnee was mortally wounded. Simon Kenton treated his wound and questioned him as he lingered on the edge of death for days. His name, he said, was Leaning Tree and he remembered well when Bahd-ler was brought captive to Mackachack.

Some of the settlers were for executing and scalping him at once but Simon would not permit it, and for this Leaning Tree was grateful and answered the frontiersman's questions readily. When asked if it was Girty who had led the attack on this station, Leaning Tree said no. The party had been led by a Kispokotha named Chiksika and his younger brother, Tecumseh. It was the latter, Leaning Tree said, who would one day do great things for the Shawnees, for already his exploits were the pride of the entire nation.

When Leaning Tree finally died at the end of the fourth day, Simon buried him unscalped along Limestone Creek and then returned to the interior to recruit more men to come back with him and not only build a new and better blockhouse but remain in the area and put down their own roots there.

In July, Simon's brother Mark arrived from the east on a farewell visit to his family. He was dying; a horrible consumption had taken hold of him and he coughed constantly and spat up great gobs of bloody material. He stayed only long enough to visit a day or so at the Salt River cabin shared by his mother and sister, a single day at John Kenton's cabin and a day at the frontiersman's station. And when he paddled off to the north, he left behind him a great sadness, for the family knew they would never see him again.

Along with the growth of Kentucky population came civil problems. It soon became apparent that Kentucky County was too large and would have to be broken into smaller counties administered each by a county lieutenant and a sheriff. Two large counties were formed, Fayette and Bourbon, and Daniel Boone, dissatisfied with the way things were going at Boonesboro, moved to Lexington and reluctantly accepted the office of sheriff of Fayette County.

And now, for the first time, serious land-claim problems were rising. In more cases than not, claims badly overlapped one another and sometimes two or three or even more individuals claimed the same tracts. Arguments broke out and then fights, and sometimes men involved in disputes simply disappeared and were never heard of again. On August 1, the Virginia Legislature ordered the establishment of an office in Louisville for the reception of locations and surveys for lands south of the Ohio. All claimants were advised to write out descriptions of the tracts they had claimed and file them at this office. There were many who knew the wisdom of this and did so immediately, but there were as many or more who were illiterate, unable to claim in any other way than by making their mark upon a tree. Simon Kenton was of this group. He might perhaps have taken the time to have someone help him do this if he hadn't been quite unexpectedly and very thoroughly distracted.

It happened on October 1, when a large new group of emigrants from eastern Virginia arrived at Limestone to settle. Among them was the sister of William Kenton's wife, Mary Cleland Kenton. She was the widow of Thomas Dowden and had come to the Kentucky country with her four children to be near Mary. Her two sons were Jack Dowden, who was seventeen, and Archibald, twelve. The daughters were Jane, fifteen, and Martha, fourteen. It was the latter who so distracted the frontiersman. Never had he been so instantly attracted to anyone as he was to this beautiful dark-haired girl. Without being asked, he did the lion's share of the work in erecting a cabin for the Dowdens close to his brother John's place, just so he could be near Martha — at first merely to look at her and feel himself go rubbery inside at the exquisite loveliness of her and, later, to talk with her and tell her stories of how he came to this country and what he had done here.

Martha was enthralled with whatever he said, sympathizing with him for the trials he had undergone and exulting with him in his victories. To him, her laughter was the sound of angels and the touch of her hand on his arm was enough to make him flush and burn with an inner fire that blocked out everything except his love for her.

For a long while he refused to admit even to himself that he was in love with her. He was, after all, nearing thirty — more than twice her age. He even went away for a few days in an effort to convince himself that it was wrong for him to feel this way about a girl hardly more than a child. But it didn't work. The longing and need to hear her voice, to see her and feel her touch, drove him back; and so, desperately afraid of what her answer might be and yet unable to keep from saying it, he asked her to be his wife.

Martha Dowden accepted, feeling as deeply for Simon as he did for her. But it was the judgment of the widow Dowden which prevailed. She was sure, she said, that Simon Kenton would make an admirable husband for her daughter but she had grave doubts that a fourteen-year-old had maturity enough to make such a decision and she could not approve the marriage at this time. She saw no objection to permitting the courtship to continue, within reasonable bounds, since the pair were so obviously in love, but there could be no marriage now and that was final. If, in a couple of years, both of them still felt the same, then they could marry with her blessings. In the meanwhile she urged that both of them, Simon in particular, show restraint and common sense. And, though it was a disappointment for them, they both agreed.

The influx of settlers continued and now there were more family groups than ever. Charles Scott, his wife and three sons settled at the new station of Versailles just west of Lexington and the Abner Overfield family took up residence at Kenton's Station, followed almost immediately by the last contingent of Kenton's family to come from the east — his older sister Mary with her husband, Cornelius Rains, and their children. The families of Bethel Owen, William Maddox, Job Masterson and William Henry all arrived the same day and put down their roots at Limestone. George Berry and his family came from Kenton's childhood home area to settle at Limestone, too, and when George's brother Elijah, who had come to Kentucky with the Kentons, heard about it, he moved his own family from Salt River to Limestone to join him. The woods were alive with the sound of axes ringing against trees and saws ripping into wood.

The arrival that surprised Simon more than any other, however, was that of his old rival, William Leachman, on December 12. Living up to the promise he made him over a year ago in Fauquier County, Simon immediately presented him and his son with a hundred good acres near John's place, which Leachman accepted as his due, without thanks.

The final party to arrive in 1784 was welcomed heartily, for it provided Limestone, Kenton's Station and the settlement growing near John Kenton's place with something they needed very much, an ordained minister of the Gospel. The party was led by William Wood, Baptist preacher, and arrived at Limestone about noon on the last day of December. He brought with him not only his own family but those of Benjamin Fry and James Turner. Their intention had been to go on to Louisville but the river was beginning to freeze and the floating ice made further travel in their three small boats too dangerous.

A large delegation of settlers from the three communities, led by the three Kenton brothers — Simon, William and John, along with William's son, Thomas — now approached the party. As spokesman for the group, Simon bade them welcome and then told them of their need for religion here and urged them to stay.

"I'll sell you land here," Simon said, "as good and as cheap as could be got in Kentucky."

Wood, Turner and Fry said they would consider it and inspected the area thoroughly, were pleased with what they saw and felt they could not do better. They decided to stay and bought from Simon four hundred acres of ground in the area of John Kenton's settlement and immediately laid out a town which they named Washington, in honor of the general of whom every American was justifiably proud.[8]

And so, in the face of a bitterly cold winter and repeated minor Indian attacks, the Kentucky country's population continued to grow. At this same time, nearly half a continent away, the streets of the young nation's largest city thronged with jubilant people who had just heard the news: the Continental Congress had made New York City the capital of the United States of America.

CHAPTER VII

[*January 21, 1785 — Friday*]

THE chiefs, sachems and warriors of the Wyandot, Delaware, Ottawa and Chippewa nations sat in stony silence at the great meeting being held at Fort McIntosh on the Ohio River below Pittsburgh. Their expressions altered not in the least as the essential elements of the proposed new treaty were explained to them by the fastidiously dressed delegate from New York through his interpreter.

The Americans, he said, having emerged victorious in their recent war with the British, were anxious to establish a permanent and lasting peace with these assembled Indians. The Americans, he asserted, believed they could live in peace and harmony, possibly even friendship, with these assembled Indians. But — and this was the "but" which every man present knew was coming — in order to prevent arguments which might lead to warfare, it was necessary to establish boundaries between them which were clearly defined and understood by both sides. Unfortunately, boundaries established in the past had somehow not held up well, probably through vagueness or lack of understanding on the parts of some people. This was something the Americans wished to avoid in the future and this was why he had been sent here as an emissary of peace. He would make the new boundary clear to these assembled tribes so that there could be no misinterpretation which might result in conflict in the future.

"The boundary," he declared, "is to begin at the mouth of the river Cuyahoga and to extend up said river to the portage between that and the Tuscarawas branch of the Muskingum; then down the Tuscarawas to the crossing place above Fort Laurens, then westerly to the portage of the Great Miami — or Omee — River and down the southeast side of same to its mouth.[1]

East of this line would be American territory and to the west it would belong to these assembled tribes. The only exception to this being that the Americans reserved the right to a parcel of land six miles square at the mouth of the Great Miami and a similar amount on the portage between the Great Miami and Auglaize Rivers and the same amount on Sandusky Bay, and also a parcel of land two miles square on each side of the lower rapids of the Sandusky River. These areas were to be reserved so that the Americans could establish trading posts thereon. Did these assembled Indians now clearly understand the boundaries?

They understood far more clearly than he imagined. They were painfully aware, for example, that the two thirds of the Ohio country which this new boundary gave to the Americans contained little land claimed by any of them. This was mostly territory belonging to the Shawnees and Miamis and some of the Mingoes. Yet, no Shawnees or Miamis or Mingoes had been invited to this treaty.

They were equally aware that once more, as had happened time and again, their own boundaries had been pushed back — this time from western Pennsylvania to central Ohio — and that as soon as this land was filled with settlers there would come more fighting and more treaty talk and once again they would be pushed farther to the west.

Treaty papers meant nothing and so why not sign this one if it kept the Americans happy for a little while and allowed the Indians assembled here to live in peace temporarily? It would not last, of course, but it would last longer than if here and now they refused to accept these terms.

And so they signed and shook hands and parted . . . and not one of them really expected to live happily ever after.

[*April 30, 1785 — Saturday*]

They had been awake since before the dawn but now, with the first shafts of sunlight leaking through tiny holes and spearing the gloom of the *wegiwa* with cheery light, Wabethe pushed Blue Jacket up from her and smiled at him as he knelt beside their low bed. Her words were playful, yet with a thread of seriousness woven in them.

"Were it up to you, my husband, you would have me in child all the time, with no emptiness in between." Her dark eyes were suddenly deep with longing. "Would that I could bear you more."

Blue Jacket grinned, showing strong white teeth and slapped his hand down upon her flat naked belly. At her sharp exclamation he threw back his head and laughed. "It has been four years since the last one," he said. "My little Swan, it is obvious that all you have left here," he moved his hand lower, "is pleasure. But do not think I will discard you. No! For that pleasure I would keep you if your hair became white and all your teeth fell out." His voice softened. "What warrior would not keep a woman such as you? You have given me a son and two daughters. You are a part of my life. You always will be."

He leaned over and kissed her eyes and then her nose but when the heat began to rise in him again and he started to lower himself over her, she giggled and rolled over onto her stomach and cried, "Enough! You are *meshewa* — a stallion — not a man. I cannot hope to satisfy such a hunger! Go now. The sun is up and you must not be late for the grand council meeting."

Reluctantly he stood up and stepped into his leggins and pulled over his feet the fine moccasins she had made him. He was an impressive figure of a man, smoothly muscled and without an ounce of fat on his six-foot frame. His handsome face, framed by shoulder-length blue-black hair, was graven with lines of character more befitting one of fifty years than thirty. Carelessly, but with an innate grace of movement, he ducked into his fine doeskin pullover shirt and tugged it down over the broad chest. He drew his belt around him and thrust the pipe tomahawk into it and scooped up the rifle from where it leaned against the wall, automatically checking the powder for dampness. He tossed horn and pouch slings over his shoulder and then stopped for a moment beside the bed where Wabethe lay watching him. He ran his hand gently through her hair and touched his lips to her forehead. "Go back to sleep, Swan," he said. "It is early yet." Then he was gone.

The sun was nearly at its zenith when he arrived at the massive *msi-kah-mi-qui* at Wapatomica Town. The sight of the huge building, as always, filled him with pleasure. How many strange and wonderful and tragic things had he been witness to inside this heart of the Shawnee nation? And what was the reason Moluntha had called this council? There were many more horses picketed than he had anticipated and his heart beat a little faster as he entered the door.

The room was well filled with warriors of the Chalahgawtha and Maykujay septs, but here and there also were the few remaining representatives of the Kispokothas and Peckuwes and Thawegilas, such as Chiksika and young Tecumseh and the ugly old chief he liked so well, She-me-ne-to — Black Snake.

In the center of the room sat the two most important chiefs of the Shawnee tribe, Black Hoof and Moluntha, and throughout the room were most of the other chiefs and subchiefs of the various villages. Whatever the nature of this council, there could be no doubt it was tribally important.

Blue Jacket was preparing to seat himself with other warriors from his village when Black Hoof abruptly stood and pointed first at him and then at the ground at his feet.

"Weh-yah-pih-ehr-sehn-wah," the chief said, "you are to come here to sit for this council."

Puzzled, Blue Jacket obeyed. They sat quietly smoking their pipes until all had finished and placed them in their laps or on the ground beside them. Then Black Hoof arose and the faint murmur of voices stilled instantly.

"My children," he said, "we are come here for a most important matter. What will take place here today has never happened before and, I believe, will not again. It is a time of sadness and a time of rejoicing and I would ask our ancient King to tell you of it."

He reached down and took Moluntha's skeletal hand and gently helped him rise, then sat down himself. Moluntha slowly let his gaze sweep back and forth across the assemblage twice before speaking. He was becoming very frail these days and his hair had whitened and his eyes were nearly hidden in the wrinkled flesh around them. Yet his voice, when he spoke, was still rich and strong.

"My children, what Catahecassa has told you is true. This is a day of sadness and rejoicing, but the rejoicing is the greater of the two and the sadness only aids in enriching the joy. I am old and I grow weak. My eyes can no longer follow the flight of the pigeon nor my legs the trail of the deer. It is time for me to step aside as chief of the Maykujays and for this there must be a sadness in my heart and in yours.

"It is my right, not only as descending chief but as eldest of all the Shawnees, to select the warrior who will be taking my place. He must be the bravest of the brave, the boldest of the bold, but he must be much more than this. He must know when to fight and when to withdraw. He must be able and willing to think first of his people and, if necessary, to lay down his life for them. He must be proven in battle and in leadership and he must have the respect and admiration of all his fellow tribesmen. He must be wise and able to use his wisdom without pride; cruel, if necessary, but not make cruelty his master or his pleasure; kind, but not let kindness become weakness.

"The man I have chosen has all these abilities and more. Only the principal chief could overrule this decision and Catahecassa has already told me he approves my choice. From this moment forward, the chief of the Maykujay Shawnees is the man who sits beside me now — Blue Jacket!"

And the heart of the white man turned Shawnee nearly burst inside him with pride.

[*May 2, 1785 — Monday*]

The Congress of the United States did not take long to act after the Fort McIntosh Treaty was ratified. Immediately following the signing of the treaty on January 21, a bill was introduced proposing measures for the disposal of the Ohio lands to the east and south of the treaty line. The discussions were animated and on this date, just over three months later,

Congress passed such an ordinance, under which the first segment of this land was to be surveyed.

The section of Ohio concerned in this ordinance was that which was called the Seven Ranges. It was mostly within far eastern Ohio territory, where initial surveyors were apt to have little difficulty with Indians; but difficulty of some nature was expected, since these seven ranges of townships would be the first public lands ever surveyed by the general government west of the Ohio River.

The boundaries of the Seven Ranges were sharply drawn. They began at the point where the Pennsylvania line crossed the Ohio River. From this point a line was drawn due west for a distance of forty-two miles, and from here another line was drawn due south to the Ohio River almost at the mouth of the Little Muskingum River. The eastern boundary then followed the Ohio River upstream to the point of origin.

Thus, with relative quiet, the invasion of Ohio was begun.

[October 15, 1785 — Saturday]

Major John Doughty signaled for the detachment of United States troops to be called to attention and then pleasantly but firmly explained what they were doing here on the bottomland of the west bank of the Muskingum just above its mouth.

At this point, he announced, they had been given orders to erect a permanent fort. It would be a good fort, he said. Only one other American fort had ever been built on Ohio soil before and everyone here was well aware of what had happened at Fort Laurens. Constructed on the upper Tuscarawas River in September, 1778, it had been attacked by Indians led by Girty, held under siege for weeks and many of its garrison killed before it was finally abandoned in August the following year. Major John Doughty did not intend to have the same occur here.

The troops — "dime-a-day-men" as they called themselves, referring to their less than munificent wage of three dollars per month — were not happy to hear this. They would be risking their necks to build a fort to protect settlers who weren't even here yet — and for miserably low wages. But there was not a man on hand who would not work each day until his back felt broken and his hands became a mass of raw meat. There was no toleration of complaining, even less for insubordination, and the penalty for desertion was enough to make a brave man tremble. Flogging was a standard punishment for the minor offenses and a man deemed deserving of it by his superior officer might receive up to two hundred lashes. But even this was preferable to the desertion penalty: immediate execution without benefit of court-martial.

The fort, Doughty continued, would be built in the form of a regular pentagon, enclosing an area of approximately three-fourths of an acre. The walls would be constructed of large horizontal timbers and the bastions of large upright timbers fourteen feet in height, fastened to one another by strips of timber tree-nailed into each picket. And though he was anticipating next spring, the major did not mention that he planned to have these men lay out a series of fine vegetable gardens to the rear of the fort.

The completed stockade would be called Fort Harmar in honor of Colonel Josiah Harmar, to whose regiment Major Doughty was attached. It never hurt, Doughty thought, to show respect for one's superiors. Promotions always seemed to come faster when this was done.

With a rather self-satisfied little smile, Doughty dismissed the formation and the work of construction was begun.

[October 31, 1785 — Monday]

James Finley, at sixteen, was just a bit young to be writing an autobiography, but that's what he was doing each night by the light of a candle as he lay on his pallet in the loft section of his father's cabin at Washington only a hundred yards from John Kenton's place.

He was a pleasant, quiet boy and well liked by all, but he had never quite gotten over his fear of this wild land where at any given time a ferocious Indian might spring out of hiding to tomahawk him. Even Simon Kenton's assurances that he was "pretty safe" did not much ease his anxiety.

He had started the autobiography shortly after arriving here with his parents last March, and though it was really more of a diary than anything else he knew it was actually the groundwork for an autobiography he would one day write in full about his exciting life.

He admired Simon Kenton tremendously and often pictured himself as another frontiersman like him, the two of them striding through the woods together, occasionally having severe fights with the Indians but always emerging victorious. Simon Kenton was everything he thought a real man and Indian fighter should be and so it was not altogether surprising that the big frontiersman played a major role in the things he wrote.

Tonight he collected his thoughts for a few minutes and then wrote rapidly, the words coming easily to him:

Simon Kenton can write! I've really taught him how! Well, not write much, but today doing it the way I showed him how, he wrote his full name for the first time in his life. On a bond. It was jerky but you could read it. He was awful proud.

He stopped and read what he had written and, caught up in the spell of his own words, went back to the beginning of his great "book" and began paging through it, here and there reading portions. In early April he had written:

There are 22 cabins here allready and more to be built. Mr. Kenton says someday this will be a great city and I believe it. Just since we came five or six families have showed up to stay. One of them is the Washburns. They have a boy a year younger than me who is anxious to kill Indians. Allways looking for them. He has a rifle just like mine and says he'll use it if he sees any. I bet! His name is Cornelius but better not call him Cornie! Every body calls him Neil. His father's name is Jeremiah.

In the latter part of that same month he told of four families dropped off at Limestone by boats en route to Vincennes. They had been saved from Indians at the mouth of the Scioto River.

The man in charge is named Peter Patrick and he says they were starting a settlement at Scioto. Told Simon Kenton he went up Scioto a good ways and cut his initials in a beech tree, but Indians saw him and followed him back to camp and kilt two of them.[2] They are all from Redstone, Pensa. Thats where Neil comes from.

On June 12 there was an exciting entry about the Washburn boy:

Neil finly kilt him a Indian yesterday. Him and his pa were acrost the river on Eagle Creek and they heard a noise. Neil says it sounded like a bear rooting. He sneaked up bank and saw two indians side by each peeling a hickory bark with a wedge for to make a canoe. They was peeling upward, one holding bark and other pushing wedge stick up. Neil shot and kilt one. The other sprawled down in touch-me-nots for a good piece. Neil and Mr. Washburn left quick. Today they went back and got his scalp. Neil stretched it and said he will tie it on his belt. I bet!

Mr. Kenton very sad [he wrote on July 25] *because he just heard that his old friend over east of us, Mike Tygart, got hisself drownded in the Creek named after him. Horse fell whilst was crossing and he cant swim. Never seen him so sad. He still aint over that swamp fever that he gets ever so often. He gets awful put out cause no one will give him water then. They say it makes fever worser than ever. Pa says so to. But today Martha Dowden brought him some soup. Dont know why he wants to marry her like everone says, her being younger even than me. He didnt like it much when I asked him.*

On October 15, just two weeks past, it was another excited entry:

Neil went and kilt him another Indian right close by here. Seen him sneking up to steal a horse and so he snuk up hisself and when he stepped into the clear shot him. Took his scalp to so that makes two hes got now. I aint got none. I got to get busy.

Now young James Finley stopped reading and went back to the page he had started writing and began a new paragraph:

Mr. Kenton has an amazzing way about him in respect to laying off lands. Today he dictated a deed which I wrote for him which was the description of a parcel of land of 320 acres near his station which he was selling to Wm. Wood and Arthur Fox. How he remembers all those things I dont know but when checked out its allways right. He describes deeds by saying so many steps to this hackberry and so many poles to that sugar tree and so many steps to a hiciory and so on.

Today we finished the O'Bannon cabin. Thats 31 cabins here in Washington now not counting the one where Reverend Wood does his preaching. Getting to be a regular town for sure! Even got a wagon road through the cane alls the way into Limestone. Mr. Kenton kept lookout for danger whilst we worked. He is a truly great adventurer. He is truly the master spirit in this region and he means a lot to us here. Everbody here looks on him as the great defender, always on the alert, and ready to fly at a moments notice to a place of danger for the protection of the scattered familys in this wilderness. He is the teacher and captain of all the young boys in these parts and I regard him as the prince of pioneers of this region of the country. Pa says he considers him as a man raised up by Providence for a special purpose because of the miraculus way he was delivered up from perils and he says he is for certain a Child of Providence.

There was good reason to believe it true.

[*January 3, 1786 — Tuesday*]

The small party of Shawnees led by Chief Blue Jacket showed remarkable restraint in masking their anger and disgust at the conditions of the treaty they were being asked to sign at this new little fort. The blatant incongruities in the articles were almost laughable, yet both sides pretended ignorance of their existence; the whites because they believed they were deluding "these ignorant savages" and the Indians because objection at this time could have served no other purpose than to endanger themselves. They were painfully aware that although the colonel and his men treated them with a forced respect, each man in the company, with the exception of the colonel, carried a rifle. The twenty Shawnees were outnumbered nearly ten to one and so now was a time to show neither the anger nor the scorn they felt at these proposals.

Colonel Richard Butler and his fellow commissioners, Captains Ephraim Lewis and Ebenezer Zane, had arrived here several weeks ago, just as Fort Finney was nearing completion. Located on a bottomland along the Great Miami River three fourths of a mile upstream from its mouth, the fort had been built with nervous speed under direction of its commander, Major Robert Finney, and his adjutant, Captain David Zeigler.

The treaty being offered these Shawnees was simple and deceptive. Without ever mentioning the treaty with the northern Indians or the fact that already the Seven Ranges was being surveyed, it reaffirmed the Ohio River as the borderline between Shawnees and whites. The only exceptions were the two forts and their sites — Fort Harmar at the mouth of the Muskingum and this fort. Their purpose was not one of invasion, Colonel Butler said blandly, but merely as guard posts to turn back any whites who might attempt to settle on the Ohio side of the river. The treaty proclaimed a new and everlasting friendship with the Shawnees, stating that "differences of opinion" between the two factions could now at last "be put aside for all time."

The officers were surprised at the fluency with which Chief Blue Jacket spoke English and even more amazed when, with a distinct flourish, he signed the treaty with his Shawnee name, Weh-yah-pih-ehr-sehn-wah, and then added in parentheses, Chief Blue Jacket. When Colonel Butler casually asked him who taught him to speak and write English so well, Blue Jacket smiled faintly and replied only that his teachers had been good but that he had later come to despise them.

After leaving the fort the Shawnee band rode upstream nearly twenty miles before camping for the night. A light snow had commenced falling and the chief sat close to the fire beside Chiksika and Tecumseh. He spoke softly but his voice was bitter as he told them that he had never hated the whites as much as he did today. They were deceitful, treacherous, implacable enemies and never to be trusted in word or writing or deed and they should be destroyed. They *would* be destroyed, he promised the brothers. Not now, for their own party was too small and the weather too bad to launch an attack. But in the Green Moon they would return here in force, kill all these soldiers and burn this fort whose presence was an insult to their dignity and intelligence.

[*April 9, 1786 — Sunday*]

They had collected their gear and moved out just in time. Standing now on high ground to the west of the swollen river with their company stretched out behind them, Major Finney and Captain Zeigler watched gloomily as the waters of the Great Miami River inundated the fort bearing the major's name. The flood had come swiftly and now only the top of the blockhouse and the last eight inches of the wall pickets still showed above the swirling yellow waters.

With a disgusted grunt, Major Finney stood high in the stirrups and gave his men the command to march, leading them west toward the north side of the Ohio River opposite Louisville. Here he planned to build a new fort which would take the name of the abandoned one. But this one would be built on high ground above flood level. No cruel hand of nature would destroy *this* one!

Not one of the near two hundred men in that column realized that the "cruel hand of nature" that had just destroyed the fort had also just saved their lives. At this very moment, less than thirty miles away, Chief Blue Jacket was leading a force of over five hundred warriors to storm the fortification and wipe out its garrison.

[*July 30, 1786 — Sunday*]

For young James Finley, the glamour of writing his great "autobiography" had worn a little thin these days. Nevertheless, he kept at it doggedly, though his entries became terse. Some, in fact, over the past months, were stark in their matter-of-factness:

> . . . *Awful lot of Indians marawding this Spring, many coming from Wabash River country. Mostly horse stealing cept for that fight at Limestone April 13. Mr. Kenton says Blue Jacket struk with over 100 warriors with him when he hit us. Word from Louisville that may-be 400 more attackted them bout the same time. Col. Christian was kilt here and SK says one of six Indians we kilt was little chief Black Wolf* . . .
> . . . *So much Indian trouble theres talk Genl Clark will mount expedition against Indians in Wabash country. May-be in September. Mr. Kenton has organized party of minute men here to proteck us from Indians when necessary. K is captain and John Masterson is lieutenant. Washburn jined up. Pa says I can't* . . .
> . . . *Clark got orders to march against Wabash Indians. Him and Ben Logan to lead army acrost river soon.* . . .
> . . . *Lot Masterson and Hezekiah Woods kilt on Sunday by Indians* . . .

[*September 14, 1786 — Thursday*]

"General," said George Rogers Clark, "no commander likes to lose his good right arm. To me, that's what you are. But now it appears there's no help for it." He paused to light his pipe.

Brigadier General Benjamin Logan said nothing, knowing Clark would continue in a moment. He suspected it had to do with the information their spies had just brought in from the north.

They were at the exact same camping place where, during the invasion in November of 1782, Clark had put him in charge of the detachment to go against the upper Great Miami River towns while the general led the main body against Chillicothe. The larger creek that until now had no name and was joined just below their campsite by the one they had named

Little East Fork, was now called Todd's Fork in memory of Colonel John Todd, who was killed at Blue Licks.

Their plan had been to move directly northwestwardly from this point with their seven hundred troops against the Wabash River Indians whose young confederacy was beginning to worry Congress. This confederacy, led by Chief Little Turtle of the Miami tribe, was reported to be growing rapidly and already included some five thousand warriors or more of the Piankeshaws, Weas and Little Turtle's own Miamis.[3]

But now, it seemed, the army's plans were changing. General Clark blew out a cloud of blue-white smoke and then pointed the stem of his pipe at Logan.

"Ben," he said, "the spies have just brought word that a lot of Maykujay Shawnees are moving northwest to join up with the confederacy. We're going to have to do something to show them this isn't a good idea and to draw them back to the Mackachack Towns. I want you to leave right away, tonight. Go back to Kentucky and raise as large a force as you can. We've got most of the militia here right now, so you're going to have to call for volunteers. But if you don't get enough response, start drafting men. As soon as you have five hundred or more, move against those towns to the north and destroy them. I don't need to tell you that the faster this is done, the better."

[*October 17, 1786 — Tuesday*]

Although the Kentuckians had not shown any great interest in joining George Rogers Clark's expedition to march against the far-distant Wabash River Indian tribes, it was a different story where General Logan's campaign was concerned. The Shawnees remained the especial enemies of these settlers and volunteers had flocked to answer Logan's summons. The rendezvous was to be at Limestone within two weeks and never before had such a mass of people gathered here.

Seven hundred ninety men there were, of whom five hundred had supplied all their own needs — horse, weapons and rations. The remaining two hundred ninety were provided government mounts. Fifty fat cattle were assembled to be driven along at the rear as food, and for two full days the women at Washington, Kenton's Station and Limestone did nothing but parch corn and bake johnnycake for their men to take along. Most of the men also carried with them a little bit of bacon and a gallon-sized pouch containing a mixture of finely ground corn meal and maple sugar. When this was mixed with water it made a remarkably good beverage, rich in energy and food value.

All night and all the next day on September 29–30 the crossing of the Ohio River had been made. The assembled army had then marched only a short distance before camping for the night near Eagle Creek on the very same spot in the gap of the river hills — now called Logan's Gap — where Simon had been captured by Bo-nah eight years before.

The march had gone well until, on the evening of October 4, a gawky, serious young newcomer to Kentucky named Willis Chadley decided that it was wrong for them to march against defenseless Indians. He confided to a friend that he was going to desert and go to the Mackachack towns to warn the Shawnees there of the army's approach. Within an hour of his riding off, word of his desertion spread through camp and General Logan summoned Simon, George Nokes and Hugh Ross. They were, he directed, to follow Chadley's trail and bring him back. If nothing else, they were given leave to kill him before he could get to the Shawnees. Logan, in the meanwhile, would lead the army on a forced march so that even if Chadley were successful in giving his warning, the army would be upon them before they had time to prepare.

The camp, ever afterward called "The Deserted Camp," was on the upper waters of Todd's Fork and it was still about sixty miles to Mackachack.[4] But the scouts had a difficult time following the deserter's trail at night, and they didn't catch up with him until two hours after dawn on October 6. It was too late. Seething with frustration, they watched from cover as the deserter boldly entered Mackachack, holding aloft a white kerchief.

Several Shawnees had rushed out menacingly and he appeared to have difficulty making himself understood. A few more men came out and one took his arm and pulled him not too gently off his horse. This one, it seemed, could speak English and they talked for several minutes. At a surreptitious signal from the warrior questioning the white man, one of the other warriors moved behind him and abruptly slammed his tomahawk into the deserter's skull, killing him instantly.

Simon and his two companions withdrew and hastened back toward Logan. They weren't quite sure what had happened back there, but it had to be one of two things: either the Indians hadn't believed Chadley at all, or he had succeeded in convincing them and then been executed because of their hatred for any man, white or Indian, who would betray his own companions in such manner. In either case, Logan must be advised immediately.

The general had wasted no time in following the trail of his scouts and in less than an hour the trio came upon the army being guided by Boone. As soon as they reported, Logan said they'd have to assume Chadley had given them away. They would continue the approach now with all speed and attack on three fronts: Colonel Robert Patterson, backed up by Captain Hugh McGary, would lead the left wing; Colonel Thomas Kennedy, with Captain Christopher Irvine, would command the right wing; Colonels Henry Lee and Richard Trotter would command the rear to protect the cattle and supplies; and the main body of the army, under Logan, would strike in the center, this formation to be led by Colonel Daniel Boone and Major Simon Kenton.

They came in sight of Mackachack at 10 A.M. and immediately moved to the attack at a gallop, howling and shouting ferociously. There was not much to fight. Here and there a lone Indian warrior scampered along, crouching in the tall prairie grasses or taking cover behind isolated thickets or in islands of trees. But the fighting, what little there was, became mainly a faint scattering of shots and a few weak skirmishes. It became obvious at the outset that there couldn't be more than twenty-five warriors here and that mostly there were just squaws and small children. Eight or nine warriors were downed in the first onslaught but those that remained fought with a fury that made many of the whites thankful there were not more on hand.

The squaws fled shrieking in frightened bevies and Colonel Kennedy spurred his horse after them, swinging an old Scotch broadsword he had honed down to a razor edge. His blade sank into the skull of the first squaw he overtook and her falling nearly jerked the weapon from his grasp. Regaining his balance, he galloped after a cluster of seven other squaws and one by one chopped them down, killing all but one who had thrown up a hand to ward off the blow. The blade chopped off her fingers and badly gashed her head, but did not kill her. The other small groups of squaws now fell to their knees and pleaded, "*Mat-tah tschi! Mat-tah tschi!*" Do not kill us!

Simon, a short distance away, charged after a warrior running through the deep grass at full tilt. Just as he caught up the Shawnee turned, took quick aim at the frontiersman and pulled the trigger of his flintlock. The gun snapped without firing and, before he could recover from the surprise, Simon had downed him with a tomahawk blow.

Immediately Simon galloped into the center of town and heard someone shout, "Bahd-ler! Bahd-ler!" and turned to see none other than Moluntha offering to surrender himself and his three wives to the only one of the attackers he had yet recognized.

Simon accepted Moluntha's tomahawk and then ordered a group of eight privates to stand guard over him while he went to get General Logan. When the pair returned and dismounted, Moluntha extended his bony hand in greeting and both Simon and Logan shook it. Moluntha smiled toothlessly and addressed Logan in reasonably good English.

"Moluntha," the Shawnee King said, "surrenders himself and his wives into the hands of the great white chief, Logan."

General Logan nodded. "You will not be harmed," he said. He quickly wrote out an official protection on a piece of paper, handed it to the chief and then questioned him. Moluntha said that all of the Maykujay and

Wapatomica towns were nearly deserted, their warriors — more than four hundred of them — having gone many days ago to fight against Clark on the Wabash. Logan nodded, anticipating this was what had happened, then ordered a cordon of men to surround the old chief and keep him prisoner but protect him from harm. He motioned to Simon and the two of them rode off.

Less than five minutes later, Hugh McGary rode up and, using his rank as captain, ordered the guards to let him inside the circle to question the captive. Moluntha had by this time lighted his pipe and, after puffing a few times on it himself, was passing it around among his guards. When he offered it to McGary, the captain refused it and shot a question at him.

"Were you at the Blue Licks battle?"

"Yes," Moluntha answered, "I was there."

"God damn you!" McGary shouted in instant rage. "I'll give you Blue Licks pay!"

He jerked out his tomahawk and before anyone could move to intervene, buried it to the handle in the Shawnee King's head. Moluntha fell dead without a sound. The men were so furious at this cold-blooded murder of the old man that they leaped upon McGary and began beating him, stopping only when Kenton and Logan rode up. Logan was furious, relieved McGary of his command and ordered him placed under arrest to stand trial later.

The scattered skirmishing around the village had ended and the prisoners were rounded up. There were thirty-three of them, mostly women. The army reassembled and now Logan dispatched them in companies to the other nearby towns to destroy their buildings and cornfields and bring whatever plunder was found back to this site.

There was no resistance, the other villages having been abandoned before they got there. In all, thirteen villages were destroyed: Mackachack, Moluntha's Town, Mingo Town, Wapatomica, Mamacomink, Kispoko, Puckshanoses, McKee's Town, Waccachalla, Chillicothe, Pecowick, Buckangehela's Town and Blue Jacket's Town. It would be another hard winter for the Shawnees who returned here. The destruction of the towns and cornfields took the remainder of that day and all the day following, October 7. When the plunder was collected it amounted to a valuation of just over $2,200. This was divided equally among the men. The entire campaign was hardly a credit to an army of nearly eight hundred men opposed by a couple of dozen warriors, many of whom had escaped. Only twelve Indians had been killed and this number included the squaws as well as the murdered Moluntha and a visiting Delaware Indian. Three whites had been killed.

That the men themselves were aware the whole campaign had been something of a farce became obvious as they set off on the return march on October 8. It was the custom after battle for the men to make up ballads about the fighting, singing the praises of those who had proven themselves well. The song they sang now was bitter and sarcastic and contained verses dealing with every major aspect of the campaign, beginning with the assembly at Limestone, the crossing of the Ohio, the march north and the desertion of Willis Chadley. As the ballad continued it became ever more infuriating to Colonel Thomas Kennedy and Hugh McGary, who found themselves the butt of the most bitterly sardonic lyrics:

> *Oh, our soldiers when done, in the town they convene,*
> *Where trophies of Vic'try were everywhere seen,*
> *A brave son of Mars slaps his bloody old dagger,*
> *And swears by the Lord that he made a squaw stagger.*
> *A dastardly fellow advanced to the King,*
> *Who was promised protection and brought to the ring,*
> *He soon was espied by intrepid McGary,*
> *Who just at this juncture came up from the prairie.*
> *He gave the old savage a cuss and a blow*
> *And sent him bare-skulled to the region below!*

These ten lines in particular became very popular and were sung over and over with subtle and never complimentary variations, until at length McGary's face was pinched white with anger and Colonel Kennedy shot his rifle into the air and ordered the ballading stopped or he'd kill the next man who opened his mouth to sing. An insulting silence then prevailed which lasted until they reached Limestone on October 15.

Thirty-two of the thirty-three prisoners were taken to Danville for confinement and possible trade later on for white captives. The single exception was a fine young Shawnee lad of about fourteen named Spemica Lawba — Big Horn — to whom General Logan had taken a particular shine. So much so, in fact, that Ben Logan later adopted him and gave him the name of Johnny Logan.

For a long time after the army returned, Simon Kenton was very depressed.

[October 31, 1786 — Tuesday]

Chief Blue Jacket could not understand why it should be, but it seemed that no matter what Indians the *Shemanese* crossed over the river to attack, it was always the Shawnees who bore the brunt of the destruction. This time had been no exception.

He had thought, with Clark marching against Little Turtle's confederacy, that for once the Shawnee villages would be out of the danger zone. Accordingly, he and many of his warriors had gone to meet Little

Turtle and join his engagement against Clark on the Wabash. And so what had happened? Instead of fighting they had listened to peace proposals from Clark's emissaries and the Miami chief's allies, the Weas and Piankeshaws, had agreed and convinced the reluctant Miami war chief to do the same. This had happened before the Shawnees arrived and by the time Blue Jacket got there, Clark's army was already moving down the Wabash River trail toward Vincennes and the confederacy had scattered, leaving nothing for them to do but return home. And then the shock of coming back to find thirteen of their villages reduced to ashes, their fields of grain and vegetables destroyed, their wives and children taken prisoner or dead and the old Shawnee King murdered.

Anger dictated that they turn immediately southward and retaliate, but common sense prevailed. New *wegiwas* must be built to protect the remaining squaws and children from the forthcoming winter. What little grain and vegetables remained in isolated and undiscovered fields must be harvested. Game had to be killed and brought in and the meat jerked. They needed to replenish stocks of salt, gunpowder, lead, clothing, furs; the best place to obtain these latter needs was from the boats of the white men coming up the Ohio River.

Both Blue Jacket and Black Snake immediately led parties of warriors to the Ohio, but separated upon reaching it. Once again the watercourse became littered with the wreckage of boats, with floatable debris — bobbing paddles and poles and the grotesquely bloated bodies of cattle and men. North to the Shawnee villages flowed an almost constant stream of supplies; and when the loot that reached these villages also contained bundles of scalps, these were immediately relayed to Detroit to be exchanged for more supplies.

Now, as he leaned forward and cut away the bonds holding this white man to the tree, Blue Jacket wondered again why he was relenting in this manner. By rights he should have tomahawked him in their first encounter, but what had stayed the chief's hand was the remarkable resemblance of the settler to the father of Marmaduke Van Swearingen. Even when he questioned the man and learned that his name was John May, that he was from the Limestone area now and Pennsylvania before that and was no relative after all, yet the fact that this man might have been his own father bothered him.

From the onset, May had been neither frightened nor defiant, accepting his capture by Blue Jacket as an unfortunate twist of fate. He did not want to die. No man did. But he did not beg for his life, as did so many, and this pleased Blue Jacket because this was the way he believed his own father would have reacted. And so, for the first time since becoming a Shawnee, Blue Jacket allowed mercy to prevail in his decision.

"I will turn you loose," he said, "if you will promise to go back across the mountains to the east and stay there."

John May readily agreed to do so and now he was free again, shoving his small canoe into the water of the river as Blue Jacket stood on shore with the settler's rifle. But before he was able to pull out of hearing, the Shawnee chief's voice came to him a final time.

"Do not return to this country, white man. If I ever see you again, your blood will redden the waters of this stream. Remember that."

John May was hardly apt to forget and he laid into his paddle strokes with exceptional vigor.

[*November 1, 1786 — Wednesday*]

A single lantern burned at high wick in the library of the large mansion in Trenton, New Jersey, where two men sat talking long after midnight.

"Judge," said Benjamin Stites, "believe me. Trading being my business, I've traveled all over this country. I've seen fine farmlands and valleys here in the east, as well as to the south and north of here. But never *anywhere* have I seen land as rich and beautiful as that to the north in Ohio straight across from the mouth of the Licking."

Judge John Cleve Symmes, member of Congress and a man of great wealth and influence, pursed his lips and nodded. He had known Major Stites for many years and had grown to respect the man's judgment and regard for truth. He had listened with growing enthusiasm to Stites's account: how Stites last summer had joined a party of Kentuckians at Washington and crossed the Ohio River, led by a fantastic figure of a frontiersman named Simon Kenton, in pursuit of some Indians who had stolen horses from his station; how they had gone as far north as the upper reaches of the Little Miami River to the ruins of the old Shawnee village of Chillicothe before a rainstorm forced them to give up the chase; and how they had returned, at Stites's request, through the country which lay between the Little Miami and the Great Miami Rivers and how fabulously rich the soil and forests and streams were there.

The beauty of it all was that this land was in limbo — the Indians had mostly been driven from it and there was not one settler upon it. Surely the government would sell it to them cheaply, if for no other reason than to get some kind of settlement started in the area and thus open up the country. Until now the settlers had, to a man, been extremely wary of building on the north side of the river; but if they could encourage the government to build a fort across from the Licking similar to the fort that had been built at the mouth of the Muskingum, there was every reason to believe the settlers would flock in. Look, for example, at how they were signing up for land with the Ohio Company which had just established a little land office in the shadow of Fort Harmar. And if there were a few

Indian risks involved, wasn't it worth it? After all, this area between the
two rivers bearing the same name was easily a third of a million acres of the
richest land in America.

Symmes was admittedly impressed and was inclined to believe that the
government could, indeed, be persuaded to sell them the tract, perhaps for
as little as a dollar an acre. Naturally, even at such a bargain he wouldn't
be able to buy the whole tract himself, but the success of the Ohio
Company intrigued him and others as well; it should not be difficult to
find men willing to invest in such an enterprise. He knew a number of men
with wealth, influence and imagination; men who would be able to
envision the development of this virgin land, such as his good friends Elias
Boudinot and Dr. Witherspoon, General Jonathan Dayton and William
Hubbell and William Plaskett.

It was growing light in the east when finally Major Stites rose to leave.
They shook hands and Symmes assured him he'd get busy on the project
immediately. Stites made to leave and then turned back hesitantly.

"One thing, Judge," he said. "If it goes through, I want your word that
you'll sell me ten thousand acres of the best land there at what you paid
for it."

Symmes smiled. The major was no fool. "You have it," he said.

[November 5, 1786 — Sunday]

The Dutchman, John Kinsaulla, was by no means a little man, but he was
helpless as a child in the strong grasp of the Kispokotha chief, She-me-
ne-to. Black Snake had leaped on his back and borne him to the ground
with an iron arm locked around his throat and a skinning knife at his
breast less than a minute after his fat wife had closed and barred the cabin
door behind him. He was on his way to attend the Reverend William
Wood's Baptist services, being held tonight in the cabin belonging to the
Taylors on the other side of the little village of Washington.

As soon as his initial struggles had ceased, Kinsaulla heard the Shawnee's
hoarse whisper in his ear. "You make noise, we kill. You no make noise, we
no kill." The Dutchman nodded and the grip about his throat was released
and the knife withdrawn. As he lay on his stomach his wrists were tightly
bound behind him and a rawhide tug snugged about his neck by which
they could lead him. All this while Kinsaulla's big emaciated hound dog,
Wasser, stood a few feet away, his head cocked to one side as if in
amusement. Occasionally when an Indian stepped near he wagged his
tail.

There were fourteen warriors in the party, all of them from Black
Snake's little village of Wapa-ko-neta on the banks of the Auglaize River.[5]
They were mostly very young men and for them this was something of a
training mission. Only two of them besides the chief himself had ever been

across the Spay-lay-wi-theepi before. They were excited and pleased with what they had done thus far. Kinsaulla was not the only captive; bound in similar manner were two other Washington residents, James Thomas and Ebenezer Smith.

When Kinsaulla was jerked back up to his feet, Black Snake once again whispered his threat of death and began to lead them northwest toward the Ohio River. But at the sound of singing, Black Snake raised his hand and they moved stealthily toward the Taylor cabin where a cheery yellow glow of lantern light showed through cracks in the chinking. Curiously, the chief put an eye to a small hole and studied the group of nine people inside. They were Preacher Wood himself, Mr. and Mrs. Taylor, Jane and Martha Dowden and their mother, James Finley, John Kinsaulla, Jr., and Benjamin Whiteman — the latter a sturdy seventeen-year-old newcomer to Kenton's Station who had arrived only a week ago; it was he who had volunteered to escort the widow Dowden and her daughters to the prayer meeting. Of the entire congregation — two men, two women, two girls and three youths — only Whiteman looked capable of putting up a good defense.

The ugly face of She-me-ne-to cracked in a malicious grin. "These inside," he whispered to the young Shawnees around him, "we will kill for scalps."

But the singing died away and as a droning voice came from within, the Kispokotha chief peeped in again and saw the Baptist minister standing with face raised and arms outstretched while the others stood with their heads bowed as he spoke. Black Snake asked Kinsaulla what they were doing.

"Iss vorship to Gott," the Dutchman whispered back. "Dot iss how ve pray."

At once Black Snake motioned them away from the cabin, saying, "We go. No hurt white people praying. Great Spirit would be angry."

They slipped off into the darkness and were skirting Kenton's Station just as a heavy snowfall began. Kenton's large brick home and all but one of the surrounding cabins were dark. The single exception was the outlying cabin of William McGinnis, where light shone dimly through cracks in the door. As they passed within twenty yards of it, the hound belonging to Kinsaulla, got in the way of one of the young warriors, who kicked the animal smartly. Wasser let out a startled yelp. Almost at once McGinnis opened the door to stand silhouetted on the threshold as he called out nervously, "Who's there?"

One of the young warriors threw his rifle to his shoulder and the bullet slammed through the settler's chest and sent him sprawling, half in and half out of the cabin. Behind him there was a piercing scream and then his wife showed herself briefly as she grabbed his legs and pulled him into the cabin with a frantic tug. The door slammed shut and the bar dropped with a thud, but her screams were still coming and there was no doubt they'd alert the settlement. Quickly the Indians took the McGinnis horse out of the stable shed and, without further delay, the party and their captives set off at a fast pace, Wasser dutifully trailing behind. When finally they climbed into the hidden canoes and put out from shore, the frightened horse tethered and swimming, the big skinny dog sat down and threw back his head and bayed mournfully.

Some time later, back in Washington, John Kinsaulla, Jr. returned to his cabin. When his mother asked where the elder Kinsaulla was, the fifteen-year-old was surprised. He had concluded his father had decided against attending prayer meeting tonight. At any rate, he had never shown up.

"Vasser iss vit him," the fat hausfrau said worriedly. "Doss he come back mitout your fadder, ve vill know he iss took or kilt by Inchens."

Hardly had she spoken when there came a whining and scratching at the door. Young John leaped to open it and Wasser ambled in with a half-hearted wag of his tail and sank to the floor with his head between his paws beside his master's bed.

"Oh, Gott," Mrs. Kinsaulla murmured, placing a hand to her cheek, "I vould radder haff lost two cows dan my old Chon!"

[*November 11, 1786 — Saturday*]

Former Captain Hugh McGary, a contemptuous smirk on his face, stood as ordered and faced the court. He wasn't worried in the least. No Kentuckian in his right mind would find fault in him for killing a damned Indian!

All that remained now was the verdict and he expected full absolution from the four ridiculous charges that had been lodged against him. They were:

Indictment One — The murder of a Shawnee Indian, Chief Moluntha, who was under protection of General Benjamin Logan at the time.

Indictment Two — Disobedience of Orders.

Indictment Three — Disorderly conduct as an officer, in that the accused made threats to kill Colonel James Trotter, his superior in rank and who did not approve Captain McGary's act.

Indictment Four — Abuse of other field officers for the same reason.

The verdict was a surprise and the sentence amazing. McGary was found innocent of Indictment Two, part-guilty of Indictment Four and guilty of Indictments One and Three. The sentence was almost laughable. He was suspended from command for a period of one year. That was all.

The same sneer remained on his face even as he shouldered his way out of the crowded Harrodsburg courtroom.

[*February 15, 1787 — Thursday*]

It was the first wedding celebrated at Kenton's Station and virtually everyone from every settlement within thirty miles was present and many had come from even farther. There was not enough room for them all inside the brick building and so the happy bride and groom stood on the threshold while the sonorous tones of the Reverend William Wood's voice carried well to the ears of the crowd in a large semicircle behind him.

The beautiful young bride wore a fine lacy dress that had obviously once been pure white but was now the color of ancient ivory. The groom, nearly thirty-three years old, looked extremely uncomfortable in dark wool trousers, waistcoat and jacket, knee-length white socks covering his bulging calves and his feet clamped in tight black shoes buckled over his instep. His long auburn hair was pulled back into a single neat queue, and he wore a white linen shirt with a little black string tie and ruffled collar and cuffs.

"Do you, Simon Kenton, take this woman to be your lawfully wedded wife, to love and to cherish, through joy and through sorrow, through sickness and through health, till death you do part?"

"I do." His voice cracked just the smallest bit.

Preacher Wood smiled and asked sixteen-year-old Martha Dowden the similar question and received the same answer. Wood cleared his throat and continued. "Then by the authority vested in me, I hereby pronounce you husband and wife. Whom God hath joined together, let no man put asunder. Amen. Kiss her, Simon."

And Simon did.

[*March 10, 1787 — Saturday*]

Blue Jacket could not remember ever before feeling quite so nervous as he did today. It had begun at dawn and lasted straight through until now, when the dancing and feasting were over and his warriors were preparing to leave.

It had taken many days for him to set up this day of prisoner exchange with the whites and, until this morning, he had thought the worst part of it was that initial trip across the Spay-lay-wi-theepi by himself to see Bahdler. The *cut-ta-ho-tha*, Black Hoof had instructed him, was known not to shoot an enemy if that enemy was helpless or asking peace. But Blue Jacket was not so sure. This was the man whose head he broke as he tried to escape from captivity. Would he not now shoot Blue Jacket on sight?

He took great care in his approach and, from concealment, watched Kenton's Station for more than five hours before the big frontiersman finally emerged, mounted his horse and set off alone on the wagon road to Limestone. No one else was in sight and so, when Kenton was within forty yards of him, Blue Jacket stepped from cover holding the white cloth high with one hand with the other palm held forward so that the frontiersman could see he was unarmed.

Black Hoof had made a wise appraisal. Although Simon stopped with a jerk and half brought his gun up, he abruptly realized the situation and asked Blue Jacket what he wanted. That was the start. The Shawnee had explained that the Indians wanted their people back whom the whites were holding prisoner and he was sure the whites wanted their people back who were captives of the Shawnees. Would the whites meet them on a peaceful basis directly across the river from Limestone?[6] Would the whites bring their prisoners and promise peace and surrender them up if the Shawnees did the same?

The arrangements had taken many days and this day had been set as the day of exchange. But it was a wary and suspicious group of whites who met a similar group of Shawnees. On hand for the whites were Kenton, Logan, Boone, Robert Todd, Robert Patterson, Ben Whiteman, George Hany and Luther Calvin, along with half a hundred others. Blue Jacket was in charge of the Indian side of the negotiations, but also on hand were Black Snake, King John, Captain Billy, Me-ou-se-ka, Black Beard, Captain Wolf and more than sixty warriors.

The white prisoners had not yet been brought up from a place far back in the woods, nor had the Indian prisoners been brought across the river. They stood on the Kentucky shore in a cluster whose silence spoke more of hope than any words they might have uttered.

Blue Jacket felt almost revolted at the protestations of friendship he had to give. Friendship! What could the treacherous whites know of this? They promised the same, but Blue Jacket told Black Snake in an undertone that they would see evidence of white treachery before this day was done.

For their parts the whites, with Benjamin Logan acting as spokesman, offered the same and promised to bury forever, from this day forward, the enmity between their peoples.

A well-hidden rage swept through Blue Jacket when King John rose to speak. A very minor Maykujay chief in whose village there lived only sixty warriors and ninety women and children, he had never proven himself as any kind of fighter. When the Shawnee nation had split years ago, he had almost gone with them and many times since then had expressed the wish that he had. Now he gravely told the whites that the Shawnees did indeed want peace, so desirous of this was he that lest the men from his own village violate it, he would leave to join their brothers in the Missouri country soon after the exchange and all those of the village who wished to go with him were welcome.

This was weakness before an enemy and Blue Jacket felt shamed for his people. But he said nothing and the tension in the air eased somewhat.

The prisoners were assembled and the exchanges made and it was a time filled with cries and tears of gladness and sorrow. John Kinsaulla was there and at sight of him his son broke down and wept aloud and through his tears told his father that Mrs. Kinsaulla was waiting and praying on the other side.

There was a white girl of about sixteen who didn't know who she was or where she had been captured and she looked at the white men assembled there and once or twice called out querulously for her papa, but fell silent when there was no reply.

The two sons of Major George Hany, taken two years ago on the Kentucky River, were returned now and the reunion was a joyous one. It was a different story when a mother was brought across the river to identify a girl of about nine. This woman had lost her child to the Shawnees when the girl was barely a toddler, but she knew there would be a triangular-shaped scar at the hairline where her daughter had once fallen. It was there! But though the mother screamed for joy, the daughter screamed in anguish, stretched out her arms to the squaw who had raised her as her own and cried out, "*Nik-yah! Nik-yah!*" — Mother! Mother! — begging the squaw not to give her up. Finally the Shawnee woman had to run into the woods with her hands over her ears and her eyes blinded with tears.

On the Indian side the emotion was no less intense, but it was better contained. Warriors who had not wept since they were children now felt tears slide down their cheeks as they were reunited with wives or children, sisters or brothers or friends.

Only one Indian showed any reluctance to leave the whites and this was Johnny Logan — Spemica Lawba — the adopted son of Benjamin Logan. He had come to like his life as a white. He had learned English swiftly and was going to school and the elder Logan had treated him with great kindness and consideration at all times. They embraced one another for a long moment and the general could not speak, but Spemica Lawba whispered, "To my white father I will always be Johnny Logan and I will never raise my hand against him or his army."

When the exchange of prisoners was completed without any form of ransom in money or goods being demanded by either side, and an agreement made that all hostilities should cease for the day, a huge barbecue was begun of several fine beeves and a pair of elk. The Indians were requested to stack their guns and, as the whites set the example, they did so, keeping their knives and tomahawks in their belts. More of the whites came over the river, including many of the women, and quite a few of the people on both sides relaxed a little and enjoyed themselves. Dancing was begun and the Shawnees smiled and nodded at the light-step reels and then the whites watched with open-mouthed wonder the circular shuffling dance punctuated by occasional hoppings as performed by the Indians.

Toward late afternoon, Luther Calvin suddenly recognized William

McGinnis's mare among the Indian horses and with that the levity ceased. He swore he would get it "if I have to scalp every Injen here to get it!" Tempers were beginning to flare and, in an attempt to settle things down, Boone and Kenton bargained with Black Snake and bought the mare for a keg of whiskey. While everyone on hand watched, they swam it back across the river and delivered it to Widow McGinnis.

Calvin was not altogether mollified. He and a group of men got their heads together and after a while moved out of sight. The feasting and dancing continued but the spark of levity refused to be re-ignited and after about an hour the whites began moving back to the Kentucky shore.

The last three boats were going across when abruptly there was a fierce howling from the Shawnees. Gunfire sounded and little spurts of water erupted around the boats. The men in them were wise enough not to throw down their paddles and start shooting back, but to continue rowing for all they were worth until out of effective range.

Blue Jacket, his face once again set in surly lines, finally ordered the shooting to halt and the warriors to head back for their villages with the liberated prisoners. It was no satisfaction to him that his earlier prediction to Black Snake had been borne out. While the dancing and feasting had been going on, Calvin and his men had overpowered two Indians on guard and escaped across the river with fourteen Shawnee horses.

The peace had been a short one.

[December 31, 1787 — Monday]

Relations between Shawnees and whites degenerated rather than improved over the rest of the year. Scarcely a week passed throughout the summer and fall and even deep into the winter when Indian raiding parties did not cross the Ohio to burn isolated cabins, kill cattle, steal horses and, where possible, take prisoners or scalps. It became necessary for the whites to post guards whenever there was any field work to be done — and even then the killings increased.

Time and again Simon Kenton and his volunteer Limestone minutemen mounted up to chase parties of Indians in efforts to recover stolen horses and goods, but actual encounters were few; the Shawnees planned their strategy well and got far out of range rapidly. They seemed to have an especial knack for utilizing inclement weather. A bad rainstorm or heavy snowfall soon covered tracks and baffled pursuit.

On at least two occasions it was fortunate indeed that the pugnacious little party of whites led by Kenton did not catch up to the Indians they were trailing, for they were outnumbered six or eight to one. On other occasions they did manage to catch smaller parties off guard and take back goods that were stolen.

Late in summer Simon Kenton and Daniel Boone led a party as far north as the prairies near where Chillicothe used to be along the Little Miami River. They would certainly have wiped out the smaller Indian band they were chasing had not the Shawnees set fire to the dry grasslands and caused a great wall of fire between themselves and their pursuers, behind which they escaped.

Colonel John Bowman was back again and his campaign against the upper Great Miami River towns in July proved abortive. The nearer they approached their objective, the colder became his feet. When within striking distance, Bowman ordered the army into retreat without having seen any of the enemy except for a group of squaws picking blackberries; thus "Bowman's Blackberry Campaign" became a term the colonel would live with for the rest of his life.

But while these expeditions and swift retaliatory trips across the Ohio had little effect upon the Indians, the news that white men were crossing into the Ohio country quite frequently without disaster encouraged settlers both here and in the east to begin to think seriously about claiming some of this fine land as their own. Everywhere, here on the frontier as well as in the east, land deals were being consummated; and while, for now, it was mostly on paper, these matters must before long cause a massive emigration of whites into the Ohio country.

The biggest news of the year was the official establishment by the federal government of the Northwest Territory by ordinance. In this Ordinance of 1787, all land to the north and west of the Ohio River, clear to the Canadian border, was organized into a commonwealth — the first in the world whose organic law recognized every man as free and equal. It was an amazing document and so unique in its establishment that wherever posted, and that included points along the entire frontier border, it was for weeks the single most important topic of discussion. It provided, among other things, for the appointment of a governor and other territorial offices, for the establishments of both civil and criminal laws, for the laying out of counties, the setting up of a general assembly, the authorization of a delegate to Congress who would have the right to debate but not to vote during the temporary government. The Ordinance further prohibited the molestation of any man because of his mode of worship or his religion; it provided the benefits of the writs of habeas corpus and of trial by jury; that there would not be permitted in this Territory either slavery or involuntary servitude; and that "Religion, morality and knowledge being necessary to good government and the happiness of mankind, schools and the means of education shall forever be encouraged."

Article V of the Ordinance declared that this Northwest Territory was to be divided into no less than three nor more than five states. The westernmost state in the Territory was to be bounded on the west by the Mississippi River, on the south by the Ohio and on the east by the Wabash River as far upstream from its mouth as Vincennes and then, from there, on a line due north to the Canadian border. The middle state's southern boundary would also be the Ohio River and its eastern boundary a line drawn due north from the mouth of the Great Miami River to the Canadian border. The easternmost state of the Territory would take in the rest of the land to the east of that line, and to the north and west of the Ohio River and Pennsylvania border to the Canadian border as established by the Treaty of Paris.[7]

But the portion of the Ordinance of 1787 which most flabbergasted and outraged the Kentuckians was Article III of Section 14, which declared in part:

. . . *The utmost good faith shall always be observed towards the Indians; their lands and property shall never be taken from them without their consent; and in their property, rights, and liberty they shall never be invaded or disturbed, unless in just and lawful wars authorized by Congress; but laws founded in justice and humanity shall, from time to time, be made, for preventing wrongs being done to them, and for preserving peace and friendship with them . . .*

What this amounted to, as the frontiersmen saw it, was that it now became illegal for the whites to mount further retaliatory parties against the Indians who came south of the river to steal and burn and kill. It was one portion of the Ordinance which no red-blooded Kentuckian had any intention of obeying.

The Ordinance had far-reaching effects. In New York, sales of parts of the Seven Ranges amounting to almost $73,000 were made, and in Salem, Massachusetts, Dr. Manasseh Cutler and Winthrop Sargent, who were agents for the Ohio Company which had been formed in that eastern state for the purpose of the settlement of Ohio, immediately made a contract with the government to buy, for no less than a dollar per acre, a chunk of Ohio nearly a million acres in size. The deal was consummated only ten days after the Ordinance was enacted.[8] As is frequently the case in buying land sight unseen, however, the Ohio Company had bought something of a lemon. The land purchased, with few exceptions, was the most hilly and sterile countryside of any tract of similar size in the entire Ohio country.

John Cleve Symmes had lined up his backers, too, and quickly petitioned for the purchase of the land between the two Miami Rivers. Before the sale was legally consummated, he sold to Matthias Denman, of Springfield, New Jersey, a tract of seven hundred forty acres of land directly opposite the mouth of the Licking River. Denmen paid him five shillings per acre in Continental scrip, or about fifteen pence per acre in specie, which amounted to less than $125 for the entire plot. Here Denman planned to build a port settlement — one which he envisioned would, in years ahead, become one of the greatest ports on the entire Ohio

River. But to begin this project he would need help, and so he journeyed to Lexington where two good friends — John Filson and Robert Patterson — lived. Perhaps they would be interested in forming a partnership.

Expecting a sharp increase in settlement, another land office was opened on August 1 at Louisville; this one for the reception of locations and surveys made *north* of the Ohio River. The Virginia Legislature, recognizing now the growing importance of Limestone as a port city, also approved of the city layout on one hundred acres of land, "the property of John May and Simon Canton," and incorporated it not as the city of Limestone, but as the city of Maysville. John May also established a new settlement eight miles south of Washington on the buffalo road to Blue Licks and this he named May's Lick.

Fort Harmar, at the mouth of the Muskingum, was now well established, as was the new Fort Finney across the Ohio River from Louisville; and the construction of a large and very impressive two-story walled fortification was begun just east of the mouth of the Muskingum and this was being called Campus Martius. On October 28 Colonel Josiah Harmar received the welcome news that he had received his commission as brigadier general and immediately he left Fort Finney with his troops for Fort Harmar. There was a strong rumor that next spring or summer he would march his men against the Shawnees and wipe them out for good.

Hardly noticed at all amid all these matters of great significance was the thin little wail of a newborn child in late November at Kenton's Station, where seventeen-year-old Martha Kenton and her husband became the parents of a fine little daughter who was named Nancy, after Simon's sister.

And far to the north and west, along the Mississippi River just across from the mouth of Apple Creek, Tecumseh and Chiksika and their band of twelve young warriors made a good winter camp after having spent four months as the guests of the great chief of the Miami tribe, Little Turtle, along the Mississinewa River. It was good to be far from the constant harassment of the whites; but even so, Tecumseh often stood alone and faced toward the rising sun which he knew was shining down at that moment on the land along the Little Miami River that he loved so much — a land he missed more than anyone suspected.

[*January 12, 1788 — Saturday*]

It had been a long time since anyone had seen Daniel Boone smile, much less explode with great laughter as in days gone by. His eyes seemed now to carry a sorrowful, faraway look and he seemed not to know what to do with himself. Since leaving his job as sheriff of Fayette County and taking up residence in the cabin at Maysville that Simon Kenton had helped him build, he had been at loose ends — a man unsure of what he should do.

Increasingly over the passing months he had been called into court to testify in land disputes and, as with Kenton himself, more and more of his land was whittled away because of overlapping and faulty claims. Visiting Henry Lee at his little station southeast of Maysville, Boone commented glumly on the situation. "Henry," he said, "over and over I've been robbed of my lands here. I'm constantly being called on to give depositions in land claim cases and told to sign papers and then later find out I've signed away the rights to my own land. These lawyers are always trying to make me falsify my oath."

Lee nodded sympathetically. Boone was not the only individual having such troubles here. The sharp landgrabbers were making killings preying on the ignorance and illiteracy of the frontiersmen who opened this land. He wished he could help but knew there was nothing he could do.

"By God, Henry," Boone continued, growing angrier the more he thought of it, "it's bad enough to be stripped of my land without being abused and being accused of falsehood. From now on, no one need send to me for a deposition. All my own lands are gone and others will just have to take care of their own."

He paused reflectively for a moment, then added, "I believe I'm going west of the Mississippi where it ain't so all-fired crowded. I won't live in a country where I can't fell wood in my dooryard." His eyes widened and his voice registered something between surprise and consternation. "Why, at Bryant's Station they have to haul wood a half mile!"

"That's Spanish land west of the Mississippi, Dan'l," Henry Lee cautioned. "It's still all wilderness and the Indians are moving out there. They might not take too kindly to your coming to settle."

To Lee's surprise, Boone chuckled at this; and Lee could have sworn there was a note of keen eagerness in the sound.

[*March 29, 1788 — Saturday*]

TO: *Governor Beverly Randolph*
Governor of the Continental Western Territory
Richmond, Virginia

Sir:

By Captain Rogers, who will forward this, we inform the executive that the Indians for some time past, have discovered a disposition to prosecute a war against us with uncommon ardor and usual barbarity. They have, since the commencement of the present year, at different times, taken, we think, not less than thirty horses from the counties of Fayette and Bourbon. They have repeatedly fired upon the inhabitants of these counties and several have been killed. Last week they made an attack on the house of Mr. Shank on the frontier of Bourbon, adjoining Fayette, in the night. They killed five of this family, destroyed the property, and burnt the house. This but too common, they escaped without adequate punishment. In the last attack and pursuit, two of the enemy were killed and one wounded. The inhabitants on the frontier of each of these counties are alarmed and moving, and when this once begins it is hard to say where the evil will terminate, or what part may be a frontier.

> I am, Sir, Yr Mst Humble & Obdt Svt,
> Levi Todd, Colonel
> Lieutenant, Fayette County

March 29th Inst.
1788

[April 13, 1788 — Sunday]

"Little brother," Chiksika had said yesterday, placing his hand on Tecumseh's shoulder, "what I say now will come to be. Just as our father knew that he should die in that battle with the *Shemanese* where the Kanawha and Spay-lay-wi-theepi meet, so I know that I will die tomorrow during the midst of our little battle. When the sun is at its highest, then will a bullet from the whites strike me here," he had placed a finger to his forehead midway between his eyes, "and my life will be ended. But do not let them falter. Lead them on with an attack at once and they will emerge victorious."

And now, as they rode toward the frail fortification behind which the whites lay, a devastating sorrow drained Tecumseh of strength and will as he followed Chiksika wordlessly toward the destiny his older brother had predicted.

He thought again of the years they had shared and the warmth they had always held for one another. Not even their sister, Tecumapese, whom he loved so dearly, filled as great a part of his heart as did Chiksika; the certainty that this day he would lose all that made him want to cry out in anguish and hug his brother and force him to go away with him somewhere so this would not happen. But he knew he could not.

The winter camp they had shared on the Mississippi in the northern Illinois country had been a good camp, the closeness of Chiksika bringing as much warmth within as the fires brought without. And when, during the Hunger Moon, they had started south at a leisurely pace, hunting and exploring along the way, untroubled by encounters with whites or other Indians, the world had seemed a good and full place.

Tecumseh wished he could disbelieve his thirty-one-year-old brother's prediction, but he could not. How many times in the past had Chiksika predicted exactly what would happen and when? Too many times to count. Even on the trip south they had laughed together when Chiksika had told Tecumseh that though he was a better hunter than himself or any other of the dozen Kispokotha warriors with them, in three days he would fall from his horse and break his hip as he attempted to down a buffalo. But it had happened just as he said. Two months ago, they had charged a small herd and Tecumseh had thundered up beside the largest bull, prepared to strike, when the animal's shoulder had bumped his horse, throwing it off stride. The horse had slipped and fallen, throwing Tecumseh from its back, and he had lain there filled with admiration for Chiksika's prophetic ability, even as the waves of pain from the broken hip bone throbbed through him.

Only during the last week had he been able again to mount and ride with any degree of comfort and ability. They had met old friends among the Cherokees and stayed with them in their village on the Tennessee frontier and it was a good stay, filled with story telling and exploits and renewed friendships.

But as the Shawnees were having their troubles with the *Shemanese* in the Ohio country, so too were their Cherokee friends here. A new little settlement not far away was causing the most trouble and it had been decided to ride against it. Though not asked to do so, the party of Shawnees had said they would ride with them, for were they not the guests of the Cherokees? Had they not eaten from the same cookpot with them?

And then last night Chiksika had told Tecumseh of his presentiment and abruptly the world had become cold and hard and alien. So sorrowful at Chiksika's prediction was he that Tecumseh scarcely heard his older brother's further prediction.

"Tecumseh," he said, "you must carry on for our people and become for them a leader. You will do this, I know. I have looked ahead and seen you not only as the leader of the Shawnees, but as the greatest and most powerful chief any tribe has ever known. I have seen you journey to far lands and I have watched you bring together under your hand a confederation of Indian nations such as has never before been known."

But Tecumseh found little comfort in the words. His own mind was filled with words that would never be spoken and his heart with a pain that would never be eased. He vowed to stay by his brother's side during the engagement.

The fight began late in the forenoon and it was a hot one, the whites defending their little stronghold with unexpected tenacity. Only gradually were the settlers picked off and the Indians able slowly to advance. The Cherokee chief three times led a charge and three times had been forced to retire, but each time less emphatically than the last. Now, out of effective rifle range, he stood high and called his tribesmen and Shawnee friends to rally behind him for a final charge that would bring them victory.

Chiksika unexpectedly placed his hand over Tecumseh's and squeezed it. He pointed to a hickory sapling, its branches bare but for swelling buds. It stood arrow straight in the ground and the sun made the shadows of the branches a spiderwork pattern on the ground about the trunk, but there was little trunk shadow, for the sun was at its zenith.

"Happy am I," Chiksika said softly, "to fall in battle and not die in a *wegiwa* like an old squaw."

He and his younger brother then joined the Cherokee chief and suddenly, even before the sound of the distant shot came, there was a heavy thunking sound and Tecumseh whirled to see Chiksika just beginning to topple sideways, a hole nearly the diameter of his thumb between his brother's eyes in the middle of the forehead. Tecumseh leaped forward and caught him and gently lowered him to the ground. As he did so, the Cherokee chief exhorted his men to charge the whites, but they were shocked at the bullet having traveled so incredibly far and so accurately to kill their northern ally and considered it a bad sign. Even though Tecumseh begged them to charge again, telling them that Chiksika had said they would win and that he would lead them beside their chief, they refused to fight more.

As the entire party withdrew, Tecumseh's shoulders slumped far more with the weight of sorrow than with the weight of his brother's body in his arms.

[*April 24, 1788 — Thursday*]

Even though the bullet wound in his left side was not yet entirely healed, and he was more tired than he was willing to admit, Blue Jacket was pleased that he had come. None would have thought the worse of him had he elected to stay behind in his *wegiwa*, rather than lead his men on this raid deep into Kentucky country, but he would not hear of it.

Three weeks ago he had received the wound as he stood high on a rocky outcrop upstream on the Ohio from the mouth of the Scioto and watched a large flatboat drift downstream in the swift current toward Maysville. It was a good lookout point, one called Hanging Rock, and from it a great vista of the Spay-lay-wi-theepi could be seen in both directions. Blue Jacket was nearly a half mile from the boat and had even smiled at the little puffs of smoke; at such range, and from a moving boat, they could not hope to hit him. But then had come the tremendous blow in his side and the faint cheers from the men as he fell.

He had quickly plugged the wound with buzzard down and pulled himself onto his horse and headed home, though he was somewhat foggy about the trip and remembered nothing of falling unconscious from his mount just as he entered the village. Wabethe had probed and found the bullet, removed it and dressed her husband's wound and for four days a great fever had ridden him. But her ministrations had been good and he recovered quickly. And when he heard of the projected raid to get horses from across the Ohio, there was nothing else to do but take leadership of the party, despite Wabethe's protests.

She had bound him tightly about the middle and begged him not to move suddenly, nor stretch, nor engage in running or jumping lest he break open the wound and the red fire-in-the-flesh which he knew as infection should attack and kill him.

The night before they left she had presented him with an unusual but beautiful gift — a special hat she had labored over during nearly all the time he had been convalescing, a talisman to keep him safe from all harm. It was a jet-black affair made of the feathers of crows meticulously sewn to a kind of skullcap. A thin band of rawhide held it securely under his chin. Partially extended wings stuck out, one from each side, and tail feathers hung down from the rear. He accepted it gravely and told her he believed in its powers. He had worn it all during the raid in which his party of fifteen braves took thirty horses from Strode's Station. At once they started home.

About noon, when they reached the Ohio River shore near the mouth of Cabin Creek five miles above Maysville, a cold misty drizzle had begun falling. Feeling reasonably secure from pursuit, Blue Jacket had ordered the horses be taken across and driven to their village. He would stay here to rest a few hours and then follow. Unwilling to leave their chief alone in his weakened state, however, two of the warriors returned after the horses had been taken across; they built a fire in a relatively dry spot beneath a huge tree and sat around it with Blue Jacket. But the theft of the horses had been discovered within an hour and a dozen men, led by Jasper Hood and John McIntyre, had taken up the trail. The first the Indians even knew of their approach was when shots rang out and both warriors slumped over dead.

Instantly Blue Jacket leaped to his feet and ran, but Jasper Hood gave chase on his horse. As he overtook Blue Jacket he swung his rifle and the barrel caught the chief alongside the head, stunning him. He managed to regain his feet but, realizing the futility now of further attempting escape, surrendered. Within minutes his hands were tied securely behind him and he was driven before the men, the rumpled crow-feather hat still astride his head, with one wing now dangling.

They went first to Maysville and stayed at Boone's cabin one night. A continuous procession of visitors came to stare and jeer at the feared Shawnee chief. His capture was something to boast of and his presence something of a sideshow. With their captive securely tethered, they also stopped at Washington and May's Lick, Millersburg and Stockton's Station and finally, on the third night, reached Strode's Station again.

Weary from their exertions, the men tied the prisoner to a post in one of the cabins, placed a guard over him and retired to their own cabins to sleep before deciding what to do with him. Less than an hour later the guard had fallen asleep too and Blue Jacket wasted no time. He knew he could not free himself from the thongs which tightly bound both his ankles and wrists, but he had expanded his chest as they bound him to the stake and now these cords were loose.

Back and forth he leaned against the stake and gradually it loosened in the earth until he was able to squat and, using the chest thongs for leverage, raise the post out of the ground. Very quietly then, so as not to awaken his guard, he lay with the post on the ground and slid the thongs off the end. When he regained his feet they fell loosely to the ground.

Now he began a series of short hops, each time landing silently on the balls of his feet and poising there a moment before hopping again. He had decided to make a great bound and land with his knees in the guard's middle should be begin to awaken, but the man never stirred and his own snoring drowned out any sound made by Blue Jacket.

The Shawnee chief raised the latch with his teeth and swung the door open with his shoulder and then hopped away into the darkness. The further he got from the cabins, the greater his hops became and he did not stop until he was deep in the woods. At length, his lungs bursting and his side a mass of pain, he stopped and slumped to the ground. Although it pained his side even more to do it, he found that he could just reach the uppermost ankle binding with his teeth. It took him nearly a half hour of alternately resting and chewing to gnaw through the cord; but finally it was done and with immense relief he stretched his legs apart.

But the wrist bindings held; even rubbing them against a rock had little more effect than to tear his own skin. Since he could not afford to spend any more time in the vicinity, he set off at an easy run and before daylight reached the scattering of cabins which indicated Stockton's Station.

Crooning gently, he climbed the corral fence and stood poised there until one of the horses came close enough and he leaped lightly on its back. It reared partially for a moment but he gripped it tightly with his knees, continued his crooning chant and the horse settled down. With knee pressure he guided it to the gate and pushed off the two top bars with his foot. At an abrupt punch of his heels, the horse leaped the last low rail and Blue Jacket was on his way home.

It took four days but finally he arrived — hungry, thirsty, feverish and weak — and for the second time collapsed and fell unconscious from his horse as it entered the village. He was back home alive and the crow-feathered hat, considerably the worse for wear, was still upon his head.

[May 15, 1788 — Thursday]

Joel Barlow was delighted that his short visit from the east to "the promised land," as he was instructed to consider it, was coming to a close. How wonderful it would be to see Paris again and leave behind the roughness and coarseness and savagery of this pioneer life.

Grandiose tales had been told him of the glorious new settlement called Marietta just recently begun at the mouth of the Muskingum River. They called Marietta "a bright new city in a bright new land" and "the gateway to the richest country in the world, the Northwest Territory." Barlow hadn't really expected much but he had been rewarded with even less. The "bright new city" was no more than a few ten-by-ten rough-hewn cabins squatting in the shaky security provided by Fort Harmar and the still-under-construction Campus Martius a little way to the east.

The newly outlined Scioto Tract was land, he was told, soon to be purchased from the Ohio Company. It began "just downriver a little ways from Marietta," about opposite the Great Kanawha River and stretched far to the north as well as to the west as far as the Scioto River. The fact that the so-called Scioto Tract was thus far only a paper dream and had in no way yet been authorized by Congress or sold by the Ohio Company was not to bother him. He was hereafter to consider it land fully purchased, owned and controlled by the Scioto Company, and it was this land that he would sell in Europe.

The larceny in Joel Barlow's soul needed little watering to bloom and he saw at once that regardless of how little he liked this land, there was money to be made with it. He was not in the least bothered by scruples, nor was he the only one. The Scioto Tract had already been divided into thirty shares: Dr. Manasseh Cutler and Winthrop Sargent, as "initial proprietors," split thirteen shares between them; another thirteen very conveniently found their way into the possession of Colonel William Duer of New York, who just happened to be Secretary of the United States Board of Treasury and a man described as being "a large operator and a man of speculative turn"; and the remaining four shares were to be sold in Europe by Joel Barlow to whom, in his staggering minificence, Duer had given a one-sixtieth share.

Barlow was also given a copy of a pamphlet written by Dr. Cutler with the somewhat less than inspired title of An Explanation of the Map which Delineates that Part of the Federal Lands Comprehended between Pennsylvania, the Rivers Ohio, Scioto, and Lake Erie. This pamphlet and the map that went along with it included the endorsement of Captain Thomas Hutchins, Geographer of the United States, as to its accuracy. It was, to be blunt, extremely inaccurate.

"Your job," Barlow had been told in effect, "is to convince these poor downtrodden Frenchmen that this is a world of freedom waiting for them. No more tyrants! No more Bastilles! Here, on this wonderful new land shown on the plot diagrams we've given you, no man will be subject of any other. This is a free land for free men. Make that clear to them; it's important. Don't mention Indians! And stress this point: in anticipation of Frenchmen coming to settle here, the principal city of the Ohio Company

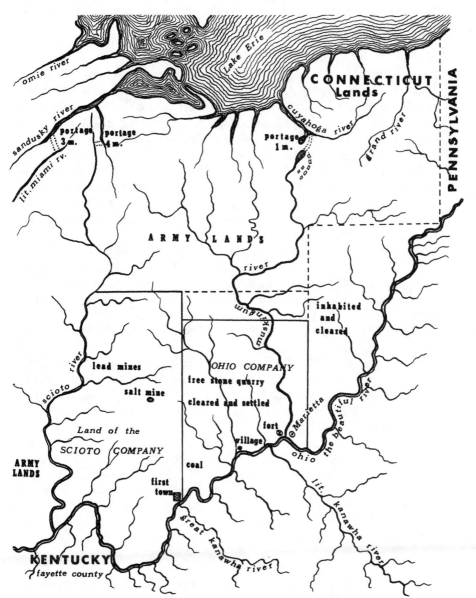

BARLOW'S FRAUDULENT MAP — showing false claims and grave
topographical errors meant to mislead French prospective buyers.

Tract has been named Marietta in honor of them and their greatest Frenchwoman, Marie Antoinette. They're emotional people. They ought to like that."

[*July 26, 1788 — Saturday*]

General Arthur St. Clair, a good man in many respects, had gone far since those days on the Pennsylvania frontier before the Revolution when he was fighting to establish the western boundary of the Colony of Pennsylvania. He was an unusually good administrator and what might well have been termed a born politician. He was also a reasonably good soldier, provided the enemy he faced stuck to the rules of the game. He was, in addition, a very good friend of George Washington and it was the latter's recommendation that had won for St. Clair, just thirteen days ago, the governorship appointment from Congress over the Northwest Territory. In that position he also became, according to the Ordinance of 1787, commander of all the western troops.

There were other Territorial appointments as well. Named as secretary under St. Clair was none other than the Ohio Company and Scioto Company land speculator, Winthrop Sargent, and shortly after his appointment came the naming of nine supreme court justices for the territory: John Cleve Symmes, James M. Varnum, Samuel H. Parsons, John Armstrong, William Barton, Rufus Putnam, George Turner, Joseph Gillman and Return J. Meigs.

It did not take St. Clair long to begin fulfilling his duties. On this date he posted his first proclamation, creating an enormous county which embraced practically half the territory; taking in all the land westward from the Pennsylvania border and the Ohio River to the Scioto River and hence northward to Lake Erie.

No one cared to comment on the fact that the northern half of this newly created county was still land which, according to the most recent treaty between the United States and the Indians, belonged to the Delawares and Wyandots. Nor was it any great surprise to anyone when Arthur St. Clair named this sprawling section of land after the man who had made his appointment possible.

Thus was Washington County established.

[*September 3, 1788 — Wednesday*]

It had been thought that the massacre of the near hundred Moravian Indians which had so incensed many whites would have been more or less forgotten as the years passed, but somehow the treachery of the deed continued to gnaw at the memory of far too many. The people still asked embarrassing questions. How can we expect the Indians to lay down their arms when it is the whites who have been guilty of the worst atrocity of all? How can we hope to have any peace with the Indians when the memory of this barbarity is a curtain hanging between us? How can our leaders let such a national disgrace go by with no attempt to make restitution, without even an official apology being offered? It was time something was done!

The voices grew louder and the requests for action turned into demands; and so on this date, six and a half years after the massacre, Congress passed an ordinance for the encouragement of the Moravian missionaries "in the work of civilizing Indians" and directed that the scattered remnants of the flock be gathered together and returned to their lands and missions, what remained of them, on the Tuscarawas River.

There was no way to atone for the lives that had been lost but, in an effort to show sincere regret for what happened, a delegation was ordered to seek out the two sons of a murdered Delaware chief, White Eyes, and invite them to come east where they would be clothed and housed, treated with great respect and honor and where they would be given, at government expense, a thorough education at Princeton College.

It was, as it had to be, a rather late and weak exchange for so many lives.

[*October 3, 1788 — Friday*]

Matthias Denman met with success upon approaching Colonel Robert Patterson and John Filson in Lexington with his plan for the foundation of a great port city on the land he had purchased from Judge Symmes directly across the Ohio from the mouth of Licking River. Both men agreed to share the cost of the venture with Denman and at once the three of them set out to inspect the property thoroughly.

Filson, not as well known as Patterson on the frontier, nevertheless had a good background for the venture. He was an explorer and schoolmaster, a surveyor and an author. Only four years ago he had published his book, *The Discovery, Settlement and Present State of Kentucky*. And he had proven his value to the partnership by surveying, during September, the entire seven-hundred-forty-acre site and laying it out in lots. It was also Filson who named the place; combining the Latin *os*, for mouth, the Greek *anti*, for opposite, and the French *ville*, for city, to coin the word Losantiville — city opposite the mouth.

Immediately following the survey, he and Patterson and Denman joined a company of sixty men, including Judge Symmes, Ben Stites and a new surveyor to the area named Israel Ludlow, to explore more of the purchase Symmes had petitioned for. They left from Maysville and landed at the mouth of the Great Miami River and explored the country for some distance inland from the Ohio.

About five miles upstream on the Ohio from the mouth of the Great Miami was the sharp bend which marked the most northerly point of the Ohio River between its junction with the Mississippi and a point more than eighty miles above the mouth of the Great Kanawha. Symmes named it North Bend and declared at once his intention of founding his own conception of a great port city which he would name Symmes City.

With two major ports in the offing, Benjamin Stites was not to be outdone. When they reached his large expanse of land just below the mouth of the Little Miami River, he declared his intention of building here his own great port city, which he would name Columbia.

For upwards of five miles back from the Ohio River the party thoroughly explored the region of Symmes Purchase between the two Miami Rivers and it wasn't until after they reached Ben Stite's proposed Columbia site that they realized Filson was gone. The explorer, schoolmaster, surveyor and author was, in fact, no longer living. His body had been dumped into a hole where a huge sycamore had blown down and his scalp now dangled from the belt of a lone Shawnee warrior en route to the north who had encountered Filson as he dallied toward the rear.

As time passed and John Filson did not reappear and the searches proved unavailing, it was assumed that the presentiment he had often voiced — that one day he would be killed by the Indians — had come to pass. And so, Israel Ludlow now accepted Filson's interests and duties in the continuing laying-out of Losantiville and became a full partner of Patterson and Denman.

[*October 12, 1788 — Sunday*]

"You won't be coming back at all?" Simon Kenton asked.

The fifty-three-year-old frontiersman before him shook his head soberly. "Ain't nothing left to come back to, Simon. My land's gone, most of my friends has got theirselves kilt, man can't move athout bumping into somebody. No, I ain't coming back. My oldest living boy, Jesse, he's got him a place near the Salt Works 'bout eighteen mile up Little Sandy. Reckon I'll hunker with him some, then head on to Missouri. Hear tell it's fine land. Wouldn't want to come along, would you?"

Simon shook his head regretfully. "Not now, Dan'l. Someday, mebbe. Send back word where you're at. Someday you'll see me show up."

They shook hands awkwardly, embarrassed by the emotions that brought hot tears to their eyes. Daniel Boone abruptly turned and paced away with that characteristic stride of backwoodsmen and Kenton watched him until he disappeared into a wooded hillside to the east.

His leaving caused a considerable regret among all the frontiersmen.

[*December 20, 1788 — Saturday*]

Maysville now became the seat of a brand new county and Kentucky took one more long stride in its development. The county was named Mason,

after George Rogers Clark's good friend, the Virginia lawyer and statesman, George Mason. It was the eighth county to be formed in the
Kentucky country by the Virginia Legislature and by far the largest of the
eight. Colonel Henry Lee had accepted the appointment as county lieutenant.

It was hard for many of the earliest settlers, such as Kenton, to realize
that less than a score of years ago this was unknown territory, described
only as Fincastle County, a sprawling deadly wilderness west of the
Appalachians. And then Fincastle had been broken up and Kentucky
became a single county of Virginia in its own right, apart from western
Virginia. Not long ago more counties had been formed and Kenton's
Station had been in Bourbon County. Now, at last, they had their own
county with Maysville as the seat of its government.

At this first forming, Mason County was in the shape of a right angled
triangle. Its base was the Ohio River from the mouth of the Licking to the
mouth of Big Sandy, a distance of one hundred fifty-two miles. Its altitude
was the Big Sandy itself and then up Tug Fork to the extreme eastern
point of Kentucky, about a hundred twenty miles.[9] And its hypotenuse
was the Licking River from mouth to source and then directly to Tug
Fork, a distance of four hundred miles.

Within its limits it contained a little over three million acres of land —
some five thousand square miles — making it a tenth the size of England,
forty times larger than London and larger than the whole of Connecticut.
And practically this whole area, particularly that bordering the Ohio River,
was regularly patrolled and protected by Simon Kenton and his company
of Volunteers from the Washington-Maysville area. It was not a labor
performed for pay, for who was there to pay them? It was simply something that needed to be done and so Simon and his men went ahead and
did it and earned, if not wealth, at least the deep gratitude of the hundreds
of people whose lives and property they saved.

Far and wide Kenton was known to the settlers not only as their pro-
tector, but their avenging angel as well, willing and able at an instant's
notice to order his company to the rescue or into pursuit. A dozen, a score,
a half hundred times and more his men had chased attackers and recovered
stolen horses and loot and, very frequently, prisoners who would otherwise
have been slain or sold to the British. Kenton, it was said, would snap erect
and mount his company at the hoot of an owl or the wail of a coyote. No
broken twig or footprint or startled bird escaped his notice and there was a
great feeling of comfort along the frontier to know that he was on hand
and ready if needed.

An example of his readiness was exhibited now. At Ben Stites's settlement of Columbia a blockhouse was being erected in urgent haste so that
it would be done before the Indians knew anything of it. On the day it was

finished the workers celebrated and during the midst of their rejoicing they fired their rifles into the air.

A few miles upstream on the other side of the Ohio, two of Kenton's minutemen were hunting and heard the shots. Fearing the worst, they immediately galloped back to Kenton's Station and reported. At once Simon called out his men, hustled them into boats and went down the river sixty miles "to the relief of Columbia." So swift had been the report of supposed trouble and Simon's response that in less than forty-eight hours after the builders had fired their guns, he was on hand with sixty men to give them the aid he thought they needed.

Little wonder that the settlers felt comfort at the knowledge that Kentucky's greatest frontiersman was close at hand.

[*December 31, 1788 — Wednesday*]

The courage, strength, ability and wisdom incorporated in the makeup of Tecumseh rapidly caused him to become the talk of the Cherokee nation. Even though most of the chiefs there were much older and more experienced in battle than he, they willingly fell in behind him, seeing in him something more, something better, something greater than any of them possessed: an intangible and indescribable influence which made him stand out as one set apart and a man to follow at any time.

The Cherokee women were especially fond of him, much more so than he was of them. But because it was expected of him and, truth to tell, because it was a rather pleasant preoccupation, he accepted the gift of a beautiful Cherokee maiden to cook for him, make and mend his clothing and provide for his carnal pleasures. He did not love her but she obviously loved him and was, except for the marriage ritual, his wife in every respect. He treated her gently and with kindness but made her understand that one day he would ride away and not return.

His taking over the leadership of the remaining Kispokotha Shawnees in the little band after Chiksika's death was so natural and automatic that no vote had to be taken, no word of acceptance given. Who among them could have offered so much? Indeed, the only one unsure of his ability to merit this leadership was Tecumseh himself. If, as Chiksika had predicted, he was to become a great leader of the Shawnees — not just this little band here in the hills of the Tennessee country, but all of his tribe — then he must be able to satisfy himself above all that he was worthy of it.

Thus began a period of many months of testing himself against staggering odds, of attacking forces far superior in number and weaponry, and of time after time emerging victorious. The Cherokees considered themselves excellent fighters, among the best in the world, if not better than the best, but now they stood in awe of this handsome young Shawnee before whom powerful enemies withered and died or fled in terror. Here he led a party of five against sixteen whites and slew all but two who escaped to spread word of this terrible demon chief who advanced and won when everything seemed to dictate he should have retreated and been glad to escape with his life. There he charged down alone upon a party of eight men, his fierce screams momentarily paralyzing them with fear and four of them falling — one to his gun, one to his tomahawk and two to his warclub — before the others could barely comprehend what was happening and flee in abject panic. Another time he led his Shawnees and one Cherokee against a new settlement and utterly destroyed it, killing every man and turning over to the Cherokees the twenty or more women and children taken prisoner.

He was possessed with an uncanny knack of assessing any situation in an instant and acting immediately in a manner which at once swung the scales in his favor. Three times his camp was attacked by surprise at night and three times he not only fought back with such ferocity that his attackers fell back, but not once was any man under his command even scratched.

The swiftness of his mind and unpreditability of his movements were fascinating. One night as he lay on a buffalo skin before a small fire, with eight of his men ranged around the blaze, his amazingly acute senses suddenly warned him that a large force had surrounded them and would attack in moments. In a conversational tone he told the others what the situation was and warned them to stay where they were until he made his move, and then to rush a certain segment of the circle drawn about them. He sat up, stretched and yawned and then casually got to his feet. Leaning over as if to straighten the huge buffalo pelt, he suddenly flung it over the fire so that in an instant all light was blacked out. In an irresistible rush the warriors smashed through the ring of thirty white men as if the enemy had been made of paper and left behind them the bodies of five of their attackers, themselves losing only a few personal items. But that was not enough for Tecumseh. Traveling swiftly in a semicircle, he led them back in a shrieking charge against the opposite side of the party of whites and, certain that they themselves were now the ones who were surrounded, the attack of the whites became a full rout of totally demoralized men. When the sound had ceased and a tally was taken, still none of the Indians was injured — but seven more whites lay dead upon the ground.

So the fame and prowess of Tecumseh grew and he was pleased to see the respect he had won here. More and more of late, however, his thoughts returned to his own people in the Ohio country. Already he and this little band had been gone for well over a year. Perhaps it was time to think about returning home.

And once again the memory of Chiksika rushed up and filled him with an overwhelming sorrow.

CHAPTER VIII

[*January 12, 1789 — Saturday*]

THE first session of Congress under the Federal Constitution, which replaced the Congress of the Confederation of States, had many problems to consider, many ordinances to pass.

Among these matters was one taken care of swiftly and passed along without objection, but yet it was one of extreme importance. It was perhaps fitting and proper that it was the First Congress of the United States which gave the Ohio Territory a permanent status among the States of the Union and thereby opened the door to statehood for Ohio in what, a great number of settlers anticipated, would be only a few short years.

[*April 1, 1789 — Wednesday*]

Simon Kenton found a wry amusement in the effrontery of the party of Shawnees in making a winter camp so close to Maysville. All winter long they had heard shooting across the river and late one night in January, after he had crossed over and eased his way carefully toward the campsite, Simon watched them around the fire, dressing hides, salting down meat and melting tallow. There were only eighteen of them camped here on Straight Creek, less than a dozen miles from Maysville, but it was evident they were a hunting party and not out to make war. The frontiersman watched them until they had retired for the night and then he slipped back out of hearing and returned to Mason County.

Except for the nervousness they caused the hunters on the Kentucky side with their shooting, the Indians seemed to be no particular hazard and Simon was inclined to leave them alone, knowing they would soon return to the north again. Indeed, he felt a stirring of sympathy for them and deduced the reason for their making camp so close to the river and its inherent danger. They could no longer winter hunt with impunity in their traditional hunting grounds on the Kentucky side of the river, so they had come as close as possible in their endeavor to follow the long-practiced customs of their people.

But what sympathy he felt quickly vanished as February became March and once again horses began disappearing from their stalls and corrals in the Kentucky settlements. In preparing to move north again, the Shawnees now had need of mounts to carry the pelts and meat they had taken.

At length Kenton called sixty of his volunteers together and this morning they had taken to boats and floated the few miles to near the mouth of Straight Creek, hid their craft and then followed Kenton overland toward the Shawnee camp. They arrived none too soon, for the horses were loaded and the camp was being struck as they came up just about noon.

Young John Kinsaulla spoiled the surprise, however, by stumbling over a root and discharging his rifle. At once the Indians began scattering. It was a long distance for accurate shooting but there was now nothing to do but fire. Three of the Indians were hit but all three regained their feet and raced on. Carefully advancing, watchful for a possible ambush, the whites entered the camp and Simon led a detachment on the trail of blood. But this trail soon ended, for the Indians had apparently plugged their wounds with buzzard down and continued their flight.

Returning to the campsite, Simon found that fifteen horses stolen from Mason County had been rounded up and the material that had been packed on each had been unloaded by the settlers. The Indians had found good hunting, for there were eight horseloads of dried and smoked deer and bear meat, nine bear pelts, thirty buckskins, several hundredweight of tallow and a dozen large bags made of whole buckskin, each filled with clear bear oil. There were also a number of blankets and other gear.

John Kinsaulla, Jr., and several other young men were extremely put out about it when Simon ordered all the meat, tallow, pelts and oil burned on the spot. They objected loudly, claiming the several hundred dollars' worth of material as plunder, but when a fierce flicker of anger began to glow in Kenton's eyes, they desisted.

"It gets burned," Simon repeated. "All of it. Ain't worth getting surprised and kilt for. Take a half hour, mebbe more, to reload it all and we ain't got time. Mebbe eighteen's all the Shawnees there was, but we got to reckon there's more a little bit away and they'll be coming back to get what they've worked for. So it gets burned. Right now!"

He ordered the furs dumped in a pile, meat tossed upon them, the tallow dumped over the meat and finally the bear oil splashed over everything. It took some coaxing to get the fire started but once it began it was a glorious blaze, sending flames shooting upward as high as the treetops and trailing off into a dense cloud of dark smoke.

Within a few minutes they were on their way. They swam the horses straight across the Ohio beside the boats and then split up, fifteen men riding the animals back to Maysville and the remainder continuing the journey by boat.

Not over twenty minutes after Simon's men left the campsite, a party of perhaps a hundred forty Shawnees stared silently at the smoldering labors of many weeks. In the eyes of all glowed anger — and in their bellies there was a hollowness.

[*May 14, 1789 — Thursday*]

If the depredations by Indians in Kentucky had seemed bad before, they grew infinitely worse now. Scarcely a day went by when surprise attacks did not occur somewhere among the settlements or isolated cabins. Nor were these attacks limited to the northern part of Kentucky along the river. Far too frequently they were occurring as deep inland as Harrodsburg and Danville and Stanford.

Boats were attacked by the scores and now it seemed the Indians were more inclined to kill than take prisoners. It was a rare week indeed when the ruins of a dozen or more boats did not drift past Maysville, mute evidence of more tragedies upstream. And who knew how many others were occurring below the city?

On the Ohio side of the river the three infant settlements of Symmes City, Losantiville and Columbia suffered frequently from attack, their posture on the north shore a highly vulnerable one. Many of the new settlers, including Robert Patterson, had been wounded and, though the settlements were still less than four months old, nine men had been killed. Had it not been for the hastily erected blockhouses, the settlements most certainly would have been wiped out.

Jake Kelsey had been wounded severely in the side and Johnny Hardin killed on the road between Washington and Blue Licks by a party of warriors led by Black Snake. Phil Skaggs was shot through the throat and scalped less than a mile from Kenton's Station, and Bill Walton was hung from an oak and disemboweled within shouting distance of Lexington. Charles Builderback — the captain who had begun the Moravian Massacre by bludgeoning to death the first fourteen victims — and his wife were captured near Cabin Creek and the woman was forced to watch as the Indians cut off, in succession, his ears, nose, thumbs and penis before his misery was ended with a tomahawk blow between the eyes and his scalp lifted.

[*November 6, 1789 — Friday*]

During his first few months in Europe, Joel Barlow was somewhat less than a smashing success as a land agent attempting to sell the alloted portion of the Scioto Tract. The internal problems in France were taking precedence over everything, and the fact that Barlow himself was not much of a salesman helped little. His enthusiasm began to ebb and he might well have slunk back to his homeland a beaten man had not two important events occurred.

The first came about when he met an engaging Londoner whom he described as "an Englishman of a bold and enterprising spirit and a good imagination." There was something perversely laughable in the fact that this individual's name was William Playfair for he was, in short, a swindler. When, over a decanter of fine wine, Barlow explained his predicament, Playfair became intrigued and expounded a few ideas on how Barlow's ill fortune could be reversed. By their third meeting the two had struck up a partnership and embarked upon a program which would result in making the Scioto Tract wholly irresistible in the minds of the Frenchmen.

The second event helped them immensely — the fall of the Bastille on July 14. Suddenly all France was in an uproar and the times had become propitious for schemes of emigration. Losing no time, the pair prepared and issued a little booklet entitled *Prospectus for an Establishment on the Rivers Ohio and Scioto*. In preparing it they leaned heavily upon the pamphlet written by Dr. Cutler and endorsed by the United States Geographer, Thomas Hutchins, which described the Ohio country. By this time Playfair had so juggled, expanded and embellished Cutler's already one-sided and not quite truthful phraseology that there was little wonder why Barlow had described him as having "a good imagination." Virtually overnight the Scioto Tract was vying with the Garden of Eden as a desirable place to be. A single example — and there were many of them — of Playfair's agile mind at work came in the paragraph which went:

A climate wholesome and delightful, frost even in winter almost entirely unknown, and a river called, by way of eminence, the beautiful, and abounding in excellent fish of vast size. Noble forests, consisting of trees that spontaneously produce sugar (the sugar maple) *and a plant that yields ready-made candles* (cyrica cerifera). *Venison in plenty, the pursuit of which is uninterrupted by wolves, foxes, lions or tigers. A couple of swine will multiply themselves a hundredfold in two or three years, without taking any care of them. No taxes to pay, no military services to be performed.*

On and on the booklet went, making of the area in question a beauty spot excelled, perhaps, by heaven but by no place else. Included with the booklet was a handsomely engraved and colored map, twelve by sixteen inches. The inaccuracies were appalling, not the least of which was the land of the Seven Ranges adjoining the Ohio Company Tract to the east, described on the map as "*Sept rangs de municipalité acquis par des individus et occupés depuis,* 1786" — "Seven ranges of townships acquired by individuals and occupied since 1786." No one in France, of course, could know that the Seven Ranges was uncleared, uninhabited and, as yet, unowned by individuals.

There was no mention in the booklet that the land allegedly belonging to the Scioto Company was hilly, rocky, and practically sterile insofar as crop-raising was concerned; that before any crops could even be planted, the forests would have to be cut down; that for a year, at least, they must bring their daily bread — or at any rate their flour — from a great distance. Nor was it pointed out that these hills were alive with large yellow timber rattlesnakes and even more densely populated with ugly-tempered copperheads; that hunting and fishing were pleasant pastimes when engaged in for amusement, but a different matter entirely when pursued for the sake of subsistence; that the area was infested not only with wolves and foxes, but with cougars, coyotes and bears.

Nor did it mention Indians.

In Paris, the imagination was too inspired by the persuasive booklet to harbor doubt or suspicion. With little difficulty, Playfair and Barlow concluded the sale of the entire portion of the tract they were authorized to sell to a firm which had been formed under five prominent Frenchmen and named itself *Companie de Scioto.*[1] The Frenchmen who made up the bulk of buyers from the firm were too ignorant or too uninformed to detect the defectiveness of the claims and they were undoubtedly swayed by the social standing of the firm's directors, who were wealthy and reputably wise. The most delightful topic of conversation at any gathering was the paradise being opened for Frenchmen in the Western world, the free and happy life to be led on the blissful banks of the Ohio and Scioto. The sales were brisk and all available land was soon gone. Single persons and whole families disposed of all their worldly goods to obtain the money to buy their tracts and flattered themselves at having made excellent bargains.

Joel Barlow swelled with pride and happiness, but William Playfair adroitly pricked his bubble of euphoria. The instant the French company gave Playfair the money for the entire tract, he disappeared forever from Barlow's life. The result was that Dr. Manasseh Cutler's Scioto Company failed and, with it, the careers of the United States Geographer, Thomas Hutchins, and the United States Secretary of the Treasury, William Duer.

As a result of all this, and for the first time in its existence, New York, capital city of the United States, reeled under the shock of a financial crisis.

[*December 7, 1789 — Monday*]

Fort Washington was undoubtedly the most encouraging and important structure yet erected on the Ohio frontier by the federal government, at least insofar as the Kentuckians were concerned. The orders for its construction had been given to General Josiah Harmar in late spring and on June 2 the actual work had commenced under the firm command of Major John Doughty, who had brought a hundred forty good men from Fort Harmar to do the job.

The site selected was just across the river Ohio from the mouth of the Licking, directly adjacent to the village limits of Losantiville.[2] The men worked hard and guarded themselves well. Although occasionally distant Indians were seen watching them, no attack was made and by early winter the fort was completed.

It was a pleasing and impressive structure which Josiah Harmar found this date when he arrived with three hundred men to take command. He wished President Washington could be here to see it, certain he would be not only impressed with its apparent invulnerability but delighted that it had been named after him.

This was a solid fort, a truly substantial fortress of hewn timber. It was a hundred eighty feet square, with excellent blockhouses at the four angles, and two stories' high. In addition, fifteen acres had been reserved around it by the government, making it by far the most extensive and impregnable military installation in the Northwest Territory.

General Harmar returned the salute of Major Doughty, complimented him on the job he had done and then advised him to prepare for the arrival next month of Governor Arthur St. Clair, who would make this his new base of operations for the continued partition of Ohio into counties. His ultimate goal: to make Ohio a new state.

[*December 9, 1789 — Wednesday*]

Arthur St. Clair winced at the pain which rose in waves from his gout. He lay down his pen and leaned over to rub his foot. All day it had been bothering him, even while he was meeting with President Washington, and once again he found himself wishing he had no foot at all rather than one which aggravated him so constantly. It would certainly be troublesome on the journey he would begin this week to Fort Washington.

After a moment he sat back in his chair and considered the events of the day in retrospect. How wonderful that, at last, President Washington was once again thinking militarily. His speeches to Congress had been extremely effective in regard to what measures could be taken to terminate the Indian menace on the western frontier. For perhaps the first time, the assembled Congress was fully apprised of the situation which existed in Virginia's Kentucky country and on the Ohio River and along the Ohio frontier. Property was being lost to the Indians in staggering quantities and hit-and-run attacks upon Kentuckians were still occurring deep inland. Consider this, said the President: in just the seven-year period ending now, *more than one thousand five hundred settlers have been killed and scalped on the Ohio River alone!*

The Congress had been extremely disturbed at this and so, before adjourning, it had finally authorized the President to call upon the Virginia, Pennsylvania and Kentucky militias to crush the tribes. It was then that Washington had summoned St. Clair and given him orders to pass on to General Harmar to launch an invasion against the Indians.

But the President was concerned lest the British still occupying Detroit consider this an invasion against them, thus reigniting the hostilities of the late war. It was important, he told the governor, to get word to the Detroit commandant and assure him that the projected assault would positively not be against him.

St. Clair now picked up the letter he had just finished writing to the Detroit commandant. Before folding and sealing it, however, he read the final paragraph once more:

The expedition about to be undertaken is not intended against the post you have the honor to command, nor any other place at present in possession of the troops of his Britannic Majesty, but is on foot with the sole design of humbling and chastizing some of the savage tribes, whose depredations have become intolerable and whose cruelties have of late become an outrage, not only to the people of America, but on humanity.

[January 2, 1790 — Saturday]

Never much inclined toward pomp and ceremony, Governor St. Clair had acknowledged with a wave and a smile the welcome given him by the paraded troops on his arrival at Fort Washington and then requested Harmar to dismiss them and accompany him to the quarters that were to be temporarily his.

Inside the small but adequate room — quite well appointed, to St. Clair's surprise — he briefly explained to the commanding general of the First United States Army the developing plan of President Washington to send a punitive force, led by Harmar, against the Indians. At this time no date had been set but it would be during the course of this year. Harmar could not hide the anticipatory light that entered his eyes at this news. They talked for nearly an hour and then, rubbing his foot to ease the pain, St. Clair said he believed he would rest now from the journey but that he would like to see the proprietors of Losantiville in the morning.

The three men, Robert Patterson, Matthias Denman and Israel Ludlow, arrived at 9:00 A.M. and greeted the governor with pleasure. They exchanged a few items of news and then St. Clair got down to business.

"Gentlemen," he said, "you have here in Losantiville the beginnings of a great American city. It will certainly be the seat of the county I will create here today. However, I must admit that I don't care too much for the name. As you may know, I am a member of the Society of Cincinnatus. I would consider it an honor and a very great favor if you would consent to renaming Losantiville and calling it, instead, Cincinnati."

None of the three ever had any particular fondness for the name coined by John Filson, but they had retained it in memory of their vanished partner. Now, however, the matter took another complexion and they discussed it quietly for a few minutes while Governor St. Clair stepped outside and asked an orderly to extend his respects to Judge Symmes and Ben Stites, both of whom were presently visiting with Harmar, and to ask them to join him as soon as convenient in the governor's quarters.

When he reentered the room, the three settlers had finished their discussion. Matthias Denman cleared his throat and smiled. "There is no reason at all, Governor, why we should retain the name Losantiville for this village. From this time forward it will be known as Cincinnati."

St. Clair expressed his appreciation and suggested that they celebrate this event with a toast of the good wine he had brought while they awaited the arrival of Symmes and Stites. The pair appeared together within ten minutes and joined their host in another toast, this one to the new county of Hamilton he was creating as of this moment, and which he was naming after his good friend, General Alexander Hamilton.

Once again, St. Clair filled their glasses and then raised his own to propose another toast — this time to the future State of Ohio.

[*April 13, 1790 — Saturday*]

Although not all boat remains drifting down the Ohio River were the result of Indian attack — some being lost in storms or while navigating treacherous waters — the greater majority by far bore the earmarks of savage assault, and the number was steadily growing.

The Shawnees had become masters at luring passing boats close to shore, sometimes even coaxing them to land before they discovered their peril. One method was to dress one of their men in the clothes of a captive and have him stand alone on the shore while the others remained hidden. The decoy would then alert passing boats with cries of "Help! I am white. Help me!" Even those boats wary of too close an approach could be chased in the Indians' own twenty-man canoes hidden in the first brush up from the river, ready for launching in a moment. Only last week they had attacked a party with three boats in this manner; the two loaded with badly needed supplies they had cut loose and captured, while the third, filled with people, rowed away faster than they would ever have believed possible.

Increasingly the names of Blue Jacket and Walking Bear, Red Fox and Black Snake, Sits-in-Shadow, Tall Oak, Reelfoot and Chiungalla were becoming synonymous with danger and destruction. Yet, some of the

settlers had to learn the hard way that carrying a rifle and a tomahawk did
not make expert frontiersmen of them. They would become bolder and
would journey across the Ohio, often never to return. More times than he
cared to remember, Simon Kenton had come across the bloated, mutilated
remains of such settlers.

And then, in the midst of all this difficulty, the state government in
Richmond, far removed from the perils of this area, pulled the props out
from under the pioneers and threw all of the frontiersmen into a deep
rage. With reluctance, Colonel Henry Lee posted in conspicuous places
throughout Mason County copies of the dispatch he had received from
Governor Beverly Randolph:

Richmond, March 20, 1790

TO: *Henry Lee, Col.*
Mason County Lieutenant

*The Governor of the Continental Western Territory has given the
Executive information of incursions having been made by parties from this
State upon tribes of Indians in amity with the United States. For conduct
like this is highly dishonourable to our national character and will inevitably draw upon individual delinquents the punishment due to such
offenses, it becomes our duty to inform you to exert your authority to
prevent any attempts of this kind in the future.*

*Should it be necessary on any occasion to call out parties to repel the
attacks of the enemy within the limits of the State, you will issue the most
positive orders, but no such party shall, under any pretence whatever, enter
the Territory either of the United States, or of any Indian tribe.*

I am, Sir, Your Obdt. Svt.
Beverly Randolph, Governor of the
Continental Western Territory

It was a devastating blow to the settlers, all the more so when it became
known that while ordering them to keep out of Ohio, the government was
going ahead with plans to attack the Indians with an army. When General
Charles Scott heard that General Harmar was planning a march with a
hundred of his soldiers from Fort Washington up the Ohio shore to the
Scioto in order to curtail Indian depredations, he raised two hundred thirty
Kentucky volunteers. They were on the Ohio shore opposite Maysville,
waiting, when Harmar's force came by. While technically an illegal move,
Harmar nevertheless welcomed Scott's force to join him for the attack on a
reported Shawnee camp at the mouth of the Scioto.

There was much hope for a general engagement, but they found the
camp deserted; the only consolation was that en route to that point they
had crossed the relatively fresh trail of a small Indian party heading south

along Ohio Brush Creek toward the Ohio River. The men clamored for a chance to follow and destroy them. Colonel John Grant and eight of his men, along with five frontiersmen — Joshua Baker, Alex McIntyre, Christopher Wood, Ben Whiteman and a new arrival to Mason County with the improbable name of Belteslazer Dragoo — were dispatched. Within ten miles they came upon the camp. Three Indians were there and a fourth was a short distance away cutting a pole. This last one was Reelfoot, so called because of his two clubfeet.

This was a find indeed, for Old Reelfoot was a deeply dreaded warrior in Kentucky. Whenever his tracks were discovered, which was frequently, it was known that scalps would soon be missing. Alex McIntyre was first to shoot and he justified his fame as an excellent marksman. Just as their presence was discovered he flung his rifle to his shoulder and snapped off a shot. Though he was a hundred yards away on a moving horse at the time, the ball passed through Reelfoot's head and slammed him to the ground in a heap.

The other whites split and galloped into the camp in two wings, while the remaining three Indians tried to escape by jumping into the creek at their backs. Before they could even react, however, one was shot near the fire and fell, another took a bullet in the back and tumbled disjointedly on the creek bank. The final warrior leaped far out into the water and four or five shots sounded while he was still in the air. The water here was breast high and instantly it turned red from blood, but the Indian regained his feet and stood there with glazed eyes, apparently dying.

Baker spurred his horse into the water to grasp him by the hair and drag him ashore, but the warrior had drawn his knife under water and as Baker came close his dazed expression vanished and he grasped the bridle and made a stroke at Baker. Only the frightened rearing of the horse barely saved him.

"Stand back, Baker," Colonel Grant shouted. "I'll fix him!"

Baker withdrew a little and Grant put his rifle to his shoulder, took deliberate aim at the panting Shawnee less than thirty feet away and put a bullet into his mouth, smashing his spine and killing him instantly.

Despite this minor victory, as they chose to term it, the frontiersmen generally remained greatly angered by Governor Randolph's order. Now the thoughts that had been mere whispers for several years became an outspoken protest. If this was the way the Virginia government was going to treat Kentuckians then, by damn, it was time Kentucky became a state in her own right!

[May 25, 1790 — Tuesday]

The Kentucky country was fast becoming a land where a lack of formal education was no great handicap in dealing with the Indians, but very much a fault where other matters were concerned. There was a growing need for learned men to manage the affairs of a burgeoning society and the illiterate frontiersmen, of whom there were many, were being passed by when it came time for individuals to accept roles of responsibility. Such was the situation in the case of Simon Kenton, who already had lost a great deal of the land he had claimed only with his tomahawk. What's more, time after time he was being discounted for important positions.

A prime example occurred when Harry Innes, special agent for George Washington in Kentucky, wrote to the chief executive and explained how effective a spy and scout system might be on the border area. He explained how a company of scouts could patrol the area regularly and how they could warn the settlers of impending attack and then follow the trail of invaders to recover stolen property and effect rescues of those taken captive. In short, he explained precisely what Kenton and his minutemen had been doing voluntarily for many seasons now, yet not once did he mention the big frontiersman or the fact that such a service was already well established.

That the idea appealed to the President became clear when Henry Lee received the following dispatch from Innes:

Whereas the President of the United States having authorized me to empower the Lieutenants of the several counties within the District to call into service Scouts for the protection of the inhabitants against the invasion of Indians; and whereas the Lieutenant of Mason County hath given me such information as induces me to believe that his country will probably be invaded by Indians; I do hereby authorize the said Lieutenant of Mason to employ six expert and active woodsmen to act as Scouts within the said County; in witness whereof I have hereunto set my hand, affixed my seal this 25th day of May, 1790.

Harry Innes

A similar proclamation was sent to each of the Kentucky counties and it was the option of Innes to name the man to command all these scouts. The obvious choice was Simon Kenton, but since there were records to keep, payment vouchers to submit and other matters involving an ability to write and figure well, Innes passed over Kenton and named Alexander D. Orr of Mason County as colonel commanding the scouts.

Henry Lee, as Mason County lieutenant, named twelve men, some of them Kenton's own volunteer minutemen, to patrol specific areas within the county, only six on duty and drawing pay at a time. The daily wage was five shillings Virginia currency.

If Simon resented this, he didn't show it. His volunteers continued to run their regular patrols, not only in Mason County but throughout the entire area bordering the Ohio River from Louisville to the Big Sandy

River. And whenever it became necessary to resort to direct action, Simon Kenton's boys, led by the able frontiersman himself, somehow always arrived first and performed best.

There was little doubt that had Simon determined to march against Detroit itself, his plucky company of volunteers would have accompanied him gladly, for no other man on the frontier instilled such confidence and commanded such faithfulness in his followers. The Kentucky District might now have a duly authorized Scout Service paid for by the government, but it was to the quiet and resourceful frontiersman named Simon Kenton that the settlers looked most for protection and assistance and salvation.

[July 9, 1790 — Friday]

The greatest thorn these days in the side of General Henry Knox, Secretary of War, was the constant friction along the Ohio River. He had little patience with safe and comfortable officials here in the east who blithely advised treading softly and turning the other cheek when the Indians attacked the Kentuckians. And as the reports of such attacks filtering to his office became ever more numerous, he decided that the time for the direct action authorized by the President was at hand.

In a dispatch to Fort Washington he directed General Josiah Harmar to confer at once with Governor General St. Clair and organize a punitive expedition against the Indians, mostly relocated Shawnees now living in towns along the Maumee and Auglaize Rivers in northwestern Ohio Territory. Harmar was to mobilize a thousand or more militiamen through enlistment or, if necessary, through a draft from Pennsylvania and Virginia, including the Kentucky District.

Four hundred regular United States troops were to be made available for the expedition and to assist in the training of less experienced militiamen. The army, General Knox concluded, would be given two months to prepare itself, the campaign to originate from Fort Washington in September.

[October 30, 1790 — Saturday]

There was only one word to describe General Josiah Harmar's expedition against the Indian forces led by the Miami chief Little Turtle and the Shawnee chief Blue Jacket, and that word was *disastrous*. Rarely had any army of its size made such an incomprehensible and unnecessary botch of a campaign. It was little wonder to the Kentuckians that Harmar had resigned his commission immediately after and been summoned to Philadelphia for a court of inquiry to determine the reason for the awful defeat experienced.

Such high hopes they had harbored in the beginning! The only thing that had really bothered Harmar at all before the expedition began was the stern order that the army must not molest or antagonize the British garrisons. After all, where did the President think the Indians were getting their guns and supplies? In his opinion, the British installations were an abomination on the countryside and nothing less than a direct insult to the United States.

Seven years ago the Revolutionary War had ended (or, to be more accurate, the Treaty of Paris had been signed which allegedly ended it). But it hadn't ended here in the Ohio Territory, nor in the Kentucky District either. Not a week went by when the army or the settlers on both sides of the river weren't having skirmishes with the Indians, and only a fool would try to deny that these very savages were being supplied with guns and ammunition by the damnable British at Detroit and in their northern Ohio forts which they tried to palm off as trading posts. And hadn't it been proven beyond any doubt that the Indians were still being paid bounties by the King for every prisoner or scalp turned in? Thus, when Harmar's army was ordered not to cast so much as an ugly look at the forts, it was nothing less than galling.

Nor was it much consolation to be aware of the reason behind the order. It had been stipulated, when the independence of the United States had been acknowledged by Great Britain, that the Americans should be held responsible for debts due British subjects — debts incurred before the war. But under the earlier form of government, the United States couldn't enforce the collection of these debts in opposition to statutes enacted by the several States to defeat the British creditor. This failure of the American government to comply with one of the stipulations of the treaty gave the British government a pretext for refusing to surrender the frontier posts, the retention of which kept the profitable fur trade in British hands and enabled the King to maintain a small but tenacious toehold in the Ohio and Michigan territories.

The turnout for Harmar's expedition had been more than gratifying. Eleven hundred thirty-three militiamen had joined with Harmar's three hundred twenty regulars at Fort Washington to form a highly respectable force of fourteen hundred fifty-three men. This promising army left the fort at 10 A.M. October 7 and marched straight into sickening disaster. A few men — regular army men, at that — later claimed through some unfathomable form of logic that the campaign was a victory, but Sergeant Ben Whiteman's reaction expressed eloquently the belief of the overwhelming majority.

"If that was victory," he said, "then I pray to God that I may never see defeat!"

Immediately following the campaign, Whiteman took it upon himself to write an account of what happened while it was still vivid in his mind.

Testimony, he knew, tended to become distorted with time. As a result, his account was quite likely the most accurate of the many to be penned.

As Whiteman explained it, most of the army was on foot, with but one troop of horsemen from Kentucky under the command of Major Fountain. These horsemen did not carry rifles. The provisions and rations for the men were loaded on packhorses; the regulars brought tents, the militia had none. The beeves were driven and were in such numbers as was supposed would be sufficient for support of the army. The principal breadstuff food was cornmeal, although a small quantity of coarse flour was taken. For artillery there were three six-pounder cannons mounted on wheels and drawn by horses.

On the seventh night the army camped at the mouth of Loramie Creek on the Great Miami River and the next morning, while some of the troops were collecting their horses, an Indian was taken prisoner. Ever since they had passed the old site of destroyed Chillicothe, Indians had been hanging around the army for the purpose of stealing horses. For some reason, however, Harmar did not have the Indian questioned until the following morning — perhaps because, as Whiteman contended, the general had been indulging too heavily in alcoholic spirits.

The Indian, after some ungentle coaxing, said that the Shawnees and Miamis were collecting at the French Store by the confluence of the St. Joseph and St. Marys Rivers, which formed the Maumee River.[3] He said that Simon Girty had gone across Lake Erie to collect forces and that if he had returned by now, the Indians would be too strong for the whites. This news seemed to worry Harmar considerably. A council of his principal officers was called and it was decided that Colonel John Hardin should select six hundred men and proceed by forced marches to take the little fort there. Benjamin Whiteman was among the number selected.

Hardin's detachment set off immediately and made a forced march of twenty-five miles. At dusk a heavy thunderstorm came up and badly confused the guides. In an effort to find the right way they continued to march until midnight before halting, with no idea where they were or whether they had been going backward or forward.

In the morning they fired off their guns in hollow trees to muffle the noise, reloaded and set off again, reaching the opposite side of the river from the French Store at noon and finding the fort on fire. A few Indians were seen and one was killed and the army encamped. The next two days were spent in reconnoitering and destroying the scattering of tiny villages in the area, all of which were deserted. Although he took much longer to arrive than Hardin anticipated, General Harmar finally came into sight again and joined the detachment at the fort.

On October 20, following the discovery by scouts of a considerable trail of Indians, Harmar directed a detachment of three hundred men under command of Ensign Philip Hartshorn to reconnoiter that way. He also sent thirty men, including Whiteman, under Captain Hughes to destroy an Indian camp and a few cabins the spies had discovered six miles up the St. Joseph River. The detachment under Hughes accomplished this objective and returned the same day, but Hartshorn found only trouble.

Eight miles from the main camp his men were ambushed and twenty killed during a veritable rout. Among the dead were Hartshorn himself and Merritt Scott, eldest son of General Charles Scott. The detachment fled back to the main camp to report and Harmar kept the army under arms all night, expecting attack hourly.

In the morning the general gave the word to prepare to move and the troops packed up, fully expecting to pursue the enemy. They recrossed the river and then, to the utter surprise of the entire army, General Harmar ordered the men to follow their own trail back toward the mouth of Loramie Creek. He was retreating! Neither to men nor officers did the general explain this extraordinary move and suddenly the ranks were heavy with dissatisfaction. What could the general be thinking of? They were still a very strong force; there had been no sudden lapse in provisions, stores, men or anything else; their artillery was in good shape and ready to fire; there was no certain information that Girty and his forces were anywhere nearby; there was good reason to believe that the force of Indians that had routed Hartshorn's detachment was no more than one hundred strong; and finally, their fallen comrades at the site of the ambush were left to lie there for the buzzards to pick, not even to be afforded a decent burial.

Irate murmurings filled the air all night after the army had camped until Colonel Hardin virtually demanded permission to select four hundred men to meet the enemy if he could be found and, in any event, to bury their dead. Again, Sergeant Whiteman was among those chosen.

Thus the detachment retraced its steps toward the fort, marching all night, and at daybreak reached the river to find the Indians encamped on the opposite shore in the same spot Harmar had vacated the day before. Their number was estimated by scouts as from eight hundred to twelve hundred and they said they had seen not only Blue Jacket and Little Turtle, but Simon Girty, wearing a long red cloak and riding a fine black horse.

Hardin called a council of his officers and it was concluded that if a retreat were undertaken, the Indians would pursue and cut them off before they could reach the main army. It was therefore determined to send an express to General Harmar for reinforcement and to attack the Indians in the meantime. The express returned on horseback and reached Harmar before the sun was an hour high. But again Harmar shocked everyone. Instead of immediately moving his men to help Hardin, he formed his troops into a defensive hollow square and swore that not a man should go to the relief of Hardin and cover his retreat. A stunned, disbelieving silence fell over the army.

Back at the river, Colonel Hardin divided his men into three wings — himself commanding the middle, Colonel McMullen the right and Colonel Horatio Hall the left. Colonel Fountain and Major Wyllys were with Hardin and Whiteman joined with Hall. The hastily conceived battle plan was for the three detachments to cross the river at the same time, with no more than three-fourths of a mile separating the left and right wings. The crossing took place just before sunrise, but the Indians were well prepared.

Ignoring his orders against spreading their forces, Colonel McMullen allowed himself to be pulled off in pursuit of a few Indians down the river, while the great body of the Indian force was directed at Hardin's and Hall's detachments. That the Shawnees who led McMullen on were a ruse became quickly evident, but it was already too late.

On the plain where the action took place a short distance below the fort, the only cover was a jumble of hazel bushes. To the left of this the detachment under Hall contended successfully for some time with a party of Indians until the latter were reinforced by those who had deceived McMullen and drawn him off into the woods. With that, Hall was forced to order a retreat across the river, the Indians screaming fiercely at their heels. As soon as Hall's men reached the opposite shore, however, they turned upon their pursuers and made a desperate resistance, killing quite a few. But then another body of warriors struck Hall's rear and within a few minutes a full third of the detachment was killed.

After McMullen was led off, the main body of the Indians had attacked Colonel Hardin and after the first onslaught, in which both Colonel Fountain and Major Wyllys were killed, the fight turned into a massacre. All but eight of the regulars were quickly killed. Shouting above the noise of battle, Hardin ordered his men to follow Hall's example and retreat across the river. This was accomplished with the Indians pressing hard, and now the two detachments were only a quarter mile apart.

As Hardin moved to merge with Hall the Indians concentrated their assault and a fantastically wild melee resulted. Hardin at once directed a retreat upstream, along the only avenue left to retreat in, and the pursuit continued for five or six miles.

McMullen, having come to grips with no more than a handful of Indians at any one time, now returned and recrossed the river where Hardin and Hall had crossed, but without opposition. Unable to see the other detachments anywhere, he ordered a retreat to General Harmar's camp, having suffered no substantial loss.

From the time the battle commenced until Hardin ordered the final retreat, three hours had passed. He had, in fact, delayed the retreat order in the vain expectation of reinforcement. He knew there were packhorses enough in camp for Harmar to have mounted several hundred men, who could have reached the scene of battle in time to turn the fortunes of the day, but General Harmar had chosen not to send succor.

It was, moreover, elementary military strategy to throw up a defensive breastwork when encamped for any period of time where enemy attack was likely; and yet, although he had been resting all day, there was still no trace of fortification at Harmar's camp.

Throughout the night stragglers from Hardin's detachment, many of them wounded, continued to show up. Finally, early in the morning, General Harmar ordered full-scale retreat to Fort Washington without any consultation whatever with his officers. This retreat was continued at the best speed possible and the army was not further molested by the Indians as it fled. The cannons had never been fired and the provisions lasted well. Some of the wounded were brought in on litters by packhorses. On the second day after reaching Fort Washington, the militia were discharged.

In concluding his account, Whiteman wrote:

Harmar had a force sufficient to have met and defeated all the Indians assembled at this point. It was certain that the men thought so and were anxious to make the trial. The largest detachment that Harmar sent out was six hundred men, and they without the cannons that had been taken out expressly to batter down the fort. Harmar was intemperate in his habits. He had never been accustomed to Indian fighting. His habits had disqualified him for the command and it was unquestionably the opinion of many of the officers and men of the army that General Harmar was panic stricken with the report made by the spies that Girty was near the fort with a large party of Indians. Had he marched with two or three hundred men to the relief of Hardin on the morning of the 22nd, it is more than probable that the Indians would have been signally defeated.

The final statistics were terrible. Killed of the federal troops: one major, two lieutenants, seventy-three rank and file. Killed of the militia: one major, three captains, three lieutenants, one ensign, twenty-five rank and file.[4] A total of one hundred nine men who would never return.

When General Josiah Harmar, a short time later, resigned his commission and turned the command of Fort Washington over to Captain David Zeigler before returning to Philadelphia, the feeling in the Kentucky District was practically unanimous: if he ever returned to the frontier again, it would be too soon.

[November 3, 1790 — Wednesday]

Catahecassa — Black Hoof — placed his gnarled hands upon the shoulders of the warrior standing before him and the pleasure that filled him now was good. His eyes were soft and a faint smile touched his lips as he saw how much the young Shawnee had changed since last they met.

The personal appearance of the brave was uncommonly fine, for though he was not particularly tall — three inches less than six feet — he had a fitness and symmetry about him that made him stand out at once in any group. His face was oval rather than angular, his nose straight and well formed and his mouth at once kind and sensitive, yet strong and determined. His eyes were direct, a clear and nearly transparent hazel, and his complexion was a smooth and unblemished tan. The hair which fell to just below his broad shoulders was a glossy black and his arms and legs were straight and well made.

The clothing he wore complimented him in every respect. His basic garments, shirt and leggins, were of the finest, softest doeskin worked to a pleasing sepia tone and over these he wore a perfectly fitted knee-length frock of the same material, the hem and seams accurately cut into frills an inch or so in length. At his wide elkhide belt he carried an elegant silver-mounted tomahawk, an excellent nine-inch razor-edged knife in a strong leather sheath, and his favorite weapon, a war club made of a heavy smooth stone the size and shape of a large goose egg sewn into wet rawhide which had dried and tightened around it to a hard finish, with a strip of this same rawhide covering a strong hickory handle. Upon his feet he wore very soft buckskin moccasins covered over by a rougher over-moccasin of heavy buffalo hide which reached nearly to his knees.

The voice of the principal chief of the Shawnees was grave as he addressed this impressive warrior for the first time in three years.

"Moneto has been kind to bring you back safely to your people. You went away from us little more than a boy and you have returned a man with the stories of your exploits in the land to the south of the Can-tuc-kee lands preceding you. It is well. You have shown the Cherokees that the Shawnee is a great warrior and your nation is well pleased with you. All of your people grieve with you over the death of Chiksika, who was also a good man and a fine warrior, and I speak for all of the Shawnees when I say welcome home Tecumseh."

There was much Tecumseh could have said, for the words welled within him now: how he knew great joy at the news of the defeat so recently of the *Shemanese*; of his sadness at the loss of the warriors who fell there; of his admiration for the strength and leadership of Blue Jacket and Little Turtle in that battle; of his deep and abiding pleasure at being once again reunited with his people; and of his great respect for Catahecassa himself. But with the simple eloquence for which he was already noted, he placed his own hands on Black Hoof's shoulders and summed up all these feelings with four words.

"My heart is filled."

[*December 31, 1790 — Friday*]

The year ended with temperatures that plummeted far below zero. In a way, this was a blessing. There had been a great fear along the frontier, particularly in the three new settlements of the Symmes Purchase, that the Indians would follow up the defeat of Harmar with an all-out assault to push the whites back across the river boundary. Had it not been for the severity of the weather, this might well have occurred.

Late in November a relatively new arrival to the frontier, Nathaniel Massie, made a declaration in Maysville, Kenton's Station, Washington and May's Lick that he was planning to erect a new station on the Ohio side of the river at Three Islands, a dozen miles upstream from Maysville. This was Virginia Military Bounty Land and Massie, an enterprising individual, had been one of the first to demand his claim.

"To the first twenty-five families who will settle in the town I am going to build," Massie announced, "I will give, as a donation, one in-town lot, one out-lot and a hundred-acre plot of ground."

It was chancy business at best to build at this time and at that place, but the offer was too good to pass up, especially for those in the Mason County settlements who had as their own only the lot upon which their cabins stood. And so Massie quickly gathered those families he needed and within a few weeks a good picket defense had been thrown up and the fifth Ohio settlement had been established.

But farther downriver on the same side there were troubles. A few miles from Cincinnati an outpost named Colerain was built on the east bank of the Great Miami River, put under the command of Colonel John Kingsbury and garrisoned with a few dozen soldiers and a single cannon. It was at this station in early December that the anticipated Indian attack occurred. Blue Jacket, accompanied by Simon Girty, led a screaming horde of five hundred warriors against it, surrounding it and desperately trying to breach the walls. All day the fight raged and had it not been for the dreadful cannon blasts, the Shawnees would surely have gained their objective.

Blue Jacket had planned to recommence the attack at dawn but the temperature dropped so terribly that he called it off. Before they pulled out, however, the Shawnees captured Abner Hunt, a settler traveling from Symmes City to Colerain, unaware of the attack there. As a warning for what lay ahead of the whites if they persisted in their encroachment into the Ohio country, Blue Jacket ordered Hunt tied to a tree within view of the fort but out of range of gunfire.

A fire was built close enough so that its heat scorched Hunt's skin and his screams filled the night. As the blaze died away, his bare stomach was

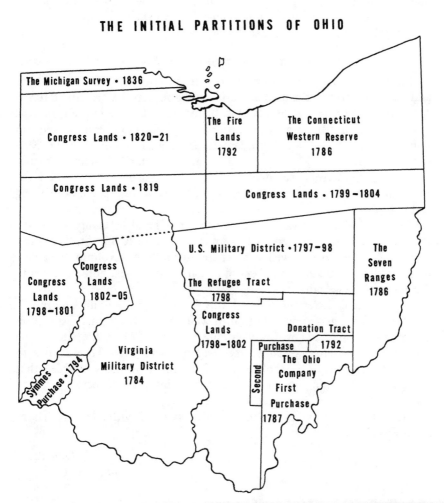

THE INITIAL PARTITIONS OF OHIO

The Michigan Survey · 1836

Congress Lands · 1820–21

The Fire Lands 1792

The Connecticut Western Reserve 1786

Congress Lands · 1819

Congress Lands · 1799–1804

Congress Lands 1798–1801

Congress Lands 1802–05

U.S. Military District · 1797–98

The Refugee Tract 1798

Congress Lands 1798–1802

The Seven Ranges 1786

Donation Tract 1792

Purchase

Symmes Purchase · 1794

Virginia Military District 1784

Second Purchase

The Ohio Company First Purchase 1787

(*Dotted line in the upper Virginia Military District and continuing solid lines to east and west state borders indicate original Indian/white boundary established by Gen. Anthony Wayne in the Greenville Treaty of 1795.*)

slit open so that his bowels tumbled forth and hot firebrands were applied to these until he died.

Almost precisely at that moment, at Kenton's Station, the big frontiersman was summoned by one of the women attending Martha to come and see the source of the lusty squalling which filled the house.

Tiny John Kenton had just been born.

[*January 16, 1791 — Sunday*]

As word of General Josiah Harmar's defeat and increasing Indian hostility and strength spread, it caused a rise in public fear in the eastern states. It came as no surprise when Harmar blamed his failure entirely on the militia, describing them as an "unruly and riotous group who would not follow orders," but it was with something of amazement that the Kentuckians heard he had been absolved of any fault for the defeat. Of this, however, the easterners cared little. What concerned them was that the First Army of the United States had been severely humiliated. Something had to be done.

George Washington was literally given a free hand by Congress to take care of this and so he turned once again to his friend, Arthur St. Clair. The governor had served him well as a general during the Revolution and now he could don the mantle of generalship again and strike a note of fear into the hearts of these Indians.

The President thereupon ordered St. Clair to begin building an army — a new one and a good one — to train it well and, with as much expedition as possible, to march north and establish a large fort at the site of the French Store, where Harmar's forces had been defeated. He was also to construct and garrison a whole series of intermediate posts between that site and Fort Washington, the object of these installations being to intimidate the Indians and thus prevent further hostilities.

The first of this news to appear in Kentucky came with the letter Harry Innes was now writing:

> *Danville*
> *January 16, 1791*

To: Henry Lee, Colonel
Commanding Officer of Mason County

    Sir: — I received a letter from Governor St. Clair on the 8th Instant dated on the 5th at the Rapids of the Ohio, by which I am informed he had come to the resolution to order out an expedition against the Indians on the Wabash and hath requested me to inform the Commanding Officers of the Militia to hold the proportions to be furnished in each County in readiness as he shall soon call for them, and that he supposes the governor of this state has made the necessary communications to you.

*The governor further observes that he is obliged to see General Harrison
on this business before he is explicit in his directions, that he is hurrying to
Fort Washington for this purpose and that you may expect to hear very
soon from him on this subject.*

I am, Sir, Yr Mst Obt. Svt.
Harry Innes

[*February 19, 1791 — Saturday*]

A new wonderful world ahead; a world free of oppression and fear; a world
where a man could raise crops in soil of incredible richness; a world of
Paradise. Little wonder that their faces shone with an inner light, that they
laughed and joked lightheartedly with one another. What a glorious
feeling it was. Surely this must have been the feeling which swept the
Children of Israel when they first embarked on their journey to the
Promised Land, the land of manna and honey.

The disposing of properties and goods had been a sad thing and the
leave-taking from beloved relatives they would almost certainly never see
again was infinitely worse; and yet, through it all there was the realization
that this was the opportunity of a lifetime. They were, just as surely as
those under Moses had been, on their way to the Promised Land.

This was the mood which prevailed among the two hundred twenty land
purchasers and their families who today left behind forever Havre de
Grace, France, to journey to their new property — that wonderful, peaceful, idyllic land on the beautiful Ohio and Sioto Rivers.

[*March 17, 1791 — Thursday*]

Colonel Henry Lee, county lieutenant of Mason, studied the two men
before him and nodded approvingly. Under orders from General Charles
Scott he had asked Simon Kenton to send him two of his best minutemen
for a special mission and now he was quite pleased with the frontiersman's
choice. Both Neil Washburn and James Ireland were widely known as men
who had survived many scrapes with Indians and who were not afraid to
take chances to get a job done.

"You both know," he said, "that so far this year we've had thirty-five
settlers killed in Mason County alone by the Shawnees. There have been at
least that many lost on the Ohio. I've received intelligence of a party of
about seventy Shawnees camped right now just above the mouth of the
Scioto. They perch up on top of Hanging Rock to keep lookout for boats
and then give them hell. I want you two to go overland to Point Pleasant
and tell Colonel Lewis about this. Tell him to notify all emigrants coming
downstream to be on their guard and not put ashore on the Ohio side for
anyone, no matter what he says.

"Tell him, too," he continued, "to advise all boating parties to lay over at Point Pleasant until a number of boats can go downstream together in a flotilla large enough that the Indians will be afraid to attack. I believe that's all."

The pair nodded and turned to leave but Lee's voice stopped them.

"One other thing. Better stop by Charlie Vancouver's place on the way and warn him. He's not very safe there by himself."[5]

[March 22, 1791 — Tuesday]

It had taken six hours, alternately running and walking, for Neil Washburn to reach Fort Randolph at Point Pleasant after leaving the Guyandotte River. He was a panting, bedraggled figure when he reported to Colonel Thomas Lewis and gave the officer Colonel Lee's message practically verbatim. He then quickly described what had happened to him and James Ireland on the way.

By the time they had reached the forks of the Big Sandy, Charles Vancouver was already in the process of breaking camp. He had gotten wind of increased Indian activity nearby and wanted to go to Maysville, but he needed help in transporting his goods there.

Ireland agreed to help if Washburn thought he could make it the rest of the way to Fort Randolph alone. Neil's grin was answer enough, so they separated. Washburn headed northeast, but just before he reached the Ohio River at the mouth of the Guyandotte, his horse suddenly staggered and nearly threw him off. An instant later came the sound of a shot and Washburn put the wounded horse into a gallop, crouching low over the animal's neck and hearing far behind the shouts of Indians.

The horse lasted no more than another mile before falling dead in midstride and Washburn set off at a hard run afoot. Within five minutes he reached the Guyandotte and, swiftly tying his clothing and gun to his head, he waded into the frigid water and swam to the other side. Shaking with cold he put his clothes back on and lay on his stomach with his rifle muzzle resting in the low crotch of a bush.

They came, as he knew they would, following his tracks right to the river's edge. He aimed carefully and shot, then smiled coldly as one of the Shawnees flopped down in a sitting position before toppling into the water. The other five separated for cover and at once Washburn was away and running.

Tom Lewis shook his head regretfully and said, "Wish you could've made it here a little sooner." He explained that yesterday morning John May, with a party of twelve men and two women, had gone downriver in May's boat after a day's stopover. A few hours later two settlers, George Edwards and Thomas Marshall, had followed in a smaller craft. And this morning, just an hour or so ago, two large canoes, one carrying the William

Hubbell party and the other a party led by Jacob Greathouse, had shoved off. All were heading for Maysville or Cincinnati.

Colonel Lewis sighed and shrugged. "Well, there's no help for it. It's in the hands of fate now."

[*March 23, 1791 — Wednesday*]

John May was very pleased with himself. In the few years since first coming to Kentucky he had amassed a fortune in land. Nor were his claims the simple and unreliable "tomahawk improvements" of many of the illiterate frontiersmen. He had filed upon tens of thousands of acres in the Louisville land office and he took a certain pride in the reputation he had earned that "once John May files a claim, it's his land for keeps." It was praise well deserved. Where such men as Daniel Boone had already lost all they had ever claimed and others, Simon Kenton for one, were constantly going to court and finding that their claims were being nibbled away, not once had a single acre of May's been given to another because of faulty title. It was, in fact, just the other way around.

Now his affairs back in Maysville needed attention and he was returning from the east where he had spent something of a vacation. The fourteen passengers in his boat were new settlers hungry for the land he would sell them, willing to take the risks involved, despite Colonel Lewis's sober warning of increased attacks on settlers — especially on boats — this year.

May was aware of the Indian method of getting boats to come to shore by wearing white man's clothing and pretending to be travelers in distress. He was confident that this boat of his would not be so easily duped. Each of the twelve men was armed with a rifle and, if necessary, the two women could load and fire as well.

He might not have been so confident in the strength of his numbers had he known what happened at the mouth of the Scioto four days ago. A number of the men still at Fort Washington who had served out their enlistment under General Harmar had begun the journey home to more civilized Virginia and Pennsylvania. They had few weapons and their baggage and provisions were placed aboard a flatboat under the command of Elijah Strong. This boat would move upstream as they kept pace with it on the Ohio shore, on condition that if attacked by Indians they would be taken aboard and transported to the other side of the river. There were fourteen men on the boat and twenty-one on shore. It was a foolish plan. At the mouth of the Scioto the entire shore party collected and waited for the boat to come and ferry them over. With horrifying unexpectedness gunfire broke out in such a barrage that only three on shore escaped. The boat was fired into at the same time and the sternsman was wounded in the arm and two of the men rowing, one on either side of Elijah Strong, were killed. Caught by the current, the boat whirled away downstream.

But of course John May knew nothing of this and now, on the Ohio shore just above the mouth of the Scioto River, they were abruptly hailed by two men who shouted that they had been prisoners of the Shawnees and had escaped. They needed help, they called. Deeply suspicious, May stayed out of range and shouted questions at them. What were their names? When were they caught? How did they get away? How could they prove that they were not Indians trying to decoy them to shore?

The men pleaded. One identified himself as David Thomas, a frail, frightened-looking man, and the other was a tough, bewhiskered man of about forty who claimed to be Peter Devine. As they explained their capture, their escape, their origin and other matters, it became clear that they could not possibly be Indians and May ordered the boat ashore to help them. As the craft ground to a halt on the gravel, May leaped off the prow to dry land and tied the rope securely around a large chunk of driftwood.

The shots came as he straightened, twenty or thirty of them at the same time, and in that single instant the lives of John May and all fourteen passengers terminated. Immediately following the volley, Blue Jacket and some seventy Maykujay and Kispokotha Shawnees emerged from the underbrush where they had been hidden and advanced on the boat. Blue Jacket stopped at May's body, which was lying face down, and turned him over with his foot. Yes, it was he — the same man he had captured four autumns ago; the man whose life he had spared because of his resemblance to the father of Marmaduke Van Swearingen; the man he had warned to leave this country and not return or he would be killed; the man who had promised he would do so.

Blue Jacket smiled grimly as he removed May's scalp.

At his command the other bodies were lifted out of the boat and tossed unceremoniously near May and scalped. There was plenty of plunder in the boat and most of this they ordered the two white captives, Devine and Thomas, to pile in a clearing in the woods out of sight of the river. When the pair uncovered two kegs of whiskey in the bottom of the boat, the tops of these were broken in with tomahawks and the warriors took turns dipping their heads down and drinking great draughts.

So absorbed were they that they paid little attention to the white men who had lured the boat ashore. Devine motioned to Thomas and they slipped off into the woods, angling toward that spot on the river where the Shawnee canoes were hidden.

Not until they were well beyond rifle range in open water did the Indians spot them. Suddenly disgusted at himself and his men for their weakness for alcohol, Blue Jacket waved off any pursuit. Let them go. The two rabbits could spread the word at the settlements and perhaps frighten more settlers into leaving the Can-tuc-kee lands. But he kicked over the kegs angrily, spilling out what liquor remained in them.

It was just about that time when George Edwards and Thomas Marshall came into view in their small boat.

[*March 24, 1791 — Thursday*]

Petersburg
March 24, 1791

Colonel Henry Lee
Cty. Lt. Mason

Sir,

I am favored with a sight of your letter to Col. Edwards respecting the approach of the enemy, which is truly alarming. The colonel informs me he has, agreeably to your request, ordered 150 rank and file to your assistance. I have given orders to Col. Todd to march 250 on Monday next 8 o'clock for Limestone, there to wait your orders. You being in the possession of intelligence will best judge how to dispose of the men. You will therefore act accordingly and this shall be your authority. You will take every lawful measure in your power to provide for those troops. Col. Edwards is also ordered to assist you in the businesss I shall throw myself forward to Lexington and perhaps to Limestone to receive intelligence from you which forward by express when emergencies require it. Save the boats and people if possible.

I have the honor to be, dear sir,
Yr. Obt. Svt.
C. W. Scott, B. G.

[*March 26, 1791 — Saturday*]

It was nearly midnight when the pounding on Henry Lee's door jolted him out of a deep sleep at his new little station four miles from Maysville. Snatching up his rifle he asked who it was and when the unmistakable voice of Simon Kenton replied, he lighted a lamp and threw open the door. With the frontiersman were three men — Ben Whiteman, Alex McIntyre and a young stranger with a bandage around his upper arm.

"Bad news, Colonel," Kenton said. "That Shawnee party upstream has hit hard. Harder'n ever. Mebbe thirty-forty dead." He turned to the stranger. "This is William Hubbell, cap'n of a keelboat. He'll tell you what happened."

The men seated themselves around a large table and Lee's wife stirred up the fire and set a kettle over it to heat water for tea as the disheveled young captain told his story.

Hubbell, a methodical man, paused occasionally as he spoke to reconsider and make certain he had left nothing out. He had come downstream, he said, from Pittsburgh with the families of William Plaskett, Daniel Light, Captain John Ray, John Stoner, a Methodist preacher he knew only as Mr. Tucker, and two other men, a Mr. Bagley and an Irishman. A German, whose name he didn't know, and that man's two daughters, traveling in a smaller boat under the command of Francis Kirkpatrick, had met them in midstream below Marietta, and the two parties had merged on Hubbell's boat.

Shortly afterwards another boat, commanded by Captain Jacob Greathouse and including his wife, twelve children and two young men, joined them and asked permission to unite with the Hubbell boat for the greater protection of all. The boats were tied together and continued floating downriver.

At dawn on Thursday morning — the twenty-fourth — the lines joining the boats had been removed and the three watercraft, two still tied together, were drifting about two hundred yards apart six or seven miles above the mouth of the Scioto when three fifty-foot Indian canoes were seen moving upstream close to the Ohio shore, each carrying twenty or more Shawnees.

The Indians, Hubbell continued, called to the boats to put in to the Ohio shore, that they would not be hurt. At this, Kirkpatrick had stood up and shouted, "Maybe the Devil will trust you, but we won't. Come on, we're ready for you!"

At once two of the canoes surged toward the Hubbell boats and the other towards that of Greathouse, bringing up the rear. They reached the Greathouse boat first and Hubbell said he saw them scramble aboard but he couldn't tell what happened because he became too occupied himself with the two that were converging on him at about twenty paces apart. Hubbell said they held off their fire until the canoes were forty yards away when Plaskett said, "They're near enough!" and the whites opened fire with seven rifles at once. Three Indians crumpled and, apparently not expecting such firepower, the others covered themselves except for those paddling and the canoes reversed direction, while the warriors in hiding sent back a terrific gunfire. Preacher Tucker, who had been kneeling on the deck praying while the others fought, was struck. John Stoner was also hit. Both were still alive but it was obvious their wounds were mortal. The German was also badly wounded, though not mortally, and Daniel Light had taken a bullet through the shoulder. William Plaskett's twelve-year-old son, William, Jr., had been creased on the forehead with a bullet.

Out of range of the whites, the two canoes followed them for thirty minutes, then gradually began to overtake them again and a general firing recommenced. The canoes were only about fifteen feet from the keelboat when the large craft began drifting near shore and the danger of becoming grounded on a bar loomed. If that happened, they were lost. Kirkpatrick snatched up a pole and began to push the boat back into the main current. He got it headed right but then a bullet smashed through his head and sent him sprawling dead between the bodies of two horses that the Indians had shot during the first onslaught. Hearing a noise below, Hubbell dashed down and found a warrior stuck halfway in the small window of the cabin. He snatched up a wooden billet and beat him to death with it, then left him hanging there as an effective block against further attacks.

He then raced back to rejoin the fighting and immediately caught a bullet in the upper arm. Another of Plaskett's sons, ten-year-old John, was also slightly wounded in the arm. But at last the Indians, having lost at least five men of their own, gave up the chase.

Now Kenton spoke again and it was obvious he was worried. Hubbell's boat and that belonging to Greathouse weren't the only ones. Elijah Strong's crippled flatboat had come drifting back too, with the story of an attack and the killing of two men in the boat and all but three of the twenty-one ashore. At Maysville they had buried Kirkpatrick, Stoner and the preacher, Tucker, as well as the two oarsmen from Strong's boat. The whole town was in an uproar.

Lee wasted no time. They would mount an expedition upstream at once. Kenton, McIntyre and Whiteman were to separate and go to all the nearby stations, ordering the militia — with Lee's written authorization — and all volunteers to assemble at once at Maysville. Lee himself would write dispatches to be carried to Colonel Alexander Orr, commander of the scout system in the Kentucky District, placing him in charge of the expedition, and also to General Scott apprising him of the situation.

The trio set off, Kenton galloping toward May's Lick, Washington and his own Station. One facet of Hubbell's story stayed with him naggingly; the fact that Jacob Greathouse had been in command of one of the boats. Everyone on the frontier, including the Indians, knew it was Greathouse who had butchered Chief Logan's family and touched off Lord Dunmore's War. He probably had changed a great deal in the seventeen years since then, but if they had captured and recognized him, the results would not be pretty.

The Shawnees reserved special forms of slow death for their greatest enemies.

[April 5, 1791 — Tuesday]

Once again, as had happened so many times in years past, the intial burning fury that had swept through Simon Kenton upon viewing the remains of Indian depredations had settled down to a steady sick rage. His hands were badly blistered from digging the shallow graves in the rocky soil in which to bury the many who had fallen and he determined to bury his own clothing when they reached his Station, knowing the sickening smell of those swollen, mutilated bodies would never leave the apparel.

Over two hundred men had ridden up the Kentucky side of the river under Colonel Orr. Colonel Robert Rankin followed with a hundred men in three flatboats but all of them had been, as expected, too late. The mounted militia had hailed and spoken with two settlers, George Edwards and Thomas Marshall, whom they had found slinking fearfully along the southern shoreline toward Maysville. The pair had miraculously escaped a "huge party of Shawnees" they had seen standing over a pile of bodies on the north shore by swiftly paddling downstream; once around a bend, they had put in to shore, sent their canoe adrift and set off overland.

The mounted men had also encountered two men encamped on the shore near Three Islands. They identified themselves as David Thomas and Peter Devine. The former was so happy at seeing the militia that he broke down and wept, confessing that they had been forced to lure ashore the party of John May and that the entire body had been wiped out.

It was the first the frontiersmen had heard of May's death and it shocked them deeply. Some of the militia were so angry at the pair for decoying the boats that, had not Colonel Orr taken firm command, they might have done them bodily harm. As it was, the contrition of Thomas was so genuine and his fear so great that Orr told them to continue downriver to Maysville and pass on word of the militia's progress. Thomas, still weeping uncontrollably, thanked the colonel and told him where the Shawnees had been, their strength and the location of their Scioto River camp, although he doubted they would still be there.

They weren't. But the remains were.

Forty-nine bodies of men, women and children, all of them scalped and most of them mutilated in some respect, lay on shore. The first eighteen discovered were those of Elijah Strong's shore party of discharged soldiers. Most had been shot to death and then scalped and severely hacked with tomahawks. They buried them quickly in a common grave and next found the thirteen men and two women of the May party, all of whom were in similar condition. The final discovery — the Greathouse party of sixteen — was worst, for it was immediately apparent that most of these had been tortured to death.

The twelve children, two young men and a young woman had been stripped and lashed to trees and beaten to death with limber hickory switches which still lay on the ground nearby. The mutilation of this form of torture was dreadful and the agonies they suffered must have been intense. All of them, down to the youngest child — a girl of about five — had been scalped. Fires at their feet had destroyed the legs and lower bodies of all.

The question Simon Kenton had asked of himself when the expedition was first organizing was now answered; the Indians had indeed recognized Jacob Greathouse and they had reserved a very special death for him and his wife.

They had been stripped, these two, and beaten terribly with switches, but not enough to kill them. What followed was simple, but not pleasant, to deduce. The ugly image of Chief Logan's pregnant sister, who had been shot, hung by her wrists and her belly slit open, had not been forgotten. Greathouse and his wife had been tethered each to a different sapling with a loop running from neck to tree. Their bellies had been opened just above the pubic hairs and a loose end of the entrails tied to the sapling. They had then either been dragged or prodded around and around so that their intestines had been pulled out of their bodies to wind around the trees as they walked. Mrs. Greathouse had apparently died before getting much more than half unwound, but Greathouse himself had stumbled along until not only his intestines but even his stomach had been pulled out and wound into that obscene mass on the tree. They had then been scalped and burning coals stuffed into their body cavities before the Indians departed.

The hatred of the Shawnee was strong, his memory long and his vengeance great. Every man on this expedition, particularly Simon Kenton, would carry the picture of this atrocity with him for the rest of his life and many a night's sleep from this time forward would be interrupted by horrible nightmares.

[April 22, 1791 — Friday]

It was not often that Simon Kenton had an opportunity to set up an ambush for Indians. Normally the reverse was true and Kenton took the leadership of his men in the resultant chase of retaliation. But this time it had been different. From the moment Ben Whiteman and Neil Washburn had reported in from their rounds, he recognized it as a golden opportunity. For once, it would be the Indians who walked into a trap set by one of the few white men who had ever been able to beat them at their own game.

On April 17, Whiteman and Washburn had been making their appointed rounds along the Kentucky shore of the Ohio River west of Maysville when, at the mouth of Snag Creek, twenty-eight miles below the town, they found four canoes hidden. Two were large wooden ones, fifty feet long, beached and covered with old driftwood. To the unsuspecting eye they would have been invisible, but not to this pair of young scouts. On closer examination they found the other two nearby, sunk in three feet of water and held down with logs. These last two were twenty-footers made of bark. All the evidence indicated that a party of perhaps fifty or more Indians had gone inland from here to raid the settlements.

The big frontiersman considered the situation carefully. In his mind's eye he could picture so perfectly the area where the boats had been located that it was as if he were standing there, seeing not only the immediate area, but the adjacent north shore of the Ohio as well. He nodded and sent out word for thirty of his men to meet at Maysville at dawn with two days' rations.

James Finley, eager to help, was dispatched to Lee's Station to advise the county lieutenant and have him send warnings to the other settlements of Mason and Bourbon Counties to be on special alert against attack and, if possible, to mount an offensive force to drive the invaders back to the Ohio River.

By sunrise the next day, Kenton was shoving off from Maysville with his party in two boats: an old keel boat in which twenty men rode and a light cedar canoe forty feet long for the other ten. They moved downstream apace and when they reached a spot along the north shore which Kenton recognized as being perhaps a quarter mile from a point above the mouth of Snag Creek, he ordered the keelboat ashore with instructions that it was to be dragged out of the water and hidden and the men were then to march downstream to assemble opposite Snag Creek. His own canoe went past the creek, ascertained that the canoes were still there, then recrossed to the Ohio side and put into the mouth of Bear Creek, a thousand yards below. As soon as they had hidden the canoe, they marched back upstream and joined the others.

A six-hour guard schedule was established and the first two men — Washburn and Whiteman — were left on shore to watch the Kentucky side for activity and the remaining party went inland several hundred yards along the Indian trail to a narrow gap where an excellent ambush could be made. Here they hid themselves at Kenton's directions, checked their rifles and settled back to wait. They were to send word immediately of any sightings and, at all costs, not to open fire or expose themselves.

For forty-eight hours with guards changing regularly, the party crouched in hiding and, as Kenton knew would happen, the patience of the men wore thin. Their rations were practically gone and they hadn't had hot food in a long while. Certain the Indians would come soon, Kenton at last permitted Washburn and Whiteman to move back into the hills to hunt for fresh meat. In a deep hollow several miles away the pair found a flock of turkeys and, firing simultaneously, downed three, Washburn's bullet killing two at the same time. The pair thereupon moved directly to the Ohio shore and followed it two miles back to where the guards were.

They saw the Indians first, three of them. Unaware that they were being watched, two were raising one of the smaller canoes and a third was tying seven horses head to tail to swim them across. Slipping along carefully under cover, the two scouts reached the point where the guards were hidden and found them blissfully asleep, back to back. Angrily, Washburn awoke them and sent them back to Kenton with the turkeys and news of the sighting. Before the Indians even began crossing, Kenton had come up with five men — Wetzel, Lemon, Boone, McIntyre and Fowler.

It was about three in the afternoon when the trio of Shawnees started across, laughing and talking as they paddled, wholly unaware of the trap. One was wearing a white shirt, and when the eight guns fired he was the only one not instantly killed. He fell, along with the others, but then raised himself and attempted to shove the boat back into the current, when another volley caught him and he crumpled.

The tired horses were easy to catch and Kenton sent Fowler and McIntyre back to camp with them. Jacob Boone and Wetzel raced out of hiding and dragged the boat ashore, scalped two of the Indians and dumped their bodies into the river. The dead man in the white shirt had long blond hair and, as Washburn began scalping him, Joe Lemon looked closely and recognized him as Bill Frame, a boyhood friend on the Monongahela whom he hadn't seen for ten years. Word was that he had become a renegade and this proved it. The shirt, full of bullet holes and bloody, did not fit him well and it was supposed he had taken it from some white captive very recently. Kenton ordered it stripped off to be taken back to Maysville with them for possible identification.

One of the men wanted to skin Frame's body to make some fine parchment and razor strops from the hide and was miffed when Kenton wouldn't permit it. Instead, the scalpless body was consigned to the river and the canoe filled with rocks and sunk. Then all but two guards returned to camp and once again the waiting began, but not so impatiently now that they had had some success and the promise of more to come.

Through the remainder of the day and night they waited; then, early in the morning on April 21, one of the guards brought word that another party of three Shawnees with six more horses was coming over. Kenton and another five men hastened to shore and nearly an exact reenactment of what had happened earlier occurred. This time, however, the man in the middle ducked down when his companions were shot and shouted, "No shoot! Me prisoner!" But John Mefford had recognized him as a Shawnee he had once locked horns with and, as the man raised his head, put a fatal bullet through his throat.

Again the horses were captured, the Indians scalped and dumped into the water. But there was a difference this time. As a warning to any Shawnees who might come this way, the head of the scarred Indian was severed and carried back to the camp where it was impaled atop a twenty-foot pole.

Kenton was certain the main body of Indians would be coming soon and all through the day they waited expectantly. At nightfall a heavy fog developed and about midnight a guard brought word of many men gathering on the opposite shore. But now things went slightly awry. Though

Kenton's party could see nothing, they could hear horses whinnying and then the Indians began hallooing, apparently expecting an answer from the north shore. When none came, an uneasy silence sprang up. In a little while they heard muttered voices and the dipping of paddles and it was about then that one of the guards accidentally dropped his rifle with a clatter. Immediately came the sound of the boat drawing away, followed by an ominous quiet. Kenton ordered the shore guards to walk a hundred-pace patrol each, moving apart, halting, then moving back together again.

They heard nothing. But on one of their walks toward one another they found a small canoe beached on shore. Some daring warrior had scouted out the camp of the whites, circled behind it, climbed high on a ridge and shouted out several times in a great booming voice, *"Puck-a-chee! Puck-a-chee! Shemanese!"* — Danger here! Long Knives!

The element of surprise now altogether lost, Kenton called for the big canoe to be brought up from Bear Creek. But before they could move across they heard gunfire from the other side; on paddling over they found that a sizable group of Bourbon County men, having received Kenton's warning, had taken up the offensive and followed the Indians. Already alerted to Kenton's trap, however, and aided by the fog, the party had scattered and escaped, leaving behind only two dead.

The ambush had not turned out to be the success Kenton's party had anticipated, but it was by no means a failure. Thirty-two stolen horses were recovered and eight of the enemy slain, while not one of their own number was even injured.

When Kenton's party returned to Maysville late this afternoon, they were in a good mood. The settlers crowded around them with questions, pleased that all had returned safely. Among them was a long-faced individual, the elderly father of Timothy Downing. Old William Downing told Simon that his son had been taken by the Indians while returning from Lexington the day after Kenton's party left for the ambush. He might have been taken captive, but both the old man and Timothy's wife feared he had been killed. Had Kenton's party seen any sign of him? He had been wearing a new white shirt.

At this, the shirt taken from Bill Frame's body was shown to the father and wife and, upon seeing it, Tim Downing's wife fainted and the old man said it was his son's beyond doubt and he broke down, certain now of his death. Simon Kenton shook his head.

"Tim's a good man," he said. "He'll be back or I've badly misjudged him."

[*April 24, 1791 — Sunday*]

The big frontiersman was right.

Two days after their return from the ambush there was a general rejoicing in Maysville at the return, by boat, of Timothy Downing. Kenton happened to be in town and upon hearing the man's story he called for his minutemen to meet again for an expedition into the Ohio country.

After being captured, Downing had related, his group of sixteen Indians had met another group of twenty-eight and they had set off for the Ohio with a few dozen stolen horses. Downing's new shirt had been taken by a blond renegade who had also wanted to kill him, but was overruled. When they came within a few miles of Snag Creek, an old Chalahgawtha chief, Meshepeshe — the Panther — along with his sixteen-year-old son, Gray Fox, and another warrior named Big Owl, had taken Downing and left the main party, moving to a point along the river a mile or so upstream from the mouth of Snag Creek. Here they had a small canoe hidden. It had been about 3:00 P.M. on the twentieth when they crossed over and, upon hearing gunfire downstream, Meshepeshe had chuckled exultantly and in broken English told Downing that the Shawnees were obviously taking another *Shemanese* boat.

On the second night, the party had camped where the picturesque Rattlesnake Creek empties into Paint Creek. It was a rainy evening and Downing was loosed of his bonds and set to making a fire. Meshepeshe sent Big Owl to the Chalahgawtha camp four miles below on Paint Creek to notify them of the success of the raid and to tell them to prepare a gauntlet line in the morning for the prisoner. The chief and his son hung a blanket for protection and the old man sat under it, facing the fire, while Gray Fox warmed himself on the other side. It was then that Downing saw the chief had removed his tomahawk and placed it on the ground slightly behind himself.

Leaping unexpectedly, Downing snatched up the weapon. Before the old man could react, the frontiersman had struck him a terrible blow on the head with it and the chief fell to the ground jerking spastically, like a beheaded chicken. Gray Fox threw himself upon Downing and they struggled in deadly silence for several minutes. Finally Downing got an arm free and buried the tomahawk in the young man's breast.

The weapon jerked out of his hand as the young Shawnee reeled backwards and began staggering off into the woods. Downing untied one of the horses, leaped to its back and was off. The rainy night confused him and he angled farther to the east than anticipated, hitting the Ohio River at dawn just below the mouth of the Scioto. As luck would have it, a boat was passing and he shouted for help. The men aboard were sure he was a decoy and bore over toward the Kentucky shore. However, there was a young man aboard who thought he might be telling the truth and he told the others that since he was the only man there without relatives he would, if they would permit him to do it, take the smaller boat and go to the stranger's rescue. They agreed and he shoved off in the canoe, his rifle in his lap. When he neared Downing he called for him to wade into the water to his chest and if this was an ambush he would shoot Downing at the first sign of it. Downing did so and was ultimately taken aboard and brought to the boat and floated with them down to Maysville.

There could be no doubt that he was an exhausted man; and yet, less than three hours after landing at Maysville, Tim Downing was guiding Simon Kenton's party of sixty men toward the Paint Creek camp of the Chalahgawthas.

[*April 26, 1791 — Tuesday*]

Less than an hour after stumbling into the Paint Creek camp, Gray Fox had died, the tomahawk still protruding from his chest and his whole front smeared with blood. Before dying he told the others what had happened and an oppressive mood of mingled sadness and fear overcame them.

Meshepeshe had not been a very powerful Shawnee chief, but to these hundred Chalahgawtha warriors and squaws he was greatly loved and his death was deeply mourned. There was no hope, in this rainy weather, of trailing the escaped white man who was now many hours gone. It was only reasonable to assume that he would return to the whites and then perhaps the greatly feared *cut-ta-ho-tha* Bahd-ler would lead an attack against them.

They would have to go but, before doing so, they must see to their chief. Under their new chief, Chiuxca, the entire group packed their horses and abandoned the scattering of *wegiwas* and marched solemnly to the site of their dead chief's camp. The fire was out when they got there and the blanket hung in a soggy belly from its poles. Partially beneath it lay Meshepeshe, face down in the mud. Many of the squaws wailed in grief at this sight and a not uncommon admixture of sorrow and hatred filled the breasts of the warriors.

During the afternoon a strange structure was built. Twenty young elms seven or eight inches in diameter were felled and the branches trimmed off to a height of twenty feet. The tops were cut off at this point and three of the straightest of these trunks were lashed together at their tips and stood on end, their bases forming a triangle. In a cone around these, the rest of the logs were leaned until the result was something of a large tepee-like structure. The entire ground area under the cone was now paved with smooth flat stones from the bed of the creek.

While this was being done, Meshepeshe's body had been stripped and bathed carefully, his hair cleansed and combed back across the gaping wound in his skull. His body was dressed in new leggins and two of the new shirts that had been among the plunder he had taken from Downing. His feet were covered with fine new moccasins and a bright blue cape of a satin material was tied around his neck and hung down his back in a peculiar splash of color.

He was then carried inside the cone hut and, on a colorful blanket spread out on the fitted slabs, he was deposited upon his back and the cape allowed to flare out around him. A fine silver necklace was placed about his throat and a headdress of a half-dozen eagle feathers attached to the lock of hair over his left ear and positioned so that the quills were up and the plumes lay across his shoulder and pointed toward his heart.

At his right hand was placed the knife with which he had taken so many scalps and the old flintlock rifle he always kept in his *wegiwa*. Along his left side were positioned a looking glass, comb, scissors, awl and a small pile of patching leather used to mend moccasins. At his feet lay a fine pipe tomahawk filled with *kinnikinnick*, beside which lay a bag of tobacco. Over everything was spread the two beautiful white linen sheets Downing had been bringing to Maysville when captured.

By nightfall the preparations were completed and the principal warriors of the tribe entered the structure and stood silently in the gloom along the sloping walls as Chiuxca gently placed on Meshepeshe's chest a leather bag filled with smaller leather pouches, each containing a different colored powdered war paint. The rest of the villagers gathered around the little building shoulder to shoulder in an ever-widening spiral. A faint, cold drizzle fell intermittently and for hours they stood thus without movement and with no sound being made, their ears shut away from any outside distraction, their hearts overflowing with grief.

About midnight a fire was built nearby and a huge kettle filled with water and herbs set over it to heat. In turn over the next few hours the Indians left their position in the lines, drank each a buffalo hornful of the steaming liquid and then returned to their places. By dawn the fire was out, the kettle emptied and repacked on a horse, the assemblage still silently mourning. The rain had stopped during the night and the clouds had broken somewhat; for twenty minutes at sunrise the area was bathed in bright light.

It was then that Chiuxca at last opened a small bag hung around his neck and removed a pinch of *nilu-famu*, the sacred tobacco, and allowed it to trickle down over the still form of Meshepeshe. He did this first facing toward the newly risen sun, then moved slowly around the body and did the same on the south, west and north sides. When he left the shelter after closing the pouch, his warriors filed out of the cone behind him and six more of the elm logs were put into place to close the opening. The crowd parted to let the men through and then fell in silently behind them and no one looked back at the lonely sepulcher.

Less than three hours later, the sixty horsemen led by Simon Kenton approached the Paint Creek village. No smoke came from the *wegiwas* and there was no sign of life. Nor was there any sunshine. Rifles at ready in case of surprise, the frontiersmen rode into the village and searched the abandoned structures, finding nothing but a few discarded pieces of raw-hide and a pile of onions. Dry tinder found in each of the huts was piled against the inside walls and set ablaze and as the column of men rode northwest along the creek, the smudge of smoke rising behind them was only slightly darker than the heavily overhanging clouds.

Timothy Downing led them to the spot where he had struck Meshe-peshe and Gray Fox and escaped and there, in the gathering twilight, they discovered the cone structure and the remains of the Chalahgawtha chief. Deliberately they knocked down the little building and gathered up the trinkets and weapons surrounding the body. They stripped him of clothing and jewelry, Simon Kenton taking the blue cape and Downing reclaiming his shirts and linen and the remainder of the men bartering among them-selves for the rest of the loot. Jacob Wetzel sliced a deep circle on the chief's head and yanked off the scalp with a savage jerk.

The nude and desecrated body was then tossed off the platform and slid a little way in the mud before coming to a stop. And as the men re-mounted and rode off toward the Ohio River, the clouds released a deluge over the still pale form of the dead chief and a wind wove its way through the budded branches overhead and the sound it made in its passage was a sound of mourning.

CHAPTER IX

[*August 1, 1791 — Monday*]

WAR was in the air. It was something that could almost be smelled on the wind and rumors of where and when sprouted, bloomed and died by the hundreds. No one seemed to know anything concrete about what was being planned except that when it came it would be the war which would not end until every Indian in the Northwest Territory had surrendered unconditionally or been killed, and that the commander in chief of this army would be General St. Clair.

The Kentuckians were delighted with contemplation of the war, since this would mean an end to their harassment; but they weren't entirely happy with the prospect of an army under the command of Arthur St. Clair. True, St. Clair had been a good fighter against the British, but the Indians didn't fight like Redcoats; they didn't make targets of themselves, which St. Clair might do with his army, but instead they hit and ran and hit again.

Simon Kenton was one of those who was disinclined to serve under the governor. He had met him upon several occasions and, while he didn't actually dislike him, he could scarcely conceive of such a man fighting Indians.

"St. Clair?" he said, when an acquaintance asked him what he thought of the governor-general. "Well sir, I'll tell you. St. Clair, he's a minister-looking man. He's well disciplined, too, but he has no brier look about him, no keenness."

When pinned down for an answer about whether or not he'd join St. Clair's army when it formed, the thirty-six-year-old frontiersman shook his head vigorously. He had had quite enough in past years of trusting his life on campaigns to men who had no conception of how to fight Indians and refused to follow advice from those who did know. He placed St. Clair in the same category as he placed Colonel John Bowman and General Josiah Harmar.

A good number of the frontiersmen felt the same and, from the looks of things, St. Clair was apt to have more trouble raising an army than even Josiah Harmar had. With Harmar's bungling campaign still fresh in their minds, they had little inclination to risk a similar campaign. Nor was this feeling diminished any when Harmar, still miffed over his own failure, predicted a similar defeat for St. Clair.

But the fact that matters of war were building to a head was evidenced by the increased traffic of supplies coming downriver from Pittsburgh to Fort Washington and by sharply increased correspondence flowing between Philadelphia, Fort Pitt, Richmond and Cincinnati. In April a federal Board of War had been established for the defense of the Kentucky District. George Washington personally appointed Benjamin Logan, John Brown, Isaac Shelby and Harry Innes as members of that board. They, in turn, issued a directive to establish an army for future defense, ordering General Scott to draft into service three hundred twenty-six privates, "properly officered, in order to relieve the guards now out and to establish several new forts." Daily rations were to be purchased with government funds at a cost of not over eight cents per ration. Hardly had this drafting notice gone out than it was followed by another requiring an additional five hundred men.

It soon was clear that Governor St. Clair was having grave difficulties, not only in getting the men he deemed necessary for this campaign, but with his quartermaster corps. It had nowhere near enough supplies and seemed hopelessly befuddled by the idea of providing during a wilderness march for an army the size St. Clair hoped to build.

In the closing days of April, St. Clair left with a significant force from Fort Pitt en route for Fort Washington. It was a disheartening trip. Stops at Wheeling and Point Pleasant, Marietta and Maysville to pick up volunteers were disappointing in the extreme. Nor did it help the morale of the men to see the wailing mob of Frenchmen who had arrived at Marietta and found their land titles worthless and the promised land an empty promise. They were given federal permission to settle temporarily at Marietta and the new Ohio settlement being formed downriver from Point Pleasant, Gallipolis; meanwhile, the government would do what it could to help them, but the stern reminder rode them constantly that this was a temporary residence and that they were a displaced people without funds or lands.

St. Clair arrived at Fort Washington on May 15, expecting to find all the remainder of supplies and troops that he needed awaiting him there so he could begin his great campaign no later than August 1; instead he saw, from the moment of landing, that if the expedition got underway before the end of October it would be a remarkable thing.

The Kentucky District draft went into effect and the younger men were pulled into service, whether they liked it or not. Most of them — men such as Neil Washburn — were incensed at this, feeling it far more important that they remain in the border country to protect their lands and families and neighbors from continued Indian incursions.

There was, somehow, a sense of foreboding involved in the formation of this army. The fact that it would be led by a general who had proven himself in battle, that it would number fully three thousand men, and that it would have half a dozen or more fine artillery pieces did little to allay this peculiar feeling. For the first time since he had come to the frontier, Simon Kenton was happy that he had not been called upon to join the expedition.

[*September 16, 1791 — Friday*]

They were the greatest assemblage of chiefs ever to meet at the mouth of the Auglaize and it was apparent from the commencement of the grand council that they had put aside whatever animosities had grown between them for past acts and were in accord with what must now be done together.

A great army was being assembled to march against them and the British, whom they had helped so much in the past, now refused to furnish them what they needed most — manpower. They would provide arms, ammunition and powder; they would even provide a few of their better Indian agents — men such as Simon Girty and Alexander McKee and Matthew Elliott — to act as advisers, but they could not afford to become publicly involved. The Americans would not need much of an excuse to march against Detroit and that fort must not fall to them.

And so it was up to these assembled chiefs to select their battle commanders and pledge their warriors and meet these whites with such power and spirit as had never been witnessed before. It took considerable discussion to establish who was to have principal command, and for a long while it balanced as a choice between Little Turtle, the Miami, and Blue Jacket, the Shawnee. But because the pair had worked so well together in the defeat of Harmar's troops last year, it was decided that they should do so again now. Little Turtle was to be principal commander, with Blue Jacket his second-in-command. Tarhe — the Crane — chief of the Wyandots, would be third in charge and, following him, Chief Pipe of the Delawares. Waw-paw-waw-qua — White Loon — would lead the Weas and Mohawks. Thus it went, down the line through the Ottawas and Mingoes, the Potawatomies, Kickapoos, Piankeshaws, Kaskaskias and Eel River Miamis. As the meeting was concluding, Simon Girty was invited to speak.

The renegade nodded and told them he had seen armies of brave warriors before, but never one so large nor so courageous. Knowing their appreciation for the unexpected, he reached into a pocket and pulled forth an egg and held it up for all to see. Its whiteness, he said, represented the whites, while the dark of his fingers stood for the Indians gathered here. What would be the outcome when they met? He held the egg high and his grip tightened abruptly. The egg crushed audibly and the roar of approval was an awesome thing to hear.

[*September 30, 1791 — Friday*]

With the boundless confidence of the very young, eighteen-year-old William Henry Harrison accepted the commission as ensign from President George Washington with the firm conviction that what he was doing was best. With the death of his father earlier in the year he had known what he would do; and now that the decision was irrevocably made, he experienced neither regret nor doubt. Despite what Benjamin Harrison had wished for his son, young Harrison had never particularly wanted to become a doctor; and so he had terminated his medical studies in Philadelphia and, with no qualms whatever, presented himself personally to George Washington. He was relying on the President's long friendship with the late Benjamin Harrison to sway him in granting this boon — and so it had.

Within the week he would leave Philadelphia for his first journey to the wild western frontier which had so long enticed him. When he presented himself to the governor-general at Fort Washington as a presidentially appointed ensign for the Tenth Regiment, his new life would truly begin. His only real concern was that even pushing ahead at top speed, he might miss the opportunity to join St. Clair's expedition.

It would be a catastrophe, he believed, to miss what might well be the most decisive campaign to be undertaken in the Northwest Territory.

[*November 14, 1791 — Monday*]

It was a decidedly unhappy army General Arthur St. Clair led out of Fort Washington. Instead of numbering over three thousand, as planned, with regular United States troops comprising four-fifths of the total, the march commenced with only seven hundred ten seasoned officers and soldiers and six hundred ninety drafted militia, for a total strength of only fourteen hundred. As if that were not bad enough of itself, there was so little food that beginning on the very first day of the march the army was placed on slightly less than half rations until the expected supply train should catch up to them. It was an inauspicious way to start a campaign, but there was no help for it.

During the late summer, week after week had passed and neither the men nor the provisions had arrived as expected at Fort Washington. With each passing day St. Clair's temper became shorter. The messages he sent by express to the Secretary of War, General Henry Knox, seemed to have no effect whatever and the invasion, originally planned for August 1, had to be delayed. New schedules were made, followed by still further post-ponements, until well over two months had passed with no definite word as to when the goods and troops would arrive. At last St. Clair decided to march whether or not the quartermaster corps delivered by the scheduled day of march. When the chosen day came and there was yet no sign of supplies, he left orders for the goods and men to be sent along at forced marches and then set off himself with the army.

In accordance with his instructions from President Washington to build a series of forts, St. Clair stopped first at the crossing of the Great Miami River twenty-three miles north of Cincinnati. Here, in a wide prairie rimming the river, he ordered the construction of Fort Hamilton.[1] But discontent, particularly among the militia, grew worse until it became necessary to keep a strong force of officers over the draftees to maintain discipline. There could be no doubt that much of their ill feeling was due to camp followers: nearly half a thousand wives, children and unattached women dogged the army's heels, disregarding St. Clair's orders that they return to Cincinnati and wait there. As was the custom, they insisted on following their militia husbands and fathers and lovers; and since these dependents had no supplies to speak of, they had to ask for handouts from the already meager rations provided to the militia. The fact that St. Clair adamantly refused to increase the militia's ration to allow for this angered the draftees even more.

Fort Hamilton was garrisoned with a detachment of twenty men and the march continued to the north in weather becoming progressively colder. Occasional Indians were spotted watching the army from a distance, a constant reminder of the possible danger that lay ahead. If these savages could scrape up even five hundred warriors with which to hit the army, the United States forces could be in serious trouble.

Although not a man in this army realized it, there was one Indian in particular most often observed, one who was constantly sending runners to the north with information about the army's strengths and weaknesses, its apparent destination and where best it could be hit. He was a twenty-three-year-old Kispokotha Shawnee named Tecumseh, and the Indian confedera-tion could not have selected a better spy.

On October 21, forty-four miles north of Fort Hamilton, St. Clair ordered another halt for the construction of his second fort near the junction of two inconspicuous little streams. The fort was swiftly erected and called Fort Jefferson.[2] But now, as another garrison of twenty men had to be left behind, a severe blow befell the general. During the night, in a

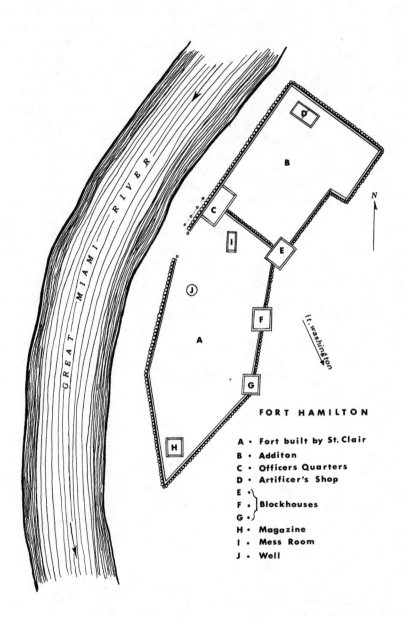

FORT HAMILTON

A · Fort built by St. Clair
B · Additon
C · Officers Quarters
D · Artificer's Shop
E ·
F · } Blockhouses
G ·
H · Magazine
I · Mess Room
J · Well

maneuver which must have been carefully planned, a full three hundred of the militia deserted en masse. Not until dawn, when they had been gone for six or seven hours, did news of their desertion reach St. Clair.

This posed far more of a problem than simply the loss of three hundred fighting men. The deserters had taken with them some two hundred of the women and children camp followers, which meant there were now five hundred hungry people on the loose. It was a distinct possibility that they would attempt to intercept and ransack the supply train which, by now, should certainly have left Fort Washington to follow St. Clair's trace. Thus, with great reluctance, St. Clair was forced to order the flower of his army, Major Hamtramck's First Regiment, to pursue and arrest as many of the deserters as possible, meet the supply convoy and escort it back to the army.

With forty men lost in the garrisoning of the new forts, with three hundred militiamen deserted, and with the strength of Major Hamtramck's regiment in hot pursuit, General St. Clair now continued the march north with a total of nine hundred twenty troops. And the farther north they marched, the worse the weather became — and the more frequently Indian sign was reported.

Unaccustomed to Indian wiles, St. Clair saw no particular cause for sending out advance scouting parties. This was a great worry to the remaining militia, all of whom had previously engaged in at least one Indian fight and most of whom had met them in battle numerous times. As a result, the militia took the initiative and began sending out scouts on its own.

It snowed during the first two days of November and the initial reports these scouts brought back made the others quail. From the amount of sign discovered in the new snow, there must be hundreds upon hundreds of Indians all around them. Finally, one of the scouts returned, breathless and unashamedly frightened, to report to a crusty old regular officer, Colonel Oldham, that he had discovered the main Indian encampment. There were "thousands of warriors assembled there," the scout estimated, whereupon Oldham, with a vague expression of interest, ordered the scout back to watch them. Incredibly, he failed to convey the intelligence of their presence to General St. Clair.

At last, on November 3, the army ground to a halt on the slushy banks of the Wabash River headwaters, thirty-seven miles north of Fort Jefferson and only three miles from the line separating the Ohio and Indiana Territories.[3] They were a miserable army — cold, hungry, exhausted — and St. Clair, now becoming more concerned over the abundance of Indian sign, announced that they would establish a camp and remain here until the supplies caught up. But, because everyone was fatigued from the march and it was already late afternoon, it was decided to wait until the morrow to erect fortifications.

It was an understandable decision but an extremely unwise one. For less than a mile away, to the north of the Wabash headwaters, more than three thousand savage warriors were, at this very moment, being given their final battle instructions by Chiefs Little Turtle and Blue Jacket.

As the soldiers built their fires and prepared camp, St. Clair took the precaution of ordering a hundred-man militia detachment and a twenty-one-man ranger outfit to establish a forward guard post a quarter mile ahead. During the night, there came a sporadic firing from the advance guard and St. Clair was awakened with the frightening report that the enemy was apparently moving into position to attack in the morning.

An hour before dawn, dressing hurriedly and pulling on his coarse capote and tri-cornered beaver hat, St. Clair ordered the army awakened and assembled at once. As the runner sped away, the general nearly groaned aloud with the severe pain from his gout-afflicted feet.

It was dawn on Friday, November 4, a mean gray morning of bitter cold with low, heavy clouds reflecting an ominous promise on the snow-covered landscape below. St. Clair raised his arms for silence, then spoke rapidly and briefly.

"From intelligence delivered to me during the night, I am led to believe that we will be attacked by the Indians today. Perhaps very soon. All men will see to their weapons at once. Artillerymen will position and load the cannons. Emergency fortifications are to be erected beginning this moment."

But the moment for such measures was already past. With fearful shriekings, an unbelievable horde of Indians sprang suddenly from cover all around them and charged. Gruesomely painted and dressed in their most resplendent battle garb, the leading chiefs — Little Turtle, Blue Jacket, Pipe, Wingenund, Black Beard, Chiuxca, Buckangehela, Black Hoof, Tarhe, White Loon and others — struck terror into the hearts of the whites. Scarcely firing a shot, the forward guard detachment abruptly panicked, threw down its rifles and ran for its life back toward the main encampment. Their contagious panic swept over the entire army and in an instant the white force was in a state of deadly confusion.

A hot fire from the first line momentarily checked the main Indian advance, but an immediate return of withering fire caused staggering army losses. St. Clair screamed for the artillery to fire but for some reason only two of the cannons went off and neither did serious damage. At once the greatest weight of Indian fire was directed toward that section, and in brief minutes practically all of the artillerymen were down, dead or dying.

Hobbling painfully, St. Clair called for his horse. But the animal was struck by a bullet and killed before he could mount — and so were two more in succession. Exasperated the general hobbled off afoot. The troops were amazed now to see their general racing back and forth on his own feet in the hottest areas of fire, calling on his men to be steady, to hold their ground, to aim well, to make every shot count. Even as he gave these orders a bullet grazed the side of his head and took a lock of his scraggly gray hair.

Upon seeing Colonel William Darke, St. Clair ordered him to lead his men in a bayonet charge and Darke forthwith rallied his men and executed the order with great spirit. Finding Colonel Oldham standing wide-eyed beside a tree, the general ordered him to a similar attack, but Oldham turned fearful eyes on him and shook his head.

"Damn it, that's suicide. I won't do it."

No sooner had he refused than he pitched forward as a bullet tore away the entire rear of his skull. St. Clair hardly paused. Rallying Oldham's men behind himself, he personally led a bayonet charge against the enemy on the left flank and repulsed them. Twice more he led similar attacks and while men about him dropped by the dozens, he remained unscathed.

Colonel Gibson of the artillery tried desperately to rally his few remaining men. "Fight them!" he shouted. "Fight them! Don't show fear. True Virginians never show fear. I'd rather die ten thousand deaths than let these savages take this field!" And in that instant he caught a bullet in the spine and was killed.

Blue Jacket seemed to be everywhere at once. Fourteen men had already fallen to his gun and tomahawk and fourteen fresh scalps were wadded together in his pouch. A regular army captain, Charles Van Swearingen, suddenly loomed and thrust a bayonet at him. As the blade slit his side, he wheeled and, with a backhand swing, sank his tomahawk in the soldier's belly. The man fell upon his back and Blue Jacket grasped his hair in one hand and felt for his knife with the other. The soldier's eyes opened in amazement as his dying gaze took in the features of the Indian chief.

"Duke?" he whispered hoarsely. "It is Duke, isn't it? It's me . . . Duke . . . it's Cha . . . Charley."

He died then. Momentarily stunned, Blue Jacket stared into his dead brother's face. No! He had no brothers but the Shawnees. With a flick of his knife he lifted the scalp and then leaped up to continue the assault, shrieking a cry that was more than merely battle lust, a cry which carried in it a trace of deep, inner pain.

The Indians now rushed both left and right flanks at the same time and these attacks were parried by St. Clair's second-in-command, Major General Richard Butler, on the right and Major William Clark on the left. Both counterattacks were successful in momentarily repulsing the enemy, but Clark died with a tomahawk in his breast and Butler had taken four bullets and now leaned against a tree, dazed and dying. All but three of his men had been killed in the counterattack. Two of these three grabbed their officer and half carried, half dragged him to the surgeon's tent. The doctor, Edward Grassen, began dressing the wounds but an Ottawa rushed in and shot him and then tried to take Butler's scalp. The dying doctor managed to reach his gun and shot the Indian. A moment later, both Butler and Grassen were dead.

St. Clair remained in the thick of the action, encouraging and directing the troops, desperately attempting to quell the panic among his men. At one point he found a half-dozen men standing in a cluster, weeping. He drew his pistol and pointed it at them, ordering them back into the fight or he would kill them on the spot. Other small groups, similarly paralyzed with fear, weaponless and bewildered, were shot where they stood by the advancing Indians. The snow underfoot in the entire battle area had become a hideous red slush. The air was filled with the triumphant shrieks of the Indians, the terrified wailings of those who had given way to panic, and the agonized cries of the wounded and dying.

Nor was the slaughter limited to the military. The women and children camp followers had fled screaming toward the south at the first attack but were cut off by Indians from behind and, weaponless, fell to their tomahawk blows. Within the span of twenty minutes over two hundred of them were killed.

St. Clair, now no longer able to walk, scrabbled about on hands and knees, still calling orders and begging someone to get him a horse so that he could direct the battle properly. At last a packhorse was found, a sluggish, recalcitrant animal that could scarcely be coaxed into anything more than a walk; but at least the general was mounted and able to traverse his lines again.

The several remaining artillerymen were continuing to get off an occasional shot, though with little effect. Most of the cannon powder simply refused to explode and the frightened cannoneers began to fall back. Captain Ford, dangerously wounded but the only one of three artillery officers still alive, screamed at them, "Stand by your guns! Die like men, not like cowards."

Other dismaying matters came to light. Labels on supply boxes were found to be inaccurate. Those marked "Flints" turned out to have gunlocks in them. Kegs of powder marked "For the Infantry" turned out to be damaged cannon powder that would barely ignite.

Now the Indians struck simultaneously on both flanks and the rear and the soldiers fell as if a great scythe had cut them down. Repeatedly St. Clair's orders were being disobeyed or ignored, not only by the militia but even by regular officers and men. The battle had been raging for the better part of three hours and already easily half the army had been killed.

The commanding general realized that if they were to avoid an absolute massacre there was only one move to make — retreat. But with the Indian forces heavily at their rear now, it would not be easy. St. Clair spurred his horse into the semblance of a trot and managed to draw together five of his officers. They must, he ordered, make a strong feint to the right flank and then abruptly turn and drive through the forces behind them. The officers spread the word and when the signal was given the maneuver was executed perfectly and a passage through the enemy lines was carved.

St. Clair remained on the battlefield to direct the move, but the word to retreat had reignited in the men their overpowering fear; now, all at once, they dropped their weapons and ran for their lives. With no strong officer up front to direct them, the retreat that was meant to be controlled and self-possessed turned into a fantastic rout with men running into one another and pushing each other aside, or trampling over comrades in frantic haste to find safety from the battle area.

St. Clair pounded the sides of his packhorse with his heels in an attempt to regain the lead of the column, but a mediocre trotting was the best he could achieve. He called on officers nearby to run to the head of the panicky men and gain control, but they ignored him and the rout continued.

All the way back to Fort Jefferson the army ran, walked or stumbled as fast as each man could manage. Hardly a man had clothing unstained by his own blood and the trail they left was that of some gigantic, wounded centipede heading instinctively for refuge. St. Clair's horse plodded along with head low and body shivering, while the general himself sat hunched in dejection on the saddle. Remarkably, he had not been wounded, although in his clothing and hat were no less than eight bullet holes.

The remnants of this army began arriving at Fort Jefferson about dusk and the influx continued all through the evening. At the fort they met the most welcome sight most of them had ever seen — the return of Major Hamtramck's First Regiment. The joy was short-lived. Not only had the regiment failed to overtake any of the deserters, even though it had traveled most of the way back to Fort Washington, it had not encountered the supply train or reinforcements. So far as was known, there were no supplies and no relief on the way.

General St. Clair called a council of his surviving field officers: Colonel Darke, Colonel Sargent, Major Hamtramck, Major Zeigler and Major Gaither (of whom both Darke and the adjutant general, Colonel Sargent, were badly wounded). Together they concluded that the risks involved in trying to remain and hold on until the supplies came, if ever, were too great; they should leave here as soon as the remainder of the stragglers were in.

At 10 P.M., the army assembled in loosely joined formation. Those unable to walk were loaded upon packhorses or carried on stretchers by their companions. Thus did the army set out, traveling all night without pause. Quite a few men died en route and were buried in snow, the ground

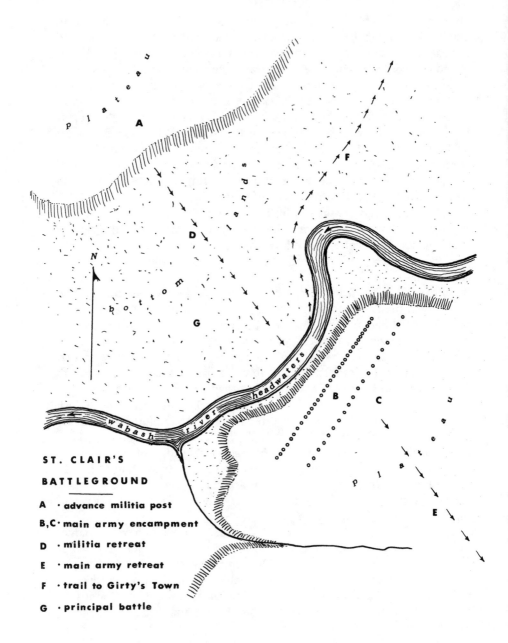

ST. CLAIR'S
BATTLEGROUND
___

A · advance militia post

B,C· main army encampment

D · militia retreat

E · main army retreat

F · trail to Girty's Town

G · principal battle

too frozen to permit a regular grave. All the food gave out and they were forced to butcher packhorses for meat.

On the third day of travel, suffering desperately from cold and hunger and more dead than alive, the army found itself south of Fort Hamilton and within eight hours' march of Fort Washington. Here, at last, they were met by the long-awaited supply train and a single company of troops — but there was little joy at the sight. Many of the men, in fact, broke down and others cursed the fresh troops and demanded to know where they had been.

It was a solemn procession indeed which finally plodded through the streets of Cincinnati. Their faces were gaunt and haunted, their eyes dazed and unseeing, their feet moving in a mechanical shuffle. There were no cheers and few tears, only a stunned and stricken silence as the residents watched the ragged remnants of the worst military disaster in the history of the young United States pass by.

The statistics alone spoke volumes: of the fifty-two officers in the battle, thirty-nine had been killed, seven wounded; of the eight hundred sixty-eight regular soldiers and militia in the battle, five hundred ninety-three were killed, two hundred fifty-seven wounded. Discounting Major Hamtrack's regiment which played no part in the battle, the final grim totals were practically beyond belief: of the nine hundred twenty men who fought on that bloody field, only twenty-four men returned uninjured; two hundred sixty-four were wounded and six hundred thirty-two were killed; plus more than two hundred camp followers who were also killed. All this compared to but sixty-six Indians killed in the same battle!

For the first time, an American frontier battle had taken on the proportions of a national disaster.

[December 31, 1791 — Saturday]

The melancholy atmosphere created by St. Clair's devastating defeat permeated the entire frontier and everything that happened in the closing days of the year seemed somehow connected with it. Most important to the Kentuckians, of course, was the fact that almost immediately following the defeat the incursions of the Indians against the settlements, particularly those along the river, became more numerous and more severe.

Few prisoners were being taken these days and settlers who had come up missing were apt to be found — a week or a fortnight or a month later — in a decomposed state in some gully or ravine or creekbed within hailing distance of their own cabins. Nor did frontier experience automatically guarantee immunity. Tobias Woods and Absalom Craig, for example, were both in their forties and both prudent frontiersmen. For five years they had run their traplines along Locust Creek. But in late November the scalpless bodies of both were discovered and there was not a frontiersman who did not shiver at the news.

As soon as word of St. Clair's defeat became known in the East, the governor-general was recalled to Philadelphia and a Congressional Committee was formed to investigate and hold a hearing at the President's request. The public, screeching for the hide of Arthur St. Clair, accused him of cowardice and bungling and worse, but George Washington knew his friend better than that; he wanted the full story told publicly so that the name of St. Clair would be cleared of blame. When he left for the East, the governor placed the command of Fort Washington under Major David Zeigler, but less than three weeks later Zeigler was summoned to Philadelphia to testify in the hearing and Lieutenant Colonel James Wilkinson, a bitter foe of George Rogers Clark, was given command of Fort Washington and its dependencies, a distinct promotion from his command of the Second United States Regiment.[4]

It was Wilkinson's outspoken belief that St. Clair had marched too far between forts; and so now he regarrisoned Fort Jefferson, which was still standing, and constructed, midway between it and Fort Hamilton, a new and sturdy installation he named Fort St. Clair.[5] In charge of the construction was Major John S. Gano, who had been at the defeat; working for him was a bright and eager new ensign, who had arrived too late at Fort Washington for the recent campaign and who was now assigned to the Tenth Regiment. His name was William Henry Harrison, a likable youth who never boasted and who, in fact, had to be asked directly before admitting that he was the son of the Benjamin Harrison who signed the Declaration of Independence, and that he knew President George Washington personally.

While the year had ended on a more satisfactory note for the Indians, there was grief in a number of the Shawnee *wegiwas* as the brave warriors lost in the victory over the *Shemanese* were mourned. The most peculiar form of mourning was that done by Chief Blue Jacket. For weeks after the battle he was silent and moody. Not even the deputation of British who came from Detroit and conferred upon him the rank of brigadier general seemed able to penetrate the gloom that enshrouded him.

With only a muttered phrase or two to his wife, Wabethe, Blue Jacket abruptly left his village on horseback and was gone for more than a week. Alone he traveled southeast to Rattlesnake Creek and traced its course to where it emptied into Paint Creek and then followed Paint thirty miles downstream to where it, in turn, emptied into the Scioto River. He crossed the larger river at the first ford and then rode down along the east bank until he reached its mouth at the Ohio River and here he turned east. He saw two boats filled with emigrants going downstream to Manchester or

Maysville or Cincinnati, but he avoided exposing himself and otherwise paid them little attention.

At length he tied his horse on a long tether at the base of a significant limestone cliff overlooking the Ohio and climbed expertly to that huge projecting shelf at the top known as Hanging Rock. Along the way he gathered an armload of sticks and tinder and on the cold bare surface of the high lookout point he built a small fire. Until it was burning well he merely squatted and gazed into the flames and then, from a small pouch around his neck, he removed the sand-colored scalp of his brother, Charley Van Swearingen.

With his knife he cut the hairpiece into small squares and individually pitched them into the fire, watching the hair singe and burn and the skin portion curl and blacken into cinder on each one before tossing in another. It took more than an hour, and when he finished the fire was low. He scattered it with a stick and, as the plume of white smoke drifted upward and dissipated in the frigid air, Blue Jacket resheathed his knife. He stood up and, with his arms crossed in front of him, looked upstream out over the broad, dark Ohio. For a long time he stood there and in his mind he was once again on that little creek bank in Virginia twenty years ago, bartering himself into Shawnee captivity for the life of his little brother. How frightened Charley had looked then and, except for growth, how remarkably little he had changed in appearance over the intervening years.

When at last the cold penetrated his reverie and he turned away from the vista below, there was a single tear on each of Blue Jacket's cheeks, the first he had shed in many years. With his foot he scuffed into space the dust and ashes and remaining embers of the little fire and then began the descent to where his horse was tied.

[*February 25, 1792 — Saturday*]

Governor-General Arthur St. Clair was exonerated.

The investigation carried out by the Congressional Committee, which was established to determine the cause of the defeat, was handled ably by the committee chairman, Virginia's James Giles. Hundreds of witnesses had been questioned and much deliberation taken and the report Giles gave to Congress was that, despite the prevailing mood of condemnation and actual detestation for St. Clair among the public, the committee believed the commanding general "was not justly liable to much censure, if any."

The report stated that St. Clair had conducted his campaign with skill and great personal bravery and that the defeat was chiefly owing to the want of discipline in the militia and to the negligence of the War Department, whose duty it was to procure and forward the provisions and military stores necessary for the expedition. The army was weakened by short allowances and desertion and by the fact that its finest fighting unit had to be sent in pursuit of the deserters. Against a force greatly superior to his own in numbers, the general had held the battlefield for an uninterrupted conflict lasting three hours, nor did he order a retreat until the field was covered with the bodies of his men and further efforts were unavailing. The general himself was last to leave the ground when retreat was ordered. And, finally, it was noted that General Arthur St. Clair "still retains the undiminished esteem and good opinion of President Washington."

But the hearings were by no means peaceful. One of the chief witnesses on behalf of St. Clair, Major David Zeigler, became so irked at the impugnment of his character and the general attitude of many of the congressmen toward the military that he resigned his commission. And not the least incensed was Secretary of War Henry Knox, who believed himself and his War Department injured by the hearing. He addressed a letter to Congress in which he complained that the committee had done him an injustice. As a result, the Congress recommitted the report to the same committee and that body, after hearing the statements and explanations of General Knox and reconsidering all of the testimony gathered, promptly rapped the Secretary's knuckles by reaffirming its first report.

Nevertheless, the damage was done. What soldiers would ever again follow into battle a man who had led his army into the worst defeat in his country's history? Exonerated or not, Arthur St. Clair's military career was finished.

[*April 3, 1792 — Tuesday*]

Excluding the great chief Blue Jacket who, as a Virginia youth, had received his early education in white schools, there was scarcely more than a handful of Shawnees who could speak English well; and among those, there was only one who could not only speak it, but read and write it with relative fluency. This was Tecumseh, and he owed the ability to two things: his insatiable hunger for knowledge and his association with Sinnanatha.

Sinnanatha — Big Fish — was, in actuality, Stephen Ruddell. He was the first captive taken by Black Hoof after the principal Shawnee chief had assumed the leadership of the tribe upon the death of Black Fish. It was in the early months of 1780 that he was taken and adopted into the tribe when Black Hoof's party returned to Chillicothe. Since he was only twelve at the time — the same age as Tecumseh — they became extremely close companions.

Ruddell adapted to Indian life well. A bright, cheerful youngster who excelled in nothing in particular, he nevertheless held his own with the other boys in the tribe. Tecumseh had become fascinated with the English tongue and worked out an arrangement whereby they would teach one another their languages — Sinnanatha making every effort to speak only in Shawnee and Tecumseh only in English, each correcting the other. None can learn so fast as a quick-minded youngster who really wants to learn and, by the end of their first year together, Tecumseh could speak English unusually well and Sinnanatha was nearly as good in the Indian tongue.

Among the plunder taken from whites, especially those emigrating downriver, books occasionally turned up. From these, Sinnanatha taught Tecumseh to read and, later still, to write. For three or four years they remained in close association, and then, as Tecumseh began accompanying Chiksika on his travels and forays, they saw less of one another. But the knowledge Tecumseh had picked up from the white youth — not only the language but much knowledge of the customs, beliefs and social structure of the whites — was always to be of benefit to him.

It was not the custom of the Shawnees to encourage captives to join war parties on raids against white settlements. But if it was the captive's own desire to go against them and the captive had been duly adopted into the tribe, it was sometimes permitted. Thus it was that when Sinnanatha asked in mid-March to be included in the horse-stealing raid into Kentucky in which Tecumseh was taking part, he was allowed to go along part way.

The party of a hundred warriors led by Chiefs Black Hoof, Black Snake and Chiuxca established a camp on the bank of Little East Fork forty miles northwest of Maysville.[6] Here they erected three huge marquee tents which had been taken as plunder from St. Clair's army. Ten warriors stayed behind at each tent, including Sinnanatha. The others, with Tecumseh riding a splendid black stallion he especially favored, crossed the Ohio River near Bullskin Creek and then separated in a half-dozen smaller parties to scour the area for any horses they could find. As soon as each of the smaller parties had gathered a good number, they were to return with them immediately to the Little East Fork campsite.

Tecumseh and his band of twelve warriors centered their activities in the area of Blue Licks, May's Lick, Washington and Maysville. When they had collected fifteen horses, most of them from the outskirts of Maysville, they set off for their initial crossing site, but not before Tecumseh had softly ripped from the wall of a cabin a notice that had been posted there. He stuffed it inside his buckskin blouse and stole away with the village inhabitants none the wiser.

The journey back to the campground was made without incident and they found that they were the last of the parties to return. A total of forty-nine horses had been captured and now there was some concern that they be on their way lest the whites, upon discovering their losses, raise a small army and trail them.

Except for the notice Tecumseh had taken from the cabin wall, the chiefs might have agreed. He had read it in the early morning light shortly after crossing the river and its contents made him feel reasonably sure they would be free from any such pursuit. It was a letter, written at Fort Washington and addressed to Colonel Lee, which Tecumseh now read:

Sir:

Wishing to spare the effusion of human blood, where it may be done consistently with the rights and interests of the nation, and moved by that humanity which distinguishes his name, the President of the United States has determined to give the misled and deluded tribes of the belligerant Indians a last opportunity to save themselves by an honorable and substantial peace.

For this purpose messages have been dispatched to the several towns with overtures of accomodation and it is deeply important, in my point of view, that whilst these overtures are pending, offensive measures should cease on the part of the United States in every quarter. It is ordered by the Honorable the Secretary of War, that you and the militia under your command do forbear all hostility other than what may be rendered necessary in your own defense, until the further pleasure of the President of the United States be made known, and govern yourself accordingly.
I have the honor to be,

> *Sir, Your most obdt., your most*
> *humble servant,*
> *James Wilkinson, Lt. Colonel,*
> *2nd U. S. Regt.; Commanding the*
> *Troops of the United States*
> *Western Department.*

When the contents of the letter were translated for the other members of the party, the chiefs were pleased and there was a general relaxing and preparations were made to spend a day or so here, eating well and resting after their labors of the past week. It was threatening to storm and none of them looked forward to herding horses a long distance in the rain. With the *Shemanese* having received such an order from their great father in the East, the chiefs agreed that there was no doubt this camp was safe from attack.

But they had not reckoned with the man they knew as Bahd-ler, the *cutta-ho-tha.*

[April 10, 1792 — Tuesday]

With many of his scouts off on patrol duty, Simon Kenton had some difficulty in rounding up sufficient men the morning after the horse thefts to follow the Indians. Only two dozen of his regular men were on hand

and, though he didn't care to, he accepted a dozen more inexperienced volunteers from Maysville.

They followed the trail to the Ohio and crossed over, going a few miles inland before setting up camp for the night. It came as no surprise to the huge frontiersman when, within minutes of crossing the Ohio, his new volunteers began fretting. What about the new order for no hostilities? When were they going to rest? What if they were ambushed? He was not altogether surprised to find, in the morning, that the twelve had sneaked away during the night, their trail leading back toward the Ohio River and Maysville. The frontiersman merely shrugged. It was better that they were gone.

Those remaining in camp mounted early and continued following the trail of the Shawnees in the moist earth. The sky was still heavily overcast, but at least it was no longer raining and the trail of so many horsemen, scarcely marred by the slight rainfall, was easy to follow. In the afternoon they heard the tinkling of a bell ahead and quickly dismounted, led their horses into hiding and concealed themselves. Moments later a horse ridden by a Shawnee brave came casually into view. The little bell was tied to the horse's neck and the Indian was chirping, apparently trying to locate a stray horse. The animal he rode was a large and beautifully proportioned black stallion.

As he came closer it became obvious he was alone and, without orders, Cornelius Washburn took aim and fired, knocking the warrior from his horse. The frontiersmen rushed up to him, and the dying Indian's eyes blazed malevolently as the whites ringed him. In Shawnee he told them that he would be avenged by Tecumseh, whose horse he had been riding. Then he died.

"Who's Tecumseh?" Washburn asked.

Simon Kenton shook his head. It was only the second time he'd ever heard the name. The first time — on that June day eight years ago — the captive Shawnee Leaning Tree had, before dying, named Chiksika and Tecumseh as the leaders of the attack on Hinkson's Fort at the mouth of Limestone Creek. He hadn't heard of him since, but now he remembered how Leaning Tree had said Tecumseh would one day do great things for the Shawnees.

Washburn took the scalp and rolled the body into the brush. When he returned to the trail the frontiersman was giving orders. Twenty-two of them were to stay here and remain at ready in case Washburn's shot had been heard. He and one volunteer would reconnoiter ahead. Knowing Kenton was angry with him for shooting, Washburn volunteered to accompany him to atone for placing them in jeopardy. Kenton nodded.

They set off afoot, still following the trail but keeping to cover, and before they had gone two miles the rain began pelting down. It was fortunate for them it did, for it drove most of the Indians into the three marquee tents and the scouts remained unseen as they peered through undercover at the encampment.

"Three, mebbe four times as many men as we got," Kenton whispered. "Mebbe more. At least they didn't hear the shot." For the better part of an hour they spied and then silently withdrew and returned to the men. Prudence indicated they should get out of there as quickly as possible and be thankful they weren't detected. The thought never entered Kenton's mind. He framed plans for an attack instead.

They would leave their mounts tied here and approach the encampment after dark. They would split into three groups of eight — Alex McIntyre and Simon's brother-in-law, Jack Dowden, to lead the right wing, Ben Whiteman and Timothy Downing to lead the center, Washburn and Kenton to lead the left. There would be no moon so they would attack about midnight and then, if they had to flee, they would have half a night's headstart before they could be followed. They would approach as near as possible to the three tents and, at Kenton's signal, fire into them simultaneously, yelling loudly at the same time. With that much of a disturbance they might succeed in making the Indians think they were a larger party and throw them into panic. If it became necessary to retreat, they would split up and each individual or small group return directly to Maysville.

It worked well, up to a point. But Simon Kenton had never before been up against Tecumseh and he was about to learn, as the whites in Tennessee already knew, that Tecumseh was wholly unpredictable and fearless.

The rain stopped about two hours after dark and by midnight the frontiersmen had worked their way to within ten yards of the tents. Abruptly an Indian came out of the shelter nearest Whiteman's wing to throw more wood on the fire. Too anxious to await Kenton's signal, Luther Calvin fired and downed him. At once the others emptied their rifles into the tenting, but the shots were staggered and Kenton realized with a sinking feeling that they sounded exactly like what they were — the shots of a small party.

Inside his tent Tecumseh came to his feet with a bound and plunged out through the flap toward the enemy screaming, "Attack! Attack! They are few!" He raced directly into Whiteman's party before any of them had an opportunity to reload and with one fierce blow of his war club, crushed Sam Barr's skull. The other men scattered as might so many quail. Warriors, rallying to Tecumseh's cries, tumbled from the tents and a general firing broke out.

Sinnanatha, almost matching Tecumseh's speed, raced out of the left tent, thrust his rifle against Kenton's chest and jerked the trigger, but it was only a flash in the pan and both men, shaken, darted off in opposite directions in the darkness.

What firing was being done had little effect, and it became obvious to Kenton that they were in serious trouble. He raised his voice in a great bellow, giving the word to scatter. Kenton and Joe Lemon, sensing they were cut off from their horses, slipped stealthily toward the east. Others fanned out similarly to west and south, none making the mistake of following the trail back to where their horses were, knowing this was the first avenue the Shawnees would check. A number of the men were able to get together after a short distance and this group — eleven men led by Washburn — struck off at a fast pace to the southeast, avoiding any trails and wading up or downstream at every little rivulet for a hundred yards or so to throw off trackers.

Only one man angled back toward where the horses had been tied. Little red-headed Alex McIntyre had no intention of leaving that fine black stallion behind. He eased his way along and practically bumped into the black horse before he saw it. Holding the bridle close to the animal's head with one hand and cupping the other over its nostrils, he led it away. He congratulated himself on his cleverness and caution, but he was not cautious enough. The rainfall had smoothed the ground they had ridden over earlier and now, though he could not see them in the darkness, both he and his horse left a trail which, until he left the path, was clear enough for even the most inexperienced tracker to find.

As this whole expedition had turned out to be, it was a serious mistake.

[April 11, 1792 — Wednesday]

The Shawnees had come out of the fight in remarkably good shape under the circumstances. Besides the brave killed while riding Tecumseh's horse and the one slain by Calvin as he tended the fire, the burst of gunfire into the tents had only killed one other Indian, although several received wounds, none of them serious.

Undeniably, the alacrity with which the warriors had answered Tecumseh's cry averted what might well have been a terrible loss. There was no possibility whatever of following the *Shemanese* until daylight and Tecumseh felt grudging admiration for the leader of the whites in selecting such a time and method of attack with so small a party. It was the type of audacity he appreciated and the kind of attack he himself might have led.

In the ominous stillness shortly following the exodus of the whites, Black Hoof, Black Snake and Chiuxca met in brief council. Should they follow in the morning and possibly overtake and capture or kill some of these whites, or would they be walking into a trap by doing so? Suppose these men had merely been the advance scouting party of another army like Harmar's or St. Clair's?

Prudence ruled and it was decided to break camp at once and head north. Tecumseh was praised for his coolness and ferocity under fire and when he asked to be allowed to remain behind with a dozen or so warriors to see, in the morning, if they could find any of the attackers, his daring was admired and his request approved. A dozen young braves, including Sinnanatha, were placed under his command.

Within the hour the main body of Indians pulled out, each of the stolen horses tethered behind an individual rider to prevent their breaking away and becoming lost in the darkness of this cloudy night. Tecumseh and his handful of men found a defensible hollow and crouched there alertly until dawn streaked the eastern sky.

Their first move upon leaving the camp area astride horses of their own was to backtrack along their trail from the Ohio River. They heard the tied horses stamping and snorting before they saw them. They eased up quietly and saw that no one had returned to take them. It was a good sign, for it meant the whites had no help coming behind them, but still they remained alert. Tecumseh ranged a little farther along the trail and suddenly exclaimed. Not only had he discovered the trail of one of the men, but a slight indentation in the right rear hoofmark indicated the horse he was leading to be Tecumseh's own treasured black.

Ordering Sinnanatha and two of the warriors to accompany him and the others to remain here to hobble the twenty-four horses so they could graze, he took up the trail at a rapid pace. It angled slightly to the southwest.

Fifteen miles ahead, weary from lack of sleep and very hungry, Alexander McIntyre had stopped and was building a little fire to cook the heel of bacon he had carried in his pouch. Since he had been able to ride rather than walk, he was certain that of all the men in the party, he was the last who would be followed. He was wrong.

The four Shawnees were coming toward him on foot less than forty feet away before he saw them. Instantly he dropped the greasy bacon rind, snatched up his rifle and ran as he had never run before. But the shortness of his stride betrayed him and he realized they were catching up. He stopped and wheeled about with his gun leveled and immediately Sinnanatha and the two braves darted behind trees. Not Tecumseh.

The Shawnee put on a burst of speed and as McIntyre's greasy hands slid on the gun and fumbled for a fatal instant, he threw himself upon the man and bowled him over, the gun going off in the air. The frontiersman was no match for the Indian. In an instant he was on his back and Tecumseh's knife was poised at his throat. McIntyre had the good sense to know when to quit.

His hands were tied behind him and he was lifted onto the horse Tecumseh had ridden here which had been brought up at once by one of the braves in the party. As Sinnanatha held the bridle, Tecumseh strode back to McIntyre's little camp and untied the black stallion. He patted its nose and let it nuzzle his hand before leaping to its back and rejoining his companions.

On the way back to the others, Tecumseh questioned McIntyre in English. The redhead said little, but at Tecumseh's evident admiration for the boldness of the attack and his curiosity as to whom their leader had been, he admitted that it was Simon Kenton. Tecumseh frowned, failing to recognize the name, but when McIntyre added that Kenton had once been prisoner of the Shawnees at Chillicothe and escaped, and that at the time he was known by the name of Butler, a faint smile touched Tecumseh's lips.

"Bahd-ler," he said, nodding. "I am pleased that it was such a great warrior as the *cut-ta-ho-tha*. He is a worthy enemy and someday I will meet him again. Soon, I think."

"Get ready to die if you do," McIntyre said sourly.

After that they rode in silence. When they arrived where the others waited beside their own horses, they were met with delighted hoots as the warriors caught sight of the black horse and the red-headed prisoner. Despite Tecumseh's assurances to the contrary, they had been worried that the whites would return for their horses and attack them. Relief was more than apparent in their voices at Tecumseh's return and they chattered like excited children as he tied McIntyre to a tree. Was there nothing this Tecumseh couldn't do?

But when the leader ordered them to round up the now somewhat scattered horses, the fear came back. Suppose, they said, the *Shemanese* had crept up in the woods and were waiting for them to split up? Why not just leave the horses and go home?

Tecumseh snorted. "What frightened sparrows! I see here no future leaders of the Shawnees. Stay together and tremble if you like. I will get the horses."

He started away and Sinnanatha joined him. The others were chagrined, but the fear they felt was stronger than the shame and they remained where they were. In a moment Tecumseh and Sinnanatha had disappeared into the woods. Their job wasn't easy. Although the hobbles did not permit the horses to move very rapidly, they had spread out considerably to find graze in these woods and it took the better part of an hour to locate and gather them and lead them back. They were unprepared for the sight which met them on their return.

From a pole stuck in the ground at the center of the trail, Alex McIntyre's scalpless head stared sightlessly at them. On another pole close by his still-dripping heart was impaled. His arm and legs had been hacked off and his body cut in two just under the rib cage and these six grotesque pieces were hung with rawhide strips from tree limbs overhanging the trail.

Tecumseh's gaze went one by one over the pieces and by the time he looked back at his men his expression had become one of great rage. When he spoke his voice was low, almost a hiss, trembling with the anger behind it.

"Cowards! Rabbits! You are not Shawnees. No! You are not even men. You are worse than the carrion birds. You disgust me with your cruelty. Are your hearts so weak? Is there no room for pity in them? Are you so afraid of your enemy that you must kill and mutilate him when he is tied and helpless in your grasp? Is this what our chiefs have taught you of courage? To destroy the weak or those unable to defend themselves? This is not courage. No! This is cowardice of the worst kind. I am ashamed for you. I am ashamed of you. And I am most of all ashamed that you are of my people!"

As if they were physical blows, the men winced at the words. They could not hold Tecumseh's cold gaze, nor could they speak, knowing what he said was true. Tecumseh stared in silence at them for a long while and finally spoke again, his voice less outraged but even colder than before.

"We will go home now where you will be safe from enemies, whether they are bound or not. Ride behind me at all times that I will not have to look upon you. It will be our last ride together. I will not bear the company of cowards."

[*April 12, 1792 — Thursday*]

George Washington was not idle in Philadelphia. He still hoped that the difficulties between the Indians and whites could be settled amicably. To carry this hope to its greatest lengths, he had personally dispatched emissaries to the chiefs of the various tribes — men such as Colonel John Hardin, who had been sent to see Chief Black Hoof of the Shawnees — with instructions to make one last strong effort to establish a truly binding peace treaty. They were to be friendly but firm. They were to let it be known in subtle fashion that while the hand the whites now extended contained a piece offering, there was another hand out of sight which gripped a club.

If these peace negotiations failed there were to be no more half measures. To succeed Arthur St. Clair, Washington had appointed Anthony Wayne to the rank of major general, giving him command of the United States Army and placing him in charge of the Indian Wars. If another campaign was to develop, it must be one which would wipe away the bitter memories of past disasters, one that must succeed. Brilliant and dashing, Wayne was considered rash and erratic by many — so much so that currently everyone called him by the name his troops had bestowed upon him during the Revolution, Mad Anthony. Nevertheless, he had already proven himself a great officer and he was the only reasonable choice.

Wayne was given a year in which to build up his army and it was to be a strong, well-disciplined force. It was to be enlarged from two to five regiments, and he was to gather and train his men at Logstown on the Ohio River sixteen miles below Pittsburgh. He was to recruit twenty-five hundred new men in the vicinity of Pittsburgh and prepare to move them as fully trained troops to Fort Washington by next spring.

This appointment of Mad Anthony was cheered by many, but for some it was cause for great consternation. The British minister to the United States, George Hammond, wrote a nervous letter to the Canadian lieutenant governor, General John Graves Simcoe, in which he observed:

General Wayne is unquestionably the most active, vigilant, and enterprising Officer in the American Service, and will be tempted to use every exertion to justify the expectations of his countrymen and to efface the Stain which the late defeat has cast upon the American Arms.

[*June 4, 1792 — Monday*]

There was good cause indeed for the jubilation rippling through Kentucky and not even the continued savage onslaughts of the Shawnees could dim it. Today was the end of a long period of dissension which had begun with that first meeting on December 27, 1784, when the matter of separating from Virginia and becoming one of the States was first formally considered.

It had been difficult to reach agreement on what the constitution of the planned state should be and during this interval, while ten conventions were held, the United States Constitution was written and ratified. Many reasons for separation were discussed at these conventions in Danville: objections to Virginia taxes, inability of Kentuckians to adapt Virginia laws to local situations, the refusal of Virginia to permit Kentuckians to pursue Indians beyond the Ohio River, and the fact that all cases appealed to higher courts had to be carried all the way back to Richmond for trial.

Some of the residents demanded that Kentucky simply become an independent state and have nothing to do with the Union. There were those who wished it to become a part of the Spanish empire. Others even wanted to remain a part of Virginia. But the loudest cries and most telling arguments were those for recognition as one of the states of the Union.

The long, bitter struggle finally came to an end at last with the framing, in April, of the Kentucky Constitution, which was modeled after the United States Constitution. Three days ago the wonderful news had exploded across the frontier — Kentucky was admitted into the Union as a state in her own right. And today at Lexington in a temporary statehouse constructed of logs — the Sheaf of Wheat Tavern — the legislature met for its first session and chose, by common consent, Isaac Shelby as governor.

[*December 31, 1792 — Wednesday*]

The peace overtures by the President came to exactly nothing. In some cases the Indians had even refused to discuss possible negotiations and in those cases where they did hear the emissary out, they were scornful of the proposals. What fools did the *Shemanese* think the Indians were? How many times in the past had they listened to such proposals? How many times had they agreed, only to find themselves pushed farther back, their land taken, their game destroyed?

In a few cases the refusals were extreme. In September, traveling under his flag of truce and trying to find the whereabouts of Catahecassa — Black Hoof — to propose peace with the Shawnees, Colonel John Hardin was met by a small party of that tribe.

It was, they said, late afternoon and still a long ride to where Chief Black Hoof was. If he would camp with them tonight they would take him to their chief on the morrow. And so Hardin had stayed with them; but, for him, there was no morrow. During the night a tomahawk crashed into his temple and his scalp was lifted, his body stripped and thrown unceremoniously into a prairie three miles west of the Shawnee village on the banks of the Great Miami River.[7]

During the summer, disregarding the continuing Indian peril, Connecticut blandly gave a half million acres of the western portion of her Western Reserve lands for the benefit of citizens who had suffered by the spoilations of the British during the Revolutionary War. This grant of seven hundred eighty-one square miles was to be distributed among the one thousand eight hundred seventy residents of nine Connecticut towns who had "suffered by fire." Thus, the tract became known as The Fire Lands.

At the moment there was no hostile activity going on here, but elsewhere the attacks grew worse. As usual, Kentucky suffered most. The attacks on boats, which had fallen off somewhat since that peak period when the John May, Jacob Greathouse and Elijah Strong parties had been exterminated, now increased again. It became unsafe for individuals to leave the confines of Columbia or Cincinnati and a dozen or more people were killed and as many captured on the few miles of road that led between the two towns.

But the final act which convinced the President that there could be no further hope for peace was the attack on the United States Army supply train of a hundred mounted riflemen escorting a similar number of packhorses between Fort Jefferson and Fort Hamilton. The attack, led by Little Turtle and Blue Jacket, took place at what was called the Forty Foot Pitch, just seven miles east of Fort St. Clair.[8] The Indian force of two hundred fifty warriors had been on its way to attack Columbia when it captured a fatigue party near Fort Hamilton cutting wood for an extension of that fort under Colonel Wilkinson's orders. Fourteen soldiers were killed and many of the prisoners were tortured.

It was the last important attack of the year and an aura of expectation now gathered along the frontier. Word had come that soon Wayne's army would be descending the Ohio to Fort Washington and that this would be the beginning of the end of Kentucky's Indian troubles.

The Kentuckians breathed a collective sigh of relief in anticipation of this event. Things looked bright for the newest state. And on December 8, the Kentucky Legislature, after considering a number of sites — including Danville, Harrodsburg, Stanford and Lexington — finally chose as the new state capital the centrally located Kentucky River town of Frankfort.

[*February 8, 1793 — Friday*]

At eighty-two, Mary Kenton was still a spry, self-possessed woman; thus, when the time neared for Simon's wife to bear her third child, she considered it her duty to be on hand to render assistance. With a kiss for her daughter, Nancy, with whom she had lived so long on Scott River, she bundled herself into a rickety wagon and with characteristic competence traveled alone all the way to the large red brick building which marked the center of Kenton's Station. Here she would stay until after the baby was born.

To Mary's way of thinking, Martha and Simon had been mismatched from the start. Martha's complaints that Simon was something less than a good father were undoubtedly justified, but this was something she should have considered before marrying him. It was no use wishing he could be like other men — farming his land and helping her raise his children — for Simon was not that kind of man. Admittedly he was a good provider and to some people's way of thinking, a wealthy man with a fortune rumored to be in the tens of thousands of dollars — a fortune which continued to grow each time he sold more of his tomahawk-claimed land to new settlers. The household actually lacked nothing of significance where material goods were concerned. No, what made Simon less than an admirable father and husband were his frequent and almost always unannounced absences.

At a moment's notice he would be up and away on an exploratory trip or a campaign or a retaliatory raid or a chase after raiding Indians. There was rarely a good-bye or even any realization he was gone until he failed to show up. No one could know the misery Martha lived through at such times. On that raid he took after the horses on the Little East Fork, everyone thought sure that he and Joe Lemon had been killed or taken captive because, with the exception of Alex McIntyre who had never come back, they were the last to return to Maysville, coming in ten days after the others.

Nor could Martha overcome the resentment she felt at his treatment of the children; he just didn't seem to want to be bothered with them. In fact — and this was getting down to the crux of the matter, the knowledge that galled her most — he showed far more interest in his ten-year-old bastard son, Simon Ruth Kenton, still living at Quick's Run, than in his own legal youngsters. Ruth Calvin had unashamedly told her son that Simon Kenton was his father. The boy idolized the frontiersman and the rare occasions when the man stopped by for an hour or so were the high points of his young life.

Mary arrived none too soon at her son's station. In the early morning hours of February 8, 1793, exactly ten years to the day after the birth of Simon Ruth, the frontiersman's new child was born — a heavy, healthy, squalling boy with an unusual amount of hair on his head exactly the same auburn color as his father's.

Simon was pleased, there was no doubt of it, and his pride was evident when he announced that the baby would be named Simon Kenton, Junior.

[*April 5, 1793 — Friday*]

Lying beside Sutawnee on one side was her father, White Wolf, and on the other side her husband, Stand-in-Water. Both were sleeping deeply, but for Sutawnee sleep would not come. She lay propped on one elbow and stared into the dying flames of the campfire. Paint Creek, rippling over the shallow ford less than a quarter mile upstream from Little Coppras Mountain, gave forth a comforting sound that lulled her into a sort of reverie.[9] How badly she had wanted to accompany these thirty warriors on this hunting expedition, and how sad she was now that Chief Sco-tach had permitted it.

In recent years, since it had become highly perilous to cross over the Spay-lay-wi-theepi to hunt, few Shawnee women had been taken along into the Can-tuc-kee lands; indeed, Sutawnee had believed she would never see the old hunting grounds again. But finally they had relented, and she had no doubt this would be her last opportunity to see it. For the same thought that had settled in many of the warriors had touched her, too; with the news that Kentucky had officially become one of the Fires of the American Union, any hope her tribe had harbored of reclaiming it was gone. The Thawegilas and Kispokothas and Peckuwes who had migrated across the Mississippi fourteen years ago had apparently been right after all. Obviously the Chalahgawthas and Maykujays had been deluding themselves all these years with the belief they'd eventually drive the *Shemanese* from their hunting grounds. But at least the hope had been there — like a driving force that kept them going. Now, even that hope was gone. Perhaps that was why Sutawnee's father had persuaded their lean old chief, Sco-tach, to let her come along this time. Had it really been twenty summers ago since she had crossed the great Spay-lay-wi-theepi and seen the tremendous herds of elk and buffalo and deer? How wonderful it would be to look upon them one last time.

But it wasn't wonderful after all. Everything had changed. Not one elk or buffalo had they seen, and where deer had once been everywhere, they saw just two — highly skittish animals which bounded away when hardly within sight. Only one black bear was seen and no panthers or wolves. And where there had been beautiful unbroken forests and canelands and prairies, now there were plowed fields and roads, cabins and towns, even a considerable number of the strange large buildings of a new type, built of regular-sized, flat, red stones fitted together into impressive and virtually impregnable walls.

The warriors had felt the same perplexity and anger over the absence of game as she. Indeed, the frustration of the hunt had set them on edge and when, as they moved back toward the Ohio River, they found the little six-cabin settlement of Morgan's Station, their hatred of the whites became a living force needing expression. They had attacked, killing several men and burning the cabins. Five horses were taken, too, and immediately they had recrossed the Spay-lay-wi-theepi and moved deep into the Ohio country before that tracking devil of a white man, Bahd-ler, could be notified and take up the trail.

Sutawnee's thoughts turned to the white man again, as they had off and on over all these years. The *Cut-ta-ho-tha* had made a lasting impression on her; even after fifteen years she could remember as yesterday how he had been strong with heat for her and had kissed and fondled her so hungrily in the Chillicothe *wegiwa*. How she had been tempted then to help him escape, and how afraid! She had felt guilty of her thoughts then and spoke to no one of them. Later, when her father told her stories of his childhood — not as White Wolf but as a white boy named John Ward — she was glad she hadn't, certain that this sympathy she had experienced for Bahd-ler was a manifestation of her white blood and something of which to be ashamed. Yet, there had been many white prisoners before and after Bahd-ler, but never one quite like him. Sheltowee, the one the whites called Boone, was similar — but not the same. No one had been quite like Bahd-ler.

(*At this instant, fifty yards or so from Sutawnee, Simon Kenton silently moved his party of thirty-two men into position for the attack, thankful for the gurgling of the nearby Paint Creek riffle which overrode the sound of their approach. He had split the group in three; Captains Joshua Baker and James Ward and their men had been sent over to the left, Captains Nathaniel Massie and Mike Cassidy and their men to the right, Kenton, Washburn, Whiteman, Ireland and six others in the center.*)

Between Sutawnee and her sleeping father, one of the camp dogs suddenly stood and cocked his head, then growled softly. She reached out and patted him and spoke gently and, as the dog settled back to where it had been, Sutawnee threw back her blanket and arose. The fire was getting low. She moved to the pile of firewood collected earlier and refueled the little blaze. As new flames blossomed from the wood, the whole camp was thrown into flickering outline.

(*Captain James Ward watched the silhouetted figure near the fire and carefully brought his rifle to bear. His finger was tightening on the trigger when Moses Fowler suddenly tapped his shoulder and whispered, "Captain, it's a woman!" Ward looked closely and, as the figure turned sideways to him, saw the outline of ample breasts under her buckskin and lowered his rifle, unaware that he had just come within a hairsbreadth of killing his own niece.*)

Sutawnee lay down again and covered herself; sleepiness came upon her at last and she drifted off. The fire continued to burn brightly and the dog that had stood up before aroused again, stretched and ambled over toward the creek. It paused for leg-lifting rituals at two shrubs and a tree and then a wafting breeze brought to its nose an alien scent; to its ears now came the faint popping of a twig and its hackles stood erect and it began barking loudly as it ran back to the camp.

White Wolf — John Ward — awakened and grunted at the dog to be quiet. When it did not, he got to his feet and picked up his rifle. It was the same weapon he had used nineteen years ago in the battle of Point Pleasant and with which he had unwittingly slain his own father. He kicked at the dog to silence it and cocked his own head to listen more closely. At that instant a dozen or more guns were trained on him.

(*On Simon Kenton's orders, as long as the Indians remained unaware of their presence, no guns were to be fired and no attack made until dawn. When the warriors arose and squatted in a group around the fire, a single fusillade might enable them to wipe out the majority of them at once. But Joshua Baker was an impatient man and one who could not follow orders well. He passed the word to his men to fire on the count of three. James Ward, knowing the majority would aim at the broad chest, himself aimed a head shot, again unaware that the figure at which he was aiming was his own brother, whom he scarcely even remembered.*)

The explosions came with frightening unexpectedness. As if a huge hand had slapped him, Sutawnee's father was slammed backwards off his feet and crumpled lifelessly. Instantly the other Indians sprang up as more shots came. Stand-in-Water pitched his blanket over the flames — a trick he had learned from the stories of Tecumseh's exploits — and in the darkness snatched Sutawnee's hand and led her to a protected spot.

(*The whites dodged for cover as a scattering of wild shots came their way from the Indians. Joseph Jones of Baker's party did not move swiftly* enough. A bullet ripped into his chest, tore through his heart and passed out his back. He fell without a word.)

Chief Sco-tach gave his braves the word to begin a move to the east across the large bottomland where, behind them, the great horseshoe course of Paint Creek at this point intercepted again. Here they would mount and ride, taking no risk of trying to save anything except themselves and the horses. The maneuver went well, even though the whites followed them slowly and continued an intermittent shooting. Just as light began to break in the east the Indians reached the other side of the bottom, leaped to their horses and thundered off to the northeast. A few futile shots were thrown their way but they escaped and no pursuit was attempted.

(Simon Kenton was furious at the failure of the attack through the disobedience of Baker and his men, but there was no help for it now. Who knew but what the Shawnees might return quickly with a hundred men or more from a nearby village or camp? There was no time to waste. He ordered the little camp plundered and a hasty withdrawal made. Since they had no spade, they tied the body of Jones high in a tree to keep it from being found and mutilated by returning warriors.)

Already several miles away and still riding rapidly on a gradually swinging curve toward the northeast, Sutawnee clung to the mane of her horse as it was led by Stand-in-Water. Blinding tears streamed from her eyes. Her grief was deep enough with the knowledge that her father had been killed, but the thought of his body having to be left behind to be mutilated by the whites was almost too much to be borne.

(Baker's party gathered around the body of the Shawnee and an argument broke out among them as to who had killed him, since, of all the guns that had fired, only one bullet had struck him, and that one directly between the eyes.

"None of you men shot him," Fowler exclaimed. "It was our captain who shot him."

At this Ward turned to him and shook his head. "Moses, you're as damned a fool as the rest. How can you know who shot him when there were twelve or fifteen fired and only one ball struck him?"

But Ward knew. No one objected when he unsheathed his knife and bent to remove the scalp.)

[June 7, 1793 — Friday]

At their first meeting, Simon Kenton liked the looks of Major General Anthony Wayne. Here was the type of man whom he would gladly serve in battle — a man with as much or more of the restless look about him of a fighter as George Rogers Clark had shown before he took to drink. Here was a man with the ability to comprehend and take action swiftly and accurately upon the most meager of information, a rigid disciplinarian who demanded and got the utmost respect and obedience from all his men, privates to field officers.

It had been quite an occasion when Wayne and his army of twenty-five hundred had arrived at Cincinnati two months ago today and met there the thousand volunteers raised by General Scott in Kentucky. There was nowhere near enough room for them all at Fort Washington, and so a huge campground was established nearby on the only level treeless section available. With the characteristic humor he displayed in most situations, Wayne named this open headquarters Hobson's Choice and began at once a thorough training of the volunteers. They were instructed in the meaning of commands, were given close-order drill, and learned to obey immediately and without question any order given by a superior officer. In a remarkably short time, they were welded into a powerful fighting force.

When Simon Kenton came to meet Wayne for the first time, he was shown into the general's quarters by his new aide-de-camp, Ensign William Henry Harrison. The general, apparently well informed about Kenton, as he seemed to be on all matters concerning Kentucky, Ohio, settlers and Indians, shook the frontiersman's hand warmly and was sincere in his delight at meeting the individual whom many people had already told him was the most remarkable Indian fighter, scout and spy ever spawned on the frontier.

"General," Kenton said, "if I'm allowed to select them, I'll provide you with a hundred of the best spies you've ever come across for your expedition."

"Mr. Kenton," Wayne said in reply, "it is a bargain, provided that you accept the rank of major and command the spy company as well as becoming my personal advance scout for the campaign."

The agreement was mutual.

[*December 31, 1793 — Tuesday*]

With the new Fort Greenville erected as winter quarters just five miles north of St. Clair's ineffectual little Fort Jefferson, the army settled down to more drill and discipline under Mad Anthony Wayne.[10] It was a much better and more defensible fort than St. Clair had built; a good stockade encompassing fifty acres, within which were erected sufficient log huts for all the men and around which a defensive ditch, virtually a waterless moat, was dug. Anthony Wayne was a man who left little to Providence.

The army had marched from Cincinnati to Fort Hamilton on October 12 and encamped on the same ground where St. Clair had camped two years before, nearly to the day. While they didn't know it immediately, they had begun the march just in time. Two days after their departure a severe smallpox epidemic struck Fort Washington, felling a third of the garrison left there. And for the first newspaper to be printed north of the

Ohio River — edited and published in Cincinnati by William Maxwell and called *The Centinel of the Northwestern Territory* — the epidemic and the expedition were practically the only two items of news meriting coverage. The appearance of this paper had the effect of providing almost as much of a feeling of security to the residents as did the might of Anthony Wayne's army.

Wayne stayed only a brief time at Fort Hamilton and then marched on to Fort Jefferson, arriving there on November 9. Finding the fort much too small and ill-placed for defensive measures, he had begun the construction of Fort Greenville, naming it after his fellow officer of the Revolution, General Nathaniel Greene.

Simon Kenton, with one of the finest corps of scouts and spies ever assembled, ranged far in all directions, having small skirmishes, taking prisoners and killing just about as many Indians as were brought in. Without rivals in the army, they competed with themselves, aiming in each excursion to outdo their former exploits. They were a proud and arrogant group, convinced of their own invulnerability and basking in the adulation of the rank and file.

Simon, however, did not lose his perspective. His wariness increased rather than abated and the scraping of a moccasin or click of a gunlock or whisper of a knife sliding out of a sheath was enough to snap him out of any slumber, regardless of his weariness.

But when General Wayne announced that Fort Greenville was to be the winter headquarters and the army would not resume the march until early summer when the weather was more propitious, Simon was disappointed. If the weather would be hard on them, a well-equipped and well-supplied army, how much more so would it be on the Indians? The time to attack, he felt, was now. The building of forts interested him not at all and when, after the completion of Fort Greenville in mid-December, Wayne announced that he would now begin construction of a fortress he would call Fort Recovery on the site of St. Clair's defeat, Kenton's discontent turned into depression.

Wayne, with a good understanding of human nature, recognized the signs in his chief scout. He sympathized with him and yet was far too good a general to be coaxed, bulldogged or prodded into offensive measures until he was altogether ready and conditions were as he desired them. Nor was Kenton the only one spoiling for action. Major Robert McMahon, a regular, also chafed at the inactivity and it was at this point that Wayne gave Kenton and his mounted scouts, along with McMahon and a force of three hundred unmounted men, permission to "go out toward Lake Erie until you find something to fight."

They found it. Near the mouth of the Auglaize, while scouting ahead with a small detachment, Kenton found enough sign to convince him that an overwhelming number of Indians was gathered ahead of them, against whom his own and McMahon's men must certainly suffer defeat. Riding back to the officer's force, he told the major what he had found and McMahon was all for attacking these Indians at once. If they didn't, what kind of sarcastic reception would they get from the other troops when they returned? But Kenton shook his head. His instinct for caution was something rarely ignored and right now it was screaming at him that such a plan was both foolhardy and dangerous.

"I don't like the looks of things, Major," he said. "I think we ought to go back with this information and forget about fighting for now. If you insist on fighting, we'll join you on one condition only: if flight becomes necessary, I will order my men to retreat. And being mounted, they must therefore leave your men far in the rear."

McMahon, though anxious for action, was no fool. He slept on this and the next morning agreed to turn back. As expected, there was some ridicule upon their return about not having entered into battle, but Wayne complimented them on their wisdom and congratulated them for being good soldiers who mixed caution with courage.

The detachment Wayne had sent forward to begin the construction of Fort Recovery arrived at the site of St. Clair's defeat on Christmas Day and met a horrible sight. Their tents were pitched on the battlefield and before they could lie down in them they had to scrape together the scattered bones and carry them outside. The next day holes were dug and the bones remaining above ground were buried, including six hundred human skulls. After this grim duty was performed, the new fort was built and on its completion one company of artillerymen and one of riflemen were left there while the rest returned to Fort Greenville.

Anthony Wayne's preparations for war did not, however, deter him from continued efforts at establishing peace with the Indians. He dispatched a dozen men or more under flags of truce to the tribes, offering peace or, if the Indians refused, total annihilation. As with George Washington's efforts, such messages were generally scorned and in a few instances the messengers never returned.

Both Indians and British remained apprehensive about Wayne's preparations for war. A great council of the confederated tribes of the Northwest and of twenty-seven tribes of Canada met with American representatives under the watchful eyes of the British and in the protection of their fort at Detroit. Negotiations broke down. Soon after that another conference was held at the Rapids of the Maumee and it also failed. It all came down to a basically insoluble problem: the Indians claimed the right to the Northwest Territory and the Americans refused to recognize that claim.

There was a good reason why the Indians were deaf to peace proposals offered now. They had defeated Harmar decisively and St. Clair devastatingly. Why would they not be able to do so with Wayne, especially if Little Turtle and Blue Jacket should again lead them? But for once Little Turtle was hesitant. He did not think it wise to oppose Wayne and urged that the confederation try to reach some peaceable compromise with the whites. That the great chief of the Miamis should speak thus was a shock to them and several of the lesser chiefs at once accused Little Turtle of becoming too old and of being a coward. Surprisingly, he did not take great offense at this. Instead he raised his hands for silence and spoke solemnly:

"We have beaten the enemy twice under separate commanders. We cannot expect the same good fortune always. The Americans are now led by a chief who never sleeps. The night and the day are alike to him and during all the time that he has been marching on our villages, notwithstanding the watchfulness of our young men, we have never been able to surprise him. There is something whispers to me that it would be prudent to listen to his offers of peace."

The discussions continued but it was obvious that now, although Little Turtle bowed to the will of the majority of chiefs and said he would fight if it was their desire, the chief of the Miamis would not be the commander-in-chief of this forthcoming battle. The Indians needed a man proven in warfare and leadership; a man with strength and cunning and ferocity; a man who had the respect not only of his own tribe, but all the other tribes. And they had just such a man.

Unanimously, Blue Jacket was appointed as commander-in-chief of the Indian forces.

[December 31, 1794 — Wednesday]

Peace!

A permanent peace at last. It was hard to believe that the Indian Wars were over forever; that from now on, so it was claimed, there would never again be Indian onslaughts into Kentucky; that Ohio River travelers would, for the first time, be safe from attack; that the settlement of the Ohio Country could now continue without harassment from hostile Indians.

There were those, of course, who disbelieved the "permanent peace" claims. Simon Kenton was one of these. True, the Indians had been soundly whipped; they were begging for peace, and preliminary treaties with General Wayne had already been agreed upon and the final papers of peace would be signed next summer. But, Simon predicted darkly, treaties had been made before — if the whites didn't break this one, then the Indians would. In either case, sooner or later there would be more strife on the frontier.

For Simon it had come as a severe blow when he had been forced to accept a discharge from the army before the battle lines had even been drawn. Early in the year the same swamp fever that had plagued him for years returned with terrible results. For over a week he hovered on the brink of death and even after the crisis had passed the fever recurred time and again in the ensuing weeks, making him unfit for any kind of duty. He lost a great deal of weight and fumed at the weakness which enveloped him so that it became tiring even to stand up and walk a few steps.

For weeks he had been cared for by a pleasant young private named Andrew McConnell, and when it became apparent to General Wayne that Major Simon Kenton was no longer physically able to participate in the planned expedition, the ailing frontiersman was given his discharge and the young private ordered to see him safely back to Kentucky.

Simon was so grateful to the youth that upon their return he gave him a hundred fine acres of land from his fourteen-hundred-acre tract on Elkhorn Creek near Georgetown and McConnell dreamed grand dreams of the wonderful estate he would build there one day. Because it seemed unimportant to Simon, the frontiersman said nothing of the litigation he had been involved in over this very land since 1788. He had no doubt but that it was his land to do with as he pleased and giving a chunk of it to this young man who befriended him gave him pleasure.

News of events to the north came with surprising regularity. Anthony Wayne had established a good line of communications between his army and Fort Washington and the news that came was good indeed, all year long. Shortly after construction of Fort Recovery, Peter Loramie's trading post was burned at Wayne's order and Loramie ordered to leave the country and cease, on penalty of death, his dealings with the Indians.

More than ever the British alarm over Wayne's presence and plans grew. It was the consensus at Detroit that the goal of the "Mad General" was Detroit itself; and so, in April, Lieutenant Governor John Graves Simcoe, accompanied by a staff of expert Indian agents, military officers and engineers, left Detroit and sailed downriver, across Lake Erie and then up the Maumee River to the foot of the rapids.[11] There, on the north bank near the ruins of the old British fort abandoned at the close of the Revolution, where agent Alexander McKee currently maintained a trading post, Simcoe ordered a fort built and manned, in distinct violation of the British-American treaty, to block Wayne's advance and protect Detroit. He named it Fort Miami after the Maumee River, which was also known as the Miami of the Lake. Almost immediately there was an influx of Indians to the King's Store in the fort to receive free arms and ammunition for the coming affray.

Throughout the spring Wayne's force continued to grow. His army of two thousand regulars and fifteen hundred mounted Kentucky volunteers was increased in April by the arrival of little Mike Cassidy leading his own company of mounted Kentucky riflemen and again in July with the arrival of General Scott and another sixteen hundred drafted Kentuckians.

The single bad news report came in late June. When a white renegade named Harry May deserted the Indians and brought word to General Wayne of a force of Indians moving toward Fort Recovery to take it, Wayne sent Major McMahon with a company of men and supplies as reinforcements. But the attack came sooner than expected, before the detachment reached the fort, and a hot battle was waged during which McMahon was killed. It was Blue Jacket, supported by McKee, who led the attack. But Wayne had built his fort well and the walls were not breached. After two days the Indians picked up their dead and left as quickly as they had come.

Finally, on July 28, Wayne took up the march. They went directly to Fort Laramie, then due north to the Auglaize River which was followed downstream toward the Maumee. The spies brought encouraging reports of the Indians fleeing from their Auglaize and Maumee villages and when Wayne arrived at the junction of the two streams, he immediately built another fort. It was completed in eight days and, after surveying its block-houses, pickets, ditches and fascines, Wayne exclaimed, "I defy the English, Indians and all the devils in Hell to take it!"

General Scott, standing at Wayne's side, remarked, "Then call it Fort Defiance."[12] And Wayne did so.

Harry May, the renegade who had deserted the Indians to join Wayne, was recaptured by the Shawnees just after their arrival there and taken to where the principal Indian encampment was located. Here were represented the Seven Nations under Blue Jacket's command — Shawnees, Delawares, Potawatomies, Miamis, Ottawas, Chippewas and Senecas — and here May was tied to a tree and a mark was made on his bare chest. Fifty Indians with flintlocks fanned out in a semicircle and at a command from Blue Jacket all fired simultaneously. No more damage could have been done to the captive had he been struck full in the breast with an eight-pounder cannonball.

Wayne continued his march down the Maumee and at a place called Roche de Boeuf erected some light fortifications as a place of deposit for their heavy baggage. He named it, appropriately enough, Fort Deposit.[13] The next morning — August 20 — fully prepared for battle, Wayne had moved against the Indian encampment at and around a hill called Presque Isle.[14] At this point they were just four miles south of the British Fort Miami. It was an area in which, some time ago, a great windstorm had uprooted whole forests of trees, leaving them in a helter-skelter scattering on the ground. The fight they were preparing to make here was, immediately after, named the Battle of Fallen Timbers.

Now the generalship of Wayne and the rigorous training he had given his men paid dividends. As his army approached the position of the enemy, Mad Anthony sent forward a battalion of mounted riflemen with instructions to feign confusion and fall back in retreat immediately upon being attacked in order to lead the Indians to ground more advantageous to the army. The plan worked perfectly and, as the battalion fled in what appeared to be virtually a rout, the Indians pursued hotly.

The morning was rainy and the army drums too muffled to communicate the concerted signals distinctly and a plan of turning the right flank of the Indians therefore failed. But the victory was nonetheless complete. The entire Indian line, after a severe contest, gave way and fled in disorder, leaving behind a hundred dead warriors. Only a brief pursuit was made, ending within sight of Fort Miami.

The British garrison watched the entire battle in silence, their gate closed, offering no assistance to the Indians even when they came to the walls and demanded it. Wayne paid the British installation little mind. He could have attacked and possibly taken the fort, but it would have been risky at best. He had the written authorization of the President to "attack and demolish the British fort of Miami" at his descretion, but on studying it closely and discovering its strength, Mad Anthony prudently declined to attack.

Immediately following the Battle of Fallen Timbers, he destroyed all of the grain and vegetables growing around the fort and burned down all the buildings surrounding it, including the house and trading post of Alexander McKee. The effrontery of this so enraged the men inside the fort that they literally groaned in frustration.

Wayne and his lieutenant, William Henry Harrison, calmly rode their horses to within eighty yards of the fort and only glanced at it momentarily when something of a noisy disturbance ensued on a parapet platform. The intelligence from a deserter the next day explained what had happened. A captain of marines had become so incensed at Wayne's arrogance that he had seized a torch and attempted to apply it to a cannon aimed directly at the pair. At this moment the commandant, Major William Campbell of the Twenty-fourth Regiment, had rushed up with drawn sword and threatened to cut down the captain instantly if he did not desist. He then had the officer arrested.

Campbell himself, however, was just as furious with Wayne and sent him a note protesting the general's near approach to a post belonging to His Majesty's troops, declaring that he knew of no war existing between Britain and America. Wayne fired off two sharp letters in reply, ordering the major to get out of American territory.

There was no doubt that Wayne wanted very much to attack the fort, but he had wisdom and restraint enough to resist risking all the fruits of this victory in so desperate a gamble. He therefore ordered his army to return to Fort Defiance in easy marches, coldly and thoroughly destroying all cornfields and Indian villages for fifty miles on either side of the Maumee River. Colonel Hamtramck, meanwhile, was sent with a detachment to the junction of the St. Joseph and St. Marys rivers where the Maumee formed and here he built a strong new fort which he named Fort Wayne after his commander.[15]

With the main body of the army, Wayne returned to Fort Greenville, arriving there on November 2 after an absence of three months and six days. But now winter became a greater foe to the Indians than even Wayne had been. They camped at the mouth of Swan Creek on the Maumee and were very hard put to stay alive.[16] With their fields and goods destroyed, they were dependent upon the British, who did not half provide for them.

The defeat and the famine were, of themselves, enough to discourage anyone but, except for a strange accident, the Indians might have attempted to see it through without suing for peace. The incident was, to their way of thinking, such a portent of evil that they resigned themselves to surrendering to the *Shemanese* at Fort Defiance and asking them for more help than they were receiving from the British.

The accident occurred late in October. Of all the white men known by the confederated Indians, none had so much influence over them nor received as much respect from them as Colonel Alexander McKee. It was he, more than anyone, who had always heretofore made certain the British lived up to their promises to provide food and firearms and various goods to them. And when these items did not arrive in time, it was McKee who single-handedly stormed Detroit and demanded the promises be met. He was a fighter as well and few major battles were fought at which he was not present and at all times in the very thick of things. Yet, never once was he wounded in any way and this lent credence to the Indian belief that he was under the special protection of Moneto. There was further belief that Moneto manifested Himself in McKee's pet deer, which followed him about with the devotion of a dog. But then, one morning while McKee was dressing, something came over the animal. As McKee bent over to thrust his leg into his trousers, the fully antlered buck charged and caught him squarely in the bare behind. It might have been uproariously funny, except for the results. The tines of the antlers plunged deeply into the flesh and one of them entered his thigh, puncturing the huge femoral artery. McKee, who had been sent sprawling with the impact, raised himself to a sitting position and with dazed eyes watched his lifeblood drain out and form a wide scarlet puddle on the floor. Within minutes he was dead.

And so, with this seemingly supernatural occurrence to add to their fear and depression, within six weeks came a whole procession of emissaries from the Seven Nations to Anthony Wayne at Fort Greenville with offers

of peace. The general accepted them, though only tentatively. An agreement was made for all the principal chiefs, war chiefs and sachems of the
Seven Nations to meet and conclude a permanent peace treaty the following summer at Fort Greenville.

The exchange of prisoners, which also took place at this time, was just
another reason for the belief that prevailed among the Kentucky settlers
that peace had come at last and that a man could till his fields or chop his
wood or pasture his cattle and horses without fear of attack by Indians.
Nevertheless, old habits were hard to break. Though actually months had
gone by without incident, still Simon Kenton walked with wariness as his
constant companion wherever he went — alert in an instant to the cry of a
bird or snap of a twig or any sudden, unnatural stillness which might
betoken an alien presence.

Back and forth through the more remote areas of Kentucky the frontiersman rambled during the latter half of the year, marking here and there
those sections of land which caught his eye and which, he felt, would one
day be valuable. By the end of this year, he had claimed settlement and
preemption rights on no less than four hundred thousand acres of Kentucky land.

Land development in the Ohio Territory continued briskly also. Even
Judge John Cleve Symmes partially resolved some of the land problems he
had been having. Unable to raise enough money to pay for the initial
mammoth land tract he had petitioned Congress for, he had closed a
contract in 1792 for one million acres, after much negotiation. But the
continual rise in government securities made it impossible for him to pay
for this and so at last, in 1795, he had closed his long-pending contract
with the government and received his patent for the land on September
13. For the bargain price of sixty-seven cents per acre, the southern portion
of the tract originally desired was purchased. The total land involved was
three hundred eleven thousand, six hundred eighty-two acres, for which
Symmes and his backers paid under $209,000, and of which the lion's
share — a quarter million acres — was owned by the illiterate frontiersman, Simon Kenton.

Three months and four days later, Israel Ludlow began laying out,
within the Symmes Purchase and adjacent to Fort Hamilton, a town which
he initially called Fairfield because of the pleasant ground upon which it
was located, but which, because of popular demand, he soon changed to
Hamilton.

Civilization — of the white variety, at any rate — was on the move.

[*April 16, 1795 — Thursday*]

There was sympathy in the United States Congress for the Frenchmen
who had been duped out of their life savings in the buying of land from a

land company which, in reality, had never owned any to sell. The displaced Europeans had not only lost the land they had bargained for while still in France, but the lands settled upon in the Gallipolis area had now been largely lost because of invalid titles.

Thus it was that the Congress smiled beatifically upon the poor immigrants and donated a tract of just over twenty-five thousand acres to the sufferers of this fraud.[17] This parcel of land, dubbed The French Grant, bordered the north shore of the Ohio River for some eighteen miles between the mouths of the Big Sandy and Scioto rivers, with Hanging Rock at about its midpoint. Surprisingly, there was little political opposition to passage of the grant. It was as if it had suddenly become important to prove to the Frenchmen and to the world (and, most of all, to themselves) that the United States had a heart.

Clear across Ohio on the northern border rimming Lake Erie, steps were being taken for the rapid development of that territory. The Connecticut Legislature sold the remainder of its Western Reserve lands east of the Cuyahoga River — just over three million acres — to a syndicate of her citizens who organized themselves into an association under the name of The Connecticut Land Company, managed by seven directors, to sell the land to sundry citizens of that and other states. The purchasers immediately proceeded to survey into townships of five square miles each the entire tract and commenced making settlements.

Kentucky was on the move with its development, but Ohio was rapidly closing the gap. If no further hostilities broke out, perhaps statehood for Ohio could be gained even before the most optimistic had expected.

[April 30, 1795 — Thursday]

One of Tecumseh's most peculiar character traits was his modesty. He accepted praise for his exploits with a pleased smile but refrained from boasting of his own prowess — a custom so common in the Shawnee society it was practically second nature. Instead, he was content to let others boast of him and let his actions speak for themselves. It was this modesty that especially endeared him to his fellow Shawnees, and soon he found himself with a large number of followers.

With the destruction by General Wayne of the villages along the Auglaize and Maumee rivers, Tecumseh announced shortly after the defeat at Fallen Timbers his intention to move to a new site, a beautiful countryside he had long admired along the banks of Deer Creek.[18] Those who cared to come along he invited to join him and several hundred did, not only members of his own Kispokotha sept, but a number of the younger men of the Chalahgawtha and Maykujay septs and a few from the remainder of the Peckuwe and Thawegila septs. All had become somewhat disenchanted with the present Shawnee leadership and saw in Tecumseh the makings of a great new chief.

The village was quickly established and Tecumseh unanimously named chief. Second in command was his younger brother, lastborn of the triplets, Lowawluwaysica, who had taken to tribal medicine, trying to learn from the Shawnee medicine men the secrets of curing sickness. The pouch he carried everywhere with him now was filled with herbs and symbolic bits of material and he had memorized many of the healing chants; he had even, from all appearances, effected a few cures. But as always, in everything he did, he looked for shortcuts to success and did not find them. Crafty, like a weasel, he discovered that craftiness alone was by no means enough to make him a good medicine man. Thus he maintained the pattern long set of being abysmally average in all his undertakings; and so where Tecumseh refused to boast of his own exploits, Lowawluwaysica would boast all the louder for him.

There was much to boast about. At twenty-six, Tecumseh was a fine figure of a man. He was five feet nine inches tall and perfectly proportioned, extremely handsome and unusually gentle and good-natured. Everything he did, save one thing, seemed to turn out well. The single exception was his marriage to the Peckuwe maiden, Monetohse. She was a slender, strong and attractive young woman with something of a domineering way about her. After she once set her sights for Tecumseh, it was not any great surprise to the others when she won him. In less than two years she had borne him a son, named Mah-yaw-we-kaw-pa-we.

But Monetohse was a rare exception among Shawnee women, caring little for her offspring and more concerned with trying to change her husband's character. Her requests became demands and she railed at Tecumseh constantly, finding fault in all he did. Because of her nagging he was soon spending more time away from his *wegiwa* than in it. Monetohse's behavior toward himself was something Tecumseh might have overlooked, but her neglect of his son was another matter. And so he invoked the ancient Shawnee marital law; he took the boy from her and put him in charge of his older sister, Tecumapese, and then ordered Monetohse away from him forever, dissolving their marriage and sending her back in disgrace to the *wegiwa* of her parents.

The other members of the tribe applauded this action, for Tecumseh had taken more from her than would have any of them. Lowawluwaysica in particular was happy to have her gone, for now Tecumseh could resume his former habits; once again he began to show interest in hunting and fishing and in the competition which plays such an important part in the life of a Shawnee.

Tecumseh had told his little brother that he would not attend the signing of the peace treaty at Fort Greenville in a few months; that he would never sign away Shawnee right to this territory; that when it became necessary he would fight again against the white man, even if he had to fight alone. But Lowawluwaysica knew there were many who felt like this, especially among the younger men, and that they would need a strong leader when the time came. He was determined that the leader should be Tecumseh and that he, himself, should be Tecumseh's lieutenant.

It was Lowawluwaysica who first had the idea of pitting Tecumseh's hunting skills against all comers in a contest. It had already been proven that few, if any, could match his brother's courage in battle and none his daring; now it was time for the whole Shawnee nation to know of his great ability as a hunter.

In recent years there had been little opportunity for games or competition and so now, as word spread and hunters began assembling from everywhere, an aura of excitement filled them. They were happy that once again they could embark upon such a contest without fear of running afoul of hostile whites. The hunt was to last three days, with each hunter returning to the village before sundown of the third day with the skins of his kill.

As Lowawluwaysica had known it would happen, Tecumseh won by a tremendous margin. Many of the warriors brought in three or four deer hides apiece and a fair number had killed five or six. Perhaps a dozen had taken ten each and three men had downed twelve. But when Tecumseh returned with the fresh hides of thirty deer, there was no doubt in anyone's mind that he was the greatest hunter among the Shawnees.

It was custom for each of the hunters, at the great feast which always followed the hunt, to tell of his own experiences and there was much laughter and admiration as, one after another, they told their tales. But when it came Tecumseh's turn, a great and respectful silence came over them, and they clung to his every word. Unlike those who had preceded him, Tecumseh spoke softly, yet in a voice which carried far, and the simple and appealing eloquence with which he expressed himself captured his audience completely. It was obvious, when he finished speaking, that every man in the audience harbored an unusually deep respect for this exceptional young man who excelled in everything he undertook.

A glow of pride and expectation filled Tecumseh's brother. When the time came for Tecumseh to take up the reins of leadership, as Lowawluwaysica was sure he would one day, he would have many followers. And at his right hand would be Lowawluwaysica.

[May 18, 1795 — Monday]

The fine red brick home which marked the heart of Simon Kenton's thousand-acre estate in Mason County reflected the affluence of its owner. Here the frontiersman lived in comfort as one of the most notable and richest men in Kentucky. Though two of his elder brothers, William and

John, lived nearby with their families, it was indisputably Simon who had become head of the Kenton clan.

A crew of Negro slaves kept the house and grounds in perfect condition and from the upper windows one could look out and see a hundred or more head of superb riding horses grazing contentedly on the slopes. The several corncribs bulged with their treasure, the product of Simon's tenant farmers who, at harvest time, put his share into the cribs. If a tenant's own provisions gave out, he could take as much as he wished from Kenton's supply without permission; his cribs were, in fact, a kind of "bank" open to any who were in need — travelers and newly arrived settlers as well as the poor or unfortunate.

By such management he never made farming profitable but more than ever he deeply endeared himself to everyone in the vicinity, even though there were those who took outrageous advantage of his generosity. Nor was this generosity limited to the giving of corn. His door was always open to friend or stranger alike. Travelers of every grade were received with kindness, treated with hospitality and pressed to stay. His table was always bountifully set. He still gave land free of charge in the vicinity of his station to those who wanted to settle there and he also established a large and well-equipped general merchandise store in Washington. But here again he was too good-hearted and trusting to make any profit. He gave friends and neighbors and often even passing strangers unlimited credit to draw supplies as they needed; thus a great quantity of guns and ammunition, clothing, tools, utensils, bedding and other goods were taken and never paid for. Only when William Ward came to Mason County from Greenbrier County, Virginia, and went to work in the store for Kenton did the operation begin to show a little profit.

Kentucky was growing with tremendous speed now that the Indian peril was ended. Packet boats made regular trips from Cincinnati to Pittsburgh and return — the round trip taking one month — and mail was becoming regular from Wheeling. A great quantity of the produce and manufacture of the east was being shipped to Kentucky and the Ohio River was perpetually dotted with boats as far upstream or down as the eye could see. It was also possible now to travel to Kentucky from the east by wagon. Under a government contract, Ebenezer Zane was laying out a fine road known as Zane's Trace from Wheeling to Maysville.[19] It passed within a hundred yards of where Simon's last skirmish with the Shawnees on Paint Creek had occurred, where Sutawnee's father had been killed and the body of Joseph Jones tied high in a tree.

With the growth of the Bluegrass State (as it was coming to be known because of the luxurious pasture grasses that grew in a wide area around Lexington), Kenton began having difficulty with his records and so he hired Israel Donalson, first-grade teacher in Maysville, as his secretary and bookkeeper in handling deeds, business papers, correspondence, records and similar paperwork. The schoolteacher, writing to a friend, said Kenton was:

> . . . *a man of noble character: entirely illiterate, he had by practise learned to make a kind of hryoglyfficks that would read Simon Kenton, but had an extraordinary memory: he once called on me to file his papers; when I went to his house he had two drawers of an old fashioned file full of papers & would come and stand by me, and when I picked up a paper, before opening would tell me what it was . . .*

The frontiersman's memory for visual details was indeed remarkable. Although he could not read any paper, he could select any one he wanted out of a number in a packet by its shape or some peculiarity in appearance, and give its gist before it was read to him for the refreshing of his mind on some detail. Another of his friends wrote about Kenton:

> . . . *his faculty of mastering the Physical geography of any region over which he passed and his recollection of its topography was something Phenomenal; for Instance. Virginia in settling her domain, had no system, such as the General Government so admirably maintains with her public lands. She issued her warrants as they were termed to the settler or speculator; those warrants were put in the hands of a surveyor or other person known as a locator, who laid off the quantity of land named in the warrant, by metes or bounds, with fixed corners and marked lines. Patents were then issued to grantees by metes and bounds as described in the surveys. In consequence of this System — or want of system — the fine lands of Kentucky were literally shingled over with patents, leading to interminable litigation . . . Kenton, although illiterate, was much employed as a locator . . . [his] testimony was frequently in demand in the land suits. On such occasions I have been told by the County Surveyor that Kenton, when accompanying him for the purpose of establishing some beginning corner, generally near some noted spring, creek, branch or other permanent land mark, would make him read over the field notes of the survey — as he read he could see the countenance of the man light up until the full train of association had been established, and then would lead the surveyor to the natural land mark — spring, creek or branch — stop — give one of his quick glances around — 'yes, yes, I am right, but no marked corners — read again the trees.' Another pause, again, 'Yes, yes,' as if speaking to himself, 'dig here, you ought to find the roots of an oak,' or ash, or maybe a walnut as the post might be. Of course, Kenton's testimony on such occasions was decisive, as in no instance, so the surveyor informed me, was he known to be mistaken . . .*

Simon's craving for acquiring land was not an avaricious one, since he cared little about personal wealth. Nor did he even care much about the land's development, although he liked it to be settled by newcomers free to do as they wished with it. He was possessed with a love for land, a need of acquisition. He spoke often and glowingly on "the fine country on the Ohio" and of spending the best energies of his life in "rescuing from barbarism so fine a country." Even as he lay almost dead at Mackachack after the gauntlet race there, he had "gazed south over the adjoining plain" which even then seemed to him "the most beautiful ever seen."

Ever since mid-February, Kenton's home had become a lively place indeed. Among the many newcomers to Kentucky was the Stephen Jarboe family, Martha's uncle and aunt and cousins. They had planned to stay over only a short while as they set about locating their own land, but when they found Martha in an advanced state of pregnancy with her fourth child, they stayed on. Simon welcomed them to stay as long as they liked, and almost at once there grew a mutual attraction between him and Martha's cousin, seventeen-year-old Elizabeth Jarboe.

Elizabeth was vibrant, intelligent, and vivacious, a black-haired, blue-eyed beauty who reminded Simon in many respects of Rachel Edgar. Her laughter was a full-throated ripple that virtually demanded accompaniment; she loved to listen to Simon's experiences almost as much as she enjoyed expressing her own perceptive views on virtually any subject under discussion. In a very short time she and the frontiersman had established a solid relationship, though each regarded this relationship in a different light entirely. To Simon, Elizabeth was an engaging, pleasant girl whose company he enjoyed and who was no more to him than merely his wife's cousin. To Elizabeth, however, Simon was easily the most fascinating man she had ever encountered and practically from their first meeting, though she kept it to herself, she fell deeply in love with him. It infuriated her to tears that Simon treated her as a child and she longed for the opportunity to prove to him that her childhood days were well behind her. With an inner ache she reconciled herself to the fact that not only was Simon married to her own cousin, but that he was forty years old — over twice her own age.

That she could handle herself as a woman, however, Elizabeth proved to Simon this day. Her mother, who was to have helped with the birth of Martha's child, fell ill and the midwifery became Elizabeth's responsibility. She shooed the menfolk and children away and performed in a manner betokening coolness and skill. And thus, in late afternoon, she emerged from the bedroom, holding in her arms the tiny swaddled form of Simon Kenton's newest daughter, Sarah.

[*August 7, 1795 — Friday*]

The Greenville Treaty was a strong document, as General Wayne had meant it to be. He was determined that this treaty would not be broken by either side on grounds of ignorance or absence. He had long felt that this was the greatest failing of past treaties — that usually the Indians who should have been there were not and that the terms agreed upon between the parties were nebulous at best. Mad Anthony Wayne was going to see to it that the Greenville Treaty was not only direct and clearly stated, but that it was presented to the authorized representatives of the twelve tribes concerned.

Throughout the Indian nations preliminary councils had been held — among themselves and with Wayne — beginning in late January. By runner, word had been sent throughout the Northwest Territory that each chief or representative, with his own entourage, should assemble at Fort Greenville in mid-June.

But the chiefs were not to be rushed into anything nor told what to do by the white general. They would come, but at their leisure. Fortunately, Wayne understood enough of the Indian pride to be patient on this point. The council fires were lighted on June 15, but the only tribe on hand was the Delaware nation. All day the fires were burned and when, by the next morning, none of the other chiefs had arrived, Wayne addressed those who were there, accompanied by William Henry Harrison and several other military men, a few emissaries from President Washington and a number of frontiersmen, including Simon Kenton and Isaac Zane.

"I have," he told them, "cleared the ground of all brush and rubbish, and have opened roads to the east, the west, the north and the south, that all your nations may come in safety and with ease to meet me. The ground on which this council house stands is unstained with blood and is as pure as the heart of General Washington, the great chief of America, and of his great council; as pure as my heart which now wishes for nothing so much as peace and brotherly love. The heavens are bright, the roads are open, we will rest in peace and love and wait the arrival of our brothers. In the interim we will have a little refreshment, to wash the dust from our throats. We will, on this happy occasion, be merry without passing the bounds of temperance and sobriety. We will now cover up the council fire and keep it alive till the remainder of the different tribes assemble and form a full meeting and representation."

Teteboxti, aged King of the Delawares, arose and smiled at the general and said, "All my people shall be informed of the commencement of our friendship and they will rejoice in it and I hope it will never end."

Wampum belts were at once exchanged between them and the two factions returned to their own positions to wait. Such belts were now, as they had always been, extremely important, at least insofar as the Indians were concerned. They were used to impress indelibly the desired points embodied in the message of the speaker delivering them. The belts were usually made of tubular shell beads strung into strings about eighteen inches in length and skillfully woven by the women into plain or figured rectangular bands three or four inches wide and a yard long. A peace belt could be twice this size.

Contact with the whites over the years had worked something of a revolution in the construction of the wampum belts. The beads were originally cut from either fresh water or ocean mussel shells and were about an eighth of an inch in diameter and twice as long, with a hole drilled through the center of the length with a slender flint drill. This was a slow and laborious process, usually relegated to certain skilled workmen. But when the whites came with their ready-made beads, a significant change occurred. Because these beads meant so much to the Indians, they became an enormously profitable item of trade for the white men.

A black wampum belt was generally a signal of war talk, whereas the white was considered auspicious, signifying peace, health or prosperity of some kind. Violet, which could also signify war, generally showed hostility, sorrow, death or disaster. In order to make the message plain, figures would be woven into the belt to form squares, diamonds, parallel lines, trees, houses, animals, celestial objects or human beings.

The belts exchanged now between Teteboxti and Wayne were the important white chain belts, which were powerful signs. The Indian orators had a wide stock of metaphors to express their ideas. To make war was to raise the hatchet and a design of this nature was incorporated into the appropriate belt. To deliberate was to kindle the council fire; to cover the bones of the dead was to make reparation and gain forgiveness for killing them; a state of war and disaster was typified by a black cloud and a state of peace by brilliant sunshine or by an open path between two nations. The Indian orator seldom spoke without careful premeditation and his memory was refreshed by belts of wampum, which he delivered after every major point in his harangue as a pledge of the sincerity and truth of his words. The white belts which the American general and Delaware chief now exchanged bore figures of an Indian and a white man holding a chain of friendship between them.

Gradually the other Indian contingents began to arrive and each was greeted by General Wayne and presented with similar white wampum belts in solemn ceremony. Through the latter part of June they arrived and during the first two weeks of July, stately and proud, dressed in their most ceremonial garb. The Delawares made up the largest single Indian contingent, numbering three hundred eighty-one individuals, led by Teteboxti, Peke-tele-mund and Buckangehela. There were also two hundred forty Potawatomies under chiefs New Corn, Asimethe and Sun, and a hundred eighty Wyandots under Chief Tarhe, the Crane. Black Hoof, Black Snake and Blue Jacket showed up in a party of a hundred forty-three Shawnees and Little Turtle arrived solemnly leading seventy-three Miamis, including twenty-two Eel River Miamis under Chief LeGris. Forty-six Chippewas attended under chiefs Massas and Bad Bird, while the forty-five Ottawas were represented by Chief Augooshaway. A dozen Weas and Piankeshaws came under the leadership of Chief Reyntwoco and ten Kickapoos and Kaskaskias arrived under Chief Keeahah.

Twelve tribes totaling eleven hundred thirty men had finally taken their places and the council fires were rekindled and the negotiations begun. They went slowly, with much oration and passing of wampum belts, each belt being accepted by the chief being addressed who, in turn, gave it to the keeper of the tribal archives to deposit carefully in the tribal council bag with copies of former treaties, wampum belts and other valuable documents.

The slowness of this method was not unexpected and General Wayne allowed them all the time they needed to deliberate fully, so as to be in accord with one point before moving on to the next. But at length the terms of the new treaty became clear to all assembled. Anthony Wayne had begun by stating that the permanent treaty was to be based, in part, upon the treaty lines established by the Fort McIntosh Treaty of January 21, 1785. The Indians would be permitted to retain the privilege of hunting and fishing throughout the Ohio country to the Ohio River. But the dividing line between Indian and white territories in this treaty he read to them slowly and explained carefully:

The general boundary line between the lands of the United States and the lands of the said Indian tribes shall begin at the mouth of the Cuyahoga River and run thence up the same to the Portage between that and the Tuscarawas branch of the Muskingum, thence down that branch to the crossing place above Fort Laurens, thence westerly to a fork of that branch of the Great Miami River running into the Ohio, at or near which stood Loramie's Store, and where commenced the portage between the Miami of the Ohio and St. Marys River, which is a branch of the Miami which runs into Lake Erie [Maumee River]; thence a westerly course to Fort Recovery, which stands on a branch of the Wabash; thence southerly in a direct line to the Ohio, so as to intersect that river opposite the mouth of the Kentucke or Cuttawa River.

In addition to this, Wayne explained, the United States would claim sixteen different tracts of land for government reservations *within* the Indian territory. Most of these tracts were to be six miles square each and located at such strategic spots as near the former site of Loramie's Store, near Girty's Town, at the head of the Auglaize River, and similar places.

By the terms of this treaty the Indians were to cede to the United States about twenty-five thousand square miles of territory, plus the sixteen tracts for reservations. For these cessions the Indians would receive goods to the value of $1,666 for each of the twelve tribes represented here, plus an annual allowance to each of the tribes of $825.

This was not at all an easy treaty to put across. Chief after chief spoke at great length and at first there were strong opponents — primarily Blue Jacket, Little Turtle and Black Snake — but these three were painfully aware that they had little choice. It would be better, perhaps, for all the chiefs to sign this document and make the best of it, adhering closely to its limitations and seeing to it that the whites did the same, thus salvaging both land as well as pride. To continue in a hostile vein would be to lose everything. None had any doubt of this; moreover, they were tired of war and longed for peace.

Thus, on August 3, each chief had signed the treaty, as did Wayne; and today, August 7, the signed treaties were exchanged and Chief Tarhe of the Wyandots was given permanent custodianship of the document on behalf of the assembled Indians.

In his farewell address to the Indians, Wayne said: "I now fervently pray to the Great Spirit that the peace now established may be permanent and that it now holds us together in the bonds of friendship until time shall be no more. I also pray that the Great Spirit above may enlighten your minds and open your eyes to your true happiness, that your children may learn to cultivate the earth and enjoy the fruits of peace and industry."

And thus, officially, ended the Indian Wars. Or so, at least, everyone claimed.

[*August 16, 1795 — Sunday*]

Although Tecumseh had been invited to attend the treaty negotiations at Greenville, he had scornfully refused to enter into any agreement with the whites. Such agreements, he said, had always been and would always be wholly worthless. But the fact that the young chief's prestige had risen greatly in the Shawnee nation became evident when Blue Jacket personally made a special trip to the Deer Creek village immediately after the treaty was concluded to tell Tecumseh the details.

The son of Pucksinwah listened in silence until Blue Jacket had finished. By the terms of the treaty, this very land they were on now belonged to the whites. He shook his head, saying he and his people would remain there until the corn was harvested and the winter hunting finished. Only then, when melting snow swelled rivers, would he move to the upper waters of the Great Miami River. His voice was low and bitter in conclusion:

"My heart is a stone: heavy with sadness for my people; cold with the knowledge that no treaty will keep whites out of our lands; hard with the determination to resist as long as I live and breathe. Now we are weak and many of our people are afraid. But hear me; a single twig breaks, but the bundle of twigs is strong. Someday I will embrace our brother tribes and draw them into a bundle and together we will win our country back from the whites."

Blue Jacket looked Tecumseh over slowly and then dipped his head. "I think maybe you will."

[*December 31, 1795 — Thursday*]

The year ended with peace in the land and the real settlement of Ohio began in earnest. Almost overnight cabins blossomed throughout southern Ohio and east of the Cuyahoga in the Western Reserve lands. In a wide area around the principal settlements — Marietta and Gallipolis, Manchester and Cincinnati and Hamilton — as well as throughout most of the Symmes Purchase, the countryside became checkered with new farms and the atmosphere was constantly made bluish-white with the smoke of clearance fires.

On October 7, Governor Arthur St. Clair — back in Ohio again in his official capacity — along with General Jonathan Dayton and Colonel Israel Ludlow, bought an excellent section of land at the confluence of the Mad, Stillwater and Great Miami rivers and at once ordered it surveyed by Daniel C. Cooper and Captain John Dunlap. On November 4, Israel Ludlow himself laid out a town on the site and named it Dayton, after the general.

Cincinnati was growing quite rapidly now, with a permanent population (exclusive of the garrison at Fort Washington) of some five hundred people. Besides numerous stores, stables and other business establishments, ten new frame houses had joined the ninety-four cabins already in the village limits.

By order of General Wayne, William Henry Harrison was promoted to the rank of captain and given command of Fort Washington. A short time later, after something of a whirlwind courtship, the handsome young captain married Anna Symmes, the judge's daughter.

The Greenville Treaty was presented to the United States Senate on December 9, and thirteen days later it was ratified. Throughout the entire frontier area there was an aura of optimism stronger and more promising than any of the frontiersmen had ever known.

But Simon Kenton remained among the dwindling number who were unconvinced of this so-called "permanent peace."

CHAPTER X

[*October 7, 1796 — Friday*]

THE corn and vegetable crop had been good and the hunting during the winter excellent and so, despite the restlessness that seemed to rule him these days, it was with genuine regret that Tecumseh ordered the Deer Creek village abandoned and led his followers in March to the headwaters of the Great Miami where a new village was established and new crops planted.

During the winter Tecumseh had taken a wife. She was an older woman, named Mamate, whom he had married not because he was in love with her but because he had been urged to do so by his friends. A chief should have a wife to bear him children and set an example for the rest of his followers.

But for Tecumseh, Mamate was little more than an embodiment of physical gratification and it was without emotion that he greeted the news of her pregnancy. During the summer she had become sick and when the baby was born she was so weak that soon afterward she died in the night. The infant boy, who had been named Nay-tha-way-nah — A Panther-Seizing-Its-Prey — survived and Tecumapese cared for it tenderly, as she was still caring for her brother's other son.

Tecumseh's restlessness, meanwhile, grew rather than abated, and he took to wandering alone, mostly in the Ohio Territory but also in the southern portion of the Indiana Territory. Along the banks of the White-water River, near where East Fork joined it, he found a location that appealed to him.[1] He had become quickly disenchanted with the village site on the upper Great Miami and so now, with the corn crop harvested, he once again ordered the abandonment of the village and the establishment of a new one at the Whitewater location.

Still the move was not enough to satisfy him. Sometimes with his village medicine man brother, Lowawluwaysica, but more often alone, he continued to roam through the countryside he loved more than any other — the area surrounding the site of the long ago destroyed and abandoned Chillicothe. It was here, as a boy, that he had wrestled and hunted and played games with the other Shawnee youngsters. It was here, in the Little Miami River, that he had won his *opa-waw-ka*, the stone he still wore around his neck, and where he had lived in a *wegiwa* with Chiksika. And there was the trail along which they had borne the body of Chief Black Fish for burial. Bits of this former Shawnee existence still lay exposed on the surface of the ground — the cornerposts of the old *msi-kah-mi-qui*, an occasional arrowhead, a shard of broken pottery, a bit of rotted buckskin, a rusted tomahawk, a corn-grinding stone, a hide scraper.

Often Tecumseh would crouch on the rise where the big *msi-kah-mi-qui* had stood and stare unseeingly over the fertile fields now grown up in weeds. What he saw instead was hundreds of *wegiwas* and the bustle of a numerous, proud, carefree and happy people, tending crops and tanning furs and sitting about the fires telling the wonderful stories of life here long ago.

At such times an overwhelming sadness arose in him and with it came the determination that somehow, in some way and at some time, the Shawnees *must* reclaim this land that was rightfully theirs.

[*December 13, 1796 — Tuesday*]

The face of the Ohio Territory was rapidly changing. Early in the year had come the sale in Pittsburgh and Philadelphia of other parts of The Seven Ranges for nearly $50,000 and eager settlers were flocking to their new land. To the west, along the Great Miami River, the first of the settlers had begun to arrive at Dayton, both by land and by water. The first party came by boat and was led by Benjamin Van Cleve, arriving on April 1, ten days after putting out from Cincinnati.[2]

East of the Scioto River a massive stretch of land comprising four thousand square miles was appropriated through an Act of Congress on June 1 and called United States Military Lands. This area of two and a half million acres would be used to satisfy the claims of officers and soldiers of the Revolutionary War. It was quickly surveyed into townships five miles square and then divided into quarter townships two and a half miles square, each containing four thousand acres. Finally, even these were further divided into forty lots of a hundred acres each to accommodate soldiers whose warrants entitled them to only that much land.

On August 3, Colonel Nathaniel Massie laid out a new town at the mouth of Paint Creek just a short distance from where one of the early Chalahgawtha villages had stood. At first he called it Massie's Town by popular demand, but later, taken by the name of that Shawnee town, he renamed the town Chillicothe.[3] Twelve days after the town was established, Governor St. Clair issued a new proclamation establishing the third Ohio county and named it after General Wayne. But there was something ominous in the formation of Wayne County because, despite the Greenville Treaty, the territory included in this county was made up almost entirely of Indian land, taking in the area westward from the mouth of the Cuyahoga, a large segment of the northeastern part of the Indiana Territory and the whole of the Michigan Territory. Once again, it appeared, the insidious encroachment had commenced.

Along Lake Erie, in September, the general agent of the Connecticut Land Company, General Moses Cleaveland, surveyed and mapped a new city at the mouth of the Cuyahoga. Settlement began almost at once in the new village named after him.[4]

By the end of November nearly a thousand of the new, well-built flatboats called Broadhorns had passed Marietta loaded each with dozens of emigrants bound for the more attractive regions of southwestern Ohio, and not one of the boats was even threatened, much less attacked by Indians.

Simon Kenton had spent nearly all that summer making tomahawk improvements in the Ohio country, ranging from the Great Miami River in the west to the Scioto in the east. But Martha was expecting again and so, as winter closed in, he turned his steps back toward the big brick home along Lawrence Creek. He was not in time.

At twenty-six, Martha was feeling more weary from this pregnancy than she had from any of the previous four. She slept frequently during the day and, to avoid climbing stairs, had directed her Negro servants to bring her bed downstairs. Here she lay for most of each day while the Jarboe family saw to matters about the house. On December 13, however, the Jarboes had gone to Maysville and the servants were all outside. To keep Martha comfortably warm while they were gone, the fireplaces had been freshly replenished with firewood. But whoever had put the wood on the fire in the room directly above where she lay had neglected to replace the protective screening. A small gas pocket in one of the pieces of burning wood popped and shot a flaming bit of wood onto a bed, setting it afire. Quickly the flames spread to the floor, and the dry planking began to burn furiously. Soon a large segment of the floor caved in, showering Martha's bed with flaming debris.

The frontiersman's wife awoke with a terrified scream and tried desperately to escape from the fire, but the timbers had pinned her. Her screams were heard finally and several of the servants rushed in, smothered the blaze and freed her. But the damage was done. It was a melancholy household to which Simon Kenton returned. Martha had given birth to a stillborn baby an hour after being rescued and, herself severely burned, had followed the infant in death before the night was out.

[December 31, 1796 — Saturday]

The most momentous news for Americans during the year came on July 11 when the British finally gave up their fragile hold on United States territory and turned over to the army both Fort Miami and Detroit. The ceremony was somewhat reminiscent of the scene enacted over thirty-five years previously when France had yielded Detroit to the British. Two American ships, carrying General Wayne and his army, crossed Lake Erie and sailed up the Detroit River, landing near the fort.[5]

Wayne was a very ill man. An acute attack of gout had seized not only his feet but also affected his liver, kidneys and heart most seriously. It was impossible for him to take part in the ceremonies and so, while he stayed aboard ship, a company of his men under Captain Moses Porter marched up to the fort and were met there by the Detroit commandant, Colonel Richard England. A large crowd of spectators looked on soberly, including Chief Little Turtle and a hundred or more of his Miami warriors.

Reluctantly, yet proudly, Colonel England lowered the British ensign and Captain Porter raised the flag of the United States. Salutes were fired and the transfer made official. At once the colonel led his Redcoats across the Detroit River into Ontario and marched them to Fort Malden at the mouth of that river where Lake Erie forms.[6] With them went hundreds of British and Loyalist citizens.

Meanwhile, Mad Anthony Wayne was carried into Detroit for treatment. Severe cramps doubled him up and his heart pounded frightfully and erratically in his breast. He could eat but little and the functions of defecation and urination became moments of extreme agony. For months he lay there recuperating and then, late in the year, when he was feeling somewhat better, he boarded a small schooner bound for Buffalo. From there he planned to return overland to Philadelphia for better medical treatment; but such was not to be. On December 15 he suffered an even more serious attack; the craft quickly put in at the port of Erie, Pennsylvania, and he was gently carried into the fort at Presque Isle. Before the sun had set, one of the most brilliant and resourceful generals in American history had breathed his last.

With little fanfare his remains were quietly laid to rest beneath the fort's flagpole and the year closed on a note of gloom at the passing of this great man.

[March 29, 1797 — Wednesday]

James Galloway wore a deeply satisfied smile as he emerged from the trees and saw before him the beautiful fields bordered to the north and west by lines of trees where the streams flowed. He swiveled in the saddle and told his family behind him that the long trip from Lexington was over at last.

His wife and five-year-old daughter Rebecca looked where he pointed and recognized the landmarks he had so often told them about, although they had never seen them before. Ever since he had joined with George Rogers Clark in his second expedition to this site in 1782, James Galloway had known that one day he would return.

Spreading out from that rise over there, he told them, had been the hundreds of *wegiwas* that had formed the Shawnee village of Chillicothe. At the central point of the rise had stood the impressive council house which they had burned during the campaign; and on the other side of the rise, at the foot of the slope, was the wonderful bubbling spring that had provided more than enough sweet fresh water for the whole village. Beyond that lay the expansive, marshy ground which stretched a quarter mile west to the Little Miami River. It was to the north of that principal rise, along the riverbank, where they would build their home and these fields would produce their crops of corn and fruit and vegetables. For fifteen years Galloway had dreamed of this and now that dream would become a reality.

As they approached the rise, however, Galloway suddenly spotted a lone, squatting Indian watching them. With a sharp word for them to remain where they were, he left his family and galloped to the Indian who stood as he approached.

The Shawnee appeared peaceable and Galloway greeted the buckskin-clad man in English. To his amazement, the Indian responded in excellent English, his voice gentle, though slightly wary. Galloway then explained that he intended to settle here with his family; that he had never seen such beautiful land and that he admired the Shawnees for having picked such an excellent site for their village. He could understand well why the Indians had been loath to leave it and he sympathized with them. It was land, he said, that a man might willingly die for.

The Indian nodded and replied that this had once been the site of his village and that he frequently came back to remember again those days of his childhood here. He welcomed the settler and said that he was glad the first white man to come here was a man who loved the land and wanted to live on it and care for it — not merely to grab it up so that later he might break it into pieces and sell it to others.

As they conversed, Galloway beckoned his family to join them and the Indian smiled at the introductions and told Galloway his wife had the brightness about her of the sun and his daughter the soft loveliness of the moon. He pointed to the southeast where a cluster of trees grew and said that there, where a large spring burst forth the year around, was where he had been born. His pointing finger moved to the south and he said that was where the great Shawnee chief, Black Fish, had been buried and that it was hallowed ground which should be left undisturbed. For more than an hour they conversed and when, at last, the Indian said he must go now to return to his people, Galloway spoke up quickly and asked him to return often.

"Our home will be built soon," he added. "It would honor us to have you visit. The door will never be closed to you nor to any of your people."

The Indian nodded and offered his hand to Galloway. "For my people and for myself, I am grateful. You and your family are good people and you need never fear harm will come to you from the Shawnees. I will come back."

He dipped his head again and strode away toward the southwest without looking back. Little Rebecca, fascinated by the visit, watched him go and when she returned her attention to her father her eyes were large and bright with excitement.

"What did he say his name was, Daddy?"

"An unusual man," Galloway muttered, appearing not to have heard her. "Most unusual. He said he lives now over on the Whitewater River in the Indiana Territory. I wonder where he learned to speak English so well." He caught himself and smiled at his daughter. "Excuse me, Becky. He said his name is Tecumseh."

[December 1, 1797 — Friday]

It took Simon Kenton a long time to realize it, or at any rate to admit it to himself, but now there was no doubt about it as he rode the final short distance toward home from Maysville: the most wonderful thing about coming back home again after these excursions through the Ohio country was seeing Elizabeth Jarboe. After Martha's death, the Jarboes had stayed on and cared for his four youngsters as if they were their own. Elizabeth, in particular, had become something of a mother to them, even though she was only nine years older than Simon's eldest daughter, Nancy. He felt a strong debt of gratitude to the Jarboes for this help, but what he felt for Elizabeth was considerably more than appreciation. The nineteen-year-old beauty had stirred in him feelings similar to those he had felt for Martha Dowden in those early days of their courtship, but with a difference. It seemed to him that this time there was more of a depth to the feeling, a greater strength than before and more of a real need.

He turned to the west off the Maysville-Washington Road to ride the final mile to his station and thought about how things had changed since the days of his first courtship. Look at how the nation was growing and new leaders were replacing the old. Wayne was gone, dead and buried. John Adams had moved into the Presidency by just three votes over his opponent, Tom Jefferson, who had become Vice President. Even the face of the land itself had changed; forests were felled and cabins built; towns grew and were tied together by spiderweb roads through the wilderness.

The once impenetrable Indian country of Ohio was being partitioned into more counties — the two newest ones being named after the new President and Vice President. Everything, it seemed, was subject to change except man's basic nature.

The door to the brick house flew open as he rode up and Elizabeth rushed to meet him. He swept her up in his arms and they lost themselves in the nearness of one another.

[*April 30, 1798 — Monday*]

For the second time, Parson William Wood had officiated at a wedding in which Simon Kenton was the groom. He pronounced the frontiersman and Elizabeth Jarboe man and wife on March 27 and immediately afterwards the couple, leaving Simon's children in care of her parents, set off on their wedding trip to Missouri Territory. They made the trip by horse and raft, the only means available, exploring the country as they went and camping wherever night found them. It was an idyllic time.

Shortly after passing the mouth of the Ohio and crossing the Mississippi, they entered the Missouri area, that part of the Louisiana Territory stretching far to the north. The area they entered first was known as Cape Girardeau, a place of uncommon beauty. Its name was familiar to most of the frontiersmen, for this was where, nearly a score of years ago, Peter Loramie had led the migrating Shawnees after the septs had split. Overlooking a wide majestic curve of the Mississippi River, the land had a charm and beauty about it that was wholly unspoiled and Simon resolved that someday he would return to this general area and claim — or buy, if it was already claimed — a large piece of land. As ever, the lust for acquiring more land was a ruling factor in his character.

A few months ago Nathan Boone had come down the Ohio River with most of the Boone family to join their father and had stopped off long enough to tell Kenton where Daniel had settled. Simon and Elizabeth had little difficulty finding it. They followed the west bank of the Mississippi northward past the French settlement of St. Louis until the great Missouri River from the west joined it. From this point it was only a matter of fifteen miles or so upstream on the north bank of the Missouri, not far from another French fur trading village called St. Charles, that they found the lonely little Boone cabin.

The reunion was a happy one. Elizabeth had never met the famous frontier comrade of her husband, but she had heard a great deal about him. Somehow she had expected them to be more or less cut from the same cloth, but almost at once their differences were apparent and became more striking as the days and weeks passed.

Boone, a restless man, hunter and trapper, had come to the wilderness by choice; for Simon it had been a fugitive necessity. Both men, though illiterate and uneducated, were masters of wilderness lore; each was daring and courageous and both had shown themselves to be exceptional leaders of men at times of difficulty or danger. Time and again both had displayed a willingness to lay down their lives in defense of inexperienced emigrants and their families, and both were efficient promoters of the settlement of the wilderness.

But here the similarities ended. The refined person might have been shocked at the commonness of the rugged and vigorous Boone, but no man ever heard from the lips of Simon Kenton an obscene word or licentious comment. Kenton did not paradoxically detest the very settlements he had helped promote, as did Boone. He did not grow restless when game became scarce and Indians even scarcer, when fields became safe enough for planting without men to guard the planters, when pastures became safe enough for fine herds of cattle and horses to roam and graze in peace. Unlike Boone, Kenton enjoyed seeing the new towns spring up and grow into thriving little cities, and he took pride in the fact that he had contributed substantially to their establishment.

Boone was the lone wolf type to an extreme, whereas Kenton enjoyed visiting with the settlers and feeling people near and around him. Boone thrived in loneliness, exulted in the sense of freedom he knew in the untrammeled wilderness; to Kenton, this same wilderness was something to conquer and bend to his will. If Boone's love of wilderness meant that his family must suffer a self-imposed ostracism in order to be with him, then that was the way it had to be. But Simon never lost his love of his own kind; moreover he wanted very much for his own children to have the education that he himself had foregone.

Frontiersmen they were, Boone and Kenton, but from a different mold entirely. For this, Elizabeth Jarboe gave thanks.

[*May 5, 1798 — Saturday*]

Buckangehela, principal chief of the Delawares, smoked his pipe quietly and gazed at the little fire before which he sat in Tecumseh's *wegiwa*. As always on the rare occasions when he met this young Kispokotha Shawnee chief, he was impressed by him and by the subtle aura of power which seemed to surround him.

He had come to find out why it was that Tecumseh had more or less separated himself from his tribe. Most of the Shawnees had now taken up residence far to the north, along the Auglaize and Maumee and even as far north as Detroit. Why was it that Tecumseh had brought his followers here to the Whitewater River?

Tecumseh explained his inability to agree with Black Hoof that the Greenville Treaty was binding and that they should bury the hatchet for all time. Tecumseh respected his chief and had always admired him, but surely Black Hoof could not really believe the *Shemanese* would live up to the agreement, could he? He could, and so they had drifted apart, Tecumseh taking with him many of the younger men who felt as he did — who sensed that all trouble had not come to an end and who dreamed of one day reclaiming their rightful land.

Buckangehela listened quietly, only now and then nodding. Black Hoof was right in his way, but so was Tecumseh in his. The Delaware had heard consistently more of this young chief who was so strong in all ways and he admired him. There would come a day, perhaps, when a strong young war chief such as Tecumseh would be needed again.

Buckangehela addressed the Kispokotha seriously. The Delawares were living now on the White River in this Indiana Territory, farther to north and west. The Delawares were opening their *wegiwas* and their arms and their hearts to Tecumseh and his followers. Would Tecumseh and his people come and live with the Delawares, hunt with them, reside in peace with them at that place? And would Tecumseh, if such time came, lead the Delawares against any enemy who might threaten them?

Tecumseh would.

[*November 18, 1798 — Sunday*]

For the Kentons, the sojourn with Daniel Boone and his family in the Missouri country had been a pleasant interlude. While he didn't say so to Boone, Simon was not too favorably impressed with the Missouri lands, even though the two men had ranged far together through them and Simon had claimed several large tracts. The soil was of considerably poorer quality than that found in Ohio and much of Kentucky, as reflected in the seemingly endless forests of scrub oak scarcely more than twenty or thirty feet tall.

The time for leaving had come at last and all during their journey back to Kentucky, Simon and Elizabeth had serious discussions about their future. Finally they reached a decision: they would leave Kentucky and emigrate to the Ohio country. It was a decision not entirely unexpected. After all, Kenton's Station had been the home of Simon and Martha, and Elizabeth didn't care to compete with her dead cousin. Also, within another couple of months Elizabeth would bear her first child for Simon. Would not Cincinnati be a fine place for this baby to start life?

Simon was delighted that Elizabeth felt this way, and immediately upon reaching Kentucky again, he began getting his affairs in order. It was no easy task. Men in Kentucky who owned one hundred thousand acres of land were called capital landholders and Simon Kenton had earned such a title easily four times over. From the time in 1779, when he had claimed settlement and preemption rights to those fourteen hundred acres on Elkhorn Creek, he had never ceased claiming lands. His Kentucky entries ranged from a smallest claim of a hundred fifty-two acres to many of fifteen thousand acres all through Mason, Fayette, Lincoln and Bourbon Counties. But he was dreadfully tired of the interminable litigation which owning such land had brought about.[7]

To Simon's great pleasure, one of the most nagging of his land suits had just been cleared up. Since 1788 he had been in and out of courts in regard to double claims on the land he had marked along Elkhorn Creek. His gift of part of this land to Andrew McConnell, the young man who had helped him home from Wayne's army when the fever struck him, hadn't helped at all. Instead of developing it himself, McConnell had sold the hundred acres to another party. When a double claim arose for this portion it was not McConnell but Kenton, by law, who had to make restitution to the buyer or else have the case tried in court.

The frontiersman could have paid off with no difficulty at all, but it was the principle of the thing that most irked him. If he, who could afford it, did not fight this threat, then the land of so many of his companions who could *not* afford to fight was jeopardized. Nor did he concede defeat when the first court found against him and for the plaintiff. He took it to the Kentucky Court of Appeals and the fight went on.

The court's first decision against him ultimately involved all but the dissenting judge in a scandal of high degree and a year later the decision was reversed in Simon's favor. But still that did not end it. Twice more his opponent appealed, but each time the decree in Kenton's favor stood confirmed and unaltered. Had it been otherwise, the possessions of practically every Kentucky pioneer would have been endangered, for any decision of the early Virginia commissioners could have been questioned and, by the splitting of fine legal hairs, home after home could have been taken away from the men who held Kentucky during the first three years of its settlement.

In rapid succession, Simon now sold off the lion's share of his Kentucky land holdings. And that which he didn't sell — amounting to one hundred forty-five thousand acres — he assigned in trust to his brother, John, with which to meet his engagements. He also retained his land around and including Kenton's Station.

And so it was that on November 18, after twenty-eight years and after having been among the first of a handful of white men to thrust their way into the uncharted canelands, Simon Kenton left behind him a quarter-million citizens of a peaceful and settled and civilized state and struck out once again for the frontier fringe.

Daniel Boone might be content to hunt and trap and wander alone in the Missouri wilderness for years to come, and George Rogers Clark might be content to vegetate on his Mulberry Hill across the river from Louisville, but for Simon the only thing that had changed was the location of the frontier. At the age of forty-three, he had no intention of letting it leave him behind.

[*December 31, 1798 — Monday*]

William Henry Harrison was still not at all certain what it was he wanted out of life, but of this much he had no doubt: a life of idleness and dissipation in command of a remote garrison, however important Fort Washington might be to the frontier, was not to his liking.

This country was opening up as if it were a basket of ripe fruit and the wise individual would snatch his plum now, before it was too late. The Ordinance of 1787 had declared that when the free male population of the Ohio Territory reached five thousand, and eight separate counties had been formed, the territory would be eligible for a change in its form of government; in short, statehood. Already more than the requisite number of free males lived here and, with Governor St. Clair's proclamation on August 20, establishing the sixth Ohio County (Ross), the final goal was nearing.[8]

Thus, when he was offered an opportunity to resign his military commission and become Secretary of the Northwest Territory under St. Clair, Harrison accepted with alacrity. He had come a long way for a man of only twenty-five years, but as far as he was concerned, this was only the beginning.

[*January 23, 1799 — Wednesday*]

Shortly before midnight, Simon Kenton's sixth child — and Elizabeth Kenton's first — announced her arrival in their snug Cincinnati cabin with a piercing little squall. As her parents had decided weeks before, in case it was a girl, Elizabeth named her Matilda.

Unfortunately, Simon was not on hand. For the past fortnight he had been exploring in the vicinity of the old Shawnee village of Chillicothe. This was land he had been intending to claim and it had come as a distinct shock to him when he arrived to find a sturdy two-story log building built by James Galloway already there and much of the land claimed. The home was only a short distance from where the council house had stood.

Hiding his disappointment, Simon stayed with the Galloways for a few days, having now decided that he would look over the good land to the east of where old Piqua Town had stood.[9] There, in a level, rich-looking area where a substantial spring-fed stream rushed to merge with the Mad River, he began claiming land.[10] As he approached the spot he started a magnificent buck that had been drinking from the creek just above its mouth and so he immediately named the stream Buck Creek.[11]

The more the frontiersman looked over this land, the more pleased he became with it. No less than a score of large, clear springs bubbled forth in the plain, which in itself was considerably larger than the one where Chillicothe had been located. It was a fine looking land where twenty or more large farms could be laid out and still leave plenty of room. Kenton's thoughts leaped ahead to envision the development of the area and for the first time in many years he thought of his old benefactor in Warm Springs, Virginia, Jacob Butler, for whom he had worked and whose name he had taken for so long. Butler had made an excellent living with his mill. If farmers came into this Ohio area in the numbers Simon expected — and he had no doubt they would — they'd soon be needing a gristmill. What a wonderful mill could be built here on Buck Creek! A man could make his fortune with such an operation.

It was food for thought.

And far to the south, along Quick's Run, sixteen-year-old Simon Ruth Kenton was dreaming his own dreams. As with his father, a dream was only the first step in the making of reality. But his dreams were not of the frontier, nor were they of acquiring lands. His dream lay with the sea, with gliding down the Ohio and Mississippi to New Orleans and joining a crew of privateers. To him the names of buccaneers such as Captains John "Long Ben" Avery and Bartholemew Roberts and Edward "Blackbeard" Teach carried far more glamor and promise of adventure than the names of men such as James Finley and David Duncan, Daniel Boone and James Harrod . . . or even Simon Kenton.

[*April 5, 1799 — Friday*]

The Kenton party did not settle at the mouth of Buck Creek, even though the big frontiersman had already claimed it. With the coming of spring the complexion of the land had changed from that bleak January scene. It was even nicer, but there was another site nearby that Simon had good reason to remember and it was here that he meant to settle.

The spot was located nearly five miles up the Mad River from the mouth of Buck Creek. Here poised a picturesque rolling hill in the midst of an expansive prairie less than a mile east of the river. It was bordered by fine groves of wild plum, cherry and crab as well as excellent hardwoods and — its most important aspect — in the center of the thousand-acre tract Simon claimed there gushed forth the clearest, coldest, finest spring he had ever seen.[12]

The site wasn't hard to find. Even had not the well-beaten Indian trail led directly there, memory alone would have sufficed for Simon. For it was here, after he had run the gauntlets at old Chillicothe and Piqua Town and was being marched to an uncertain fate at Mackachack, that Bo-nah and his other Shawnee captors had camped for the night twenty-one years ago. As he had lain here bound and tortured with pain, still he had known that someday he would return — if he lived.

The party the frontiersman led here was a large one, including not only himself, Elizabeth and five Kenton children, but also Elizabeth's family, the Jarboes, Martha's family, the Dowdens, the Elijah Berry family, the William Ward family, the John Humphries family and twelve Negro servants. It was a strange procession they made out of Cincinnati. No roads permitted wagon travel and so they followed the Indian trails on horseback, and from the deep pockets of huge saddlebags hung on each side of the horses peered the faces of wide-eyed little children.

They rode with care and alertness at Kenton's instructions. The Greenville Treaty had made this no longer Indian land, but Simon knew that in the Shawnee mind they were trespassers. He rode in front, rifle at ready and eyes constantly flickering from side to side and ahead as well as to the ground in front of them, watching for sign. His brothers-in-law, John and Archibald Dowden, flanked him on either side and slightly behind, themselves scanning horizon and ground for Indian sign as the frontiersman had trained them.

But though occasional glimpses of Indians were seen, the party was left in peace and on this day arrived at the site that was to be their Ohio home. For Simon Kenton, more than for any of the others, it was a moment of great personal triumph and he savored the taste of it.

[*May 25, 1799 — Saturday*]

If the plans of Ben Van Cleve, the Reverend William Hamer and some of the other settlers in Dayton had worked out as expected, it might have resulted in a good bit of revenue and fame coming to the new frontier settlement. Throughout most of last fall they had helped at building a large and well-fashioned flatboat. In early winter they had launched it in the Great Miami and tied it fast to await the swelling of the streams with spring rains. From that time until mid-March they had concentrated on getting the cargo gathered for a maiden voyage to New Orleans.

Over two thousand excellent fur skins — bales of beaver, otter, muskrat, bear, raccoon, skunk and mink pelts — constituted the bulk of the cargo and the remainder was made up of five hundred extra-good smoked venison hams, pickled pork, smoked bacon and a hundred large deerskin bags filled with shelled corn. Visions of Dayton becoming a major frontier shipping port danced in the settlers' heads.

Everything went well at first. The rains came when expected and on March 25 the flatboat had shoved off with a crew of ten, commanded by David Lowry, the man who designed the craft. It was an interesting though basically uneventful trip. In fact, the only occurrence of note came when they picked up an unexpected passenger — a youth clinging doggedly to a little homemade raft about ten feet square. His destination, he said, was New Orleans, so they took him on and he paid for his passage by providing them at each camp stop with fresh game downed under his flintlock rifle.

But the big impression the settlers had hoped to make in New Orleans failed to materialize when they arrived two months after leaving Dayton. The cargo was sold easily enough, though for hardly as much as expected, and an attempt to pole back upstream met with such difficulty that they wound up selling the flatboat also and returning to Ohio on horseback.

The youth they had picked up in midstream did not return with them. He wandered about, dazzled with the excitement of this extravagant, bustling city which was more colorful than his imagination could possibly have pictured. During that first evening he struck up an acquaintance with a youth three years his senior who seemed knowledgeable about the sea. They ate together at a crowded, dirty pub and the young traveler very nearly choked, much to his companion's amusement, on the first mug of rum he had ever drunk.

Not until their third mug each, when both were feeling heady and not a little silly, did the sixteen-year-old from upriver realize that he didn't even know his companion's name, nor that youth his. He stuck out his hand and grinned lopsidedly and his voice was a bit slurred when he spoke.

"By the way, my friend, my name's Kenton. Simon. What's yours?"

The older youth took his hand and shook it strongly. "Welcome to New Orleans, friend," he said. "Mine's Laffite. Jean Laffite."

[June 7, 1799 — Friday]

There could be no doubt that Tecumseh's sphere of influence was expanding. It took in not only his Shawnee followers and the Delawares with whom they had taken up residence on the White River, but other of the Ohio tribes. His natural eloquence held audiences spellbound and many of the older chiefs of the Wyandot and Chippewa and Seneca nations were saying that never before had any chief of any nation been such a speaker.

He seemed to take a deep delight in addressing his audiences, depending not on gestures or blatant emotionalism to hold them, but saying simply and well what was in his heart and expressing it in such manner that each hearer was inclined to remark to himself, "That is how I have felt inside but I have never been able to say it."

At this council being held now on the spot where the trails from Deer Creek and old Piqua Town converged, as they headed north toward Blue Jacket's Town, he addressed an audience of seventy, mostly Wyandots and Ottawas.[13] He had been speaking for well over an hour, drawing a comparison of what this country had been to what it was now and the word pictures he used touched them deeply.

"My brothers," he told them in conclusion, "how can our people continue to deceive themselves with their foolish belief in the supposed strength of the white chief Wayne's treaty signed at his fort of Greenville? The only difference between this treaty and the hundreds before it is the boundary line. Each time we have been told, 'This, Indian brother, is the last Treaty, the one that will be honored by red men and white alike for all time.' Such lies make the vomit burn in my throat. This is *not* the last treaty. There will be another. And another after that. And others to follow. And each time it will be the Indians, your people and mine, who will be pushed back, not the whites. At this very moment an hour's easy ride to the south is the newest of the white settlements. The cold spring there that has always before flowed for us, now satisfies the whites living in the fourteen cabins they have built by it. Soon other whites will come and build. And will all of these be content to stay behind Wayne's boundary? On my tongue is the harsh laughter of mockery. Think on this, brothers. Put aside your anger. Put aside your fear. Put aside your vain hopes. Think without prejudice of what I have said here and it will become clear to you as it is to me why the very leaves of the forest drop tears of pity on us as we walk beneath. And after you think on it, remember this: any child can snap with ease the single hair from a horse's tail, but not the strongest man, not the wildest stallion, can break the rope woven of these same hairs."

[*August 30, 1799 — Friday*]

The fact that a band of about two dozen roving Cherokees had suddenly decided to camp a few miles southeast of Kenton's new station and that numerous Indian councils were being held to the north, some as near as eight miles away, made the settlers uneasy to say the least. Nor did the knowledge that the Greenville Treaty permitted the Indians to hunt or camp anywhere they liked in Ohio relax their fears.

Simon Kenton was sure they were peaceful, but just to be safe he ordered a small blockhouse erected near the spring. In just these few short months since their arrival here, a score or more other settlers had come, some erecting cabins on Simon's land near the spring and even more on his land close to the mouth of Buck Creek. But these were basically unprotected cabins and, if trouble should loom, all would need a safe fortification in which to assemble. The blockhouse, capable of holding upwards of a hundred people, was built without delay.

The speaker at all these councils, the frontiersman had heard, was the young chief Tecumseh. It was Chiuxca and Coonahaw, two friendly Shawnees, who told him of this. They also said there was no need for the whites to worry; Tecumseh was not preaching war. He only spoke of what had been and what was now and what might come.

The name Tecumseh bothered Kenton, however, and he probed his memory until suddenly the incident came to him: the fight on Little East Fork. His plan of shooting into the Indian tents and thereby throwing them into a panic had failed because of the warrior named Tecumseh, who had charged instead of run and who had crushed Sam Barr's skull with his war club and captured Alexander McIntyre.

So now he was a chief. If he decided to take up the tomahawk again, things might become very bad for them here. Then, a few weeks ago, William Ward had rushed up to him and breathlessly read aloud the clippings a newcomer had given him from the new *Cincinnati Journal* newspaper:

CINCINNATI — *May 21, 1799 — The following important and alarming intelligence was handed in a few days ago for publication:*

Fort Washington
May 15, 1799
By a letter dated 4th May, 1799, I am informed from Col. David Strong, commanding at Detroit, that there is a report of a body of Indians collecting, who are meditating some hostile operations against some parts of the frontier. I am requested to make it known to the public.
Edward Miller
Captain Commanding

At once Simon and Ward mounted up and set off for Detroit. Arriving there they attempted to visit the nearby Ottawa towns where the Shawnee chief Black Snake and six other chiefs had been holding council, but they were turned away. Ward then wrote a letter to Black Snake, asking him if his intentions were hostile, as the whites had heard. They remained at Detroit several days until the runner returned with a long letter which he said had been dictated by Black Snake. It professed innocence of any idea of taking up the hatchet against the whites and reaffirmed their friendship, inviting Kenton and Ward to meet with them. The letter ended with the comment:

Brothers [the Shawnees], *being the last to make peace at Greenville with our father General Wayne, we would be the last to break this peace. Brothers, we regret that you have received a false alarm from some bad person.*

The letter was shown to Colonel Strong who immediately sent it on by express to be published in its entirety in the next issue of *The Western Spy* and, with it, another letter written by William Ward and signed by both Kenton and Ward which was to be published beneath Black Snake's letter:

The above is a copy of a letter received in answer to one sent by us to search the truth of the report respecting the attack from the Indians. The public will draw what conclusions and security they see proper from it. We are this day going to meet some of the chiefs; any of the information we may receive shall be communicated in some channel.

Simon Kenton
William Ward

Satisfied with the truth of Black Snake's letter, the pair returned home. So, despite minor incidents such as this, it appeared that all the Indians were adhering closely to the treaty. Simon wondered just how long it would last.

[*September 24, 1799 — Tuesday*]

When Governor Arthur St. Clair called the meeting in Cincinnati on September 16 to establish the now authorized territorial legislature, the two principal questions in the minds of all on hand were who would be elected speaker and who would become the territory's delegate to Congress?

It took eight days for representatives to be chosen and for the two houses to organize themselves for business. Then came the anticipated moments. By a unanimous vote, the very popular Dr. Edward Tiffin of Chillicothe was elected speaker; and taking eleven of the twenty-one votes cast for delegate to the United States Congress was the young Jeffersonian Party candidate whom everyone said was sure to go places — William Henry Harrison.

[*September 12, 1800 — Friday*]

Never before in the history of the Shawnees had there been such amity between Indians and whites. Not only were guns no longer raised when they met one another unexpectedly on the trail, in many cases firm friendships sprang up between them. Just as whites were welcomed to visit the Indian villages, so the Indians were welcomed in the cabins of many whites, often staying over as visitors under their roofs for days, sometimes weeks. Tecumseh, for example, and Blue Jacket, too, had become good friends of the James Galloway family and stayed at his home frequently.

Two Shawnees — Coonahaw and the minor Maykujay chief Chiuxca — visited Simon Kenton numerous times and when, in June, they arrived with their families and set about building their *wegiwas* within a stone's throw of Kenton's house, the frontiersman welcomed them. He liked both men a great deal and was pleased that they had honored him in this manner. On many evenings thereafter they held impromptu meetings of the three families — Kenton's, Chiuxca's and Coonahaw's — either before

Simon's huge stone fireplace in the large cabin or else outside around a campfire.

Here they talked at length of many things. Chiuxca, soon after his arrival, told of the death dance that had been held in Detroit in May for Alexander McKee, even though the British agent had been killed by his pet deer six years before. It was an impressive ceremony with several hundred Shawnees and numerous other Indians present, along with many of McKee's former friends, such as Simon Girty and Matthew Elliott. Never before in Chiuxca's memory had such an honor been bestowed upon a white man, for the two-day dance of death was traditionally held only for men of great distinction.

In many cases these two Shawnees knew more about what the whites were doing in Ohio than did Simon himself. It was they who told him of the construction of Fort Industry by the United States Army at the mouth of Swan Creek on the Maumee River.[14] And it was Chiuxca who first told Simon that he had heard the Indiana Territory was soon to have its own government, apart from St. Clair's, and that the soldier-turned-statesman, William Henry Harrison, was rumored to be the man whom the great white chief, Adams, was picking for the job of governor. This bit of information bothered both Shawnees considerably. The Indiana Territory was just what its name signified: territory of the Indians. It was theirs according to the boundaries established in the Greenville Treaty and they were worried lest such a move by President John Adams open old wounds.

Simon, in turn, passed news on to the Indians. Three more counties, he said, had been formed in the Ohio Territory this year — Trumbull, Fairfield and Clermont. With their formation, Ohio was now fully eligible for statehood. Connecticut had ceded to the United States her jurisdiction claims to the Western Reserve lands — where already over a thousand white men had settled and seven hundred miles of road had been built — setting a pattern immediately followed by Massachusetts and New York with similar cessions of Ohio lands to the federal government. He also told them that the nebulous seat of Ohio government, which had bounced back and forth between Marietta and Cincinnati, was now fixed temporarily at Chillicothe — that is, the white man's Chillicothe — at Paint Creek's mouth.

It was customary among the whites at this time to consider Indians as emotionless people utterly devoid of feelings of love, compassion or a sense of humor; but, as Simon Kenton and others of the whites were learning, such was not the case at all. They loved every bit as deeply as the whites and pity was certainly not unknown to them. Few people enjoyed a good joke more, whether verbal or physical, and often they went to great lengths to perpetrate pranks or hoaxes upon one another, or even upon the whites.

Not for many a year, however, had as great a coup been pulled off in this vein as the one so adroitly engineered by Blue Jacket beginning last spring. One of the prevailing puzzles among the pioneers was the question of where the Shawnees mined all the silver they used for their ornaments. That they had a fantastic supply of it was obvious, for rare indeed was even the lowliest of Shawnee warriors who did not own many beautiful hand-beaten armbands, necklaces, medallions and other objects of the purest quality silver. The man who could find this hoard would undoubtedly stake his claim on a small piece of land which would be worth millions of dollars.

The Shawnees, however, refused even to discuss the matter with the whites. But then, in late spring, an avaricious individual named Jonathan Flack came up from Kentucky and spent several months with the Shawnees at their villages and hunting camps, trying to induce Blue Jacket to divulge the location. With a show of extreme reluctance, Blue Jacket finally agreed, providing his people were compensated enough. He said he would meet Flack on a specified date at the home of James Galloway on the site of old Chillicothe and there they could discuss terms.

Flack galloped back to Kentucky, gathered a group of backers and formed what he called the Blue Jacket Mining Company. On the appointed date he was back at Galloway's house with a dozen men. Two days of negotiations passed, during which Blue Jacket considered their proposals at length, his demands rising in proportion to their growing eagerness to possess the knowledge which would bring them all untold wealth.

A bargain was finally consummated: horses, goods and a great deal of money were turned over to the chief who, in turn, distributed them among the Shawnees. Hesitantly, then, he told them the location. The mines were in Kentucky along the Red River, a tributary of the Kentucky River. The information stunned them. Tradition among the whites had it that the fabulous mines were located somewhere in the vicinity of old Chillicothe, most likely in the deep glen to the northeast a few miles. No wonder they'd never been able to find it!

Blue Jacket and his squaw, Wabethe, were escorted in grand style to Kentucky where they were feasted and feted in the most flattering manner, with all their wants anticipated and liberally supplied. In due time, and with all possible secrecy, they reached the "sacred area" and here Blue Jacket demanded seclusion so that he might purify and humble himself through fasting and thus appease the Great Spirit so as to get His permission to disclose the whereabouts of the mines.

Time passed — a great deal of it — until finally Blue Jacket returned and the search began. But somehow Blue Jacket was unable to locate the right area. He blamed this on the dimming of his eyes with age and suggested that if the company would wait here, he and Wabethe would return home and send back their son, Little Blue Jacket, whose eyes were clear and who also knew the location of the mines. The white men agreed readily.

The Shawnee chief departed and the members of the Blue Jacket Mining Company waited . . . and waited.

Two hundred miles to the north the word spread among the Indian nations of the greatest practical joke in decades and around their campfires, as they discussed it, the Shawnees were convulsed with glee.[15]

[*December 31, 1800 — Wednesday*]

Throughout the long winter nights in the White River village, the Shawnees and Delawares slept peacefully, unaware for the most part that in the *wegiwa* of Tecumseh a momentous long-range strategy was evolving. Sometimes in company with his weasel-like younger brother, Lowawlu-waysica, but more often by himself, Tecumseh spent night after night seated before his fire, planning for the future.

The more he considered his plans and the more he improved and elaborated on them, the more certain he became of their eventual success. This was no hastily drawn strategy. What he envisioned might take ten or twelve years of concentrated effort to consummate, but he knew he had the ability to pull it off, and the self-confidence as well. Should this plan culminate in success — and it must! — the detested *Shemanese* would be driven back not only across the Spay-lay-wi-theepi, but even beyond the mountains to the east.

Tecumseh knew as well as any man alive that, given equal arms and equal numbers, no white force could stand up to the fearlessness and savagery in battle of Indians. How many times had mere handfuls of Indians routed greatly superior white forces? How few times had the Indians themselves been defeated, and then only through the greater manpower and weaponry of the enemy? The victory over Harmar's army had shown what a small Indian army could do to a large white force. The victory over St. Clair had shown what a superior Indian force could do to a white army smaller in number, regardless of its armament.

Beginning in spring, according to his plan, he would commence welding the tribes together, not in a confederation but in a great and powerful amalgamation. There had been confederations before, such as those formed under Pontiac and Thayendanega and, more recently, under Little Turtle. But all of these had eventually failed for two prime reasons: first, because the leadership had eventually disintegrated; and, second, because the confederacies had not initially been united strongly enough to forget their petty intertribal jealousies.

This amalgamation Tecumseh would forge must be stronger than any ever seen before. It would not be made up of a half-dozen or so tribes loosely united to fight the common enemy. He himself would range far and, using the great gifts of eloquence and prescience with which Moneto had endowed him, he would take his time and convince the different tribes of the necessity of joining together if they were to survive. He would tell them in such manner that they would stamp their feet and shout and chafe at any delay in carrying out the amalgamation. He would draw together a tightly interwoven force of fifty or more different tribes. They would not meet the whites as a number of tribes totaling five hundred or a thousand or even five thousand warriors. When the *Shemanese* were confronted it would be by a single, unified body of thirty or forty or fifty thousand warriors, perhaps even more. What he envisioned with such a force was a demand to the whites for a return of their lands. He would, if at all possible, avoid warfare with them. But if it came to that, he would not turn aside.

The travels Tecumseh had made as a boy, and later as a young man, with Chiksika had shown him the strength of the various tribes. By themselves they were strong in their individuals but too weak tribally to oppose the whites. In small confederations, each still retaining its own tribal form and its own leadership, they were stronger and could hold their own — but not for long. But in an amalgamation such as Tecumseh now envisioned, which joined them all under a single, strong leadership against the most deadly peril in any of their histories, the enemy would be swept away as the autumn leaves before the gale that springs from the west.

He would start his unification with at least fifty tribes. There were more, of course, and Tecumseh was sure that once they saw the value of the amalgamation's strength and power, they would all hasten to join. To the northeast there would be what remained of the Iroquois Confederation — the Mohawks and Oneidas, the Onondagas and Cayugas and Senecas. Right here, in the Northwest Territory, there would be the Delawares and Wyandots and Potawatomies, the Miamis, Eel Rivers, Muncies, Tuscarawas, Illinois, Kaskaskias and, of course, the Shawnees. To the north he would collect the Hurons, the Ottawas and Chippewas and, a little farther to the northwest, the Winnebagos and Foxes, Sacs, Menominees, Kickapoos; perhaps even the Dakotas and Mandans and the Cheyennes. And due west of the Mississippi, from whence much of the amalgamation's numerical strength would come, there were Poncas and Pawnees, Iowas and Omahas, the mighty Sioux and Otos and the Missouris and Osages, Kansas and Wichitas.

There were many tribes to the southwest, but he would concentrate at first on the more powerful; the Quapaws and Yazoos and Natchez, the Caddos, Hasinais, Kitchais and the Tawakonias. And to the south, there were his good friends and admirers, the Cherokees and, adjoining them, the Choctaws and Chickasaws, the Alabamas and the Biloxis and the Upper Creeks.

And finally, to the southeast, there were the remainder of the scattered Santees and Catawbas and Calusas. And there were also the Lower Creeks and their brothers, the Seminoles.

With his gift of prophecy, he would give them signs in which to believe. He would call on their honor, their pride, their religion, their superstitions. Every argument, every force he could bring to bear, he would do so without hesitation. And he would use, especially here in his own country, the single great talent of Lowawluwaysica — his ability to agitate, to anger, to stir to a fury against the *Shemanese* the thoughts of every Indian.

All this would not be done in a week or a month or a year. Perhaps not even in a decade. With some of the tribes he would have to move slowly, carefully, gradually gaining their confidence, their respect, their willingness to follow. With other tribes it would go swiftly, with only a word or two needed for the war belts to begin circulating and the tomahawks to be struck into the war posts.

And most important of all, while this was going on they *must not show it*. They must adhere to their treaties at all costs. They must, when the time came, as come it would, overlook infringement of their rights by the whites. They must profess a peaceable intent in all things until they were ready. If there was any possibility of accomplishing their aims without warfare, then this must be the course followed. But, war or not, it would be done. This fact must be kept from the whites and no outsider must ever be allowed to sit in on the councils. The Indians must faithfully, honestly and forever bury whatever past hostilities and animosities had risen between themselves and each man must treat every other, regardless of his tribal affiliation, as no more nor less than a fellow Indian fighting at his side for the same cause.

They must place an inviolate prohibition on the consumption of any alcoholic beverage and, though their pipes could still be filled with *kinnikinnick*, they must cease to smoke the tall green weed which brought strange dreams and weakness.[16] They must study closely, seriously and unobtrusively the way of the whites, their strengths and weaknesses. They must break whatever alliances presently existed between themselves and the whites — be they Americans, British, French or Spanish. They must be encouraged to take anything of value which the whites might offer them in the form of gratuities or annuities, but they must join no white man to fight another white man, for in this direction lay ruin. With past alliances, Indians had been used, manipulated like tools, to promote only the welfare of one white faction over another. Let the whites fight among themselves if they wished. It would weaken them. But let not any Indian bind himself to any white man or any white cause or any white ideal.

They must, in some cases, swallow their fierce pride temporarily and, if necessary, fall back when the *Shemanese* nudged them. They must turn their cheeks and pretend docility and under no pretext must they take up the hatchet against the whites until, and unless, there was no other choice — and then not until he, Tecumseh, gave the sign. This would be a sign that would come to all of these tribes on the same day and at the same time.

And when the period of waiting and building and growing was over, they would demand the return of their lands. With such a united force to back the demand, there was every reason to hope that the whites would vacate peaceably. But if they would not, Tecumseh would give the signal — and when that unmistakable sign was given, then this irresistible wave of warriors would wash across the face of the land to drown every white man who did not flee to the east of the mountains.

[*January 10, 1801 — Saturday*]

When on this day William Henry Harrison was sworn into office as governor of the Indiana Territory, he was still a month away from his twenty-eighth birthday. Few men his age had ever achieved such a position; moreover, in appointing him to this seat, President John Adams had given him such powers as had never been bestowed upon any other individual, civil or military, since the organization of the nation. In this office Harrison became virtual king of the territory, responsible only to the President himself and that only to a minor degree. He was able at will to enact any law and he held within his grasp the power of life and death over anyone within the territory, Indian or white. And among the many powers he had was the right to treat with the Indians on behalf of the United States in any manner he saw fit.

It was an enormous responsibility and, in the hands of a lesser man, might well have caused irreparable damage. But the President had selected well. In just the short time Harrison had been secretary of the Northwest Territory under St. Clair, he had acquired a reputation for strength, decisiveness, fairness and extraordinary ability.

At this time the Indiana Territory extended all the way from the Ohio Territory line to the Mississippi River and in all this area there were only three white settlements: Clark's Grant at the Falls of Ohio opposite Louisville; Vincennes, on the River Wabash, where the new governor would make his headquarters; and an area extending along the Mississippi River which took in both Kaskaskia and Cohokia. Total population was about five thousand, but the settlements were so distantly separated that it was impossible for them to contribute to one another's defense if the need arose.

And chances were that it would.

[*March 4, 1801 — Wednesday*]

The Presidential election had resulted in a tie: both Thomas Jefferson and Aaron Burr had received equal votes. It became the duty of the House of Representatives to select the one who would become President. There

could be no doubt that it was the voice of the still extremely influential
Alexander Hamilton that swung the balance to the Republican candidate,
Jefferson, even though he differed in many of his views with the man. The
Federalist candidate, Burr, was in Hamilton's sage opinion, "undepend-
able."

Today Jefferson took his oath of office and became the first President of
the United States to be inaugurated in the nation's new and permanent
capital, Washington, D.C.

[December 31, 1801 — Thursday]

The year continued to see the rapid settlement of lower Ohio. On March
17 a new town had been laid out near where Kenton had blazed his land at
the mouth of Buck Creek, and Elizabeth Kenton was asked to name it.
Delighted at having been chosen for this honor, Elizabeth thought carefully and then said, "On account of the many delightful and valuable
springs within and around this place located for the town, I'd like to
suggest it be called Springfield."[17] And so it was.

On May 4, to attract even more settlers, Congress authorized the
opening of lands east of the Scioto, south of the United States Military
Lands and west of the fifteenth range of townships of the Seven Ranges.
This tract was to be brought into the market and offered for sale by the
government to the general public, and was thereafter known as the
Congress Lands.

A land office was opened at the new settlement of Steubenville on the
far eastern border of the Ohio Territory for further sales of parts of the
Seven Ranges and the seat of government of the Territory, which had
jumped back and forth between Marietta and Cincinnati and had finally
gone to Chillicothe, was now reestablished at Cincinnati with passage of a
bill by the Legislature on December 19.

One of the most spectacular events of the year came on August 27 when
the first sea vessel equipped for ocean travel — a five-hundred-ton ship
built at Marietta — cast loose and passed down the Ohio River carrying a
cargo of produce for New Orleans. The riverbanks resounded with cheers
from huge crowds which gathered as the great lumbering craft slipped
quietly past Manchester, Maysville, Cincinnati and Louisville.

But not all the changes that came about were pleasant — at least not for
Simon Kenton. He suffered a severe financial blow when Judge John Cleve
Symmes was finally forced to admit to the government that he was unable
to pay for his long-pending purchase. Congress at once canceled the sale
and Symmes lost everything, including the money various buyers had paid
him for lands within the purchase. Overnight, Simon Kenton's quarter
million acres within this Symmes Purchase area vanished. When it became
obvious to the frontiersman that there was nothing he could do about it,

he shrugged with characteristic calmness and turned his interests elsewhere.

Springfield was growing quite rapidly, as was Dayton, twenty-four miles southwest. Already a wagon road had been cut between the two towns and it was time, Simon realized, to get moving on that gristmill he envisioned on Buck Creek. He claimed a suitable piece of ground some distance up the swift little watercourse from its mouth and named it Lagonda, after the name the Shawnees had given to the creek.

His next step was to send back East for the materials he would need, which included a number of good saws from Pittsburgh and some quality millstones cut at Laurel Hill in Pennsylvania. These he had hauled twenty-five miles to Redstone Old Fort on the Monongahela, there to be put aboard a flatboat and floated down the Ohio. In early fall he enlisted the aid of Chiuxca and his strong son, Spy Buck, to help cut a road he was already calling Kenton's Trace directly from Lagonda to Newmarket, a tiny new settlement on the Ohio almost opposite Maysville. Over this road the heavy millstones and other equipment would be wagoned to the mill site. It was slow work hacking a road through the tangled undergrowth and it was really not much of a road when finished, barely wide enough to accommodate the wheels of a wagon. However, it was enough; time and travel would take care of further widening and clearing of it.

Late in the fall, when the flatboat arrived and the wagons were loaded and started north, Simon did not accompany them. Elizabeth was soon to have another baby; still, he reasoned, he could make a quick trip into Kentucky with Spy Buck to see about his holdings there and return in time.

But the frontiersman's troubles were by no means over. Not only had his brother John lost practically all of the lands left in his care, but those of Simon's lands not already gone were involved in a morass of lawsuits almost beyond belief. So serious were these troubles that he wound up selling even his land and fine old brick house at Kenton's Station to a man named Samuel Tebbs.

And then came the crowning blow. The same fever that had knocked him out of Wayne's campaign at Fallen Timbers now struck again and laid him low in extremely serious condition. He was unaware of anything when Betsy bore him her second daughter on December 6 and named her Elizabeth after herself.

Leaving Kenton in the care of a good friend in Washington, Spy Buck recrossed the Ohio and struck out for the frontiersman's home to let them know that Simon was dying. And thus the year ended, with the frontiersman clinging tenaciously to life, nearly a hundred miles away from his wife and family.

[*April 17, 1802 — Saturday*]

Despite having just borne a child, Elizabeth Kenton lost no time in getting to Kentucky to help care for her husband. She arrived there on January

2 — the same day that Cincinnati was incorporated by the Territorial Legislature and David Zeigler appointed president, or mayor, of the city.

The crisis for Simon passed and recuperation began, but it was a slow recovery at best. Perhaps it may have fogged the frontiersman's thinking some, for as he lay regaining his strength he developed a plan quite bold in conception but not at all logical. With much of his land here in Kentucky gone, with his entire Symmes Purchase tract gone, he turned his thoughts to the possibility of establishing an empire all his own. He remembered how Richard Henderson, in his Watauga Treaty with the Cherokees, had bought the whole of Kentucky for the purpose of establishing the empire he wanted to call Transylvania. Although Virginia had promptly declared the title invalid, at least Henderson had been permitted to keep a sizable portion of the claim.

The question now was with whom he should establish his treaty; he decided upon the Shawnee chief he had heard was gaining so much prominence among the Indians, Tecumseh. Thus it was that when his recuperation was finished and he returned to Springfield with Elizabeth in late March, Simon set out again without a word to anyone for the White River village of the Delawares where Tecumseh was currently residing. He arrived there just in time to catch the Shawnee chief before he left on an extensive journey of his own.

Tecumseh was surprised to see the *cut-ta-ho-tha* here, but he remained expressionless and listened quietly as Simon explained what he wanted. If he was amazed at the effrontery of the proposition, he didn't show it. The frontiersman produced a treaty he had had written up by one Abey Clark, in which Simon agreed to give the Indians "considerable goods and provisions," including the promise to "pay more money or goods as long as grass grows and water runs." In exchange, Tecumseh was to give Simon most of the land lying between the Great Miami and Wabash River — an area of close to five thousand square miles.[18]

It was, of course, prohibited by Congress for any unauthorized private person to treat with the Indians in matters of land — a fact both Kenton and Tecumseh knew. But the frontiersman apparently thought he could pull it off, and Tecumseh looked upon it as something of a great joke, similar to the one his good friend Blue Jacket had pulled off with the Blue Jacket Mining Company. In fact, had Kenton wished to buy the moon from him, Tecumseh would probably have sold, knowing such a sale would be considered no more valid than this one. Furthermore, it was in keeping with his own established plan of taking anything the whites might offer. Tecumseh accepted.

Throughout the countryside the Indians rocked with laughter over this tremendous joke; it bested even Blue Jacket's exploit, and once again Tecumseh's prestige rose significantly among all the Indians who heard of it. For his own part, Simon returned home elated with his success; though

he talked little about it, his eyes gleamed with something akin to fanata-
cism the more he thought about his "empire." The millstones and other
equipment ordered from Pennsylvania lay waiting for him at Lagonda, but
his enthusiasm for the mill project had been replaced. Ever more frequently he turned his eyes to the west. He would not be content until he
had thoroughly explored the entire area he had purchased.

In mid-June, again without a word to anyone, he strode off into the
wilderness with nothing but his rifle and tomahawk and the clothing he
wore. And once more, as was becoming his habit, he left behind a pregnant
wife.

[*May 18, 1802 — Tuesday*]

Ever since they had become friends following Wayne's campaign, William
Henry Harrison had felt a bond of affection for the minor Delaware chief
named Beaver. He was a rather fat, jovial man, slow to anger and with an
engaging personality. His wife, nearly as fat as he, was a slow and ungainly
woman who had lost most of her teeth and was so afflicted with rheuma-
tism she could scarcely walk.

Since becoming governor of the territory, Harrison had visited numerous
times with the chief in this little village of Wapakoneta in the Ohio
Territory.[19] He had taken quite a liking for the chief's ten-year-old son, also
named Beaver. But unlike the other visits, this was a melancholy one. For
some reason never made adequately clear to Harrison, Chief Beaver had
been accused of practicing sorcery. The charge had come from Ku-la-qua-ti,
the tribe's medicine man, and a council of Delaware chiefs had met and
sentenced Chief Beaver to death.

When the time for the execution came, Chief Beaver had dressed
himself in fine clothing and, before leaving the *wegiwa*, embraced his wife
and son and shook hands with the governor. He asked Harrison if he
would watch over little Beaver for him, and Harrison went even further —
he offered to take the boy back to Vincennes with him and raise him.
Chief Beaver nodded approvingly, instructed his son to consider Harrison
as his new father and left the *wegiwa*.

Harrison knew enough not make any attempt to stop the execution.
This was strictly an Indian affair. But it appalled him to think that the
superstitions of these people were so strong that they would resort to such
measures.

Most of the men of the village, plus a number of visitors from other
villages and a few from other tribes, were on hand to witness the execution.
Flanked by two men, Chief Beaver walked casually toward a little rise at
the edge of the village. He conversed in a pleasant manner with the pair at
his sides until they reached the appointed spot. Then he bade them
farewell, stepped a pace or so forward and turned his back to them, facing

the setting sun. One of the warriors removed a war club from his belt, raised it high and brought it down on the chief's skull in a blow so savage that it crushed the whole top of his head. The execution was that quick and simple.

Shaken by witnessing such a thing, Harrison left the village immediately after the shallow-grave burial. Behind him on the same horse rode ten-year-old Beaver. The boy's face had been a mask all through the day but now, as they left the village behind in darkness, he leaned his head against Harrison's back and silent tears streamed from his eyes.

Back in the Indian village, a visitor sat before the fire, neither talking nor listening to what was being said. Lowawluwaysica had come here to begin the first subtle preachings of Tecumseh's doctrine and had found a most receptive audience. Moreover, the execution of Chief Beaver had planted a provocative seed in his mind which was already sprouting. As with the Delawares and most other tribes in the Northwest Territory, the Shawnees had a position in their society equivalent to a spiritual leader and head medicine man, or, more familiarly, a prophet. He was a man who could not only cure illnesses, invoke secret spells and have, to some degree, the ability of a seer, but a man whose sense of sociological values was advanced to the point where he was able to perform well as a tribal conscience and moral reformer among his people. As such, he could wield enormous power which, on occasion, rivaled or possibly even superseded that of the principal chief.

Within the Shawnee tribe, the man who now filled this important and extremely influential post was a frail, almost century-old Chalahgawtha Shawnee named Penegashega — The-Change-of-Feathers — whose own health had been faltering of late and who must certainly die before long. His high office was not acquired by mere succession, but through self-assertion by the Shawnee who had, in the recent past, exhibited the most qualities for the job. This was usually one of the minor doctors or medicine men of the tribe, of which Lowawluwaysica was one, even though not a very good one.

Suppose, mused Lowawluwaysica, he and Tecumseh were to combine their talents — he providing the medical knowledge and innate craftiness the office called for and Tecumseh providing the prophecy. Lowawluwaysica was well aware that Tecumseh had always been a better prophet than Penegashega could ever have hoped to have been. In the privacy of their *wegiwa*, Tecumseh could give him the prophecies and Lowawluwaysica could announce them as his own. It would be natural, then, when Penegashega died, for him to step into the exalted office, from which he could wield great power as the tribe's prophet and conscience. His voice added to Tecumseh's would provide just that much more strength in encouraging the tribes to embrace the plan; and if there were some who remained reluctant, perhaps a little encouragement in the form of executions for witchcraft would help. It was exciting food for thought.

[*August 11, 1802 — Wednesday*]

Each time he addressed one of these councils, Tecumseh felt a great exaltation as he saw how his words caught and held his listeners; how easily, with the proper turn of a phrase, he could stir in them emotions of anger and hate, love and pleasure, regret and sorrow. Each time he began to speak he was never really sure exactly what he would say, but then the words came to him, rolling fluently from his tongue and never failing to stir deeply all who listened.

He was much pleased with the way things had gone thus far. All during spring, summer and fall of last year he had gone from village to village, journeying as far eastward as western Vermont and Massachusetts. This past spring, as soon as he had concluded the laughable treaty with the *cut-ta-ho-tha*, he had ranged across upper and western New York State and northwestern Pennsylvania. All of the remaining Iroquois Confederacy had been deeply inspired by the plan and they looked upon the speaker with something very akin to reverence. They had pledged their faith and their secrecy and, most important, their help when the great sign should be given.

This great sign that Tecumseh spoke of wherever he went always remained the same, and his telling of it never failed to awe his audiences. When the period of waiting was over, he told them, when tribal unification had been completed, when all was in readiness, then would this sign be given: in the midst of night the earth beneath would tremble and roar for a long period. Jugs would break, though there be no one near to touch them. Great trees would fall, though the air be windless. Streams would change their courses to run backwards, and lakes would be swallowed up into the earth and other lakes suddenly appear. The bones of every man would tremble with the trembling of the ground and they would not mistake it. No! There was not anything to compare with it in their lives nor in the lives of their fathers or the fathers before them since time began; when this sign came, they were to drop their mattocks and flesh scrapers, leave their fields and their hunting camps and their villages and join together and move to assemble across the lake river from the fort of Detroit. And on that day they would no longer be Mohawks or Senecas, Oneidas or Onondagas or any other tribe. They would be Indians! One people united forever where the good of one would henceforth become the good of all.

So it would be!

[*November 29, 1802 — Monday*]

There was excitement this day in Cincinnati.

In accordance with the act passed by Congress last April 30 authorizing the call of a convention to form a state constitution for Ohio, the meeting had begun on Monday, November 1, and from all over the territory came county delegates who were to make up the membership of this body.[20]

As expected, the speaker of the territorial legislature, Dr. Edward Tiffin of Ross County, was chosen president of the Constitutional Convention. Under his very able hand matters moved well and the articles of the constitution were swiftly drawn. But a fuse that had been ignited during the last session of the territorial legislature at Chillicothe caused an explosion that, on November 22, had rocked the convention.

During that session, there had been heated disputes about the proposed boundaries for the soon-to-be-organized state of Ohio and a mob had assembled one night in the streets. The next morning, an angry Governor Arthur St. Clair came into a room occupied by Hamilton County representatives Jeremiah Morrow, Francis Dunlevy and Edward Foster, all of whom had frequently opposed his moves in previous sessions. Attributing the mob's presence to political disputes, St. Clair, in decidedly blunt terms and with a remarkable degree of indiscretion, abused the democratic institutions of both the nation and the territory and expressed the emphatic opinion that they could not last. The country must soon return to a stronger form of government, he insisted, such as had made England a model among nations.

Morrow, Dunlevy and Foster were too stunned to reply immediately, but upon St. Clair's departure, Francis Dunlevy sat down and drew up in writing a faithful report, as nearly verbatim as possible, of the governor's declarations. The three men signed the paper before a justice of the peace and Dunlevy at once dispatched it by special courier to his good friend, President Thomas Jefferson.

The bomb that had burst in the Constitutional Convention was the announcement that President Jefferson had relieved St. Clair of his governorship and all other authority, effective immediately, and was appointing as acting governor, Charles Willing Byrd of Hamilton.

Immediately St. Clair's friends and supporters charged the removal to party intolerence and proscription of Republicans, and claimed that St. Clair was being removed to gratify the malice of his enemies by the very man who had been his friend and adviser, Thomas Jefferson. The opposition claimed otherwise, saying that Republicanism in its purity was on trial for the first time in history; that the men who had brought this action about were the real Republicans because they had faith in Republican institutions; that the facts had been spread before President Jefferson and he had no choice but to act as he had.

Whichever was true, the matter was summed up succinctly by Territorial Judge Jacob Burnet, who noted that the removal of St. Clair "was one of the first evidences given by the new administration that politics were stronger than friendships and partisan services more availing than talents."

But at last the furor died down and the convention continued. And today, November 29, 1802, a constitution of state government — without being referred to the people of the state for approbation — was ratified and became the fundamental law of the state by act of the convention alone.

[*March 3, 1803 — Thursday*]

Simon Kenton had been a long time gone, and what he returned to was most certainly not what he had left. When he went out to explore his new empire, Ohio was a territory. Now it was the seventeenth state of the Union.

A general election on January 3 had made Dr. Edward Tiffin its first governor, even though the Congress did not approve the constitution and recognize Ohio as a state until February 19. Nor was it any longer a state of just nine counties — the First Ohio General Assembly had met and enacted a large number of laws and just two days ago created eight new counties: Gallia, Scioto, Franklin, Butler, Columbiana, Warren, Greene and Montgomery.

There was bad news awaiting the frontiersman, too. His land troubles in Kentucky had grown even worse; not only were most of his holdings there lost but he was being held liable for certain damages. In the months since he left home many a stranger had knocked on the Kenton door trying to collect money which the Kentucky courts claimed the frontiersman owed.

What was worse, the fears that had been growing in him all these months now became cold, hard reality: not one single person had any intention of recognizing his purchase of the "empire." He had been bilked out of everything he had paid for it, and all he could do was chalk it up to experience.

Although it was not his happiest homecoming by any stretch of the imagination, there were two things which worked wonders for Simon: one was the fact that he returned in perfect health again, his eyes clear and bright, his step firm, his strength prodigious. He even decided to resume work on his mill at Lagonda — a building he planned to make eighteen feet square and quite tall, with a well balanced waterwheel on one side. The other matter that pleased him was the fact that he had arrived home just in time for the birth of another daughter, whom he named Mary, after his mother.

[*May 1, 1803 — Saturday*]

It was the first court to be held in newly formed Greene County and it was a proud day for Benjamin Whiteman. He had been named an associate judge in the county court under Francis Dunlevy and he reached the log cabin "courthouse" simply bursting with enthusiasm.

A fair-sized crowd was there and congratulations went the rounds, but as it came time to call court into session, it came as something of a disappointment to learn that there were no cases on the docket to be tried.

There was, however, a barrel of whiskey to celebrate the opening of the court and a good supply of tin cups. In a remarkably short time the whiskey level had become quite low and the crowd proportionately high. Songs were sung and more was drunk and then one bleary-eyed settler squinted at another and, for some obscure reason, mumbled, "You know somethin'? You ain't no better'n a hog thief!"

The man so accused reached into his pocket and took out his purse. He turned to Whiteman with a tight smile.

"How much will it cost me, Judge, to beat hell out of a damn liar?"

Immediately a wild melee broke out and the first court day in Greene County turned out to be a roaring success after all. Eighteen cases of assault and battery were tried.

[*May 20, 1803 — Friday*]

As had many of the earliest settlers, when once a frontier town took on some semblance of civilized respectability, James Harrod had grown discontent with life in Harrodsburg. In the early days, he had enjoyed making the settlement, defending it from Indians and gradually watching it grow into a fine city bearing his name. But now the city was self-sufficient. A man no longer had to carry a rifle wherever he went and the element of danger was gone. Worst of all, the sense of being needed was gone.

And so James Harrod struck out on his own again, possiby this time to begin another settlement in the Ohio country that would one day grow into a city that might perhaps become another Harrodsburg. Uncertain as yet where he would locate, he decided to stop off in Ross County, Ohio, to visit a day or so with his old friend, Nathaniel Massie. Perhaps that pioneer might have some ideas as to where an important frontier town could be established.

From a treeless hillside he looked down at the town of Chillicothe. It surprised him with its size — seventy or more sturdy cabins, along with perhaps a dozen well-built frame homes. An impressive church spire punctured the sky and even from a mile or so away he could see a number of stores and a large, public-type building. With Paint Creek meandering past its very doorstep to merge with the Scioto River, it made a picturesque scene. Massie must be very proud of what he had accomplished; moreover, Harrod admired the man for advocating that the town be named Chillicothe rather than some form of his own name, as it had been in the beginning. Not many a man would have been willing to see such a significant memorial to his name changed.

Pleased at the thought of meeting his frontier companion again after such a long time, Harrod gripped his rifle, reshouldered his pack and took a step toward the town. In that instant there came the crash of a shot from close behind him and a bullet the size of the first joint of his thumb slammed into his back, ripped through his heart and left a hole the size of his fist where it exited from his chest.

There would not be another Harrodsburg.

[*May 23, 1803 — Monday*]

Waw-wil-a-way was sincerely thankful that the warfare between Indians and whites was over. It had been far too long since the Shawnees had enjoyed such peace. He was grateful, too, that Chief Black Hoof had not been talked into accepting that fantastic, hopeless plan Tecumseh was brewing, as had so many of the younger Shawnees and other Indians. It could only bring bloodshed and a worsening of the Indians' lot. A troublemaker, that's what Tecumseh was. How fortunate for the Shawnees that Black Hoof was still vigorously alive at seventy-seven to oppose the young chief. Without the old chief's counsel, many more Shawnees would have joined Tecumseh by now.

In the years since he had attached himself to Nathaniel Massie, Waw-wil-a-way had become a familiar figure in and around new Chillicothe. He had made many friends there and found great delight in strolling into the town to be greeted by whites who knew and liked him, who sometimes visited him in his own *wegiwa* and who even invited him into their homes to eat. Now he was on his way to join Massie on a long-planned turkey hunt and his steps quickened in anticipation.

The three shabbily dressed men saw the Indian before he saw them. They were sitting on a log at the edge of the woods and he was walking across the prairie. The leader of the trio was known by the name of David Wolfe, and his companions were loutish men whom Wolfe addressed as Williams and Ferguson.

They had been discussing the death three days ago of James Harrod. The popular pioneer's body, stripped of all its goods and scalped, had been found in the early evening and a great fear had swept Chillicothe that Indian hostilities were beginning again. But wiser, calmer men were not so sure. Massie, who viewed the body of his old comrade, had declared his belief that Harrod was killed by marauding whites, averring that no Indian would have made such a butchery of scalping his victim as had Harrod's murderer. Nevertheless, the town remained alarmed.

At sight of Waw-wil-a-way walking toward them, Wolfe smiled and nodded and his cohorts showed yellowed teeth in answering grins. They checked their rifles and then began a careless walk that would intercept the Shawnee.

Waw-wil-a-way dipped his head as they neared and then shook hands with each man in turn. He asked after their health and that of their families and then inquired where they were going. It was Wolfe who did the talking. He said that, as a matter of fact, they had been on their way to see Waw-wil-a-way, that Wolfe had been wanting to find a different gun and thought Waw-wil-a-way might want to make a swap.

Waw-wil-a-way shook his head but, at Wolfe's request, let the white man see his rifle, at the same time accepting Wolfe's to inspect it. Partially hiding the Indian's gun from view, Wolfe emptied the priming from the pan and then shook his head, handed the gun back to the Shawnee and said he liked his own better. Wolfe's next remark startled Waw-wil-a-way.

"You Shawnees back on the warpath against the whites?"

"No, no!" he answered, believing they were referring to Tecumseh's activities. "The Indians and the white men are now all one — all brothers."

"That a fact? Then who shot and scalped Jim Harrod two-three days ago?"

Surprised and concerned, Waw-wil-a-way at first doubted the story, but when they convinced him it was true, he shook his head thoughtfully and said perhaps Harrod had an argument with someone. "May be whiskey," he said. "May be too much drink was cause of quarrel."

"Harrod had no quarrel with the Indians."

"May be," Waw-wil-a-way said softly, "some bad white man kill Captain Harrod."

The trio exchanged startled glances at the comment and then Wolfe said they had to be going. Once again Waw-wil-a-way shook hands all around and turned to go. He had taken no more than three steps when Wolfe jerked up his rifle and shot him in the back.

Waw-wil-a-way fell but almost instantly was back in a crouch with his rifle centered on Wolfe. He pulled the trigger but the gun only snapped. Without pause he dropped it and whipped a huge hunting knife from his belt and threw himself toward Wolfe, stabbing downward. Wolfe scrambled to get out of the way and the blade just skimmed past his belly and then sank to the hilt in his thigh.

Wolfe dropped his gun and screamed and Williams and Ferguson plunged in to attack. Snatching up Wolfe's rifle, Waw-wil-a-way swung it in a vicious arc which connected with Ferguson's head and shoulder at the same time and dropped him with a thud.

Wolfe's gun wrenched out of Waw-wil-a-way's grasp with the blow and now he dived to get Ferguson's weapon, rolled over and came up with the muzzle centered on the breast of Williams, who was just raising a tomahawk to strike. A bullet the size of the first joint of his thumb left the muzzle of the gun and caught Williams in the middle of his chest, lifted him clear off his feet and slammed him dead to the ground on his back.

Slowly, wearily, Waw-wil-a-way got to his feet and stood there swaying, his vision rapidly dimming. A faint smile touched his lips and then he crumpled in a lifeless sprawl atop the body of Williams.

[*July 3, 1804 — Tuesday*]

The Sioux are a great and numerous nation, Tecumseh told the assembled chiefs, proud of their heritage and jealous of their country and rightly so. Long had the stories been told in their tepees and before their council fires of the troubles brought upon Indians east of the great mother of rivers by the white men. No matter whether the Indians had offered peace or war, yet they had been pushed back out of their lands.

The times it had happened were too many to number. Had not the Delawares lost their home on the shores of the great eastern sea and been thrown back to the Ohio country? Had not the Onondagas finally split in the mountains of New York and those who had not remained there come to this Missouri country? Had not the same thing happened to the Shawnees, who long ago had been forced away from their warm coastal territory in the land called Florida, then forced to move again and again until finally, in the Ohio country, they too had split and most of them crossed the mother of rivers to seek peace? And what of the Cherokees and the Tuscarawas, the Pamlicos and Powhatans, the Susquehannas, Narragansetts, Cayugas and Senecas and a hundred other tribes? Had not all of them been pushed back? Were not all of them still being pushed back?

The Sioux must peel back the husks from their eyes and see what was coming. No longer was the great mother of rivers a barrier to hold back the white flood. No! Until last year there had come only a few scattered Americans, alone or in small parties, to penetrate deep into their country — coming in peace, they said, to trap and trade and no more, as the Frenchmen who were already there along the Mississippi were doing. But now the great white chief, Jefferson, had bought from the French, who had no just title to it, all this land and more and would soon be coming to claim it. At this very moment, as the Sioux were aware, a large force of whites under the young captains Clark and Lewis moved upstream on the Missouri to find their way across the great mountains far to the west and reach the western sea.

And heed well this fact: this young Captain William Clark was the brother of the white chief George Rogers Clark who had helped take Ohio lands from the Indians, as all assembled here knew. Other men would follow. It was always thus. Thirty summers ago the lands of the Shawnees had seen the same; and though they had fought, yet they had seen their game destroyed, their forests leveled, their prairies burned, their lands taken, their villages ruined, their warriors killed. And now the Can-tuc-kee country and the Ohio country had become part of the Seventeen Fires — individual States in the Union of the whites.

So it would happen here west of the mother of rivers. Not *might* happen. *Would* happen. Unless the union of the Indians became too strong for the whites. Already many tribes are ready, when the great sign is given, to join together in such union as one people; Senecas and Oneidas, Mohawks, Ottawas, Wyandots, Winnebagos, Sacs, Foxes, Kickapoos. There are more. There will be many more than that. Fifty nations or a hundred joined into one to hold and protect what is theirs and to reclaim what has been taken from them. When the great sign is given, the Sioux should take up their weapons and come. Would they?

The Sioux would.

[*December 31, 1804 — Monday*]

On the whole, 1804 had been a quiet year for the Ohio settlers. The matters of business and government continued at a quick pace, settlers continued to arrive in large numbers and towns grew rapidly. Springfield became a bustling village and, log by log, Kenton's mill on the north bank of Buck Creek at Lagonda and a general store he was building close by were going up.

On the first of March the growing list of Ohio counties had been added to by the formation of Muskingum County. Four days later, in Cincinnati, David Zeigler was appointed by President Jefferson as the first United States Marshal of the Ohio district.

As James Harrod had become discontented with life in the city of his founding and sought new frontiers, so too did Colonel Robert Patterson. On May 8 he removed from Kentucky forever and settled on an excellent tract of land a mile south of Dayton. During the summer Major Isaac Bonser and Uriah Barber were busy at work building a state road along the Ohio River from Nathaniel Massie's new little town of Portsmouth at the mouth of the Scioto River to the French village of Gallipolis, eighty-seven miles upstream.[21]

In September, after having settled a piece of ground on Little East Fork near the spot where he, along with Kenton's party, had attacked the camp of Tecumseh, Neil Washburn grew increasingly discontent. His imagination had been fired by stories of the far west, where white-topped mountains punctured clouds and vast herds of wild game congregated. He regretted that he had not been able to join Lewis and Clark's expedition and the more he thought of the land "out there," the more determined he became to see it. Thus, late in September, he loaded his traps and other gear onto a packhorse and rode out, with his rifle across his pommel and his eyes on the western horizon.

Virtually unnoticed in the many changes which had occurred over the countryside was the death of William Leachman, Simon Kenton's boyhood rival. On April 1, he had watched his son go to church in Maysville and after he was gone Leachman stepped up on a chair, tied a rope around the rafter and his own neck and quietly hanged himself.

On October 16, nearly eleven months after the Second General Assembly revised Ohio's militia laws, an election was held by the commissioned officers of the First Division, Ohio Militia, under orders of Major General John S. Gano. Its purpose was to elect a brigadier general for the state militia. And though he was not at the time a member of that state army, the big frontiersman of Springfield became Brigadier General Simon Kenton.

[April 18, 1805 — Friday]

For Simon Kenton it was difficult to comprehend that Ohio was scarcely considered a frontier area anymore. How quickly the border seemed to move! Ever since President Jefferson had consummated the Louisiana Purchase — eight hundred twenty-eight thousand square miles of land bought at the unheard-of bargain of about three cents an acre from France, who herself had only recently acquired much of the territory from Spain — there had been a growing movement of bordermen to the west. Great discoveries were expected from the Lewis and Clark expedition and the American flag had now been raised over St. Louis, even though many of the Frenchmen stayed on there, as well as at their other villages of St. Charles, St. Genevieve and New Madrid. And now Thomas Jefferson had ordered Zebulon Pike to lead an expedition of twenty soldiers to the headwaters of the Mississippi and take formal possession of the land there for the United States.

Nearly everyone in Ohio was talking about the far west and quite a few were deeply excited about it. Simon Kenton was certainly no exception, feeling the same tug of restlessness and desire to see new country that had been the dominant factor of his life. He was struck with a great longing to see more of this western land, perhaps to visit Daniel Boone again, or perhaps to travel as far west as the land went.

Such a trip would necessitate once again postponing the completion of his mill and store in Springfield, but that was a trifling matter and bothered him not at all. Of somewhat greater consequence was his responsibility to remain here as brigadier general in the militia. He settled that matter in his characteristically direct manner with the dictation of a letter:

Spring Field
April 18, 1805

Major General John S. Gano
First Division, Ohio Militia, Dayton

Sir:

Having taken a Resolution of making a tour through the late acquired lands of the United States, in consequence of which I think proper to resign my commission of Brigadier of the Militia, and you are hereby requested to regard this as full notice of the same, given under my hand.

Simon Kenton

The ink was hardly dry on the letter when Simon gathered up all but a very nominal amount of what remained of his cash, packed his gear and, with his fifteen-year-old son John, set off for the west.

CHAPTER XI

[*November 2, 1805 — Saturday*]

AS always happened each time he was away for a number of months
at a stretch, Simon Kenton found a great many changes upon
returning to Springfield. Shortly after his departure to the west, his good
friend Ben Whiteman had been named brigadier general in the militia
position Simon had resigned. Four new counties had been formed, three
of which — Athens, Geauga and Highland — he cared little about. But
the fourth involved Springfield, which was in Greene County when he
left but which was in the new Champaign County when he returned.[1]
During the summer another treaty was made with the various tribes at a
meeting held at Fort Industry and the Indians ceded to the United States
the tract Connecticut had set aside in 1792 west of the Cuyahoga River,
which was called the Fire Lands.

For once, however, the frontiersman did not have a new offspring
awaiting him. Thus, during the first few days he was back, he and Elizabeth rode about the country together, seeing the changes that had taken
place in Springfield and visiting the new little settlement eight miles north
of their own home which had just been established by William Ward and
named Urbana. Elizabeth was as excited as a little girl at having her
husband home again and she pressed him for details of where he'd been,
what he'd seen and done.

He told her that he and young John had first checked over the lands in
the Cape Girardeau area, gradually moving southward. About thirty-five
miles directly southwest of the mouth of the Ohio — fully sixty-five
miles if the meandering course of the Mississippi were followed — they
had found a remarkably beautiful section of country. Just a dozen or so
miles above the French village of New Madrid, it overlooked several
graceful loops of the Mississippi and seemed to have everything one could

hope for: excellent springs, impressive bluffs, fine timber, fertile bottom-lands, plenty of fish and game and a location that was absolutely superb, with river traffic available up or down the Mississippi and the whole Ohio River system virtually emptying at its shores. Here he had spent a great portion of his money buying a considerable tract of land; a place where one day he and Elizabeth would move to as their final home.[2]

After leaving New Madrid, they had gone on to visit Boone at St. Charles. The old frontiersman was seventy-one now and showing his years badly. Since he last saw Kenton he had taken one final trip into the wilderness, a journey to a wonderful land of great gray mountains capped with snow and called the Grand Tetons — the breasts of the earth. There were canyons of bright yellow stone, and a river the Indians called Snake and lakes so cold a man couldn't wade in them more than a few minutes without his feet going numb and his legs aching.

Their visit with Boone had been a nostalgic one. Simon had gone west a little way and claimed more land, but he still cared little for the looks of it and returned to Boone's. When it came time to leave, young John had begged his father to be allowed to stay "for a year or two" to explore some of this country with Nathan and Jesse Boone and Daniel Boone's grand-sons, who were now John's own age.

And so Simon had consented and returned to Ohio alone, making only one more stop — an overnight stay at the huge Kaskaskia mansion over-looking the Mississippi. Here lived John and Rachel Edgar — but of this stopover Simon seemed disinclined to elaborate.

Only one item of news remained for Elizabeth to tell Simon and it saddened him considerably. Not quite a month before, the man who had saved him from the Indians so long ago, Peter Drouilliard, had finally drunk himself into his grave on the property Simon had given him in Kentucky.

[*November 9, 1805 — Saturday*]

With already more Indian tribes aligned behind him than any other chief had ever gathered, Tecumseh was still far from satisfied when he returned to Ohio in early autumn. His wanderings had carried him far these past years, but he would have to travel much farther. There were still the nations of the southwest and the south and southeast to meet with and convince, which would take considerable time. Nor was he content to let stand the rejection of his plan by a half dozen or more tribes in the west and northwest, the north and northeast. He would return to them, as soon as matters were improved here, and flood the reluctant tribes with even more convincing arguments and prophecies, confident that eventually he would get them to unite with him as well.

The greatest disappointment was here in Ohio and in the Indiana Territory. Lowawluwaysica had not been very successful. The predictions Tecumseh had given him to relay as his own at intervals to the Indians here had come true and he had gained a certain amount of esteem as a prophet, but he had not at all persuaded them, not even his brother Shawnees, to embrace Tecumseh's plan.

The two chiefs, Black Hoof and Little Turtle, were the main reason for this failure. Both of them disliked and distrusted Lowawluwaysica and they advised their people strongly against taking him too seriously; they were especially opposed to adopting Tecumseh's plan, which they considered as being dishonorable in view of the treaty signed by their chiefs at Greenville. Even Blue Jacket, who had always been Tecumseh's friend and admirer, was not fully convinced it was the proper thing to do. That, plus the fact that Tecumseh was evidently attempting to usurp the authority of Black Hoof, angered many of the Shawnees, particularly the older men.

It was time, Tecumseh knew, to move carefully here, to gain very gradually the respect and confidence of not only the Delawares, Wyandots, Miamis and other Ohio tribes, but their own tribe most of all. How could they expect other tribes to pledge their allegiance to the amalgamation if the leaders of the movement could not even convince their own people to join?

Tecumseh instructed Lowawluwaysica in great detail about what to say and even how to say it. He provided his brother with new and more significant prophecies to give the people. That was the job of Lowawluwaysica — to convince the people. As for the chiefs, that would be up to Tecumseh. He would speak to each one quietly, individually, in the privacy of each chief's *wegiwa*. This would be no easy matter, for between himself and some of the chiefs — Black Hoof in particular — serious rifts had developed.

Just when matters seemed at their worst, an extremely fortunate event occurred for the brothers. In the process of making their rounds to the various villages, the pair had been staying for some days at the Shawnee village called Tawa on the Auglaize River. While they were there a minor epidemic of stomach sickness broke out and at the very beginning of it, the old Shawnee prophet known as Penegashega collapsed and died. At once Tecumseh and Lowawluwaysica held a hurried conference. Tecumseh said he had "seen" that this epidemic would claim three lives and that by the end of five more days, those afflicted now would have recovered. Lowawluwaysica was to assemble the villagers and tell them that three men who were evil and engaged in witchcraft would die because he, Lowawluwaysica, would not care for them, but that the rest of the afflicted he would cure in five days and at the end of that time he would ask that all Shawnees come to hear what he said, which would be something of extreme importance.

So it came about. The three died as Tecumseh had so remarkably predicted they would and the rest recovered. And when not only these villagers but quite a few others from nearby Shawnee villages, as well as a scattering of Delawares, Miamis and representatives of other tribes, showed up to hear his important message, it was the bright and shining hour of Lowawluwaysica's life.

"Hear me, Brothers!" He raised his hands and the assemblage grew still. "You have witnessed my powers of prophecy in the past. The things I have said would be have come to pass. And you have seen my skill as a doctor. Now, over these past days you have seen the three die as I predicted they would and you have witnessed the miracles I have performed in casting out the sickness which threatened your own lives.

"You have known me by the name of Lowawluwaysica, but no longer! From this day forward I shall be known to all men as Tenskwatawa — One-with-Open-Mouth — and my mouth will be open with words which will lead you to a better life, to better health, to a better future. Penegashega the Prophet is dead. I say to you now that henceforth I am your Prophet and that there is none other who qualifies, none other who can do for you what I can do. Do I hear you say that you wish me to take this high office?"

He paused and cupped a hand behind each of his ears in an exaggerated posture of listening and there was a roar of approval. A crafty glint appeared in his eyes as he waited until the cries were silenced and then he made his demand:

"My people speak and call on me to serve them as Prophet. But such must first be approved by the Shawnee Council. Since those wise men are here among us today and since our Prophet is dead and there is little time to waste in lengthy discussion, I call on them now, here and at this moment, to say whether or not I am the Shawnee Prophet!"

Taken unawares and confused at the speed with which all this had come about, the Council members bent to the will of this assemblage and nodded in turn as the speaker pointed at them. A great exultation arose in Tenskwatawa's breast. They had done it! Just as Tecumseh had said they would. He smiled, raised his arms for silence and spoke again, this time at considerable length, going carefully over the points Tecumseh had instructed him to make.

He told them that he was a true Prophet, a man who could see into the future without the need for such superstitious implements as little stones and pieces of bones and small bags of fine sand to sprinkle and stir on a piece of cured skin, such as Penegashega had needed. This, he said, was a form of witchcraft, of evil sorcery, which depended upon the help of Matchemenetoo — the Devil — rather than the Great Spirit. He told them he would lead the Indians away from such superstitious beliefs and that those who practiced such lore were themselves bewitched and would neither go to the good Afterworld nor ever see Moneto. He then denounced drinking with great vehemence:

"On the day that Penegashega died," he said, "I went up into the clouds and the first place I came to was the dwelling of Matchemenetoo; here I saw all who had died as drunkards, with flames of fire issuing from their mouths. Yes, previous to this revelation I myself drank, but this has so frightened me that I will never drink again and I say to you gathered here that neither must you drink."

He continued orating in this vein for some time and then went into another topic with a great deal of earnestness. The Indians, he said, must keep their women from intermarrying with whites, for this was one of the great causes of unhappiness and the means by which the whites had long been attempting to destroy the pure strain of Indian blood. The blood of Indian woman and white man must not be allowed to mix, under threat of most severe penalty.

For over three hours he spoke as he had never spoken before, holding his audience spellbound. He stressed the importance of Indians becoming one people united to common goals — much as the United States, whose people were English, French, Irish, German and other races but who were first of all Americans. He said that the property of one Indian must become the property of all Indians, that each of them must work for the common good of all; that the duty of the young at all times was to support and cherish the aged and infirm; that innovations of dress, especially adopting clothing standards of whites, were detestable practices which should stop and that no Indian should wear linens or woolens but must dress as his father had in the skins of animals; that the Indians must return to the habits of their fathers and the fathers before them, adhering to them and rejecting habits adopted from the whites; that they must not eat the flesh of hogs or sheep or cattle, since Moneto had created the deer and buffalo and other wild creatures for food; that they must not make bread of wheat but of Indian corn; that they must believe, as was true, that the Indian race — not one tribe or another, but the whole Indian race — was superior to any other race on earth; that they had now begun, with his appointment as Prophet, to travel the trail which would show their superiority to the entire world; that no Indians who believed in the power and protectiveness of Moneto and had confidence in himself and in his people need ever look up to any man of another race; that there must be, beginning now, a return to more stringent religious principles and greater respect and admiration for the many gifts and blessings Moneto had bestowed upon all of them; that the Great Spirit had revealed to him why it was that in the past, no matter whether they had lost battles or won them, the Indians had always found themselves on the side where lands and crops and lives had been lost, and that he had been shown how all this could be changed.

"As I take on my duties as Prophet, as I begin a life of devotion to the cause and the principles of the Indian people, this now I say to you: a tremendous power has been given to me by the Great Spirit to confound our enemies, to cure all diseases and to prevent death from sickness or on the battlefield. I am your prophet — Tenskwatawa!"

Rarely had his listeners ever heard such inspired speaking. Tecumseh himself was deeply impressed and pleased. He had not known Lowawlu-waysica was going to change his name to Tenskwatawa, but he approved of the timeliness of it.

A strange transformation had come over the self-proclaimed Prophet as he spoke. He was still the unusually ugly little man with none of the dignity or other noble characteristics of his elder brother; he was not courageous or truthful or above cruelty if it benefited him; he had not lost his cunning or his showy smartness. But yet, in some intangible way, he had become possessed of powers of persuasiveness and plausibility at least equal to those of Tecumseh. The reason, perhaps, was that on this day, at this place, Tenskwatawa had believed in what he was saying; had believed in *himself* more firmly than anyone yet believed in him.

During the speech Tenskwatawa told his listeners that he and Tecumseh would leave on the morrow to establish a new village — not a Shawnee village but an *Indian* village — near Fort Greenville. All who believed in him as Prophet and in Tecumseh as the chief who would lead them to greater glory than they had ever known were welcome to come along.

And it was apparent at once that a very large number of them, more by far than they had any reason to hope for at first, would be joining them.

[*March 24, 1806 — Monday*]

Although it was a long time in coming, the edge of fear that now sliced through the Ohio settlements had not been dulled by over eleven years of peace. In fact, the specter of Indian uprising was all the more frightful after such a lapse and scarcely a frontier town did not immediately see to its defenses: to erect blockhouses if it had none, to improve them if it did. There began something of an exodus of women and children on horseback, returning to friends or relatives in Kentucky until the trouble should pass.

Tecumseh had known long ago that eventually the whites must realize something peculiar was in the wind. It couldn't be helped. He knew also that they might consider the signs they detected as evidence of uprising. That, too, was unavoidable. As a matter of fact, he was mildly surprised that it had not come sooner than this. The important thing was that they not find out the details of the grand plan.

The Stony Creek Council was the one to ignite the fires of suspicion.

Tecumseh made a temporary camp here on the headwaters of the Great Miami, about ten miles northeast of Blue Jacket's Town and several miles south of Indian Lake, as he had made in many places whenever enough people had gathered to hear him speak.[3] The council had been in progress for nearly a week when it was discovered by Simon Kenton.

Jim McPherson and the frontiersman were out riding a dozen miles or so north of McPherson's new little cabin at Urbana when Simon abruptly forced Jim's horse into cover, told him to wait there and vaulted from the saddle. He disappeared soundlessly in the woods and was gone for just under half an hour. His expression, when he returned, was deeply troubled. Carefully, clinging to cover as much as possible, the pair moved to the northeast. Every now and again Kenton would grunt meaningfully as he detected some significant sign, but not until afternoon when they were peering from hiding at the Stony Creek campsite a quarter-mile distant did Simon explain that it was a war council. A war post had been planted in the midst of the camp and was being struck frequently with toma-hawks and clubs. A number of black war belts were being passed around. Tecumseh was speaking but, at this distance, they could not even be sure of his identity, much less hear what was being said. Frequent runners came and went along the trails which led toward Wapatomica, Upper Sandusky, Wapakoneta, Girty's Town and Greenville; most of these runners also carried belts of black wampum.

After studying the scene for some while, Kenton touched McPherson's shoulder and they returned to where they had hidden their horses and rode south. The frontiersman had no doubt but that the situation was serious enough to warrant sending out a general alarm to the settlers. They promptly set about it, stopping at each isolated cabin to tell the forbidding news. When they reached Urbana and the residents of the little town had been informed, the pair split up, Kenton riding down the east bank of the Mad River and McPherson the west. Unlike the clustered settlements of early Kentucky, the cabins here had been strung out chainlike on each side of the river between Urbana and Springfield.

The pair continued to warn the settlers at each cabin they passed, advising them to go to the strongest house in the immediate area or, better yet, to head out for the safety of the blockhouse at Springfield.

For four days they forted up, awaiting attack. When none came, Kenton, McPherson, Charles McIlvain and Major Thomas Moore decided to press the matter by going to the Stony Creek camp openly under a flag of truce to determine exactly what was going on. Before leaving, however, McIlvain wrote a brief deposition explaining the situation, swore to it before Sam McCulloch, the Champaign County judge, and then returned to Major Moore who said he would have one of his men take it on the mail run to Chillicothe and deliver it to Governor Edward Tiffin there. Moore read the deposition and then decided they had better inform the governor of the proposed trip to the council. He wrote a hurried letter, enclosed it with McIlvain's document and left orders for its delivery. The party set off before dawn and did not return until nightfall, at which time Moore, considerably disturbed, fired off another letter to the governor, this one by special mounted courier:

February 18, 1806

To Gov. Tiffin
  From Thomas Moore, Major
  State of Ohio, Champaign County

Sir:
  I went to the Council accompanied by Capt. McPherson, General Kenton & Mr. McIlvain we arrived at the Indian Town about two o'clock when we attempted to go to the Council the[y] sent a man to tell us not to come there at all (when we was at about 40 yards Distance) but said the[y] would come to us at another place we immediately mounted our horses and started for we considered ourselves very unwelcome guests we had not gone farr before the[y] called to us to Stop and talk we got off our horses again the[y] came to another house we went in with about 18 Indians whare the following Discourse took place viz. we your friends Conceive we have just Reason to be much alarmed from the information we Receive from our white friends and your Neighbors The[y] are leaving their homes and Flying into the Settlements and we your Brothers are come to see you on the action and wish for nothing but trew Friendship . . . the Chief . . . s'd the[y] Intended know harm and thanked the great Spirit above that we their Brothers Still wished that trew friendship might subsist we then appointed to meet them on the 21st of this Instant in the Settlement then and there to see if we can compromise and all parties be satisfyed but when we went to take our Leave the[y] allmost all give us their Left hand in a very cool manner Capt. McPherson is a gentleman that has been well acquainted with the manners of the Indians for upwards of 15 years and he says that he verily believes their intentions is not good for these Reasons 1st being their not Letting us into their council and 2nd the Number of panted fiethers which we Never Saw the Like amongst them accept in time of war we Therefore trust that you in your Wisdom will consider our infant Settlement for we are in no ways able (though willing to do what we can) to stand in our defense.
  To the Governor

I am, Sir, Respectfully yours,
Thomas Moore, Maj.

Upon receipt of the deposition from Charles McIlvain and the first, short letter of their intentions from Moore, Edward Tiffin showed a remarkable lack of alarm, although he did confer with some officers immediately after reading it. Then he wrote the major a reply and gave it to his aide, George Bennett, to deliver to Moore, since Bennett had been planning to go to Springfield anyway:

February 19, 1806
Chillicothe

Major Thomas Moore

Sir:

I have this morning received yours of the 16th Inst. covering the deposition of Charles McIlvain taken before Judge McCulloch, relative to the fears apprehended from the Shawnee Indians. From your letter and the deposition it appears that the Indians are preparing for war, but it does not appear that their object is war against the white people — neither does it appear that any violence has been offered to our citizens. I have councilled with some of the officers here on the contents of your communication and from a variety of considerations we are of opinion that those Indians can never be so mad as to wage war against the people of the United States. I am much pleased with the very prudential measure you inform me you are undertaking, that of your visiting the Indian council with . . . McPherson. This I wish to be done if it should not have taken place before this reaches you, and in my name request the chiefs to state explicitly whether their object in thus preparing for war arises from any complaints against our people, if so, to state their complaints and they shall be immediately attended to — if they have no cause of complaint against us, you need not urge your inquiries any further. I am led to think their object is against another quarter. However, you will please to use every means to ascertain their object if the above mode shall fail of success — Keep an eye on their conduct, endeavor to quiet the minds of the people as much as possible, and if anything occurs really alarming, inform me immediately thereof: the greatest prudence should be observed in all your measures and nothing of a hostile nature appear in our part, until dire necessity compels it.

Yours respectfully
Edward Tiffin

But the governor's concern increased sharply when, less than three hours later, he received Moore's second letter by express. He, too, used a special courier to send the major his reply:

Chillicothe
February 19, 1806

Major Moore

Dear Sir:

I wrote you this morning by Mr. Bennett, since which time I have received another communication from you giving me an account of the conduct of the Indians when you visited their council in company with Capt. McPherson, General Kenton and Mr. McIlvain. From the contents of this communication we can only, as well as from the other, gather that the Indians appear to have hostile views, but we cannot yet ascertain their object is certainly to make war upon us. I hope, and cannot help believing, that they will not dare to commit any acts of violence against our people. I have enclosed a speech to the chiefs and a large belt of white wampum, which you will please deliver to them, and I hope we will get such satisfaction as will enable you to quiet the minds of our people. I feel sensibly for them in their defenseless situation and if it can be certainly ascertained that the Indians are determined to wage war upon us, I shall use every exertion for their immediate relief. I send you the act to provide for organizing and disciplining the Militia. In the 50th Section you will see that if any sudden invasion is made by the Indians in any county within the State, the commanding officer of the Militia of such county is authorized to call out the whole, or such part, of the Militia as he may think necessary as well as call in the commanding officers of the adjacent counties and give immediate information to the Governor. If, therefore, contrary to my hopes and beliefs, the Indians should make any attack upon our people, you will, if you are the senior officer in Champaign County — or if you are not, present this to the senior officer — who will call out such part of the Militia as circumstances may require and call in General Whiteman of Greene County for assistance from the whole of his Brigade, at the same time giving me immediate information of the situation of affairs, and every effort shall be used in behalf of our frontier brethren.

But I hope and request that the utmost caution and prudence will be observed — and in no case whatsoever should violence be first exercised by our people. We are only authorized to repel violence when actually inflicted — and only then after every effort to preserve peace proves abortive.

I remain with great respect,
Your Obt. Svt.
Edward Tiffin

The "speech" he enclosed for Moore to deliver to the Indians was a fine example of the diplomacy for which the governor was noted; brief, yet much to the point without ever becoming insulting:

To the Principal Chiefs of the Shawnee Indians

Friends and Brothers

I have received information from our respectable white brothers settled on the waters of the Mad River, that from the hostile appearances manifested amongst our Red Brothers they have cause to be alarmed, and some of them are leaving their homes and requesting assistance to protect them. I cannot believe that our Red Brothers will be so far lost to a sense of their duty and best interests as to entertain a desire to disturb the peace and friendship which so happily subsists between them and us; on our part we sincerely wish to brighten up the chain of peace and friendship in token of which I herewith present you a fine white belt — but as our people are distressed to know your determinations — and as I wish to quiet their fears, and to prevent our people from injuring our Red brethren, I do request that you will expressly state to our respectable Major Moore, who will present you with this letter, if you have any cause of complaint against our people. If you have, make it known to me, and if you have not I shall then be able to prevent any serious consequences that might otherwise happen both to you and to us. In hopes that the Great Spirit will incline your hearts and the hearts of your people to peace, I remain your friend,

Edward Tiffin, Governor of
the State of Ohio

Chillicothe
February 19th, 1806

When Major Moore delivered the wampum belt and speech to Tecumseh on February 21, the Shawnee chief told the officer to return home, that no attack would be made on any white settlement and to tell Governor Tiffin he would receive a letter from the Shawnees in one moon.

He smiled as Moore rode off and then retired to his *wegiwa* to consider carefully how he would reply. The faint worry that had ridden him these past few days since the first deputation of whites had tried to enter the council was now eased. The possibilities of hostilities breaking out before he was ready for them were now ended. In fact, the whole chain of events had provided him with an unexpected opportunity to imbue the white government with a sense of reestablished security. By waiting a month to send his reply, the governor would feel sure the letter was the result of long and careful deliberation by the full Shawnee Council.

This was the first opportunity Tecumseh had ever had to repay in kind the many devious and deceitful communiqués the Shawnees had received over the years from the whites. It was very pleasant, for once, to be on the giving rather than the receiving end of such a document. He felt no guilt over what he eventually wrote, and though his written word was not a model of literary style, still it put across very well the assurances he wished to convey:

To the Governor of the Chillicothe, taken from the Shawnee Chiefs in Publick Council at the Head of Big Miami, 20th March 1806.

Friend and Brother
Never a speech was received with more joy than yours handed to us by Major Moore. We were all in great trouble at that time for the sake of

your people, and we would not account for it, for we were entirely inno-
cent of what they wanted to impute on our nation, was absolutely out of
our knowledge.

We have immediately return our prayers to the Great Spirit above, for
you, and will never forgotten your goodness towards us, and we thanks him
for having given us such a good and wise man. We were very much please
of one part of your speech saying you didn't believe that we wished to
cause any disturbance with the white people. No be well assured it never
was our intention, nor never will be in our part. We have more things of
more important than that to mind, which is believe in God. We will tell
you what was our intention when we were blame incorrectly. We had got
all our young men and young women together to try to larn them good
things, to worship the Great God above us and to fixt ourselves in a good
place for to raiz shanty full grain for our women and children. We thought
we were doing well, particularly when it was requested by our Father
Jefferson to do so and expected to be safe or protected by all our brothers,
the white people of the United States, but to our sorry and great surprise,
we were interrupted and all the people of Mad River or about were pre-
paring to come against us to destroy the whole of us. Upon foolish lies
that bad people had told them. So that our women are all in fears, and we
do not know what to do for to secure them in a peaceable place that we
might have happy with all our neighbors. We believe that some of the
principal men are to easly belonging of the Militia Department. Good men
should be appointed, particularly those that wish to have war of us, and
that they may keep peace and not to make a great noise without founda-
tion. We beg you may publish the contrary of this bad news to all your
people that for the future we might not be disturbed any more and that
you may punish those bad men that wish to break the chain of friendship
that ties our hands together. Four our good chain will always be bright on
our side. We have no more to say at present, only to assure you of our
sincerity towards you and beg you may continue to do as good and that you
may have along life in great prosperity and happiness and we may love one
another like to brothers out to do.

> *from your friends the*
> *Shawnees*

Governor Edward Tiffin finished reading the poorly scrawled letter and
then leaned back in his chair, a deep sigh of relief escaping him. He'd been
right from the beginning after all. The settlers had been running from
shadows again, just as they had that time when James Harrod had been
killed. When would they realize that Indian wars in the United States
were over for all time?

[*April 28, 1806 — Saturday*]

Ever since that day he had taken the office of Prophet at Tawa, the prestige and power of Tenskwatawa had grown. For months there had come a constant procession of Indians from an ever-expanding radius of tribes to hear him speak. A great many of them were being converted to the new doctrine and had agreed to unite under Tecumseh when the great sign should be given. When they returned to their villages they spread the word of what had transpired and a sort of chain reaction was occurring. Tecumseh's village at Greenville now had some four hundred permanent residents, and already more than two thousand other Indians had come to hear the inspired Prophet speak. Tenskwatawa, vain and deceptive though he was, really believed in the benefits to be gained by what he preached. The moral precepts of the Shawnees, of all the tribes, had slipped during the years of association with the whites and it was up to him to lead them back — to abolish whiskey drinking and female intermarriage with whites, to destroy witchcraft and return them to a stronger reverence of the Great Spirit. Only through Tecumseh's grand plan could the Indians ever regain fully that which they had lost. The visitors to Greenville sensed this self-belief in Tenskwatawa and it reassured them, except for an occasional few who failed to see any chance of such a plan succeeding. Others were plainly jealous of the power both Tecumseh and Tenskwatawa were gaining, while still more refused to cease being a proud Shawnee or Delaware or Wyandot in favor of becoming, instead, simply an Indian. Some of these objectors were vigorous in their denunciation of both the Prophet and his brother — Black Hoof, Little Turtle and Tarhe were notable examples of this — and they were having a certain amount of influence on those who might otherwise have adopted the new programs. To Tenskwatawa it was obvious that now was the time for something of an inquisition to begin; slowly at first, to see what the reaction would be, then more vigorously if it went well. Perhaps fear could accomplish for some what arguments could not.

In his speeches Tenskwatawa now took to becoming angry, shouting tirades at those who would stand in the way of all their brothers. He announced that such people were obviously possessed by evil spirits which had to be destroyed. And he was delighted when there was muttered agreement among the listeners.

The first execution was that of an old woman. A childless widow of a Delaware subchief, Tenskwatawa knew her to be constantly carrying a medicine bag holding various charms. Without warning he accused her of being bewitched and declared that she must be burned to death for her crime. The same day a dozen warriors of her own tribe bound her, placed her atop a large pile of wood and burned her alive. No one voiced anything but approbation for ridding the tribe of this witch.

Intensely gratified, Tenskwatawa the next day went a little further. He charged Teteboxti, the ancient Delaware chief, with similar witchcraft and ordered his execution. The Prophet was still incensed with the alacrity with which Teteboxti had met with General Wayne at Greenville to sign the treaty of peace. At once resigned to his fate, Teteboxti arrayed himself in his finest clothing and then even assisted in the erection of his own pyre. To the many who were wavering in acceptance of the Prophet's true ability, this was a highly convincing display. They admired the benevolence of this Prophet who took pity on the white-haired old chief and permitted him to be killed first by a tomahawk blow before being burned.

A Wyandot who called himself Joshua — a Christian convert — was the next victim of the inquisition. Once again no word of protest was raised against what was happening, lest the protester himself be accused of being possessed of evil spirits and ordered executed.

Such matters could not be kept from the whites forever, and soon several unimpeachable sources reported the Prophet's activities to Governor William Henry Harrison at Vincennes. Deeply disturbed at the intelligence — and clearly remembering the execution of his good friend Beaver on witchcraft charges — Harrison at once sat down and composed a remarkable letter to the chiefs of the Delaware nation:

MY CHILDREN:

My heart is filled with grief, and my eyes are dissolved in tears at the news which has reached me. You have been celebrated for your wisdom above all the tribes of the red people who inhabit this great island. Your fame as warriors has extended to the remotest nations, and the wisdom of your chiefs has gained you the appellation of grandfathers from all the neighboring tribes. From what cause, then, does it proceed that you have departed from the wise counsels of your fathers and covered yourselves with guilt? My Children, tread back the steps you have taken, and endeavor to regain the straight road which you have abandoned. The dark, crooked, and thorny one which you are now pursuing will certainly lead you to endless woe and misery. But who is this pretended prophet who dares to speak in the name of the great Creator? Examine him. Is he more wise and virtuous than you are yourselves, that he should be selected to convey to you the orders of your God? Demand of him some proofs at least of his being the messenger of the Deity. If God has really empowered him, He has doubtless authorized him to perform miracles that he may be known and received as a prophet. If he is really a prophet, ask of him to cause the sun to stand still, the moon to alter its course, the rivers to cease to flow, or the dead to rise from their graves. If he does these things you may believe that he has been sent from God. He tells you that the Great Spirit commands you to punish with death those who deal in magic, and that he is authorized to point them out. Wretched delusion! Is then the Master of Life obliged to employ mortal man to punish those who offend Him? Has He not the thunder and the power of nature at His command? And could He not sweep away from the earth a whole nation with one motion of his arm? My Children, do not believe that the great and good Creator of Mankind has directed you to destroy your own flesh; and do not doubt that if you pursue this abominable wickedness His vengeance will overtake you and crush you.

The above is addressed to you in the name of the Seventeen Fires. I now speak to you from myself, as a friend who wishes nothing more sincerely than to see you prosperous and happy. Clear your eyes, I beseech you, from the mist which surrounds them. No longer be imposed upon by the arts of an imposter. Drive him from your town, and let peace and harmony prevail amongst you. Let your poor old men and women sleep in quietness, and banish from their minds the dreadful idea of being burnt alive by their own friends and countrymen. I charge you to stop your bloody career; and if you value the friendship of your great father, the President; if you wish to preserve the good opinion of the Seventeen Fires, let me hear by the return of the bearer that you have determined to follow my advice.

Your friend and adviser,
William Henry Harrison
Governor—Indiana Territory

That the white chief of all the Indiana Territory should send such a letter as this to them both excited and bothered the Delawares. Supposing what he said was true? Supposing the Prophet was an imposter and they were being duped? Perhaps the signs that the Prophet had shown them were really mere accidents or clever deduction. The white father had sent a direct challenge to Tenskwatawa and it was a good one. It did not come from the Delawares, so they would not be in jeopardy should it turn out that Tenskwatawa was, after all, the true Prophet; the challenge would be upon the white chief's head, not theirs. Let the Prophet take it up; they would demand it. If he failed, they would know that he was indeed a false Prophet. And as Harrison had advised them, if the Prophet succeeded, then they would know beyond any doubt that he was a true Prophet who must be followed and obeyed.

A party of forty Delawares led by Chief Peke-tele-mund left the White River village straightaway for the village at Fort Greenville; they found Tenskwatawa in deep discussion inside his *wegiwa* with Tecumseh, who had only lately returned from Stony Creek. The two brothers came outside and heard the message in silence and then, at a faint sign from Tecumseh,

Tenskwatawa told the Delawares to rest and eat, that he would retire to his *wegiwa* to meditate on this to see what action, if any, the Great Spirit would direct.

Within the privacy of the structure, however, the veneer of calmness dropped from the Prophet and his eyes showed alarm as he asked his elder brother what they should do now, expressing the fear that this might well undermine all that they had established. Tecumseh shook his head sorrowfully at his brother's fears. After all this time, did Tenskwatawa still not believe Tecumseh could foretell what would occur, just as Chiksika had done and their father, Pucksinwah, before them?

Less than an hour later the pair emerged and Tenskwatawa ordered that all in the village — the resident four hundred as well as a number of transients on hand and the forty Delawares — assemble at once. When they had done so he stood before them and voiced a bitter denunciation of the whites in general and Harrison in particular, expressing scorn for any Indian who might believe what a white man said or wrote. The Great Spirit was angry and he would give them a sign so that any lingering doubt over the Prophet's authority would be dissolved:

"Fifty days from this day there will be no cloud in the sky. Yet, when the sun has climbed to its highest point, at that moment will the darkness of night cover us and the stars shine round about us. The birds will go to roost and the night creatures will awaken and stir. Then you will know, as the white chief Harrison has said, that your Prophet has been sent to you from Moneto."

[*June 3, 1806 — Tuesday*]

Tecumseh had always been a more than welcome visitor at the James Galloway household on the Little Miami River near the site of old Chillicothe, but his travels had kept him away considerably over the past few years. Now, however, he began spending a great deal more time in visiting here. He took considerable interest in the household comforts that were a part of the pioneer's life and one of his greatest joys was discussing at length with Galloway matters of politics, religion, ethics and past Indianwhite treaties, of which his knowledge was practically photographic.

There were about three hundred volumes in Galloway's library, embracing many of the best publications of the period; books that had been carried by wagon or horseback across the Allegheny Mountains and by boat down the Ohio River to Stoner Creek and Lexington and finally by packhorse to this very house. To Tecumseh they were a great treasure and *Hamlet* very quickly became one of his favorites. Frequently Galloway read aloud from the Bible and was pleased to see the studiousness with which Tecumseh followed the words. The Shawnee was most fascinated by the

story of the exodus of the children of Israel. The miracle of the parting of
the waters was of great interest, too. An exodus tradition with crossing of
waters, he informed Galloway, was an important part of his nation's
history.

For his own part, Galloway never ceased to be amazed at the fact that
Tecumseh asked the blessing of Moneto before each meal and followed his
eating with a prayer of thanks. Somehow the settler had never considered
Indians doing such acts. The Galloways were religious people and the
household usually gathered about the family altar for prayer before each
day's work and always before each night's retiring. Tecumseh was at all
times deeply respectful of the Scotch Associate religious customs and
fundamentalism of this host and his family, but at no time did he consider
adopting such beliefs as his own. His belief was unshakable that the Great
Spirit in His ministrations to His Indian children had given them spiritual
truths they could better understand and interpret for their own guidance
in daily duties and obligations.

Tecumseh was especially impressed with the white man's development
of printing, whereby the thoughts and philosophies of great men could be
preserved accurately for all time in books. Such a method had great advantages over anything the Shawnees possessed for recording and communication. And while he could speak English quite adequately and both read
and write it passably, yet there was much about these abilities of his which
needed improvement. It was to this task that Rebecca Galloway, now
fourteen, applied herself.

An attractive girl, Rebecca was highly educated for her age and able to
deliver remarkably astute commentary on any number of subjects. She was
a prodigious reader and enjoyed reading aloud, and so she and the
Shawnee, whom she playfully called "Mr. Tikomfa Chief," often sat for
long periods as she read aloud. He would listen carefully and then they
would discuss in depth the subjects covered. She naturally became interested in his use of English and, as she was the daughter of a family
accustomed to correct expression, she spent long hours teaching him the
better use of her own tongue. It gave her keen pleasure to witness the
aptitude for learning Tecumseh showed. Rarely did he need to be cor-
rected a second time on any kind of error in speech or writing.

There was one thing of which James Galloway was extremely curious:
what was going on at all these Indian council meetings at which Tecumseh
was apparently playing such a large part? He was burning with a desire to
know more about them but, respecting the Shawnee's privacy, did not
inquire. If Tecumseh wanted him to know about such matters, he would
volunteer the information.

But Tecumseh did not enlighten him.

[*June 17, 1806 — Tuesday*]

It was the fiftieth day; the day that had been eagerly awaited by both the supporters and opponents of the Shawnee Prophet. Word of the white father Harrison's challenge to Tenskwatawa and the Prophet's acceptance of it and subsequent prediction had spread all throughout the Ohio country and beyond.

At precisely noon there was a total eclipse of the sun.

In the areas where the darkness fell it lasted for varying periods, but over Greenville, where the greatest totality of the eclipse passed, the darkness lasted for about seven minutes. Stars of the first and second magnitude were visible, as were some of the planets. Birds settled in confusion in the trees and many nocturnal animals, aroused, left their dens.

The Prophet, standing in the midst of the village, now shouted triumphantly: "Behold! Did I not prophesy truly? Darkness has shrouded the earth!"

Throughout the Indian nations there was fear and awe and a new and deeper respect for this Prophet who had arisen among the Shawnees. Before the day had ended, a thousand and more Indians had begun preparations for a pilgrimage to Greenville to see and hear this great man who commanded even the sun.

[*August 22, 1806 — Friday*]

Simon Kenton's mill at Lagonda on the north bank of Buck Creek was operating quite well now, as was the adacent general store and trading post he had established. Most of the goods for the store were procured in Kentucky and shipped to Lagonda in wagons along Kenton's Trace from Newmarket on the Ohio. There were, however, a number of items in the store he had gotten in trading with the Shawnees now living at the rapids of the Maumee River — fur skins, tanned hides, ginseng root and cranberries. With his businesses operating so well, it appeared that Simon might be on the road to recouping the losses suffered on his land suits.

But, as in Kentucky, the frontiersman proved himself a poor businessman, allowing far too many people to buy goods on credit or promises to pay "later" for the grain they wanted milled. Finally, as he had done with his store in Washington, he was forced to hire a young man named James Robinson to handle his business affairs for him. His judgment of Robinson's character was about as good as his business sense.

As soon as Kenton was gone to continue his usual ramblings over the countryside, secure in the belief that his new man would guard his interests, Robinson began a wholesale defrauding of his employer. He was in cahoots with a clique of drunken, rowdy men whom he outfitted in anything they wanted from Kenton's store in exchange for their collecting, by force if necessary, the debts owed Kenton. It was a job for which they were well suited, and in an unusually short time they had collected quite a large amount of money and turned it over to Robinson. And, lest the frontiersman return and crimp his plans, Robinson outfitted himself from the store, took all the money and set off for parts unknown.

When Simon came back and found practically all his merchandise gone and learned about the debts having been collected, a murderous rage grew in him. For all intents and purposes, his business was ruined and all the money he had invested in it gone. But if Robinson thought Kenton would just overlook it, he was rather a fool.

Simon began questioning people and before long had determined that Robinson, mounted on the chestnut mare Kenton had loaned him, had headed southward toward Maysville. The frontiersman immediately packed essentials in a bed roll, tied it behind his saddle and headed toward the south himself with his rifle across the pommel. A quarter mile from his cabin he encountered his eleven-year-old daughter returning home from Springfield.

"Sarah," he told her, "tell your mother I've gone away."

And with no more notice than that, he took up the month-old trail of James Robinson.

[April 6, 1807 — Monday]

The naming of Simon Kenton's new son, born on February 12, was postponed until his father returned from wherever it was he had gone. There were those who shook their heads and said the frontiersman would never be seen again; that this time, somewhere in a deep forest, he had met with disaster. Elizabeth didn't believe it. At fifty-two her husband may have slowed down a bit, but he was still more than a match for a scoundrel like Robinson. He would be back.

She was right, but proof of it was a long time in coming. Simon was gone nearly eight months when one day he appeared on horseback in the distance and the children excitedly shouted the news. Elizabeth ran to meet him, and he leaned over and circled her small waist with a strong arm and lifted her up, breathless and tearful with joy. Thus they rode the remaining short distance to their home.

Limping slightly, Simon followed his wife inside, refusing to answer any questions until he saw his new son. He smiled with evident pleasure at the health and alertness the infant boy exhibited and thereupon named him William Miller Kenton — the first name after his elder brother, the second after his mother's maiden name.

Now the family pressed him for details of his journey, especially Simon, Jr., the most vociferous of the lot. At fourteen he was coming to look almost exactly as his father had looked at that age: a tall, strong, handsome boy with auburn hair, a devil-may-care grin and an easy affability about him. He also had a man-sized bump of curiosity, and a flood of questions ensued.

The frontiersman gave terse answers and no amount of coaxing could make him elaborate. He had gone through Kentucky, Tennessee, Georgia and Florida on Robinson's trail before finally encountering him. He limped because he was still recuperating from a broken leg which was the outcome of that encounter. He was content with the way things worked out, because he had gotten some of the money back which Robinson had not yet had time to spend and, he assured them, Robinson would never steal from another man. That was all he would say about it.

Now the frontiersman asked for news of the home area and Betsy quickly brought him up to date. In January another new county, named Miami, had been formed from Montgomery County, with the little settlement of Staunton selected as county seat.[4] Governor Tiffin had ordered troops out to take Blennerhasset Island in the Ohio River a mile or so downstream from the mouth of the Little Kanawha River, thereby effectively nipping in the bud some sort of grandiose scheme of Aaron Burr's to set up a separate western empire. For this the governor had received a special commendation from President Jefferson and then, last month, he had resigned his gubernatorial seat to become a United States senator and Thomas Kirker became acting governor.

But the most important matter was the chill of impending Indian hostilities overhanging the state. That Shawnee man called the Prophet had made a series of fiery speeches up in the Detroit area and was now once again preaching his (and Tecumseh's) doctrine over Greenville way. Indians from tribes Elizabeth had never heard of — from the far west and northwest, north and northeast — had been coming to Greenville in droves to hear him speak. It was rumored that already over twenty men who opposed him and Tecumseh had been accused of witchcraft and executed by their own people. The government was getting very worried about what all this was leading up to.

Griffith Foos, who had laid out Springfield, was now busy turning his home into a fort. He said he expected war pretty soon; if not with the Indians, then with the British. Everyone had heard how the British ship *Leopard* had fired upon and boarded the United States frigate *Chesapeake*; English agents were also known to be moving among the Indians, inciting them to join forces against the Americans. Ohio residents had been passing resolutions of loyalty and forwarding them to Governor Kirker and Ben Whitemen had just recently discovered a huge Indian gathering at Yellow Springs and was seeking permission from Kirker for a general calling out of the militia.

Tecumseh was reported to be busy traveling about speaking, but apparently mostly to his own tribesmen. Word had gotten around that a very serious rift had developed between him and the principal Shawnee chief, Black Hoof, and that some kind of trouble was coming, though no one knew exactly what. Since all this problem seemed to stem from the Greenville area, Governor Kirker had asked a delegation from the Shaker Society at Lebanon to attend some of the Prophet's speeches and report their feelings about him and what possible threat he and Tecumseh represented for the whites.

Betsy Kenton smiled nervously as she watched Simon eat and asked if he thought there would be Indian trouble again. Simon grunted scornfully. He would talk with Ben Whiteman, he said, and maybe take another small party of men on his own to Greenville to try to see what was brewing. Ever since Wayne's Treaty was signed there in 1795 he'd said there would be trouble by the bucketful someday, but people hadn't chosen to listen. Elizabeth knew he was right when he added, "Ain't often I misjudge what Injens are up to."

[May 17, 1807 — Sunday]

Tecumseh thoroughly disliked Anthony Shane, the half-breed Shawnee who worked for the whites out of Fort Wayne; thus, six days ago when Shane had arrived with an important message from William Wells, the Indian agent, he listened with barely concealed contempt.

William Wells he considered something of a traitor. As a small boy he had been rescued from the Ohio River by Little Turtle after his father had been shot and killed. Little Turtle had adopted and raised him, teaching him, he thought, to be a good Miami Indian. Wells had remained with the Miamis as long as times were fair and the Indians had their victories over Harmar's and St. Clair's armies. But as soon as the tide had changed with Wayne's victory, he changed sides. Soon after the Battle of Fallen Timbers he had asked Chief Little Turtle to walk with him in the woods and, when they were alone, had pointed to the sky and said, "When the sun reaches the meridian I leave you for the whites; and whenever you meet me in battle, you must kill me as I shall endeavor to do by you." Broken-hearted, because he had come to love this young man as if he were his own son, Little Turtle had permitted him to return in peace to the whites. As a reward for his knowledge of Indians and the Indian tongue, Wells had been made the principal Indian agent at Fort Wayne, with the military rank of captain.

With the present stir among the Indians increasing, Wells was very worried. He estimated that already this year more than fifteen hundred Indians had passed and repassed Fort Wayne alone on their way to and from Greenville and there was no way of estimating how many hundreds or thousands had gone there by different routes. Many, he knew, were from very remote nations and great numbers of councils were being held constantly. He knew that messengers were being sent from tribe to tribe with pipes and belts of wampum and that the object of all this was being kept entirely secret from the Americans and Indian chiefs who were considered unalterably friendly to the American cause. His spies had reported that Tecumseh and the Prophet now had no less than eight hundred Indians who had accepted their leadership and taken up residence in the village.

William Wells was not a brave man and Tecumseh was aware of this. And so when Shane came to Greenville with the "important message" from Wells, Tecumseh was not impressed. Still he allowed a council to be called and Shane delivered his message, which was a request for Tecumseh and the Prophet, along with two of their other chiefs, to visit Wells at Fort Wayne in order that he might read to them a letter he had just received from their great father, the President of the United States.

Tecumseh did not even deign to consult with the other chiefs sitting about the fire in his *wegiwa*. He arose and stabbed Shane with a fierce gaze and said, "Go back to Fort Wayne and tell Captain Wells that Tecumseh has no father who is called President of the United States. The sun is my father; the moon is my mother. I know none other. Tell Captain Wells that my fire is kindled on the spot appointed by the Great Spirit above and that if he has anything to communicate to me, *he* must come *here*. I shall expect him in six days from this time."

It was all he would say and the half-breed was obliged to return to the Indian agent. Wells, knowing Tecumseh's dislike for him and all too aware of the executions that had already taken place at Greenville and elsewhere, was afraid to go. Instead, at the appointed time, he sent Shane back with a copy of the President's communication.

And now, deeply indignant because Wells had not showed up personally, Tecumseh listened in hard silence as the message was read aloud to the council. The substance of it was that the President wished them to remove themselves from the Greenville area, since this was now American land in accordance with Wayne's Treaty. It was a gently persuasive letter and suggested that if they would move beyond the boundaries agreed upon at the treaty, assistance would be given them by the government until they were established in their new home.

When Shane finished, Tecumseh stilled with an outstretched hand the murmur that arose from the assembled chiefs. He got to his feet in a fluid movement and his eyes were hot with the anger reflected in them. At once he went into something of a discourse on the injuries the Indians had received at the hands of the whites and of how their lands had been taken and were still being encroached upon.

"These lands are ours," he said then. "No one has a right to remove us, because we were the first owners; the Great Spirit above has appointed this place for us on which to light our fires, and here we will remain. As to boundaries, the Great Spirit above knows no boundaries, nor will his red people know any. If the President of the Seventeen Fires has anything more to say to me, he must send a man of note as his messenger. I will hold no further intercourse with Captain Wells."

[*May 29, 1807 — Friday*]

The Shaker Committee requested by Governor Kirker to witness and report on the speeches of Tenskwatawa was made up of three men — David Darrow, Ben S. Youngs and Richard McNemar, the latter a well-educated Presbyterian minister who joined the Shaker Society after prominent leadership in a series of notable revivals in 1800 and 1801 in both Tennessee and Kentucky.

The committee was impressed, to say the least. As usual, Tenskwatawa harangued against the sins of witchcraft, the beating of wives because they will not have children, stealing, adultery, lying and, with special emphasis, whiskey drinking. He continued to declaim against Indian women contracting interracial marriage and advocated return to ancient customs of dress and community property and asserted the duty of all young Indians to love, honor, cherish, support and respect the aged and infirm fathers and mothers of their nation.

The comments of the committee report to Governor Kirker were reassuring. In part it said:

On this occasion our feelings were like Jacob's when he cried out "surely the Lord is in this place, and I knew it not . . ."

Although these poor Shawnees have had no particular instruction but what they received from the outpouring of the Spirit, yet in point of real light and understanding, as well as behavior, they shame the Christian world . . ."

The report was a long one and in every respect reflected the Greenville meetings in a favorable light. It was a great relief to Governor Kirker, and its effect was not diminished by a letter received a short time later from four settlers who had also gone to Greenville and whose impression varied remarkably in some respects from that of the Shaker Committee. In part it said:

. . . When we arrived there we found . . . that the Shawnee chiefs were all away from that place, mostly gone to Detroit, and that there was there a number of Pottawattamies and other forreign Indians at that place . . . seen some parties coming in and some few returning so . . . could not tell what number was there . . . many spoke a language never

before heard, nor was there an [Ohio] *Indian at that place who understood them, except by their interpreter who was of the Sauky nation. The Puttawattamies said they were of a nation that was called Wynapaas, and that they had been three months and a half constantly traveling, coming from their homes. They all had rifles and were nearly naked. On parting they all gave us their left hand, resolutely refusing the right. The reason given by the Indians for coming to Greenville, is to listen to the Prophet.*

Signed,
Simon Kenton
James McPherson
James M. Reed
Wm. Ward

[*June 30, 1807 — Tuesday*]

Tecumseh, whenever he could, continued to visit the Galloways. Although he said nothing about it on this occasion, he was not pleased to see that close by the site where the fine old Chalahgawtha *msi-kah-mi-qui* had stood, several settlers had built their cabins. They were calling the location Old Town in reference to the Shawnee village that had once stood there.[5]

As usual, Tecumseh spoke with James Galloway at length on various topics and together they smoked again the ceremonial pipe of peace which Tecumseh had long ago presented the white man. It was something of a ritual with them, to reaffirm without ever saying so the friendship that had developed between them and to reestablish their long-continuing pact of peace.

Fifteen-year-old Rebecca waited with poorly hidden impatience for them to finish so that she could have her turn to be with the fascinating Indian chief. This time the impatience was occasioned by more than just an eagerness to converse with him. Some time ago Tecumseh had given her, as a token of friendship, a beautifully constructed bark canoe to use on the Little Miami that flowed past their dooryard. He had instructed her in the use of the light craft and she had been as quick to learn from his instruction as he from hers. Now she wanted to take him for a ride to show how adept at paddling and maneuvering her practice had made her since his last visit.

The two men, however, had gone into a discussion of the changes in Ohio, a discussion occasioned by Galloway's mention of the fact that earlier in the month, on June 7, another three counties had been formed: Cuyahoga, Ashtabula and Portage. From this they fell to talking about the possibly ominous future facing the whole Northwest Territory.

Rebecca, aware that such a discussion could stretch out for hours, became exasperated with the delay and, snatching the canoe paddle from the wall rack, called to Tecumseh to come with her and see a new kind of tree about a mile up the river. She had found some strange new flowers growing nearby that she wanted to transplant to her flower bed.

A look of uncommon concern appeared briefly on Tecumseh's face, but vanished before either the girl or her father noticed it. He smiled at her as he stood up and asked gently if the tree she spoke of was near the river-bank at its second bend above the house.

"Why, yes," she replied, surprised. "You seem to know something about it. Come on. Stop talking about things that ought never to happen. Come on and let's go to the tree. What was it that made you ask about its location, Mr. Tikomfa Chief? You have to tell me all about it when we get there, all about it. Now mind! Not half around, please, like you Indians do when you don't want your paleface friends to know your secrets."

For a moment Tecumseh paused as if to reply, but then he merely nodded and followed her silently down the pathway which led to a natural pier: a magnificent sycamore with great branches stretching out over the river and a huge emergent root that reached out into the water so as to make a natural walkway and port for the canoe resting alongside it.

"You get in first," Rebecca told him. "I'm going to show you I can do real well at paddling. Then you'll be proud of your pupil even if her face is pale."

They lapsed into silence as Rebecca's strong young arms skillfully paddled them into the main current and then upstream. As they rounded the second bend in the river she angled the boat neatly to a landing and Tecumseh held it as she stepped lightly out. He pulled it up a little way so it would not drift off and turned to find her smiling quizzically at him.

"Come," she said, "the tree is just around the hill and the flowers are there, too. Maybe you'll know what they are. I don't. Anyway, there's nothing like them that I can find in the woods."

In a short distance she cried, "Here they both are. See the blossoms on the tree, how beautiful they are, and the flowers there, what are they? I never saw anything like them." She stooped and picked up a fruit and handed it to Tecumseh and then picked up a stone to use as a hammer. "This looks good enough to mash and eat. I believe I will."

With a quick movement the Shawnee chief was at her side, a grave expression on his face. "I didn't expect you'd ever find them," he said. "You shouldn't know the tree and flowers are here; they are nowhere else near. Why didn't I kill what might do my pale friends harm? Come over to this stone and sit down and I will tell you something. Will you listen, then forget?"

Rebecca, confused and a little awed at his demeanor, merely nodded. She sat looking up into his strong face while he paused for a considerable time, as if trying to determine exactly what he should say. At length he released a breath and shook his head slightly.

"The tree and the flowers," he declared, "shall be destroyed so that no harm may come to you or your family. It is the pact of peace. Now you are in our care, no harm can come to you."

The girl frowned, a little frightened by the unexpected comment. Her voice was higher pitched than she meant it to be as she said, "Tell me what it is and what you mean! What kind of a tree is this? Are it and the flowers poison?"

In a tone of authority she had never heard him use before, he asked, "Will this I tell you be for you and you only?"

"Yes," she replied instantly, then added, "it is your wish and it will be for my ears — and, should you consent, for one other — only."

For perhaps five minutes Tecumseh did not speak. He seemed to have become remote, his thoughts far away from this place and this time, his face somewhat sorrowful. When at last he caught himself and began to speak, it was more as if he were talking to himself than addressing her.

"It is the Indian's secret! He suffers pain as you palefaces do. He fears the wound, the torn arm and leg. But this you have found, if prepared right, quiets pain. The red man takes the powder of the flowers and leaves, or of that other fruit you held in your hand, into battle with him. If the bullet bites or the arrow pierces, the potion quiets the pain. If the warrior falls in battle, it eases him. What you had in your hand is best. With it, the pain of the fire at the stake is little. If wounded, the warrior can be removed to a place of safety without pain. The powder is as powerful to quiet pain as your opium is, but does not do the harm it has done. No paleface knows its power. It is our secret. If the Indian loves, he speaks the truth; but if he does not, he is silent."[6]

Rebecca did not know what to say and so, after a little while, the pair walked silently back to the canoe. As she stepped into the little craft she went by the paddle and left it for him to use. With a few strong strokes he drove the slender boat skillfully into midstream and there did little more than guide it as the current swept them back to the pioneer home. It was evident from the expression she wore that Rebecca had been profoundly impressed with the secret she had promised to keep, as well as with his willingness to confide in her.

"Do you recollect," she said at last, "the things next to my heart that we talked about during your last visit here? I want to talk about them again. I shall keep the secrets you gave me today, and reveal them at last to some one of my own blood who may be worthy, and through him in the same way of succession, and so await the time your Great Spirit speaks for their release for humanity's sake; but you must promise me whatever conditions of war or conquest may arise in the future, that, as your sister Tecumapese and I have so earnestly beseeched you, you will throw all your power against the massacre of women and children, and of men who have surrendered or who are hopelessly overpowered."

The trees above and along the shores slid by quietly and he did not speak. In fact, not until the little canoe touched the natural pier and came to a stop did he finally utter the words she so longed to hear.

"I promise, little paleface girl, I promise."

[*July 7, 1807 — Tuesday*]

Through the years, New York–born Christian Schultz had been a great admirer of Anthony Wayne, seeing in the late general one of the greatest figures in American history. When Wayne had died and been buried at Erie, Pennsylvania, eleven years ago, Schultz had promised himself that one day he would visit the shrine.

It was only now that the New Yorker had finally been able to reach Erie, and with a deep sadness and reverence he approached the grave. But what he saw stunned him and he wept. The flimsy wooden palings around the grave were almost entirely rotted away; the only marker for this great American hero was a misshapen stone that had obviously been found in the rubbish of the fort. Upon this stone, faintly scratched with a nail or some other object, were the initials A. W.

Schultz's sorrow quickly turned to anger and he took out his penknife. Directly beneath the initials he carved boldly in the rather soft rock: *SHAME ON MY COUNTRY.*

[*August 2, 1807 — Sunday*]

Jethro Fisher, trader for long years with the Indians, was somewhat startled when he returned to Greenville after an absence of many months. The tiny village that had been established here by Tecumseh and Tenskwatawa had now grown into one of the largest Indian towns he had ever seen, with easily eight hundred *wegiwas* already erected and more being put up. A large council house had been built and several log cabins were under construction. The whole place was a beehive of activity and it seemed that every Indian he saw carried a brand-new rifle of British make.

Concerned with the possible future of his business with the Indians should hostilities break out, Fisher sought out the Prophet, with whom he had always been on friendly terms. He asked him if he wasn't worried about the Americans clamping down on them to make them move back into their own territory. The Americans, he told the Prophet, were strong and terrible enemies to have.

An ugly smile creased Tenskwatawa's ferret face. He replied, "I can bring darkness between the Americans and us; more, I can bring the very sun under my feet! What white man can do this?"

He picked up a bowl of water and tossed the contents to one side in a spray. "I can overthrow the Americans as easily as this. Do you want to know how much I care for Americans?"

Before Fisher could reply, the Prophet bent over at the waist and slapped a palm to his behind and at this same moment discharged an enormous and noisy blast of gas.

"That," he said, breaking into cackling laughter, "is how much I care for Americans!"

[*September 19, 1807 — Saturday*]

When a settler by the name of Myer was killed and scalped a few miles west of Urbana, the aura of fear in Springfield and the surrounding country bloomed again.[7] At once some of the settlers began sending their wives and children back to Kentucky for safety. General Ben Whiteman was alarmed enough to ask and receive Governor Kirker's authorization to mobilize several companies of militia and to send emissaries to both Tecumseh at Greenville and Black Hoof near Fort Wayne to ask them to deliver up the murderer.

Tecumseh's group blamed the death on Black Hoof's followers and Black Hoof in turn blamed Tecumseh's. After lengthy parleys, both Indian groups agreed to meet in council with the whites in Springfield during early September. The meeting place decided upon was an open space near Kenton's Mill and both factions arrived heavily armed.

In accordance with a plan previously agreed to, the hundred seventy Indians under eighty-one-year-old Black Hoof left their tomahawks with Major Thomas Moore and carried only their rifles. It was agreed that when they arrived at the council ground, all armed men not taking part in the talks should stand well away in the rear, each on his own side, while the principal whites and chiefs, none of them carrying weapons, should advance to the center and speak.

However, Tecumseh and his hundred thirty men came by a different route, not passing Major Moore's place in Urbana, and arrived at the council ground armed with both guns and tomahawks. At the insistence of the whites, all of the Indians, including Black Hoof's, stacked their arms to one side — except, that is, Tecumseh, who refused to surrender his pipe tomahawk. There was something of a chilling humor in his eyes when he commented that he might want to use one end or the other of it before the day was out.

At this Parson James Pinchard approached Tecumseh with a dirty, long-stemmed clay pipe and suggested that if the chief wanted to smoke for peace, he might use this. Tecumseh took it and then gave Pinchard such a penetrating stare that the little man backed off hastily in evident fear. Faintly smiling, Tecumseh gingerly sniffed at the bowl of the pipe, turned up his nose in a ludicrous expression and pitched the pipe over his head.

Both Indians and whites howled with laughter and the tension of the meeting was eased. With reluctance, Tecumseh then handed his tomahawk to one of his men who bore it away.

Tecumseh was undoubtedly the outstanding figure at the meeting. He greeted the whites, especially Simon Kenton, in a decidedly friendly fashion and almost at once set the entire assemblage to laughing again by asking if there were any whites on hand who would like to buy Ohio. As the brunt of this joke, the frontiersman grinned in a shamefaced way and then set the audience to further peals of laughter by saying that if anyone did, he would sell it to them, since he had already bought it.

Tecumseh then asked Kenton who the general was and Simon explained it was Ben Whiteman, who had been a member of his party which attacked Tecumseh's camp on Little East Fork fifteen years ago last April, the engagement in which Tecumseh killed Sam Barr. Tecumseh nodded and, his face expressionless but his eyes twinkling, he hailed Whiteman and said, "Are you a big man?"

Taken somewhat aback at the question, Whiteman hesitated and then answered, "Yes."

"Well, I am a better man than you."

"That," replied Whiteman, "is yet to be tried."

"Oh no," the Shawnee chief said quickly, slapping Whiteman's shoulder in a friendly manner, "I whipped you when we were boys. Maybe I'll do it again."

Again the laughter broke out at this repartee; and thus the council got down to business in an unusually and unexpectedly good mood. The whites were represented by Kenton, Whiteman, Ward, McPherson and Moore; Black Hoof's contingent by himself, Blue Jacket and Captain John, a young brave devoted to the elderly chief. Tecumseh's faction was represented by himself, Black Snake and Roundhead, the latter a Wyandot chief who had long ago thrown himself fully behind Tecumseh's plan.

There had been a general feeling that trouble might come when Tecumseh charged Black Hoof with the murder of Myer or vice versa, but Tecumseh surprised them all by not only claiming no knowledge of Myer's death, but also stating that he was certain Black Hoof knew nothing of it either. This greatly pleased the old chief, who said he agreed and felt for the first time in too many moons that the gap between himself and Tecumseh was closing. After much counciling, it was decided that the murder of Myer had been committed by some unknown passing Indians, of which there were many lately.

But having so many of Black Hoof's followers here was an opportunity Tecumseh could not let pass and he went into a long and forceful speech about what he and Tenskwatawa were doing and how they hoped to uplift the Shawnees as well as the other Indian nations with their doctrine. Quite a number of Black Hoof's men expressed approval with nodding heads for such a worthy objective. Tecumseh was particularly pleased when, as the meeting broke up, Blue Jacket came to confront him, shook his hand and promised his support.

About the time the council was breaking up, Governor Kirker, displeased with the variance of reports from different whites and wishing for confirmation from the Indians personally before discharging the militia, sent Thomas Worthington and Duncan McArthur to Greenville to invite Tecumseh and other chiefs there to attend a banquet in their honor in the Ohio capital city, Chillicothe.

Tecumseh came, along with Blue Jacket, Roundhead and Panther, the latter a sachem of the Unami sect of the Delaware tribe. At a record-breaking mass meeting presided over by the governor himself, Tecumseh gave a moving address in English which was at once able, magnetic and convincing. Worthington and McArthur had already submitted a report to the governor which was entirely favorable to the Prophet's program, with no evidence to indicate it was a covert war movement. With that report and the assurance by Tecumseh personally that the Indians desired to live in peace with the whites, the pioneer unrest was set aside and hostile feelings abated. Governor Kirker ordered the discharge of the militia that had been called up and hundreds of men who listened to Tecumseh's eloquent speech with close attention returned to their homes relieved of their fears that another Indian war was impending.

However, there were still a few who were far from convinced. Among them was Simon Kenton, who claimed to be able to see more deeply into the Kispokotha Shawnee than any of the settlers.

"I propose," he said seriously, "that we kill Tecumseh. He is getting too much power. If we let him live, he's going to raise the devil all over the Northwest.

But no one heeded the frontiersman.

[*December 15, 1807 — Monday*]

In her ninety-sixth year, still living with her son John in Washington, Kentucky, Mary Miller Kenton died quietly in her sleep.

It was a deep sadness for Simon when word of it came and he immediately made plans to go there. Since Indian matters in Ohio had settled down somewhat, he might even go out to take another look at his New Madrid lands and visit Boone in Missouri. It was time, anyway, to bring his son John home.

The sojourn in Kentucky was not a pleasant one. An unexpectedly deep grief welled up in the frontiersman as he stood beside his mother's final resting place and he mentally berated himself for not having paid more attention to her and visited her more over these years. Then, although he did not know how to do it well and had never been religiously inclined, he offered up a quiet prayer for her.

His brother John's mismanagement of the remaining property Simon owned in Kentucky had, over the past decade, resulted in the loss of the greater majority of the land. John insisted that Simon take back into his own responsibility the residue. This Simon did, at once selling practically all of it for $36,000 before leaving for Missouri. At New Madrid, more than ever pleased with the land there, he bought another tract for a cash down payment of $16,000 and a promise to pay $8,000 more.

The visit with Boone was brief but pleasant. Nearly seventy-four now, Boone was more feeble than ever, but still mentally alert and greatly pleased to see his old comrade again. They reminisced over old times and discussed at length the development of this western country. A man who had the money to invest in it, Boone asserted, could set up a string of stores along the new wagon trails that were forming and quickly make a fortune.

A fortune is precisely what young John Kenton was interested in having. His eighteenth birthday just past, he had become something of a dreamer, and the predominant dream was that of acquiring a great fortune and living in luxury the rest of his days.

Following their stay with the Boones, the two Kentons stopped off in Kaskaskia to visit the Edgars. Roads now led from all directions to this place where, a generation ago, Simon had helped pilot Clark's ragtag army through an unmarked wilderness. John and Rachel Edgar were overjoyed at seeing Simon again and delighted at meeting his son. Together they feasted and talked at great length in the Edgars' palatial home.

John Edgar had always been a good businessman and knew particularly well how to establish and operate profitable frontier trading posts. Almost as if he had eavesdropped on Kenton's recent discussion with Boone, John Edgar described how a sharp individual with money to invest could make his fortune quickly with such stores. That clinched it. Nothing remained but that young John Kenton try his hand at it. If his father would set up the business capital, he would get it going and attain that pile of wealth.

The plan was to open two stores, but not along the frontier, where Boone and Edgar suggested. John decided instead to have one in St. Louis and the other in St. Charles. With $18,000 from Simon he immediately went about making his plans, listing everything that would be called for in the trade of the times: corn, whiskey, tobacco, knives, needles, beads, threads, garters, leggins, moccasins, vermilion, kegs, lead, paints, powder, guns, blankets, white goods, pork, meal, flour, flints, knife handles, gun screws, shirts, wampum belts and the like. Great plans were made and out of the very first profits they would liquidate the $8,000 debt still owed on the New Madrid purchase.

With the arrangements all settled, the frontiersman once again headed back to Ohio alone.

[February 25, 1808 — Thursday]

Because the great number of Indians who had come to hear the Prophet were running out of provisions and faced serious famine, Governor William Henry Harrison dispatched an order to Fort Wayne for Captain William Wells to distribute food to them from the public stores there. With this act he left himself open for considerable criticism for being so charitable; but it was not the quality of mercy alone upon which this move of Harrison's was motivated. While no one had yet been able to come up with any proof, he was still certain that Tecumseh and Tenskwatawa were up to no good. He was also aware that anger and violence took root and grew more rapidly in an empty stomach than in a full one. He meant to prevent this, if possible.

Wells was irked, not only because he felt that giving the Indians food was "aiding the enemy," but because Harrison had figuratively rapped his knuckles by bluntly and coldly rejecting a plan Wells had advanced — that of setting a trap to catch the brothers and imprisoning them to prevent further agitation. But Harrison said that such an act would undoubtedly do more than anything else to unite the tribes and cause an outbreak of war.

And he was quite right, for the following of Tecumseh in Ohio and the Indiana Territory had grown significantly over the winter. Even those Indians who were not publicly supporting him were showing indications of sympathy for the doctrines he promoted. To arrest him would be all the encouragement many of them would need to throw their full weight of support behind him. Tecumseh, Harrison said, would remain free.

[May 15, 1808 — Sunday]

Although it should have been apparent to James Galloway long before now, it came as a decided jolt to him when Tecumseh, with great dignity and his customary directness, requested the hand of Rebecca in marriage. At once it became clear to the settler that the many gifts the Shawnee chief had brought his daughter — including the beautiful canoe and an elegant silver comb of considerable weight — were more than mere gifts of friendship; they were tokens of the deep love that had grown in him for the beautiful Rebecca Galloway.

A multitude of thoughts raced through Galloway's mind as he casually filled the ceremonial calumet with tobacco, lighted it, took a few puffs and handed it to Tecumseh. So far as he knew, Rebecca had not thought of Tecumseh except as a brilliant, interesting and quite exciting occasional visitor. How might she react to a proposal of marriage? This was an acute situation which must be handled with great delicacy.

When the settler finally did speak, it was with gentleness and great kindness. Tecumseh, he said, certainly was aware of the many problems such a union would necessarily engender. Not only the most apparent problem of racial difference, but the fact that Rebecca was only sixteen, while he was forty. And what of the lingering, even growing animosity between Ohio whites and Indians? What of adaptability; could Rebecca fit into his way of life or Tecumseh into hers? Furthermore, she had never shown any indication to either himself or her mother, through word or action, that she loved Tecumseh. Though still quite young, Rebecca was possessed of rare intelligence and individuality, and whether or not Tecumseh could marry her was a decision which must come not from her father, but from herself. Galloway personally had no objection to Tecumseh, and he had the settler's unqualified permission to speak to his daughter on the matter.

Tecumseh spoke to her at once.

Although she was surprised and certainly flattered at Tecumseh's proposal, Rebecca was not as shocked by it as her father had been. For a good many years now she had deeply admired her "Mr. Tikomfa Chief" and found in him more attractive attributes than she had ever seen in any other man — except, perhaps, her own father. The idea of having such a man for a husband had undoubtedly crossed her mind before, and she must have considered some of the benefits and disadvantages briefly. She had not believed him romantically inclined toward her until after his last visit; then she had reflected on what he had told her about the medicinal tree and flowers and the remark she kept coming back to time and again was: "If the Indian loves, he speaks the truth; but if he does not, he is silent." For her own part, she felt a strong emotion for this man in whom she saw so much power and ability; but whether or not such emotion was truly love was something of which even such a mature sixteen-year-old girl as she could not be sure.

On only two specific matters did she comment at this time: highly as she regarded him, it would be impossible for her to adapt to the life, labor and limited environment of the women of his tribe; and polygamy, while not encouraged by the Shawnees, was not unknown among them, whereas to her it was an abhorrent custom. What of these things?

They were problems of little moment to the chief. He told her that she would be his only wife, that there could be an agreeable combination of tribal life and the life to which she was accustomed; he would not expect her to do the work usually required of Shawnee women.

Rebecca said she must consider this carefully and Tecumseh nodded. He had expected no decision now. In another moon he would return and then she could state her decision.

With that, Rebecca rejoined her mother in the kitchen and Tecumseh sat with her father. The matter of marriage was not again referred to during this visit, nor did Tecumseh hasten his departure. The usual agreeable relationship with the entire family was maintained as though nothing out of the ordinary had occurred. There was light banter and much laughter and enjoyment at dinner, and afterwards Tecumseh and Galloway sat and talked at length of many things. Because he trusted them, Tecumseh spoke this evening with more directness than ever before with any white man of the great events that were shaping in this country; of the first rumblings of the terrible storm which might break into a fury of battle over this land; and, to some degree, of Tecumseh's part in all this.

James Galloway had always strongly admired Tecumseh's manner of conversing — the colorful, sometimes poignant, sometimes angry, reflective way he expressed himself. In past meetings he had discussed at length the injustice of tribal treatment by the United States, in which as little as a single penny per acre was all the Indians had realized from the land treaties. He had spoken of the refusal of the government to permit the Indian himself to sell his land to individual purchasers. He had talked of the bland disregard of the government for overlapping tribal interests in Indian land treaties. He remarked bitterly on the ever-growing migration of white men pushing westward over the Alleghenies to settle on Indian land, regardless of treaties. And recently he had spoken of the cloak over the white man's treaties; a cloak which too often covered the hand of the aggressor, and of the desperate need of a protective confederation of tribes to save his people from the inevitable losses which threatened them.

But this evening Tecumseh spoke to the whole Galloway family of the new village he and his brother had established. Antagonism against their continued presence in Greenville had reached a point where to stay would have been to invite open hostilities, and he did not wish that. When, in March, the Potawatomies and Kickapoos had joined in an invitation to Tecumseh and Tenskwatawa to remove to a tract of land they would give them on a branch of the Wabash called the Tippecanoe River they had accepted. The town was now even larger than it had been in Greenville and far removed from the influence and interference of the white man. It was being called Prophet's Town and at this site Indians from an ever-widening radius were assembling to hear him and his brother speak.

Soon now his immediate work with the chiefs of the Delaware and Wyandot and Shawnee nations would be completed and then he would be gone for a long period, during which he would travel far to the southwest and the south and the southeast to meet and speak with the chiefs of the tribes who held these lands.

Abruptly, as if catching himself before he should say too much, Tecumseh rose, bade the host and his family good-bye and promised to see them again in one moon.

Only after the door had closed behind him did the full significance and portent of Tecumseh's visit break over the family. What they were facing here was not a theory but an imperative reality. The situation in this household had changed in a day. Tecumseh the guest had become Tecumseh the suitor and if the situation could not be met favorably then it must, at all costs, be handled with great care. So great, indeed, was the respect of the family for this Shawnee chief, that to follow any course which might wound his feelings was unthinkable.

A serious family conference was held and all aspects of the matter discussed until late into the night. But it was counsel and wisdom that was given to Rebecca, not orders or demands. Both parents agreed that it was she, not they, who must decide what to do; she must, in her own way and in her own time, determine and announce her decision. No further discussion would be held among them about it unless Rebecca herself brought up the matter.

At last they assembled before the family altar. A psalm was sung, followed by a reading from the Scriptures, and then they knelt together and offered a prayer of supplication that Divine direction be extended to the one who now greatly needed God's hand to lead her through a difficult way.

Later, as she lay awake in her dark room with the house quiet and peaceful around her, Rebecca felt a burning tear slide across her cheek, and for the first time she fully realized that she was very much in love with Tecumseh.

[*June 2, 1808 — Thursday*]

The feeling that now filled the frontiersman was a good one. It was nice to be back in Ohio again, to see Betsy and the children and to settle down again, for a little while at least, to more mundane matters. It was good to know, too, that Tecumseh and the Prophet had left Greenville and moved deep into the Indiana Territory.

Simon Kenton was not bothered at all by the fact that most of his cash fortune had disappeared, that his Kentucky lands were gone, that none of the Ohio claims he had so laboriously staked out were being honored, and that his large purchase in the Indiana Territory continued to be a huge joke on the frontier. Such matters scarcely touched him, for there were other very good things to consider: his Missouri claims and purchases were still in excellent shape, particularly those in which he was most interested near New Madrid; furthermore, he had faith that young John would make a good showing with the new stores in St. Louis and St. Charles. Who knew but what this enterprise alone might not repay him for all he had lost in his land deals?

There was still hope, as well, that his brother, William, would be successful in his mission to Washington, D.C., where he had gone soon after the frontiersman left for Kentucky and Missouri. William hoped to get Congress to grant an extension act whereby the settlers in the Mad River area could save their jeopardized Symmes Purchase lands by paying, annually for eight years, one eighth of the amount due under the contract. Even though William had not yet returned to Ohio, an atmosphere of hope prevailed among the settlers.

News of Simon's purchase of additional lands at New Madrid had circulated around the state and one Ohio land speculator made a special trip to see him. He had not long ago seen those very lands himself and been highly impressed with them, and so now he offered the frontiersman a trade: in exchange for the New Madrid area lands Kenton had bought, he would give him "several thousand dollars in cash and sixteen hundred acres of choice land near the new village of Columbus, Ohio, in Franklin County, very rich." He also agreed to take over the payments still due on the New Madrid lands.

But Simon Kenton refused. This was the land where he now dreamed of creating his Kenton empire and, as ever with Simon, the dream was only a step or so away from the reality.

[June 15, 1808 — Wednesday]

The month had not been an easy one for Rebecca Galloway. How she envied the young women to whom a proposal of marriage was such a simple matter, demanding only a yes or no answer and with little real concern for what the future might be, regardless of which answer was given. Such simplicity was denied her in the decision which must be made now. The problems to face if she answered yes were staggering and the possible consequences if she were to answer no were not pleasant to contemplate.

A hundred times at least she wished she could read the future, to know what would be, not only between herself and Tecumseh, but between red men and white. And yet, though she was certainly no seer, she was gifted with a keen logic and the same sense of prescience which many women possess. She knew beyond any doubt that Tecumseh was a powerful man now and would continue to grow in power among his people. She knew, as well, that this power must, sooner or later, prove dangerous to her own people and highly fateful to his.

And while she tried to keep from thinking of it, she continued to consider the possibility that this incident of love between herself and the Shawnee chief might, in some way, be made to change future events; events which, as she had listened to his discussions with her father in their home, seemed not only impending, but inevitable. With a woman's intuition she knew, after grasping the meaning of these discussions, that a terrible ordeal was in store and that she, an unknown sixteen-year-old girl of the frontier, had it within her power to alter the very course of history.

Foreordination is a strong doctrinal tenet of the Scotch Associate communion. It unconsciously influences its members in the daily relationships of life and very consciously influences them in the serious emergencies which they encounter. And so, despite her resolution not to think along these lines, Rebecca's thoughts turned to what she might do to stop the storm she knew was approaching. Was it not altogether possible that if she gave her consent to marry Tecumseh — as she was naturally inclined to do because of the love she felt for him — she could turn the power of this unusual man from war to peace? No one but she and Tecumseh could ever truly know what calamity would be thereby averted.

There were, then, these strong inducements for her to give an answer of yes, but there were even stronger inducements for a negative response. What of the relationship between her people and his? What of the lives of the children who might be born of this union? What of religion? And even — though she considered this the least of the problem — what of their age differential?

At last, a week before the moon of waiting was up, she reached her decision and, having reached it, again enjoyed peaceful sleep. Although her parents realized that she had made up her mind, they did not ask her what the answer would be and she did not tell them, reserving that declaration for the one most greatly to be affected by it.

At the appointed time, Tecumseh arrived at the Galloway home and found the usual warm hospitality extended to him. For a long time he sat and conversed pleasantly with James Galloway, but the basis for his visit hung tangibly in the air, and at last Rebecca made her appearance. Her eyes sparkled with somewhat more than usual interest as she listened to the conversation and she seemed almost to glow with the symphony of romance that filled her.

As the evening wore on, Rebecca finally went to Tecumseh's side and softly suggested that they take a ride in her canoe upon waters shimmering beneath the full moon. Tecumseh smiled faintly and nodded and they left the house together.

The night was warm and peaceful, filled with the concerto of fiddling crickets and the perfume of honeysuckle. The paddle moved softly in the water under Tecumseh's hands and they slipped quietly through the deep shadows of the trees lacing the watercourse. From a long distance came the stirring, lonesome hooting of an owl, and from nearer at hand the throaty lilt of a whippoorwill. It was a matchless setting for the expression of one of life's great sentiments, and now she gave him her answer.

"I will marry you, Tecumseh."

The orb of moon seemed brighter after her words, the sounds of the night sweeter and the scents more enriching. They were both silent for a short time and then she spoke again, repeating herself and adding to what she had said.

"I will marry you if, on your part, you will adopt my people's mode of life and dress."

Tecumseh continued his silence, which did not surprise her, for she knew she had asked of him a tremendous sacrifice. For a half hour longer they paddled and drifted and when, at length, they moored their little craft at the huge sycamore and returned to the house, Tecumseh had still not spoken. At the door he held her close to him for a long while, and then his warm and gentle voice touched her ears.

"I will return with my answer at the next moon."

She nodded and they entered the house. After a little more conversation with the whole family, the Shawnee chief said he must leave. Before doing so he asked James Galloway to smoke again with him the calumet, and when this ritual was performed the two of them went to the door and Tecumseh paused there a moment before leaving. When he spoke his words indicated that, regardless of how well they had hidden it, he had sensed the dread of possible harm that must have haunted the family should Rebecca have refused his proposal. And the very tone of his voice indicated understanding and forgiveness of them for it.

"You and your family," he told the settler, "need have no fear from my race."

He looked past Galloway at Rebecca, standing on the other side of the room beside her mother. Again he smiled faintly and said, "Next moon." And then he was gone.

The decision was now Tecumseh's.

[*July 2, 1808 — Saturday*]

"The white chief Harrison," Tenskwatawa declared, "has a responsibility to provide the people of my village with provisions. These cannot be consistently withheld from me, since the white people have always encouraged me to preach the word of God to the Indians and it is in this holy work that I am now engaged."

The reasoning may have been faulty but the demand was clearly stated to William Henry Harrison by the delegation the Prophet sent down the Wabash to Vincennes to deliver his speech. Except for the demand for provisions, the speech contained little that was new to the governor; a denial of all the unfavorable representations that had been circulating among the whites about his purposes; a reiteration that both he and Tecumseh wished to live in peace with the white people; a promise to visit the governor personally before long. The messenger who had brought this speech to the governor stayed and broke bread with the white chief and told him during a private conference:

"I have now listened to that man upward of three years and have never heard him give any but good advice. He tells us that we must pray to the Great Spirit who made the world and everything in it for our use. He tells us that no man could make the plants, the trees and the animals, but that they must be made by the Great Spirit, to whom we ought to pray and obey in all things. He tells us not to lie, to steal, nor to drink whiskey; not to go to war but to live in peace with all mankind. He tells us also to work and make corn."

It sounded fine, but William Henry Harrison was unconvinced.

About this time, a few hundred miles east, William Kenton returned to Springfield with good news: Congress had granted the extension act he had petitioned for, so that now the Mad River settlers would not lose their homes and lands provided they could meet the annual payments.

And far to the south, across the Ohio and along the banks of Tygart Creek, birds that had been startled into silence by a sudden loud crash gradually resumed their evening songs, paying little attention to the overturned buggy with one wheel still revolving slowly by its own centrifugal force; uncaring that beneath the buggy lay the crushed and lifeless remains of John Kenton, brother of the frontiersman who had once claimed this very land.

[*July 15, 1808 — Friday*]

That Tecumseh and Rebecca Galloway made a handsome couple was undeniable. She was of medium height and erect, her body full and well formed with the bloom of young womanhood, her features smooth and decidedly pleasant to look upon. The appearance of Tecumseh was uncommonly fine, too, his face more oval than angular and his nose aquiline and well molded. His mouth was firm and strong and his eyes a clear transparent hazel with mild expression. His skin was a rich tan rather than the reddish-bronze cast so many of his tribesmen possessed. He, too, stood quite erect and walked with a brisk, vigorous step.

Now, as invariably, he was clad entirely in buckskin as he and Rebecca walked from the Galloway house to stand together beneath the great black oak tree a short distance away. The mellow orb of the moon shone through the leaves and spread out in little puddles of light on the ground around them.

For a long moment the Shawnee chief held her close. He pressed his lips first to her right eye and then to her left and then kissed her lips tenderly. But his voice, when he spoke, was heavy with regret.

"I will not come back again, Rebecca. I cannot take you as my wife under your conditions. To do as you require would lose for me the respect and leadership of my people."

He held her close again, briefly, then turned and disappeared soundlessly into the forest.

And Rebecca Galloway wept.

[*August 20, 1808 — Saturday*]

In the past two weeks, during which time he had held frequent interviews with Tenskwatawa, here in Vincennes, William Henry Harrison had undergone an almost complete reversal of opinion regarding the Prophet. His first impulse had been to laugh in the face of the little Indian who had come to demand supplies of him; but as the days passed and he listened to the Prophet speak, not only to himself but to the large crowd of Indians who had accompanied him here or come later, he began to find himself in sympathy with him.

Could this be the man everyone had warned him about? Could this be the man whose supposed threat overshadowed all the whites of the frontier? Could it be that the stories told about him were wrong and that the Shaker Committee had been right — that the Prophet and Tecumseh had, after all, only the welfare and betterment of their people by peaceful means as a goal?

Apparently the little Shawnee had nothing to hide. The governor's friends among the Indians assembled here assured him that the speeches Tenskwatawa gave now were no different in delivery or intent than those he had been giving for years; that he dwelled most often and most earnestly upon the great evils resulting from war and the use of liquor.

As the opinion of Harrison for the Prophet grudgingly swung to the favorable side, he frequently tested the little Indian's influence over his followers by holding private conversations with small numbers of them and offering them whiskey, but it was always firmly refused. Long interested in what was to be done with and for the Indians, Harrison had many times himself urged the government to pass laws prohibiting the supplying of liquor to Indians. For the first time, he now began to have real hope that this Shawnee preacher of temperance was on the right track and might better the conditions on the frontier for both Indians and whites; thereupon he authorized the further distribution of goods to the Prophet's people.

In his last visit with the governor before departing for Prophet's Town on the Tippecanoe, Tenskwatawa spoke with great earnestness:

"Father, it is three years since I first began that system of religion which

I now practice. The white people and some of the Indians were against me, but I had no other intention but to introduce among the Indians those good principles of religion which the white people profess. I was spoken badly of by the white people, who reproached me with misleading the Indians, but I defy them to say that I did anything amiss."

Tenskwatawa fixed Harrison with a sorrowful gaze. "Father, I was told you intended to hang me. When I heard this, I intended to remember it and tell my father when I went to see him and relate the truth. I heard, when I settled on the Wabash, that my father, the governor, had declared that all the land between Vincennes and Fort Wayne was the property of the Seventeen Fires. I also heard that you wanted to know, my father, whether I was God or man, and that you said if I was the former I should not steal horses. I heard this from Mr. Wells, but I believe it originated with himself."

The Prophet paused and frowned as if displeased with the memory and then continued in a gentler tone. "The Great Spirit told me to tell the Indians that he had made them and made the world; that he had placed them on it to do good and not evil. I told all the redskins that the way they were in was not good and that they ought to abandon it; that we ought to consider ourselves as one man, but we ought to live agreeably to our several customs, the red people after their mode and the white people after theirs; particularly that the red people should not drink whiskey, that it was not made for them but for the white people who knew how to use it and that it is the cause of all the mischiefs which the Indians suffer, and that they must follow the directions of the Great Spirit and we must listen to Him, as it was He that made us; determine to listen to nothing that is bad; do not take up the tomahawk should it be offered by the British or by the Long Knives; do not meddle with anything that does not belong to you, but mind your own business and cultivate the ground, that your women and children may have enough to live on."

For a long moment the Prophet hesitated, and then he continued: "I now inform you that it is our intention to live in peace with our father and his people forever. My father, I have informed you what we mean to do, and I call the Great Spirit to witness the truth of my declaration. The religion which I have established for the last three years has been attended by all the different tribes of Indians in this part of the world. Those Indians were once different people; they are now but one; they are all determined to practice what I have communicated to them, that has come immediately from the Great Spirit through me.

"Brother," he continued, slipping from the highly respectful term of father to the more equal form of address, "I speak to you as a warrior. You are one. But let us lay aside this character and attend to the care of our children, that they may live in comfort and peace. We desire that you will join us for the preservation of both red and white people. Formerly, when we lived in ignorance, we were foolish, but now, since we listen to the voice of the Great Spirit, we are happy.

"I have listened to what you have said to us. You have promised to assist us. I now request you, in behalf of all the red people, to use your exertions to prevent the sale of liquor to us. We are all well pleased to hear you say that you will endeavor to promote our happiness. We give you every assurance that we will follow the dictates of the Great Spirit. We are all well pleased with the attention you have shown us. Also with the good intentions of our father, the President. If you give us a few articles, such as needles, flints, hoes, gunpowder and the like we will take the animals that afford us meat with powder and ball."

Harrison nodded. The bit of wheedling for even more supplies was characteristic of Indian speeches and it did not surprise him. But he was quite agreeable to it. If this little bit of help could prevent further hostility along the border, then certainly it was worth it. The thing that most impressed him was the very obvious sincerity of Tenskwatawa. There could be no doubt in anyone's mind who heard him that he deeply believed in everything he said. The execution of those accused of witchcraft was a regrettable thing, but perhaps it was not as bad as he had been led to believe. After all, these changes that Tenskwatawa was promoting — the reformation of morals and the general enlightenment of the Indians by the removal of old prejudices — were bound to have some violence connected with them. Perhaps, when all was considered, this was a case where the end truly justified the means.

[*October 26, 1808 — Wednesday*]

Although Simon Kenton was not a religious man, neither was he irreligious. He had lived too long in the woods and been in too close contact with nature not to feel that there was some higher power behind it all. But he could never quite understand what it was that got into people like the Shakers who manifested their contact with God in the strangest of ways.

For many years, ever since the rise of the Shakers in Kentucky, he had seen scores of his neighbors "quickened" by religious jerkings until the individual went into something of a trance and was thrown, seemingly by some power other than his own, violently to the ground where he flopped about uncontrollably, as would a fish pulled from a stream and tossed onto the riverbank. He had seen it often, but had never himself felt the slightest manifestation of such a power.

Kenton frequently went to church, though in the Kentucky days with Martha it was more often as lookout and sharpshooter — guarding the congregation against Indians — than as a devout participant in the ceremonies. Since coming to Ohio, however, it had become a regular practice of his to attend the camp meetings with Elizabeth when the autumn season rolled around. Thus, when a religious meeting was called by the Methodist Episcopals under the leadership of the Reverend Bennett Maxey, he and Elizabeth attended, along with other members of the family. For several days they camped at Voss's campgrounds on Buck Creek a few miles above Springfield, listening to the sermons and watching as friends and neighbors were saved. But this time the big frontiersman showed a marked interest; an interest which became particularly pronounced on the camp meeting's first Sunday, September 25, when several of his relatives had professed their sins, accepted the Lord and been saved.

Not even minor deviations in the respectability of the services took the edge off for him — such as at one point when, during the midst of his sermon, the minister abruptly stopped, scanned the top of a nearby tree and said, "I want to remark right here that yonder is one of the best forks for a pack saddle I ever saw in the woods. When services are over, we'll get it."

The next day Simon kept more or less to himself, a troubled expression on his face, until finally he approached the Reverend Maxey.

"Mr. Maxey," he said slowly, "I'd take it kindly if you'd walk out into the woods a bit with me."

The preacher readily assented and the two men strolled together through the woods until the sound of the camp meeting was lost behind them. Finally Kenton stopped and faced the minister.

"Mr. Maxey, I am going to communicate some things to you which I want you to promise to me you will never divulge."

"If it will not affect any but ourselves," Maxey replied immediately, "then I promise to keep it forever."

With the preacher thus pledged to secrecy, the frontiersman sat on a log and broke into a long and detailed confession of the things he had done with his life, of the wrongs he had committed. He spoke of White Rock Ridge and Quick's Run, of Detroit and Kaskaskia and Florida, and of those times on the battlefield when he put to death Indians held helpless beneath him. God had been merciful to him, he said, in preserving him amid all the dangers and conflicts of his years on the frontier wilderness. Could God — *would* God — accept such a one as he? He was getting up in years, fifty-three now, and one day the hand of death would close over him. Was there anything for him to look forward to? Could he still, at such a late stage of life, ask for and receive the forgiveness of God for his sins and the redemption the minister preached? His lip quivered as he spoke and his sincerity was such that tears laid wet furrows down his craggy cheeks.

At Maxey's direction, both of them fell to their knees there in the wilderness and prayed aloud to God for mercy and salvation as Maxey beseeched Jesus, the Almighty Savior, to help this man. And as he did so, a great transformation came over the frontiersman; an inner glow suffused him and he came to his feet with a joyous cry that rang through the woods. And then he ran, leaving Preacher Maxey behind, leaping over logs and bushes and bellowing with a fierce exultation. He burst from the woods into the campgrounds and, when the startled crowd had gathered around him, told them all in a roaring voice of his being saved. He was joining the camp of God at last!

Soon the Reverend Bennett Maxey made his way to the inner ring of people encircling the frontiersman and, during a pause in Simon's enthusiastic outpourings, said, "General, I thought we were to keep the matter a secret."

Kenton shook his head violently. "Oh, it's too glorious for that." His voice rang out above the murmur of the crowd, "If I had all the world here, I would tell of the mercy and goodness of God!"

But except for this remarkable outburst, there was really only one significant change in the frontiersman's behavior. He was still, as before, greatly beloved by friends and neighbors. He continued, as before, to play with the children and tell them stories and they idolized him. His manner with women and children retained the same courtesy and tenderness it had always had, and the expression he wore remained mild, his voice low and gentle. There was never a taint of wrongdoing attached to him and he never indulged in even the temperate use of liquor and utilized tobacco only as snuff or in an occasional pipe. As one neighbor put it in describing the frontiersman's simple and unsophisticated everyday life, Simon Kenton, "for a man without scholastic culture, was remarkably chaste in his behavior and conversation."

The single important change was that now, for the first time since leaving the home of his benefactor, Jacob Butler, in Warm Springs in 1771, he lay down his rifle. Carrying the death-dealing weapon had become such an ingrained habit with him that it was not an easy change to make. As something of a compromise, he fashioned a fine staff over five feet in length and this he carried with him wherever he went, grasping it about a foot from its upper end.

It was a change that no one had ever really expected to witness in Simon Kenton.

[*December 31, 1808 — Saturday*]

Ohio continued to grow.

Stark and Delaware and Tuscarawas counties had been formed in February and these were followed by Licking and Preble and Knox counties. On October 11, Samuel Huntington of Trumbull County was elected governor and, two months later, took over his office from Governor

Kirker. And during the final session of the state congress for the year, the Muskingum County delegation was assured by the legislature that if Muskingum County would, at its own risk, furnish suitable buildings for the use of the legislature, a law would no doubt be passed making Zanesville the new state capital.

While Ohio continued to grow, so did the plans of the Shawnee brothers, Tecumseh and Tenskwatawa. Tecumseh had expanded his activities again, frequently making long trips for one- or two-day speeches to the Winnebagoes or Sacs, Sioux or Iowa, Huron or Chippewa tribes, leaving Tenskwatawa behind to continue his preachings, providing him with a whole new set of minor predictions to maintain his authority as Prophet, leaving him with two prime requisites to adhere to in his absence: a continuation of the abject secrecy from the whites of the "grand plan" and a refusal to join the British who had begun to show signs of asking the Indians to once again join them in a struggle against the whites.

A subtle change had taken place in the Prophet, a change which even Tecumseh did not recognize. In Tenskwatawa's eyes, Tecumseh was still a great leader, a great war chief, a personification for other Indians of admirable qualities, but he was not quite the absolute leader Tenskwatawa had long considered him. Who was it, he asked himself, that gave these people a strong religion? Who was it that kept them from the vices of theft and drunkenness and promiscuousness with whites? Who was it that foretold for them the future? Yes! It was Tenskwatawa, not Tecumseh. Let his elder brother, if he wished, continue to believe that the Prophet was his man, controlled and ordered by him. Let Tecumseh continue to give him prophecies to pass on to their people; were not these prophecies merely verification of the events he had already foreseen in his own mind? He was indeed the greatest Prophet ever known to the Indians and he would, in time, lead his people to the restoration of all that they had lost at the hands of the whites. Tecumseh was right — they did not need the hand of the British to help them. They would overcome by themselves and, when the time came, they would know that it was the Prophet, not his brother, who was the guiding and redeeming factor for all the Indians.

Thus, when a large British delegation came to visit him in Tecumseh's absence, to invite the Indians to make war on the Americans, he all but laughed in their faces and sent them away.

Tenskwatawa needed the help of no man. He was supreme, invincible, second only to the Great Spirit Himself.

He was the Prophet!

[*December 31, 1809 — Sunday*]

The watchword of the year was suspicion. Everyone, it seemed, was suspicious of something.

Early in the year Tecumseh became suspicious that the Sacs, Foxes and Kickapoos, worried about the increase of whites in their territory, were preparing to attack them and he went to them quickly. They must, he told them, have patience. Should one or two or only a handful of tribes attack the whites before the appointed time, it could only result in disaster for the tribes involved and for the grand plan in general. If necessary, they must hold their pride in check and turn the other cheek; their entire energies must be held in reserve for that one great wave of retaliation from the Indian amalgamation, which would drive the whites forever from their lands.

No sooner had this suspicion been alleviated than a new one cropped up. His own brother, Tenskwatawa, was engaging in war talk with the Indians gathered under him on the Tippecanoe, actively urging that they strike Vincennes soon in force and destroy it. As a result of this, some of the Indians already at Tippecanoe were becoming alarmed and returning to their own villages, while other tribes who had been on the verge of joining the Tippecanoe assemblage were holding off.

Furious, Tecumseh returned to Tippecanoe with all haste and went into private council with Tenskwatawa, castigating him for his ambition and warning him to follow orders or he would soon be answering to Tecumseh himself in a manner he would not find pleasant. Then, accompanied by a minor Shawnee chief who had long ago adopted the name Captain Lewis, Tecumseh journeyed to Upper Sandusky to attend the council of Wyandots and Senecas and once again made his strong inducements for these tribes to abandon for the time their Ohio homes and take up residence in Prophet's Town on the Tippecanoe. He told them that the country on that river was better than that which they now occupied, that it was farther removed from the whites and that they would have more game and be happier there.

Tarhe, chief of the Wyandots, was not so easily swayed. The experience suffered by both the Wyandots and Senecas during Wayne's campaign had given them a wholesome fear of offending the Seventeen Fires.

"Tecumseh," said Tarhe, "I fear that you are working for no good purpose at Tippecanoe. We will wait a few years. If then we find you happy and contented, we will probably join you."

The fires of suspicion were ignited in Captain William Wells, too. The information brought to him at Fort Wayne by his spies was disturbing and he passed it along at once to Governor Harrison, informing him that, according to reports, the Indians had been required by the Prophet to take up arms against the government, not only to exterminate Vincennes, but also the settlements along the Ohio. The Prophet, Wells reported, was telling his followers that this was the order of the Great Spirit, who threatened destruction to those who disobeyed. He also reported that

Chippewas, Potawatomies and Ottawas were deserting the Prophet in consequence of this order. Wells added that there were not more than a hundred warriors remaining with Tenskwatawa.

Harrison, who had his own spies and his own suspicions, knew better. At the very time that he was getting this information from Wells, there were camped within fifty miles of Vincennes no less than five hundred devoted followers of Tenskwatawa or Tecumseh or both. Whether or not they meant mischief he did not know, but he immediately organized two full companies of volunteer militia and garrisoned them at Fort Knox, just two miles above Vincennes. When no attack came, he was convinced that this show of strength had put a stop to it.

The Indians were suspicious of Harrison and greatly angered with him when it was learned that in March he had held council at Greenville with a select few peaceable chiefs of the Miami, Eel River, Delaware and Potawatomi tribes. For some token payments of food and material goods, he had gotten them to put their thumbprints to a treaty which irrevocably transferred to the United States a large tract of land lying east of the Wabash River — land upon which more than a dozen tribes were now living. At the treaty, Harrison had called out, asking if all the Indians were present who were considered to have any claim on this land. He was assured they were. Even though this was not true, the treaty was nevertheless signed and another great chunk of Indian land was gobbled up by the United States.

In midsummer, Tenskwatawa and forty of his men from Prophet's Town again journeyed to Vincennes under a flag of peace and the Prophet and Harrison conferred at length. Tenskwatawa meekly denied any part in the suspected plan to attack Vincennes and, falling back on what Tecumseh had told him, claimed that the plot was confined entirely to the tribes of the Mississippi and Illinois rivers and that it was he, the Prophet, who had made his influence known and prevailed upon them to put aside their warlike ideas. That William Henry Harrison was not to be so easily deceived by Tenskwatawa a second time was evident in part in the letter written by the governor to the United States Secretary of War while the Shawnee was still in Vincennes:

. . . I must confess that my suspicions of his guilt have been rather strengthened than diminished at every interview I have had with him since his arrival. He acknowledges that he received an invitation to war against us from the British, last fall, and that he was apprised of the intention of the Sacs and Foxes, &c., early in the spring, and was warmly solicited to join their league. But he could give no satisfactory explanation of his neglecting to communicate to me circumstances so extremely interesting to us and towards which I had a few months before directed his attention,

and received a solemn assurance of his cheerful compliance with the injunctions I had impressed upon him. The result of all my inquiries on the subject is that the late combination was produced by British intrigue and influence, in anticipation of war with the United States. It was, however, premature and ill-judged . . . The warlike and well-armed tribes of the Pottawatomies, Ottawas, Chippewas, Delawares, and Miamis, I believe, neither had nor would have joined in the combination; and although the Kickapoos . . . are much under the influence of The Prophet, I am persuaded that they were never made acquainted with his intentions, if they were really hostile toward the United States.

Despite all the suspicions in the air, the year closed without open hostilities erupting anywhere. The United States, under its new President, James Madison, continued to be suspicious of the British; Harrison continued to be suspicious of Tecumseh and the Prophet; many of the Indian chiefs continued to be suspicious of the amalgamation of tribes; Tecumseh continued to be suspicious of the growing insubordination of his brother; the settlers continued to be suspicious of all Indians; and Tenskwatawa continued to be suspicious of everything and everybody.

The Prophet's work in helping to unite the tribes behind his movement was, on the whole, a big disappointment to Tecumseh. These tribes — the Delawares, Miamis, Wyandots and, in particular, the Shawnees — must be convinced to join. Without their active support, the entire grand plan might collapse. Yet, instead of uniting them, Tenskwatawa had succeeded only in alarming them and driving them away with talk of immediate attack on Vincennes and the river settlements, and by his suggestions that the Great Spirit would destroy any who did not join in to help. It was a maddening development and, before he set out again to visit each of these chiefs, Tecumseh held long conferences with his younger brother and gave him strict orders to follow.

Tenskwatawa was to begin immediately to regain some of the prestige he had lost during the year. He would retire alone to the woods and there make a large number of sacred slabs which he was to tell the assembled Indians he had made under direction of the Great Spirit. The directions for their construction were explicit.

Each slab was to be of the same length, thickness and taper and each was to have carved, on one side only, the same symbols. The slabs were to be made of red cedar and each was to be accompanied by a bundle of thin red sticks. Each of the red sticks was to represent one moon and, when the bundle and slab was given to a particular chief, he would be directed to throw away one of the red sticks at each full moon until only the slab itself remained, at which time he must prepare for the great sign to be given soon.[8]

THE SACRED SLAB

PUBLIC MEANING   SECRET INTERPRETATION

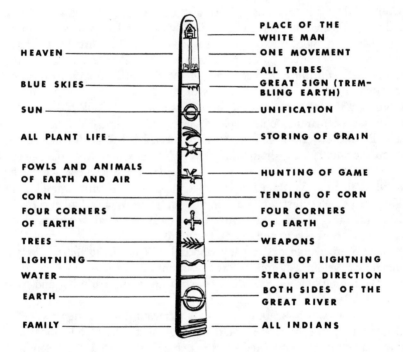

PLACE OF THE
WHITE MAN

HEAVEN — ONE MOVEMENT

ALL TRIBES

BLUE SKIES — GREAT SIGN (TREM-
BLING EARTH)

SUN — UNIFICATION

ALL PLANT LIFE — STORING OF GRAIN

FOWLS AND ANIMALS
OF EARTH AND AIR — HUNTING OF GAME

CORN — TENDING OF CORN

FOUR CORNERS   FOUR CORNERS
OF EARTH   OF EARTH

TREES — WEAPONS

LIGHTNING — SPEED OF LIGHTNING

WATER — STRAIGHT DIRECTION

EARTH — BOTH SIDES OF THE
GREAT RIVER

FAMILY — ALL INDIANS

(Sacred slab is read from base to top)

The symbols on the slabs were to have a double meaning — one to tell any curious whites who might see them, the other to be the true meaning. For the whites, these were to be described as heaven sticks — symbols which would guide them to the happy Afterlife. The symbols, reading from bottom to top were *family*, which was the most important single factor in everyday Indian life, the *earth* upon which they lived, followed by the principal features of the earth: *water, lightning, trees, the four corners of the earth, corn, fowl and animals of the earth and air, all plant life, the sun, the blue sky* and all of these things having to be experienced and understood before the *people* could reach the uppermost symbol, *Heaven*.

The actual meaning of this symbolism, however, was considerably different and much more menacing. It was for all the *Indians* on *both sides of the Mississippi River* to come in a *straight direction* toward Detroit at *lightning* speed with their *weapons*; coming from the *four corners of the earth*, leaving behind the *tending of corn* or *hunting of game* or the *storing of grains* to become *united* when the *great sign* was given so that *all the tribes* might, in *one movement*, by peaceable means if possible but by warfare if necessary, take over the *place of the whites* which had been usurped from them.[9]

CHAPTER XII

[*June 11, 1810 — Monday*]

ONCE again the fear.

Throughout the settlements the throb of it was heard in every voice. In the new Ohio capital, Zanesville, muttered discussions and meetings were held and echoed in Frankfort, Vincennes, and Washington, D.C. Rumors circulated everywhere — that a great union of Indians was being molded by Tecumseh, greater by far than any Indian confederacy ever heard of or imagined before; that one day without warning a bloodthirsty horde would sweep down upon the white settlers and destroy them and all they had worked and fought to acquire.

Yet, if true, why then should the oldest and most powerful Shawnee chief of all, Black Hoof, deny it? Not only did he refuse to recognize Tecumseh's leadership, he continued to profess peace between his own people and the whites. If Tecumseh could not lead even his own people in such an uprising, what need to fear that he would lead other tribes, many of them tribes with whom the Shawnees had long been enemies?

Hearing of the reports of Black Hoof's refusal to unite in any alliance under Tecumseh, William Henry Harrison dispatched a messenger to the Shawnee chief's Auglaize River village with a letter congratulating the principal chief for his wisdom and strength, praising his refusal to aid Tecumseh, and warning of the great destruction which must strike the red men if they went to war. The messenger returned with news that the Shawnees were well pleased with the governor's letter and reaffirmed their friendship under the terms of the Greenville Treaty.

But this was the only ray of hope in an otherwise grim atmosphere. A trader, after some time in the Tippecanoe area, informed Harrison that no less than a thousand permanent residents were assembled there, at least four hundred of whom were warriors burning with the fire to make war.

They refused, he said, to buy ammunition from him because he was American, adding that they had a plentiful supply and could get more from the English without paying for it.

Less than a month later came the report that now there were at least eight hundred warriors at Prophet's Town, with more coming all the time, and that another huge council of the unallied Indians was gathering on the St. Joseph River. At once Harrison sent an appeal to the assembled chiefs through his friends, the Delawares, exhorting them to remain untainted by the influence of the Shawnee brothers, pointing out the inevitable destruction of those tribes who would take up the hatchet against the whites. He also warned them of the great danger to the friendly tribes should war break out, since the whites would be unable to distinguish between friendly Indian and foe.

But the message had an unforeseeable effect. The powerful Wyandot nation, which had always carried so much influence among the Indians, took this to be tantamount to a declaration of war and reversed their decision to stand apart. They vowed their allegiance to Tecumseh and vowed equally to adopt the principles being taught by the Prophet. Almost overnight the attitude of the remaining reluctant chiefs changed. If their revered "uncles," the Wyandots, venerated for all time for their talents and vigor, were adopting the new doctrine, might it not be well for all of them to do the same?

Chief Roundhead of the Wyandots, in particular, had long been enthusiastic over Tecumseh's grand plan. When he learned that his fellow Wyandot chief, Leatherlips, had taken his men away from the council and refused to take any part in a war against his friends, the whites, he so informed Tenskwatawa. Immediately a council of the remaining Wyandot chiefs was called, with the Prophet presiding. It was determined that Leatherlips, living in the Ohio country, had been among the chiefs who last year sold the land east of the Wabash to Harrison, and it was voted that he be executed for witchcraft and treason.

Roundhead was named by Tenskwatawa to head a party of five executioners, who set off straightaway for Leatherlip's village on the Scioto River a dozen miles above the little settlement of Columbus. Upon their arrival, a council was called and Roundhead spoke with heat and bitterness of any chief who should so ignore the cause of his fellow men and followers. Leatherlips was permitted to reply and he was calm and dispassionate. It was no surprise to him when, after deliberating two hours, the council reaffirmed the death penalty.

Leatherlips walked slowly to his *wegiwa*, ate several strips of jerked venison, washed himself thoroughly and dressed in his best apparel. As a final touch he painted his face with whorls and lines from small pots of white and blue and vermilion dyes. Tall and gray-haired, decorated and finely dressed, he made a distinguished picture of a graceful and command-ing Indian.

When the hour for the execution arrived, the chief shook hands with many of his villagers and a few white spectators from nearby Columbus, then turned and walked from the village chanting the melancholy melody of the death song. He was followed closely by Roundhead and the other five in the execution party to a shallow grave some eighty yards distant; there, at the edge of the grave, he knelt in an erect posture and solemnly raised his voice in prayer to Moneto. As soon as he was finished, Roundhead knelt beside him and prayed in similar manner and, when he was finished, Leatherlips prayed again.

With the conclusion of the prayers, Leatherlips remained silently in his position, looking straight ahead. As Roundhead stepped back, one of the warriors removed from under his shirt a bright new tomahawk and stepped up behind Leatherlips. For a long moment he held the weapon high and then he struck down with all his strength and the blade sank into the crown of the chief's head.

Leatherlips collapsed, jerking spastically. Gradually his movements slowed and then stopped. He was sprawled half in the grave, but no move was made to roll him the rest of the way into it; instead, the Indians stood around silently for perhaps fifteen minutes before Roundhead moved closer to inspect the chief. Continued welling of blood and beads of perspiration on his cheeks and neck indicated he was still alive. Roundhead smiled broadly. Such perspiration was proof that Leatherlips had been guilty. He nodded at the executioner, who quickly approached and methodically smote Leatherlips three times on the head with the stained tomahawk. With the skull virtually collapsed, there was now no more doubt that he was dead. The body was rolled into the grave, hastily covered with soil and the party left.

Justice — Wyandot style — had been meted out.

When word of the execution spread and, with it, knowledge of the fact that the Wyandots had now adopted the principles of Tecumseh and Tenskwatawa, the unallied Indians were considerably moved. Perhaps the Wyandots were right. Perhaps they, too, should join this great alliance. Were not the Wyandots a wise and proud tribe? Did they not possess the original copy of the Treaty of Greenville? Did they not also possess the war belt which had once united many tribes into one nation? And had they not admitted in open council with Tenskwatawa that they were tired of the white-man situation and looked upon everything that had been done since the Treaty of Greenville as nothing? Most of all, had they not publicly and proudly announced that they would adopt Tecumseh's grand plan?

Having agreed to turn over to the Prophet the war belt of which they

had been custodians for so long, a large segment of the Wyandot population now joined together in a huge party to carry the belt back to Prophet's
Town. On the way they held a conference with Little Turtle and the other
Miami chiefs, showed them the great belt and reproached them for having
united with the whites against their Indian brothers. So impressed were
the Miamis that they immediately joined the procession and, because the
Miamis had been swayed, so too did the neighboring Weas join in.

News of this movement came quickly to Governor Harrison. Grosble,
ancient chief of the Piankeshaws, who was deeply afraid of the impending
war, broke up his village at once to migrate west of the Mississippi. On the
way he stopped off to inform Harrison that there were now fully three
thousand warriors encamped within a thirty-mile radius of Prophet's
Town; all were carrying on a great deal of secret counciling and there was
talk that simultaneous attacks were to be made on Vincennes, St. Louis,
newly formed Chicago, Fort Wayne and Detroit.

And then, just last week Harrison had sent a boat up the Wabash with
salt for the Indians as part of their annuities, but the Prophet had refused
it in Tecumseh's absence, insulting the men who had brought it and telling
them to go back to Vincennes.

Tecumseh, had he been there, would probably have approved his
brother's action; but at the moment he was again in the Auglaize River
village, making one last attempt to convince Black Hoof to adopt his plan
and thereby swing the whole weight of the Shawnee nation behind him.
But Black Hoof, now eighty-four years old, refused even to go into council
with Tecumseh. Ever since the disastrous defeat by Wayne, he had been
convinced of the futility of all attempts, no matter how grandiose, to drive
back the whites. He showed Tecumseh the letter he had received some
months ago from Harrison, praising him for his peaceful disposition.
Tecumseh took the letter from his skeletal hand and scornfully threw it
into the fire.

"If your Governor Harrison were here," he said, his voice brittle, "I
would serve him in the same way." His glance took in the chiefs and
warriors of the village standing around them. "Can you people here not see
that the whites are deceiving you? For my part I will never put any
confidence in them. Look around you. How well have you been treated by
them? How much have you gained by the treaties you have signed in the
absence of those who wished to save our land? As to you chiefs here who
sold land to the white chief Harrison, my words of you my mouth is too
ashamed to speak. Dogs and skunks have not so little mind as those who
did this. If only I had been here, not one inch of our land would he have
bought. And every Indian who has put his thumb to it should have his
thumbs cut off!"

Without further word, Tecumseh stalked away.

[*June 26, 1810 — Tuesday*]

François Dubois, special agent from Governor Harrison to spy on Tecumseh and Tenskwatawa at Prophet's Town, returned early this afternoon with his report. The strength of the brothers, he related to the governor, still grew rapidly. There were those among the assemblage in and around Prophet's Town who boasted that, if the need arose, Tecumseh could raise ten thousand men in a week and twenty thousand in a month. Indian nations Dubois had only heard of vaguely, far to the west and northwest, had given Tecumseh their hands and promises.

Not all of these western and northwestern nations had done so, he added. The Osages, it was said, and the Meremacs, the Cheyennes and the Mandans and the eastern Dakotas had refused. But for each who had refused, a dozen or more had joined in pledges and some of them, such as the Fox and Sac tribes, were impatiently awaiting the word to sink their tomahawks into the war post. All of the pledged tribes, it seemed, were waiting for some mysterious sign to be given, which Tecumseh had promised them, upon which they would pick up their weapons and march to meet him.

Tenskwatawa, Dubois continued, was growing more emphatic in his denunciation of the whites, particularly Harrison himself. He was rousing his followers to fever pitch by telling them they had been cheated of their lands; that to be valid, a sale of Indian lands must be sanctioned by all the tribes involved, and that no such sanction had ever been given by all the tribes.

It was not at all a pleasant report. The only encouraging news Dubois had to offer, in fact, was rather nebulous in its ramifications: one of the Shawnee chiefs, a dreaded enemy of the whites and a great and fearsome warrior who lately had leaned toward Tecumseh and might soon have convinced Black Hoof and the rest of the Shawnee nation to adopt Tecumseh's measures, had died of a fever in his village.

This chief, so it was said, was the one named Weh-yah-pih-ehr-sehn-wah, better known to the whites as Blue Jacket.[1]

[*July 4, 1810 — Wednesday*]

James Daleigh, Shaker minister at the little mission in the settlement just above Vincennes, was at first a little disconcerted and then gradually delighted when a handful of Kickapoo warriors, followers of the Prophet, entered the building out of the night and stood in the rear by the door. It seemed apparent that they had come to hear the service and, after a bit of stammering, the Reverend Daleigh waxed enthusiastic upon the way of the Lord to lead the stray heathen to the path of Righteousness.

The Kickapoos listened intently, but when the distant hooting of an owl came softly during a pause in the preacher's vigorous peroration, the Kickapoos smiled, bobbed their heads and slipped out the door.

Five minutes later, as the congregation left the church building upon completion of services, it came as a distinct blow to discover that every one of the horses that had been tied to the rail in front was gone.

The articulation upon this discovery was scarcely of a devout nature.

[*July 10, 1810 — Tuesday*]

For almost a year the shadow of imprisonment had hung over Simon Kenton. Numerous land claim cases were on file against him in the Kentucky courts and it was apparent that if he crossed to the south side of the Ohio River again, he would undoubtedly be arrested and jailed for noncompliance with court orders for his appearance.

Simon had no intention of returning to Kentucky. In fact, he was prepared to leave his home north of Springfield and move somewhere else — possibly to another location in Ohio, maybe even to Missouri. His farm here had never amounted to much, and the mill and store were practically ruined anyway. Kenton was not businessman enough to get them back on their feet after the disastrous blow dealt them by James Robinson's embezzlement.

As it turned out, the decision to move was more or less taken out of Simon's hands. One of the Kentucky land claimants got wind of the frontiersman's land purchases in Missouri and, lest Kenton move out there beyond his reach, sent his lawyers into Ohio to collect settlement from him. Considering the claim unjust, Simon refused to pay and immediately the claimant's lawyers invoked the old debtor's law, whereupon Simon was ordered seized and held by the Champaign County authorities until a judgment was made.

Urbana was the site of the jail; and since Champaign County had been settled largely by good friends and relatives, steps were taken to give him as little discomfiture as possible. With alacrity the residents were polled and Simon was elected county jailer. It was just as well, since Kenton was not about to be taken by force. In fact, during the first court held in Champaign County, a writ of *capias* was issued against Kenton and Phillip Jarboe for the recovery of this Kentucky debt. On this writ the sheriff had penned: *Found Phillip Jarboe and have his body in court; found Simon Kenton, but he refused to be arrested.*

It wasn't likely that there was a man in the county who could arrest Simon if he would not allow himself to be — and so he wasn't. The court smiled as he took his time about closing up his mill and store and disposing of his farm. Then he moved with his family to Urbana, where he took up temporary residence at the home of his former Kentucky frontier minuteman, Joe Lemon, with whom he had escaped back to

Maysville in April of 1792 after their attack on Tecumseh's camp. Within a few weeks he took the oath of office for his new position and moved into the county jail with his family. It was really quite a nice arrangement; with "five rooms above and one below" for his own residence, right in town.

As his own jailer he was, of course, not confined to a cell. Urbana had "town bounds" through which a prisoner might roam at will if he had been properly bonded. George Fithian, William Fyffe and Zephaniah Luce became Kenton's bondsmen and the frontiersman observed the boundaries with strict formality. With his staff in his right hand he would walk from end to end of his bounds, bringing himself to a quick military halt at the limits, turning and marching back.[2]

Nothing could make him break his bounds — not even the sudden death through illness of his eight-year-old daughter, Elizabeth. He attended the funeral services in the family room below and went with the funeral procession as far as possible without crossing his bounds. But the cemetery lay beyond them and at the line he stopped and stood, sadly watching the column wend its way through the prairie to the grave. Simon was a firm believer now in the quotation that "the Lord giveth and the Lord taketh away"; with Elizabeth gone, taken away by the hand of the Lord, it was time now for the Lord to give. And so, a short time later, when Betsy gave birth to another daughter, this one, too, was named Elizabeth. Such, said he, was the way of the Lord.

[*July 14, 1810 — Saturday*]

William Baron, special messenger to Tenskwatawa and Tecumseh from William Henry Harrison, was not at all prepared for the reception he got when he arrived at Prophet's Town on the Tippecanoe River. Some distance outside the village he was met by a large party of warriors who escorted him ceremoniously to a huge chair in the midst of the *wegiwas*, in which Tenskwatawa sat, a deep scowl making his face even uglier than usual. He was left standing alone about ten feet in front of the quasi-throne for several minutes while the Prophet simply stared at him without sign of recognition, though he knew Baron well. At last, holding his flowing robe around him, Tenskwatawa stood and spoke angrily.

"For what purpose do you come here? Brouilette was here; he was a spy. Dubois was here; he was a spy. Now *you* have come. You, too, are a spy." The Prophet raised one arm and pointed a bony finger at the ground near Baron. "There is your grave. Look on it!"

Tecumseh abruptly emerged from the doorway of a large *wegiwa* nearby, tossed an impatient glance at his brother and then walked up to within a couple of feet of Baron. He greeted the man coldly.

"Your life is in no danger," he said. "But what is your reason for coming here? Speak!"

"I have been sent to you by Governor Harrison," Baron replied. "He has asked me to read to you and to the Prophet a letter." He reached into his shirt and withdrew some folded pages which he opened and began to read aloud:

William Henry Harrison, Governor and Commander-in-Chief of the Territory of Indiana, to the Shawnee Chief and the Indians Assembled at Tippecanoe:

Notwithstanding the improper language which you have used towards me, I will endeavor to open your eyes to your true interests. Notwithstanding what white men have told you, I am not your personal enemy. You ought to know this from the manner in which I received and treated you on your visit to this place.

Although I must say that you are an enemy to the Seventeen Fires, and that you have used the greatest exertions to lead them [the Indians] astray. In this you have been in some measure successful; as I am told they are ready to raise the tomahawk against their father, yet their father, notwithstanding his anger at their folly, is full of goodness, and is always ready to receive into his arms those of his children who are willing to repent, acknowledge their fault, and ask his forgiveness.

At this, a look of bitter scorn flashed across Tecumseh's features, but he did not speak and Baron continued reading:

There is yet but little harm done, which may be easily repaired. The chain of friendship which united the whites with the Indians may be renewed, and be as strong as ever. A great deal of that work depends on you — the destiny of those who are under your direction depends upon the choice you make of the two roads which are before you. The one is large, open, and pleasant, and leads to peace, security, and happiness; the other, on the contrary, is narrow and crooked, and leads to misery and ruin. Don't deceive yourselves; do not believe that all nations of Indians united are able to resist the force of the Seventeen Fires. I know your warriors are brave, but ours are not less so. But what can a few brave warriors do against the innumerable warriors of the Seventeen Fires? Our blue-coats are more numerous than you can count; our hunters are like the leaves of the forest, or the grains of sand on the Wabash. Do not think that the red-coats can protect you; they are not able to protect themselves. They do not think of going to war with us. If they did, you would in a few moons see our flag wave over all the forts of Canada. What reason have you to complain of the Seventeen Fires? Have they taken anything from you? Have they ever violated the treaties made with the red men? You say they have purchased lands from those who had no right to sell them. Show that this is true and the land will be instantly restored. Show us the rightful owners. I have full

power to arrange this business; but if you would rather carry your com-
plaints before your great father, the President, you shall be indulged. I will
immediately take means to send you, with those chiefs you may choose, to
the city where your father lives. Everything necessary shall be prepared for
your journey, and means taken for your safe return.

For once Tenskwatawa had little to say. Tecumseh, however, replied at
some length to the messenger. His voice was level, emotionless, but his
demeanor not unfriendly to the white man as he spoke.

"Mr. Baron," he said, "I do not intend to make war, but it is impossible
to remain friends with the United States unless they give up the idea of
making settlements farther to the north and west and unless they will
acknowledge the principle that the Western Country was the common
property of all Indian tribes.

"The Great Spirit," he continued, "gave this great island to his red
children. He placed the whites on the other side of the big water. They
were not contented with their own but came to take ours from us. They
have driven us from the sea to the lakes. We can go no farther. They have
taken it upon themselves to say that this tract of land belongs to the
Miamis, this to the Delawares, and so on; but the Great Spirit intended it
as the common property of all. Our father tells us that we have no business
upon the Wabash — the land belongs to other tribes; but the Great Spirit
ordered us to come here, and here we will stay."

Tecumseh stopped abruptly. This was not the man to whom he should
speak. It was Governor Harrison himself who should hear these words
firsthand.

"I am pleased with the white chief's speech," he concluded. "I have
never been to see him, but I remember him as a very young man sitting by
the side of General Wayne. I have never troubled the white people much,
but now I will go to Vincennes and show the governor that he has been
listening to bad men when he is told that we are meditating war against
the United States. I will arrive there in one moon with some of my principal men and probably a large number of the young men who are fond of
attending upon such occasions."

[*August 12, 1810 — Sunday*]

Captain George R. Floyd, commanding officer of Fort Knox, just above
Vincennes, set the lamp on his desk and resumed writing the letter he had
begun earlier in the day:

. . . *Nothing new has transpired since my last letter to you except that*
the four hundred Shawnee Indians have come; they passed this garrison,
which is two miles above Vincennes, on Sunday last, in eighty canoes.
They were all painted in the most terrific manner. They were stopped at

the garrison by me, for a short time. I examined their canoes, and found them well prepared for war in case of attack. They were headed by the brother of the Prophet, Tecumseh, who perhaps is one of the finest looking men I ever saw — about six feet high, straight, with large, fine features, and altogether a daring, bold looking fellow. The governor's council with them will commence tomorrow morning . . ."

[August 15, 1810 — Wednesday]

From the very beginning, on Monday, the council had gone poorly. Not only was there a mutual distrust between Tecumseh and Harrison, but there was an equal lack of understanding. The governor had intended the meeting to take place on the portico of his own fine home, where seats had been fitted for this purpose. It was here, attended by the Supreme Court judges, a number of military officers, a thirteen-man platoon from Fort Knox under command of a sergeant, and quite a few citizens of Vincennes, that Governor Harrison sat awaiting Tecumseh's arrival.

At the appointed time, Tecumseh left his camp outside Vincennes and approached to within about five hundred feet and stopped. Harrison immediately sent out a man with a request for the chief and his men to take seats on the portico, but Tecumseh refused, considering this an ill place to hold a council and preferring a grove of trees a short distance from the house. The governor shrugged upon hearing this. He had no objection other than the fact that there were no seats out there.

"Bring out chairs enough to accommodate your own people only," Tecumseh said. "The earth is my mother and upon her breast I will repose."

Chairs, benches and a table were set up at once in the grove and the whites took their places, Harrison in a large armchair in the middle with the friendly Potawatomi chief, Winnemac, beside and slightly behind him. Winnemac had long been a foe of Tecumseh's, jealous of the Shawnee's power, and he scorned even his own people for having joined him. He was here now as an interpreter for Harrison. When the whites were all settled, the Indians sat cross-legged upon the ground — all except Tecumseh, who remained standing. Now he began his address:

"Brother, I wish you to listen to me well. As I think you do not clearly understand what I before said to you, I will explain it again . . . Brother, since the peace was made, you have killed some of the Shawnees, Winnne- bagoes, Delawares and Miamis and you have taken our land from us and I do not see how we can remain at peace if you continue to do so. You try to force the red people to do some injury. It is *you* that are pushing them on to do mischief. You endeavor to make distinctions: you wish to prevent the Indians doing as we wish them — to unite and let them consider their lands as the common property of the whole; you take tribes aside and advise them not to come into this measure; and until our design is accomplished, we do not wish to accept your invitation to go and see the President. The reason I tell you this; you want, by your distinctions of Indian tribes in allotting to each a particular tract of land, to make them war with each other. You never see an Indian come, do you, and endeavor to make the white people do so? You are continually driving the red people; when, at last, you will drive them into the Great Lake, where they can't either stand or walk.

"Brother, you ought to know what you are doing with the Indians. Perhaps it is by direction of the President to make those distinctions. It is a very bad thing, and we do not like it. Since my residence at Tippecanoe, we have endeavored to level all distinctions — to destroy village chiefs, by whom all mischief is done. It is they who sell our lands to the Americans. Our object is to let our affairs be transacted by warriors.

"Brother, this land that was sold and the goods that were given for it were only done by a few. The treaty was afterwards brought here and the Weas were induced to give their consent, because of their small numbers. The treaty at Fort Wayne was made through the threats of Winnemac; but in the future we are prepared to punish those chiefs who may come forward to propose to sell the land."

A cold hard glare passed between Tecumseh and Winnemac, but it was Winnemac who dropped his eyes, whereupon Tecumseh continued: "If you continue to purchase of them, it will produce war among the different tribes and, at last, I do not know what the consequences will be to the white people.

"Brother, I was glad to hear your speech. You said if we could show that the land was sold by people who had no right to sell, you would restore it. Those that did sell did not own it. It was me. These tribes set up a claim, but the tribes with me will not agree with their claim. If the land is not restored to us, you will see, when we return to our homes, how it will be settled."

The vague menace in Tecumseh's words abruptly became a more clearly stated threat. He spoke slower now, emphasizing each point. "We shall have a great council, at which all the tribes will be present, when we shall show to those who sold that they had no right to the claim that they set up; and we will see what will be done to those chiefs that did sell the land to you. I am not alone in this determination; it is the determination of all the warriors and red people that listen to me. I now wish *you* to listen to me. If you do not, it will appear as if you wished me to kill all the chiefs that sold you the land. I tell you so because I am authorized by all the tribes to do so."

A fierce pride, rare in Tecumseh, now crept into his words and the grove rang with his voice. "I am the head of them all! I am a warrior and all the warriors will meet together in two or three moons from this. Then I will call for those chiefs that sold you the land and shall know what to do with them. If you do not restore the land, you will have a hand in killing them!"

He paused for a long moment, and a frightened muttering arose among the white citizens listening. But as Harrison raised his hand they quieted and Tecumseh continued:

"Brother, do not believe that I came here to get presents from you. If you offer us any, we will not take. By taking goods from you, you will hereafter say that with them you purchased another piece of land from us . . . It has been the object of both myself and brother to prevent the lands being sold. Should you not return the land, it will occasion us to call a great council that will meet at the Huron village, where the council fire has already been lighted, at which those who sold the lands shall be called and shall suffer for their conduct.

"Brother, I wish you would take pity on the red people and do what I have requested. If you will not give up the land and do cross the boundary of your present settlement, it will be very hard and produce great troubles among us."

The Shawnee chief slapped a hand to his thigh in seeming exasperation, realizing he was repeating himself but sensing he was not really getting through to Harrison. Not a whisper of sound came from any of the listeners now, neither Indian nor white, and after a moment Tecumseh continued:

"How can we have confidence in the white people? When Jesus Christ came on earth, you killed Him and nailed Him on a cross. You thought He was dead, but you were mistaken. You have Shakers among you and you laugh and make light of their worship. Everything I have said to you is the truth. The Great Spirit has inspired me and I speak nothing but the truth to you . . ."

Harrison continued to sit with his eyes locked upon Tecumseh's, his face a mask, his hands still on the table before him. There was no indication of his relenting as Tecumseh concluded:

"Brother, I hope you will confess that you ought not to have listened to those bad birds who bring you bad news. I have declared myself freely to you and if any explanation should be required from our town, send a man who can speak to us. If you think proper to give us any presents — and we can be convinced that they are given through friendship alone — we will accept them. As we intend to hold our council at the Huron village that is near the British, we may probably make them a visit. Should they offer us any presents of goods, we will not take them; but should they offer us powder and the tomahawk, we will take the powder and refuse the tomahawk. I wish you, Brother, to consider everything I have said as true and that it is the sentiment of all the red people that listen to me."

As soon as Tecumseh had taken a seat at the head of his people, Governor Harrison arose and, following Tecumseh's lead, he minced no words. His first statement was to deny that the Indians were one nation, and that when the white people came to America, the Miamis occupied all the country on the Wabash and the Shawnees lived in Florida and Georgia, from which place they had been driven by the Creeks. These lands, he declared, had been bought from the Miamis, who were the owners. It was ridiculous to declare the Indians all one people. If the Great Spirit had meant this to be true, why then had he given them different tongues?

The thought must have occurred to some of his audience that this very accusation held equally true for the Americans, who spoke English, French, Italian, German, Spanish and many other languages. Yet were they not all Americans and one people? But while the thought may have been there, no word was spoken and Harrison continued.

The Miamis, he said, thought it in their best interest to sell part of their land for a further annuity, the benefit of which they had for a long time experienced in the promptness with which the United States had paid them. The Shawnees had no justification to come from a distant country and try to control the Miamis in the disposal of their own lands.

With this, Harrison sat down again while his interpreter began to translate the speech into Shawnee for the assembled Indians who had not understood English. But Tecumseh had understood, and for one of the few times in his life he lost his temper. Leaping to his feet he shouted aloud in violent Shawnee, gesticulating wildly at each sentence. Harrison was surprised and looked behind him to see Chief Winnemac priming his pistol in such manner that the Indians would not see what he was doing. General Gibson, who understood the Shawnee tongue, muttered to Lieutenant Jennings, "These fellows intend mischief. Better bring up the guard." Jennings sprinted off at once.

At this the whole body of Indians sprang to their feet in a semicircle behind Tecumseh, all but the chief himself brandishing tomahawks or war clubs. Harrison quickly drew his sword from its scabbard while at the same time Captain George Floyd, to his right, drew a dagger and Winnemac, to his left, cocked the pistol. Many of the white citizens were picking up clubs or showing other weapons and the Methodist Reverend Winans ran to the door of the governor's house, snatched up a rifle and stood there to protect the family if need be. All during this flurry of activity, an unreal silence prevailed. And when Lieutenant Jennings came running up with the guard holding their guns at ready, only a fragile thread remained to prevent outright warfare from bursting forth with terrible results.

The governor stayed the guard with an upraised hand and then asked the interpreter what Tecumseh had said and was informed that the interruption was a cry to the effect that Harrison was a liar, that everything he said was false and that the Indians had been cheated and imposed upon by him and by the Seventeen Fires. Harrison fixed Tecumseh with a baleful stare and frostily told him that he would have no further communication with him.

"You and your people may go in safety," he said, "since you have come under my protection to the council fire, but you must leave immediately."

And so the first council had been an utter flop, and it appeared there would not be another. But later, back in his own camp outside Vincennes, Tecumseh grew angry with himself for having lost his temper; if war was not to break out and spoil all the work that had been done to inaugurate the grand plan, then he must make some attempt to patch things over.

In the morning he sent for the interpreter and asked him to deliver to the governor his regret over the incident and to ask that he be given an opportunity to explain his reaction. Most of all, the governor must be made to realize that no threat had been intended against the whites attending this council.

Harrison, after some deliberation, agreed to another council and a meeting similar to the previous day's was called. There was a difference this time, however, for each white man at the scene was armed with a gun. Harrison opened the discussion. "Do you," he asked Tecumseh, "intend to prevent the survey of the land on the Wabash?"

Cool and dignified now, Tecumseh replied softly. "I am determined that the old boundary shall continue."

Harrison moved his glance to take in the other chiefs in turn and, in succession, the Wyandot, Kickapoo, Potawatomi, Ottawa and Winnebago chiefs arose to state the same fact: that they had united as Indians; that they had joined Tecumseh; that they had accepted Tecumseh as their leader; that they would support Tecumseh in all ways. Harrison nodded as the last of them sat down again.

"Since you have been candid in acknowledging your intentions," he told Tecumseh, "I would be so, too. I will send to the President a faithful statement of what you have said in disputing the claim to the lands in question. I will tell you what the President's answer is when I receive it. However, I am sure the President will never admit these lands to be the property of any other than those tribes who have occupied them since the white people came to America. Since we have come to title of them by fair purchase, then I am sure that these titles will be protected and supported by the sword. I hereby adjourn this council."

Now it was Harrison's turn to do a bit of pondering on his own; and the more the thought of what had transpired, the more he felt it might be to the advantage of both sides if he and Tecumseh could have a private discussion. Accordingly, the next morning he appeared alone at Tecumseh's camp and the Shawnee chief received him politely.

"Are your intentions really as you stated them in council?" Harrison asked.

"They are. It would be only with great reluctance that I would make war upon the United States, since I have no complaint against them except their purchase of Indian lands. I am anxious to be at peace with the Americans and if you will prevail upon the President to give up the land in question and agree never again to make a treaty without the consent of all the tribes, I will be your faithful ally and assist you in all your wars against the British."

Tecumseh stirred the fire with a stick and, after a moment's silence, continued speaking quietly. "I know that the British are always urging us to war for their own advantages. Certainly not for the good of the red man. They urge us to attack the Americans as one might set a dog to fight. I would rather be a friend of the Seventeen Fires.

"However," and now his voice grew noticeably harder, "if the President does not comply with my terms, I will be obliged to take the other side."

Harrison blew out a great breath of annoyance and frustration. Was there no way to make this savage see? He sighed. "I will tell the President of all your propositions. But again I say, there is not the least probability that he will accede to your terms."

Tecumseh nodded gravely. "Well, as the great chief is to determine the matter, I hope the Great Spirit will put sense enough in his head to induce him to direct you to give up this land. It is true, he is so far off he will not be injured by the war; he may sit in his town and drink his wine, while you and I will have to fight it out."

And each man knew, if it came to that, he would be facing an adversary who was stronger, wiser and better than any he had ever faced before.

[*May 2, 1811 — Thursday*]

The very instant that Simon Kenton was released from his debtor's bounds, he resigned his position as Champaign County jailer and set off at once for St. Louis. It was not a happy arrival. As son John's letter had forewarned, not a trace remained of the St. Louis store in the Kenton name — he had been as poor a businessman as his father and had sold out what remained of it, which was not much. The same held true for the store in St. Charles.

Intent on recouping the loss, John had taken some of the money from the sale and bought a hundred traps and started up the Missouri, thinking that perhaps in two or three years of trapping he could repay the loss to his father. But apparently his plans had become known, along with the fact that he still carried a fair amount of cash in his poke, because along the

way he was ambushed, knocked unconscious and robbed of everything —
money, traps, horses, supplies, even his shoes, and very nearly his life.

Thus, with everything gone in Missouri except his New Madrid lands,
Simon Kenton once again headed his horse east to return to his family.
And as he rode along the Ohio River he was witness to an event of
immense importance to the whole west: the voyage, from Pittsburgh to
New Orleans, of the first steamboat ever launched upon the western
waters. It was the opening of a new era.

But the craft was an object of interest to Kenton only while it was in
sight, and his thoughts soon returned to John's letter. The message had
been brief and phrases of it, read to him by Betsy, haunted the frontiersman all the rest of the way home:

. . . *everything lost . . . everything . . . going away . . . going to the*
southwest . . . Sante Fe . . . maybe Mexico . . . never return until the
$18,000 has been made up . . . will repay somehow . . . sorry . . . so
very very sorry . . .

[*June 26, 1811 — Wednesday*]

It was the matter of the second salt shipment which really opened William
Henry Harrison's eyes to the vulnerability of Vincennes. He had dispatched a boatload of salt up the Wabash early in the spring for distribution among the various tribes camped along the river, wondering vaguely if
the Prophet would do as he had done last year and refuse to accept his
share. He wasn't long in finding out. Instead of refusing it, Tenskwatawa
had seized it all and then had the gall to send the boatmen back with a
message to the effect that the governor should not be angry because, after
all, the Prophet and Tecumseh had two thousand men to feed and hadn't
received any salt for two years.

The boat, a reasonably large one, had made it down to Vincennes in just
thirty hours from Prophet's Town. The boatmen reported seeing many
hundreds of canoes lined up on the banks there, all ready to be launched,
and that with strong men at the paddles a canoe could easily make it from
Tippecanoe to Vincennes in twenty-four hours. Harrison suddenly realized
that should Tecumseh lead a force of even a thousand men in canoes,
which could approach with greater speed and silence than any overland
force might be able to accomplish, he could take Vincennes with ease.

This was a highly disconcerting thought, and for the first time a needle
of fear punctured the governor's normal composure. At once he sent an
express to Washington, D.C., requesting both reinforcements and the
authority to act offensively against the Indians if it could be determined
that they were definitely hostile and an outbreak was imminent.

All through the spring troubles continued to blossom between settlers
and the Indians, though even Harrison had to admit that the greater

majority of these incidents were provoked by the whites. Not only had horses been stolen but there had also been isolated instances of both whites and Indians being killed. The settlers were becoming trigger-happy, sometimes striking out against the most innocuous of Indians. As Harrison himself put it in a letter to Secretary of War William Eustis:

I wish I could say the Indians were treated with justice and propriety on all occasions by our citizens, but it is far otherwise. They are often abused and maltreated, and it is rare that they obtain any satisfaction for the most unprovoked wrongs.

A case in point occurred when one Muskogee Indian, on a peaceful visit to Vincennes after visiting Tecumseh, was shot and killed by an Italian innkeeper without any just reason. Angered by such disregard, not only for human life but for the powder keg upon which the whites were perched here, Harrison had the innkeeper arrested and tried for murder. But such was the antagonism and fear felt by the settlers for Indians in general that the jury acquitted him practically without deliberation.

On another occasion, two Potawatomi warriors killed two white men who, without any provocation, had shot and seriously wounded a pair of Wea warriors in the Vincennes area. It was only through exerting his influence to the utmost that Tecumseh was able to prevent further retaliation by his followers.

With such incidents occurring more and more frequently, it was little wonder that the Shawnee chief refused to turn over to Harrison on demand the Delaware warrior named White Turkey, who had robbed the house of a settler named Vawter. Tecumseh declared that not until the whites who had murdered Indians were punished would any Indian be turned over to the governor for white man's justice. Still, in disobeying the explicit dictates of Tecumseh and Tenskwatawa against theft, White Turkey had made a serious mistake. A council was held and the Delaware was executed for his crime.

Harrison sighed with relief when his requested reinforcements arrived: the entire Fourth United States Regiment from Pittsburgh, under command of Colonel Charles Boyd. The colonel had received his orders directly from President Madison and his army had been augmented, as it moved down the Ohio, by sixty-five Kentucky volunteers.

With this additional strength behind him now, Harrison dispatched one of his aides, Captain Benjamin Wilson, with a strong letter to the Kispokotha Shawnee brothers on June 17:

BROTHERS: Listen to me. I speak to you about matters of importance to both the white people and yourselves; open your ears, therefore, and attend to what I shall say. Brothers, this is the third year that all the white people in this country have been alarmed at your proceedings; you threaten us with war; you invite all the tribes to the north and west of you to join against us.

Brothers, your warriors who have lately been here deny this, but I have received information from every direction; the tribes on the Mississippi have sent me word that you intended to murder me, and then to commence a war upon our people. I have also received the speech you sent to the Pottawatomies and others to join you for that purpose; but if I had no other evidence of your hostility to us, your seizing the salt I lately sent up the Wabash is sufficient. Brothers, our citizens are alarmed, and my warriors are preparing themselves, not to strike you, but to defend themselves and their women and children. You shall not surprise us as you expect to do; you are about to undertake a very rash act. As a friend, I advise you to consider well of it; a little reflection may save us a great deal of trouble and prevent much mischief; it is not yet too late.

Brothers, what can be the inducement for you to undertake an enterprise when there is so little probability of success? Do you really think that the handful of men that you have about you are able to contend with the Seventeen Fires, or even that the whole of the tribes united could contend against the Kentucky Fire alone? Brothers, I am myself of the Long Knife Fire.[3] As soon as they hear my voice you will see them pouring forth their swarms of hunting-shirt men, as numerous as the mosquitoes on the shores of the Wabash. Brothers, take care of their stings. Brothers, it is not our wish to hurt you; if we did, we certainly have the power to do it. Look at the number of our warriors to the east of you, above and below the Great Miami; to the south on both sides of the Ohio, and below you also. You are brave men, but what could you do against such a multitude? — but we wish you to live in peace and happiness.

Brothers, the citizens of this country are alarmed. They must be satisfied that you have no design to do them mischief, or they will not lay aside their arms. You have also insulted the government of the United States by seizing the salt that was intended for other tribes; satisfaction must be given for that also. Brothers, you talk of coming to see me, attended by all your young men; this, however, must not be so. If your intentions are good, you have need to bring but a few of your young men with you. I must be plain with you; I will not suffer you to come into our settlements with such a force.

Brothers, if you wish to satisfy us that your intentions are good, follow the advice I have given you before: that is, that one or both of you should visit the President of the United States and lay your grievances before him. He will treat you well, will listen to what you say, and if you can show him that you have been injured, you will receive justice. If you will follow my advice in this respect it will convince the citizens of this country and myself that you have no design to attack them.

Brothers, with respect to the land that was purchased . . . I can enter into no negotiations with you on that subject; the affair is in the hands of the President. If you wish to go and see him, I will supply you with the means.

Brothers, the person who delivers this is one of my war officers. He is a man in whom I have entire confidence. Whatever he says to you, although it may not be contained in this paper, you may believe comes from me.

My friend Tecumseh, the bearer is a good man and a brave warrior. I hope you will treat him well. You are yourself a warrior, and all such should have esteem for each other.

> *William Henry Harrison, Governor*
> *Cmdr In Chief; Indiana Territory*

Tecumseh, just back from a successful visit with both the Iroquois and Wyandots, had always respected a brave man, whether white or red, and he treated Captain Wilson with particular cordiality. He conversed peacefully with him and gave him food and then wrote a reply to be given to Harrison:

Brother: I give you a few words until I will be with you myself. Brother, at Vincennes, I wish you to listen to me whilst I send you a few words, and I hope they will ease your heart. I know you look on your young men and young women and children with pity, to see them so alarmed. Brother, I wish you now to examine what you have from me. I hope it will be a satisfaction to you, if your intentions are like mine, to wash away all these bad stories that have been circulated. I will be with you myself in eighteen days from this day.

Brother, we cannot say what will become of us, as the Great Spirit has the management of us all at his will. I may be there before the time, and may not be there until the day. I hope that when we come together all these bad tales will be settled. By this I hope your young men, young women and children will be easy. I wish you, brother, to let them know when I come to Vincennes and see you, all will be settled in peace and happiness. Brother, these are only a few words to let you know that I will be with you myself; and when I am with you, I can inform you better. Brother, if I find I can be with you in less than eighteen days, I will send one of my young men before me to let you know the time I will be with you.

> *Tecumseh*

[July 6, 1811 — Saturday]

Where the rumor started — if rumor it really was — no one seemed to know, but almost overnight the Indiana frontier was thrown into a state of alarm, especially Vincennes. According to so-called "reports," a whole string of murders of white men by Shawnees had taken place in the Illinois country, both on the Kankakee River and the Des Plaines River. This, so the story went, was merely a diversionary tactic preceding an impending assault upon Vincennes. Many of the newer settlements immediately sent out official letters, both to Governor Harrison and to William Eustis, Secretary of War. They all said essentially the same thing: if the government did not take steps to protect them, they would take up arms and protect themselves.

Harrison himself wrote to Secretary Eustis and reported that while fear was rampant among the settlers, he was convinced that it was more a fear based on falsehoods than on facts, but that he would keep a close watch on the situation. Then he discussed the forthcoming visit of Tecumseh:

. . . *Upon being told that I would not suffer him to come with so large a force, he promised to bring with him a few men only. I shall not, however, depend upon this promise, but shall have the river watched by a party of scouts after the descent of the chief, lest he should be followed by his warriors. I do not think this will be the case. The detection of the hostile designs of an Indian is generally, for that time, to defeat them. The hopes of an expedition, conducted through many hundred miles of toil and difficulty, are abandoned frequently upon the slightest suspicion; their painful steps retraced, and a more favorable moment expected. With them, the surprise of an enemy bestows more éclat upon a warrior than the most brilliant success obtained by other means. Tecumseh has taken for his model the celebrated Pontiac, and I am persuaded he will bear a favorable comparison in every respect with that far-famed warrior . . .*

[July 15, 1811 — Monday]

Tecumseh's escort for the trip down the Wabash to Vincennes was as small as he could gather together and still retain the dignity befitting his rank and position as leader. Normally he would have taken many more, but he had in mind the governor's request that he hold the numbers down lest the settlers misconstrue the intent of the party; thus he settled for a retinue of about three hundred, ten per cent of whom were women and children.

They camped outside Vincennes where they had camped during the last council and all of the chiefs and a number of select warriors — a group totaling about one hundred and eighty men — accompanied Tecumseh to the arbor Harrison had had built especially for this council. There was unusual solemnity on both sides: the whites, Governor Harrison in particular, seemed unnerved by the large number of armed men with Tecumseh; the Indians were, in turn, disturbed by the large body of soldiers in full battle dress who had deliberately marched back and forth across the parade ground prior to the meeting's commencement in an ostentatious show of strength. It was peculiarly like the meeting of two strange dogs approaching one another, stiff-legged and with hackles raised, willing to be peaceable but ready to fight if necessary.

The governor had opened the council on Sunday, July 14, without delay and with little finesse. He referred at once to the alleged murders of whites in the Illinois country and the considerable alarm Tecumseh had caused by descending the Wabash for this meeting with such numbers, after promising to bring only a minimum retinue. As he spoke, Tecumseh's face hardened into harsh lines.

Perhaps Harrison had done so deliberately, perhaps he had done so through fundamental failure to grasp the red man's psychology, but however he did it, he dealt Tecumseh a tremendous insult with those words. That this minimal number of people making up Tecumseh's escort was declared to be "far too many" was a direct wound to the chief's self-respect and dignity and the prestige in which his people held him. Probably at no other time in his life had William Henry Harrison been so close to death without knowing it.

Apparently not sensing Tecumseh's injured pride, Harrison had moved right along with his speech. He promised to listen to anything further that Tecumseh or the other chiefs might have to say about the Wabash land purchase, but that he would enter into no negotiation about it since, as he had already explained in his letter, the matter was in the hands of the President. He then brought up the matter of the seizure of the salt and demanded an explanation.

Sarcasm was heavy in Tecumseh's voice as he replied: "The salt that was taken was taken in my absence, just as the salt that was refused the previous year was refused in my absence. It seems to me that it is impossible to please the governor. Last year you were angry because the salt was refused and this year you are just as much displeased because it was taken!"

It was all he had to say and Harrison abruptly found himself angrier than he knew he should become. Without further ado he adjourned the meeting until the next day. It was hardly an auspicious beginning.

Today — Monday — when the council convened again just after noon, the chief of the Weas, Wa-paw-waw-qua — White Loon — opened with a long speech tracing in detail the many treaties made by Harrison with various Indian groups. The inference that deceit had been utilized on the part of the whites was clearly evident.

As soon as he was finished, Harrison immediately changed the subject without any comment whatever upon what White Loon had said, thereby delivering a substantial insult to that chief, too. Instead, the governor now asked Tecumseh to turn over to him the two Potawatomi warriors who had slain the white men, so that he could have them tried in the white man's court for murder. If Tecumseh did this, Harrison added, it would show the governor he was sincere in his professions of friendship for the United States.

Tecumseh's reply did not surprise him. The Shawnee chief said that he had taken great pains to unite the northern Indian tribes under himself and that the whites were unnecessarily alarmed at this. Had not the United States itself set the example for them by establishing a union of Seventeen Fires? The Indians did not complain of this. Why then should the whites feel justified in complaining when the Indians united? Was it not as fair for one as for the other? As for the Potawatomies Harrison asked for, Tecumseh would not deliver them up. The whites who died had not been murdered; they had been executed, bringing this fate upon themselves by shooting two Wea Indians without provocation. He added that he had long since set the whites an example of forgiveness of injuries and that now they ought to imitate him.

"Soon after this council is concluded," Tecumseh said, "I will leave this country to visit the tribes to the south to ask them to become a part of our Indian union. A great number of Indians will be coming back to settle on the Tippecanoe with us. We will make them welcome. But the land you falsely purchased on the Wabash is our finest hunting ground and we will need it to secure food for these people. I hope that nothing will be done by the whites toward settling this hunting ground before my return next spring. At that time, when our union is complete, then will I be ready to visit the President and settle all difficulties with him."

By this time night had fallen and the moon was up. Entirely displeased with the way the council had gone, Governor Harrison closed it on a sharp warning note. He pointed to the celestial orb and said, "The moon you see would sooner fall to the ground than the President would suffer his people to be murdered with impunity, and I will put petticoats on my soldiers sooner than give up a country I have bought fairly from its true owners!"

[July 18, 1811 — Thursday]

The twenty warriors who were to accompany him to the south sat astride their horses and patiently waited for Tecumseh to emerge from the *wegiwa* where he and Tenskwatawa had been in close discussion for over an hour.

Inside, Tecumseh placed his hands upon his younger brother's shoulders. Everything here, he said, was being left in trust with Tenskwatawa. The Prophet should continue to preach their doctrine and he should continue to maintain the peace. This was extremely important now. Within another five moons the amalgamation would be powerful enough to stand by itself and make its demands. The great sign would be given then and this would be the turning point in the fortunes of all the Indians of this great island.

But it was imperative that, between now and then, no open hostilities break out between Indians and whites. Harrison was a shrewd man who knew something was in the wind and who would leap on any excuse to open actual warfare. Tecumseh may have given them a slight margin by making Harrison think he would not be back until next spring when, in reality, he hoped to return before winter. Tecumseh was sure Harrison would attempt something in his absence and he stressed the point to his brother: *this must not be allowed!* If it was necessary to make concessions for the sake of maintaining the peace, then these concessions were to be made. If it became necessary to swallow pride, then the pride must be swallowed. If actual attack was made by the whites, the Indians must scatter and withdraw without engaging the enemy, melting into the forest until it was safe to return, even should Prophet's Town itself be destroyed. The village could be easily rebuilt. The amalgamation could not.

Tenskwatawa smiled crookedly. Tecumseh had nothing to fear about matters here, he said. In the hands of the Shawnee Prophet, all would go well. He bade his brother farewell and stood in the doorway of his *wegiwa* and watched as Tecumseh nimbly mounted his horse and led his small party southward.

When they had disappeared from sight, Tenskwatawa reentered the *wegiwa*. Tecumseh had not given him any prophecies, but it was just as well — the Prophet had plenty of forecasts to make and he didn't need Tecumseh's help to see the future.

[*July 26, 1811 — Friday*]

In his fine home at Vincennes, Governor Harrison was just finishing the report he would send about the recent council with Tecumseh to Secretary of War Eustis. He ended it with a rather shrewd analysis of the Shawnee chief's strength and sagacity and a final sentence which subtly indicated that his own sagacity was not lacking:

. . . The implicit obedience and respect which the followers of Tecumseh pay him are wonderful. If it were not for the vicinity of the United States, he would perhaps be the founder of an empire that would rival in glory Mexico or Peru. No difficulties deter him. For four years he has been in constant motion. You see him to-day on the Wabash, and in a short time hear of him on the shores of Lake Erie or Michigan, or on the banks of the Mississippi; and wherever he goes he makes an impression favorable to his purpose. He is now upon the last round to put a finishing stroke to his work. I hope, however, before his return, that that part of the work which he considered complete will be demolished, and even its foundation rooted up.

I remain, Sir, Yr. Mo. Obt. Svt.,
William H. Harrison

[*August 28, 1811 — Wednesday*]

To each of the southern tribes he visited, Tecumseh presented a sacred slab, along with a bundle of the red sticks. But where once these stick bundles had been large, now they were unusually small. The one he had given to the Cherokees a few weeks ago when they had agreed to assemble under his leadership had only four sticks. And when, three days ago, he had concluded his talks with the Seminoles, their bundle had contained only three sticks.

Everywhere he went he was listened to eagerly. His fame had spread far; few indeed were those who could not relate exploits of the great Shawnee chief, Tecumseh, or who failed to be impressed deeply by the scope of his amalgamation. Thus, they readily pledged themselves to join him when the great sign came. Along with the Cherokees and Seminoles and Lower Creeks, there were the smaller and more scattered tribes — the Santees and Calusas and Catawbas and the slightly larger Choctaws and Biloxis, the Chickasaws and the Alabamas.

Occasionally one or another of the tribes would require a show of proof from Tecumseh — some small sign to show that he was, indeed, under the auspices of the Great Spirit. In most cases, minor prophecies sufficed, such as in the case of the Seminoles. When they had hesitated to join him, he told them that in two days there would come to Florida's coast an ocean vessel which would be filled with arms and supplies for the Seminoles. They assembled at the point he indicated and at dawn on the given day they discovered a British ship at anchor in the bay and its smaller boats coming ashore laden with gifts of guns and powder and tomahawks, cloth and jewelry and foodstuffs. There was no further hesitancy among the Seminoles to join Tecumseh.

Now the great Shawnee leader was beginning his swing northwestward through the Alabama country to seek the important alliance formation with the powerful Upper Creek nation. From there he would move west, heading into the Mississippi lands and Louisiana, then again northward on the west side of the mother of rivers to Missouri again. And along the way he would stop to win over the Natchez and Yazoo, the Tawakonias and Caddos and others.

But first the Upper Creeks. Big Warrior, principal chief of the Upper Creeks, listened with a disapproving frown as Tecumseh told his people of his great plan, its near culmination and the part he wished them to play in it. There could be no doubt of his jealousy of this Shawnee who could come from hundreds of miles away and sway his people so swiftly with his reputation and his elocution. Great numbers of the Upper Creeks had come to this village called Tuckabatchee located on the Tallapoosa River to hear the chief; but no matter how earnestly and convincingly Tecumseh spoke, Big Warrior refused to pledge his people. Sensing his jealousy, Tecumseh became scornful. He looked first at the large crowd and then his gaze swung to Big Warrior.

"Your blood is white!" he said. "You have taken my talk and the sticks and the wampum and the hatchet, but you do not mean to fight. I know the reason. You do not believe the Great Spirit has sent me. You shall know. I leave Tuckabatchee directly and shall go . . . to Detroit. When I arrive there, I will stamp on the ground with my foot and shake down every house in Tuckabatchee!"

Impressed in spite of himself, Big Warrior thereupon agreed to come and join the amalgamation — if and when the houses of Tuckabatchee all fell down. Tecumseh nodded. The Upper Creeks would come. What now could stop this mighty force he had joined together?

[*September 2, 1811 — Monday*]

When the seven young warriors came to him to ask advice and permission for the planned escapade, Tenskwatawa was pleased. Not only because they had come to him with great respect, honoring him as he had always hoped to be honored, but because two of the seven were Shawnees, two were Kickapoos and one each was Eel River, Potawatomi and Wyandot — living proof of Tecumseh's dream that the Indians could cast aside tribal designations and embrace one another as brother Indians.

In practice for events which might come, they asked the Prophet if it would be all right for them to slip quietly down to the white settlements to see if they could steal away a horse apiece without being detected. The Prophet hesitated. Were Tecumseh here he knew permission would be denied. But there was more here than met the eye; more than just the matter of eager young braves stealing horses. Here would be wonderful proof that individuals of various tribes could depend upon one another as they depended upon their own tribesmen. Moreover, Tenskwatawa formed no mental picture of this little escapade causing any harm; after all, he was the Shawnee Prophet and if there was any danger involved, it would have been revealed to him in a vision by now.

He nodded gravely and, whooping wildly, the seven dashed away. Tenskwatawa smiled and found himself almost wishing he could go along.

In five days they returned victorious, riding their stolen mounts and boasting of their prowess and how they had taken them away from beneath the very noses of the whites. But the jubilation lasted only a day. The next afternoon a party of fifteen armed white men arrived at the village, having followed the hoofprints of the horses, and demanded of Tenskwatawa their return.

The Prophet, a bit disconcerted at their sudden appearance, agreed immediately and merely laughed it off as something of a joke. The white men refused to crack a smile, however, and rode off silently, leading the seven recovered horses.

Tenskwatawa retired to his *wegiwa* to give this some thought and perhaps get a vision about it. When he emerged an hour later his face was screwed into an ugly frown. The Great Spirit, he told the assembled villagers, had revealed to him that those horses were rightfully the property of the Indians and that no harm would befall them if a large party was to go in pursuit and take them back. Within a few minutes fifty warriors thundered off on the trail.

It was well after dark when they spied the flicker of the white man's campfire. The Indians made no attempt to sneak up, but rode bodly into camp, some of them holding the whites at bay with leveled rifles while the others rounded up not only the seven original horses but the fifteen the men had been riding. The whites were directed to go back where they belonged and not come again to the Prophet's Town if they valued their lives.

No shots were fired, no lives lost. It was a wonderfully easy victory. How simple it was when the Great Spirit was on your side and His amazing Prophet directed your movements.

[*November 7, 1811 — Thursday*]

Nothing could have suited William Henry Harrison better than the double theft of horses from the settlers. Ever since Tecumseh's departure he had been poised to strike the Indians, awaiting only some hostile movement by them to justify an offensive measure.

This was it.

Three weeks after the horse-stealing incident, the governor's army of nine hundred men was outfitted and ready for the attack they had so long anticipated. Certain supplies still were needed, but they could follow behind later. And so, on September 26, with the thirty-eight-year-old governor leading the column, they marched out of Vincennes with the cheers of the populace ringing in their ears.

At a place where, according to Indian tradition, a great battle was once fought between the Illinois and Iroquois confederations, he made camp on the banks of the Wabash River and ordered the erection of a substantial fort, which he named, with something of a lack of modesty, Fort Harrison.[4] Then he sent a deputation to the Delawares, who, more than any other tribe, seemed disinclined to make war with the whites. Harrison wanted some of their chiefs to act as missionaries to the different tribes implicated at the Tippecanoe village. Eager to try to help settle this dangerous situation, all the Delaware chiefs who could walk set out immediately for Fort Harrison. They were cut off by a small war party from Prophet's Town, however, whose spokesman was none other than Winnemac, the Potawatomi chief who had sided with Harrison at the Vincennes councils, and who was now apparently a strong follower of the Prophet.[5]

"Will you or will you not," he asked without preamble, "join us in this war against the Seventeen Fires? We have taken up the tomahawk under direction of the Prophet and will not lay it down but with our lives."

The Delawares attempted to maintain a position of neutrality, but Winnemac would not stand for it. He cut off the Delaware speaker with a savage wave of his hand. There could be no middle people here; it was one side or the other.

"The Prophet," he said, "has given us positive assurance of victory. There is no doubt about it. In his visions, which have always been true before, he has seen us emerge victorious. Weigh this carefully among you, because when we have beaten the Americans, those tribes which have refused to join us will have cause to repent it."

The Delawares held a muttered conference and dispatched a runner to Harrison to tell him of the meeting, while the chiefs changed course to accompany Winnemac back to see Tenskwatawa. While this took place, Harrison was given more cause for attacking Prophet's Town. One of his sentinels on guard duty was ambushed, shot and seriously wounded. Had all his supplies been on hand, the governor would have attacked immediately; but the example of St. Clair's defeat had shown him the foolishness of attempting an attack without supplies, and so, fuming at the delay, he bided his time.

It had come as something of a disappointment to realize that these Indians were really serious about making a fight of it. The fact that Tecumseh was not here to lead them, and that so many of the tribes had for so long vacillated before siding with the Shawnee, had assured the governor that the advance of his army would demoralize them into desertion or submission, either of which would shame them into abandonment of further resistance.

On October 27, the Delaware chiefs who had detoured to Prophet's Town finally arrived at Fort Harrison. They were extremely angry with Tenskwatawa and immediately announced their intention to side with Harrison fully and have nothing further to do with Tecumseh, the Prophet or the tribal amalgamation.

The Prophet, they reported, had insulted them with contemptuous remarks, received them badly, treated them worse and finally dismissed them after verbally castigating the governor. They reported that the Tippecanoe Indians were war dancing every night while the Prophet, who swore to burn the first prisoners taken, frequently retired in solitude to practice "strange infernal rites."

Soon after talking with the Delawares, Harrison drafted a message to be taken to the Tippecanoe village, demanding that the Potawatomies,

Winnebagoes and Kickapoos who were there should return at once to their own tribes, that the stolen horses should be returned and that the murderers of the whites be delivered up. When his own messengers showed a strong disinclination to carry the message into the enemy camp, the governor accepted the offer of some of the Delaware chiefs and a few friendly Miamis to accomplish the errand. They left and were never heard of again.

The anticipated supplies reached Fort Harrison on October 28, and the next day the governor marched his army. Two routes were used by the Indians for reaching Prophet's Town by land; the trail on the southeast side of the river was shorter, but it was very narrow and went through some stretches of deep woods much too favorable for ambush. And so Harrison decided to use the trail on the other side; but to fool the Indians, he had the southeast trail cleared and opened for a distance and started his wagons along it. The army marched this way for a little distance and then abruptly crossed the river and took up the other trail. It was a good deceptive move and no Indian scouts were seen.

On the night of November 5, the army encamped within ten miles of Prophet's Town. Still no Indians were seen, although there were traces of scouting parties everywhere. The next morning, only five miles from the village, some Indian parties were seen and the interpreters in front of the army were directed to communicate with them. The only replies to their calls were insulting gestures. About a mile and a half outside the town, Harrison established a camp for the night and decided on one last attempt to persuade the Indians to submit without having to resort to battle. After all, the scouts had reported over two thousand warriors in the village and his own army had only nine hundred men. Captain Dubois was then sent forward with a flag of truce, but it was not honored and an attempt was made to cut him off from the army which very nearly succeeded. Despite the nearly three-to-one odds against them, Harrison resolved to attack.

But Tenskwatawa was just beginning to open his black bag of tricks. With an effrontery that was astonishing, a deputation of three of the Prophet's men advanced under a truce flag and very innocently inquired why the army was moving in on them. Tenskwatawa, they said, wished only for peace. Hadn't the Delaware chiefs returned with this message to the governor? No? A shame. Apparently they had returned on the southeast side of the Wabash and had thus missed the army.

After some consideration, Harrison agreed to suspend hostilities and treat for peace with the Prophet's assemblage in the morning. He told the Prophet's three men he would encamp on the edge of the Wabash, and then marched toward the town to find a good camping spot. As they neared the village, however, the order of troops was changed to allow for the

uneven nature of the terrain; immediately the Indians became alarmed at
this maneuver and positioned themselves for defense. But Harrison rode
forward, called some of the Indians to him and explained that he had no
intention of attacking. Soon the army reached a good campground and
the men were ordered to sleep with their guns in their hands, although
quite a number of them were already grousing over the possibility of being
cheated out of the battle they had marched so far to fight.

They needn't have worried. The Indians were worked up to a high pitch
of fanatical zeal inspired by their Prophet. After all that Tenskwatawa had
foretold of their invulnerability, how could they possibly be harmed? All
the chiefs on hand attended the council Tenskwatawa called early in the
evening to form a battle plan. It was a simple and treacherous one.

The chiefs would go next morning as planned to meet in council with
the whites and would agree to all of Harrison's proposals. They were then
to retire a short distance away, to where the warriors were stationed, but
two of the chiefs, both of whom were Winnebago volunteers, would not go
back with the other chiefs. They would linger behind in Harrison's vicinity
until the chiefs reached their own lines and then they would swiftly jerk
out their weapons and assassinate the governor. At that point the real
battle would begin.

The night was cloudy and very dark and soon a cold drizzle set in, but
still a large cluster of Indians surrounded Tenskwatawa, who made many
mysterious movements and muttered strange words. After repeating several
incomprehensible incantations, in what appeared to be a state of trance, he
suddenly jerked to awareness and raised his arms for silence.

"One half of the white chief's army," he told them emphatically, "is
now dead. The other half is now crazy. It will be a small matter to finish
them off with our tomahawks."

But somehow, during the night, the entire plan was changed and by 4:00
A.M. the muddy ground was aswarm with Indians creeping up on the
sentries of the American camp. They had waited too long, however, for it
was Harrison's practice to arouse his men long before daylight so that they
would be on the alert until the sun rose. And now, on this November 7, he
had just risen and was pulling on his boots before a campfire, conversing
with several of his officers while the men were being awakened, when with
startling unexpectedness a single shot rang out and a thousand or more
voices screeched out the terrifying Indian battle cry. The shot had come
from the gun of a sentry who had spotted an Indian sneaking up on him
and dropped him in his tracks.

The battle was on in full now and the Indian forces charged in a frenzy,
led by White Loon and Stone Eater. The guard was forced to give way
before the first onslaught, but the soldiers had gotten their guns ready with
dismaying swiftness. The campfires having been extinguished, the fighting

in such total darkness became a terrifying experience; it was virtually necessary to feel with outstretched hand the person encountered to determine whether he was friend or enemy. A hideous cacophony of screams filled the air, punctuated by gun blasts and the ugly sound of tomahawks thunking home.

Harrison had leaped to his horse at once and all during the battle rode from one side of the camp to the other, encouraging and directing his men. He was urged not to expose himself so, and one officer even took hold of the bridle to detain him, but he jerked free and persisted in galloping into wherever the firing was hottest. His hat rim was perforated by a bullet and another grazed his hair, but he was not struck. Without his example of great courage, it was quite possible that panic would have swept the army.

On a small hill nearby — but not too near — Tenskwatawa perched himself and chanted a war song, absolutely certain the whites were going down to utter massacre and that his predictions were all being borne out. His confidence was reflected in the battle actions of the Indians who fought.

For one of the first times in a battle between Indians and whites, the Indians rushed boldly and openly to clinch with the enemy, not even taking advantage of cover where it was available. What need was there to do that in view of Tenskwatawa's prophecies: that all the American bullets would rebound harmlessly whenever they struck Indian flesh; that the whites would be in thick darkness while the Indians would be able to see as under the light of noonday; that half the army was already dead when they attacked and the other half insane. What need for cover under such circumstances?

But soon after the battle began, messengers raced up to the Prophet to tell him that his followers were dying in the most natural way. He shook his head in annoyance.

"Fight on!" he ordered. "Fight on! It will take a little while for the prophecy to be fulfilled. I will raise my voice to encourage it!"

His wildly inspiring war chant then rose clearly above the cracking of rifles and Indian war whoops and the Indians fought on with renewed faith. Never had Indians been known to fight in so exposed a manner or with such complete abandon. Under the influence of the fanaticism Tenskwatawa had roused in them, they actually rushed right into the bayonets of soldiers.

But as the chilling gray light of dawn crept over the battlefield, a horrible awareness came to them that they were being killed, that Tenskwatawa was no longer chanting and that he was, in fact, gone from his little hill. And though they far outnumbered the whites, the very fact that the bullets did not bounce from them and that they were being killed — and that their Prophet had deserted them — so demoralized them that the whisper raced among them that all who did not flee at once would be slain.

Within minutes the Indians had melted out of sight into the surrounding woods. One hundred eighty-eight corpses lay strewn across the campground. Of these, only thirty-eight were Indians; and yet it was a victory for the army.

Thus ended the Battle of Tippecanoe.

[*November 10, 1811 — Sunday*]

As though a great stone had been dropped into a quiet pool and the concentric rings spread rapidly in all directions, so the Tippecanoe Indians scattered and, with them, the news of the disaster. In all of them there was a great fear of what would happen now and a great anger at the man who had called himself a Prophet and led them into this.

A strong core of Indians dedicated not to the Prophet but to Tecumseh established a camp on Wildcat Creek some miles from where Prophet's Town had stood. That town stood no longer. The army had started marching back to Vincennes soon, but not until the town was ransacked and burned. The only plunder taken was a large number of rifles, many not yet even unpacked from their British wrappings, discovered in a storage *wegiwa*.

Chau-be-nee — the Coalburner — a Sac chief who was a favorite of Tecumseh's, and Black Partridge, a fierce Winnebago chief strongly dedicated to Tecumseh's plan, had taken over joint leadership of these remaining Indians. Despite the flight of so many of their own and other tribesmen, they would remain here to await the return of Tecumseh.

The pair had exerted themselves greatly to hold as many of the Tippecanoe Indians as possible here, but the defeat had destroyed the faith of large numbers of them. Advance parties of Sioux, Huron, Ottawa, Iowa, Iroquois, Fox and Cherokee Indians and many others, who had filtered in before the battle to be on hand when Tecumseh's great sign should be given, now slipped away to return to their tribes to tell of what had happened here and to discourage their people from joining Tecumseh when — and if — the great sign came. If Tecumseh could not even control his Prophet brother, how then could he lead a united nation of warriors?

And so all that remained here at the Wildcat Creek camp of the over two thousand who had been at Tippecanoe, were perhaps forty warriors, a number of whom were still on the verge of leaving. And in the very center of the camp was a little rat-faced man tied securely to a post. It was Tenskwatawa, who had returned the day after the battle. The self-confidence had been stripped from him and he had moved furtively, fearfully, through the camp to Black Partridge and Coalburner.

There had been some mistake, he declared, some error in the compounding of his concoctions and in the expression of his incantations. The fault was not his; there was an evil spirit that had settled among them. The erstwhile Prophet spoke in a whining voice and, though he stood erect, he seemed to cringe before the two leaders.

Coalburner coldly accused him of being a coward, a murderer and a betrayer of all Indians, then directed some of his own men to bind him. He said Tenskwatawa must die for what he had done and Black Partridge nodded in agreement.

"You are a liar," the Winnebago told Tenskwatawa. "You are a false prophet. You told us that the white people were dead or crazy, when they were in all their senses and fought like the Devil! For this you must pay."

But then, this morning, there came a great joyful cheering and the entire company sprang to their feet to welcome the party of horsemen approaching, with Tecumseh at their head. The Shawnee's face was frozen in hard lines and he looked neither to right nor left as his horse plodded into the center of the encampment. The hopeful half-smile that had appeared on the face of Tenskwatawa faded away as Tecumseh halted his horse, dismounted and then stepped over to where his brother was tied and stood looking down at him for a long time. Tenskwatawa's eyes widened as Tecumseh's hand went to his belt and pulled from the sheath his razor-edged hunting knife.

Tecumseh stooped and took Tenskwatawa's hair in his left hand and jerked his head back so that his throat was exposed. He lay the edge of the blade against the flesh and moved it very slightly. A trickle of blood slid down the captive's neck and stained his collar.

"It would be a favor to you, Tenskwatawa," Tecumseh said, "were I to let my hand have its way. But I will not kill you. That would be too easy, too honorable a fate."

He took the knife away, cut his brother's bonds and returned the knife to its sheath. Hesitantly, Tenskwatawa got to his feet. Without another word, Tecumseh reached out and gripped the hair above each of his brother's ears and shook him so violently that Tenskwatawa felt his scalp must be ripped away and his neck broken. His nose began to bleed and a long painful wailing erupted from him.

At last Tecumseh thrust him away and Tenskwatawa slumped to the ground. The Shawnee chief turned his back and strode to where Black Partridge and Coalburner were standing. He clasped their hands silently in turn and his face softened. He had heard how they had brought together those who had not fled in panic and for this he was grateful. Henceforth they would be his left hand and his right hand.

As for Tenskwatawa, death was too good for him. In a day he had virtually destroyed what it had taken a decade to build. He was a liar and a

cheat and, even worse, a man so filled with ambition that he would destroy
the hope of all Indians. So far as Tecumseh was concerned, Tenskwatawa
was dishonored as no man had ever been before. He was no longer his
brother. He was no longer a Shawnee. He was no longer an Indian. He was
no longer even a man. Yes, death would be too easy for him, too honorable. From this time forward he would live in scorn and hate, disgust and
distrust. He would be a man without a family, without friends, without a
people, living as one despised on the fringe of the villages of those he had
sought to rule in his lust for power. His death began this day but it would
be years in coming, for each day henceforth he would die a little more until
at last he would be gone and no living creature would care.

Tecumseh now dismissed Tenskwatawa from his mind as if his brother
had never existed. He called for an immediate council of all who remained
and a large fire was built and they gathered around it. Tecumseh spoke for
many hours, telling his people where he had gone and what he had done,
of the many alliances he had formed and of the fact that when word of the
defeat on the Tippecanoe reached their ears, a majority of them would not
honor their pledges, even though the sign would come.

This fact made necessary a significant change in the grand plan. There
would not now come enough tribes to unite, and they would not have the
strength to back up their demand that the whites leave these lands. They
would, therefore, have to do what Tecumseh had very much not wanted to
do; they would have to accept the British as their ally and join with the
Redcoats in destroying the Americans. Once this was done, then would be
time enough to consider what should be done with the British in their
lands. But now the British-Indian alliance was essential, for neither faction
was strong enough of itself to overwhelm the Americans.

Though the Indian cause had suffered a severe setback, Tecumseh said,
there was belief in his heart that many who had panicked could yet be
brought back into this union to fight for what was theirs. There was no
hope now of taking back what they had lost by peaceable means. It would
have to be through battle; but, with the arms and strength of the British to
support them, it could be done.

All that were here assembled would now mount themselves and disperse.
They would return to their villages by the swiftest routes and tell what had
transpired here, to assure their tribes that all was not lost; that with the
united nation of Indians they could still regain what they sought. The
Prophet had failed them, but Tecumseh would not. The great sign he told
them would come was on the way and would be given as he had said.

All of the tribes, he told these followers, who had received bundles
of red sticks, had but one of these sticks left. In six days a preliminary
sign would be given to the tribes. It would be the sign under which he had
been born and named. A great star would flash across the heavens and this

would indicate that Tecumseh was still guided by the hand of the Great Spirit. The sign would be clearly visible to all the tribes and when it came they were to take that last red stick and cut it into thirty equal pieces. Each day thereafter one of these pieces was to be burned in the light of dawn. But the thirtieth piece was to be burned in the midst of the night and when the last of these had been burned, then would come the great sign of which he had personally told them all. And when this sign came, all who believed in Tecumseh and in the future of the Indian nation would take up their weapons and strike out at once for the British fort that was called Malden, located on the north side of the head of the lake that was called Erie.

[November 16, 1811 — Saturday]

Under a crisp cloudless sky the Indians crouched. No fires had been lighted, lest this drive away or interfere with the sign. There was no moon this night and the stars twinkled with almost tangible brightness in their deep black background. With blankets held over their shoulders to hold back the bite of the cold air, the Indians waited: in southern Canada, from the great falls of the Niagara to the great Lake-of-the-Woods they watched; in western New York and Pennsylvania they watched; in Ohio and in the Indiana Territory and in the land that pushed north between the two great lakes and in the land to the west of the lakes they watched; along the Mississippi and Missouri and even farther west they watched; in the Tennessee and Alabama and Mississippi country they watched. And the principal chief of each tribe held in his hand the final red stick of his bundle.

Just before the midpoint of night it came — a great searing flash from out of the southwest; incredibly bright with a weird greenish-white light, incredibly swift, incredibly awe-inspiring. And the heads of a thousand, ten thousand, a hundred thousand Indians swiveled to watch its fiery progress across the heavens until it disappeared in the northeast. And they were deeply moved by it.

Many of the chiefs broke their sticks over their knees and threw them away and hid their fear in anger. But there were some who retired to their wegiwas or tepees or hogans, lay the red stick upon the ground before the fire and carefully measured, marked it off with a bit of charcoal and cut it into thirty equal lengths.

And then they waited.

[November 22, 1811 — Friday]

Captain William Wells was surprised that so many of the Indians had shown up here at Fort Wayne for the distribution of Indian annuities. Many of those present, he was positive, were among those who had battled against Governor Harrison on the Tippecanoe, yet now they were here, professing friendship with the whites and denying any participation in what had occurred on the Wabash tributary.

The Delawares were here, and the Miamis. So, too, were the Potawatomies and Shawnees, the Weas and Wyandots and Eel Rivers, all eager to accept the handouts offered to help carry them through the winter — flimsy cloth to take the place of animal hides no longer available, spoiled beef to take the place of wild game no longer existing in numbers enough to support them, salt to make up for the salt they were no longer allowed to make for themselves at their traditional salt springs and licks, cheap blankets to take the place of heavy buffalo robes for warding off the winter cold.

Wells questioned each party before he distributed the goods. What of the Prophet? What of Tecumseh? What of the effort to unite all the Indians as one? And since their chief aim at present was to secure these annuities, they answered in a manner they knew would give him pleasure: Tecumseh had not returned; the amalgamation of Indian tribes had collapsed at the Battle of Tippecanoe; the Prophet was imprisoned and under sentence of death.

Black Hoof told him they wanted to live in peace with the United States and the aged Little Turtle agreed that he was strongly in favor of peace, too. White Loon said he wished harmony with all men and Tarhe declared that he still held high the wide white wampum of peace.

At hearing these professions, Wells was pleased. The governor, he knew, would also be glad to hear them. He quickly distributed the annuities and the Indians departed — Black Hoof back to his Shawnees, over whom his influence seemed to have slipped some since the comet appeared; Little Turtle back to his Miamis living on the banks of the Mississinewa fifty miles northeast of Greenville, where at this moment Tenskwatawa lived in freedom, if not in happiness; White Loon to his Weas along the Wabash, who each morning burned with some ceremony one of the thirty pieces of wood into which he himself had divided the red stick; and Tarhe back to his Wyandots to engage once more in tribal council in an effort to quell the again-rising admiration for Tecumseh.

[*December 16, 1811 — Monday*]

At 2:30 A.M. the earth shook.

In the south of Canada, in the villages of the Iroquois, Ottawa, Chippewa and Huron, it came as a deep terrifying rumble. Creek banks caved in and huge trees toppled in a continuous crash of snapping branches.

In all the Great Lakes, but especially Lake Michigan and Lake Erie, the waters danced and great waves broke erratically on the shores, though there was no wind.

In the western plains there was a fierce grinding sound and a shuddering, which jarred the bones and set teeth on edge. Earthen vessels split apart and great herds of bison staggered to their feet and stampeded in abject panic.

To the south and west tremendous boulders broke loose on hills and cut swaths through the trees and brush to the bottoms. Rapidly rushing streams stopped and eddied and some of them abruptly went dry and the fish that had lived in them flopped away their lives on the muddy or rocky beds.

To the south whole forests fell in incredible tangles. New streams sprang up where none had been before. In the Upper Creek village of Tuckabatchee every dwelling shuddered and shook and then collapsed upon itself and its inhabitants.

To the south and east, palm trees lashed about like whips and lakes emptied of their waters, while ponds appeared in huge declivities which suddenly dented the surface of the earth.

All over the land birds were roused from their roosting places with screams of fright and flapping wings. Cattle bellowed and kicked, lost their footing and were thrown to the ground where they rolled about, unable to regain their balance.

In Kentucky and Tennessee and the Indiana Territory, settlers were thrown from their beds and heard the timbers of their cabins wrench apart and watched the bricks crumble into heaps of debris masked in choking clouds of dust. Bridges snapped and tumbled into rivers and creeks. Glass shattered, fences and barns collapsed and fires broke out. Along steep ravines the cliffside slipped and filled their chasms, and the country was blanketed with a deafening roar.

In the center of all this, in that area where the Ohio River meets the Mississippi, where Tennessee and Kentucky, Arkansas and Missouri and Illinois come together, fantastic splits appeared in the ground and huge tracts of land were swallowed up. A few miles from the Mississippi, near the Kentucky-Tennessee border, a monstrous section of ground sank as if some gigantic foot had stepped on the soft earth and mashed it down. Water gushed forth in fantastic volume and the depression became filled and turned into a large lake, to become known as Reelfoot Lake. The whole midsection of the Mississippi writhed and heaved and tremendous bluffs toppled into the muddy waters. Entire sections of land were inundated and others that had been riverbed were left high in the air. The Mississippi itself turned and flowed backwards for a time. It swirled and eddied, hissed and gurgled, and at length, when it settled down, the face of the land had changed. New Madrid was destroyed and tens of thousands of acres of land, including virtually all that was owned by Simon Kenton, vanished forever; and that which remained was ugly and austere.

Such was the great sign of Tecumseh.

This was the earthquake which occurred where no tremor had ever been recorded before; where there was no scientific explanation for such a thing happening; where no one could possibly have anticipated or predicted that an earthquake would happen. No one except Tecumseh.

And though they were only a small percentage of those who had pledged themselves to do so, nevertheless quite a number of warriors of various tribes gathered up their weapons and set out at once to join the amazing Shawnee chief near Detroit.

[*April 1, 1812 — Wednesday*]

The earthquake of December 16 was only a starter. It lasted, intermittently, for two terror-filled days; and at the end of that time the atmosphere was so choked with dust and smoke that for a week afterwards the sun shone sickly reddish-bronze through an ugly haze.

The second earthquake struck on January 23 and the third hit four days later. And finally, on February 13, came the last and worst of them — a hideous grinding and snapping which lasted for only an hour but caused about as much damage as the other three combined.

This was powerful medicine — more powerful than the Indians had ever seen. Those who had deserted Tecumseh now began to reconsider. Although most were in no hurry to rejoin the Shawnee chief, the inclination was there; if, as Tecumseh had predicted, there would definitely be war with the whites, why not make the most of it right where they were?

And so began the hostilities.

At first they were isolated cases mostly, but too serious to be overlooked; a horse theft here, a cabin burned there, a small herd of cows shot to death with bow and arrow elsewhere. Once again settlers carried their rifles to the fields with them and their eyes carried the look of the hunted.

And soon began the attacks upon people. The killings were done quietly — bow, knife or tomahawk rather than the noisy gun. One man was killed near Springfield and another near Urbana; a soldier at Fort Recovery went out to hunt deer and was found four days later spreadeagled and scalped; three men following the Detroit Trace were captured near Fort Defiance, tied to trees and used for knife-throwing contests, then scalped and beheaded.

Near the fort at Greenville a half dozen or more settler cabins and a mill had been built; here the settlers enjoyed a greater sense of security than elsewhere on the frontier because of the proximity of the garrison. Andrew Rush, one of three brothers to settle in the area, stopped off while on his way to the mill that day just before noon to see his nearest neighbors, Dan

Potter and his wife. After chatting awhile, Rush prepared to leave and Cora Potter asked if he wasn't afraid the Indians might waylay and kill him.

"No, ma'am," he said, laughing and sweeping off his hat, "I had my wife just this morning cut my hair so short that they couldn't get my scalp off."

Half an hour later, close to the mill, Rush suddenly jerked erect at the blow that struck his back and with unbelieving eyes saw protruding from the center of his chest the chipped flint head and part of the shaft of an arrow, all of it scarlet with his own blood. It was the last thing he ever saw.

He slid from the saddle and a trio of Potawatomies raced up. As one caught the horse, another slammed his tomahawk into the back of Rush's neck. The third had to work hard at it, but he finally managed to get the scalp off.

[*June 14, 1812 — Sunday*]

Indian or white, there was now no doubt in anyone's mind that war must soon break out. William Hull, who had won honors as an officer of the Revolution when he fought beside Anthony Wayne at Stony Point, and who was now governor of the Michigan Territory, was extremely conscious of the buildup of Indians under Tecumseh. Hull's spies had reported "scores of savages" camped outside the British Fort Malden and it was said that the Shawnee chief was conferring regularly with Major General Isaac Brock, who was providing the warriors with new guns. In numerous letters, Hull urged Congress to authorize the invasion and seizure of Canada before the forces there had become too strong to control. He succeeded in creating considerable apprehension in the capital.

In April, President Madison issued orders. In addition to regular troops, twelve hundred of the Ohio militia were to be called up for a year's service, to meet at the headquarters in Dayton and there to be fitted out with new muskets and uniforms of bright blue with scarlet collars and cuffs and a white-feather cocked hat for each. Hull himself was commissioned as a brigadier general to command them.

No accommodations had been provided for in Dayton and so the troops bivouacked on the Common.[6] When this area became too full, the troops bivouacked at the mouth of Hole's Creek. On May 6, Ohio governor Return J. Meigs arrived to inspect the troops and Hull arrived soon afterwards, setting up his headquarters in McCullum's Tavern. By May 26, the Northwestern Army, as it was designated, numbered twenty-five hundred men and on that date, in an impressive ceremony virtually dripping with esprit de corps and flowery elocution, Hull accepted the command from Governor Meigs.

"This army," Meigs orated, "is honored to be under the leadership of this able hero, this Superintendent of Indian Affairs and Governor of

Michigan, who is so well fitted to conduct them to speedy and complete victory."

Hull, scarcely the soldier he had been nearly two-score years ago, glowed under the praise. Fat and sluggish now, and decidedly confused in mind and spirit, he rose to the occasion nonetheless and responded with a grandiose speech about the hallowed ground over which they were to march, and about the British "system of oppression and injustice which that nation has continually practiced, and which the spirit of an indignant people can no longer endure!"

On the first day of June the army marched north, arriving in Urbana six days later. A number of young men in the area immediately enlisted, among them a handsome nineteen-year-old named Simon Kenton, Jr. His father had been tempted to go along, too, but a touch of the old fever and the leg break still bothered him, and so he decided to sit this one out. He had, since resigning his job as Champaign County jailer, taken up residence in a cabin on King's Creek, not far from Taylor's Mill. There, living on the same ground with him and his family, were his two devoted Shawnee friends, Chiuxca and Coonahaw. This morning — June 14, 1812 — shortly after religious services, a group of soldiers who had heard about the two Indians decided that now was the appropriate time to draw first blood for the American forces. In something of an ugly mood they tramped to Kenton's place and banged on his door. Simon answered it.

"They's a couple Shawnee devils camped right over yonder," one of the men told him. "We don't much like the idee of you harborin' the enemy an' we aim to wipe 'em out right now."

Simon looked over the dozen men and then nodded slowly. He raised a hand for them to wait a moment, indicating he'd join them, and disappeared into the room. In a moment he was back with the rifle he hadn't carried for years. He slammed the door behind him, marched a few paces from the house and suddenly spun about with the weapon leveled waist high at them.

"Pay close attention," he said softly, "cause I ain't going to repeat. Mebbe you'll massacre them Injens, but not whilst I'm alive. And if you aim to kill me, they's a few other white men present who'll be took off suddenlike first!"

Under such circumstances the soldiers abruptly lost their taste for the adventure and turned away, grumbling. Fifty yards from the cabin one of them looked back at the big form of the frontiersman still standing there and remarked to a companion: "That there fellow don't have much to say, but what he *does* say is sure as hell impressive!"

[August 19, 1812 — Wednesday]

War with Great Britain was declared on June 18.

For a long time President James Madison had been urging Congress to authorize the declaration — not, as the frontiersmen chose to believe, because of British aid to the Indians in Ohio, but because of troubles at sea. The sweeping system of blockades established by the British to prevent other nations from bringing essential supplies to this country was not only galling, it was endangering the lucrative American commerce with France. That these blockade methods widely overstepped legal limitations was obvious, but extensive protest through diplomatic channels had helped not at all. And so Congress had authorized the Declaration of War.

Had James Madison made every effort possible in that direction, it is highly doubtful that he could have selected a more incompetent and inadequate commander for the Northwestern Army than Brigadier General William Hull. On June 15, Hull's army left Urbana and struck out for Detroit, and now the going got rough. There were no roads north of Urbana, only sodden trails, and the traveling was slow and arduous. Much of this area was forest and swamp and when the army wasn't hacking its way through heavy brush, it was wading knee-deep through miasmic marshes. Malaria and ague felled many of the men and the hard-driven supply-train animals were pushed beyond capability, dozens of them falling dead in their traces. Ill-trained and poorly disciplined to begin with, the men became stupid and quarrelsome with exhaustion. It took the army more than a fortnight just to reach the Maumee Rapids, ninety-five miles distant, and it arrived there in miserable shape.

Hull was well aware of the British naval dominance on Lake Erie. Nevertheless he commandeered the little United States schooner *Cuyahoga* at the foot of the Rapids, placed aboard it all his supplies and baggage and many of his sick and ordered it to proceed down the Maumee, across the western end of Lake Erie, past Fort Malden and up the Detroit River to Detroit itself. Meanwhile he would lead the men afoot the rest of the way to that city.

Not unexpectedly, the *Cuyahoga* failed to make it. She was taken easily by a British gunboat, her crew and passengers made prisoner and all supplies and baggage confiscated. Nor was that the worst of it. For some ungodly reason, Hull had also put aboard the ship all his papers and plans for the campaign and these were immediately forwarded to Major General Isaac Brock.

Of course, Hull was unaware of this until he reached Detroit on July 5. Fort Malden, he was assured by his spies, was very weak, since its reinforcements had not yet arrived. If he struck at once, his vastly superior force could take it handily. Without delay the general led his troops across the river to Sandwich, Ontario.[7] But on arriving there, just sixteen miles from Fort Malden, doubts assailed him. What if the assault should cost too many lives? What if the seventy Indians under Tecumseh were to rise and massacre the nonmilitary whites around Detroit? What if the American Army should lose its general?

And now word had come that far to the north the tiny but important garrison at Fort Mackinac had surrendered to a detachment of Brock's men. Hull found it unnecessary to dwell on the uncomfortable thought that the fort had fallen with such incredible ease because the United States government and the commander of its Northwestern Army had neglected to inform its commandant that war had been declared two months previously. And so, despite the fact that his officers and men were in a fever to attack, he ordered an about face and recrossed the river to Detroit.

While this was going on, a rather large council of Indian chiefs inclined to neutrality had assembled at Brownstown, in the Michigan Territory across the Detroit River from Fort Malden. A deputation of chiefs was sent to Tecumseh to invite him to attend, but he grew indignant over it.

"No!" he declared. "I have taken sides with the King, my father, and I will suffer my bones to bleach upon this shore before I will recross that stream to join any council of neutrality."

Having settled down and established his headquarters in the fort in Detroit, General Hull now dispatched a detachment of six hundred men under Major Thomas B. Van Horne to escort the mail, open communications with Ohio if possible and meet a supply convoy under Major William Brush at the mouth of Raisin River.[8] But Tecumseh, leading his own seventy warriors and forty soldiers under Captain James Muir, met them instead. In the first land action of the War of 1812, Van Horne was decisively defeated and sent in hasty retreat to Detroit with severe losses.

Elated with Tecumseh's victory over Van Horne's greatly superior force, Brock commissioned the Shawnee chief a brigadier general. Tecumseh, who had been slightly wounded in the attack, as was Captain Muir, immediately sent runners to all the tribes with the news that already a battle had been fought and won, the American Fort Mackinac had been taken, Tecumseh himself had won the rank of general and that soon Hull's entire army would be in British hands. If any of the braves wished to share in the plunder, they must join his forces at once. Immediately seven hundred Indians, already inclined to join the Shawnee chief and equally susceptible to the influence of success, snatched up their weapons and flocked to his side.

Hull now realized that Indian uprisings would soon spread all over the frontier and that the smaller garrisons were in grave danger. He dispatched an express to Captain William Wells at Fort Wayne directing him to hurry to Fort Dearborn and order the evacuation of that garrison as well as the little adjacent village of Chicago. But the order was too late. Chicago was already fairly well surrounded by hostile Potawatomies, Foxes, Sacs and Winnebagoes, awaiting only a word from Tecumseh to strike.

Wells and Tecumseh's runner arrived at Chicago about the same time and the Indians, led by the Winnebago chief Black Partridge and the

Potawatomi chief Blackbird, immediately attacked the fleeing throng. The whites hadn't a prayer of a chance.

William Wells had lived long enough as the adopted son of Little Turtle to know that a lingering and terrible death was in store for him if he fell into their hands alive. He moistened some gunpowder and blackened his face with it as a symbol of defiance, then galloped his mount directly toward the Indians, calling them miserable squaws and shouting the most terrible insults he knew at them. The plan worked and he was shot and killed by Blackbird himself. Reverting to an old tribal custom, Blackbird slit open Wells's chest, ripped out his heart and ate a large portion of it raw. The rest of the Fort Dearborn troops, with but a few exceptions, were then massacred.

At Fort Malden, General Brock had become keenly aware of General Hull's indecision and fear and the daily weakening of the American army through lack of supplies, and he had no intention of letting such a splendid opportunity pass by. Calling Tecumseh to him, Brock asked what kind of country they must pass through to reach Detroit if they crossed from here directly to the American side. Tecumseh took a roll of elm bark, spread it on the ground and fastened the corners with four stones. With his scalping knife he drew an amazingly accurate map of the country, showing its hills, woods, springs, rivers, swamps, ravines and roads. Few generals ever possessed more thorough knowledge of enemy terrain than he.

Having decided the Canadian side would be better, Brock moved his army of seven hundred thirty soldiers — a third the size of Hull's force — north to Sandwich on August 13. Unaware of this, Hull dispatched three hundred fifty men, under Colonels Duncan McArthur and Lewis Cass, in an attempt to reach the convoy supposedly coming up under Major Brush. Then, on August 16, Brock began lobbing a few random cannonballs across the river into the fort. When there was no answering fire, Tecumseh crossed over to Spring Wells on the American side with his warriors and Brock followed.

Hamstrung with fear and befuddlement, Hull met Brock and surrendered Detroit and the Northwestern Army to him without firing a single defensive shot. His own men could not believe it true, and when the full realization of it struck home, many of them threw down their weapons in rage and wept at the disgrace of it.

A day or so later McArthur's detachment returned unsuccessful, prevented from reaching their destination for want of provisions and having had nothing to eat for several days. Great was the astonishment at finding the British flag flying over Detroit and Indians engaged in killing the cattle belonging to the Americans. Any resistance in their own weakened state was hopeless, and so McArthur sent in a flag of surrender. When he and his fellow officers saw the articles of capitulation, Colonel Cass broke into indignant tears, thrust his sword into the ground and snapped it in two.

Living up to his promise made long ago to Rebecca Galloway on the Little Miami River, Tecumseh issued stern orders to all his Indians that they were not to abuse the captives in any way. "Kill the enemy if possible and leave none to be captured," he told them, "but if prisoners fall into your hands, treat them humanely." It was a disappointment to his warriors, to whom the butchery of captives had always been a sweet fruit of victory, but no attempt was made to disobey the great chief. However, this did little to salve the minds of the American soldiers. They were shocked, stunned, outraged; their mood exemplified in the letter written by one of Hull's men, Private Nathaniel Adams:

> Detroit
> August 19, 1812
>
> My Dear Brother,
>
> I have only time to inform you that our army surrendered to the British under Gen Brock on the 16th. We could have whipped hell out of the rascals but Gen. Hull has proved himself a traitor and a coward.[9] On the 12th of July, we crossed the river at this place and encamped at Sandwitch in Canada, with the object of driving the red coated devils away from Malden . . . Gen. Hull was informed there that Fort Mackinaw above Detroit had surrendered to the British and Indians, who were rushing down the river in numbers sufficient to crush our people. Old Gen. Hull became panic struck, and in spite of the entreaties of his officers and private Soldiers run us back to this place where we were made to submit to the most shameful surrender that ever took place in the world. Our brave Capt. Harry James cursed and swore like a pirate, and cried like his heart would break.

In this grand manner commenced the War of 1812.

[September 1, 1812 — Tuesday]

With Hull's army taken so abysmally, the entire frontier erupted in an orgy of blood skirmishes between Indians and whites, and warriors of the Miami tribe joined Tecumseh practically en masse.

Nor were they the only ones. Sacs came, too, and so did more of the Winnebagoes, Potawatomies and Ottawas, as well as scattered bands from the Sioux, Cherokee, Upper and Lower Creek, Delaware, Eel River, Kickapoo and Shawnee tribes. The smell of victory was in the air and the tribal amalgamation so severely damaged by the ambitious Prophet was beginning to re-form.

Important councils were held and now the words of Tecumseh were revered as if they were the words of Moneto. The principal obstacles now standing between them and their regaining complete control of Ohio, the

Shawnee chief said, were Fort Harrison on the Wabash and Fort Wayne at the head of the Maumee. Therefore, the Potawatomies and Ottawas, aided by Tecumseh and the British, would capture Fort Wayne, which was now commanded by Captain Oscar Rhea; while Fort Harrison, under command of young Captain Zachary Taylor, would be taken by the Miamis and Winnebagoes.

For the whites the situation, especially around Detroit, had become horrible. Despite Tecumseh's instructions, the Indians, in their chief's absence, committed all sorts of depredations against the settlers along the Detroit River. The British, flanked by their Indian allies, moved south from Detroit to Frenchtown at the mouth of Raisin River where they built a large stockade to command the land approach to Detroit.

But for all their fear and anger, the Americans were not standing still. A battle lust comparable to days when the frontier was in their own backyard now swept the Kentuckians and they enlisted in the militia in great numbers. And though it was contrary to law, since he was not any longer a citizen of that state, William Henry Harrison was appointed brevet major general of the Kentucky Militia, to lead them against Detroit.

Somewhat chagrined that Kentucky had gained the edge here, the federal government quickly commissioned Harrison as brigadier general of the United States Army. Thus, when Hull surrendered and it became necessary to name a new commander of the re-forming Northwestern Army, everyone naturally assumed the choice would be Harrison. After all, his defeat of the Tippecanoe Indians was still a matter of great national pride.

But the government, with inexplicable stubbornness and a seeming inability to learn from past mistakes, chose instead General James Winchester, another old-line Revolutionary soldier. For the past thirty years Winchester had been in retirement on his Tennessee farm and what little skill he had possessed as a young soldier was now decidedly gone. He was hardly a better choice than Hull had been.

The lament of the military was loud and long. Winchester embodied just about everything they detested in a leader. He was old, fat, stubborn, overbearing and exceedingly pompous. Worse, he knew nothing of strategy, was very dense, refused to listen to any officer subordinate to him and was unbearably dictatorial. It was only with the greatest of difficulty that Harrison — who, as something of an afterthought, had been placed second in command — was able to keep his men from deserting when they learned Winchester was the new top man.

But Harrison merely smiled. He had a pretty good idea that General James Winchester wouldn't take very long to prove himself a miserable choice.

[*September 12, 1812 — Saturday*]

The attacks upon Fort Harrrison and Fort Wayne began simultaneously on September 3, but they shouldn't have. Tecumseh had told them to wait, especially in attacking Fort Wayne, until he could get there to direct matters. But the Indians were flushed with the success of the war thus far and eager for more victories and for the eventual takeover of Ohio from the Americans.

Fort Wayne was a sturdy bastion insofar as construction went, but its garrison had a fatal flaw. Commanding the seventy soldiers here was Captain Oscar Rhea, a man inclined to very heavy drinking.

After having kept the fort under heavy siege for over a week, the Indians under Chief Winnemac devised a clever plan for entry. With a large concentration of warriors hidden in a semicircle around two sides of the fort, he and four other chiefs draped in blankets would openly approach the gate under a flag of truce and ask to be permitted inside to discuss a peace proposal. When Captain Rhea had gathered his officers together, they would suddenly pull the hidden pistols from under their blankets and kill the three lieutenants, sparing only the captain. They believed, because of his predilection for drink, that he was a weak man and that once his officers were dead and his own skin threatened, he would agree to open the gates and surrender the fort.

But just as they were about to enter the bastion, two Shawnees and a white man rode up. The latter was William Oliver, scout for General Harrison who was at this moment marching toward Fort Wayne. One of the Shawnees was Bright Horn, and the other was Spemica Lawba, better known to almost all the American soldiers as Johnny Logan. This was the same Shawnee who, as a boy many years ago, lived at Mackachack when Benjamin Logan's army attacked and Chief Moluntha, after surrendering, had been murdered; he was the same Shawnee whom Ben Logan had taken under his wing and adopted and taught the ways of the white man; the same Shawnee who had taken the name Johnny Logan in honor of his adopted father and through all these years had remained faithful to his benefactor and to the Americans.

Spemica Lawba had been a boyhood friend of Tecumseh's and still saw him occasionally. In fact, just before this war had broken out, he had sat with the Shawnee chief before the fire for an entire night while Tecumseh tried to talk him into espousing the British cause in the coming war; and Spemica Lawba had tried as vigorously to persuade Tecumseh to side with the Americans. Neither was successful, but they had nonetheless parted on good terms.

Certain that Harrison's army must be close behind them, Winnemac sullenly shook hands with the trio and said he had decided not to talk peace after all. With that, the five chiefs turned and walked back into the woods; at once a heavy firing broke out and the three newcomers ducked inside the fort.

Unless someone got word to Harrison right away, the fort might well be taken. Bright Horn and Johnny Logan volunteered to go. At a break in the firing, the pair thundered out of the gate and swept past the enemy lines, barely ahead of the converging Indians, who were unmounted. Johnny Logan raised an arm in a wave and let out a triumphant yell, as the entire garrison cheered heartily in reply. The two men reached Harrison in good time with the urgent news.

Back at Fort Wayne, the attackers kept up their firing, several times setting the walls afire with flaming arrows. Lieutenant Joseph Curtis, who had relieved Captain Rhea of command and placed him in confinement for drunkenness, then furnished every man able to shoot with several stands of loaded weapons and ordered them to hold off firing until the enemy came close. It worked well. The Indians made a concerted rush but fell back under the withering fire, leaving eighteen dead warriors behind.

Just before Harrison's army reached the fort on September 12, the Indians attempted one last trick. First they built several great fires at a distance so that the billowing smoke might lead the forted soldiers to think a battle was in progress. Then, in great disorder, acting the part of a routed force, they fled past the gate. The object was to draw the garrison out in pursuit and lead it straight into a trap, but the men inside were content to stay put and await Harrison. With that the siege was lifted and the enemy vanished.

Tecumseh's men succeeded no better at Fort Harrison on the Wabash, where Captain Zachary Taylor had only fifty men, a third of whom were sick.[10] On September 3 a body of Miamis and Winnebagoes, supported by a handful of Kickapoos, came with their squaws and children to the fort and asked admittance to hold council. They claimed to have desperate need for provisions. Taylor was suspicious. He lowered food to them over the walls, but refused to open the gates. The party lingered, professing friendship. But the next day they set fire to one of the blockhouses set in the walls, and as a section burned away and a large gap appeared in the wood, a small army of Indians lying in ambush opened fire through it.

The fire did not catch well, however, and the flames began to die away of their own accord. But the gap was large enough now for passage and the Indians charged. As the garrison opened fire and held them off, Taylor directed a work party in the swift completion of a breastwork of logs over the gap. It worked admirably. For eight days more the Indians hovered about and when at last they left, angry and frustrated, they went directly to the white settlement at Pigeon Roost, a branch of the White River, and here they massacred twenty-one men, women and children.

[*September 15, 1812 — Thursday*]

On August 31, Simon Kenton, Jr., prisoner at Detroit just as his own father had been thirty-four years previously, stood at attention before the new British commandant and listened with the rest of the prisoners of war to what the officer was saying. It was very apparent that Major General Henry Proctor, who had replaced General Brock, did not relish what he was telling them.

All of the men of General Hull's army, he declared, were to be paroled and permitted to return to their own homes, in accordance with long-practiced British rules of war — rules, he observed sourly, which he would do his utmost to have changed. If it were up to him, he would turn them over to the Indians for scalping parties or ceremonies at the fire stake. However, and he sighed regretfully, he had no choice in the matter. Each man would be given a safe-conduct pass which would see him through the Indians to his own country.

The general's voice sharpened. These paroles were granted only when the men swore under oath that they would hereafter refuse to join any army, militia, war party or private company whose object was to fight the British or damage Crown property. Any man recaptured in such capacity would be summarily hanged without benefit of trial or appeal. Any man here who did not wish a parole under such circumstances should raise his left hand now.

No one did.

Proctor grunted and told them all to raise their right hands and repeat after him. Line by line he read off the oath, waiting at the end of each phrase for the prisoners to repeat it. And when he finally finished with the last line and looked up to ask them if they solemnly swore to the oath they had just repeated, every man there replied, "I do."

But Simon Kenton, Jr., had held his left hand behind him with the fingers crossed. And now, just fifteen days later at Fort Wayne, the nineteen-year-old son of the frontiersman had his right hand raised again, but this time his fingers weren't crossed. He was enlisting again, in William Henry Harrison's command.

[*October 21, 1812 — Wednesday*]

Naval Lieutenant Jesse D. Elliott was not a man to let opportunity pass him by. Ever since early September, when the United States government had given him orders to get a navy yard in operation on the upper Niagara River, he had been working with great haste. For weeks now the yard construction had been progressing in the shelter of Squaw Island about three miles below Buffalo, but it was far from completed and it was a long time beyond that before any good ships could be finished.

But now had come word that the British brig *Detroit* and the schooner *Caledonia* had sailed down Lake Erie to anchor under the protective guns of Fort Erie, Ontario, across the mouth of the Niagara River from Buffalo. Jesse Elliott meant to have those ships.

With a hundred men in two boats — the second under command of Sailing Master George Watts — Elliott embarked from Buffalo at 1:00 A.M. and slipped quietly across the waters. Two hours later, he and his men scrambled up the sides of the *Detroit* and in ten minutes had possession of it at the cost of one man killed and another wounded.

Watts's party, meanwhile, boarded the *Caledonia*, took it over, cut the cables and sailed the vessel over to the American shore where they beached her. It would not be much of a job to get her unstuck when the need came.

Elliott labored hard to get the brig across, too, but the heavier ship could not buck the winds and currents. Instead, he was swept straight toward the Canadian shore and was forced to drop anchor in point-blank range of Fort Erie's guns. As soon as dawn broke the fort began to shell him. Elliott fired all the ship's ammunition back at the fort and then drifted down to Squaw Island in his own little boat while the shore batteries made a wreck of the *Detroit*.

The exploit helped some, but the guns of Fort Erie still commanded the channel between Black Rock and Lake Erie. Until they were silenced, the little American fleet under construction at Black Rock would be effectively bottled up. There was only one answer — Fort Erie would have to be taken.

[November 25, 1812 — Wednesday]

Death came slowly and painfully for Johnny Logan — Spemica Lawba — but he met it with laughter on his lips.

General Harrison, still at Fort Wayne, had come to rely heavily upon the scouting skill of this remarkable Shawnee; early in November he directed him to take two good men and reconnoiter the country down toward the Maumee Rapids. The warrior selected his old friend, Bright Horn, and another trustworthy Shawnee, Otter, grandnephew of Black Hoof.

As the three neared the rapids they encountered a huge party of British and Indians and were chased. Only through great exertion and skill were they able to escape and arrive safely at Fort Winchester. Here they reported to General Winchester himself and his aide, a Kentucky officer, Major Price.

With absolutely no grounds for making such a statement, Price flatly accused Johnny Logan of infidelity and with giving information to the enemy. Had the accusations come from another Indian, the Shawnee would have killed him on the spot for such an insult, but he realized he could not do this with an American officer. Drawing himself up proudly, he announced that he would prove his loyalty beyond any doubt. His white friend, William Oliver, was at the fort and Johnny Logan sought him out and told him what had transpired. Oliver cautioned him against being rash, telling him he wasn't obliged to prove anything, but Johnny Logan shook his head.

"My pride and my word are at stake. I'll start from here in the morning and either leave my bones bleaching in the woods or return with such trophies from the enemy that never again will any man accuse me of unfaithfulness."

The next morning — November 22 — he started down the Maumee again with his two companions. About noon, while resting, they were surprised by a party of six mounted Potawatomies and a British officer. The Indians were led by Chief Winnemac and the Redcoat was Captain Matthew Elliott, longtime friend of Simon Girty. With no show of surprise or consternation, Johnny Logan greeted Winnemac with pleasant words and a friendly handshake.

"These two and me," he told the chief, indicating his comrades, "are tired of Americans. We have left them for good and are on our way now to throw ourselves behind Tecumseh and General Proctor."

Winnemac grunted suspiciously and ordered the trio disarmed. He positioned men all around them and the whole group set out for the rapids. Johnny Logan, a bright and friendly person by nature, chattered away amicably as they walked. Gradually Winnemac relaxed, and by the time the afternoon was half gone the Shawnee had talked him into restoring their rifles.

About dusk they made camp on the bank of Turkeyfoot Creek, about twenty miles from Fort Winchester. Four of the Potawatomies ambled off to search the nearby woods for some black haws before it became too dark, and suddenly Johnny Logan knew they would never have a better opportunity. At a nod of his head the three men fired simultaneously. Chief Winnemac and Matthew Elliott fell dead, and the other warrior was killed on the fourth shot.

By now shots were buzzing in from the four who had gone in search of black haws and had come sprinting back at the sound of gunfire. Almost immediately a bullet shattered Bright Horn's shoulder. The four Potawatomies had spread apart so as to place the three in a crossfire, but Otter killed one of them and Johnny Logan another. The remaining two, realizing the odds had suddenly shifted, decided on a retreat. They ran off, pausing only once to fire a final volley back into the camp. They never realized that one of the bullets had caught Johnny Logan in the stomach.

With no wasted time, Otter boosted his wounded companions onto Winnemac's and Elliott's horses, took one of the others for himself and led them out. Moving along at a steady pace, he managed to reach Fort Winchester by midnight; soon word had spread through the garrison that Johnny Logan's wound was undoubtedly mortal, and a deep sadness filled the soldiers. The Shawnee had been very much a favorite of theirs, and now the hatred they felt for General Winchester and Major Price grew proportionately and became an almost palpable emotion.

For three days Johnny Logan writhed in an extreme of agony. At the end, he opened his eyes and noted the melancholy expression on the face of William Oliver, who sat in a chair beside the bed.

"Do not grieve, good friend," he whispered. "I am not sorry. I prize honor more than life. I die satisfied."

He fell silent for a long time and then his lips spread in a wide grin. Abruptly he laughed aloud, despite the pain it caused.

"What is it, Johnny?" Oliver asked softly.

"I was just remembering," the Shawnee replied, "the unusual way Otter took the scalp from Winnemac, while at the same time trying to look in all directions." He laughed aloud again.

"How was he doing it, Johnny?"

But there was no answer. Spemica Lawba was dead.

He was the only Indian in Ohio history to be buried by United States Army officers with full military honors.

CHAPTER XIII

[*January 2, 1813 — Saturday*]

THE letter was extremely difficult for Elizabeth Kenton to read, obviously having been written by some barely literate person who had probably spent long hours composing just the few tragic lines it contained. It was neither dated nor signed and the wonder was that it had been delivered at all, addressed as it was simply to "Mr. Kenton of Ohio."

The writer told of being a friend of John Kenton's. The frontiersman's son and he had joined a revolutionary party in Mexico and were fighting with the Mexicans against Spanish tyranny. John had risen to commander of a small force, but he had, unfortunately, been killed while scaling the enemy's walls.

Simon Kenton remained silent for some time after Betsy had finished reading. At last he leaned forward in his chair and poked the coals in the fireplace with his staff, its end long blackened from this practice.

"Although I am sad over the loss of my son," he told her after settling back in his chair, "I'm glad the lad showed some of his father's spirit and died a man."

[*January 22, 1813 — Friday*]

That General James Winchester fancied himself a great strategist was evident to every man serving under him, just as it was equally evident to them that he was not what he fancied. Therefore, there were groans of dismay when, after a prolonged spell of intensely bitter weather, he posted orders at Fort Winchester that the army would begin at once to march across the frozen surface of Lake Erie to take Fort Malden by surprise.

The army of eight hundred fifty men marched downstream along the north bank of the Maumee until, on January 10, they reached the site of Wayne's Battle of Fallen Timbers nineteen years before. Here, at the foot of the Maumee Rapids, they camped — cold to the bone and thoroughly disheartened. This same day a horseman galloped into view with an urgent message from the American settlers living in Frenchtown at the mouth of Raisin River. A party of three hundred British and Indians who had occupied the town were now threatening to burn it down and carry off the people as prisoners.

Sensing an excellent opportunity for an easier victory, Winchester at once sent a detachment of six hundred men to liberate the town while he and the remaining two hundred and fifty men stayed here "in reserve." Pleased with the abandonment of the plan to walk across Lake Erie, the detachment moved out with alacrity for the thirty-mile hike to French-town, where they knew they would find sturdy homes and warm fireplaces. They performed well, surprised the enemy and drove them from the town after a brief, sharp battle.

General Winchester, elated by the news, marched his remaining men to the town at once, showing the same disregard for fundamental military strategy that Hull had exhibited last summer. It was of little concern to him that Fort Malden, with its highly significant force of British and Indians, was only a day's march away — eighteen miles across the hard-frozen mouth of the Detroit River.

The American Army, spent from having lived outside in subfreezing, often subzero weather for over two weeks, was not at all prepared for the fierce attack which came at 5:00 A.M. the next day — January 22 — when General Henry Proctor arrived with a force of two thousand soldiers and Indians. Tecumseh was at this time on the Wabash collecting more warriors, and so the Indians were led instead by Chiefs Roundhead and Walk-in-Water.

From the first volley, it was obvious that the Americans had little chance, especially when it became known that Proctor had brought cannons with him. Greatly frightened, a number of Winchester's men — the general among them — tried to escape, not realizing they were sur-rounded. Fifty of them were tomahawked and scalped and the rest captured. Winchester was taken prisoner and brought before Proctor.

Despite its inferior numbers, the remainder of the army still in the town lay down a withering fire and managed to hold the more exposed enemy at a distance. Proctor thereupon directed Winchester to order a surrender or he would bombard the town with his artillery and permit the Indians to destroy all who survived. Winchester capitulated, but the troops still did not lay down their arms until they received a promise from Proctor himself that their wounded would be cared for and that all of them would get protection from the Indians. Proctor promised.

Gathering up his own wounded and the six hundred unwounded Ameri-can prisoners, Proctor set out for Fort Malden. His promise was worthless.

He left just one British officer behind to "protect" the two hundred or so wounded Americans still in the town under Indian guard. Another promise given which he had no intention of keeping was that he would send for the wounded as soon as his own men had been treated at Fort Malden.

Roundhead and Walk-in-Water, with the heat of battle and their hatred for Americans still strong in them, waited until Proctor's force was out of sight before they held a council on what should be done. After more than a quarter century, the specter of the Moravian Indian massacre at Gnadenhutten had not faded and so, in a long-delayed act of vengeance, the hundred wounded who were ambulatory were assembled outside and the two houses containing a hundred other bedridden wounded were put to the torch. The screams of those inside were horrible and some who attempted to crawl out were felled or forced back with rifle fire.

When the roasting of the hundred was finished, the Indians set off toward Fort Malden with the remaining wounded, most of them poorly dressed and many even shoeless. All but a small handful of these wounded gave out on the march and, as each collapsed or fell behind, a hole was batted in his skull with a tomahawk and he was scalped and left on the ice.

And so, the second major battle of the War of 1812 repeated the results of the first — a monumental defeat for the American forces.

[*January 30, 1813 — Saturday*]

Though the fortunes of war were definitely going against the Americans and ever more Indians were joining Tecumseh, the eighty-seven-year-old principal chief of the Shawnees remained staunch in his promise to adhere to the Greenville Treaty. The word of Black Hoof had been given long ago on it and no vow was more sacred to him than his given word. It took tremendous courage for him to stick by what he said, for under present circumstances it was obvious that if the Americans lost there would be little future for him and his remaining Shawnees.

Now, because serious rumors were circulating that he had weakened in his conviction, Black Hoof decided to visit General George Tupper at nearby Fort McArthur and reassure him of his fidelity.[1] It was, he felt, an act of courtesy and respect that would be appreciated.

Arriving in the early evening, he dined with the general and a few other officers in the headquarters tent and afterwards they smoked the calumet together as Black Hoof reiterated his firm and continuing friendship. A lantern threw the shadows of the men in bold relief on the tent walls; outside, a private who held that any Indian was worth hating, raised his pistol and aimed at the unmistakable silhouette of the Shawnee chief.

The explosion was loud and the ball plunged through the canvas and struck Black Hoof in the head. Entering his cheek at an angle, the bullet glanced along the bone and came to rest firmly embedded in the chief's neck. The Indian slumped to the floor.

Such was the reward for unwavering loyalty.

Instantly the camp erupted with men and a diligent but fruitless search was made for the would-be assassin. Realizing that the whole Shawnee nation would turn against them if their chief died, Tupper called for the camp surgeon, who immediately operated and removed the misshapen bullet. When it was over, the doctor told Tupper that although it was a very serious wound, especially in view of Black Hoof's advanced years, there was a chance he could pull through if given very good care.

At once a permanent guard was set up; surely no Shawnee ever received better care at the hands of the United States Army.

[*February 17, 1813 — Wednesday*]

It was a long time in coming, but the two swift and disastrous defeats had finally aroused the federal government to the importance of the war being fought along the western front, rather than just the war at sea. Something had to be done quickly and it was evident that the primary concern now must be to find two excellent commanders — one to become commander-in-chief of the Northwestern Army and the other to see to the suddenly menacing naval situation on Lake Erie.

William Henry Harrison was the only conceivable choice for the former position and he was named to it at once. Without hesitation, he ordered the erection of several forts, the most important of which was Fort Meigs on the south shore of the Maumee River at the foot of the rapids, opposite and a little upstream from the old British Fort Miami. Colonel Wingate was placed in charge here. Then Harrison set off to the south to find what men were available at Cincinnati, Dayton, Springfield and Urbana, meanwhile broadcasting an urgent appeal for more volunteers from both Kentucky and Ohio. What limited number of men were already in reserve he equipped well and moved to Fort Meigs, hoping to strike Fort Malden a blow which would in some measure retrieve the fortunes already lost. Among the young men in his command was Simon Kenton, Jr., eager for another try at the British.

The man chosen for the Lake Erie campaign would have to be the very best available, because he would be forced to begin with virtually nothing and yet gain control of the lake. The officer finally selected could hardly have been a better choice — he was twenty-seven-year-old Oliver Hazard Perry.

Ever since the Declaration of War last June, Perry had busied himself in the training of his crews in gunnery. By assembling gunboats and dividing them into opposing squadrons and conducting sham battles, he had gained unusual ability in devising swift, decisive strategy. There was one other qualification which set this man slightly apart from other, more experienced officers — a certain well-directed rashness. For the job at hand it would be an essential quality; challenging British naval power on Lake Erie was no light undertaking. American shipyards at Sackets Harbor, Oswego and Niagara would be unable to help; moreover, Lake Erie was three hundred feet above Lake Ontario — unreachable by large boats built below. Nor were the young American ports above the falls, at Black Rock, Buffalo and Erie, yet equipped for extensive shipbuilding; there were few supplies to draw from, and few experienced shipbuilders available.

The beached *Caledonia* could be put into service but, other than that, Perry would have to start from scratch. He would have to build, arm and man a fleet superior to that of the British, which meant at least ten strong ships. It was a formidable job.

But then, Oliver Hazard Perry was a remarkably able man.

[May 4, 1813 — Tuesday]

William Henry Harrison paid scarcely any attention to the dispatch which had arrived from Washington notifying him of his promotion to the rank of major general. He had more important matters to concern him, not the least of which was the expectation of a full-scale assault on Fort Meigs. He had begun to expect it as the ice in Lake Erie went out. Fort Meigs had become the principal depot for all military stores for the Americans in this quarter and he was sure the enemy knew it. He was also certain General Proctor was aware that if he could take this largest of all frontier forts, American land defenses would collapse and the whole western front could be lost to them. For this reason, Harrison sent another urgent request to the governors of both Kentucky and Ohio that they send reinforcements at once.

As usual, he had analyzed the situation correctly. On April 26, two thousand Redcoats and Indians under General Proctor and Tecumseh appeared on the north bank of the Maumee and at once began to erect artillery batteries on a high bank sixty feet above the river. Included among the artillery were two fearsome twenty-four-pounder cannons, which Proctor assured the Indians would promise an easy conquest.

Tecumseh was confident that Proctor was not merely boasting. The Shawnee chief had a healthy respect for artillery and especially for the explosive cannon shells which he called "double balls." By the last day of April he had moved almost all of his Indians across the river to surround the fort at a safe distance and wait for the batteries to split open the fort.

The erection of these batteries was, to the Americans, a frightening move, one that might well be disastrous for them. With the British advantage of height, concentrated artillery fire lobbed over the river into the fort might easily kill most of the garrison. Some good defensive scheme had to be devised. And so it was.

On Harrison's order, all of the large tents were erected side by side in a long line for the entire length of the fort. Behind these tents, hidden from view of the observers across the river, the men dug furiously, throwing up two huge traverses. The first embankment, called the Grand Traverse, was twelve feet high, twenty feet wide at the base and nine hundred feet long. The second traverse ran parallel to the first and was about seven hundred feet long. Various rooms for protection were dug at angles from the bottom of the great trench that resulted from the removal of the earth for the traverses. It took twenty-four hours of concentrated work by every person inside the fort, but they were finished before the British batteries could open up.

As dawn broke on the first day of May, the big guns commenced firing and the quiet spring morning was shattered by the scream of shells and their explosions as they struck within the fort, sending bits of whining, whistling shrapnel in all directions. The Americans sent a few shots back at them from their own cannons, but not many. Cannon ammunition was not plentiful enough to open up a real barrage.

To Tecumseh and his Indians, this shelling of Fort Meigs was a wonderful sight and they yelled with fierce delight, positive that the shells bursting inside the walls must be destroying scores of the enemy. With scarcely a pause, the bombardment continued through the first, second and third of May.

Word was soon brought to General Harrison that a British mortar battery was being readied on the American side of the river, two hundred fifty yards east of the fort. At once Harrison ordered a series of short earth traverses thrown up to protect batteries, command posts and the magazine against shells lobbed from this direction.

To encourage, as well, the recovery of re-usable shot, General Harrison announced that the magazine keeper had been authorized to give a gill of whiskey for every cannonball turned in to him that had come from across the river. By the end of the third day, over a thousand gills of spirit had been earned by the soldiers.

Normally the destruction of men under such cannonading would have been enormous, probably amounting to half a thousand or more; but such was the protection provided by the traverses and trenches that only eighty men were killed and several dozen wounded. The dead were all removed to the rear traverse and quietly buried each night, and the wounded were placed in the large hospital tent.

This morning, all enemy guns remained silent and a British officer appeared bearing a white flag. He was admitted to the fort and at once requested an audience with the commanding general. His manner had

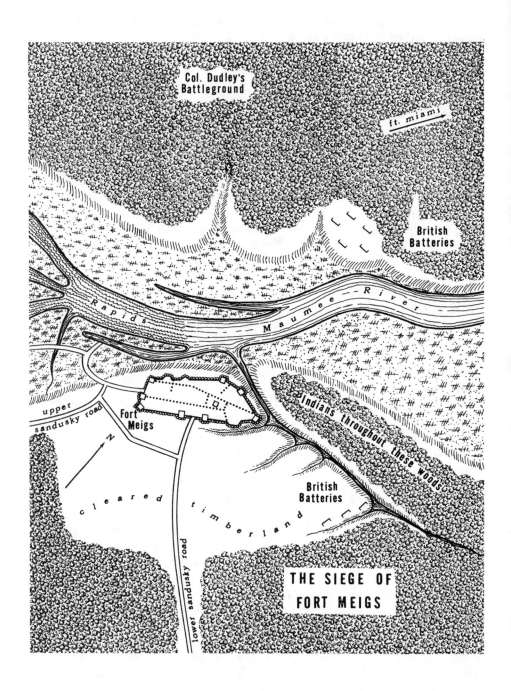

Col. Dudley's
Battleground

ft. miami

British
Batteries

Rapids — Maumee — River

upper
sandusky road

Fort
Meigs

N

Indians throughout these woods

cleared   timberland

British
Batteries

lower sandusky road

THE SIEGE OF
FORT MEIGS

been smug at first, but when he saw no sign of dead bodies scattered about and, in fact, nothing to indicate anyone had even been badly wounded by the heavy shelling, a look of consternation appeared in his eyes. He was led to the grand battery position where Harrison was standing and came to a stiff, respectful attention before the general.

"Sir," he said, "I am Major Chambers. General Proctor has directed me to demand the surrender of this post. He wishes to spare the effusion of blood."

Harrison smiled mirthlessly. "The demand, under present circumstance," he commented, "is a most extraordinary one. As General Proctor did not send me a summons to surrender on his first arrival, I had supposed that he believed me determined to do my duty. His present message indicates an opinion of me that I am at a loss to account for."

Chambers was at once apologetic. "General Proctor could never think of saying anything to wound your feelings, sir. The character of General Harrison as an officer is well known. General Proctor's force is very respectable, and there is with him a larger body of Indians than has ever before been embodied."

"I believe I have a very correct idea of General Proctor's force," Harrison said, his expression now frigid. "It is not such to create the least apprehension for the result of the contest, whatever shape he may be pleased hereafter to give it."

With a nod at one of his officers to show Major Chambers back to the gate, Harrison's tight little smile returned and he added, "Assure the general, however, that he will never have this post *surrendered* to him upon any terms. Should it fall into his hands, it will be in a manner calculated to do him more honor, and to give him larger claims upon the gratitude of his government, than any capitulation could possibly do."

As the gate closed behind a considerably crestfallen Major Chambers, a tremendous cheering erupted inside the fort.

[*May 7, 1813 — Friday*]

Throughout the months following the capture of the *Caledonia* and *Detroit* from the British and the subsequent loss of the *Detroit*, Fort Erie had harassed the shipyard at Black Rock by lobbing occasional artillery shots across the Niagara River. The range was too great for much damage to be done, but the whistling and booming of shells was a constant reminder to the Americans that if they meant to get their new ships out onto Lake Erie proper, these British guns would have to be silenced.

After weeks of planning, the army and navy engaged in a surprise assault and landing. Storming the trouble spot, they drove the British out of Fort Erie and off the entire Niagara Peninsula. Within days of this triumph, the five boats were made ready to move to the lake. This in itself was no easy business. The Niagara River at Black Rock has a current speed of three knots and the prevailing winds are in a downstream direction. It is therefore seldom possible to sail up the river to Lake Erie. To overcome this hurdle, lines were attached from the ships to teams of oxen on shore and the vessels were towed one by one up to Buffalo Creek.

The five craft, carrying a total of seven guns, were the schooners *Tigress* and *Somers*, the supply ship *Ohio*, the sixty-ton sloop *Trippe* and the captured and refitted *Caledonia*. It was not much of a navy but, together with the five ships under construction behind the protection of the long breakwater sand bar of Presque Isle at Erie, Pennsylvania, it just might be a force strong enough for the upcoming mission of Commodore Oliver Hazard Perry.

[*May 9, 1813 — Sunday*]

At midnight last night, after five consecutive days of shelling, a messenger arrived outside of the gates of Fort Meigs, whispered the password and was admitted. It was Captain William Oliver, returning with good news for General Harrison.

The young officer was extremely fatigued, not having slept since he left on the third night of the siege; but he saluted his commander smartly and reported. Less than two hours away, just above the head of the Maumee Rapids, General Green Clay had arrived with twelve hundred militiamen from Kentucky, having floated down to that point in boats from Fort Defiance. He was awaiting further orders.

Harrison, considerably pleased, ordered Oliver to bed and called in Captain Vernon Hamilton to carry orders back to Clay. The Kentucky general was to continue by boat through the rapids. Upon arriving at the fort, eight hundred of the men were to land on the north bank, there to charge the gun emplacements and spike the cannons. At the same time the remaining four hundred were to land on the south bank and join a detachment from the fort to spike the cannons of the British to the east. As soon as these jobs were done, all twelve hundred were to return to the fort. The message from Harrrison concluded: *I take occasion to warn you against that rash bravery which is characteristic of the Kentucky troops, and if persisted in is as fatal in its results as cowardice.*

Acting upon these orders, Clay gave command of the north bank detachment to Colonel John Dudley and the entire party started downstream. They reached the foot of the rapids just after dawn and underwent heavy rifle fire from both Proctor's and Tecumseh's men.

The operation went smoothly to a point, with the landing on both sides of the river effected according to plan. Dudley's men charged directly into strong resistance and forced the enemy to retreat. Two hundred fifty men from the fort streamed out to meet General Clay to spike the eastern cannons. This detachment was led by Colonel John Mills, and it included one platoon led by Sergeant Simon Keaton, Jr.

Mills's detachment came under more fire from Indians than from the British and took considerable losses, but managed to spike the heavy guns and return to the fort. Dudley's men accomplished the same objective on the north side of the river, but instead of retiring as ordered after the cannons were spiked, he instructed his men to pursue the enemy. It seemed an opportune thing to do, for a band of perhaps fifty straggling Indians shot at them and then, in seeming confusion and fear, took to their heels. This was a neatly executed ruse engineered by Tecumseh.

General Harrison and a group of his officers watched from the grand battery inside the fort, saw what was happening and frantically waved for them to return. The men chose to ignore the recall and pressed on. Harrison groaned in anguish.

"They are lost!" He clenched his fists in frustration. "They are lost! Can I never get men to obey my orders?"

For nearly two miles Dudley's eight hundred men swarmed after the elusive enemy through woods and swamps. And then, with devastating abruptness, they found themselves in a ravine, surrounded by double their own numbers. Triumph turned into hysteria as whole swatches of them were mowed down. Many simply dropped their rifles and threw up their hands in surrender. When finally the dust had settled, six hundred fifty of Dudley's men were killed or captured.

The dead were scalped and the captured herded to Fort Miami, while Tecumseh and two thirds of his Indians returned to the battle area. As the captives were marched along, many of them were shot or tomahawked by the exultant Indians. Those who survived to reach the fort were herded into a sort of low, outdoor pen.

In a few minutes General Proctor came up, resplendent in his red and gold. He viewed the captives with unveiled hatred and then gave the remaining Indians leave to select any man each of them wanted and kill him in any manner desired. The Indians fell to with a vengeance and it was a gruesome time. Some were shot, others tomahawked, others knifed or struck with arrow or war club. Soon the carnage was out of hand as the Indians became possessed with a fierce desire to kill all they could reach, and the pen became something of a huge slaughter yard.

Thus far Colonel John Dudley had been unharmed, but now, just as Tecumseh came thundering up on his horse, two of the Indians grabbed him. One held him and jerked his head back by the hair and the other made ready to stab him.

His face dark with rage, Tecumseh slammed to a halt and leaped from his mount, brandishing his war club. In three strides he reached the men and knocked the knife-wielder over with a push. He turned to the other man and ordered him to turn the prisoner loose. Instead, the Indian reached to his belt, whipped out his knife and slashed it across Dudley's throat, severing the jugular vein. Tecumseh leaped forward and struck the Indian a smashing blow on the head with his club, killing him. Then he spun around and shouted at the others to stop, which they did, falling back in confusion and shock at seeing their own chief strike down an Indian. They became silent as Tecumseh thrust his club back into his belt and addressed them scathingly.

"Did we not direct in council that prisoners at our mercy were not to be slain? Did we not acknowledge that such cruelty was the act of frightened men? Where is your bravery now? What has become of my warriors?"

He paused and his glance fell on General Proctor, who had been watching with pleasure the slaughter of these Americans. The Shawnee chief pointed a finger accusingly at him.

"Why have you allowed this massacre?" he demanded.

"Sir," replied Proctor, "your Indians cannot be commanded."

Tecumseh's lip curled contemptuously. "Begone!" he said. "You are unfit to command. Go and put on petticoats!"

The two men stared at one another with naked malice for a full minute before Proctor turned and walked away without a word. Tecumseh placed the remaining live prisoners under guard of four warriors, warning them that if any more were killed or abused, all four would be executed. He then ordered the others to mount up and follow him back to where brave men, not cowards, were needed.

More prisoners were brought in at intervals for the next few hours. Throughout a wide area surrounding Fort Meigs, individual Americans or small groups of them who had become separated from their detachments were endeavoring to regain the safety of the fort. Two of these were Sergeant John Wilson and Sergeant Simon Kenton, Jr. leading a platoon of fifteen men. Abruptly surprised by forty Indians, all but three privates and the two sergeants were killed in a single volley. Two of the privates raced off in one direction and the other private and two sergeants in another.

As the latter trio neared the river and were momentarily out of sight of the Indians, the private ran up a leaning tree with the agility of a cat and crouched terrified in the branches. Kenton and Wilson leaped into the knee-deep water and began thrashing away.

"If we're taken prisoner," gasped the frontiersman's son, "remember to call me Tom Johnson. If they find out my real name, my neck's good for hemp!"

Wilson nodded, and just then the Indians broke from cover. Guns barked and little geysers of water sprang up all around them. At least five bullets struck Wilson in the back and he dropped but, amazingly, young

Simon was untouched. It was all over now and he knew it. He jerked to a stop and raised his hands, turned and waded back to the Indians, thus becoming a prisoner of war for the second time in less than a year.

The worst part of this whole day was that these nearly seven hundred deaths had all been in vain. The spikes hurriedly driven into the cannon vents were pulled out or rammed through without much trouble and the barrage continued. Throughout the daylight hours on the fifth, sixth, seventh and eighth the shelling of Fort Meigs continued.

But now Tecumseh saw that his warriors were becoming disgusted and some were beginning to leave and so he once again confronted General Proctor. Why had not the British split open the fort which he had boasted would be a quick and easy capture? Why did the general and most of his men stay hidden and leave to the Indians the unhealthy business of rushing the fort afoot in an attempt to breach the walls? Where was this great strength the British boasted of having?

Proctor made no attempt to answer. Instead, he called in his officers for orders and in the early morning light of this day — May 9 — the British and Indians raised the siege and withdrew to Fort Malden.

[*June 20, 1813 — Sunday*]

Because the United States had loudly and bitterly decried for so long the British use of Indians in their battles against the Americans, it was only with the greatest of reluctance that the federal government itself now accepted help from the Indians. William Henry Harrison, again in the interior of Ohio beating the bushes for more troops, was well aware that Indians could be a considerable asset and so had convinced the President to let him make use of them where possible. Although he had been gone from Fort Meigs for only a few weeks, leaving it in command of General Clay, word had come of a suspected second attack building up; he would have to make arrangements to return before much longer.

First, however, he held a council with the neutral chiefs of the Delawares, Shawnees and Senecas.

"It is now time," he told them with unmistakable firmness, "for all the neutral Indians to take up with one side or the other in the war being waged. General Proctor has sent a message to me in which he said he will trade his American prisoners for the Indians friendly to the United States. This looks as though General Proctor has received some hint that you are willing to take up the tomahawk against the United States.

"Your father, the President, wants no false friends. You must either prove your friendship by moving far into the interior or else by joining me in the war."

The chiefs held a muttered conversation and then Tarhe — the Crane — principal chief of the Wyandots, said, "We have been waiting many moons for an invitation to fight for the Americans. I speak on behalf of all the tribes present when I profess our friendship. We have agreed, without any dissension, to join you."

Harrison was pleased. "I will let you know when you are wanted. But you must conform to our mode of warfare. You are not to kill defenseless prisoners, old men, women or children." When the Indians nodded, he continued: "General Proctor, I have been told, has promised to deliver me into the hands of Tecumseh if I am captured. Now, if I can succeed in taking Proctor, you shall have him for your prisoner, provided you will agree to treat him as a squaw and only put petticoats on him, for he must be a coward who would kill a defenseless prisoner."

[*July 28, 1813 — Wednesday*]

One thing was now certain about General Henry A. Proctor: he was not a fighter. Whenever possible he would send Indians to do his fighting for him while he stayed far to the rear. For this he earned the overt scorn of Tecumseh.

The second siege of Fort Meigs — if siege it could be called — began on July 20. For several weeks prior to this, growing concentrations of Indians had been seen in the vicinity of the fort. General Clay, with no intention of leaving protective cover for them to hide behind within rifle range, sent out work parties to clear off the trees and burn the trunks which had been left on the ground earlier. Several skirmishes resulted while this was being done and a handful of men were killed.

But on July 20, English and Indians came back in force — five thousand of them. The Redcoats camped at Fort Miami and the Indians stayed out of range to the south of the American fort. During the night Clay sent an express to Harrison, who was now at Fort Stephenson in Lower Sandusky.[2]

On July 23, Tecumseh led eight hundred mounted Indians up the Maumee River and it was assumed that he meant to attack Fort Winchester. Two days later, the British moved to the Fort Meigs side of the river and camped behind a point of woods. From this General Clay suspected they meant to storm the fort again, but once more nothing happened. It was perplexing.

When Clay's express reached Harrison, the comander in chief felt that Tecumseh's move toward Fort Winchester was a feint and that the real objective was the small and virtually untenable post at Fort Stephenson. Its only real defense, other than the rifles of the troops, was a six-pounder cannon. In discussing this matter with Major George Croghan, the sharp young commander of the fort, Harrison told him, "Should the British troops approach you in force with cannon and you can discover them in time to effect a retreat, you will do so immediately, destroying all the public stores.

"You must," he added soberly, "be aware that the attempt to retreat in the face of an enemy force would be in vain. Against such an enemy your garrison would be safe, however great the numbers."

Still uncertain which of the forts would be struck — Meigs, Stephenson or Winchester — Harrison left this little post and headquartered himself at Fort Seneca, eleven miles upstream on the Sandusky River from Fort Stephenson.[3] From this point he could move with alacrity to the relief of whichever fort was attacked. He also sent a message to Clay telling him that he was informing the Ohio governor of their situation and relief troops would not be too long in coming, though not to expect them immediately.

Because of Proctor's reluctance to engage in a strong offensive, Tecumseh now planned one of his own; a stratagem by which to decoy the American forces from Fort Meigs. On the afternoon of July 26, soldiers in the fort heard a heavy firing of rifles and Indians yelling. In the distance on the Sandusky Road could be seen a body of Indians attacking a column of men. At first the column seemed about to fall apart, but then it rallied and the Indians gave way. Gradually the fight moved toward the fort and inside Fort Meigs the soldiers became extremely excited and set up a cry, eager to go out and help their comrades. But General Clay would not permit it. The dispatch received from Harrison expressly stated that no relief would come immediately and he suspected a ruse. He ordered the cannons fired a few times on the combatants and, when this was done, all of them quickly disappeared — together.

On July 28 the siege was again lifted. The British sailed back down the Maumee River and the Indians set out to the east on foot. Clay suspected they were on their way to attack Fort Stephenson.

[*August 3, 1813 — Tuesday*]

Although he was yet only twenty-one years old, Major George Croghan was well deserving of his rank. Intelligent, sensible, alert, he was a good leader of men and a courageous individual. He was also the nephew of General George Rogers Clark and noted for his ability to "use his head" in times of trouble. This was a good thing, for he never had more trouble to face than right now.

It began when General Clay's message reached Harrison, confirming the commander in chief's suspicion that Fort Stephenson would be the next post attacked. He called a meeting of his officers, who were unanimous in their opinion that the little fort must inevitably fall if attacked and, as it was a relatively unimportant post whose loss would not matter greatly, that the garrison should not be reinforced but withdrawn and the place destroyed.

General Harrison dispatched a message to Croghan, ordering him to abandon and fire the fort, then come upstream to join him at Fort Seneca at once. But the messenger somehow got lost and it was fully twenty-four hours before he found his way to Fort Stephenson. By then there were already a number of Indians hovering about and, remembering Harrison's previous comment to him to hold the fort if the Indians came by land, Croghan discussed the matter with his officers. The consensus was that it would be a risky business to leave and that the fort could be maintained against the enemy at least until further orders could be received from Harrison. Croghan thereupon sent back this message:

Sir, I have just received yours of yesterday, 10 o'clock P.M., ordering me to destroy this place and make good my retreat, which was received too late to be carried into execution. We have determined to maintain this place, and by heavens we can.

In writing this strong and improprietous note, Croghan had a view to the probability of it falling into enemy hands. But it got through, and when Harrison received it — not fully understanding the circumstances and motives under which it had been written — he became livid with rage. Within minutes he had an order prepared which removed Croghan from his command. He sent it to the officer in the morning with Colonel Wells, escorted by Colonel Ball and his corps of dragoons.

July 30, 1813

SIR — The general has just received your letter of this date, informing him that you had thought proper to disobey the order issued from this office, and delivered to you this morning. It appears that the information which dictated the order was incorrect; and as you did not receive it in the night, as was expected, it might have been proper that you should have reported the circumstance and your situation, before you proceeded to its execution. This might have been passed over; but I am directed to say to you that an officer who presumes to aver that he has made his resolution, and that he will act in direct opposition to the orders of his general, can no longer be entrusted with a separate command. Colonel Wells is sent to relieve you. You will deliver the command to him and repair with Colonel Ball's squadron to this place.

By command &t
A. H. HOLMES
Assistant Adjutant General

Dismayed at the manner in which General Harrison had taken the intent of his letter, Croghan turned command over to Wells and immediately returned with the squadron to headquarters. It took some explaining, but at last Harrison realized that the young officer had acted not out of deliberate disobedience but in the best interests of his men. He treated the major cordially and returned his command to him in the morning.

Croghan's first move upon returning was to send out a party to reconnoiter. Toward evening it discovered the approach of British by water. They watched from concealment throughout the night and returned to the fort about noon the next day. A few hours later the whole force of five hundred Redcoat regulars and twenty-eight hundred warriors approached the tiny fort defended by a hundred and sixty men. Tecumseh's remaining force of two thousand Indians was still hovering near Fort Meigs.

As usual, the Indians were first to show themselves over the hill at Fort Stephenson. They were greeted by a blast from the six-pounder and immediately scrambled back out of sight. Half an hour later the first British gunboat hove into view and a great horde of Indians appeared from all directions.

The puny six-pounder spat a few cannonballs at the ship and was answered by the more powerful artillery on the vessel. Anchorage was made a mile below the fort and the British disembarked with one field piece, a five-and-a-half-inch howitzer.

Two men approached from the British force carrying a flag of truce. One was the same Major Chambers who had demanded the surrender of Fort Meigs from Harrison. The other was the British Indian agent, Ralph Dickson. They were met by Major Croghan's spokesman, Ensign Shipp of the Seventeenth Regiment. The usual introduction ceremonies were observed and then Major Chambers got down to business.

"I am instructed, sir, by General Proctor, to demand the surrender of this fort. The general is most anxious to spare the effusion of human blood, which he cannot do should he be under the necessity of reducing it, by the powerful force of artillery, regulars and Indians under his command."

"And I, sir," Ensign Shipp replied levelly, "am instructed to advise you that the commandant and garrison of this fort are determined to defend it to the last extremity. No force, sir, however great, can induce us to surrender. You may advise your commander that we are resolved to maintain our posts or to bury ourselves in its ruins."

"Oh, don't be stupid!" Dickson put in sharply. "There is an immense body of Indians here and if we succeed in taking your fort — they will not be able to be restrained from murdering the whole garrison."

When the ensign made no comment, Dickson struck his fist into his palm angrily. "Sir, for God's sake, surrender and prevent the dreadful massacre that will be caused by your resistance."

"Mr. Dickson," Ensign Shipp's voice shook just the faintest bit, "when — *and if* — the fort is taken, there will be none to massacre. It will not be given up while a man is able to resist."

At this moment a Potawatomi who had crept up in a nearby ravine, raced up behind Shipp and attempted to wrest away the sword at the officer's side. At once Dickson shoved the Indian aside and sharply ordered him to behave himself.

Seeing that there was no further use in discussion, the ensign shook hands with Dickson, saluted Major Chambers and walked briskly back to the fort. He was under no illusion that the Potawatomi attack was anything but an elaborate scare scene planned well in advance.

Within a quarter hour the British opened fire with the howitzer on shore and a larger artillery piece still aboard the ship, but although the firing continued at intervals all night, it had little effect. With his ammunition scarce, Croghan fired his six-pounder only occasionally, each time from a different location so that it would appear he had a number of cannons.

Since the British fire was concentrated on the northwest angle of the fort, Croghan was sure that this was where they meant to storm his works. He had the cannon moved secretly to a blockhouse where it could command this angle. Then he masked the embrasure so it would not be apparent from outside except through close-up scrutiny, and finally loaded the gun.

Shortly after dawn the British opened up with the howitzer and three six-pounders they had planted in the woods during the night. In the afternoon they again concentrated their shots on the northwest angle. This made Croghan even more positive the attack would be made here and he had the whole interior strengthened at this point with bags of sand and flour.

By now the smoke of firing lay so heavily around them that they could see little. Eyes watered constantly from the acrid air. Several minor rushes were made at the southern angle of the fort but Croghan shook his head, certain these moves were feints. He maintained his troops at the northwest angle.

And then, quite suddenly, breaking through the shroud of smoke within twenty paces of this point, came three hundred fifty men in a body. Croghan at once gave the word for rifle fire and a heavy fusillade of shots threw the attackers into confusion. They fell back a considerable distance. These troops were led by Colonel Short, a good fighter who quickly rallied his men, re-formed them and led a second attack at once. The barrage of rifle fire from the fort was even worse this time and Colonel Short directed his men to take cover in the ditch nearby, just as Croghan had suspected he might. This ditch lay directly down the line of fire from the cannon. When the ditch was full, Croghan opened the masked embrasure and one blast of grape shot wrought such havoc that few escaped. The assault turned into a rout. Colonel Short was dead, as were no less than a hundred fifty of his men, and most of the others were wounded. Inside the garrison, one man had been killed and seven were wounded.

Night fell soon after the attack and the wounded in the ditch could not be fully relieved by either side. Most of those who could walk, crawl or squirm returned to the English lines. Croghan lowered buckets of water over the walls to the wounded who remained. He even had a ditch opened under the palisades and a few of the wounded managed to squirm inside to receive treatment and be taken prisoner. During the night the Indians crept in to reclaim their dead, making an accurate estimate of their losses impossible, though it was expected to be in excess of a hundred.

And then, amazingly, Proctor's fears overwhelmed him and he ordered a full retreat shortly before dawn. A small boat was left behind, containing some clothing and stores and seventy stands of arms. Pistols were scattered all over the ground outside the fort's walls and these were retrieved when it was determined that the enemy had really gone.

Proctor retreated so precipitously because, he said, he expected an attack from Harrison's force; but Harrison had not marched to Fort Stephenson's relief because he had learned from spies that only light artillery was being used. As soon as he heard of the retreat, however, he arrived on the scene with a company of dragoons.

Deciding against pursuit, lest Tecumseh should take this moment to attack Fort Meigs or the column of Ohio reinforcements Harrison was expecting, the general nevertheless sent a small party of Wyandots after them. The Indians succeeded in surprising and capturing a few of the English soldiers and brought them back. The Wyandots strutted about proudly, apparently considering themselves deserving of extraordinary commendation for having abstained from cruelty. They were often seen telling the story to other warriors and laughing uproariously over the terror of their captives, who had expected nothing better than death at the stake.

In his official report of the attack on Fort Stephenson, General Harrison wrote: *It will not be among the least of General Proctor's mortifications that he has been baffled by a youth, who had just passed his twenty-first year. He is, however, a hero worthy of his gallant uncle, Gen. George R. Clarke.*

Immediately upon hearing the news, President James Madison bestowed upon this remarkable young soldier the brevet rank of lieutenant colonel and Congress authorized the presentation of a gold medal for extraordinary valor.

After the defeats of Fort Mackinac, Detroit and Raisin River and the siege at Fort Meigs with its numerous American deaths, this wonderful little victory at Fort Stephenson was the stimulus the whole country needed to go on to bigger and better things.

[*August 8, 1813 — Sunday*]

The Indian cause was irrevocably lost.

With the certainty with which he had known of the coming of the eclipse, the comet, the earthquake and other matters, Tecumseh now knew that the Indians could do nothing to regain what they had lost, nor even to retain what they still had. The knowledge had come to him unmistakably as he journeyed with several thousand of his followers around the western end of Lake Erie to meet again with General Proctor in Fort Malden, where the British officer had sailed immediately following the humiliating debacle at Fort Stephenson.

But though he knew this, Tecumseh was not sure whether or not it would be a good thing to tell his followers. Which was better, to sit back and cede defeat with the certain knowledge victory could not come, or to continue fighting when there was only one possible end for it? In one case lands would be lost, along with homes and goods — and self-respect. In the other, lands and homes and personal goods would be lost — along with life itself. Which was better, death with honor or life without? And even if he made his own choice, did he have the right to speak for all Indians in such a great matter? It was a problem to consider deeply and at length.

First, however, there were other things to attend to. Among the many traders he had known, Tecumseh had liked best the little Frenchman of Detroit, Edouard Le Croix. Here was a man of honesty and integrity in all matters, a man to whose tongue a lie was an abomination and whose heart was good and pure. A man whose friendship was unwavering.

Whispers had come to Tecumseh that he was gone; arrested by General Proctor and put aboard a ship lying at anchor off the fort, which would soon take him to Montreal for imprisonment. His crime, it was said, was speaking the truth. Proctor had been keeping from the Indians the fact that elsewhere, besides here in the Northwest Territory, the British were losing ground to the Americans. It was this information that Le Croix had spoken of to some chiefs, and which he intended to tell his friend Tecumseh. Yet, these were only whispers; there might be no truth in them.

Upon arriving at Fort Malden, therefore, Tecumseh went immediately to Proctor. The fat, red-faced general smiled as the Indian chief entered, but it was a lip-smile only; his eyes were cold and wary. Tecumseh spoke first.

"What do you know of my friend Le Croix?"

The Shawnee saw the lie forming on the general's lips even before it was spoken and he raised his hand in a sharp, halting gesture. "Before you answer, General, consider this: if I ever detect you in a falsehood, I, with my Indians, will immediately abandon you."

Proctor paused, then shrugged and admitted he was holding Le Croix prisoner. He was startled at the murderous flicker that sparked in the Indian's eyes.

"I tell you now, General, set that man free."

Again the officer paused. Abruptly he sighed, dipped his goose quill into the ink pot and scrawled an order for the release of the prisoner, adding:

The King of the Woods demands it and it must be done. He wrote the words with the intent of sarcasm, but he knew they were true.

He said nothing to Tecumseh about the defeat at Fort Stephenson, nor did Tecumseh comment on it, but the contempt that flowed from the Indian's eyes to enshroud the British commander could almost be felt. Without another word, Tecumseh turned his back and left the room.

Two days after this encounter, Tecumseh assembled a large council of the chiefs and warriors who had been fighting under his command.

"When we took up the tomahawk and joined our father, the King, we were promised plenty of white men to fight with us," he told them, "but the number is not now greater than at the commencement of the war. We are treated by them like the dogs of snipe hunters; we are always sent ahead to start the game. It is better that we should return to our own country and let the Americans come on and fight the British."

By far the greater majority of Indians present murmured assent and nodded their heads, but then there arose the chiefs of the Sioux and Chippewa factions. They spoke earnestly and at length, and what they said was essentially the same: that Tecumseh had induced them to join in the war and it was he who had been first to unite with the British; therefore, he ought not to leave them now.

Tecumseh stood immediately and told them that this was true, and that he had no right to leave as long as an Indian still fought for the British. He would remain.

But though many of his followers stayed with him here at Fort Malden, an even greater number slipped away in the night and returned to their homes and their people and their lands. And Tecumseh was glad they had gone.

[*August 19, 1813 — Thursday*]

"Shelby's comin' through!"

That was the word which swept across the country around Urbana and folks from as far as fifty miles away came riding in to the Champaign County seat to see their old comrade-in-arms from Kentucky days. Isaac Shelby — frontiersman, settler, officer of the Revolution, first governor of Kentucky and now general in the War of 1812. For many of the Ohio settlers, it was the first time they'd seen him in a dozen years or more.

The general had brought with him an army of Kentucky volunteers and there was scarcely a man in the Ohio country who didn't have an old friend or partner or relative among those troops. None knew more nor had more joyful reunions than Simon Kenton. Tears welled in the frontiersman's eyes and a huge lump formed in his throat and the heart within him felt fit to burst with nostalgia and pleasure.

General Shelby wrung the frontiersman's hand in a grasp which spoke more than any mere words could, and when he asked Simon if he would come along to whip the British and Indians again — "just like old times" — a glow came to Simon's cheeks and a gleam to his eye that had been missing for many a year.

Would Simon come along, Shelby continued, not as an enlisted man nor even as an officer; would he come along as a respected counselor, as a treasured adviser, as a beloved friend, to amble from company to company, to mess with old friends, to ride again into who knew what?

Aye, Simon would come along.

Then came the objections from the family: he still limped on his bad leg; he could no longer stand the rigors; and after all, he was fifty-eight years old, not thirty. To silence them, Simon gave them the impression he would not go, and they breathed a collective sigh of relief. When at last the company marched out of Urbana to the north, all the Kentons thought the matter was fully resolved — as indeed it was.

A few hours later the frontiersman saddled his horse, flung a blanket and a sack of corn across it and rode casually away, presumably to the mill. A few miles out of town he met a neighbor and asked him to relay word to his family that he was on his way "to Proctor's Mill."

Simon Kenton had a lot of reasons for going on this campaign. To see and be with old friends, yes; to see again the old sites far to the north, yes; to help in some small way to bring the enemy to its knees, yes. But there was another reason, at least as powerful as any of the others. A soldier who had been with his son had stopped by and told the family he had seen Simon Kenton, Jr., captured by the Indians. Whether or not he was still alive, he did not know.

Simon Kenton, Sr., aimed to find out.

[*September 5, 1813 — Sunday*]

It would be the first time in many years that Beaver had seen William Henry Harrison. Not once in those years since his father had been executed for witchcraft and Harrison had taken him away to Vincennes had he forgotten the debt he owed this great white chief. The governor had become a second father to him and it was a sad parting when time came for him to return to his own people and take up the life of a Delaware Indian again.

Now, with his tribesmen, he headed for Fort Seneca on the Sandusky River to offer his second father the strength of the Delaware arm in the struggle ahead. They had not yet reached Fort McArthur when a young Shawnee joined them.[4] No one seemed to remember what his name had been long ago, for when his idolized chief, Blue Jacket, died of a fever, he had adopted the same name and been called by it ever since, though it was obvious that he would never measure up to what that name had once meant in Ohio.

Because Beaver was easily one of the most promising warriors in the Delaware nation, the young Blue Jacket talked with him at length as they marched — far more than was prudent. When Beaver learned the reason this Shawnee had joined with them, he had difficulty controlling his facial expression. Blue Jacket intended to profess friendship for Harrison and the desire to help him. Then, when the time came that he could approach the great white general without his motives being suspect, he would draw out his tomahawk and assassinate the great man.

Conflicting loyalties tore at Beaver throughout the rest of the day. That night, as they sat around the fire, a sense of peace flooded over him as he made his decision. He stood up and placed himself before the young Blue Jacket, who sat nearby on a log. His expression was more sad than angry as he looked down at the would-be assassin.

"You would murder our father, the American chief," he said, "and bring disgrace and mischief upon us all. You shall not do it. I will serve you as I would a mad dog."

With these words the hand that he had been holding behind him raised high and, even as the light of comprehension flashed in young Blue Jacket's eyes and he scrambled to get out of the way, he was too late. The blade of the tomahawk caught him high on the forehead and split his skull to the bridge of his nose.

There would be no assassination of General William Henry Harrison.

[*September 10, 1813 — Friday*]

In the early sunlight of this crisp, clear day, the six British ships that had been lying at anchor off Amhurstburg and Fort Malden prepared to leave. Under the orders of the one-armed captain, Commodore R. H. Barclay, they weighed anchor, unfurled their sails and moved into formation for the short trip across Lake Erie to the islands.[5] The sleek little seventy-ton schooner *Chippewa* led the pack, followed by the rebuilt four-hundred-ninety-ton ship *Detroit*, the hundred-eighty-ton brig *General Hunter*, the four-hundred-ton ship *Queen Charlotte*, the two-hundred-thirty-ton schooner *Lady Prevost* and the ninety-ton sloop *Little Belt*. They made a colorful spectacle, with the vessels all freshly painted in orange and black, and acres of white sail bellying out in the gentle breeze. All battle flags were raised.

Commodore Oliver Hazard Perry was ready for them. Sick and flushed with the fever that had dogged him for months, he was equally afire with anticipation for this crucial contest to begin. In the final conference with his officers last night, he had impressed upon them the importance of keeping the United States fleet in close formation and pressing for action so that the short-range guns could be used with effectiveness. Then, with a flair befitting his nature, he exhibited a new blue flag upon which white muslin letters had been sewn to quote the dying Lawrence in Boston harbor: DON'T GIVE UP THE SHIP.

"When this flag shall be hoisted to the main royal masthead," he told them, "it shall be your signal for going into action."

And now that time had come. Quickly he formed his line and stood down on Captain Barclay's advancing fleet, ran up the blue signal flag and heard the cheers of his men.

The breeze was too light, the maneuvers too slow. Not until fifteen minutes before noon did the vessels close to firing range near Middle Sister Island. With her long guns, fearsome in their brutal power, the *Detroit* fired first. In five minutes she connected with a cannonball that blasted through the side of Perry's flagship *Lawrence*; the slaughter had commenced.

It was another five minutes before Perry's ship could come within range of the first of the British vessels, and ten minutes more before her cannons could reach the *Detroit*. All during this time the British shots were ripping her to shreds. By 2:30 P.M. eighty-three out of her one hundred three men were killed or wounded and every brace and bowline shot away, every gun rendered useless.

Behind the *Lawrence*, one of the *Scorpion*'s two guns had blown down the hatch, killing several of the crew and, even worse, one of the guns aboard the *Ariel* had exploded with more disastrous effects. At this moment the battle seemed lost to Perry.

But, heaving to, he made a dramatic dash through a gauntlet of shot to the *Niagara* and transferred to her. In five minutes he was pressing her toward Barclay's line. The one-armed Barclay was severely wounded and his *Detroit* a wreck. And now it was Perry who delivered a devastating broadside fire with the big guns while his crew raked the decks with pistol and rifle shot. Ten minutes later — at 2:50 P.M. — the British fleet could stand no more; every commanding officer and his second had either been killed or so severely wounded as to be unable to stay on the deck. Barclay lowered his flags and the guns ceased firing. Perry received the surrender on the bloody, littered deck of the *Lawrence*.

A little while later he scribbled a note to General William Henry Harrison on the back of an envelope:

DEAR GENERAL: *We have met the enemy and they are ours — two ships, two brigs, one schooner and a sloop.*

> *Yours, with great respect and esteem,*
> OLIVER HAZZARD PERRY

[*September 18, 1813 — Saturday*]

From the shoreline at Fort Malden, Tecumseh and his Indians had been most interested in the distant thunder of battle between the two fleets. It was not possible to tell who was winning, but the booming of the cannons rolled over the water to them for nearly three hours and at times great clouds of smoke hid the whole fleet.

When the silence had come at last, and it became apparent that the British ships were not returning to the Amhurstburg port adjacent to the fort, the Shawnee chief became suspicious that perhaps things had not gone well — despite General Proctor's loud claim that no navy on earth could stand up to the British fleet.

Three days later, when still no ships had come, Tecumseh confronted Proctor. As usual, the bewhiskered general was extremely edgy in the presence of this difficult Indian ally. Imperious and willful, it was natural for Tecumseh to rule, not to submit. His straightforward manner and directness of speech always unnerved Proctor and never failed to make him feel less sure of himself. Indeed, although he would never admit it to the chief, he knew that Tecumseh was superior to him in almost every way and that, by rights, he should be subordinate to Tecumseh. Because of this, Proctor feared the Shawnee's outspoken disapproval and dealt with him through a cringing and maneuvering policy which was not only transparent to Tecumseh, but roused his indignation and dislike for the British officer even more.

In answer to Tecumseh's query, General Proctor now made a show of being busy and his comment was brief:

"My fleet has whipped the Americans," he said, "but the vessels have been heavily damaged. They have gone into Put-In-Bay in the islands to refit themselves. They will be back here in a few days."

But the belief that the battle had been lost was strong in Tecumseh and he demanded to know why, if what the general said was true, the garrison here at Fort Malden was beginning to pack up its gear. Proctor told him this was merely a precautionary measure and that he was preparing to send his valuables and papers up the Thames River.

Tecumseh was not convinced and demanded that the general meet him and all his Indians in council. Not daring to refuse, lest the chief become even more suspicious about the battle on the lake and thus desert him, Proctor grudgingly agreed.

So now they were assembled and if, in those first few days after the naval battle, there had been some doubt about what Proctor's intentions were, there was little remaining now; it was quite obvious that he was preparing a full-scale retreat.

Tecumseh stood in the space between Proctor and his officers and the large assemblage of Indians seated on the ground. He held up his hands and the murmur of small conversations ceased as those gathered here waited expectantly.

"Father, listen to your children," Tecumseh began, "you have them all before you."

He was addressing his remarks directly to General Proctor, but his voice carried clearly to all who were present. One of Proctor's aides sat at a small desk nearby and swiftly wrote down Tecumseh's speech as he gave it. Having suspected what Tecumseh was going to say, the general wanted to have a written copy of the speech to preserve so that later he could show his superiors and his colleagues "the insolence to which I was forced to submit in order to prevent that chieftain's withdrawing from the struggle."

Tecumseh continued: "The war before this, our British father gave the hatchet to his red children when our old chiefs were alive. They are now dead. In that war our father was thrown on his back by the Americans, and our father took them by the hand without our knowledge. And we are afraid that our father will do so again this time.

"Summer before last, when I came forward with my red brethren and was ready to take up the hatchet in favor of our British father, we were told not to be in a hurry, that he had not yet determined to fight the Americans.

"Listen! When war was declared, our father stood up and gave us the tomahawk and told us that he was ready to strike the Americans; that he wanted our assistance; and that he would certainly get our lands back which the Americans had taken from us.

"Listen! You told us at that time to bring forward our families to this place and we did so. And you promised to take care of them and they should want for nothing while the men would go and fight the enemy; that we need not trouble ourselves about the enemy's garrisons, that we knew nothing about them and that our father would attend to that part of the business.

"You also told your red children that you would take good care of your garrison here, which made our hearts glad. Listen! When we were last at the Rapids it is true we gave you little assistance. It is hard to fight people who live like groundhogs.[6]

"Father, listen! Our fleet has gone out. We know they have fought. We have heard the great guns. But we know nothing of what has happened to our father with one arm."

The tone of the chief's voice became rather sarcastic now and he locked his eyes on those of the British commander. "Our ships have gone one way and we are very much astonished to see our father tying up everything and preparing to run the other without letting his red children know what his intentions are.

"You always told us to remain here and take care of our lands. It made our hearts glad to hear that was your wish. Our great father, the King, is the head, and you represent him." And now the sarcasm deepened and the words Tecumseh spoke were heavy with contempt and insult. In his eyes, Proctor was guilty of one of the worst possible crimes — cowardice.

"You always told us you would never draw your foot off British ground but now, Father, we see that you are drawing back and we are sorry to see our father doing so without seeing the enemy. We must compare our father's conduct to a fat dog that carries its tail on its back but, when affrighted, drops it between its legs and runs off.

"Father, listen! The Americans have not yet defeated us by land. Neither are we sure that they have done so by water. We therefore wish to remain here and fight our enemy should they make their appearance. If they defeat us, we will then retreat with our father.

"At the Battle of the Rapids last war, the Americans certainly defeated us.[7] And when we returned to our father's fort at that place, the gates were shut against us.[8] We were afraid that it would now be the case but, instead of that, we now see our British father preparing to march out of his garrison."

The words of Tecumseh now became an entreaty: "Father, you have got the arms and ammunition which our great father sent to his red children. If you have an idea of going away, give them to us and you may go and welcome. For us, our lives are in the hands of the Great Spirit. We are determined to defend our lands and, if it be His will, we wish to leave our bones upon them."

As Tecumseh finished his speech he stepped back and stood with arms folded across his chest, waiting to hear the long speech of the general. Proctor, however, was extremely brief. He made no mention of the insults Tecumseh had paid him. In fact, all he said was that this movement he planned was to get them farther away from the force of the American army so that when, along the River Thames, they stopped to wage battle, it would be on grounds familiar to them and strange to the enemy and where the enemy would be weak from having traveled so far.

At this Tecumseh once again threatened to leave the English service if this was their way of fighting a war. But now, as they had done before, the Sioux and Chippewa chiefs arose and objected to leaving the British when they had given their word to fight for them. Tecumseh capitulated.

"My home," he said, "is on the battlefield and I have no fear of death. I will stand by them if you insist."

[*September 26, 1813 — Sunday*]

The Thames River of Ontario empties into the southeast corner of Lake St. Clair about twenty-five miles east of Detroit which, itself, lies at the southwestern corner of the lake. It is a substantial river which bisects the lower peninsula of Ontario between Lake Erie and Lake Huron, twisting its way upstream to the northeast for a hundred thirty miles or more. And it was up this stream that General Proctor had directed the retreat be made. They would march north from Fort Malden to opposite Detroit, then eastward along the southern shore of Lake St. Clair to the Thames.

The nearly one thousand mounted Redcoats and seventeen hundred Indians left the fort this morning and when they reached a rising ground a few miles to the north, Tecumseh pulled up and looked back and his chief aide, Chau-be-nee — the Coalburner — and Tecumseh's brother-in-law, Wasegoboah, stopped beside him.

Below and behind them the flames licked hungrily at Fort Malden and sent a billowing column of lead-colored smoke high into the air. It was a melancholy sight at best.

"My brothers," Tecumseh said softly, "I feel well assured that we shall never return."

[*October 2, 1813 — Saturday*]

General Isaac Shelby's thirty-five hundred Kentuckians joined Harrison's army of five thousand soldiers and two hundred Indians about the same time that Colonel Richard M. Johnson's mounted regiment arrived. Harrison directed the latter force to ride around the western end of the lake, cross the Detroit River and meet him at Fort Malden where they would engage the enemy. The commander and the remainder of the army would be carried across Lake Erie from the islands by the American fleet.

The maneuver went as scheduled, with the troops landing at Bar Point and moving on the fort without delay. But it came as a considerable surprise to find Fort Malden only a pile of smoldering ashes and no one there to fight. General Harrison was highly encouraged by the sight, since it indicated considerable fear on the part of the British; a frightened enemy, he knew, was more susceptible to defeat.

There was nothing salvageable at the fort, only broken guns, cannonballs, rubbish, and garbage. However, Harrison had no intention of remaining here; at once pursuit was begun in forced marches.

The army was less than five miles upstream from the mouth of the Thames when they were approached by a party of sixty Wyandots led by Chief Walk-in-Water, who was carrying a flag of truce. He was taken to Harrison.

"We have left the British and our deluded Indian brothers forever," Walk-in-Water told him. "We wish only peace hereafter with the Americans. What would you have us do?"

"It is good you have abandoned Tecumseh," Harrison replied curtly. "Now all you need do is go home and stay out of the way of the American army."

They were terms far better than the Wyandot chief had expected and he accepted them readily and hastened away to return to Ohio.

Some miles ahead of the army, Proctor and the Indians were moving along at a somewhat slower pace. Tecumseh was extremely impatient to find a suitable position to make their stand. At least half a dozen times Proctor had promised to stop at one place or another, only to change his mind when he got there. Finally, at Dalson's Farm, a place where an unfordable stream falls into the Thames, Proctor decided to give battle and Tecumseh was pleased with the location.

"It is a good place," he commented. "When I look at these two streams they remind me of the place where the Tippecanoe enters the Wabash in our home country."

But after reconsidering, Proctor's fears got the best of him and he changed his mind again and ordered the army to move on. Thoroughly disgusted now and hungering for the action long denied him, Tecumseh decided to stay here with a small party for a preliminary skirmish with the army. They hadn't long to wait. It was a brief fight and casualties were light on either side. The Indians held their ground until ten small cannons were brought up and then Tecumseh ordered a return to the British, himself having suffered a minor wound in the arm.

They moved back at top speed and found Proctor had stopped near a Delaware Moravian Indian town — the same Moravian Indians who so many years ago had fled Ohio, fearing the approach of Colonels Crawford and Williamson. It was on this spot now that Tecumseh confronted Proctor, accused him sharply of the worst kind of cowardice and told him that if he wanted the help of the Indians at all, he must stop here and now to hold battle, as the Indian forces would go no farther with him. And Proctor agreed, though very reluctantly.

The site was well situated for defense, protected on one flank by a large marsh and on the other by the river. It was a place in which to fight . . . and perhaps to die.

[*October 4, 1813 — Monday*]

In the center of the Indian encampment, off to one side from Proctor's army, Tecumseh sat before the fire, not joining in the conversation but merely smoking his pipe. Close by sat Wasegoboah, husband of his sister Tecumapese, and beside him was Chau-be-nee, his most trusted lieutenant. Although there was some excitement in the eyes and talk of many of the younger men over the impending battle, none of this was reflected in the forty-five-year-old Tecumseh.

One of the younger Indians, known by the name of Billy Caldwell, spoke eagerly to Tecumseh. "Father, what are we to do? Shall we fight the Americans?"

Tecumseh nodded slowly. "Yes, my son, on the morrow we will be in their smoke."

He was silent for a handful of minutes more, and then, as if reaching a decision he had been long considering, he stood. At once the assemblage came to respectful silence.

"My children," he said, "hear me well. Tomorrow we go into our final battle with the Americans. In this battle I will be killed."

There was an instant murmur of consternation among them, but Tecumseh silenced it and went on. "You are my friends, my people. I love you too well to see you sacrificed in an unequal contest from which no good can result. I would dissuade you from fighting this fight, encourage you to leave now, this night, for there is no victory ahead, only sorrow. Yet, time after time, even until tonight, you have made known to me that it is your desire to fight the Americans here and so I am willing to go with my people and be guided by their wishes."

He then began to remove every sign of rank which he wore: medals, bracelets, necklaces, insignia, the two-feathered headband. They watched him in silence as each item was removed until, finally, he stood before them in his simple tanned buckskins — leggins, frock shirt and moccasins. His knife he gave to Chief Roundhead. His tomahawk went to Black Hawk.

His sword he handed to Chau-be-nee and said, "When my son Pugesha-shenwa becomes a noted warrior and able to wield a sword, give this to him."

He looked around at the others now and the sad gentleness of his face affected them deeply, for all wore mournful expressions and the eyes of many were bright with tears still unshed. All he had retained of his possessions was his favorite weapon, the war club he had carried since the early days of fighting beside his brother Chiksika. He told them that he was now divested of all rank and ornamentation which might identify him as Tecumseh. Then he took the ramrod from his rifle lying nearby and handed it to Wasegoboah.

"When you see me fall," he instructed, "fight your way to my side and strike my body four times with this rod. If you will do so, I will then arise and, with my life renewed and charmed against further harm, will lead you to victory. But should I fall and this cannot be done, then retreat at once, for further fighting will be useless."

With a sense of awe, Wasegoboah accepted the ramrod and promised that he would stay close to his chief and that when Tecumseh should fall, he would come to his side at once and strike the four blows as directed.

Not one of the Indians present had any doubt that if Tecumseh did fall and his body was struck with the rod, he would arise as he had indicated. They had long ago learned to accept the mysterious predictions from their chief without question. After all, had they not always come true?

[October 5, 1813 — Tuesday]

With the first light of the dawning, General Harrison moved his army to engage the enemy. The British and Indians, according to the spies, had set up their battle lines on the opposite side of the river on higher solid ground between a marsh and the stream.[9]

The army crossed the river at the first ford and in a rather singular style, each mounted man carrying behind him an infantry soldier. It was near noon when they came within sight of General Proctor's battle lines. General Harrison conferred with Colonel Johnson and drew up the plan of battle, determining to try to break through the British at the onset with a smashing charge of the mounted regiment.

When Johnson formed his men in accordance with the general's wishes, he saw that there would not be room for more than the first battalion of his regiment to attack between river and marsh. He therefore decided to take the second battalion under his own lead and attack the Indians, who were in battle position on the other side of the marsh.

The United States Army advanced until the first mounted battalion, led by Colonel Johnson's brother, was fired upon from a distance. This started the horses and produced some confusion, giving the English time to reload and deliver a second volley. But the mounted men, now fully in motion, charged. They broke through the English lines with ease and almost before it was begun, the British surrendered and the battle at this point was over.

With the Indians it was another matter. The mounted battalion came bravely on but, in accordance with Tecumseh's preliminary instructions, the Indians held fire until the flints in the American guns could be seen. Then Tecumseh sprang forward, the blood-chilling Shawnee war whoop bursting from his lips. A thousand Indian guns fired almost as one from a thousand different hiding places and nearly the entire advance line of Johnson's men was cut down in its tracks.

Johnson himself came charging up with a sword in one hand and his pistol in another. An Indian dressed in simple buckskin ran toward him with nothing but a warclub in his hand and sprang up in an attempt to knock the officer from his horse with a killing blow. Johnson had only time to thrust his handgun forward and jerk the trigger as the barrel of the gun connected with the Indian's chest. The blast was muffled and the Indian slumped to the ground, dead. Johnson spurred on.

Another warrior, brandishing the ramrod of a rifle, ran toward his fallen companion through the thick grass at the edge of the marsh and the bullets from three different guns cut him down in midstride.

And suddenly, as if they had melted into the ground, the Indians were gone. Here and there was a fleeting glimpse of one or another, and then none. It was incredible. For some time the soldiers, both afoot and on horseback, milled about confusedly, looking for someone to fight. Could it be that this long-anticipated battle was over in five minutes? Unbelievable!

Unbelievable, perhaps, but nonetheless true.

Not concerned with the "cowardly Indians" who had turned tail and run, General Harrison became deeply involved with seeing to the British. Only once did he reflect a moment and then look up to ask his aide, "Is Tecumseh dead?"

The aide departed to wander through the field of dead Indians, but he had no idea what Tecumseh looked like and neither, it seemed, did anyone else. But word was passed around that there was one man here who knew Tecumseh very well and could identify him — the old frontiersman, Simon Kenton.

A runner was sent to fetch him and a number of the Kentucky militia began whetting their knives to get "souvenirs" from the body when it should be pointed out to them. Within the hour Simon Kenton appeared and began walking among the many bodies. Some three hundred Indians had been killed and it was necessary to stop at each one, turn him over if necessary and study the face beneath the paint. Although it was years since Simon had seen Tecumseh, he was sure he would recognize him.

And he did.

His eyes widened slightly when he turned the body over. He hadn't expected it to be Tecumseh, for there was nothing about it to indicate that it was any more than an ordinary warrior without rank. But there he was, his buckskin blouse clotted with a great smear of blood from the bullethole in his chest.

The frontiersman's face was expressionless and he moved a short distance away to another body, which he also recognized. This was Roundhead, who had fallen with a fatal bullet wound in the temple and lay on his back almost as if sleeping. Fine silver armbands encircled his upper arms and a necklace of bear claws and silver beads was around his neck. Beautiful beadwork fringed his garb and his whole appearance made it clear to the most impartial viewer that this was most definitely a chief.

"Ah," Simon muttered, squatting beside the body and staring closely at the face. He nodded confidently and then stood up and the soldiers crowded around him eagerly.

"Is it him?" someone yelled, and another voice said, "That *is* Tecumseh, ain't it, Simon?"

The frontiersman stepped back a little and pursed his lips. "Been years since I've seen him and there's a great deal of change in appearance between a live man and a dead man," he said, but then he nodded again and added, "Yes, that's Tecumseh."

There was a babble of voices: "So *that's* Tecumseh! . . . By God, we got the Devil hisself at last . . . He's a good Injen now, ain't he boys? . . . I claim that necklace . . . Me the bracelets! . . . I want them there beaded moccasins . . ."

In moments the body was stripped of every particle of clothing or ornamentation, but they did not stop there. Now the knives came out and they went to work with a vengeance. The scalp was first to go, then strips of flesh four or five inches wide were cut off from neck to legs, both from chest and back, in order to make razor strops from them. One man cut off the large humps of skin covering the buttocks, to make a bag out of them. Another slit the face and took the cheek skin to make a little change purse and still others cut long strips from the legs to use in making belts.

Kenton watched them, his eyes bleak, more than ever glad that he had pointed out the wrong body. No man deserved such degradation and certainly not as great a warrior, as great a man, as the powerful Chief Tecumseh.

Disgusted by the wreck of the body of Roundhead, he turned and walked back to where Tecumseh lay. Very gently he turned him back over into the position in which he had fallen. He straightened, glanced over at the remains of Roundhead, and then back at Tecumseh.

"There have been cowards here," he murmured.

[*October 6, 1813 — Wednesday*]

It was almost 2:00 A.M. when the Shawnees came. They slipped from cover to cover, carefully stepping around the bodies of their fallen comrades. There was no hesitation in them, no confusion as to where to go. The spot where Tecumseh had fallen was indelibly graven on their memories, not only for tonight, but forevermore.

They found him there, lying stiff and cold in the position in which he had fallen and they lifted him gently and carried him back to where the horses had been left. One of the men mounted his horse and the other two raised the body of their chief and he took it from them, cradling it in his arms.

They rode a long way, to the edge of a sweet clear creek, and a sadness almost too great to be borne rode with them. On a high bank beneath the branches of a fine young tree with a long life ahead of it, they dug his grave and laid him tenderly in it.

And when they were finished, they raised their voices in the lonesome, longing notes of the death chant.[10]

Among the Shawnees there are many traditions, but none so sacred as that which was born this night:

Tecumseh will come again! In that hour of the second coming, there will be nakude-fanwi udawa *— "one town of towns." It will mark the end of strife, wars and contentions among all Indian tribes. Then the celebration will consummate all that the Great Spirit intends for His red children. It will begin in the spring and continue without ceasing, from tribe to tribe, until the season closes.*

The sign of this second coming will be a star appearing and passing across the sky, as it did at the time of Tecumseh's birth, and Tecumseh will again be born under the same circumstances, to lead his people to this "one town of towns" for all Indians.

Tecumseh will come again!

EPILOGUE

[*April 29, 1836 — Friday*]

SIMON KENTON was dying.

The long bony figure of the frontiersman lay quietly in the dimness of the little cabin along the headwaters of the Mad River. The years had passed swiftly, as in retrospect they always do. Yet, this last score of years had flashed by even faster, it seemed. They were years filled with a multitude of stories — some bright and cheerful, some gray and glum. Some of these stories had just begun. Many of them had ended.

The War of 1812 had been won by the Americans and, with it, the Northwest Territory. Now there was a newer, wider frontier far to the west, where an older and more stable government would deal with other Indians — no more wisely, perhaps, and no less harshly, but certainly much more summarily.

It was a safe world east of the Mississippi now, where the worst enemy a man had to face was his own kind. The fiercely proud Indians were gone, except for pitiful little reservations of them, and names such as Shawnee and Chippewa, Wyandot and Delaware, Ottawa and Seneca and Huron were the names of places rather than people.

Yes, some of the stories had only begun and others had ended:

. . . Simon Kenton, Jr., had returned unharmed from his captivity and Simon Ruth Kenton from his privateering . . . the frontiersman's last child, Ruth Jane, was born in his sixty-first year, 1816, and his first child, Nancy, died the following year . . . two of his oldest friends, Simon Girty and George Rogers Clark, had died in 1818 . . . the same year Simon, Jr., had wed . . .

. . . and there were others whose stories had ended . . . old Daniel Boone had breathed his last on his Missouri farm in 1820, and two years later Rachel Edgar was gone . . . Robert Patterson died in 1827 . . .

. . . even the seemingly indestructible Black Hoof, principal chief of the Shawnee nation, finally gave up at the age of one hundred five in 1831, and Black Snake — She-me-ne-to — had followed him into the Shawnee After-world in twenty months . . . and in the little Kansas reservation into which had been herded the once proud and free Shawnees, a bitter, lonely old Indian died, still despised by his own people — the man who had started life named Lowawĺuwaysica, lived it for a while as the Prophet, and left it in 1834 as Tenskwatawa . . . and in that same year a rugged frontiersman to the end, Cornelius Washburn was killed by an Indian on the banks of the Yellowstone River . . .

And now it was the turn of the frontiersman.

His faded blue eyes opened briefly and settled upon Elizabeth, who sat quietly beside him, waiting. A flickering ghost of a smile moved his mouth fractionally and he closed his eyes again. After several minutes his lips parted slightly and his voice strained to be heard, his whisper a faint sound in the stillness which filled the room:

"I have fought the last battle and it has been the hardest of them all."

And there, at the age of eighty-one years and twenty-six days, the frontiersman died. Few lives had ever been as eventful, few men as important to an era. And upon his headstone is engraved in eloquent simplicity:

Full of Honors, Full of Years

CHAPTER NOTES

THE sheer number of sources consulted in the preparation of *The Frontiersmen* precludes any hope of listing each one individually. A complete listing of all the books, letters, logs, official reports, records and other sources would itself require a volume. But because of the outstanding nature of one particular source and its extensive use in the research for this book, it is only fitting that it be expressly commented upon.

This source, as mentioned in the Author's Note, is the Lyman C. Draper Collection of some 500 volumes of original manuscript material, described by many historians as being unsurpassed in historical value for the period and geographical area encompassed.

Lyman Copeland Draper began his collection in 1838 and continued adding to it without interruption until his death in 1891. Deeply concerned about the alarming number of romanticized and highly fanciful narratives that were beginning to appear concerning border warfare, frontier scouts, Indians and Indian fighters and the opening of this nation from the Appalachians to the Mississippi, Dr. Draper began his lifelong search with the primary mission of preserving the facts of this time and place.

He began with an unusually extensive correspondence with the actual survivors of the border periods, but this was not enough for him and two years later he embarked upon his famous series of personal visits to such people, both Indian and white. He visited and interviewed at length not only the survivors themselves but just as frequently their friends and relatives. He took down notes literally by the pound in these travels through the areas known now as Iowa, Illinois, Indiana, Ohio, Kentucky, West Virginia, Virginia, Pennsylvania, New York, Michigan, Wisconsin, Minnesota and south-central Canada. Traveling mainly by horseback or buggy, he covered well over 60,000 miles. Besides being possessed of a great inquisitiveness and dedication to truth, he had a pronounced ability to draw people out and a remarkable knack for following leads, exposing discrepancies and establishing the accuracy of historical fact.

Sixteen years after beginning his collection, Dr. Draper became head of the Wisconsin State Historical Society and three years later he computed that his manuscript collection contained 5,000 pages of original manuscripts, diaries, notes and journals, thousands of letters and fully 10,000 pages of his own notes of the recollections of Indians and pioneers, taken down accurately from them as they spoke: such men as Daniel Boone, Tecumseh, George Rogers Clark, John Sevier, Thayendanega (Chief Joseph Brandt), Simon Kenton, William Henry Harrison, Robert Patterson, Blue Jacket, and John Cleve Symmes. Yet this calculation was made when his collection was only nineteen years old and the fruits of another thirty-four years of collecting were destined to be added to it!

At the close of his life, Dr. Draper's manuscript collection was catalogued into fifty series of material — Boone papers, Kenton papers, Clark papers, and so on — and these came to a staggering total of 486 volumes of material — material valuable beyond description to the history of this nation.

While the benefit of that collection to this book has been enormous, it must be stressed that this was only one of a great number of sources consulted, the collections of a multitude of libraries — private, municipal, county, state and federal — proving of great benefit also.

In the individual chapter notes which follow, each chapter listing begins with a brief bibliography of the principal sources for the development of that chapter, and those sources utilized for quoted dialogue, for heretofore unpublished historical facts and for material which may be considered debatable due to its divergence from previously accepted belief.

Following the bibliographical listing for each chapter are the notes, keyed directly to the text, with a new set of numbers for each chapter.

* * *

PROLOGUE

PRINCIPAL SOURCES

Drake, Benjamin, *Life of Tecumseh and His Brother, the Prophet* (Cincinnati, 1841), pp. 66, 202.
Galloway, William A., *Old Chillicothe* (Xenia, 1934), pp. 164, 181.
Harvey, Henry, *History of the Shawnee Indians from the Year 1681 to 1854 Inclusive* (Cincinnati, 1855), pp. 134–191.
Kenton, Edna, *Simon Kenton: His Life and Period, 1755–1836* (Garden City, 1930), pp. 16–17.
McClung, John A., *Sketches of Western Adventure* (Covington, 1832), pp. 95–96.
Marshall, Humphrey, *History of Kentucky* (Frankfort, 1824), pp. 214–217.
American Pioneer, I (June, 1842), 205; (Sept., 1842), 332.
Ohio Archaeological and Historical Quarterly VII (1897), 79–81; XIII (1904), 271; XV (1906), 494–496; XXVII (1918), 430.

U.S. Bureau of Ethnology Bulletin, XXX, No. 14.
Draper MSS. (unpub. collection, Archives, Wisc. State Hist. Soc., Madison): *Brant Miscellanies*, D–4–G–84; *Draper's Notes*, D–21–S–252–254; *Simon Kenton Papers*, D–1–BB–1–6; D–5–BB–99; D–6–BB–1–17; D–8–BB–152; *Thomas S. Hinde Papers*, D–2–YY–12, 120; D–11–YY–4, 8, 17.

NOTES

1. Present location of this site is the northeastern section of Fauquier County, Virginia; a county formed in 1759 when Prince William County was partitioned.
2. There has always been some degree of confusion in regard to the location of the Shawnee village Chillicothe, mainly because five different Shawnee towns went by this name in Ohio. The principal town of each Shawnee sept (or clan) was named after the sept. When such a sept moved to a new location, the town it built was known by the same name. The particular Shawnee town in question here was the fourth of five Shawnee villages to be so designated after the Chalahgawtha sept. It was located at the present site of Oldtown, Greene County, Ohio, near the junction of Massie's Creek and the Little Miami River, three miles north of the present county seat, Xenia. The other four Chillicothes were: (1) on the site of the present city of Piqua; (2) near the village of Westfall, four miles down the west bank of the Scioto River from present Circleville; (3) on the site of present Hopetown, three miles north of present Chillicothe in Ross County; and (4) on the north fork of Paint Creek ten miles northwest of present Chillicothe on the site of present Frankfort.
3. Chiksika (occasionally spelled Cheeksekah or Chiksekau) was also known by the name Pepquannahek, meaning "Gunshot."
4. Methotasa (also Methotase and Methoatase), contrary to statements by some early writers, was not a Cherokee Indian.
5. There were numerous spellings and pronunciations of the five sept names. Thawegila was also known as Sawakola, Sawokla, Sawokli, Assiwikala, Swickly and Sewickley. The Peckuwe sept was also called Piqua, Peckuwetha, Pequea, Pechoquealin, Pecquealin, Pickawillany, Pickaway. The name of the Chalahgawtha sept had the least number of variants, becoming most widely known as Chillicothe. Maykujay is also written Maquck, Mequck, Muquck, Macqueechaick, Mackachack, Mecquachake, Machachach, Macqueechek and Maykujayki. The English derivation now used in the area where the Maykujay towns were located is Mac-o-chee. Kispokotha was also Kispugo, Kispocotha, Kiskapooke, Kiskapoke and Kispugoki.
6. This spring is presently on the grounds of a state fish hatchery of the Ohio Division of Wildlife, District Six Headquarters, Xenia.
7. Variously spelled Tikomfi, Tikomfa, and Tecumtha, but the most commonly accepted form is Tecumseh.

CHAPTER I

PRINCIPAL SOURCES

Bennet, John, *Blue Jacket, War Chief of the Shawnees* (Chillicothe, 1943), pp. 28–32.
Coleman, Robert T., "Simon Kenton," *Harper's*, XXVIII (Feb., 1864), 289–304.
Galloway, William A., *Old Chillicothe* (Xenia, 1934), pp. 177–179.
Grills, William, *Journal of William Grills* (Baltimore, 1808), pp. 107–113, 135–138, 180–183, 191–209.
Howe, Henry, *Historical Collections of Ohio* (Cincinnati, 1888), II, 580.
Kenney, James, *Journals of James Kenney, 1758–1770* (Philadelphia, 1816), II, 71; III, 21–24.
Kenton, Edna, *Simon Kenton: His Life and Period, 1755–1836* (Garden City, 1930), pp. 21, 25–26, 28–30, 33.
Ruddell, Stephen, "Journal of Stephen Ruddell," unpub. narrative written in 1882 for Benjamin Drake, in Galloway Papers, Xenia Lib. Coll.

Smith, Col. James, "A Pilgrim of Ohio One Hundred Years Ago," in James W. Taylor, *History of Ohio, 1650–1787* (Sandusky, 1854), I, 580–582.

American Antiquarian Soc., *Archaeologia Americana* (Philadelphia, 1818), pp. 278–279, 287–292.

Draper MSS. (unpub. coll., Archives, Wisc. State Hist. Soc., Madison): *Simon Kenton Papers*, D–1–BB–7–9, 44–46; D–5–BB–97–125; D–10–BB–40–40[1-2].

NOTES

1. Kispoko Town was located about two miles downstream from present Circleville, Ohio, on the west bank of the Scioto River.
2. Much information on Tecumseh originates from the unpublished journal of Stephen Ruddell who, as a boy, was captured by the Shawnees, adopted into the tribe and given the name Sinnanatha, meaning "Big Fish." He was adopted into Tecumseh's family and since he was Tecumseh's age, the two became very close companions.
3. Some doubt exists that the first two names were given to the first two born of the triplets. There exists the possibility that these are merely variations of the names of Tecumseh and Lowawluwaysica and that history has never recorded what the other two were called. Sauwasekau was also known by the name of Elkskwatawa.
4. Present vicinity of Richwood, W. Va.
5. These two streams are presently known respectively as Jackson River and Back Creek.
6. The point of their contact with the Greenbrier River was in the vicinity of present Cass, W. Va.
7. The party crossed the Great Kanawha River at a ford near present Leon, W. Va.
8. Presently called Whiteley Creek. Provance Settlement was just west of present Masontown, Pa.
9. In the Shawnee: *Tagi nsi mvci-lutvwi mr-pvyaci-grlahkv, evga mvtv inv gi mvci-lutvwx, gi mvci-ludr-giev gely. Walv uwas-panvsi inv, wacigaanv-hi gol-utvwu u kvgesakv-namv mani-lanvw-awewa yasi golutv-mvni geyrgi.*
   Tagi bemi-lutvwi walr segalmi mr-pvyaci-grlahkv, xvga mvtv inv gi bemi-lutvwv, gi bemi-ludr-giev gely. Wakv vhqualami inv, xvga nahfrpi Monetu ut vhqualamrli nili yasi vhqualamahgi gely. (Courtesy of Thomas Wildcat Alford, late Head Committeeman and Custodian of the Tribal Records of the Absentee Shawnees, and great-grandson of Tecumseh.)
10. Fort Pitt, named after William Pitt, was begun by the English in 1754 but taken over by the French before completion, finished by them the same year and named Fort DuQuesne. The English drove out the French in November 1758 and renamed it Fort Pitt.
11. This area is presently known as Mingo Bottoms.
12. Site of present Wheeling, W. Va.
13. Now called the Hocking River.
14. This stretch of harsh rapids was soon to be called Letart's Falls.
15. Site of present Charleston, W. Va.

CHAPTER II

PRINCIPAL SOURCES

Galloway, William A., *Old Chillicothe* (Xenia, 1934), p. 142.

Graham, Christopher C., "Simon Kenton," *Louisville Monthly*, I (March, 1879), 127–132.

Grills, William, *Journal of William Grills* (Baltimore, 1808), pp. 209, 211.

Howe, Henry, *Historical Collections of Ohio* (Cincinnati, 1847), p. 260.

——, *Historical Collections of Ohio* (Cincinnati, 1888), I, 190–191, 391, 679, 693, 961–963; II, 144, 346, 408–409.

Kenton, Edna, *Simon Kenton: His Life and Period, 1755–1836* (Garden City, 1930), pp. 43, 45, 59–60, 129–130.

McClung, John A., *Sketches of Western Adventure* (Maysville, 1832), pp. 98–99, 107–108, 212–220.

McDonald, John, *Biographical Sketches* (Dayton, 1852), pp. 198–203.

Ruddell, Stephen, "Journal of Stephen Ruddell," unpub. narr. written for Benjamin Drake in 1882, in Galloway Papers, Xenia Lib. Coll.

Seelye, Elizabeth E., *Tecumseh and the Shawnee Prophet* (Chicago, 1878), pp. 37–38.

Thomas, Abraham, "Reminiscences of Abraham Thomas," in *Troy* (Ohio) *Times*, n.d., 1839.

Wood, Norman B., *Lives of Famous Indian Chiefs* (Aurora, 1906), pp. 173–188.

University of Kentucky, *Kentucky* (New York, 1939), p. 178.

Ohio Archaeological and Historical Quarterly, XIII (1904), 1–39, 281.

Pennsylvania Archives, Old Series, IV (Harrisburg), p. 811.

Pennsylvania Colonial Records, X (Harrisburg), pp. 227–228.

Virginia Gazette, Feb. 4 and Feb. 11, 1775 (Williamsburg).

Draper MSS. (unpub. coll., Archives, Wisc. State Hist. Soc., Madison): *Simon Kenton Papers*, D–1–BB–5–35, 51, 119; D–2–BB–11, 61²⁻³; D–4–BB–50–53; D–5–BB–97–125; D–6–BB–1–17; D–9–BB–59¹.

NOTES

1. Present site of Boaz, W. Va.
2. *Shemanese* in the Shawnee meant, literally, the Long Knives, alluding to the swords carried by colonial soldiers, but the term quickly came to embrace the American frontier settlers as a whole, as opposed to the British.
3. The Falls of Ohio was that stretch of the Ohio River where steep rapids tumbled past the site of present Louisville, Kentucky.
4. One might speculate if perhaps the mysterious white people these Indians referred to as Azgens were in reality the members of Sir Walter Raleigh's colony of Roanoke, who disappeared without trace in 1587. One of the leading colonists of that party was an individual named Richard Darigem. Is it not possible that the Indians, learning his last name, assumed it was the generic name for the whites and subsequently corrupted it to Azgens?
5. This point, and the city built upon it, are still known as Point Pleasant, W. Va., although there is some question as to whether Kenton named it.
6. Three Islands is in the Ohio River adjacent to the site of present Manchester, Ohio. One of these islands has since been eroded away, but two remain.
7. Limestone Creek, named by Lt. Hedges of Capt. Bullitt's party of surveyors, retains this name.
8. Crooked Creek, Lewis County, Ky.
9. Tygart's Creek.
10. Coal Branch.
11. Site of present Greenup, Ky.
12. Site of present Lewisburg, W. Va.
13. Near present Steubenville, Ohio.
14. Two miles downstream from present Wellsville, Ohio.
15. The Forks of the Muskingum is the site of present Coshocton, Ohio.
16. The disputed area included the region now constituting southwestern Pa. and northwestern W. Va.
17. Pronounced Wee-shee-cah-too-wee, with accent on first and fourth syllables.
18. This resolution, made at Ft. Gower at the mouth of the Hockhocking River, came as the result of a meeting held there of all the troops to consider the grievances of British America. An unidentified American officer present addressed the meeting in the following words: "Gentlemen, having now concluded the campaign, by the assistance of Providence, with honor and advantage to the Colony and ourselves, it only remains that we should give our country the stronger assurance that we are ready at all times, to the utmost of our power, to maintain and defend her rights and privileges. We have lived about three months in the woods, without any intelligence from Boston, or from the delegates at Philadelphia. It is possible, from

the groundless reports of designing men, that our countrymen may be jealous of the use such a body would make of arms in their hands at this critical juncture. That we are a respectable body is certain, when it is considered that we can live weeks without bread or salt; that we can sleep in the open air without any covering but that of the canopy of heaven; and that we can march and shoot with any in the known world. Blessed with these talents, let us solemnly engage to one another, and our country in particular, that we will use them for no purpose but for the honor and advantage of America and of Virginia in particular. It behooves us then, for the satisfaction of our country, that we should give them our real sentiments by way of resolves, at this very alarming crisis." (H. Howe in *Historical Collections of Ohio*, II, 407.) The meeting immediately made choice of a committee to draw up and prepare resolves for their consideration. This was accomplished in quick time and the resolves were then read and ordered to be published in the *Virginia Gazette* (Feb., 1775) as follows: "*Resolved, that we will bear the most faithful allegiance to his majesty, King George the Third, while his majesty delights to reign over a brave and free people; that we will, at the expense of life and everything dear and valuable, exert ourselves in the support of his crown and the dignity of the British Empire. But as the love of liberty and attachment to the real interests and just rights of America outweigh every other consideration, we resolve, that we will exert every power within us for the defence of American liberty, and for the support of her just rights and privileges, not in any precipitous, riotous, or tumultuous manner, but when regularly called forth by the unanimous voice of our countrymen. Resolved, that we entertain the greatest respect for his excellency, the Right Honourable Lord Dunmore, who commanded the expedition against the Shawanese, and who, we are confident, underwent the great fatigue of this singular campaign from no other motive than the true interests of the country.*

*Signed by order of and in behalf of the
whole corps.*
Benjamin Ashby (Clerk)

19. Though the boundaries of the so-called Northwest Territory were constantly changing, they were at this time, generally speaking, drawn to enclose the present states of Ohio, Indiana, Illinois, Michigan, Wisconsin and parts of Minnesota and south-central Canada.

CHAPTER III

PRINCIPAL SOURCES

Collins, Richard and Lewis, *History of Kentucky* (Louisville, 1874), p. 187.

Galloway, William A., *Old Chillicothe* (Xenia, 1934), pp. 29–34, 38, 49, 170–206, 287–288, 309–310.

Hatcher, Harlan, *Lake Erie* (New York, 1945), p. 52.

Howe, Henry, *Historical Collections of Ohio* (Cincinnati, 1888), I, 467.

Kenton, Edna, *Simon Kenton: His Life and Period, 1755–1836* (Garden City, 1930), pp. 45, 60–70, 83–85, 89–90.

McClung, John A., *Sketches of Western Adventure* (Covington, 1832), pp. 108–111.

Montgomery, D. H., *The Leading Facts of American History* (Boston, 1899), pp. 167–168, 187.

Robertson, James Rood, "Petitions of the Early Inhabitants of Kentucky to the General Assembly of Virginia," in *Filson Club Publication*, XXVII (Louisville, 1914).

Wood, Norman B., *Lives of Famous Indian Chiefs* (Aurora, 1906), pp. 188–189.

Kentucky General Assembly Minutes, 1769–1792 (Frankfort, Ky.).

Draper MSS. (unpub. coll., Archives, Wisc. State Hist. Soc., Madison): *Draper's Life of Boone*, D–4–B–21–24. *Boone Papers*, D–4–C–61; D–12–C–121–127. *George Rogers Clark Papers*, D–4–J–31–34. *Draper's Notes*, D–8–S–5–7. *Simon Kenton Papers*, D–1–BB–17–18, 47, 51, 51[1-3]; D–6–BB–18–29, 33, 107–108; D–7–BB–63; D–8–BB–198–216; D–10–BB–15[2], 118[3]; D–11–BB–118[3], 121[2]; D–12–BB–117–117[1-3]. *Robert Patterson Papers*, D–1–MM–9–19.

NOTES

1. Later, when concerted attack by the Indians could not overpower this fort, they called it Standing Fort, and this name was eventually corrupted to the present name of the city, Stanford, Ky.
2. McClelland's Station later became present Georgetown, Ky.
3. Present U.S. Highway 68 follows this same trail.
4. The site of this camp was nearly opposite the present Lexington (Ky.) Cemetery.
5. February.
6. April.
7. From *wegiwa* comes the familiar term, wigwam, which has become practically synonymous with teepee. They were not at all the same. The Ohio Shawnees never lived in teepees (tipis, tepees) but rather in the better-built, not-portable *wegiwas*.
8. At this time Goschachgunk (phonetically pronounced Go-schock-gunk) was the principal town of the Turtle sept of the Delaware tribe. Its name has now been modernized to Coshocton, the present Ohio city still on the same site, and seat of Coshocton County, Ohio. The Delaware village occupied the site of the city's present lower streets stretching along the river bank below the junction of the Tuscarawas and the Walhonding Rivers. There were five other Delaware towns in the nearby vicinity.
9. Leestown was located on the Kentucky River just a little below present Frankfort, Ky.
10. The boundaries of Kentucky County, established this date, are the same boundaries of the entire present state of Kentucky.
11. "*Used to gather nettles,*" wrote Col. Nathan Boone, son of Daniel Boone, to Dr. Lyman Draper, "*a sort of hemp, towards spring when it became rotted by the wet weather, and spin them, very strong — in rich lands grows four feet high: nettles the warp, and buffalo wool spun the filling — both spun. For socks the buffalo wool alone was used — quite soft and wears very well.*"
12. The governor's full name was Phillipe François Rostel Sieur de Rocheblave.

CHAPTER IV

PRIMARY SOURCES

Bailey, Thomas A., *The American Pageant* (Boston, 1956), p. 119.
Beatty, Erkuries, *Diary of Major Erkuries Beatty* (Maysville, 1821), entry for Sept. 1, 1786.
Burnet, Jacob, *Notes on the Early Settlement of the Northwest Territory* (Cincinnati, 1847), pp. 460–468.
Butterfield, Consul Willshire, *History of the Girtys* (Cincinnati, 1890), pp. 79, 172–174.
Coleman, Robert T., "Simon Kenton," in *Harper's*, XXVIII (Feb., 1864), 289–304.
Finley, James B., *Autobiography of Reverend James B. Finley* (Cincinnati, 1853), pp. 26–33.
Galloway, William A., *Old Chillicothe* (Xenia, 1934), pp. 114–115.
Howe, Henry, *Historical Collections of Ohio* (Cincinnati, 1888), II, 581–582.
Kenton, Edna, *Simon Kenton: His Life and Period, 1755–1836* (Garden City, 1930), pp. 53, 100–101, 107–110, 112–117, 122–127, 130, 132–136.
Ruddell, Stephen, "Journal of Stephen Ruddell," unpub. narr. written for Benjamin Drake, in Galloway Papers, Xenia Lib. Coll., pp. 114–115.
Thomas, F. W., "A Day's Ramble: A Visit to Simon Kenton, the Old Pioneer," in *Cincinnati Mirror*, Dec. 7, 1833.
Amer. Antiquarian Soc., *Archaeologia Americana* (Philadelphia, 1818), pp. 287–292.
University of Kentucky, *Kentucky* (New York, 1939), p. 39.
Ohio Archaeological and Historical Society Quarterly, XIII (1904), pp. 1–39, 263–277, 281, 483–484.
Draper MSS. (unpub. coll., Archives, Wisc. State Hist. Soc., Madison): *George Rogers Clark Papers*, D–8–J–299. *Draper's Notes*, D–8–S–5–7; D–19–S–128. *Simon*

Kenton Papers, D–1–BB–60[45], 87–88; D–2–BB–11, 18, 37, 42; D–3–BB–29; D–5–BB–97–125; D–7–BB–44, 63, 63[1-42], 65, 73, 77; D–8–BB–12; D–10–BB–50[11-16], 153[1-17]; D–11–BB–113[5-9].

NOTES

1. The river was reached just below present Morrow, O.
2. This tributary is present Massie's Creek.
3. Todd Fork.
4. This branch is Little East Fork, which they crossed near present Williamsburg, Ohio.
5. The gap through which they passed is now known as Logan's Gap, through which now runs U.S. Highway 68, en route to Ripley, O.
6. This village was located on a flat, fertile ground five miles west of present Springfield, O., between present George Rogers Clark State Park and the Mad River. The old village site is now bisected by Interstate Expressway 70.
7. Site of this spring is about three miles north of present Springfield and seven miles south of present Urbana, along U.S. Highway 68.
8. This was at King's Creek, four miles north of present Urbana, in Champaign County, Ohio.
9. Buckangehela's Town was located three miles north of present Bellefontaine, Ohio. Blue Jacket's Town was on the site of present Bellefontaine. McKee's Town was on a beautiful ridge by a small stream now bearing his name, two and a half miles southeast of Bellefontaine. Mingo Town was on the site of present Mingo, Ohio. Girty's Town was on the site of present St. Mary's, Ohio. Moluntha's Town was located a mile east of West Liberty, Ohio. Wapatomica was two miles southwest of Zanesfield, O., and Mackachack Town was a mile east of Moluntha's Town along the stream now known as Mac-o-chee Creek.
10. Upper Sandusky, still bearing that name, is in Wyandot County, Ohio, 135 miles south of Detroit and 20 miles northwest of present Marion, Ohio.
11. The prisoners were seven children who were subsequently adopted by the Shawnees, and a Mrs. Rachel Kennedy. They had been captured near the waters of Raccoon Creek in Washington County, Pennsylvania, between present Burgettstown and Florence.
12. The lake retains the same name today, although it has been enlarged through the construction of a dam and much of the former surrounding marshland has been inundated. Logan's camp was located on a ford of the upper Scioto River near the present village of Pfeiffer, Hardin County, Ohio.
13. This was a common monetary term of the day, still in use at present. A buck was, of course, the skin of a deer and each buckskin was valued at one dollar.
14. Lower Sandusky was on the site of present Fremont, Ohio.

CHAPTER V

PRINCIPAL SOURCES

Cattermole, E. G., *Famous Frontiersmen, Pioneers and Scouts* (Chicago, 18??), pp. 169–202.

Collins, Richard and Lewis, *History of Kentucky* (Louisville, 1874), II, 442–450.

Drake, Benjamin, *Life of Tecumseh and His Brother, The Prophet* (Cincinnati, 1841), pp. 40–41.

Galloway, William A., *Old Chillicothe* (Xenia, 1934), pp. 50, 70, 76–79, 79n.

Howe, Henry, *Historical Collections of Ohio* (Cincinnati, 1847), p. 192.

Howe, Henry, *Historical Collections of Ohio* (Cincinnati, 1888), I, pp. 388, 467, 480.

Howe, Henry, *Historical Collections of Ohio* (Cincinnati, 1888), II, 693–694.

Kenton, Edna, *Simon Kenton: His Life and Period, 1755–1836* (Garden City, 1930), pp. 146–148.

McBride, James, *Pioneer Biography* (Cincinnati, 1869), I, 210–211.

Roosevelt, Theodore, *The Winning of the West* (New York, 1890), II, 94.

Townsend, J. W., "Historical Notes on Kentucky," in *Western Miscellany* (San Francisco, 1932), pp. 97–98.
Springfield (O.) *Gazette*, August 9, 1880.
Virginia Gazette, July 10, 1799.
Illinois Hist. Soc. Colls., VIII (Springfield), pp. 451–453.
Ohio Archaeological and Historical Quarterly, XIII (1904), 1–39, 281.
Draper MSS. (unpub. coll., Archives, Wisc. State Hist. Soc., Madison): *George Rogers Clark Papers*, D–8–J–136. *Simon Kenton Papers*, D–1–BB–18, 87–88; D–2–BB–47, 60[45], 101; D–3–BB–9[3, 6-7]; D–5–BB–1–20, 105, 117, 175; D–6–BB–17; D–7–BB–4, 71, 71[3], 78; D–8–BB–19–20, 39–40; D–9–BB–60[39-45]; D–10–BB–2[4], 16[2-3]; D–12–BB–117[1-3], 119[4-5], 137[4].

NOTES

1. Near the site of present Port Washington, Ohio.
2. Village near site of present Wheatland, Indiana.
3. Fort Nelson had been newly erected at the site of present Louisville, Ky.
4. Located presently in the bend of the Baltimore & Ohio Railroad line approximately 200 yards upstream on Shawnee Creek from where that stream crosses present Hawkins Road, just northwest of Xenia in Beavercreek Township, Greene County, Ohio.
5. Despite claims by some biographers that Andrew Jackson was born in the Waxhaws District, Lancaster County, South Carolina, on March 15, 1767, there is good cause to believe this to be erroneous and that Jackson was, in fact, born at sea while his parents, Andrew and Elizabeth Hutchinson Jackson, were immigrating to America from County Antrim, Ireland, thus making him legally ineligible for the office of President of the United States, which he later assumed. Simon Kenton, in his own reminiscences, given verbally to Judge John James, who took them down in writing in Kenton's home in 1833, discussed his meeting and fight with Andrew Jackson in the autumn of 1779. At different points in this narration, Kenton told Judge James that (1) "Jackson was certainly twenty-odd years at that time" and (2) "Jackson was one year older or younger than myself, I don't remember which." This would, of course, mean that Andrew Jackson was born in either 1754 or 1756. General Henry Lee in his notes in the Draper Collection fully corroborates Kenton's remarks and the fact that he was in Kenton's company during that encounter in 1779. Had Jackson been born, as biographers claim, in 1767, he would at this time have been only 12 years old and hardly apt to have been in command of a team of packhorse men (all of whom he had allegedly whipped) and employed in running the North Carolina/Virginia survey line. To further narrow down and authenticate the earlier date, this quotation from an article in *Historical Magazine*, issue of May, 1859, by the same Judge James:

"*In September, 1840, when General Harrison was coming to Urbana from the Western countries to attend one of the large meetings of that day, I was requested to attend the committee of arrangements and meet him at the border of the county, as I was personally known to him and they not. I was accompanied by John Chambers of Kentucky, who took a seat with me, and I drove him to Urbana. Among the many things said during that drive, this statement by him is most vividly remembered: 'There is in my neighborhood an old woman, of humble rank, but a member of a church, and very much respected, who says that she came to America in the same ship with Gen. Jackson's parents, and that Jackson was born at sea, three days from land. She said, "I received him in my own hands."' Mr. Chambers said he had intended to have her statement reduced to writing, and verified, but he had neglected it. Her statement was doubtless known to others in Kentucky.*"

Simon Kenton met Jackson only once after 1783. This was in June, 1819, when President Monroe was making his tour through the Western states. Monroe, accompanied by General Jackson, stopped over at the home of Richard C. Anderson at Bear Grass, near Louisville, Kentucky. Marshall Anderson, son of Richard C.

Anderson and brother of Governor Charles Anderson of Ohio, was present and states in his notes that while all the other gentlemen were on the porch or in another room, his father (Richard C. Anderson) and General Jackson were talking alone about matters of early history. He stood by and listened to them and at that time his father asked this question: "General Jackson, where were you born?" And Jackson's answer, immediately given, was, "I was born at sea." In view of these comments recorded at the time by persons not in contact with one another, there is very good reason to believe that Andrew Jackson was not a native American and that his age has been altered by twelve years; that he was not, in fact, born after his father's death, nor was he born in South Carolina, but instead was born in a ship at sea in 1755, the year his parents were immigrating from Ireland to America, and this birth occurred either three days after the ship left the Irish shore or three days before it reached American soil. It is probable that when Jackson became an important American figure militarily and politically, he realized that his foreign birth made him constitutionally ineligible for the Presidency and so, to overcome this, thereafter gave his birth date as being twelve years after he was actually born. This would indeed clarify many puzzling discrepancies about where Andrew Jackson was and what he was doing during the early years of his life. (For full details see: Kenton, Edna, *Simon Kenton; His Life and Period, 1755–1836* (Garden City, 1930), pp. 146–148; *The National Intelligencer* for February 7, 1859; *Historical Magazine* for May, 1859, and the Draper Manuscript Collection, *Simon Kenton Papers*, D–4–BB–28, D–5–BB–97–125 and D–9–BB–60$^{39-45}$.)

6. In addition to Simon Girty there were his brothers, George and James. George Girty had deserted from the Continental Army the preceding May to join his brothers in renegade-inclined activities among the Indians. At the time of his desertion he held the rank of lieutenant.

7. Site of present Defiance, Ohio.

8. Site of present Wapakoneta, Ohio.

9. Site of present Covington, Kentucky.

10. Gray's Run was forded where it empties into the South Licking River at present Cynthiana, Ky.

11. Three miles below present Paris, Ky.

12. This structure built on site of present Cincinnati, O.

13. As taken from the Shawnee Tribal Records and as related by the now-deceased Thomas Wildcat Alford, great-grandson of Tecumseh.

14. This is not the present Piqua, Ohio, referred to here, which was the site of the last Shawnee village of that name. The Piqua which Chief Black Hoof referred to here was located on the north side of the Mad River, five miles west of present Springfield, O., by the present site of George Rogers Clark State Park.

15. The gorge described is Clifton Gorge, east of Yellow Springs, Ohio. The tributaries are Massie's Creek, Yellow Springs Creek and Caesar Creek. For additional details, see the following note and also note 15, Chapter X.

16. This treasure, never recovered by the Shawnees, apparently still lies hidden somewhere in that marsh area, which has since been drained and is now cultivated. The old oak has long since disappeared and while certain marshy areas remain, the extensive bog is gone. According to reports made to the author by present residents of the area, a deputation of Shawnees from Oklahoma comes to the area at irregular intervals to pay homage to the birthplace of their great chief, Tecumseh, and to once again walk in the fields of their ancestral homeland. Invariably these parties are observed spending considerable time searching about the old marsh site, allegedly for the unrecovered Shawnee deposit. One of the older Indians who comes has several maps which he consults frequently, but which he shows to no one else. The author himself, with the aid of a mine detector, has gone over some of this ground but has located only a scattering of artifacts and nothing of a spectacular nature. Long sought, too, by the residents of this area, has been the silver mine where the Shawnees originally obtained the valuable mineral. Some decades ago an exploratory shaft was sunk in the cliffside of Clifton Gorge. No heavy deposit of silver was

located and the shaft was abandoned and sealed off when it showed signs of collapsing. However, some years later, a geology student collecting samples of rock in the gorge found several pieces of ore quite rich in silver.

17. What few buildings had not been fully destroyed at Chillicothe before his arrival, Clark rekindled and destroyed. Although here Clark describes Picaway (Piqua Town) as being on the waters of the Big (Great) Miami, it was actually the Mad River he meant.

18. The Frenchman, unnamed, had been taken some weeks earlier on the Wabash River by the Shawnees. He had slipped away from them during the action and was found hidden in the loft of one of the *wegiwas*.

19. The former site is present Piqua, Ohio.

CHAPTER VI

PRINCIPAL SOURCES

Bennet, John, *Blue Jacket, War Chief of the Shawnees* (Chillicothe, 1943), pp. 77–78.
Butterfield, Consul Willshire, *History of the Girtys* (Cincinnati, 1890), pp. 161–189.
Galloway, William A., *Old Chillicothe* (Xenia, 1934), pp. 84–85, 130–131.
Hatcher, Harlan, *Lake Erie* (New York, 1945), p. 55.
Howe, Henry, *Historical Collections of Ohio* (Cincinnati, 1888), II, 682–685, 886–890, 892.
Kenton, Edna, *Simon Kenton: His Life and Period, 1755–1836* (Garden City, 1930), pp. 163–164, 173–175, 236–237.
Seelye, Elizabeth E., *Tecumseh and the Shawnee Prophet* (Chicago, 1878), pp. 55, 142–144.
University of Kentucky, *Kentucky* (New York, 1939), p. 170.
Illinois State Hist. Soc. Coll., XIX (Springfield), p. 151.
Ohio Archaeological and Historical Quarterly, XII (1903), 322–323.
Ohio Archaeological and Historical Quarterly, XXXIV (1925), 117–131.
Draper MSS. (unpub. coll., Archives, Wisc. State Hist. Soc., Madison): *Daniel Drake Papers*, D–14–0–73. *Draper's Notes*, D–12–S–133–139; D–14–S–158; D–7–S–111. *Simon Kenton Papers*, D–3–BB–31; D–4–BB–133; D–5–BB–49–50, 113, 120–122, 164; D–8–BB–226; D–10–BB–1. *Robert Patterson Papers*, D–1–MM–162; D–2–MM–6.

NOTES

1. Just below present Steubenville, Ohio.

2. Present location is the community of Crawford in Crawford Township, three miles southeast of Carey, O.

3. Wingenund was speaking here of Dr. Knight, who was later turned over by the Delawares to the Shawnees, from whom he subsequently escaped. Later he published his famous narrative which effectively branded Girty as the worst renegade in history.

4. Although Knight's narrative portrayed Girty as an unspeakably inhuman beast, yet there can be no doubt that Girty did all he could to save Crawford.

5. The two creeks here are Todd Fork and Little East Fork at the site of present Clarksville, Ohio.

6. The forty included: Simon's parents, Mary and Mark Kenton, Sr.; Simon himself; his sister Nancy and her daughter Lucy; his brother William and his wife Mary and their six children, Philip, Thomas, Jane, Mary, Elizabeth and Sarah; neighbor Thomas Laws and wife Jane and their five children, Nancy, Charlotte, Mary, Sarah and James; Laws's three brothers, Jeremiah, Mason and William; neighbors Elijah Berry, wife Susan and their two children, Enoch and Clara; neighbor James Whitehouse, wife Sarah and their three children, John, Thomas and Mary; neighbor John McGraw and his wife Sarah; and three slaves — Simon's new servant, William; Berry's servant, Jim; William Kenton's servant girl, Prissy. (This list prepared on Feb. 25, 1857, by the last surviving member of the party, Elizabeth Kenton Arrowsmith.)

7. New Store is now Elizabeth, Pa.
8. Beginning about this time, Kenton gave away as gifts little of his land. Instead, he sold it at reasonable prices. However, he retained a 1400–acre tract adjacent to Washington, Ky., which he "let out" free of charge in 5-acre plots to anyone who would settle there, to use as long as they wished to live on or cultivate it, but to revert to Kenton when abandoned; and also some similar 5-acre plots adjacent to his station.

CHAPTER VII

PRINCIPAL SOURCES

Beatty, Erkuries, *Diary of Major Erkuries Beatty* (Maysville, 1821), entries for May 15, 1786 through June 5, 1787.
Bennet, John, *Blue Jacket, War Chief of the Shawnees* (Chillicothe, 1943), pp. 114–116.
Finley, James B., *Autobiography of Reverend James B. Finley* (Cincinnati, 1853), pp. 13, 29, 74, 124, 211, 235–238, 309, 346, 358, 367, 393, 419, 441.
Galloway, William A., *Old Chillicothe* (Xenia, 1934), pp. 91–94, 131, 294–299, 318.
Howe, Henry, *Historical Collections of Ohio* (Cincinnati, 1888), I, 746–747.
Howe, Henry, *Historical Collections of Ohio* (Cincinnati, 1888), II, 98–99, 411, 738–756.
Kenton, Edna, *Simon Kenton: His Life and Period, 1755–1836* (Garden City, 1930), pp. 175, 179–180, 185–186, 189.
Wood, Norman B., *Lives of Famous Indian Chiefs* (Aurora, 1906), p. 322.
Draper MSS. (unpub. coll., Archives, Wisc. State Hist. Soc., Madison): *Joseph Brandt Papers,* D–11–F–61. *Draper's Notes,* D–7–S–111; D–12–S–133–139; D–14–S–158–160. *Simon Kenton Papers,* D–1–BB–92; D–3–BB–33; D–4–BB–11–14, 17, 27, 79, 87–88, 181; D–5–BB–158; D–7–BB–39; D–8–BB–11, 46–49, 88–90; D–9–BB–1²⁶⁻²⁷, 2, 19, 57¹⁻⁶, 60⁴⁻⁵, 60¹⁸⁻²⁰, 62¹; D–12–BB–7⁴. *Kentucky Papers,* D–1–CC–3–4.

NOTES

1. Roughly, this follows a line from present downtown Cleveland, south through Akron and Massillon to just below Nevarre, then almost due west clear across the state to west of Indian Lake and then south through Dayton, Middletown and Hamilton, ultimately to the point where the Great Miami joins the Ohio River eight miles west of Cincinnati. This takes in approximately two thirds of the present state of Ohio.
2. These initials, later discovered on that tree by settlers, resulted in the naming of present Pee Pee Creek and Pee Pee Township in Pike County, Ohio.
3. The main town of the Piankeshaws was located along the lower Wabash River near Vincennes, Ind.; the chief town of the Weas was Ouiatenon, near present Lafayette, Ind., also on the Wabash; the chief village of the Miami tribe at this time was Little Turtle's own village of Kekionga, located near the junction of the St. Joseph and St. Mary's rivers where the Maumee River is formed and where Fort Wayne, Ind., is now located.
4. Although Kenton did not name this "rather particular acquaintance" of his, there is some evidence, though not conclusive, which leads the author to believe it was Ignatius Ross, brother of Kenton's scouting companion, Hugh Ross.
5. Present site of Wapakoneta, Ohio. The Shawnee name for the river, Auglaize, means "Fallen Timbers."
6. At the site of present Aberdeen, Ohio.
7. These boundaries are basically today's boundaries of the states of Illinois, Indiana and Ohio.
8. The land in question here was bounded by the Ohio River from the mouth of the Scioto to the intersection of the Seventh Range of Townships then being surveyed; thence by said boundary to the northern boundary of the Tenth Range of Townships; thence by a due west line to the Scioto and back to the beginning point.

Initially 1,500,000 acres was petitioned for, but this was subsequently diminished to 964,285 acres.
9. Tug Fork is now known as Tug River.

CHAPTER VIII

PRINCIPAL SOURCES

Finley, James B., *Autobiography of Reverend James B. Finley* (Cincinnati, 1853), pp. 207–218.
Galloway, William A., *Old Chillicothe* (Xenia, 1934), pp. 126, 131.
Hatcher, Harlan, *Lake Erie* (New York, 1945), pp. 58–59.
Howe, Henry, *Historical Collections of Ohio* (Cincinnati, 1888), I, 223, 669, 747.
Kenton, Edna, *Simon Kenton: His Life and Period, 1755–1836* (Garden City, 1930), pp. 203–212.
Ruddell, Stephen, "Journal of Stephen Ruddell," unpub. narr. written in 1882 for Benjamin Drake, in Galloway Papers in Xenia Lib. Coll., pp. 86–87.
Seelye, Elizabeth E., *Tecumseh and the Shawnee Prophet* (Chicago, 1878), pp. 57–58.
Ohio Archaeological and Historical Quarterly, XX (1911), 89–96.
Draper MSS. (unpub. coll., Archives, Wisc. State Hist. Soc., Madison): *Draper's Notes*, D–7–S–111. *Simon Kenton Papers*, D–4–BB–23, 70–72, 74–76, 87, 179; D–5–BB–118; D–6–BB–83–85; D–8–BB–87; D–9–BB–1[18], 1[27-31], 20–36, 58[29], 61[1-2]; D–10–BB–26[1], 46[8-10]. *Kentucky Papers*, D–13–CC–217.

NOTES

1. The five Frenchmen were M. Gouy de Arsy, M. Barond, M. St. Didier, M. Maheas, M. Guibert Chevalier de Coquelon.
2. Present location in downtown Cincinnati, Ohio. Losantiville was begun with the erection of four cabins, the first of which was built on Front St., east of and near Main St. The lower table of land was then covered with sycamore and maple trees and the upper with beech and oak. Through this dense forest the streets were laid out, their corners being marked upon the trees. This survey extended from Eastern Row (now Broadway) to Western Row (now Central Avenue) and from the river as far north as Northern Row (now Seventh Street). Fort Washington was erected a little east of Broadway and where Third St. now crosses it.
3. Site of Fort Wayne, Ind.
4. Rank of the dead is permanent rank, not temporary, brevet or honorary, such as in the case of Col. Fountain.
5. Charles Vancouver, who had built a cabin at the forks of the Big Sandy River on the site of present Louisa, Ky., was brother of the great English navigator, George Vancouver, who, a year from this time, discovered the Vancouver Islands located off the northwest coast of America.

CHAPTER IX

PRINCIPAL SOURCES

Bennet, John, *Blue Jacket, War Chief of the Shawnees* (Chillicothe, 1943), pp. 71, 113.
Flint, Timothy, *Life and Adventures of Daniel Boone* (n.p., 1868), p. 249.
Frost, John, *Border Wars of the West* (Cincinnati, 1853), pp. 71–77.
Hatcher, Harlan, *Lake Erie* (New York, 1945), pp. 60–61.
Howe, Henry, *Historical Collections of Ohio* (Cincinnati, 1888), I, 532, 544–545; II, 222–225, 230–232.
Kenton, Edna, *Simon Kenton: His Life and Period, 1755–1836* (Garden City, 1930), pp. 230–231, 234–239.
Ruddell, Stephen, "Journal of Stephen Ruddell," unpub. narr. written for Benjamin Drake in 1882, in Galloway Papers in Xenia Lib. Coll., p. 94.

Seelye, Elizabeth E., *Tecumseh and the Shawnee Prophet* (Chicago, 1878), pp. 96–97.
Ohio Archaeological and Historical Quarterly, XX (1911), 87–88.
Draper MSS. (unpub. coll., Archives, Wisc. State Hist. Soc., Madison): *Draper's Notes*, D–7–S–111. *Simon Kenton Papers*, D–1–BB–19; D–3–BB–33³⁻⁴, 99, 110, 113–119; D–4–BB–76–79, 96, 99, 110–120; D–10–BB–16–20, 49⁴⁻⁶, 50⁷⁻¹³.

NOTES

1. On the site of present Hamilton, Ohio.
2. Site of the town of that name in Darke County, Ohio, five miles south of present Greenville. The two streams, at the junction of which Fort Jefferson was built, are presently called Mud Creek and Prairie Outlet.
3. Present site of Fort Recovery, Mercer County, Ohio.
4. In exchanges lasting for some years, Wilkinson and Clark locked horns and, partially because of Clark's propensity for drink, Wilkinson succeeded in thoroughly discrediting Clark and having his military standing and reputation stripped from him. Not until some eighty years after his death was it discovered that during this time Wilkinson had been accepting money from the Spanish government and acting as a spy for Spain and traitor to his own government.
5. Site of present Eaton, Preble County, Ohio.
6. Present location two miles below Lynchburg, Ohio.
7. Three miles west of Sidney, O., present site of Hardin.
8. Site of Ludlow's Springs just east of Eaton, Ohio.
9. Present site is three fourths of a mile downstream from where U.S. Highway 50 crosses Paint Creek, three miles east of present Bainbridge, Ohio.
10. Present location of Greenville, Ohio.
11. The foot of the Maumee Rapids is at the present site of Perrysburg, about twelve miles upstream from present Toledo.
12. Site of present Defiance, Ohio.
13. Just south of the present Waterville, Ohio.
14. Two miles south of present Maumee, Ohio.
15. Site of present Fort Wayne, Ind.
16. The city bears the same name today.
17. Actually, the initial grant given in March, 1795, was for 24,000 acres, but this was increased by 1,200 acres on April 16 when the initial grant proved insufficient to supply the demand.
18. In the vicinity of present London, Ohio.
19. Zane's Trace eventually became part of the present federal and state highway system from Wheeling to Zanesville to Circleville to Chillicothe to Bainbridge to Maysville.

CHAPTER X

PRINCIPAL SOURCES

Drake, Benjamin, *Life of Tecumseh and His Brother, the Prophet* (Cincinnati, 1841), pp. 40–43.
Ellet, Elizabeth F., *Pioneer Women of the West* (New York, 1852), pp. 428–434.
Filson Club Publ. No. 17 (Louisville, 1902), *The Old Masters of the Blue Grass*.
Filson Club Publ. No. 33 (Louisville, 1925), *Old Kentucky Land Grants*.
Filson Club Publ. No. 34 (Louisville, 1926), *Old Kentucky Entries and Deeds*.
Galloway, James, Jr., *Journal of James Galloway, Jr.* (Xenia, 1849), p. 61.
Galloway, William A., *Old Chillicothe* (Xenia, 1934), p. 121.
Howe, Henry, *Historical Collections of Ohio* (Cincinnati, 1888), I, 396, 706; II, 276, 491, 758.
Kenton, Edna, *Simon Kenton: His Life and Period, 1755–1836* (Garden City, 1930), pp. 246, 250, 255, 258–259.
Seelye, Elizabeth E., *Tecumseh and the Shawnee Prophet* (Chicago, 1878), pp. 97–100.
Ohio Archaeological and Historical Quarterly, XXVI (1917), 114–116.
Ohio Archaeological and Historical Quarterly, XXXIV (1925), 117–131.

Draper MSS. (unpub. coll., Archives, Wisc. State Hist. Soc., Madison): *Draper's Notes*, D–7–S–111. *Simon Kenton Papers*, D–4–BB–138; D–5–BB–97–125; D–9–BB–1 29-31.

NOTES

1. Near present Brookville, Ind.
2. This landing made at foot of present St. Clair St. on southeast bank, where Monument Ave. now runs, just below the confluence of the Mad River.
3. This is the present Chillicothe, Ross County, O.
4. At some indeterminate time, the first letter "a" was omitted in the spelling and the name has ever since been spelled Cleveland.
5. Landing was at foot of present Shelby St., Detroit.
6. Site of present Amherstburg, Ontario, Canada.
7. Land patents had been issued with abandon during the early years. Anyone in Kentucky with proof of a year's residency or the raising of a single crop of corn in the area prior to 1778 could get a certificate of settlement and preemption right and make land claim entries. This guaranteed title if no other entry was valid. All shapes and sizes of areas were patented and all manner of irregular strips lay in-between. The same piece of land could be patented over and over again and some of the land cases which packed the dockets of the early Kentucky courts have not been settled to this day.
8. Ross County was named after the Honorable James Ross, former unsuccessful candidate of the Federalists for the gubernatorial seat in Pennsylvania.
9. Old Piqua Town, 5 miles west of present Springfield.
10. Site of present Springfield.
11. This creek retains the same name today.
12. This spring is located three miles north of present Springfield. The watercourse formed in part by this spring is now known as Kenton Creek. The spring is located on a farm now known as the Hunt Farm, named for its present owners, in whose family it has been since 1828.
13. Present site of Urbana, O.
14. Present site of Toledo, O.
15. The fact that the Shawnees did have large amounts of silver in a continuing supply indicates certainly an extensive and readily attainable source. Though these fabled mines, if such exist, have never been located, they are believed to be in Greene and Warren Counties, Ohio. This is based on the narratives of various white men held captive at old Chillicothe on the Little Miami River near Xenia. These prisoners were marched, always with blindfolds, for what seemed a few hours (though was probably less) upstream along the course of Massie's Creek, east from the village, where they waited under guard until they were laden with heavy sacks of what they believed to be silver-bearing ore, which they were compelled to bear back to Chillicothe. Some attempts to slip the blindfolds were, in a few cases, successful to a degree. With a map or two of "mine locations," this general area is well described by Dr. Roy S. King, University of Arizona, in an interesting article, "Silver Mines of Ohio Indians," in the *Ohio Archaeological and Historical Quarterly*, XXVI (1917), 114–116. For many years after their removal to the Auglaize Reservation, small parties of Ohio Shawnees returned every summer to Greene County and stopped for a few days' camp in the glen at Yellow Springs, now part of the campus of Antioch College. They then passed onward to the location given in Professor King's narrative and from there to well-marked locations in Warren County along Caesar Creek near present Harveysburg, where excavations (made before the advent of white pioneers) were discovered by the earliest arriving settlers. (A dam is currently being built by the U.S. Corps of Engineers at this site and by 1970 it is expected that the whole area will be beneath a large lake.) Early explorations of two similar excavations found in the glen at Yellow Springs showed vertical shafts with evidence of timbering in one of them. Excavation evidence at one site is still apparent. Geological surveys state that the Clinton limestone forming the outcropping of this glen, as well as nearby Clifton Gorge, is not ore-

bearing. Nevertheless, while he was a student at Antioch College, William Albert Galloway, lineal descendent of James Galloway, uncovered a half-inch vein by blasting near the falls on the east fork of Yellow Springs Creek, which runs through these grounds. A competent assayer in Cincinnati, to whom the residue of some specimens from this vein were submitted, found a very definite bead of high-grade silver.

16. Marijuana, which still grows wild in Ohio.
17. Present name of that city.
18. How much in monetary value Tecumseh actually received from Kenton was never recorded, but the evidence seems to indicate a sum in the vicinity of $100,000. The tract bargained for took in about three fourths of Indiana and one eighth of Ohio; beginning at the mouth of the Wabash, following it upstream past present Vincennes, Terre Haute, Clinton and Lafayette, Ind., then eastward along the same river to Ft. Recovery in Ohio, then directly to the Great Miami River, down this stream to its mouth and then following the Ohio River back to the point of origin at the mouth of the Wabash.
19. Site of present Wapakoneta, Ohio.
20. Members of the First Constitutional Convention were: Joseph Darlington, Israel Donalson, Thomas Kirker for Adams County; James Caldwell, Elijah Woods for Belmont County; Philip Gatch, James Sargent for Clermont County; Henry Abrams, Emmanuel Carpenter for Fairfield County; John W. Browne, Charles Willing Byrd, Francis Dunlevy, William Goforth, John Kitchel, Jeremiah Morrow, John Paul, John Riley, John Smith, John Wilson for Hamilton County; Rudolph Blair, George Humphrey, John Milligan, Nathan Updegraff, Bezaleel Wells for Jefferson County; Michael Baldwin, James Grubbs, Nathaniel Massie, Thomas Worthington for Ross County; David Abbott, Samuel Huntington for Trumbull County; Ephraim Cutler, Benjamin Gillman, John McIntyre, Rufus Putnam for Washington County. Thomas Scott was Secretary of the Convention.
21. Presently U.S. Highway 52 from Portsmouth to Chesapeake and State Highway 7 the remainder of the way.

CHAPTER XI

PRINCIPAL SOURCES

Ashe, Thomas, *Travels in America Performed in 1806* (London, 1808), pp. 27–42.
Drake, Benjamin, *Life of Tecumseh and His Brother, the Prophet* (Cincinnati, 1841), pp. 89–91, 144–145.
Galloway, William A., *Old Chillicothe* (Xenia, 1934), pp. 137–138, 144, 149–150, 277–283.
Hatcher, Harlan, *Lake Erie* (New York, 1945), p. 64.
Howe, Henry, *Historical Collections of Ohio* (Cincinnati, 1888), I, 879–880.
Kenton, Edna, *Simon Kenton: His Life and Period, 1755–1836* (Garden City, 1930), p. 277.
Seelye, Elizabeth E., *Tecumseh and the Shawnee Prophet* (Chicago, 1878), pp. 107, 118, 120–124, 145–149, 159–162.
Draper MSS. (unpub. coll., Archives, Wisc. State Hist. Soc., Madison): *Simon Kenton Papers*, D–4–BB–1 [12], 142; D–5–BB–28 [2]; D–7–BB–26–29, 42.

NOTES

1. Ultimately a new county was formed from Champaign, Greene and Madison counties and named Clark County after Gen. George Rogers Clark. Springfield has since that time been the seat of Clark County.
2. There is no known record of exactly how much land Kenton bought in this New Madrid area or from whom he purchased it, but there is every indication that he acquired in excess of 15,000 acres.
3. Council held on site of present Lewistown, Ohio.
4. The present seat of Miami County is the city of Troy, two miles west of Staunton.
5. The town, three miles north of Xenia, Ohio, bears this name today.

6. The validity of this rather intriguing Indian medicine is, to some degree, substantiated by the rather enigmatical quotation of a conversation which took place in 1934 between an unidentified chemist (described only as "a great chemist — a master of the *materia medica* of the American botanical field") and Dr. William Albert Galloway, A.M., M.D., LL.D., great-grandson of James Galloway, Sr. I am indebted to Dr. Galloway for the Tecumseh and Rebecca Galloway episodes reported in this book, as well as for the following:

   Dr. Galloway and the chemist, strolling in the area of the doctor's ancestral home along the Little Miami River, stopped to investigate some isolated specimens of the tree and flower mentioned here. The chemist, observing that the doctor's face betrayed his anxiety to verify the ancient tradition of the narcotic use of either or both plants, admitted that his laboratory had isolated a narcotic element from each. He pointed out an interesting and peculiar botanical structure present in the plant. "An active principle," Dr. Galloway quotes him as saying, "is obtained from the secretion of the peculiar capsule of the flower of the plant. Its structure and secretion, in that respect, are not unlike the capsule of the white poppy which, after its first incision, furnishes the juice from which the best opium of commerce is made. The plant was once indigenous to large areas of our country, and the narcotic products of its capsule unquestionably became known and used by American Indians for alleviating pain. At the date when your tradition of its use began, it was probably so long established in their *materia medica* that its date of discovery by them will never be known to us. I am anxious, however, to learn what you know of the narcotic effect of the berries of the tree, which is also indigenous to large sections of North America."

   The doctor replied: "The story of the product of the tree is almost as interesting. Its secret was evidently not so well kept by the Indians, for one of America's pioneer doctors, whose name became immortalized by his daring work in surgery, became aware of the narcotic value of the berry, ten grains of which, when properly prepared, gave his patients the same narcotic reaction as three grains of opium, and without the unhappy *sequelae*. Whether he used it as an anodyne of choice in his great operations is not known to history. Presumably, he used it in appropriate cases, as their needs required. Like the savants of another race and period, he guarded his secret as too dangerous to release to those who might easily procure it from the forests of his period, and use it to their own harm." (The doctor's reference was to the discovery by the Chinese of gunpowder more than 1000 years ago and the fact that the savants of that race believed it too dangerous to be known and therefore concealed the knowledge for many centuries.) Dr. Galloway concludes his statement with the comment: "The knowledge of the power for human harm contained in the alkaloids of the flower and the tree these two friends found growing by the roadside is forbidden release from the laboratory records of a great chemist, and from the heart of his friend, a country doctor." W. A. Galloway in *Old Chillicothe*, pp. 281–283.

7. In different accounts the slain man is identified as Myer, Myers, Meyer, Boyer and Bowyer. Myer appears in the most reliable documents.

8. The slabs were each 13½" long, ⅜" thick and tapered from one inch wide at the base to half an inch wide at the rounded top.

9. This is a liberal translation of the symbolism of the Sacred Slab, based upon the preachments of Tenskwatawa, the grand plan of Tecumseh and other events which subsequently transpired. Whether this translation is entirely accurate is subject to debate. One of these slabs still exists and is presently in the Milford G. Chandler loan collection in the Museum of Anthropology, University of Michigan at Ann Arbor.

CHAPTER XII

PRINCIPAL SOURCES

Dawson, Moses, A *Historical Narrative of the Civil and Military Services of Major General William Henry Harrison and a Vindication of His Character and Conduct as a Statesman, a Citizen, and a Soldier* (Cincinnati, 1834), 41–197.

Drake, Benjamin, *Life of Tecumseh and His Brother, the Prophet* (Cincinnati, 1841),
     pp. 144–145.
Hatcher, Harlan, *Lake Erie* (New York, 1945), pp. 73–75.
Hayden, William, *The Conquest of the Country North West of the River Ohio*
     (Indianapolis, 1896), pp. 117–201.
Howe, Henry, *Historical Collections of Ohio* (Cincinnati, 1888), I, 393, 534, 546; II,
     101.
Kenton, Edna, *Simon Kenton, His Life and Period, 1755–1836* (Garden City, 1930),
     pp. 254–255, 278, 280–281.
Seelye, Elizabeth E., *Tecumseh and the Shawnee Prophet* (Chicago, 1878), pp. 166,
     176–232, 243.
Ohio Archaeological and Historical Quarterly, XI (1902), 221–228.
Draper MSS. (unpub. coll., Archives, Wisc. State Hist. Soc., Madison): *Draper's His-
     torical Miscellanies*, D–2–Q–31. *Simon Kenton Papers*, D–4–BB–60.

NOTES

1. Little has been recorded regarding the death of Blue Jacket, although the death
   is believed to have been from natural causes, presumably cholera. Several
   varying dates, from 1810 to 1824, are given for his death, although Thwaits and
   Kellog in *The Revolution of the Upper Ohio, 1775–1777* (Madison, 1904), and
   Lyman Draper in *Simon Kenton Papers* (D–4–BB–60) concur on the 1810 date.
   Since nothing further was ever recorded of Blue Jacket's activities after this date –
   and bearing in mind that Blue Jacket was so active in all events at all times that
   some reports would almost certainly have been made had he participated in the
   most important events following this year – it is assumed that the 1810 date is the
   accurate one.
2. His limitations were from the alley on Scioto St. to High St., and from Ward to
   Reynolds St.
3. The Long Knife Fire meant Virginia.
4. Southwest of present Lafayette, Ind.
5. Though no known documentary proof exists to substantiate it, there is inferential
   indication that Winnemac may have been, at this time, still in the employ of Harrison and acting as a spy for him, or possibly even as a catalyst to make certain
   that the looked-for affray did not get settled through negotiation. It is also quite
   likely that Winnemac was simply an opportunist who just naturally gravitated
   toward the side he felt most likely to win.
6. Now Cooper Park, site of the Dayton and Montgomery County Public Library.
7. Present site of Windsor, Ontario, Canada.
8. At the mouth of Raisin River at this time was the settlement of Frenchtown, on
   the site of present Monroe, Michigan.
9. In 1814, upon charges filed by Col. Lenis Cass, Gen. William Hull was tried by
   court martial for cowardice and treason. He was found guilty of the former offense
   and sentenced to death before a firing squad. However, in consideration of his age
   and his exemplary services in the Revolutionary War, he was pardoned by President
   James Madison.
10. This is the Zachary Taylor who subsequently became the hero of Buena Vista and,
    ultimately, was elected twelfth President of the United States.

CHAPTER XIII and EPILOGUE

PRINCIPAL SOURCES

Drake, Benjamin, *Life of Tecumseh and His Brother, the Prophet* (Cincinnati, 1841),
     pp. 199–219.
Galloway, William A., *Old Chillicothe* (Xenia, 1934), pp. 152–153, 162–163.
Hatcher, Harlan, *Lake Erie* (New York, 1945), pp. 83–84.
Howe, Henry, *Historical Collections of Ohio* (Cincinnati, 1888), I, 393–394; II, 525–
     528, 573, 865n, 867n.

Kenton, Edna, *Simon Kenton: His Life and Period, 1755–1836* (Garden City, 1930), 321–326.

McAfee, Robert B., *History of the Late War in the Western Country* (Lexington, 1816), pp. 17–69.

Seelye, Elizabeth E., *Tecumseh and the Shawnee Prophet* (Chicago, 1878), pp. 272–314.

Draper MSS. (unpub. coll., Archives, Wisc. State Hist. Soc., Madison): *Draper's Notes*, D–23–S–165–169. *Simon Kenton Papers*, D–7–BB–62–63; D–10–BB–16–22; D–11–BB–18[4].

NOTES

1. Site of this new fort was approximately three miles southwest of present Kenton, Ohio.
2. Presently Fremont, Ohio.
3. This is the name of the town on that site today.
4. Fort McArthur, of which no trace now remains, was located three miles southwest of present Kenton, O.
5. Now called the Bass Islands, off Catawba Point, O.
6. Tecumseh's reference here was to Fort Meigs and the earthwork fortifications and underground compartments in which Harrison's army holed up during the siege.
7. Anthony Wayne's victory at the Battle of Fallen Timbers.
8. Fort Miami, to which the Indians were refused entry and from which no help was offered.
9. This site is a few miles from present Chatham, Ontario, Canada.
10. The location of this grave is known. But from the night Tecumseh was buried, it has been a Shawnee secret never to be entrusted to any whites. Only its general location is known by a few white men. Some years after this burial, a band of Shawnees returned to the scene to disinter the body and bear it back to their Oklahoma reservation for a reinterment suitable for the greatest leader of their race. This party, selected because it knew the precise spot of interment, found that the creek at flood times had washed away all evidence of the great warrior's last resting place. Rather than dig haphazardly, the remains were left there and the Shawnees still maintain their vigil at this spot with racial fidelity in sorrow and silence. (This is an authentic Shawnee statement of the late Head Custodian of the Tribal Records of the Absentee Shawnees, whose Indian name was written Gan-waw-pea-se-ka, but who was known to the white man as Thomas Wildcat Alford, great-grandson of Tecumseh.)

LIST OF INDIAN CHARACTERS

IN the following identification key, the individual Indian characters are listed by tribe. The Shawnees are further listed by sept (clan). For easier reference, the names are listed alphabetically; included also are other names the individual was known by, his tribal rank and, when justified, his family affiliation.

THE SHAWNEE TRIBE

Leadership of the Entire Tribe

CORNSTALK. Principal chief of all Shawnees and chief of the Chalahgawtha Sept.

BLACK FISH. Successor to Cornstalk.

BLACK HOOF. Successor to Black Fish.

KI-KUSGOW-LOWA. Chief of the Thawegila Sept.

PUCKSINWAH. Chief of the Kispokotha Sept.

BLACK SNAKE. Successor to Pucksinwah.

YELLOW HAWK. Successor to Black Snake.

MOLUNTHA. Chief of the Maykujay Sept.

BLUE JACKET. Successor to Moluntha.

BLACK STUMP. Chief of the Peckuwe Sept.

* * *

THE CHALAHGAWTHA SEPT

BLACK BEARD. Subchief of the Chalahgawtha Sept, second in command to Black Hoof.

BLACK FISH. Succeeded Cornstalk to become principal chief of all Shawnees and chief of the Chalahgawtha Sept.

BLACK HOOF. Succeeded Black Fish to become principal chief of all Shawnees and chief of the Chalahgawtha Sept. Also known as Catahecassa.

BIG OWL. Warrior.

BO-NAH. Warrior.

CAPTAIN JOHN. Warrior.

CATAHECASSA. See Black Hoof.

CHANGE-OF-FEATHERS, THE. See Penegashega.

CHIUXCA. Village chief; successor to Meshepeshe; father of Spy Buck.

COLD WATER. See Wepe-nipe.

CORNSTALK. Also known as Hokolesqua; principal chief of all Shawnees; chief of Chalahgawtha Sept; brother to Silverheels and Non-hel-e-ma; father to Elinipsico.

ELINIPSICO. Warrior; son of Cornstalk.

FROG HUNTER. Warrior.

GRAY FOX. Warrior; son of Meshepeshe.

GRENADIER SQUAW, THE. See Non-hel-e-ma.

HOKOLESQUA. See Cornstalk.

MESHEPESHE. Village chief; father of Gray Fox.

NON-HEL-E-MA. Also known as The Grenadier Squaw; village chieftainess; sister of Cornstalk and Silverheels.

OTTER. Warrior; grandnephew of Black Hoof.

PENEGASHEGA. Also known as The-Change-of-Feathers; prophet and medicine man to all Shawnees; predecessor of Tenskwatawa.

PESHEWA. Also known as Wild Cat; warrior.

SCO-TACH. Village chief.

SILVERHEELS. Warrior; brother of Cornstalk and Non-hel-e-ma.

SINNANATHA. Also known as Big Fish; a white man named Stephen Ruddell captured and adopted by Black Fish.

SPY BUCK. Warrior; son of Chiuxca.

STAND FIRM. See Wasegoboah.

STAND-IN-WATER. Warrior. Husband of Sutawnee.

STAND-UNDER-THE-TREE. Warrior.

SUTAWNEE. Squaw; daughter of White Wolf; wife of Stand-in-Water.

WASEGOBOAH. Also known as Stand Firm; husband of Tecumapese; warrior.

WEPE-NIPE. Also known as Cold Water; warrior.

WILD CAT. See Peshewa.

WHITE WOLF. White man adopted by Shawnees; white name was John Ward; warrior; father of Sutawnee.

* * *

THAWEGILA SEPT

KI-KUSGOW-LOWA. Chief of Thawegila Sept.

TE-BETH-TO-KISH-THOE. Also known as Little Moon; squaw.

* * *

PECKUWE SEPT

BLACK STUMP. Chief of Peckuwe Sept.

MONETOHSE. Squaw; first wife of Tecumseh; mother of Mah-yaw-we-kaw-pa-we.

* * *

KISPOKOTHA SEPT

A-CAT-THAT-FLIES-IN-THE-AIR. See Kumskaka.

A-DOOR-OPENED. See Sauwaseekau.

A-PANTHER-SEIZING-ITS-PREY. See Nay-tha-way-nah

A-TURTLE-LAYING-HER-EGGS-IN-THE-SAND. See Methotasa.

BLACK SNAKE. Successor to Pucksinwah as chief of the Kispokotha Sept; also known as She-me-ne-to.

BLUE JACKET. Also known as Weh-yah-pih-ehr-sehn-wah; white youth adopted into tribe; rises to rank of chief of Maykujay Sept; successor to Moluntha; husband of Wabethe; father of Little Blue Jacket; his white name was Marmaduke Van Swearingen.

BLUE JACKET. Warrior who adopts chief's name.

CHIKSIKA. Also known as Peppquannahok, meaning Gunshot; warrior; son of Pucksinwah; brother of Tecumseh.

GUNSHOT. See Chiksika.

HE-MAKES-A-LOUD-NOISE. See Lowawluwaysica.

KUMSKAKA. Also known as A-Cat-That-Flies-in-the-Air; one of a set of triplets; son of Pucksinwah; brother of Tecumseh.

LITTLE BLUE JACKET. Warrior; son of Blue Jacket.

LOWAWLUWAYSICA. See Tenskwatawa.

MAH-YAW-WE-KAW-PA-WE. First son of Tecumseh.

MAMATE. Squaw; second wife of Tecumseh; mother of Nay-tha-way-nah.

METHOTASA. Squaw; wife of Pucksinwah; mother of Tecumseh.

NAY-THA-WAY-NAH. Second son of Tecumseh. Also known as Pugeshashenwa.

ONE-WITH-OPEN-MOUTH. See Tenskwatawa.

PUCKSINWAH. Chief of Kispokotha Sept; father of Tecumseh.

PEPQUANNAHOK. See Chiksika.

PUGESHASHENWA. See Nay-tha-way-nah.

SAUWASEEKAU. Warrior; one of set of triplets; brother of Tecumseh; also known as A-Door-Opened.

SHE-ME-NE-TO. See Black Snake.

TECUMAPESE. Squaw; daughter of Pucksinwah; sister of Tecumseh.

TECUMSEH. Warrior; unofficial chief of all Shawnees; village chief; founder of great Indian confederation; son of Pucksinwah.

TENSKWATAWA. Also known as He-Makes-a-Loud-Noise, Lowawluwaysica and One-with-Open-Mouth; successor to Penegashega as Shawnee prophet and medicine man; son of Pucksinwah; brother of Tecumseh; one of a set of triplets.

WEH-YAH-PIH-EHR-SEHN-WAH. See Blue Jacket.

YELLOW HAWK. Successor to Black Snake as chief of Kispokotha Sept.

* * *

MAYKUJAY SEPT

BIG HORN. See Spemica Lawba.

BRIGHT HORN. Warrior.

ELK, THE. See Wabete.

MELASSA TEQUI. Squaw; also known as Sugar Tree.

MOLUNTHA. Chief of the Maykujay Sept;

titular king of all Shawnees; father of Young King.

SPEMICA LAWBA. Warrior; also known as Big Horn; adopted by whites and given name of Johnny Logan.

SUGAR TREE. See Melassa Tequi.

SWAN, THE. See Wabethe.

WABETE. Also known as The Elk; warrior; father of Wabethe.

WABETHE. Also known as The Swan; squaw; wife of Blue Jacket; daughter of Wabete; mother of Little Blue Jacket.

YOUNG KING. Warrior; son of Moluntha.

* * *

ADDITIONAL SHAWNEES, SEPT UNKNOWN

BLACK WOLF. Subchief.

BILLY CALDWELL. Warrior.

CAPTAIN BILLY. Warrior.

CAPTAIN WOLF. Subchief.

CHIUNGALLA. Subchief.

COONAHAW. Subchief.

KING JOHN. Subchief.

ME-OU-SE-KA. Subchief.

PLUGGY. See Pluk-kemeh-notee.

PLUK-KEMEH-NOTEE. Subchief.

RED EAGLE. Subchief.

RED FOX. Subchief.

RED HAWK. Subchief.

RED POLE. Subchief.

RED SNAKE. Warrior.

REELFOOT. Subchief.

TALL OAK. Subchief.

SITS-IN-SHADOW. Warrior.

WALKING BEAR. Subchief.

WAW-WIL-A-WAY. Warrior.

THE DELAWARE TRIBE

BEAVER. Village chief.

BEAVER. Warrior; son of Chief Beaver.

BUCKANGEHELA. Clan chief; village chief.

HAILSTONE. Village chief; war chief.

KU-LAH-QUA-TI. Medicine man of Delawares.

PANTHER. Chief of Unami Sept; village chief.

PEKE-TELE-MUND. Principal chief; third in command after Pipe and Wingenund.

PIMOACAN. Chief of sept; village chief.

PIPE. Principal chief of Delawares.

RUNNING FOX. Chief of Rabbit Sept; village chief.

RUNNING MINK. Village chief.

TETEBOXTI. Titular king of all Delawares; village chief.

WHITE TURKEY. Warrior.

WHITE EYES. Chief of Sept; village chief.

WINGENUND. Principal chief; second in command to Chief Pipe; village chief; sept chief.

THE POTAWATOMI TRIBE

ASIMETH. Principal chief.

BLACKBIRD. War chief; village chief.

NEW CORN. Principal chief; second in command to Asimeth.

SUN. Principal chief; third in command after Asimeth and New Corn.

WINNEMAC. War chief.

THE WYANDOT TRIBE

CRANE, THE. See Tarhe.

LEATHERLIPS. Village chief.

JOSHUA. Warrior; Christian convert.

ROUNDHEAD. Village chief; second in command to Tarhe.

TARHE. Also known as The Crane; principal chief of the Wyandots.

WALK-IN-WATER. Village chief.

THE CAYUGA (MINGO) TRIBE

LOGAN. Principal chief; also known as Tay-ga-yee-ta; son of Shikellimus; brother of Tay-la-nee.

SHIKELLIMUS. Principal chief; predecessor to and father of Chief Logan.

TAY-GA-YEE-TA. See Logan.

TAY-LA-NEE. Warrior; brother of Logan; son of Shikellimus.

THE CHEROKEE TRIBE

DRAGGING CANOE. Principal chief.

THE CHIPPEWA TRIBE

BAD BIRD. Chief.

MASSAS. Chief.

THE MIAMI TRIBE

LITTLE TURTLE. Principal chief.

SILVERHEELS. Village chief.

THE WEA TRIBE

REYNTWOCO. Chief.

WHITE LOON. Chief.

THE WINNEBAGO TRIBE

BLACK PARTRIDGE. Chief.

THE SAC AND FOX TRIBES

BLACK HAWK. Principal chief.

COALBURNER, THE. See Chau-be-nee.

CHAU-BE-NEE. Also known as The Coalburner; chief.

THE MOHAWK TRIBE

JOSEPH BRANT. See Thayendanega.

THAYENDANEGA. Principal chief; founder of small Indian confederacy; also known as Chief Joseph Brant.

THE OTTAWA TRIBE

AUGOOSHAWAY. Principal chief.

THE KICKAPOO TRIBE

KEEAHAH. Principal chief.

THE EEL RIVER MIAMI TRIBE

LEGRIS. Principal chief.

THE KASKASKIA TRIBE

STONE EATER. Principal chief.

THE UPPER CREEK TRIBE

BIG WARRIOR. Principal chief.

THE PIANKESHAW TRIBE

GROSBLE. Principal chief.

GLOSSARY
OF
SHAWNEE WORDS AND PHRASES

Acohqua: kettle, pot or other deep cooking vessel.

Aghqueloge: the state of being sick, especially with a fever.

Ahquoiteti: warm, hot; especially as in weather.

Ake: the earth.

Alagwa: the stars and planets.

Alwameke: bottomland; good fertile soil.

Alwe: bulk lead for making bullets.

Amaghqua: beaver.

Amatha: fish of any kind.

Anequoi: squirrel; meat of the squirrel.

Apapewee: saddle.

Apetotha: child of either sex.

Aquetteta: warm; especially as in personal comfort.

Aquewa: blanket.

Atchmoloh: speak; usually given as an order.

Calumet: the pipe of peace; strictly a decorated pipe as opposed to the tomahawk pipe. Used only in ceremonies of great moment.

Can-tuc-kee: a sacred hunting ground upon which any Indian could hunt but upon which none could take up permanent residence. It was bounded by Big Sandy River to the east, Ohio River to the north, Mississippi River to the west, Cumberland River to the south.

Cawasque: wheat.

Chalahgawtha: literally, The Place; origin of present name of Chillicothe.

Chaquiweshe: mink; especially the animal's pelt.

Cheketecaca: tomahawk.

Chobeka: medicine; actual rather than spiritual.

Cocumtha: grandmother.

Cone (or Co-o-nah): snow.

Cut-ta-ho-tha: any man condemned to death, especially by burning at the stake.

Dah-nai-tha: daughter.

Dah-quel-e-mah: love; especially marital or family love as opposed to romantic love.

Dame: corn.

Elene: man.

Englishmanake: Englishman.

E-no-ke-kah-she-ki-ki: today.

Equiwa (or S'squaw-o-wah): woman; or, literally, squaw.

E-shi-que-chi: face; countenance; expression.

Ethepate: raccoon; the animal, its pelt or meat.

Gimewane: rain.

Hahhah: yes.

H'kah-nih: bone.

H'tow-wa-ca: ear; or, less often, listen.

Il-le-nah-qui: bow.

Il-le-na-lui: arrow.

Inu-msi-ila-fe-wanu: the Great Spirit, who is a grandmother (as opposed to the

Good Spirit, or Great Good Spirit, which is Wishemenetoo).

Jai-nai-nah: brother; blood as opposed to friend.

Keewa: your wife.
Kesathwa: the sun.
Ki-be-tar-leh: tooth.
Ki-Iuh: thou.
Ki-kah-ka-mi-ka-tui: valley.
Ki-lar-ni: tongue.
Ki-leh-chi: hand or fingers or both.
Ki-neh-ki: arm.
Kinnikinnick: Indian tobacco made of various herbs and barks.
Ki-pat-te-nui: ice.
Kitate: otter; especially the animal's pelt.
Kitchecame: lake.
Kitchokema: great chief.
Ki-te-hi: heart.
Ki-tor-ni: mouth.
Ki-tschar-si: nose; less frequently, smell.
Kit-te: over; above.
Kotha: your father.

Lah-oui-ki-leh: forehead; brow.
La-nah: that.
La-neh-ke: they.
La-yah-mah: this.
Lenawawe: alive; living.

Macate: gunpowder.
Mai-ah: young.
Maketchenelu: near; close by.
Manese: knife.
Massih: a woman's genitals.
Matchele ne tha-tha: you are my enemy.
Matchemenetoo: the Bad Spirit; the Devil.
Match-squa-thi: small; little.
Matethi-i-thi: ugly.
Mat-ou-oui-sah: bad.
Mat-tah: no.
Meashethake: potatoes.
Melassa: sugar; syrup.
Melcheasiske: poor, rocky, infertile land.
Me-loh-cak-me: the season of spring.
Memequiluh: run.
Meneluh: drink.
Menethi: island.
Meniedeluh: dance.
Menquotwe: the sky; the heavens.
Mesawmi (Meesawmi): a sacred material gift of secret nature and significant power bestowed by the Great Spirit.
Meshemenake: apples.

Meshepeshe: panther; mountain lion.
Meshewa: horse; especially a stallion.
Mes-quet-wee: a cloudy day.
Metchi: many or much.
Metequeghke: trees; woods; forest.
Metequa: gun; rifle; flintlock.
Metetawawa: leggins; especially of buckskin.
Methotho: cow; female bison.
Meth-to-qui: creek; small river.
Miscoochethake: beans.
Mis-e-ken: a very large lake.
Misheolagashe: a large vessel; ship.
Miskekopke: swamp; marsh; wet ground.
Miskeque (Muskeg): pond.
M'ki-thai-nah: moccasins, especially of buffalo hide.
Moneto: the Supreme Being of All Things; God (not The Great Spirit, Wishemenetoo).
Moqueghke: hills; ridges; mountains.
Msi-kah-mi-qui: a formal council house and temple (as opposed to a house or lodge where council might sometimes be held, which is called a *Takatchemoke wigewa*).
Muga: bear; especially the black bear.

Nacamoloh: sing; chant.
Naquaga: trap (noun).
Ne wes hela shamamo: I am very well.
Neeake: wild goose.
Neegah: my mother.
Neequithah: my son.
Neeshematha: my sister.
Neetanetha: my daughter.
Neethetha: my brother.
Neewa: my wife.
Ne-kah-noh (Ne cana): my friend.
Nen-nemki: thunder.
Nenothtu: warrior.
Nenothtu oukimah: great warrior chief.
Ne-pah-loh: sleep.
Nepaka: bury.
Nepepimma: salt.
Nepwa: dead.
Nethowwe: who?
Newecanetepa Wishemenetoo: the Great Spirit is the friend of the Indians.
Ni (ne): my, mine, myself.
Nihaw kunahqa: you are my wife.
Ni-i-yah: body; physical being.
Nik-yah: mother (as opposed to *neegah*, my mother).
Ni-la: I, me.
Ni-la-weh: we, us.
Nilu famu: a sacred tobacco which, un-

smoked, is used in final sacraments at important funerals.

Nineemeh: see; look; observe.

Ni-pai-n'oui: the season of summer.

Nipe: water.

Nithichi: foot.

Nithitahlish: toes.

Niwy sheana: you are my husband.

Notha: my father (as opposed to *kotha,* your father).

Okema: chief; leader.

Olagashe: canoe.

Olame ne tagh que loge: I am very sick.

Opa-wa-ka: (also called *pa-waw-ka*) a religious token earned by the individual through which to reach and receive power from the Supreme Being, Moneto (God) and from the Great Spirit, Wishemenetoo.

Opa-wa-kon-wa: a living creature denoted as a special symbol for the individual upon which he can call for help and through whose intercession he may be able to obtain aid and inspiration from the Great Spirit. Not as powerful as the *opa-wa-ka.*

Openeake: turnips.

Oshasqua: muskrat; the animal, its fur or meat.

Oua-oui: egg.

Oui-i-si: head.

Oui-or-thi: meat; flesh.

Oui-sah: good.

Oui-shi-cat-tu-oui: strong; or, in command, be strong!

Oui-shi e-shi-que-chi: Your face is filled with strength.

Ouiske-lo-tha: any bird.

Oui-thai-quuc-quoi: bottle; vessel; flask.

Oui-thai-ah: hair (on the head).

Oui-then-eluh: eat.

Oulagequi: bark of a tree.

Ou-te-ou-wel: village; town.

Ou-thow-o-qu-quah: copper; red metal.

Pacan: nut.

Pahcotai: the season of autumn.

Pai-bai-ke-char: darkness.

Paipoun'oui: the season of winter.

Pakesemou: evening; dusk; twilight.

Pamtheloh: walk.

Papapanawe: lightning.

Pashetotha: old man.

Pasquawke: clouds; especially stormclouds.

Passah-tih: a man's genitals.

Pa-waw-ka: see *opa-wa-ka.*

P'catewah: black.

Pe-e-wah: come; follow; in this direction.

Peleneca: shirt.

Pelewa: turkey.

Peshewa: wildcat; bobcat; lynx.

Peshikthe: deer.

Petacowa: hat.

Piaitahcouthamou: morning.

Pockvano-madee-way: gossip about people, a very serious crime, for which death is the penalty.

Posetha: cat.

Poucoupeloqui: iron.

Psai-wi: big; great.

Psai-wi nenothtu: great warrior.

Ps'qui: blood.

P'thu-thoi: buffalo; bison.

Puck-a-chee: danger here; a called warning.

Quaghcunnega: the rainbow.

Quinilu-narolih: beard; facial hair.

Qui-si-qui: day.

Saketonebetcheka: bridle.

Scoote: fire.

Sepe: river.

Shakeka: flints for rifles.

Shekagosheke: onions.

Shemagana: soldier.

Shemanese: Americans; more literally, Big (Long) Knives.

Shequonur: stone; rock.

Sheshepuk: duck.

Shumaghtee: paddle (noun).

Skemotah: large net.

Skillewaythetha: boy.

Spay-lay-wi-theepi: the Ohio River.

Squithetha: girl.

S'shequoi: pine tree.

Takatchemoke wigewa: house, usually a chief's dwelling place, used to hold informal council meetings. (See also *msi-kah-mi-qui.*)

Taquana: bread.

Tawaskote: prairie.

Te-beth-ki: night.

Te-bethto-kish-thoe: the moon.

Takuwah-nepi: breadwater; a type of nutritious gruel.

Tecaca: ax.

Te-qui: tree.

Tiphicah: cup.

T'karchi: leg.

Tota: Frenchman.
Tscha-yah-ki: all; everything.
Tsi (or Tschi): kill.

Ulaoco: yesterday.
Ulethi: handsome.
Ullene: a woman's breasts.
Usketomake: melons.
Utequi: wood; wooden.
Unsoma: a notable event; an omen of good fortune.

Wabete: elk.
Wabethe: swan.
Wahbah-comeshi: oak tree.
Wahpahkeh: tomorrow.

Wahsiu: husband.
Washekee sheke: a fine day.
Wawakotchethe: fox.
Wehpetheh: go; leave; depart.
Weshe (withe): dog.
Weshecatweloo keweshelawaypa: Let us always do good.
Wigewa (wigwa): house; dwelling place.
Wishekuanwe: wind.
Wishemenetoo: the Great Spirit or Good Spirit; a great power, but not as great as the Supreme Being, Moneto (God).
Wuhkernekah: tomorrow.

Yah-ma: he.
Ya-la-ku-qua-kumi-gigi: the universe.

INDEX

Maps by the Author
Decorative Devices by Samuel H. Bryant
Design by Moses F. Carr
This book was set by American Book-Stratford Press
in 10 point Linotype Electra.
The paper is Warren's 1854 Regular Text.
It was printed offset and bound by the Vail-Ballou Press.